SEVENTH EDITION

WORK, INDUSTRY,

AND CANADIAN

SOCIETY

SEVENTH EDITION

WORK, INDUSTRY,

AND CANADIAN

SOCIETY

HARVEY J. KRAHN
University of Alberta

KAREN D. HUGHES
University of Alberta

GRAHAM S. LOWE
The Graham Lowe Group Inc.
and University of Alberta

NELSON EDUCATION
CELEBRATE LIFELONG LEARNING

1914–2014: Nelson Education celebrates 100 years of Canadian publishing

NELSON / EDUCATION

Work, Industry, and Canadian Society, Seventh Edition
by Harvey J. Krahn, Karen D. Hughes, and Graham S. Lowe

Vice President, Editorial Higher Education:
Anne Williams

Executive Editor:
Maya Castle

Marketing Manager:
Terry Fedorkiw

Developmental Editor:
Courtney Thorne

Permissions Coordinator:
Sandra Mark

Production Project Manager:
Jennifer Hare

Production Service:
Cenveo Publisher Services

Copy Editor:
Kate Revington

Proofreader:
Pushpa V. Giri

Indexer:
BIM Publishing Services

Design Director:
Ken Phipps

Managing Designer:
Franca Amore

Interior Design:
Dave Murphy

Cover Design:
Dave Murphy

Cover Image:
© Boris Lyubner/Illustration Works/Corbis

Compositor:
Cenveo Publisher Services

Library and Archives Canada
Cataloguing in Publication Data

Krahn, Harvey, author
    Work, industry, and
Canadian society / Harvey
J. Krahn, University of Alberta,
Karen D. Hughes, University
of Alberta, Graham S. Lowe,
The Graham Lowe Group Inc.
and University of Alberta. —
Seventh edition.

Includes bibliographical
references and index.
ISBN 978-0-17-653193-5 (pbk.)

    1. Work—Social aspects—
Canada. 2. Industrial
sociology—Canada. I. Hughes,
Karen D., author II. Lowe,
Graham S., author III. Title.

HD6957.C3K72 2014
306.3'60971   C2014-903697-3

ISBN-13: 978-0-17-653193-5
ISBN-10: 0-17-653193-9

ABOUT THE AUTHORS

Harvey Krahn is a Professor of Sociology at the University of Alberta, where he has served as Department Chair, Associate Dean of Arts, and Director of the Population Research Laboratory. He teaches primarily sociology of work and research methods courses. Dr. Krahn received his PhD from the University of Alberta and his earlier degrees from Western University. Prior to that, he spent several years employed as a child-care worker. Along with the sociology of work, Dr. Krahn's research interests include the sociology of education, political sociology, immigration studies, and environmental sociology. His most significant research accomplishment is a 25-year longitudinal study (1985–2010) that has tracked Edmonton high-school graduates through their transitions from school to work, from youth to adulthood, and into midlife (Dr. Graham Lowe was the co-investigator on this study from 1985 to 1999). In 2009, Dr. Krahn received the Outstanding Contributions Award from the Canadian Sociological Association.

Karen Hughes is a Professor of Sociology, and of Strategic Management and Organization, at the University of Alberta, where she teaches courses in the sociology of work and gender diversity in organizations. She holds a PhD from the University of Cambridge and has published widely on work-related issues, focusing on women's entrepreneurship and non-traditional work, paid and family caregiving, and work–family balance. Dr. Hughes is the author of *Female Enterprise in the New Economy* and a past recipient of the Social Science and Humanities Research Council's Thérèse Casgrain Fellowship for leading research on women and social change. Before becoming an academic, she held many "good" and "bad" jobs in Canada's economy. The best included leading trail rides in the beautiful Rocky Mountains as a university student. The worst included mercifully short stints in retail and accounting many years ago.

Graham Lowe is president of The Graham Lowe Group Inc., a workplace consulting and research firm. He also is a Professor Emeritus at the University of Alberta, where he was a member of the Sociology department from 1979 to 2003, and holds a PhD in Sociology from the University of Toronto.

He has three decades of organizational, labour market, and employment policy consulting experience across Canada and internationally. His books include *The Quality of Work: A People-Centered Agenda* and *Creating Healthy Organizations: How Vibrant Workplaces Inspire Employees to Achieve Sustainable Success.* He regularly contributes articles to practitioner publications, such as *Canadian HR Reporter, Canadian Business, Health & Productivity Management, HR Professional,* and *Healthcare Quarterly.* As a "thought leader" on work issues, Dr. Lowe has given hundreds of conference talks and workshops, and is a frequent media commentator. He is a recipient of the Canadian Workplace Wellness Pioneer Award.

BRIEF TABLE OF CONTENTS

CONTENTS

LIST OF TABLES AND FIGURES

PREFACE

In this seventh edition of *Work, Industry, and Canadian Society*, we have again drawn on the growing literature on work and employment, organizations, and management approaches to incorporate recent empirical findings, review new and ongoing theoretical and policy debates, and provide a more international perspective. In revisions of previous editions, the author team worked as equal partners. As individual careers unfold, however, changes in work collaborations are inevitable. Hence, this revision was largely completed by the first two authors, who continue to work at the University of Alberta. The third author, who now runs his own company, provided advice and resource material. Despite major revisions to this seventh edition, there continue to be many substantial sections originally written by the third author; after several decades, however, it is difficult to remember where or how specific ideas originated and took shape.

■ NEW TO THIS EDITION

In response to the changing contours of scholarship and public debate about work, we have significantly changed the book's structure. It now has 14 somewhat shorter chapters compared to eight long chapters in the sixth edition. In the Introduction, we outline the content of each of these new chapters. We believe this new format offers a more effective and engaging introduction to the field for students, highlighting existing themes as well as new developments in many areas, including globalization, inequality, gender and households, resistance and social movements, and theories of work. Material in all of the chapters has been substantially revised and reorganized. Because we follow the same sequence of topics, however, instructors will be able to easily adjust their teaching materials to fit with the new 14-chapter format. Almost all of the tables and figures have been updated, using the most current data available. We have incorporated nearly 400 new references (and deleted almost as many old ones). We have also added opening vignettes that personalize the topic of each chapter.

At the end of each chapter, along with Discussion Questions, we now include lists of songs and other forms of audio, and movies about work. This addition reflects our own changing work and learning environments. While bringing media into the classroom was once a laborious exercise, involving special film orders and tiny portable projectors, today's "smart classrooms" let us easily stream films, music, and news clips in ways that can greatly enrich student learning. To that end, we offer illustrative lists of resources we have used in our own teaching, that colleagues have recommended, or that we have identified through research. We enjoyed compiling these lists, but recognize that our selections of songs and movies may not suit all tastes. Valuing a broad historical understanding of work as we do (and being of a certain demographic), our choices cover a broad span of time. Quite intentionally, we have included traditional work songs and protest songs, as well as classic films, so that students learn about the historical relationship between work and popular culture. Contemporary material is also there, but we know students (including our own) will enjoy suggesting new and favourite songs and films to their instructors. We note, too, that not all the content of these songs and movies focuses *exclusively* on work, though work typically forms a strong theme. Nor is the content necessarily in line with our personal beliefs or values. In choosing material, we have been struck by how many songs and films depict work traditionally done by men or, if they feature women, place them in traditional roles. It quickly becomes apparent that the movie and music industries remain highly gendered, just like many of the workplaces described in this book. We have also been reminded that media production is a commercial activity, presenting work in often uncritical or stereotypical ways. Where possible, we have tried to identify both mainstream and independent productions, balancing this with the goal of ensuring that material can be easily accessed.

Developing these lists has brought far more material to our attention than we can include in this text. Recognizing that instructors and students may wish to explore further, we note several valuable resources here. For movies and films, Tom Zaniello's compilations—*Working Stiffs, Union Maids, Reds, and Riffraff: An Expanded Guide to Films about Labor* (2003) and *The Cinema of Globalization: A Guide to Films about the New Economic Order* (2007), both published by ILR Press—offer synopses of more than 500 films. Likewise, websites for the National Film Board (NFB), CBC's Doc Zone, Participant Media, and Why Poverty? list many interesting short and long films on work-related topics. For music, several recent books examine the fascinating relationship between music and work—in particular, Marek Korczynski, Michael Pickering, and Emma Robertson's (2013) *Rhythms of Labour,*

Ted Gioia's (2006) *Work Songs*, and Archie Green's (1993) *Songs about Work*. Together, these volumes illustrate the rich history of songs at work, as they offered rhythms to lighten loads, lift spirits, coordinate tasks, and forge bonds of collective identity. Spinning, milking, cotton-picking, weaving, seafaring, mining, and farming were just a few of many activities accompanied by what folklorists call "work songs." Industrialization silenced these work soundscapes (to paraphrase Korczynski et al. 2013), with some employers disciplining and fining workers for singing in an effort to "modernize production." Others experimented with music, piping loud tunes into factories in attempts to boost productivity, or developed company songs to inculcate corporate identity. Of course, music played a central role in labour organizing and social protest, as discussed in Ronald Cohen's (2010) *Work and Sing: The History of Occupational and Labor Songs in the United States*, and as illustrated in Utah Phillip and Ani DiFranco's album *Fellow Workers*. For those interested, these materials offer rich histories of songs at work and raise intriguing questions about the role of music in workplaces today.

Before beginning this revision, we received helpful comments from colleagues across the country. Their suggestions led to our decision to substantially reorganize the text; we appreciate their input and hope they will enjoy using this new edition in their classrooms. Along with Nelson Education Ltd., we would like to thank the following reviewers for their help in developing this seventh Canadian edition of *Work, Industry, and Canadian Society*: Greg Bird, University of Toronto; Cynthia Cranford, University of Toronto, Mississauga; David Langille, York University; Erin Phillips, University of Lethbridge; Detelina Radoeva, York University; Pamela Sugiman, Ryerson University; and David Zarifa, Nipissing University.

We also acknowledge and thank Marcella Cassiano, Will Silver, and Ashley York, doctoral candidates in Sociology at the University of Alberta, who were superb research assistants. They spent many hours locating new scholarly sources and checking references, preparing tables and charts, and compiling lists of relevant movies and songs. We also thank Statistics Canada for continuing to make available data that we have mined extensively in all seven editions of the text. We do lament the loss, however, of key data sources, such as the long-form census, and publications such as *Perspectives on Labour and Income*. At Nelson, Maya Castle encouraged us to take on another revision and challenged us to consider a significant restructuring of the text as well as the preparation of supplementary materials for instructors. She is a great team leader and motivator. Courtney Thorne managed the editorial process superbly. We have been fortunate to work with both of them. We would also like to thank Jennifer Hare, the content production manager, and Kate Revington, our copy editor, for helpful editing suggestions that have improved the text. Any errors and omissions are, of course, our own responsibility.

Professor Harvey J. Krahn, *Department of Sociology, University of Alberta*

Professor Karen D. Hughes, *Department of Sociology and Department of Strategic Management and Organization, University of Alberta*

Professor Emeritus Graham S. Lowe, *Department of Sociology, University of Alberta, and The Graham Lowe Group Inc.*

Edmonton and Kelowna, February 2014

ABOUT THE NELSON EDUCATION TEACHING ADVANTAGE (NETA)

The **Nelson Education Teaching Advantage (NETA)** program delivers research-based instructor resources that promote student engagement and higher-order thinking to enable the success of Canadian students and educators. To ensure the high quality of these materials, all Nelson ancillaries have been professionally copyedited.

Be sure to visit Nelson Education's **Inspired Instruction** website at http://www.nelson.com/inspired/ to find out more about NETA. Don't miss the testimonials of instructors who have used NETA supplements and seen student engagement increase!

Planning Your Course: *NETA Engagement* presents materials that help instructors deliver engaging content and activities to their classes. **NETA Instructor's Manuals** not only identify the topics that cause students the most difficulty, but also describe techniques and resources to help students master these concepts. Dr. Roger Fisher's *Instructor's Guide to Classroom Engagement* accompanies every Instructor's Manual.

Assessing Your Students: *NETA Assessment* relates to testing materials. **NETA Test Bank** authors create multiple-choice questions that reflect research-based best practices for constructing effective questions and testing not just recall, but also higher-order thinking. Our guidelines were developed by David DiBattista, psychology professor at Brock University and 3M National Teaching Fellow, whose research has focused on multiple-choice testing. A copy of *Multiple Choice Tests: Getting beyond Remembering*, Professor DiBattista's guide to writing effective tests, is included with every Nelson Test Bank.

Teaching Your Students: *NETA Presentation* has been developed to help instructors make the best use of Microsoft PowerPoint in their classrooms. With a clean and uncluttered design, developed by Maureen Stone of Stone-Soup Consulting, **NETA PowerPoints** features slides with improved readability, more multimedia and graphic materials, activities to use in class, and tips for instructors on the Notes page. A copy of *NETA Guidelines for Classroom Presentations* by Maureen Stone is included with each set of PowerPoint slides.

■ INSTRUCTOR RESOURCES

All NETA and other key instructor ancillaries are provided on the Instructor Companion Site at www.nelson.com/workindustry7e, giving instructors the ultimate tool for customizing lectures and presentations.

NETA Test Bank: This resource was created by Harvey Krahn, Karen Hughes, and Will Silver (all at the University of Alberta). It includes more than 275 multiple-choice questions written according to NETA guidelines. The Test Bank was copyedited by a NETA-trained editor. Forty or more short-answer questions and a similar number of essay-style questions are also included.

NETA PowerPoint: Microsoft PowerPoint lecture slides for every chapter have been created by Karen Hughes, Will Silver, and Harvey Krahn. There is an average of 15 to 20 slides per chapter, many featuring key figures and tables from *Work, Industry, and Canadian Society*, Seventh Edition. NETA principles of clear design and engaging content have been incorporated throughout, making it simple for instructors to customize the deck for their courses.

Image Library: This resource consists of digital copies of figures and short tables used in the book. Instructors may use these jpegs to customize the NETA PowerPoint or create their own PowerPoint presentations.

NETA Instructor's Manual: This resource was written by Karen Hughes, Harvey Krahn, and Will Silver. Organized according to the textbook chapters, it addresses key educational concerns, such as typical stumbling blocks student face and how to address them. Other features include suggested classroom activities to give you the support you need to engage your students within the classroom.

DayOne: Day One—Prof InClass is a PowerPoint presentation that instructors can customize to orient students to the class and their text at the beginning of the course.

■ STUDENT ANCILLARIES

Nelson Education's Student Companion Website for *Work, Industry, and Canadian Society*, Seventh Edition, provides students with opportunities to apply their knowledge and build their proficiency in critical analysis. The Companion Website at http://www.nelson.com/workindustry7e, to which students receive access with every new copy of the textbook, includes 10 multiple-choice questions per chapter, including higher-order thinking questions, providing students with immediate feedback.

INTRODUCTION

Work is undeniably an essential human activity. It is the basis for the economic survival of individuals and society. Beyond this, an individual's work activity structures much of her or his time and, one hopes, provides a source of personal fulfillment. An occupation also shapes identity and, in the eyes of others, largely determines an individual's status or position in society. Stepping back to gain a wider perspective, one sees that Canadian society and the quality of life we have come to enjoy are the historical products of the collective work efforts of millions of women and men. Thus, while the *sociology of work and industry* may, at first glance, seem as potentially boring as the part-time job you just quit at the shopping mall, it is not difficult to justify the subject's social relevance. We also believe that, once you begin reading, you will not find the subject matter boring!

A few brief definitions will be useful. First, *work* refers to activity that provides a socially valued product or service. In other words, through our work we transform raw materials as diverse as information, iron ore, and wheat into something that is needed or desired by all or part of society. The emphasis in this definition is on activity; action verbs such as *cook, hammer, clean, drive, type, teach, sculpt,* or *serve* are typically used to describe work. Obviously, such a definition is very broad: it includes both paid and unpaid work, and activities ranging from the legal to the illegal, from the highly esteemed to the undesirable and despised. Most of the material in this book focuses on paid work, recognizing the centrality of the employment relationship in modern capitalist societies; however, we also devote a whole chapter to household, caring, and community work, both because of its central importance in society and the economy and because of the many hours most Canadians spend in this unpaid, but highly valued activity.

In the last three editions of this book, which takes us back to the late 1990s, in each Introduction we began, as we do here, by commenting on the increasing pace and scope of change in Canadian workplaces, the national labour market, and the global economy. Even so, despite some remarkable developments in the local, national, and global employment contexts over the past several decades, the overall pattern of change is still best called evolutionary rather than revolutionary. When you read Chapter 1, which describes the massive social, economic, and political changes accompanying and following the Industrial Revolution, you will understand why we say this.

Nevertheless, at the level of national economy, we have seen substantial change since the beginning of this century. A decade of unprecedented economic prosperity in Canada came to a sudden halt in 2008 when the global financial system nearly collapsed, economies were pitched into one of the deepest recessions since the 1930s, and unemployment rates suddenly rose. By 2010, recovery had taken root, unemployment rates began to decline, and dire predictions of the collapse of capitalism and the need to "reset" the world economy had faded into the background. Still, the 2008–9 recession caused many individuals, families, and organizations to rethink their plans and goals—a mood of caution and uncertainty still lingers. In 2014, we are still watching to see how all of this unfolds.

Some of the prominent trends documented in earlier editions have continued, most notably increasing social inequality in Canada and in many other countries around the globe. Similarly, we are seeing further global economic integration. On the other hand, we have also begun to see more grassroots opposition as individuals and groups in many countries have become actively involved in "Occupy" and other social movements that are putting transnational corporations and national governments under greater scrutiny. Internationally, some deadly workplace accidents—the collapse of a clothing factory in Bangladesh in April 2013, which killed 1,129 workers and injured several thousand others, being the most prominent example—have drawn attention to how affluent consumers in countries like Canada benefit from the exploitation of workers in poorer countries.

New information and communication technologies continue to push the frontiers of work, both in how it is done and where, as many high-tech jobs have been outsourced to developing countries where labour costs are lower. In the manufacturing sector, China has become the new global economic powerhouse, overtaking some other Asian countries—Japan and Korea, for example—that were reshaping the world economy a decade or two ago. Today, China is flooding world markets with inexpensive but increasingly high-quality goods and showing an insatiable appetite for natural resources, including Canada's oil sands. India is also quickly establishing a global economic presence, in both traditional manufacturing and other high-tech industries. So is Brazil.

Unemployment was a leading public concern in Canada in the mid-1990s. While unemployment rates are lower now than they were then, and appear very low compared to the situation in some struggling European economies such as Spain, joblessness remains a serious concern in Canada. At the same time, employers and policymakers have been voicing concerns about labour shortages caused by the combination of a strong economy, an aging workforce, and baby-boomer retirements. Canadian immigration policies have been adjusted accordingly, with more emphasis being placed on labour market needs compared to humanitarian concerns. The rapid growth in the number of temporary foreign workers being brought into the country is the most obvious example of this policy change. While the trend toward more non-standard employment continues, it has levelled off in some respects. In other ways described in the following chapters, though, employment is becoming still more precarious. Consequently, labour market polarization continues, and social inequality has increased. With this come signs of growing public and political concern, as in the Liberal Party's current focus on the "shrinking middle class." In the United States, Democrats see minimum wages as a key electoral issue after recent "Fight for 15" walkouts in 100 cities across the nation by low-paid, fast-food workers demanding that the minimum wage rise to $15 an hour.

In this seventh edition, we once again examine these and other trends that continue to influence the work opportunities and experiences of Canadians. In particular, we are concerned with the consequences of different types of work arrangements for both the individual and society. Diversity and flexibility in jobs and work organizations remain prominent themes. As the book's title suggests, a sociological analysis of work must be grounded in its industrial context—hence, our emphasis on the underlying economic forces that have shaped and continue to shape work opportunities. But a comprehensive under-standing of the world of work also requires us to consider other features of society. For example, there are basic connections between a person's paid work and her or his family responsibilities. Society-wide value systems influence the work expectations of employees, as well as the behaviour of employers. The state plays a pivotal role in determining the nature and rewards of work through its employment standards and labour legislation, various labour market programs, and the education system. Consequently, our discussion of work, industry, and Canadian society frequently ranges well beyond the work site.

The sociology of work and industry is not a neatly defined area of scholarship, a good thing, in our opinion. More than is the case for most sociological specialties, we are forced to incorporate the insights of related disciplines. Classic sociological theory, political economy, organization and management studies, industrial relations, labour history, labour economics, macroeconomics, gender studies and feminist theory, stratification, race and ethnic relations, and social policy are some of the diverse literatures upon which we draw. Because of this scope, our coverage of the literature is far from exhaustive. Instead, we selectively examine theoretical discussions and research findings from all these areas in an effort to highlight key themes and debates in the sociology of work and industry.

The relationship between employer and employee is the cornerstone of the sociological study of work. By centring our analysis on workplace relations and the organizational and institutional structures in which these are embedded, we are able to address many of the core themes of classical sociological theory, including *inequality* and the distribution of scarce resources, *power* and how it takes shape in authority relations, and the shaky balance between the ever-present potential for *conflict* and the need for *cooperation* and *consensus*. A basic problem in all societies involves the distribution of wealth, power, and prestige. Paid work is central to this dilemma of distribution. Put more concretely, who gets the well-paying, interesting, and high-status jobs? Who is most vulnerable to unemployment? How does cooperation among employees and between management and employees occur? Are there inherent conflicts of interest between employers and employees?

Another key theoretical concern in research on the sociology of work and industry is the interplay between the actions of individuals and the constraints exerted on them by social structures. For us, the *agency–structure debate* translates into some basic and practical questions: How limiting and restrictive are today's work organizations? How much can employee actions, individually or collectively, reshape these structures? In addressing the obvious tensions between individual action and social structures, it is helpful to distinguish between *macro* (social structure) and *micro* (individual) *levels of analysis*. At the macro level, we focus on the changing global economy, labour markets, industries and occupations, bureaucracies, unions and professional associations, and a variety of institutions that *structure*, or establish, regular and predictable patterns of work activity in society. We must be careful, however, not to place too much emphasis on social structures, because in doing so, we risk losing sight of the individuals who are engaged in performing the work and, sometimes, reshaping these structures.

As a counterbalance to this macro view, an individual-level, or micro, perspective on work in Canadian society is needed. This we provide by asking questions such as these: What types of work values are held by Canadians, and what kinds of jobs do they want? How do individuals experience their work situation? What are the ingredients of job satisfaction? Or, looking at the negative side, what causes job dissatisfaction, alienation, and work-related stress? Overall, what factors contribute most to overall quality of working life as well as life away from work? In short, a micro-level analysis investigates how people experience their jobs, how they adapt to working conditions that are often far from ideal, and how, in some instances, they try to improve these conditions (that is, exert *agency*) within the confines of what is possible given existing work institutions.

To elaborate this point, while an individual's work options may be limited by social structures, there is nothing inevitable about the daily work routines, employment relationships, and legislative frameworks found in capitalist societies. Thus, we will argue throughout the book that work can be demeaning or rewarding and fulfilling, depending, in large part, on how it is organized and who has authority. Further, we will highlight some of the possibilities offered by more egalitarian and humanized forms of work. However, we stop well short of advocating a utopian vision of work. Instead, we approach the subject of work from a *reformist perspective*, arguing that even within the confines of postindustrial capitalism, the quality of working life can be improved for many. We believe that through careful theoretical reasoning and rigorous empirical research, sociologists can further the development of enlightened employment practices and public policy and help individuals create better workplaces for themselves.

It will quickly become clear that we are not presenting a strictly Marxist analysis of work. Similarly, we go beyond a simplistic Weberian approach that gives undue emphasis to employees' understandings of their work situations. We certainly do not advocate a functionalist or Durkheimian model of the work world that allows the need for social integration and stability to take on a larger-than-life presence. To varying degrees we have been influenced by these classical theoretical orientations but, as our discussion in Chapter 2 indicates, a number of influential 20th-century social theorists can also assist us in understanding the changing world of work. More than anything, our starting point is a *conflict perspective* on the social world. Thus, a Marxist or materialist perspective has informed the book's emphases on inequality, power, conflict, and control. The Weberian approach sensitizes us to the centrality of individual actors, and their beliefs and behaviours, in sociological analysis. The Durkheimian tradition reminds us that social integration, consensus, and stability within work organizations are the motivation for much management theory and practice.

Chapter 1 begins with an overview of the industrialization process and the rise of capitalism in Europe. This short history lesson provides a backdrop against which we can compare the somewhat later Canadian industrialization experience. This first chapter also introduces some aspects of the theoretical writings of Karl Marx, Adam Smith, Max Weber, and Émile Durkheim. These social philosophers developed their assessments of the problems and prospects of work in industrial capitalist societies from their observations of how Europe was transformed during the Industrial Revolution.

But the global economy, the industrial structures of advanced capitalist societies, and the employment opportunities found within them have all changed dramatically since the mid-20th century, as we explain in Chapter 2. A different constellation of rapidly growing economies, primarily in Asia, has led to a reshaping of the international balance of power. Changing technologies and expanding markets for new services have created demand for different skills and have shifted the locations where work is completed. In this chapter, we also discuss the writings of social theorists who have helped us understand the emergence of postindustrial society and the changing forms of work and work relationships within it.

In Chapter 3 our focus shifts from history and theory to a detailed empirical overview of the major industrial, labour market, and labour force trends in Canada. We begin by examining changes in the composition of the labour force over the past few decades: the workforce has become older and more educated, while immigration and a growing First Nations population have reshaped Canada's demographic profile. We then turn our attention to changing labour force participation patterns before documenting the emergence of a service-dominated economy with a very different distribution of industries and occupations than what we would have observed a century ago.

Chapter 4 introduces an evaluative component to our empirical overview, as we describe the varying quality of jobs within Canada's contemporary labour market. Central to this chapter is a detailed discussion of the rise of nonstandard forms of work (temporary and part-time, for example) which has led to a more precarious employment situation for many working Canadians. In this chapter we also examine unemployment trends and patterns within Canada and in other countries.

Labour markets are central institutions in the contemporary work world, basically determining who gets the good jobs and who ends up in the less desirable ones. Chapter 5 examines how the Canadian labour market operates by comparing recent research findings with the predictions of two competing theories: the human capital model and the labour market segmentation approach. This chapter also focuses directly on the problem of growing labour market polarization and increasing social inequality.

The growing labour force participation of women, clearly one of the most significant social changes of the last five or six decades, has been woven into our discussions in Chapters 3 through 5. Chapter 6 provides a more in-depth analysis of gendered work, work organizations, and labour markets. This chapter outlines the transformation of women's economic roles over time and explains how gender has become a source of entrenched divisions within the labour market and within work organizations. It also examines theoretical explanations of and policy responses to gender inequality in the workplace.

Chapter 7, new to this edition, focuses on household, caring, and community work, much of which is typically unpaid. Recent research on the household division of labour, on mothering, fathering, and eldercare, and on volunteer work is discussed, as are studies of work–family balance. An examination of different theoretical approaches to understanding caring work helps link this discussion to themes discussed in other chapters that examine primarily paid work.

The organization and management of paid work, and how they have changed over time, are the core topics in Chapters 8 and 9. In the first of these two chapters, we describe the emergence of large bureaucracies and assembly-line factories in the early 20th century, along with the management problems they created. The "modern" solutions—"scientific management" and the "human relations" approach—generated their own problems. Chapter 9 describes and critiques the variety of new managerial approaches that, over the past four or five decades, have been implemented to try to solve some of the problems of bureaucracy, decentralize authority systems, and generally improve working conditions, while increasing productivity and profits for owners.

Chapter 10 is, in some ways, a debate with the mainstream management approaches. Our starting point is the labour process perspective, a much more critical assessment of employer–employee relationships in capitalist society. We examine different methods managers have used to control and gain compliance from workers, and ask whether, on average, workers today are using fewer or more skills in their jobs than was the case a half century earlier. We also discuss the link between changing technologies and shifts in skill use, worker decision-making, and patterns of social inequality.

Unions receive some comment in earlier chapters, but Chapter 11 is devoted to this subject. We discuss various theories about the origins and functions of unions and document the development of the organized labour movement in Canada as well as in the United States. We also describe the legal framework—the industrial relations system—that has emerged for regulating union–management relations. The chapter concludes by examining strike patterns, over time and cross-nationally, to see how they are linked to changes in industrial structures, labour market processes, and management approaches, as discussed in earlier chapters.

Chapter 12 invites readers to step back from the current pattern of labour–management relations and institutionalized conflict described in previous chapters and look for alternatives. We begin by asking whether unions represent a revolutionary or a reformist collective response by workers to the greater power of employers. We then describe current approaches to addressing health and safety concerns in the workplace since, to some extent, they require co-management by workers and management. We then go further afield to discuss different forms of industrial democracy as well as examples of worker ownership, arguing that these approaches to organizing and managing work do have something to offer.

The last two chapters of this book shift our attention from the largely structural analysis in the previous chapters to an examination of how individuals experience work. In Chapter 13, we discuss society-wide work values and how they vary across time and culture. We then examine work orientations, asking what individual employees seek to obtain from their work. Are their work orientations (or preferences) perhaps shaped by the work opportunities available to them? Equally important, are we seeing the emergence of new work orientations in response to growing employment insecurity and income inequality? Chapter 14 presents summaries of the research literature on job satisfaction, a parallel social psychological approach to understanding alienation from work, and the large multi-disciplinary body of research on work-related stress. A major theme developed in this chapter is that negative work experiences can have serious and lasting effects on individuals.

Finally, in Conclusions, we raise important questions about the future of work in Canada. As the 21st century unfolds, a number of trends concern us. Corporate and public-sector downsizing, the outsourcing of jobs, and continued growth in some forms of nonstandard work mean that, for a large minority of Canadians, work is precarious and economic well-being is insecure. Unemployment rates remain unacceptably high. Some sub-groups of the Canadian population are much more likely than others to be unemployed, underemployed, or inadequately rewarded for their work. In short, social inequality is slowly increasing, as is polarization in the quality of working life. New human resource management strategies and new technologies hold out some possibilities for creating better and fairer workplaces. But they could just as easily have negative effects on the quantity and quality of work. We do believe, however, that we have some control over our destiny. In our opinion, what Canada needs is more public debate among employers, governments, unions, and other collective organizations to determine how best to balance the interests of workers, who want both a decent standard of living and an improved quality of working life, with the economic growth sought by employers and government. Yet public debate is only the first step. We also need political leaders to put in place and maintain policies and legislation that will ensure that these goals are balanced. It is our job, as citizens, to push them to do so.

HISTORICAL PERSPECTIVES ON WORK (1700–1950s)

"Canada was a country that depended on workers.... How did our work-ancestors live a hundred years ago? It is very hard to generalize across a century in which remarkable stability in the value of money concealed enormous changes in every other economic and social factor. An unskilled day-labourer in 1867 might earn a dollar a day for a ten-hour day, six days a week. A highly skilled craftsman might earn three times as much. A woman's wage would be half that of a man—as little as thirty-five to sixty cents a day. A child earned as little as twenty-five cents. Employers offered no paid holidays, and they rarely felt obliged to make provision for sickness, injury, or old age except to dismiss or reduce the wages of workers who were past their prime. Until 1877, masters and servants acts allowed the courts to send disobedient or absentee workers to jail at an employer's request.... Working people in good times could afford to live in a two- or three-room cottage with a pit privy outside but usually without running water. They ate an adequate but monotonous diet heavily dependent on bread, potatoes, and cheese. Any surplus was all too likely to be spent on liquor because Canadians were notoriously hard-drinking people.... Everything depended on good times. A working-class family lived always in the shadow of disaster. Work was heavy and often dangerous. Severe and crippling injuries were commonplace in almost every trade."

Source: Desmond Morton. (2007). *Working People: An Illustrated History of the Canadian Labour Movement*, 5th ed. McGill-Queen's University Press, pp. 1–6.

◼ INTRODUCTION

In the early 1870s, John Henry Lincoln, known as Harry, travelled from his home and birthplace in Huntingdonshire in England to New Haven, Sussex, to attend the wedding of his sister to Fred Waters. There he met Fred's sister, Anne, and that was the beginning of it all, for they soon married. Harry was 23 and a master boot maker by trade. Anne was from a well-to-do family, and her desire to marry a craftsman caused something of a stir. After marrying, Harry set up his own boot-making and repair shop, while Anne devoted herself to raising their family. Together, they would have 11 children.

In the early 1900s, the family left to homestead in Canada. Packing their possessions into 10 trunks, they travelled two weeks by sea to Montreal, then 1,700 miles by train to Manor, Saskatchewan. Once the family settled, a younger son, Arthur, moved further west to Alberta, where he homesteaded, married, and raised three children. A resourceful man, he survived two world wars and the Great Depression, working in farming, sales, and then his own business. In the postwar prosperity of the 1950s, he saw his daughter move to the big city of Edmonton and juggle a career, marriage, and motherhood at a time when few women did. Her three baby-boom children would all go on to university, the youngest eventually teaching there and collaborating on the book you are now reading.[1]

Reflecting on this story, it is hard not to be struck by the huge change that has occurred in just a few generations. Families with 11 children are not the norm. Farming has been replaced by factory work, and then again by white-collar, retail, and knowledge-based jobs. Canada still relies on immigrants to fuel its economy, but not primarily those from Britain as was once the case. Although people still migrate for work, work itself is increasingly mobile, with production being spread across the globe. This book examines these changes and the types of paid work now done by Canadians. Today, most work for wages or a salary in bureaucratic organizations. In most two-adult households, both partners are employed outside the home. In a labour force of nearly 19 million individuals, three in four workers are in the service sector. Compared to the past, fewer workers are full-time employees. More than one in four is working in either a temporary or a part-time job; roughly one in six is self-employed. For every 12 employed Canadians, one is unemployed.

These labour market realities become more interesting when we realize that only a generation or two ago, some of these trends had just begun to emerge. And going back over a century, as we have seen, the differences in work patterns are huge. What social and economic forces led to the shifts from agriculture to manufacturing, then to services? Why did bureaucracies develop? Why has education become more important? Why are women, Aboriginal people, and visible minorities underrepresented in better-paying jobs—and what are the social consequences? To answer these and many related questions, we look back in history and at other societies to examine the complex process of industrialization. This historical and comparative approach will help us to understand present patterns and trends, assess their significance for individuals and society, and respond to the future challenges they pose.

Industrialization refers to the technical aspects of the *accumulation* and processing of a society's resources. *Capitalism* is a term used to describe key aspects of the economic and social organization of the productive enterprise. In an *industrial society*, inanimate sources of energy, such as coal or electricity, fuel a production system that uses technology to process raw materials. But labelling a society "industrial" tells us little about the relationships among the individuals involved in the productive process. In a *capitalist system of production*, a relatively small number of individuals own and control the means for creating goods and services, while the majority have no direct ownership stake in the economy and are paid a wage to work by those who do.

Studying the rise of capitalism requires us to make sense of large, complex processes spanning generations and leaving no aspect of daily life unaffected. The theoretical writings of Adam Smith, Karl Marx, Émile Durkheim, and Max Weber help us to explain, not just describe, the causes and consequences of capitalist development. As we will see, the sociological concepts of *power, control, inequality,* and *conflict* that these early social scientists used to analyze changes in their times continue to be central to today's debates about the nature of 21st-century postindustrial society. Therefore, this chapter provides vital history that we can build on in subsequent chapters to address questions such as these: Has the rise of knowledge-based, high-tech economies benefited some groups more than others? How are new mobile technologies transforming the content and organization of work? Is economic globalization increasing the power of transnational corporations at the expense of national governments? And with global economic changes such as the rise of China and India, the collapse of the Soviet Union and uneven transitions of Eastern European countries toward market-based economies, and the changing prospects in many established economies, do we need to rethink long-accepted explanations of capitalist development?

THE ORIGINS OF INDUSTRIAL CAPITALISM

Capitalism and industrialization dramatically reshaped the structure of European society economically, socially, and spatially. These changes occurred over centuries, with a different pace and pattern in each country. While the details of these changes differed internationally and regionally within countries, the result was profound change in how, where, for whom, and under what conditions individuals worked.

The emergence of capitalism in Europe consisted of two basic periods: *mercantile* or *commercial capitalism*, which began in the 1500s, and *industrial capitalism*, which evolved somewhat later.[2] In the mercantile period, merchants and royalty in Spain, Holland, England, and France accumulated huge fortunes by trading internationally in a variety of goods, including spices, precious stones and metals, sugar, cotton, and slaves. An elaborate trading network evolved, linking Africa, Asia, and the American colonies with Europe. This global trade and the pillage of cultures (slaves from Africa, for example, and vast amounts of gold and silver from Central and South America) provided wealth that would subsequently fuel the growth of industrial capitalism in Europe (Beaud 1983).

These early signs of capitalist commercial activity emerged out of a *feudal society*—the *Industrial Revolution* had not yet begun. Most people still lived in the countryside. The class structure of these agrarian societies consisted of a relatively small aristocracy and merchant class, most of whom lived in the cities, a rural landowning class, and a large rural peasantry. Work typically involved peasants farming small plots of land they did not own. Landowners received rent, usually in the form of agricultural produce, little of which was sold for cash. Generations of peasant families lived and died on the same feudal estates.

Thus, feudal Europe was predominantly a *pre-market* economy in which the producer was also the consumer. It was also a *pre-capitalist* economy because wage labour was rare and a business class had not yet become dominant. Feudal lords accepted rent and expected services in the form of manual labour required for the upkeep of the estate. In return, they allowed historical tenancy relationships to continue and provided some protection, if necessary, for their tenants. Feudalism was thus built upon a system of mutual rights and obligations, reinforced by tradition. One's social position was inherited. The society was relatively stable, but it stifled economic progress.[3]

Did the decay of feudalism lead to the rise of capitalism, or was it the other way around? Scholars are divided on this question. Some argue that factors internal to feudal society, such as growing rural populations, deterioration of land, and landlords demanding more rent, forced people off the land and into the cities where they could form an urban working class. Others counter that, as mercantile capitalism developed in urban areas and as the market economy slowly began to make an impact on rural life, cities began to attract

4

landless serfs. This debate is difficult to resolve, since the two processes influenced each other (Hilton 1976; Aston and Philpin 1985). What is undisputed is that capitalism brought with it an entirely new social order.

Early Capitalism

Industrial capitalism began to emerge in the early 1700s. The production of goods by artisans, or by the home-based *putting out system* in which merchants distributed work to peasant households, led to larger workshops (manufactories) that made metal, cloth, glass, and other finished goods (Beaud 1983). By the late 1700s, various inventions were revolutionizing production techniques. James Hargreaves's spinning jenny transformed work in textile industries. Growth in trade and transportation, the construction of railways, and military demand for improved weapons encouraged new techniques for processing iron and other metals. Inventors also were devising ways of harnessing water and steam, as exemplified in James Watt's steam engine.

These early inventions facilitated a new form of work organization: the *industrial mill*. A technical breakthrough that involved harnessing many machines to a single inanimate energy source, the mill also had immense social implications, consolidating many workers under one roof and the control of managers (Beaud 1983: 66–67; Burawoy 1984). A growing class of impoverished urban wage-labourers endured horrific working conditions in early industrial mills. Some workers resisted this trend, particularly artisans who previously had controlled their own labour. Episodes of destroying textile machinery occurred between 1811 and 1816 in a number of British communities. The unemployed craftsmen involved (called "Luddites") were not unthinking opponents of technological innovations, but skilled workers frustrated by changes that were making their skills obsolete. These uprisings were quashed by the state; some participants were jailed or deported, while others were hanged (Beaud 1983: 65; Grint 1991: 55).

The emergence of industrial capitalism also changed the *gender-based division of labour*. While women, men, and children had done different types of work in feudal times, much of it at home, they were often engaged in parallel work activities (Middleton 1988). The putting out system, particularly in the textile industries, brought many women into the paid labour force along with men, since they could work out of their home and still carry out domestic work and childcare. Early textile factories also employed men, women, and children (Berg 1988). But as manufacturing developed and expanded, it became the preserve of men. While a gendered division of labour had long existed, it became more pronounced with the rise of industrial capitalism.[4]

The Great Transformation

In only a matter of decades, factory production dominated capitalist societies. The urban landscape also changed as manufacturing cities grew to accommodate the new wage-labour force. Mechanization and the movement to factory-based production proceeded even faster in the 1800s than it had in the previous century. Manufacturing surpassed agriculture in its annual output. Industrial production in Britain, for example, increased by 300 percent between 1820 and 1860. The portion of the labour force employed in agriculture in Britain, France, Germany, the United States, and other industrializing countries declined, while employment in manufacturing and services rose rapidly. By the end of the 19th century, industrial capitalism was clearly the dominant system of production in Western nations.

According to Karl Polanyi, the *great transformation* that swept Europe with the growth and integration of capital, commodity, and labour markets—the foundation of capitalism—left no aspect of social life untouched.[5] The struggle for democratic forms of government, the emergence of the modern nation-state, and the rapid growth of cities are all directly linked to these economic changes.

Along with new technologies, the replacement of human and animal sources of energy with inanimate sources, and the emergence of an integrated market system for finance, commodities, and labour, this era saw dramatic changes in how work was organized. Over time, the relatively stable landlord–serf relationships of feudalism were replaced by wage-labour relationships between capitalists and labourers. Employers paid for a set amount of work, but also determined exactly how, and under what conditions, work would be done. Previously independent artisans lost out to the factory system. In the end, the result was a higher standard of living for most residents of industrialized countries. But the interrelated processes of change that created a market economy also led to new problems of *controlling, coordinating*, and *managing* work—central themes in this book.

● CANADA'S INDUSTRIALIZATION

The process of industrialization in Canada lagged behind that in Britain and the United States, and can be traced back to the mid-1800s.[6] As a British colony, Canada had been expected to provide raw materials, rather than to produce finished goods that would compete on world markets with those of the mother country. Canadian economic elites focused on traditional activities, such as exporting *staple products*, including timber and fur, to sell on world markets, and developing transportation networks (particularly railways) that could link the resource-producing regions of the country with the port cities involved in export trade.

Work in Pre-industrial Canada

The first half of the 19th century, then, was a pre-industrial economic era in Canada. Canada still had a pre-market economy, since most production and consumption took place in households. In fact, given the peculiarities of a colonial economy dependent on Britain, even land was not really a marketable commodity. By the mid-1830s, less than one-tenth of the vast tracts of land that had been given by the French, and later British, monarchy to favoured individuals and companies had been developed for agriculture.

At the same time, more people from Europe were arriving. Shortages of land for small farmers, potato famines in Ireland, and dreadful working conditions in many British factories fuelled immigration to the New World. Large numbers of immigrants landed in Canada, only to find shortages in urban factory jobs and little available agricultural land. As a result, most of these immigrants sought employment in the United States, where factory jobs and land were more plentiful (Teeple 1972).

Some of the immigrants who stayed in Canada were employed in building the Welland and Rideau canals—the first of many transportation megaprojects—in the first half of the 19th century. The influx of unskilled workers created a great demand for such seasonal jobs, which often involved 14 to 16 hours a day of hard and poorly paid work. Consequently, poverty was widespread. In the winter of 1844, the *St. Catharines Journal* reported that

> the greatest distress imaginable has been, and still is, existing throughout the entire line of the Welland Canal, in consequence of the vast

accumulation of unemployed labourers. There are, at this moment, many hundreds of men, women, and children, apparently in the last stages of starvation, and instead ... of any relief for them ... in the spring ... more than one half of those who are now employed must be discharged.[7]

The Industrial Era

By the 1840s, Canada's economy was still largely agrarian, even though the two key ingredients for industrialization—an available labour force and a transportation infrastructure—were in place. Prior to Confederation in 1867, some of Canada's first factories were set up not in Ontario or Quebec, as we might expect, but in Nova Scotia. Shipbuilding, glass, and clothing enterprises were operating profitably in this region before the Maritime provinces entered Confederation (Veltmeyer 1983: 103). After 1867, manufacturing became centralized in Ontario and Quebec, resulting in the *deindustrialization* of the Maritimes. A larger population base, easy access to U.S. markets, and railway links to both eastern and western Canada ensured that the regions around Montreal and Toronto would remain the industrial heartland of the country.

At the time of Confederation, half of the Canadian labour force was in agriculture. This changed rapidly with the advance of industrialization. By 1900, Canada ranked seventh in production output among the manufacturing countries of the world (Laxer 1989). The large factories that had begun to appear decades earlier in the United States were now springing up in Toronto, Hamilton, Montreal, and other central Canadian cities. American firms built many of these factories to avoid Canadian tariffs on goods imported from the United States. This initiative began a pattern of direct U.S. foreign investment in Canada that continues today.

These economic changes brought rapid urban growth and accompanying social problems. Worker exploitation was widespread, as labour laws and unions were still largely absent. Low pay, long hours, and unsafe and unhealthy conditions were typical. Workers lived in crowded and unsanitary housing. Health care and social services were largely nonexistent. In short, despite economic development in the decades following Confederation, poverty remained the norm for much of the working class in major manufacturing centres (Copp 1974; Piva 1979).

The Decline of Craftwork

Traditionally, *skilled craftworkers* had the advantage of being able to determine their own working conditions, hire their own apprentices, and frequently set their pay. Some worked individually, while others arranged themselves into small groups in the manner of European craft guilds. But this craft control declined as Canada moved into the industrial era. Factory owners were conscious of the increased productivity in American factories, where new technology and "modern" systems of management were applied. Dividing craft jobs into many simple tasks allowed work to be performed by less skilled and lower-paid employees. Mechanization further cut costs while increasing productivity.

As these systems entered Canada, the job autonomy of craftworkers was reduced, resulting in considerable labour unrest. Between 1901 and 1914, for example, more than 400 strikes and lockouts occurred in the 10 most industrialized cities of southern Ontario (Heron 1980; Heron and Palmer 1977). Although these conflicts may look like working-class revolt, they are more accurately seen as a somewhat privileged group of workers resisting efforts to reduce their occupational power. While large numbers of skilled workers experienced the "crisis of the craftsmen" (Heron 1980), there were larger numbers of unskilled manual labourers whose only alternative to arduous factory work was seasonal labour in the resource or transportation industries, or unemployment.

There were, in fact, thousands of workers employed in the resource extraction industries throughout Canada, and many others worked on constructing the railways. In *The Bunkhouse Man*, Edmund Bradwin estimates that up to 200,000 men living in some 3,000 work camps were employed in railway construction, mining, and the lumber industry during the early 20th century. These workers were from English Canada and Quebec, as well as from Europe and China. Employers considered immigrants to be good candidates for such manual work, as they were unlikely to oppose their bosses. This hiring strategy often did ward off collective action, although immigrants sometimes were the most radical members of the working class.[8]

The creation of a transcontinental railway led to a high demand for coal. Mines were opened on Vancouver Island and in the Alberta Rockies, with immigrants quickly taking the new jobs. Mine owners tried to extract a lot of work for little pay, knowing they could rely on the military to control unruly workers. It has been estimated that, in the early 1900s, every 1 million tons of coal produced in Alberta took the lives of 10 miners, while in British Columbia, the rate was 23 dead for the same amount of coal.[9] These dangerous conditions led to strikes, union organization, and even political action. In 1909, Donald McNab, a miner and socialist, was elected to represent Lethbridge in the Alberta legislature. The same year, the Revolutionary Socialist Party of Canada elected several members to the British Columbia legislature (Marchak 1981: 106). Nonetheless, although the labour movement took root in resource industries, it never had the revolutionary spark that some of its radical leaders envisioned.

● THEORETICAL PERSPECTIVES

Now that we have some historical background on industrialization and capitalism, we can examine major explanations of the causes and consequences of these changes. The next sections discuss classical theories of social and economic change. In Chapter 2, we explore contemporary theories. After we have acquainted ourselves with the theorists and their analytic concepts, we can apply their insights throughout the book when considering specific work issues.

Karl Marx on Worker Exploitation and Class Conflict

Karl Marx (1881–83) spent a lifetime critically examining the phenomenon of industrial capitalism. His assessment of this new type of society was presented within a very broad theoretical framework. He called the overall system of economic activity within a society a *mode of production*, and he identified its major components as the *means of production* (the technology, capital investments, and raw materials) and the *social relations of production* (the relationships between the major social groups or classes involved in production).

Marx focused on the manner in which the ruling class controlled and exploited the working class. His close colleague, Friedrich Engels, documented this exploitation in his 1845 book, *The Condition of the Working Class in England*. Engels described one of London's many slum districts, noting that other industrial cities were much the same:

> St. Giles is in the midst of the most populous part of the town, surrounded by broad, splendid avenues in which the gay world of

London idles about.... The houses are occupied from cellar to garret, filthy within and without, and their appearance is such that no human being could possibly wish to live in them. But this is nothing in comparison with the dwellings in the narrow courts and alleys between the streets, entered by covered passages between the houses, in which the filth and tottering ruin surpass all description.... Heaps of garbage and ashes lie in all directions, and the foul liquids emptied before the doors gather in stinking pools. Here live the poorest of the poor, the worst paid workers with thieves and the victims of prostitution indiscriminately huddled together.[10]

It was from such first-hand observations of industrializing Europe that Marx developed his critique of capitalism.

Class conflict was central to Marx's theory of social change. He argued that previous modes of production had collapsed and been replaced because of conflicts among class groups within them. Feudalism was supplanted by capitalism as a result of the growing power of the merchant class, the decline of the traditional alliance of landowners and aristocracy, and the deteriorating relationship between landowners and peasants. Marx identified two major classes in capitalism: the capitalist class, or *bourgeoisie*, which owned the means of production, and the working class, or *proletariat*, which exchanged its labour for wages. A third class—the *petite bourgeoisie*—comprising independent producers and small business owners, would eventually disappear, according to Marx, as it was incorporated into one of the two major classes.

Marx argued that capitalism would eventually be replaced by a socialist mode of production. The catalyst would be revolutionary class conflict, in which the oppressed working class would destroy the institutions of capitalism and replace them with a *socialist society* based on collective ownership of the means of production.

Marx sparked ongoing debate on the nature of work and of class conflict in capitalist societies (Zeitlin 1968; Coser 1971). Ever since, social, political, and economic analysts have tried to reinterpret his predictions of a future worker-run socialist society. No capitalist society has experienced the revolutionary upheavals Marx foresaw. And the collapse of the Soviet communist system in Eastern Europe ended speculation that communism would evolve into true socialism. In fact, Marx probably would have been an outspoken critic of the Soviet communist system, given its extreme inequalities in power distribution and harsh treatment of workers. He would also have condemned the inequalities in today's capitalist Russia.

Marx's critique of capitalism has also shaped research in the sociology of work and industry, as analysts try to refine or refute his ideas. First, Marx emphasized how the capitalist profit motive is usually in conflict with workers' desires for better wages, working conditions, and standards of living. Second, Marx argued that the worker–owner relationship led to workers losing control over how they did their work and, hence, to the dehumanization of work. Third, Marx predicted that the working class would eventually organize to more actively oppose the ruling capitalist class. In short, Marx wrote about inequality, power, control, and conflict. His enduring legacy for sociology was this more general *conflict perspective*. He recognized that the relations of production in industrial capitalist society typically are exploitative, with owners (and their representatives) having more power, status, and wealth than those who are hired to do the work. Almost all of the debates about better ways of organizing workplaces and managing employees, the need for unions and labour legislation, and the future of work in our society stem from this basic inequality.

Adam Smith: Competition, Not Conflict

Adam Smith (1723–90) wrote *The Wealth of Nations* in 1776, during the early Industrial Revolution in England, extolling the wealth-producing benefits of capitalism. Thus, he is often portrayed as the economic theorist whose ideas outlasted those of Marx who, writing some time later, predicted the eventual downfall of capitalism. Even today, Adam Smith's ideas are frequently used to call for less government intervention in the economy, the argument being that "the unseen hand of the market" is best left alone.

It is important to note, however, that Adam Smith did not condone the exploitation of workers. He recognized that working conditions in the industrializing British economy were far from satisfactory and argued that higher wages would increase the productivity of workers and the economy as a whole (Weiss 1976; Saul 1995: 150). But Smith was clear about what he saw as a key underlying principle of capitalism. *Competition among individuals and enterprises*, each trying to improve their own position, led to growth and the creation of wealth. As he put it, "It is not from the benevolence of the butcher, the brewer, or the baker, that we expect our dinner, but from their regard to their own self-interest" (Smith [1776] 1976: Book 2, Chapter 2: 14).

Thus, for Adam Smith, the "profit motive" was the driving force of capitalism. Individuals and firms in aggressive competition with each other produced the "wealth of nations." Where Marx (some decades later) saw conflict, exploitation, and growing inequality, Smith saw competition leading to greater wealth.

These different perspectives continue to underpin arguments for, on the one hand, restructuring employment relationships to reduce inequality and, on the other, eliminating barriers to competition that are perceived to be holding back the creation of wealth. These counter-positions highlight a central contradiction of capitalist economies. Many people like to believe that the "marketplace" is best left unchecked if greater wealth is to be produced. At the same time, it is clear that social inequality increases without labour legislation, employment insurance, and other programs that smooth the rough edges of capitalism. The question, then, is what kind of society do we want?

Diverse Perspectives on the Division of Labour

Human societies have always been characterized by a basic *division of labour*—essentially, how tasks are organized and distributed among workers. In primitive societies, work roles were assigned mainly according to age and gender. But with economic development, these roles became more specialized, and the arrival of industrial capitalism further intensified this process. Once a certain scale of production was reached, it was much more efficient to break complex jobs into their component tasks.

Pre-industrial skilled craftworkers are often idealized. C. Wright Mills, for example, emphasized the personal satisfaction derived from being involved in all aspects of the creation of some product, being free to make decisions about how the work should be done and to develop one's skills and abilities (1956: 220). Obviously, not all pre-industrial workers were fortunate enough to be craftworkers, but it is clear that such opportunities were reduced with the growth of industrial capitalism. Part of the change was due to the loss of control over work that accompanied the spread of wage-labour. Equally significant was the division of work processes into simpler and smaller tasks, each done by an individual worker.

In *The Wealth of Nations*, Adam Smith identified the division of labour as a key to capitalism's success. Using the example of a pin factory, he described how productivity could be greatly increased by assigning workers to specific tasks such as stretching wire, cutting it, and sharpening it. Whereas individual workers might produce 20 pins a day each by doing all of the operations themselves, with a well-defined division of labour, 10 people could make 48,000 pins a day. The greater productivity, Smith reasoned, came from the increased dexterity a worker could master in repeating a single task over and over again, the time saved in not having to change tasks and shift tools, and the added savings obtained from designing machines that workers could use to repeat the single task (Smith 1976; Braverman 1974: 76). The real advantage of this form of work organization would be realized only when factories made large quantities of a product—precisely the goal of industrial capitalism.

In 1832, Charles Babbage translated Smith's principles into practical cost-cutting advice for entrepreneurs. By subdividing tasks, he argued, less skill was required of any individual worker. Consequently, employers could pay less for this labour. Workers with fewer skills cannot demand as high a reward for their work (Braverman 1974: 79–83). The early history of industrialization is full of examples of this basic economic principle at work. The advent of factories with detailed divisions of labour invariably replaced skilled craftworkers with unskilled factory workers who were paid less—just the sort of outcome that Marx criticized.

Returning to Mills's description of the craft ideal, we can easily see some of the problems. A central feature of *craftwork* was the degree to which one individual was involved in all aspects of the creation of some product. The resulting sense of pride and self-fulfillment was an early casualty of industrialization. Furthermore, the minute subdividing of tasks in an efficient mass-production factory or administrative system inevitably led to repetitious, boring work. Little wonder, then, that many craftworkers actively resisted factory-based production.

Marx's discussions of work in capitalist society focused on the negative consequences of an excessive division of labour. For him, capitalism itself was the source of the problem. The division of labour was simply a means to create greater profits from the labour of the working class. The development of huge *assembly-line factories* in the early 20th century epitomized this trend. Henry Ford, the inventor of the assembly line, took considerable pride in recounting how his Model T factory had 7,882 specific jobs. Ford calculated that about half the jobs required only "ordinary men" and 949 required "strong, able-bodied men"; the rest, he reasoned, could be done by women, older children, or men who were physically disabled. These observations do not reflect a concern for workers with disabilities; instead, they highlight the extreme fragmentation of the labour process, to the point that even the simplest repetitions became a job.[11]

Émile Durkheim: Interdependence and Social Cohesion

Émile Durkheim (1858–1917), an early French sociologist, provided an alternative, conservative assessment of capitalist employment relations, particularly the division of labour. He noted that industrial societies contained diverse populations in terms of race, ethnicity, religion, occupation, and education—not to mention differences in beliefs and values. Durkheim pointed to evidence in European industrialization of group differences creating conflict over how scarce resources should be distributed, over rights and privileges, and over which beliefs and values set the standard. Durkheim saw the division of labour as a source of *social cohesion* that reduced this potential for conflict.[12] He reasoned that individuals and groups engaged in different tasks in a complex division of labour would recognize their mutual interdependence. In turn, tolerance and social harmony would be generated.

Durkheim believed that individuals in modern society are forced to rely on each other because of the different occupational positions they fill. In simple terms, lawyers need plumbers to fix their sinks while plumbers need teachers to educate their children. By the same logic, capitalists and their employees are interdependent. Without cooperation between the two groups, the economy would grind to a halt. We will see in later chapters how Durkheim's positive assessment of the division of labour shaped management theories that assume shared interests in the workplace. While Marx has influenced conflict perspectives on work in modern society, the conservative assumptions of Durkheim's general model are the backbone of the *consensus approach*.

Max Weber on Bureaucratic Organizations

Max Weber (1864–1920), a German sociologist writing in the early 20th century, addressed yet another major change accompanying capitalist industrialization: *bureaucracy*. Weber noted that Western societies were becoming more rational, a trend most visible in the bureaucratic organization of work. Informal relationships among small groups of workers, and between workers and employers, increasingly were being replaced by more formal, impersonal work relations in large bureaucracies. Rules and regulations were now determining workers' behaviour. Although Weber was concerned about the resulting loss of personal work relationships, he believed that this development was far outweighed by greater organizational efficiency. For Weber, bureaucracy and capitalism went hand in hand. Industrial capitalism was a system of rationally organized economic activities; bureaucracies provided the most appropriate organizational framework for such activities.

What defined Weber's "ideal-type" bureaucracy was a precise division of labour within a hierarchy of authority (Weber 1946: 196–98). Each job had its own duties and responsibilities, and each was part of a chain of command in which orders could be passed down and rewards and punishments used to ensure that the orders were followed. But the power of the employer could not extend beyond the bureaucracy. The contract linking employer and employee was binding only within the work relationship. Also necessary for efficiency were extensive written records of decisions made and transactions completed.

Recruitment into and promotion within the bureaucratic work organization were based on competence, performance skills, and certifications such as educational credentials. Individual employees could make careers within the organization as they moved as far up the hierarchy as their skills and initiative would carry them. Employment contracts assured workers a position so long as they were needed and competently performed the functions of the office. In short, rationality, impersonality, and formal contractual relationships defined the bureaucratic work organization.

Yet bureaucracies were not unique to 19th-century capitalism. A somewhat similar form of centralized government had existed in ancient China, and European societies had been organizing their armies in this manner for centuries. What was unique, however, was the extent to which workplaces became bureaucratized under capitalism. At the beginning of the 20th century, increased competition and the development of big, complex industrial systems demanded even more rationalized production techniques and worker-control systems. Large bureaucratic work organizations would become the norm throughout the industrial capitalist world. But bureaucracy also became the norm during the 20th century in industrialized communist countries of the former Soviet bloc. So, while closely intertwined, bureaucracy and capitalism are, in fact, separate phenomena.

● CONCLUSION

From feudalism to early capitalism to the rise of industrialization in Canada, we have covered a lot of ground in this chapter. We began with a historical overview of the origins and development of industrial capitalism, then considered various theories that explain and evaluate the causes and consequences of this complex process. As economies and societies continually evolve and the nature of work is transformed, new social theories have emerged (see Chapter 2). Here, we have highlighted the most important social and economic changes unleashed by the Industrial Revolution in Europe. As feudalism gave way to capitalism, markets grew in importance. A new class structure evolved, and a predominantly rural society became urban. Factory-based wage labour became the norm, while craft-work declined. Larger workplaces demanded new organizational forms and, in time, bureaucracies evolved to fill this need. And while industrial innovations led to substantial increases in productivity, it was some time before the standard of living of the working class began to reflect this increase. These far-reaching social and economic changes were the focus of early sociologists such as Karl Marx, Émile Durkheim, and Max Weber, as well as economists like Adam Smith. Many of the key questions they raised—over capitalism's capacity to generate inequality and conflict, or greater prosperity and interdependence—continue to be debated today. Although late to industrialize, compared to Britain and the United States, Canada faced many similar concerns. Having had a brief look at the changing worlds that these social theorists were observing, we are now better equipped to understand how their concerns and conclusions carry into the present day.

● DISCUSSION QUESTIONS

1. What is industrial capitalism, and how did it differ from previous ways of organizing work?
2. How did industrial capitalism develop in Canada? In what ways did Canada follow the path of other countries, such as Britain? In what ways was the Canadian experience unique?

3. How did Karl Marx, Adam Smith, Émile Durkheim, and Max Weber believe industrial capitalism would affect workers? What are some of the main differences in their ideas?

4. How does the nature of work in early industrializing Canada compare to work today? Thinking broadly, what would be some of the essential similarities and differences?

ADDITIONAL RESOURCES

WORK AT THE MOVIES

- *Margaret's Museum* (directed by Mort Ransen, 1995, 114 minutes). Adapted from the book *The Glace Bay Miners' Museum* by Canadian Sheldon Currie, this film explores the impact of mining on individuals, families, and communities in 1940s Cape Breton, as seen through the eyes of Margaret MacNeil (played by Helen Bonham Carter).
- *The Grapes of Wrath* (directed by John Ford, 1940, 129 minutes). Based on John Steinbeck's novel, this film follows the Joad family who lose their Oklahoma farm during the Great Depression and become migrant workers in search of new opportunities.
- *The Voyageurs* (directed by Bernard Devlin, 1964, 19:50 minutes). This short historical film re-creates scenes of 19th-century fur-trade work in Canada. It is available through the National Film Board of Canada: www. nfb.ca/film/voyageurs.
- *Why the Industrial Revolution Happened Here* (produced by Charles Colville, 2013, 57:55 minutes). This BBC documentary examines the economic, social, and political conditions that sparked the Industrial Revolution in Britain and led to a massive transformation of the British economy.

SOUNDS OF WORK

- "Dust Bowl Refugee" (Woody Guthrie). Based, in part, on Guthrie's own experiences in the American Dust Bowl in the 1930s, this song tells the story of the travelling migrant workers of that era.
- "John Henry" (Traditional/Bruce Springsteen). Springsteen's rendition helps preserve the legacy of American folk hero, John Henry, who perished during the construction of a railroad tunnel.

- "Peg and Awl" (Traditional). This tune conveys how the Industrial Revolution brought new technologies that caused the demise of many pre-industrial crafts.

NOTES

1. Abridged from Joyce Doyle's (1980) *Our Family History*.
2. Beaud's (1983) history of capitalism is a major source for our brief discussion; see also Grint (1991: 48–83) on pre-industrial and early industrial work patterns.
3. Over the centuries, however, technological innovations did lead to important changes in work patterns. See, for example, White's (1962) detailed historical analysis of the impact of draught horses and the wheeled plough on agriculture, and of the effects of the invention of the stirrup on the practice of warfare.
4. Grint (1991: 69–73). Cohen (1988: 24) concludes that industrialization in Canada did not lead to a sharper gender-based division of labour since (as was not the case in England) such segmentation already existed.
5. Polanyi (1957). See Boyer and Drache (1996: 8–12) for an application of Polanyi's ideas to the current era.
6. This discussion is drawn from a variety of sources, many cited individually below. For a useful overview of this period in Canadian history, see Ryerson (1968), Laxer (1989), Kealey (1995: Part 1), Palmer (1992), and the Canadian labour studies journal, *Labour/Le Travail*.
7. Bleasdale, Ruth. (1981). "Class Conflict on the Canals of Upper Canada in the 1840s." *Labour/Le Travail* 7:9–39, p. 13. See Wylie (1983) on the building of the Rideau Canal.
8. Bradwin (1972); see Avery (1995) and Creese (1988–89) on strikes and radical behaviour among immigrant workers.
9. Mine accidents that took the lives of many miners at one time are mainly responsible for these high averages. For example, 189 miners died in a mine explosion in Hillcrest, Alberta, in 1914. A memorial to these miners and background on the disaster can be found at http://coalminersmemorial.tripod.com/hillcrestminedisaster.html. See McCormack (1978: 9) on British Columbia and Caragata (1979: 16–21) on Alberta coal miners during this era.
10. Engels, Friedrich. (1971). *The Condition of the Working Class in England*. Oxford: Basil Blackwell, p. 63. (Orig. pub. 1845.)
11. Toffler (1980: 50) provides the quote from Henry Ford.
12. Durkheim (1960) did allow that a "forced" division of labour, where individuals have no choice over how they participate in the productive system, would not lead to increased social solidarity. He argued, however, that this and other "abnormal" forms of the division of labour would disappear as industrial capitalism matured further.

CONTEMPORARY DEBATES ON WORK (1950s TO PRESENT DAY)

"A fire killed 10 people at a garment factory in Bangladesh about six months after a factory building collapse that killed 1,100 people exposed the harsh and often unsafe conditions in an industry that is the world's third-largest. Authorities and global clothing companies have pledged to improve safety standards in Bangladesh's garment industry after the Rana Plaza collapse and numerous other fatal accidents. The cause of the fire at the Aswad garment factory in Gazipur outside Dhaka was not immediately known, but the government was investigating...."

"Another garment factory fire last November killed 112 workers in a building authorities said did not have enough exits. Bangladesh earns $20 billion a year from garment exports, mainly to the United States and Europe. The sector employs about four million workers, mostly women."

Source: CBC News (2013, October 9). Used with permission of The Associated Press. Copyright © 2014. All rights reserved.

● INTRODUCTION

Today's global economy offers some starkly contrasting images of work. In cities such as Toronto, Vancouver, New York, and London, we can observe well-dressed, mobile professionals streaming through bustling airports and gleaming office towers, working their cellphones while hailing cabs or boarding planes, en route to the next destination. Surrounding them, in fast-food courts, restaurants, hotels, and taxis, are legions of service workers—often youth or immigrants—rustling up meals and scrubbing floors, all for minimum wage. Halfway around the globe, in countries such as Bangladesh and China, young workers—typically women—stitch the latest fashions or assemble laptops, working long days in poor conditions that eerily resemble the early factories and sweatshops just discussed in Chapter 1.

Such images highlight the dramatic, and uneven, changes taking place as a result of innovative new technologies and the global flow of workers and work. In recent decades, new occupations and ways of working have sprung up. New economic regions and new forms of globalized production have also emerged, along with political arrangements favouring freer trade, globalization, and the deregulation of labour markets. Together, these developments raise important questions. How is the nature of work and inequality changing, both within Canada and others nations, and between the global North and South? Are we witnessing fundamental, "epochal" changes in the world of work? Or are recent developments more incremental, mixing elements of continuity and change? Building on our historical discussions in Chapter 1, this chapter examines developments from the 1950s to the present, including postindustrialism, globalization, economic restructuring, and the rise of new economic regions. We also discuss new forms of work, such as interactive service work and emotional work, and consider how more recent thinkers, such as Ulrich Beck, Pierre Bourdieu, and Michel Foucault, may help us understand contemporary workplace and economic change.

■ CHANGING ECONOMIES IN THE 20TH AND 21ST CENTURIES

The Managerial Revolution

Despite being a late industrializer, Canada had a strong resource- and manufacturing-based economy by the early 20th century. Large corporations had also begun to dominate business affairs. Formerly, most manufacturing enterprises had been owned and controlled by individuals or families. Then came the joint-stock companies in which hundreds, sometimes thousands, of investors shared ownership and profits. Such a diverse group of owners obviously could not directly control the giant corporation in which they had invested. Consequently, a class of managers who could run the enterprise became essential (Berle and Means 1968).

As this pattern spread, observers began to question the Marxist model of industrial capitalism that portrayed the relations of production as a simple two-class system: capitalists who owned and controlled the means of production versus workers who had little choice but to exchange their labour for a wage. An alternative model became popular. The *managerial revolution* theory predicted a new era of reduced conflict and greater harmony in the workplace (Burnham 1941). The theory held that *managers*, who were salaried workers and not owners, would look beyond profits when making decisions: the good of both the company and the workers would be equally important. Since ownership of the firm was now diffused among many individuals, power and control of the enterprise had essentially shifted to a new class of professional managers (an occupational group that has grown dramatically in size, as we discuss in Chapters 3 and 4).

Many decades of debate and research later, it is generally agreed that this perspective on industrial relations in capitalist society was overly optimistic and exaggerated the degree of change (Zeitlin 1974; Hill 1981). First, family ownership patterns may be less common, but they have not disappeared. In Canada, the prominence of names such as Molson, McCain, Bronfman, and Weston (as in Galen Weston Jr. in the Superstore commercials) demonstrate the continuing role of powerful families in the corporate sector. Furthermore, while ownership of corporations involves more individuals, many corporations are still controlled by small groups of minority shareholders. Individuals who serve as directors of major corporations are linked in a tight network of overlapping relationships, with many sitting on the boards of several major corporations simultaneously. Another postwar trend has been the corporate ownership of shares. Concentration of ownership increased as a few large holding companies replaced individual shareholders. Thus, the belief that the relatively small and powerful capitalist class described by Marx has virtually disappeared is not supported by current evidence.[1]

Advocates of the managerial revolution theory also must demonstrate that, compared with earlier capitalists, the new breed of managers is less influenced by the bottom line of profit. But research continues to show that senior managers and corporate executives think and act in much the same way as capitalist owners. They share similar worldviews, often come from the same social backgrounds as owners, and hold large blocks of shares in the corporation, where they frequently serve as directors, as well. In brief, the optimistic predictions of an era of industrial harmony brought on by new patterns of corporate ownership and management are largely unfounded.

■ POSTINDUSTRIALISM

Postindustrial Society

In the latter half of the 20th century, continuing social and economic change led some social scientists to argue that we had moved out of the industrial era into a *postindustrial society*. Daniel Bell, writing in the early 1970s, was among the first to note these transformations in the U.S. occupational structure.[2] The Industrial Revolution had seen jobs in the manufacturing and processing sectors replace agricultural jobs. After World War II, jobs in the service sector became much more prominent. The number of factory workers was decreasing, while employment in the areas of education, health, social welfare, entertainment, government, trade, finance, and a variety of other business sectors was rising. White-collar workers were beginning to outnumber blue-collar workers.

Bell argued that postindustrial societies would engage most workers in the production and dissemination of knowledge, rather than in goods production as in industrial capitalism. While industrialization had brought increased productivity and higher living standards, postindustrial society would usher in an era of reduced concentration of power (Bell 1973: 358–67). Power would no longer merely reside in the ownership of property, but also in access to knowledge and in the ability to think and to solve problems. *Knowledge workers*—technicians, professionals, and scientists—would become a large and important class. Their presence would begin to reduce the polarization of classes that had typified the industrial age. In contrast to the managerial revolution thesis, which envisioned a new dominant class of managers, Bell felt that knowledge workers would become the elite of the postindustrial age.

Creative Economies

In the early 2000s, Richard Florida (2002) has added to this line of thinking in *The Rise of the Creative Class*. Like Bell, Florida sees the shift from goods to knowledge production as a crucial change. But for Florida, knowledge and information are simply the tools and materials for what really drives growth in a postindustrial age—*creativity*. Mapping the U.S. economy, Florida suggests there is an emerging *creative class* that accounts for roughly one-third of workers. At the top is a *super creative core* of scientists and engineers, poets, professors, novelists, entertainers, and artists. A second layer includes *creative professionals*, who possess high levels of human capital and formal education, and work in a range of fields, such as business, finance, and law. According to Florida, these workers are transforming the economy through a new work ethic that places high priority on interesting work, flexible forms of organization, and creative places in which to live.

But what about those left out of this elite group? Writing about this in *The Flight of the Creative Class*, Florida (2005) acknowledges a growing divide between creative workers and a "service class" who provide cleaning, childcare, and other services for them. Other writers such as Robert Reich (2000) in *The Future of Success* have also noted that the knowledge economy offers great opportunities for well-educated, creative workers. But at the other end of the economic spectrum, job quality has eroded sharply through declining pay and job security and increased demands for continual effort. Reflecting on this economic divide, Reich remarks, "Not for a century has America endured, or tolerated, this degree of inequality" (2000: 107). Likewise, Florida notes that today the United States is the most unequal of all industrialized nations, with inequality rates nearly double those of Sweden and Japan (2005: 186). McGuigan (2009) also offers a critical perspective on creative economies in his book, *Cool Capitalism*.

Why the optimism in the early theories of postindustrial society? These explanations of social and economic change were developed in the decades following World War II, a time of significant economic growth in North America.[3] White-collar occupational opportunities were increasing, educational institutions were expanding, and the overall standard of living was rising: hence, the optimistic tone of the social theories being developed. Yet, as we discuss at various points in this book, other commentators paint a negative picture of the rise of service industries and an expanding white-collar workforce. These critical perspectives point to job deskilling, reduced economic security, the dehumanizing impact of computers, and widening labour market polarization—trends that have become more pronounced since the early 1980s (Beck 1992, 2000).

These themes have also been revisited in debates about the *new economy*, which essentially refers to industries based on new information and communication technology, especially the Internet. As Don Tapscott (1996: 43) has argued, what distinguishes the old industrial economy from the new "digital economy" is that the latter is "built on silicon, computers, and networks" and its main inputs and outputs are information. Thus, the new economy is also a knowledge-based economy. Taking stock of these trends, sociologist Manuel Castells (1996, 1998) concludes that a new technical–economic paradigm, or model, has emerged: a networked society. As old boundaries imposed by time and space have broken down, opportunities to organize our collective and individual lives in more flexible ways emerge, with profound implications for society. The big unanswered question, of course, is who the winners and losers will be. There are growing concerns about a "digital divide," based on social groups or communities that are included in or excluded from the technology and knowledge of the new economy. Research continues to assess how information technology affects working conditions and rewards (Hughes and Lowe 2000; Sciadas 2002), an issue we return to later in this chapter and in subsequent chapters.

Industrial Restructuring and Precarious Work

Technological change continues to accelerate at a time when the global economy is also undergoing dramatic change. In the early 1980s and early 1990s, economic recession, fierce international competition, multinational free trade arrangements, and the spectacular growth of other economies had a major impact on Canada. In the 2000s, Canada likewise felt the brunt of the 2008 global downturn, though to a lesser extent than many other countries around the world. With growing economic interdependence, it is becoming more difficult to think in terms of discrete national economies. In the words of Robert Reich, "Money, technology, information, and goods are flowing across national borders with unprecedented rapidity and ease" (1991: 6). This *globalization* of economic activity continues to bring about fundamental read-justments in the Canadian economy and labour market, including plant shut-downs, job loss through downsizing, corporate reorganization and mergers, and the relocation or expansion of company operations outside Canada.[4]

But are these trends new? Writing in the early 20th century, economist Joseph Schumpeter considered *industrial restructuring* a basic feature of capitalism. According to Schumpeter, this process of "creative destruction" involves breaking down old ways of running industry and building up more competitive, efficient, and high-technology alternatives.[5] North American industry clearly is engaged in this process today. But while necessary for the economy as a whole, industrial restructuring can also diminish the quality and quantity of work for individuals. Job losses may be part of the process for some, while others may experience reduced job security.

Industrial restructuring involves interrelated social, economic, and technological trends. Crucial is the shift from manufacturing to services. Canada's service industries have rapidly grown in recent decades, compared with declining employment in agriculture, resource, and manufacturing industries. Indeed, both Canada and the United States have experienced *deindustrialization*. This concept refers to declining employment due to factory closures or relocation, typically in once-prominent manufacturing industries: steel, automotives, textiles, clothing, chemicals, and plastics. Once mainstays of the Canadian and U.S. economies, these industries are now sometimes referred to as "sunset industries" because they have failed to adapt quickly to shifting consumer demands. Factories have been sold off, shut down, or relocated to areas such as Mexico, China, or other developing nations where labour is cheap and employment rights and environmental standards are lax.

Canada has been vulnerable to processes of deindustrialization. In the 1990s, dozens of large multinationals, encouraged by the Canada–U.S. free trade agreement, announced or implemented plant closures in central Canada, seeking cheaper labour and fewer regulations. For example, after purchasing the Bauer hockey equipment company, Nike announced in 1997 that it was closing the Ontario factory.[6]

But Canadian-owned firms have made similar moves. As Canadian corporate giants like Bombardier have become global competitors, they have shifted more of their operations and, therefore, job opportunities out of the country to low-wage countries such as Mexico and China. Today Canada's once-strong manufacturing sector is increasingly vulnerable, with many workers facing layoffs and unemployment (Bernard, 2009, Vrankulj, 2012).

▉ GLOBAL TRANSFORMATIONS

Globalization

The term *globalization* has become part of everyday language, but what does it really mean, and can evidence document such a trend? The basic idea is not new; in Canada's colonial past, the masters of the British empire no doubt envisioned their reach as global. Yet searching for a definition of *globalization*, one is struck by the great many meanings it conveys. Advocates of globalization echo ideas discussed later in this chapter: notably, the "logic of industrialism" view, which sees the spread of capitalist markets and national convergence as inevitable. As Gordon Laxer explains, globalization typically refers to four interrelated changes:

> *Economic changes* include the internationalization of production, the harmonization of tastes and standards and the greatly increased mobility of capital and of transnational corporations. *Ideological changes* emphasize investment and trade liberalization, deregulation and private enterprise. *New information and communications technologies* that shrink the globe signal a shift from goods to services. Finally, *cultural changes* involve trends toward a universal world culture and the erosion of the nation-state.[7]

Corporations and often governments promote globalization as a means by which expanding "free markets" will generate economic growth and elevate living standards. Signs of an increasingly global economy are visible in multinational trade agreements, financial markets, and economic treaties. Examples include the North American Free Trade Agreement (NAFTA), the European Union, and the Association of Southeast Asian Nations (ASEAN); international regulatory frameworks such as the World Trade Organization (WTO); and the integration of financial markets through information technology. Critics—and there are many—detect more sinister aspects of globalization. For example, the protesters at the Summit of the Americas in Quebec City in April 2001 (where government leaders from Canada, the United States, and Central and South America discussed creating a free trade area of the Americas by 2005) raised concerns that such treaties threaten national cultures, workers' rights, the environment—and ultimately, democracy. In the 2000s, activists have organized through vehicles such as the World Social Forum (WSF) and the Occupy movement to voice their concerns. Even mainstream commentators such as Nobel Prize–winning economist Joseph Stiglitz recognize basic challenges (Stiglitz 2006, 2012). Thus, as Thomas Friedman writes in his book on globalization, *The Lexus and the Olive Tree*:

> Any society that wants to thrive economically today must constantly be trying to build a better Lexus and driving it out into the world. But no one should have any illusions that merely participating in

this global economy will make a society healthy. If that participation comes at the price of a country's identity, if individuals feel their olive tree roots crushed, or washed out, by this global system, those olive tree roots will rebel.[8]

Community-based opposition is only one reason why a globally integrated economic system remains largely an ideal. In a truly global economy, corporations would operate in a completely transnational way, not rooted in a specific national economy. But research suggests that there are few such corporations (Hirst and Thompson 1995). While McDonald's, IBM, and General Motors may do business in many countries, operating vast networks of subcontractors and suppliers, they remain U.S. based. The United States and the European Union still account for a significant part of world trade (both goods and services) through corporations located mainly in those countries, though China now plays a leading role (WTO 2012). While multinational corporations account for 25 percent of the world's production, they employ only 3 percent of the world's labour force (Giles 1996: 6). Even so, computers, software, clothes, shoes, cars, and a vast range of other goods are produced by global business networks that span several continents. Some observers argue that large corporations' sustained power will depend on creating and controlling these networks or "business alliances" (Harrison 1997). However, Anthony Giles (1996: 6) cautions, "Beyond the obvious technological, economic and logistical hurdles, there are a host of cultural, legal, political and linguistic factors which complicate the development of genuine globally integrated production systems."

It is much easier to imagine production systems spanning several continents than it is to envision a largely global labour force. Despite expanding international markets for some goods and services, labour is still a local resource. According to Hirst and Thompson (1995: 420), "Apart from a 'club-class' of internationally mobile, highly skilled professionals, and the desperate, poor migrants and refugees who will suffer almost any hardship to leave intolerable conditions, the bulk of the world's populations now cannot easily move." In fact, Canada plays an important role in this regard, being one of the few nations to accept relatively large numbers of immigrants annually.

Picking up on this theme, Saskia Sassen (2002) argues that mainstream accounts of globalization have overemphasized the export of low-wage work to developing nations while ignoring the growing role migrant workers play in the industrialized North. As Sassen points out, the managerial, professional, and technical elite who live in global cities are increasingly dependent on low-paid service workers to maintain the infrastructure that allows them to do their work. Office buildings need to be cleaned; young children and elderly parents need to be cared for. Groceries must be purchased, meals made, and dishes done. Much of this work, as well as other vital services, is done by migrant women, many of whom have moved in search of work to support their own families back home (see also Stasiulis and Bakan 2003; Zimmerman, Litt, and Bose 2006).

Although labour might not become part of a truly global market, globalization may still have an impact on labour practices, notably through the public's growing concern about the labour practices of nationally based firms operating in developing countries (one could say the same about environmental practices). Global media coverage has helped to raise North Americans' awareness. In the past, multinational corporations such as Nike and Liz Claiborne have been the targets of public campaigns because of their global labour practices. More recently, in response to devastating tragedies involving garment workers—for example, the 2012 fire in the Tazreen Fashion Factory and the 2013 collapse of the Rana Plaza in Bangladesh, which, together, claimed over 1,200 lives—there is growing public and political pressure for compensation, improved working conditions, and stronger legal protection of workers. Despite efforts of many organizations, such as the International Labour Organization and the Clean Clothes Campaign, however, only a few of the corporations involved in these tragedies have agreed to participate in compensation funds set up for families of the victims.[9]

Canada and Free Trade

Since the late 1980s, Canada's economy has been increasingly shaped by free trade agreements. The 1989 Free Trade Agreement (FTA) with the United States and the 1994 North American Free Trade Agreement (NAFTA), which included Mexico, committed Canada to a policy of more open, less regulated markets. While claims of massive job losses directly from the FTA and the NAFTA have not been borne out, the permanent factory closures and job losses that occurred in central Canada in the early 1990s have been partly linked to free trade. Nevertheless, new job creation and growth in Canada and the United States have offset these losses. Significant industrial restructuring was already taking place, but the FTA probably accelerated the process, allowing the individuals and communities negatively affected less time to respond. Between the first quarter of 1990 and the second quarter of 1991, Canada lost 273,000 manufacturing jobs, a decline of 13 percent in the industry as a whole. As the Economic Council of Canada (1992: 4) concluded, "Many of the jobs that were lost will not return." These issues are presumably being monitored, since NAFTA includes both an accord on labour and a commission for labour cooperation, which is mandated to track labour market trends in the three NAFTA countries and to address complaints about workers' rights, collective bargaining, and labour standards.[10]

To put NAFTA in perspective, the three participating countries had a combined labour force of approximately 223.4 million in 2012, with about 70 percent in the United States (154.9 million), 22 percent in Mexico (49.7 million), and 8 percent in Canada (18.6 million) (United States Department of Labor 2013). In the early 2000s, all three countries had roughly similar levels of growth in Gross Domestic Product (GDP), ranging from 2.3 to 2.6 percent (see Table 2.1). In the post-2008 period, however, Mexico has had slightly higher rates of GDP growth. In the United States, the question of NAFTA became a point of debate in the 2008 U.S. Democratic Party primaries with then-senators Hillary Clinton and Barack Obama both promising to reopen and renegotiate core provisions of the treaty, including existing side agreements on labour and environmental issues (Alexandroff, Hufbauer, and Lucenti 2008). Although Obama quickly backtracked on this issue in the primaries, he did voice concerns over the impact of free trade on the U.S. economy after becoming President: he argued for the need to increase U.S. exports in order to spur domestic growth and job numbers (*Washington Post* 2010). In the United States, a trend to "reshoring," or bringing back production to the United States from other countries, has emerged, though the share of jobs involved is small. For instance, firms such as GE have recently relocated some of their production from China to Kentucky (*Economist* 2013).

What has been the impact of NAFTA? At the outset, the migration of jobs from Canada or the United States to Mexico was a major concern of NAFTA opponents. In the 1990s, there was little doubt that the *maquiladora* factories along Mexico's northern border were booming; indeed, from

1990 to 2000, the number of *maquila* plants and employees saw dramatic growth, effectively doubling in numbers, though levels have tailed off since (Commission for Labor Cooperation 2003: 81; Scott, Salas, and Campbell 2006: 44). Were these "new" jobs or jobs relocated from high-wage countries, such as Canada or Japan? From available evidence, it seems that fewer jobs than expected have migrated south.[11] And much of the new foreign investment in Mexico is due not just to NAFTA but to the proliferation of global trade and production, with firms based in Japan, East Asia, and Europe seeking a Mexican base from which to supply the North American consumer market. Over time, maquilas have also become more diverse, as auto and pharmaceutical manufacturers such as Volkswagen, Honda, Eli Lilly, and Mercedes Benz have set up operations.

Jobs may be migrating south, but only in some manufacturing industries, and if firms seek low wages, they will likely relocate to China, Bangladesh, Vietnam, and other "low-cost" countries, not Mexico. There is just as much concern that competitive pressures from NAFTA in some manufacturing industries, such as auto and auto parts manufacturing, have accelerated the trend toward *nonstandard or contingent* work in the United States and Canada (Roberts, Hyatt, and Dorman 1996). This kind of work can be part time, temporary, or contract. Workers in Canada's resource industries have also benefited less than they could, given U.S. refusals to comply with NAFTA rulings on ongoing softwood lumber disputes.

Others would argue that the group most negatively affected by NAFTA is Mexican workers. While maquila workers' low pay, lack of rights, and working conditions may be deplorable by Canadian standards, they are part of an emerging middle class in Mexico and relatively advantaged compared to the majority of Mexicans: the rural poor. The Zapatista uprising in the rural state of Chiapas in 1994 briefly drew the world's attention to those who are not benefiting from NAFTA. Though maquila workers face an uphill battle, they have had some success organizing for better pay and benefits (Kopinak 1996: 199). More recently, they have worked with Canadian and U.S. labour and student groups to bring complaints about labour rights violations under NAFTA's labour side agreement. The Maquiladora Solidarity Network (MSN) in Canada and the United Students Against Sweatshops (USAS) are just two examples of emerging global solidarity networks that help monitor and challenge labour violations.

◼ RETHINKING INDUSTRIALIZATION

Contemporary changes, such as globalization, have prompted rethinking of traditional ideas about industrialization. Although countries differ in the timing, pace, and form of industrialization, there appear to be some similar underlying dynamics and processes. Industrialized countries tend to be highly urbanized; production typically takes place on a big scale using complex technologies; workplaces tend to be organized bureaucratically; and white-collar workers make up most of the workforce. Citizens are reasonably well educated, and generally an individual's level of education and training is related to her or his occupation. Such similarities led American social scientists in the 1950s to claim:

> The world is entering a new age—the age of total industrialism. Some countries are far along the road, many more are just beginning the journey. But everywhere, at a faster pace or a slower pace, the peoples of the world are on the march towards industrialism.[12]

This is the *logic of industrialism thesis*, a deterministic and linear argument about the immensity and inevitability of industrial technology. It contends that industrialism is such a powerful force that any country, whatever its original characteristics, will eventually come to resemble other industrialized countries. In current debates about globalization, the same argument has been restated as a *thesis of economic, political, and cultural convergence.* Yet, as we will see in later chapters, comparisons of work patterns in various industrialized countries do not support this prediction. For example, there are pronounced cross-national variations in unemployment rates, innovative forms of work organization, unionization and industrial relations systems, and education and training. And as noted below, globalization also is not a standardized process, but rather is playing out quite differently at national, regional, and community levels.

Our historical overview in Chapter 1 illustrates that Canada's industrialization occurred later and was shaped by its colonial status; that immigration was a major factor in creating a workforce; and that resource industries played a central role. Other countries such as Sweden and Japan also industrialized later, but their experiences differed from Canada's. In recent decades, many nations have undergone rapid industrialization. For example, Central and South American nations such as Mexico and Brazil have seen rapid industrialization as well as pronounced inequality (Milanovic 2011; Stiglitz 2012; Piketty 2014). In each case, however, the process has varied. Likewise, the experiences of the "tiger nations" of East Asia, and the more recent and rapid expansion of China, India, and the former Soviet Union, highlight significant diversity in how change unfolds, as we discuss shortly. Other than at the broadest level of analysis, there does not appear to be an inherent *logic of industrialism* (Rodrik 2007; Whyte 2009).

This observation becomes clear when we compare the 23 countries presented in Table 2.1. Keep in mind that comparing nations at different phases and levels of development presents challenges because perfectly comparable data are lacking. However, the World Bank and other organizations have constructed basic comparative measures that are as precise as we can get, so we use these in Table 2.1. Canada provides a useful benchmark for interpreting the relative socioeconomic conditions in other countries. After noting which countries are included in Table 2.1, scan each column to get a sense of the huge differences in population, urbanization, per capita income, annual economic growth, education, female labour force participation, and inequality (measured by the GINI coefficient, where 0 is perfect equality and 100 is maximum inequality). Keep in mind that, in many developing nations, significant economic activity still occurs in informal sectors of the economy, so it may not be captured in the official government statistics presented in Table 2.1 (Jütting and de Laiglesia 2009; Portes 2005). Still, these basic social and economic development indicators raise a host of questions about the underlying historical, cultural, and political contexts in which countries industrialize.

We should also be attuned to matters of timing and the changing fortunes of national economies. For instance, in the period after World War II, Japan attracted great attention due to its rapid growth—the "Japanese miracle"—and unique management practices. We discuss Japan in Chapter 9. In the 1980s, attention shifted to other countries, for example, the "Asian Tigers," and more recently, China, India, Russia, and Brazil. We discuss these countries here in order to highlight how processes of economic development differ.

The East Asian Tigers

In the final decades of the 20th century, one group of countries that attracted significant attention from scholars, businesses, and politicians alike was the

Four Tigers of East Asia—Singapore, Hong Kong, Taiwan, and South Korea. In a short time span, these economies underwent rapid industrialization, either surpassing or fast approaching per capita incomes in the major Western industrial nations. While it took Britain 58 years (1780 to 1838) and the United States 47 years (1839 to 1886) for per capita gross domestic product (the total output of the economy) to double, it took South Korea only 11 years (1966 to 1977) (World Bank 1991). In the same region, another set of *newly industrializing countries* (NICs)—Thailand, Indonesia, and Malaysia—were following just behind the Four Tigers. The Four Tigers and the NICs exhibited impressive economic growth rates through most of the 1990s, but a major financial crisis in 1997–98 shook the foundations of many of these economies. Although recovery and renewed expansion occurred as of 2000 for a decade, strong economic growth was tempered by events such as the 2001 dot-com crash, the devastation of the 2004 tsunami (which affected parts of Indonesia and Thailand), and the 2008 global downturn (World Bank 2005b).

Signal features of the "East Asian miracle" were spectacular growth rates and greater reductions in income inequality than in other developing nations (World Bank 1993: 277). But other factors were important, too; these included rising output and productivity in agriculture at the same time that a manufacturing export sector was developing, steep declines in birthrates so that population growth was constrained, heavy investment in human resources through the expansion and improvement of educational systems, and a bureaucratic state run by a career civil service.

But this summary overstates the similarities among these nations; in fact, there are striking differences between them. For example, capitalism has taken distinctive forms in the Four Tigers.[13] A few giant diversified corporations, called "chaebol," have close ties to the state, dominating the South Korean economy. Taiwan's dynamic export sector is sustained by a network of highly flexible small- and medium-sized manufacturing firms with extensive *subcontracting systems* that often extend into the informal sector of the economy. In Hong Kong (and also Taiwan), the main organizing unit of business is the Chinese *family enterprise*. These firms give utmost priority to the long-term prosperity and reputation of the family—a very different concept than the rugged individualism of North American capitalism. Singapore is set apart by the prominent role of the state in setting the direction of industrialization, which has involved much greater reliance on direct investment by foreign multinational corporations.

TABLE 2.1 Social and Economic Indicators for Selected Countries

Country	Population in Millions (2011)[a]	Urban Population as % of Total (2011)[b]	GNI (PPP) per Capita in US$ (2011)[c]	Average Annual GDP % Growth[d]			% of Labour Force with Tertiary Education (Latest Available)[e]	Adult Female (15 years+) Economic Activity Rate (2012)[f]	GINI Coefficient (Latest Available)[g]	Unemployment Rate as % of Total Labour Force[h]	
				2002–8	2009–12	2009 Only				2009	2012
Canada	34.5	81	39,710	2.4	1.2	-2.8	47	62	32.35	8.29	7.33
United States	311.6	82	48,820	2.3	1.1	-3.5	22	58	37.82	9.28	8.23
Brazil	196.7	85	11,420	4.0	2.7	-0.3	9.3	60	50.10	8.08	6.00
Mexico	114.8	78	16,720	2.6	2.0	-5.9	17	44	47.55	5.45	4.80
Chile	17.3	89	16,300	4.4	4.0	-1.0	26	47	49.40	10.83	6.64
India	1,241.5	31	3,620	7.4	7.1	8.5	10	29	33.38	—	—
China	1,351.2	51	8,390	11.0	9.2	9.2	—	68	47.40	4.30	4.10
Indonesia	242.3	51	4,500	5.4	5.9	4.6	7	51	34.10	7.87	6.20
Thailand	69.5	34	8,360	5.1	3.0	-2.3	17	64	40.02	1.50	0.68
Korea (Republic)	49.8	83	29,920	4.4	3.1	0.3	35	49	40.02	3.65	3.30
Singapore	5.2	100	59,380	6.4	5.1	-0.9	28	57	47.80	3.03	2.13
Japan	127.8	91	34,670	1.2	0.1	-5.5	41	49	32.92	5.05	4.51
Russian Federation	143.0	74	21,210	6.8	1.1	-7.8	54	56	40.11	8.40	6.00
Ukraine	45.7	69	7,040	6.7	-1.3	-14.8	—	53	26.44	8.84	7.80
United Kingdom	62.7	80	35,950	2.6	-0.6	-4.0	37	56	33.00	7.45	8.13
Germany	81.8	74	40,190	1.4	0.7	-5.1	28	53	29.00	7.74	5.21
Sweden	9.4	85	42,210	2.7	1.4	-5.0	33	59	24.40	8.30	7.50
France	65.4	86	35,910	1.6	0.2	-3.1	32	51	30.80	9.50	10.14
Switzerland	7.9	74	52,530	2.2	1.0	-1.9	33	61	29.70	3.71	3.38
Saudi Arabia	28.1	82	24,700	6.3	5.7	0.1	—	18	—	10.46	—

United Arab Emirates	7.9	84	47,890	6.0	1.2	—	44	—	—
Egypt	82.5	43	6,120	5.0	3.5	4.7	24	30.77	—
Nigeria	162.4	50	2,290	10.4	7.0	7.0	48	48.83	19.70

a: Source: World Bank. Available at http://data.worldbank.org/indicator/SP.POP.TOTL.

b: Source: World Bank. Available at http://data.worldbank.org/indicator/SP.URB.TOTL.IN.ZS.

c: Source: World Bank. Available at http://data.worldbank.org/indicator/NY.GNP.PCAP.PP.CD. Gross national income (GNI) per capita based on purchasing power parity (PPP). PPP GNI is gross national income (GNI) converted to international dollars using purchasing power parity rates. An international dollar has the same purchasing power over GNI as a U.S. dollar has in the United States. GNI is the sum of value added by all resident producers and any product taxes (less subsidies) not included in the valuation of output plus net receipts of primary income (compensation of employees and property income) from abroad.

d: Source: World Bank. Available at http://data.worldbank.org/indicator/NY.GDP.MKTP.KD.ZG. Annual percentage growth rate of gross domestic product (GDP) at market prices based on constant local currency. Aggregates are based on constant 2000 U.S. dollars. *GDP* is the sum of gross value added by all resident producers in the economy plus any product taxes and minus any subsidies not included in the value of the products.

e: Source: World Bank. Available at http://data.worldbank.org/indicator/SL.TLF.TERT.ZS. Due to availability reasons, percentages refer to different years: percentages for Thailand, Singapore, United Kingdom, Germany, Sweden, France, and Switzerland refer to 2010; percentages for Canada, Mexico, Chile, Indonesia, Japan, and Russia refer to 2008.

f: Source: United Nations Statistics Division, "Social Indicators" section, "Work" subsection. Available at http://unstats.un.org/unsd/demographic/products/socind/default.htm.

g: Source: World Bank, OECD, Eurostat, or National Bureaus of Statistics, depending on the country. The data for Canada, United States, Mexico, Chile, and Japan were compiled from the OECD data bank. Available at Fact Book, Country Statistical Profiles, 2011 edition section: http://stats.oecd.org/Index.aspx?QueryId=26068. The data for Republic of Korea, Indonesia, Thailand, Russian Federation, Ukraine, Egypt, and Nigeria were compiled from the World Bank data bank. Available at http://data.worldbank.org/indicator/SI.POV.GINI. The data for United Kingdom, Germany, Sweden, France, and Switzerland were compiled from Eurostat. Available at http://epp.eurostat.ec.europa.eu/tgm/table.do?tab=table&init=1&language=en&pcode= tessi190&plugin=0. The data for Brazil was compiled from IBGE (Brazilian Institute of Geography and Statistics). Available at http://saladeimprensa.ibge.gov.br/en/noticia?view=noticia& id=1&busca=1&idnoticia=2222. The data for Singapore was compiled from Statistics Singapore, "Key Household Trends Report 2012." Available at http://www.singstat.gov.sg/Publications/ publications_and_papers/household_income_and_expenditure/pp-s19.pdf. The data for China was produced by National Bureau of Statistics (NBS) and sourced from the *People's Daily*. Available at http://english.peopledaily.com.cn/90778/8101702.html. Due to availability reasons, GINI coefficients refer to different years: Canada (2010), United States (2010), Brazil (2011), Mexico (2010), Chile (2010), India (2005), China (2012), Indonesia (2005), Thailand (2009), Republic of Korea (2009), Singapore (2012), Japan (2010), Russian Federation (2009), Ukraine (2009), United Kingdom (2011), Germany (2011), Sweden (2011), France (2011), Switzerland (2011), Egypt (2008), and Nigeria (2010).

h: Source: International Monetary Fund (IMF). Available at: http://www.imf.org/external/pubs/ft/weo/2012/01/weodata/index.aspx.

These variations in business systems account for diverse industrialization paths and approaches to work organization within firms.

The Rise of Capitalism in the BRIC Economies (Brazil, the Former Soviet Union, India, and China)

Most recently, attention has turned to the most populous countries in the world—China and India —as they undergo unprecedented economic and social change. Media reports abound with stories of rich "peasants" in China buying German luxury cars, India's thriving "Silicon Valley," and the garishly lavish lifestyles of Russia's new entrepreneurs. How is economic change transforming these countries? Social scientists have examined this question, seeking to understand the complex shifts occurring in "transitional economies." Recent research looks beyond markets in a narrow economic sense, striving to present a more comprehensive explanation of what influences the economic behaviour of individuals in these societies. Factors such as a society's culture, norms, and customs, as well as existing social networks, state policies, and work organization, all influence how markets take shape and how individuals pursue new opportunities within them (Basu 2004; Jha 2002; Rodrik 2007; Whyte 2009; Winters and Yusuf 2007).

China is a case in point. Since introducing market reforms in the late 1970s, the Chinese economy has grown at an astonishing rate of nearly 10 percent per year (*Economist* 2009; World Bank 2005a). From 2002–8, China's average annual GDP growth rate was 11.0 percent, vastly outpacing that of Canada, the United States, and other industrialized countries (see Table 2.1). Even in the post-2008 context, as Table 2.1 shows, growth averaged 9.2 percent from 2009–12. As the world's most populous nation, with 1.35 billion inhabitants, China is seen by corporations as a huge market to conquer. Its workers are also being integrated into the global economy, especially in its "special economic zones," which attract foreign firms such as Wal-Mart and The Gap. "Made in China" now appears on a growing number of consumer items that Canadians buy. Indeed, China is a leading recipient of foreign direct investment by multinational corporations, with more than half of its trade now controlled by foreign firms (*Economist* 2009; Whyte 2009).[14] It is also making significant investments in the West, in particular, in the oil industry, including Canada's resource sector.

Is communist China being overtaken by capitalist free enterprise? The short answer is no, and the democratic reforms many hoped would flow from economic change have not taken root. But remarkable social and economic transformations are occurring, especially in coastal industrial regions in the south. Notably, the Chinese version of an entrepreneurial spirit is deeply rooted, and it can be seen in the rich and powerful dynasties established by mainland Chinese families who migrated throughout Asia around a century ago (*Economist* 1996, March 9: 10). Chinese-style capitalism, influenced, of course, by the Western version, built Singapore, Taiwan, and the former British colony of Hong Kong, which has now reunited with mainland China.

Unlike the former Soviet Union, where privatization is now widespread, state ownership of property remains dominant in mainland China—though changes are occurring here, too, as ownership rules open up in some sectors. Bureaucratic systems of state-run work units and the Communist Party remain important influences on income levels and access to housing for many workers. But some rules have changed: farming has shifted from collective farms to households, giving farmers full return on anything they produce over a set quota. And while state-owned enterprises are still prominent, at the local level, hybrid corporations straddling the state and private sector are permitted. Although the Communist Party and state institutions still strongly influence individuals' occupational rewards, market reforms have coincided with rising social inequality—across occupational, urban–rural, and regional lines—sparking debate over the implications and causes of such change (Wu and Xie 2002; Feng 2008). Debate also continues to focus on whether economic reform may lead to political reform and the eventual emergence of a democratic state.

India is another country that has received enormous attention. Like China, it has a huge population: more than 1.2 billion. With its higher birthrate and growing life expectancy, India is projected to surpass China's population by 2035 (World Bank 2005a; *Economist* 2009). Despite high levels of poverty and illiteracy, India has invested heavily in computer engineering and science, creating a two-tiered economy where highly skilled, cutting-edge knowledge services sit alongside a subsistence agriculture sector that employs most of the country's poor. India's technological savvy has attracted great interest, fuelling rapid economic growth of 7.4 percent from 2002–8, and 7.1 percent from 2009–12 (see Table 2.1). White-collar outsourcing has been central to India's growth, whereas manufacturing has played a minor role (as compared to

China). In *The World Is Flat*, Thomas Friedman (2005) cites a litany of jobs now being done in India for North American and European firms—from call-centre work to software engineering, income tax preparation, and the reading of CAT scans. India's attraction is not simply cheaper labour costs and time differences that facilitate 24/7 production, but a deep pool of highly skilled technology workers and fluency in English as a legacy of British colonialism.

As in China, India's economic growth has come through conscious state planning, especially in the mid-1980s under Rajiv Gandhi, who sought to make India highly competitive in the high-tech sector. But because India is a democratic society, with an increasingly fragmentary political system, there has been difficulty furthering reform, especially at the local level (Jha 2002; Basu 2004; Parthasarathy 2004). Thus, companies such as Dell, Microsoft, and IBM employ an elite group of knowledge workers in specially created "campuses" or software technology parks (STPs). For example, at InfoSys campus, the "jewel" of India's IT sector, employees enjoy a resort-size swimming pool, putting greens, restaurants, and a health club (Friedman 2005: 4). India is also home to a burgeoning call-centre industry (Mirchandani 2012). Outside the gates of InfoSys, however, other parts of the economy remain untouched. Today a significant portion of the population continues to live in poverty, and rates of adult literacy and life expectancy remain low.

Compared to China and India, the former Soviet Union has taken a much different course. As Robert Brym observes, a "strange hybrid of organized crime, communism and capitalism grew with enormous speed in the post-Soviet era" (1996: 396). Private enterprise, or market liberalization—introduced in the mid-1980s—was a relatively chaotic process, ensuring that competitive capitalism as we know it failed to emerge. The reason, in Brym's view, is that the old Communist Party elite, along with organized criminal gangs that had prospered in the corruption of the Soviet economy, were well placed to take advantage of any new opportunities. The result is a predatory form of capitalism that has enriched a small elite, or oligarchy, while breeding corruption and making life worse for ordinary Russians.

Despite an emerging private sector and successive state policies aimed at reform, the Russian Federation has not seen the development of a vibrant, diversified, entrepreneurial sector or reductions in social inequality. This reality is contrary to *market transition theory*, which was developed to explain recent social and economic changes in China and the former Soviet Union.

Strong growth of 6.8 percent from 2002 to 2008 slowed abruptly to average growth of 1.1 percent in 2009–12 (see Table 2.1). But this latter average reflects a large drop in 2009 (–7.8% growth), followed by positive growth of 3–4 percent in recent years. Russia's economy relies heavily on oil and gas. Income inequality is a significant issue, as are demographic pressures sparked by plummeting male life expectancy and an aging population (*Economist* 2009; Gerber and Hout 1998).

A broadly similar pattern is typical of other Eastern bloc nations. Former Communist Party elites, who still control state resources and have good business networks, continue to benefit in the post-Soviet era, while living standards for the majority have declined (Rónas-Tas 1994; Szelényi and Kostello 1996). Unlike earlier transitions to capitalism in Western Europe and North America, what is occurring in the former Soviet bloc does not involve the rise of a new economic elite or the creation of a working class—both of which existed in different forms under communism. Thus, Polanyi's "great transformation" from feudalism to a market economy in 19th-century Europe represented a unique experience of social and economic change. Subsequent transformations to market-based capitalism have taken some unexpected twists and turns.

■ NEO-LIBERALISM AND THE ROLE OF THE STATE IN TODAY'S ECONOMY

Clearly, the information technology revolution, industrial and labour market restructuring, and economic globalization have proceeded in a political context dominated by laissez-faire beliefs that advocate free markets with little or no government interference.[15] In a sense, this political environment is also a key determinant of Canadians' future employment prospects. These trends have the potential to either improve employment opportunities for Canadians or lead to further labour market disruptions. It is difficult to predict just what their ultimate impact might be, but it is important to consider how these forces could be shaped to our collective advantage. Public policy in other industrial countries in Europe and Asia has been more proactive in trying to influence the course of technological, labour market, and economic change.

The FTA and NAFTA were negotiated by governments and have been hotly contested political issues in all three countries affected. These trade agreements underscore the evolving role of the state (or government) in the economy and the labour market. The history of industrial capitalism is replete with instances of different forms of state intervention. For example, in the early Industrial Revolution, the French government forced unemployed workers into factories in an effort to give manufacturing a boost. We noted in Chapter 1 that in the early 19th century the British government dealt harshly with the Luddite protests against new technologies. And the Canadian government adopted its National Policy in 1879 to promote a transcontinental railway and settlement of the West.

In fact, as Canada industrialized, the government heavily subsidized the construction of railways in order to promote economic development. It also actively encouraged immigration to increase skilled labour for factory-based production and unskilled labour for railway construction. At times, it provided military assistance to employers combating trade unionists and introduced laws discriminating against Chinese and other non-white workers. But the Canadian government also passed legislation that provided greater rights, unemployment insurance, pensions, and compensation for workplace injuries. Although some might argue that these initiatives were designed mainly to ensure industrial harmony and to create an environment conducive to business, it remains true that these labour market interventions benefited workers.

A consensus, or compromise, was reached between employers and workers (mainly organized labour) in the prosperous post–World War II period. Acting on *Keynesian economic principles* that advocated an active economic role for the state, the Canadian government sought to promote economic development, regulate the labour market, keep unemployment down, and assist disadvantaged groups—in short, to develop a "welfare state." While the Canadian state was never as actively involved in the economy and the labour market as some European governments, it still played an important role.[16]

But industrial restructuring has been accompanied (some would say "facilitated") by conservative political doctrines based on free-market economics (Marchak 1981; Saul 1995; Kapstein 1996). In the 1980s, Ronald Reagan in the United States, Margaret Thatcher in Britain, and Brian Mulroney in Canada argued that economies would become more productive and competitive with less state regulation and intervention. Public policy was guided by the assumption that free markets can best determine who benefits and who loses from economic restructuring. The ideas of Adam Smith were used to justify the inevitable increases in inequality. High unemployment came to be viewed as normal. In some jurisdictions, labour rights were diluted, social programs of the welfare state came to be seen as a hindrance to balanced budgets and economic competitiveness, and government-run services were privatized: changes that directly or indirectly affected employment relationships.[17] As John Ralston Saul (1995) argues, these free-market ideologies erode democratic freedoms, threatening to bring about what he calls "the great leap backward." Similarly, with many rapidly developing economies, governments routinely use economic imperatives to restrict individual and collective rights.

Thus, in today's economic climate of globalization and restructuring, proponents of free-market economics seem to have more influence. But as we noted when discussing the ideas of Adam Smith, an unchecked marketplace generally leads to greater inequality. So, what kind of society do we want? When answering this question, we will have to determine the role of the state in achieving the desired society. Looking back, we can see that differing government policies have interacted with economic globalization to produce different effects at the local level. Looking forward, there is no fixed trajectory for globalization. Political choices by citizens and their governments undoubtedly will continue to shape the process in diverse ways. Canadians are concerned about labour market inequalities, employment, workers' rights, and employers' responsibilities to communities. The extent to which governments are held accountable for these issues will determine the impact of global economic forces on our daily economic lives.

■ GREAT TRANSFORMATIONS REVISITED

To this point our discussion has focused largely on economic and political change. But equally important since the 1950s have been dramatic shifts in gender, family, and household life. While we examine these changes in greater depth in Chapters 6 and 7, a key point for our discussion here is that postindustrialism and globalization have unfolded alongside dramatic shifts in women's paid work activity, as well as the growing "marketization" of household work (e.g., cooking, cleaning, caring). Speaking to this, U.S. sociologist Arlie Hochschild (2009) argues that contemporary households offer another example of Polanyi's "great transformation," with family relationships coming under the sway of market forces and new forms of paid work emerging as a result (see also McDowell 2009; Reich 2000; Lair and Ritzer 2009; Anderson and Hughes 2010). Here we highlight some key consequences, returning to these issues in later chapters.

Interactive Service Work, Caring Work, and Emotional Labour

Perhaps one of the most notable outcomes of this shift is the rise of *interactive service work*, which involves significant contact with clients or customers (McDowell 2009). Some work may be tightly routinized, requiring workers to follow scripts, while, in other cases, workers may have far more autonomy and discretion (Leidner 1993). Many such jobs (though certainly not all) also involve *caring work*—activities necessary for the sustenance of human life. Serving meals, providing paid childcare, driving elderly seniors to appointments, and cleaning homes are all examples of such work (Hochschild 2009; Lair and Ritzer 2009). A unique feature of these jobs is that many also involve *emotional labour*—the management of one's emotions to conform with employer-defined rules (e.g., "service with a smile"). To the extent that emotional control (often thought of as a private matter) becomes a requirement of the job, it becomes work: hence the term, *emotional labour*.[18]

One of the most influential, early studies on emotional labour—Arlie Hochschild's (1983) *The Managed Heart*—found that workers (in this case, flight attendants) used "feeling rules" to determine appropriate emotions on the job, engaging in "surface acting" (simply projecting required emotions, such as a smile) or "deep acting" (where they actively tried to change what they were feeling). Of concern to writers such as Hochschild was whether harnessing emotions for market purposes created "emotional dissonance," with workers developing a sense of distress or self-estrangement due to the emotional demands of their job. Since then, many studies have examined the concept of emotional labour (now often called "emotion management") in order to understand the extent to which service work and emotional labour can be scripted or regulated; how different types of workers experience such work; and how the nature of service, caring, or emotional work might vary across diverse sectors and work settings. For instance, some studies suggest distinctions between an "emotional proletariat" (low-skilled jobs with high emotional demands and little control) and "privileged emotional managers" (high-skilled jobs offering autonomy); see Bolton (2005) and Wharton (2009) for reviews of such work.

The rise of interactive service work also raises important questions about the growing role of customers in controlling worker behaviour, through instruments such as customer feedback forms. Some writers contend that the traditional dyad of employer–employee control has been replaced by a "triangle of power" comprised of customer, employer, and employee (for discussions, see Korczynski and Macdonald 2009).[19] Our purpose here is not to settle these debates—we return to them in later chapters—but simply to highlight the growing complexity of work in contemporary economies.

Mobile Workers and Mobile Work

Earlier we noted how globalized production practices have meant the outsourcing of work to other countries. But this outsourcing is just one dimension of increasing work-related mobility. Globally, we also see growing mobility of workers, both between and within countries, although we would emphasize that mobility remains the exception, not the norm. In Canada, the United States, and European countries, however, we do see a growing reliance on "transnational caregiving," where workers—typically women, but also men—migrate temporarily or permanently from the global south to work as nannies, personal care attendants, caregivers, or housekeepers in private homes, childcare centres, or long-term care centres (Zimmerman et al. 2006; Ehrenreich and Hochschild 2002). "Temporary foreign workers" have also become more common in fast-food service, cooking, cleaning, health care, and agricultural work, prompting heated public debate (D. Thomas 2010). Professional workers are also increasingly global, although this remains a tiny elite (Elliott and Urry 2010).[20]

Mobility is not simply global, however. Nationally, in Canada, we have strong interprovincial mobility—for example, between Newfoundland and Fort McMurray—where workers travel between a permanent home (where their family resides) and work sites (where they work 14 days and then have 7 days off). Capturing this trend, a CBC *Ideas* program profiled *mobile workers* in the oil sands. An ongoing project, *On the Move*, documents the growing range of employment-related mobility in the country.[21] Within local settings, some workers are highly mobile, either due to their occupation (e.g., couriers) or the need to travel to different employers to secure a full week's work (Vosko 2005). Of note, recent changes to *Employment Insurance* require workers to become increasingly mobile by accepting jobs within a one-hour commute from home, which is more than twice the average commuting time in Canada (Statistics Canada 2013g).

Beyond mobile bodies, mobile technologies are also altering how work is done, allowing more "knowledge work" to be carried out, coordinated, and monitored across geographical space. Some workers, for instance, no longer go into the office but instead *telecommute* (working partly from home), *hot-desk* (using desks at clients, suppliers, or employers), or work in *virtual teams* (where members are spread across different cities, regions, or countries). Spurring this trend are increasingly affordable, powerful laptops, iPads, and cellphones, as well as a plethora of apps, that allow workers, managers, and customers to connect with their data and with one another. As these technologies become more common, some routine rituals of the workplace, such as face-to-face meetings and water-cooler conversations, are replaced by Skype, FaceTime, and Google Chat. That said, such change also appears to be more selective and slower to catch on than predicted (Noonan and Glass 2012).

We return to these issues in later chapters, but what is germane to our discussion here is the way that virtual work extends both the temporal and spatial boundaries of the workplace. Whereas the office tools of the mid- to late-20th century—for instance, typewriters or large mainframe computers—stayed put at the end of the day, today's mobile technologies allow work to be accessed *anywhere, anytime.* With this come demands for 24/7 availability, as well as greater potential for work–family conflict (Perlow 2012), drawing our attention again to the shifting boundaries between home and work. Highlighting the benefits and downsides of virtual work, a study of 30,000 Canadian office workers found that while virtual work boosted productivity and generated more interesting work, it also increased stress and workloads. Work–life balance proved to be harder to maintain, with it being "easier" and "too easy" to work from home (Towers et al. 2006). Of note, some technologies, such as e-mail, may be more stressful for workers (compared to face-to-face meetings or hallway conversations), since they accumulate regardless of time or place, making workers feel mentally taxed and less in control (Barley, Meyerson, and Grodal 2011).

● CONTEMPORARY THEORETICAL PERSPECTIVES

Just as the rise of capitalism and industrialization sparked theoretical analyses from early sociologists, such as Marx, Weber, and Durkheim (as discussed in Chapter 1), ongoing economic change has captured the attention of more recent thinkers. Casting an eye over a diverse range of theorists—for example, Jürgen Habermas, Michel Foucault, Pierre Bourdieu, Ulrich Beck, Zygmunt Bauman, and Anthony Giddens—we see that many have engaged with central work-related themes, such as *power, control, inequality, consensus,* and *conflict*—albeit in new ways (Korczynski, Hodson, and Edwards 2006; Hancock 2009). Thus, despite suggestions that sociology's attention has shifted largely to questions of identity, culture, and consumption, it appears that sociological thinking about work and economic issues remains alive and well. Below, we offer a brief and selective sampling of contemporary ideas; those interested in reading further can consult a number of valuable books and discussions.[22] In later chapters, we examine additional theories on specific topics, for instance, feminist theory as it addresses gender and work (see Chapters 6 and 7).

Michel Foucault on Surveillance and Self-Discipline at Work

One writer who has influenced contemporary thinking about work and organizations is Michel Foucault (1926–84), a French theorist often associated with postmodernist thought (though Foucault himself did not claim that label) (Burrell 2006). While Foucault's primary interests were not explicitly on work and economic matters—but rather, psychiatry, medicine, the penal system, sexuality, and knowledge—a unifying interest was in understanding how power operates. Foucault's ideas on power are distinct; rather than viewing power as a resource wielded by individuals or social groups, he argued that power was diffused, operating through discourse and knowledge to "produce" the reality of everyday life. His interest, then, was not in the "organization of production," but in the "production of organization" (Burrell 2006). Not surprisingly, some scholars have found his concepts of *power, discipline,* and *surveillance* highly relevant, using them to study issues of team work, electronic surveillance, and human resource management practices (Burrell 2006; Townley 1994).[23]

One of Foucault's most important contributions comes from *Discipline and Punish* (1975), a historical examination of penal systems. Using the metaphor of the Panopticon, a prison design conceived by Jeremy Bentham, a U.K. philosopher and social reformer, Foucault develops his ideas about how power operates in society. Physically, the Panopticon is circular in design, with a central watchtower, surrounded by concentric circles of cells (with windows facing outwards only). Because all prisoners fall under the *gaze* of a single guard, the Panopticon thus maximizes external *surveillance*. Moreover, because prisoners cannot see the watchtower or one another, they do not know if or when they are being observed. They thus control their own behaviour, becoming (to use Foucault's language) *self-disciplining*.

Applying these ideas to contemporary organizations, writers such as Sewell and Wilkinson (1992) examine teamwork (discussed in Chapter 9), showing how worker control is maintained through peer surveillance and self-discipline. Other writers use Foucault's ideas on *discourse* and the *body*. For instance, Townley (1993) shows how human resource management (HRM) can be seen as a discourse of what is "acceptable" and "unacceptable" at work, thus producing workers who can be measured, analyzed, and compared against an "ideal." HRM practices such as job descriptions and performance appraisals operate to rank, discipline, and sequester workers. Studies of specific types of work, such as secretaries (Pringle 1989), show how HRM systems emphasizing "service with a smile" bring the body into the service of the corporation (Burrell 2006).

Pierre Bourdieu: Work, Practice, and Social Reproduction

Another influential thinker in discussions of work and social inequality is Pierre Bourdieu (1930–2002), a French anthropologist and sociologist, and contemporary of Foucault's. Bourdieu's work is equally wide-ranging, but focuses more explicitly on work-related themes. Early in his career, Bourdieu carried out fieldwork in Algeria, leading him to move away from a purely philosophical approach to embrace sociological and anthropological methods. This, and subsequent work on education and social reproduction, as well as capital, class, and cultural distinctions, have led to many of his ideas being used to examine issues of workplace practices, organizational culture, and economic and social inequality (Everett 2002; Lizardo 2012).

Like Foucault, Bourdieu was interested in how power operates in society. But he came to his own distinct point of view. His most important concepts are *field*, *habitus*, and *capital*, which developed over the course of his career. *Fields* are sites of structured social relationships where struggles occur for position and access to resources (Everett 2002). *Habitus* is best described as the dispositions, lifestyles, and values of social groups that are acquired as part of belonging to that collectivity. Applying these ideas, we can think of workplaces and organizations as fields, where individuals earn a living and build relationships, reputations, and careers. Likewise, we can see habitus as the commonsense idea of how things are done in a particular work setting. For instance, studies show how workers as diverse as servers at McDonalds and litigators in law firms come to understand expected workplace behaviours (Leidner 1993; Pierce 1995). Finally, *capital* is central for determining one's position in the field and for establishing habitus (or what can be thought as the rules of order).

For Bourdieu, there are several types of capital. *Economic capital* (material wealth such as cash, land, and other assets) is the most fundamental; however, it can be converted into other forms of capital—specifically, *social capital, cultural capital*, and *symbolic capital* (Bourdieu 1986; Everett 2002). *Social capital* involves relationships and networks between individuals that generate resources. Here we can think of senior executives who work and golf together, exchanging information about business opportunities. *Cultural capital* involves cultural facility and knowledge, and ranges from formal credentials and degrees (institutionalized cultural capital) to possessions such as books, paintings, and music (objectified cultural capital) to ways of speaking, dressing, and presenting one's self (embodied cultural capital). In some professions, such knowledge can be critical for moving ahead. Finally, *symbolic capital* comes through honours or recognition, such as winning an Oscar or Grammy. Together, these forms of capital operate to position individuals within a society, and within the workplace.

To date, scholars have taken Bourdieu's ideas in many directions. For instance, Bauder (2003) shows how the *cultural capital* of immigrant workers coming to Canada is devalued, leading them into lower-tier work. Likewise, Ross-Smith and Huppatz (2010) show how female managers use *gendered capital* to build their careers. In later chapters we return to Bourdieu, discussing some of his ideas further.

Ulrich Beck: The Risk Society

A final thinker who is important for understanding contemporary economic trends is Ulrich Beck (1944–), a German social theorist born towards the end of World War II. Along with other prominent social theorists, including Anthony Giddens, Zygmunt Bauman, and Scott Lash, Beck has argued that recent decades have seen a transition from a "modern society" to a "risk society," where individuals increasingly navigate more complex and risky work and life trajectories.[24] Central to these changes, as outlined in his book *Risk Society: Towards a New Modernity* (1992), Beck sees two interrelated processes. The first involves the shifting relationship between capital and labour that dramatically alters labour markets and economies. The second is greater *reflexivity* and *individualization*, creating more varied paths through the once predictable life course from childhood to career, marriage, parenthood, and retirement.

With respect to the economic changes, Beck highlights—as have other writers—a shift away from full-time, secure, "career" opportunities toward more flexible labour markets, offering part-time, temporary jobs, with poorer pay, career prospects, and security. Equally important is growing global competition for jobs, heightened skill and credential requirements, and the erosion of traditional social safety nets (e.g., unemployment insurance), along with a decline of state- and employer-sponsored training (as evidenced by rising tuition and decreased workplace training). Bundled together, these changes operate both to heighten economic risk and download it onto workers—thus "individualizing" risk. In Western economies, Beck argues, the result is to dramatically erode the quality of work, bringing it in line with poorer countries. Describing this in *The Brave New World of Work*, Beck states:

> Equally remarkable is the new similarity in how paid work itself is shaping up in the so-called first world and the so-called third world; the spread of temporary and insecure employment, discontinuity, and loose informality into Western societies that have hitherto been the bastion of full employment. The social structure in the heartlands of the West is thus coming to resemble the patchwork quilt of the South, characterized by diversity, unclarity and insecurity in people's work and life.[25]

Building on Beck's work, studies have explored questions about growing risk and insecurity in a variety of settings, from youth labour markets to freelance and manual workers: see Mythen (2005) and Fevre (2007) for valuable reviews and critiques. While some see great merit in Beck's ideas, others suggest they overstate the degree of change. In Chapters 3 and 4, we will have some opportunity to consider their merit in the Canadian context.

◼ CONCLUSION

From the managerial revolution to postindustrialism, globalization, and the rise of new economic regions such as China and India, we have covered many significant developments in this chapter. Our discussion has focused on trends since the 1950s to the present, exploring how new technologies, trade agreements, globalized production, and changing modes of work and family organization have reshaped economies and the nature of daily work. We have also considered how some contemporary theorists, specifically Foucault, Bourdieu, and Beck, add to our understanding of economic and workplace change.

Our overview highlights some key changes over the past half century and more. Much larger workplaces, new technologies, a more complex division of labour, growth in white-collar occupations, and a new class of managers were among the changes observed as industrial capitalism matured in 20th-century Canada. Once again, these changes generated new ideas and concerns about the impact of technology, social inequality, skills, knowledge, and labour–management cooperation and control. But the optimistic predictions of reduced inequality and conflict in a postindustrial era have not been well supported by the data. Instead, as we will see in Chapters 3 and 4, contemporary employment trends raise questions about a growing gap between more and less advantaged workers—with risk and insecurity being distributed unequally, both on a national and a global scale.

We have also highlighted a number of global economic and technological forces now re-shaping employment patterns. Like other advanced capitalist societies, Canada has become a service-dominated economy. New technologies are having a major impact on both the quantity and quality of work in the Canadian labour market, as are processes of industrial and labour market restructuring. The eventual outcomes of these trends are still unclear. We will also have to confront the limits to growth, as environmental sustainability becomes a more pressing global problem (World Commission on Environment and Development 1987; Gomez and Foot 2013). We may see a general improvement in the standard of living and the quality of working life, or the benefits may go primarily to those who already have better jobs, thus contributing to increased polarization in the labour market and in society as a whole. In subsequent chapters, we will return frequently to these fundamental questions.

DISCUSSION QUESTIONS

1. What is meant by the "logic of industrialism" thesis? Using three countries discussed in the text, how would you evaluate the merits of this idea?

2. What is a postindustrial society? Based on material you have read in this chapter, would you characterize Canada as postindustrial? Why? Why not?

3. Drawing on your reading in this chapter, discuss how free trade, globalization, and industrial restructuring are re-shaping the Canadian economy. What do you see as the most important changes taking place?

4. What are some new types of work that have emerged in Canada? What has led to their development?

5. In your opinion, how do the contemporary theories of Beck, Foucault, and Bourdieu explain current workplace trends in Canada and other countries?

ADDITIONAL RESOURCES

WORK AT THE MOVIES

- *El Contrato* (directed by Min Sook Lee, 2003, 51:11 minutes). This NFB documentary outlines the experiences and working conditions of people from Central Mexico who migrate each year to tend Ontario's tomato farms. It is available through the National Film Board of Canada: http://www.nfb.ca/film/el_contrato.
- *The Best Exotic Marigold Hotel* (directed by John Madden, 2011, 124 minutes). This British comedy about retirees in India explores a wide range of themes, including the globalization of call-centre work, retirement, and health care.
- *For Man Must Work or the End of Work* (directed by Jean-Claude Burger, 2000, 52:01 minutes). Debates over the potential impact of globalization,

economic restructuring, and technological change are explored in this NFB film, available through the National Film Board of Canada: http://www.nfb.ca/film/for_man_must_work.

- *Bombay Calling* (directed by Ben Addelman and Samir Mallal, 2006, 70: 14 minutes). This NFB documentary explores globalization in India, focusing on the call-centre industry. It is available through the National Film Board of Canada: http://onf-nfb.gc.ca/en/our-collection/?idfilm=52353.

SOUNDS OF WORK

- "Elf's Lament" (Barenaked Ladies). A lively take on globalization and working conditions in the run-up to Christmas consumption.
- "My Home Town" (Bruce Springsteen). Springsteen's song laments the impacts of economic downturn for small-town America.
- "Six Days on the Road" (Dave Dudley). Dudley sings about the realities of mobile (trucking) work and the difficulties it creates for balancing work and family.
- "On the Move to Fort McMurray" (*Ideas with Paul Kennedy*, CBC podcast, November 22, 2013). The episode looks into employment-related geographical mobility in Fort McMurray, Alberta. Available at http://www.cbc.ca/ideas/episodes/2013/11/22/on-the-move-to-fort-mcmurray/.

NOTES

1. See Grabb (2009) and Carroll (2004).
2. Bell (1973). Additional perspectives on the postindustrial society are reviewed by Krishnan Kumar (1995), Clement and Myles (1994), and Nelson (1995).
3. The managerial revolution perspective (Burnham 1941; Berle and Means 1968) was developed earlier, during an era when corporate concentration in North America was proceeding rapidly and when concerns about the excessive power of the corporate elite were being publicly debated (Reich 1991: 38).
4. See Lowe (2000: Chapter 4) for a discussion of industrial restructuring and the rise of the new economy in Canada. See also Boyer and Drache (1996) and Pupo and Thomas (2010) for critical perspectives on restructuring, globalization, and the new economy.
5. Schumpeter's views are discussed in Bluestone and Harrison (1982: 9).

6. Drache and Gertler (1991: 12–13). See Heinzl (1997) on Nike's closure of the Bauer factory. See also Mahon's (1984) analysis of restructuring in the Canadian textile industry.

7. Laxer, Gordon. (1995). "Social Solidarity, Democracy and Global Capitalism." *Canadian Review of Sociology and Anthropology* 32: 287–313, pp. 287–88.

8. Friedman, Thomas L. (2000). *The Lexus and the Olive Tree*. New York: Anchor Books, p. 42.

9. For information and reports on globalization and labour rights, see the Maquila Solidarity Network (http://en.maquilasolidarity.org/), Clean Clothes Campaign (http://www.cleanclothes.org/), and the International Labor Organization (ILO) at www.ilo.org. See also the report on "decent work" from the International Labour Office (1999).

10. See Commission for Labor Cooperation (2003). For more recent information, see the Commission for Labor Cooperation website (http://www.naalc.org), which monitors the North American Agreement on Labor Cooperation. For past assessments, see Adams and Singh (1997) and Gunderson (1998) on the impact of NAFTA on labour policies and worker rights. Vosko (1998) contrasts the different regulatory responses under NAFTA and the European Community to the spread of temporary employment. For more recent discussions, see Schott and Hufbauer (2007), who consider employment impacts, and Kay (2011), who examines labour cooperation across borders.

11. See Orme (1996: 13). Evaluations of NAFTA continue to offer widely divergent views. For earlier assessments, see Arsen, Wilson, and Zoninsein (1996) and Bognanno and Ready (1993). For more recent assessments, see Scott, Salas, and Campbell (2006), Alexandroff, Hufbauer, and Lucenti (2008), and Hufbauer and Schott (2005).

12. Kerr, Clark, J. T. Dunlop, F. H. Harbison, and C. A. Myers. (1973). *Industrialization and Industrial Man*. London, England: Penguin, p. 29.

13. See World Bank (2001), Holzer (2000), and Hsiung (1996) for accounts of economic development in the region. The argument about the critical role of a Weberian form of government bureaucracy is presented by Evans and Rauch (1999).

14. Central to China's development has been a high level of foreign direct investment within manufacturing in the "special economic zones." For example, in 2007, foreign investment accounted for 57 percent of all Chinese exports (*Economist* 2009; Whyte 2009). For valuable accounts of China's economic development, see Guthrie (2006), Sharman (2009), Whyte (2009), and Winters and Yusuf (2007).

15. See Saul (1995) for a critique of this ideology.

16. See Olsen's (1999) comparative review of changes to Sweden's welfare state.

17. See Bamber, Lansbury, and Wailes (2011) for a comparative analysis of how employment relations and labour–management relations have developed in the context of globalization.

18. For valuable discussions and reviews of interactive service work, or frontline service work, see McDowell (2009), Korczynski and Macdonald (2009), and Bélanger and Edwards (2013), among others. On caring work, see Ehrenreich and Hochschild (2002), Zimmerman et al. (2006), Yeates (2009), and Anderson and Hughes (2010). For helpful reviews and discussions of emotional labour, see Leidner (1993), Bolton (2005, 2009), Bolton and Boyd (2003), Brook (2009), Cranford and Miller (2013), Grandey, Diefendorff, and Rupp (2013), Lopez (2006), Payne (2009), and Wharton (1993).

19. For early examples of work on this topic, see Fuller and Smith (1991) and Leidner (1993). For more recent discussions, see Lopez (2010), Bolton and Houlihan (2010), and others in a special issue of *Work and Occupations*; Bélanger and Edwards (2013); and a special issue of *Work, Employment and Society*, edited by Korczynski (2013).

20. On transnational caregiving, see, for example, Ehrenreich and Hochschild (2002); Spitzer et al. (2003); Parreñas (2001); Torres et al. (2012); Yeates (2009); Zimmerman et al. (2006). For discussions on temporary foreign workers in Canada, see Thomas (2010); Fuller (2011); Taylor, Foster, and Cambre (2012); and Foster and Barnetson (2012). Elliott and Urry's (2010) *Mobile Lives* offers interesting discussions of professional work, among other topics.

21. A feature on mobile workers and the oil sands can be found on the CBC Radio program, *Ideas with Paul Kennedy*, at http://www.cbc.ca/ideas/episodes/2013/11/22/on-the-move-to-fort-mcmurray/. The episode highlights one of many projects on mobile workers in Canada undertaken through the *On the Move Project*: see http://www.onthemovepartnership.ca/. For a personal account of mobile work, see Wood (2013).

22. For students who want to know more about contemporary social theory, as well as work, organization, and economic life, we suggest reading the collection of articles in *Social Theory at Work*, edited by Marek Korczynski, Randy Hodson, and Paul Edwards (2006). Additional insightful discussions of work-related theorizing are provided by Hancock (2009), who discusses critical theory traditions, and by Burrell (2006), who discusses Foucault's reception by sociologists of work and impact on the sociology of work, labour process theory, and organizational studies.

23. Despite Foucault's relevance to work and organizations, Burrell (2006) argues that his ideas, as well as general currents in postmodern theory, have been taken

up only selectively, with some sociologists of work remaining resistant, uninterested, or highly critical of the ideas.

24. In addition to Beck, others theorists have developed compatible ideas. For instance, see Zygmunt Bauman, who develops the idea of "liquid modernity" (Bauman 2000; Clegg and Baumeler 2010), and Scott Lash and John Urry, who develop ideas about "the end of organized capitalism" (Lash and Urry 1987, 2013).

25. Beck, Ulrich. (2000). *The Brave New World of Work*. Cambridge: Polity Press, p. 1.

CANADIAN EMPLOYMENT TRENDS

"I think one of the new things that is part of this new economy is … the rise of part-time work, and as far as a pool of part-time workers, I mean students are sort of the epitome of that …"

Source: Queen's University student. Tufts, Steven, and John Holmes. (2010). "Student Workers and the 'New Economy' of Mid-Sized Cities: The Cases of Peterborough and Kingston, Ontario." In Norene J. Pupo and Mark P. Thomas, eds., *Interrogating the New Economy: Restructuring Work in the 21st Century.* Toronto: University of Toronto Press, p. 139.

"I'm in a decent job now … a good paying job with benefits. I like what I do and I'm not worried about getting laid off every 6 months. I'm glad to get out of the auto industry."

Source: Former autoworker. Vrankulj, Sam. (2012). *Finding Their Way: Second Round Report on the CAW Worker Adjustment Tracking Project,* p. 30. http://www.caw.ca/assets/images/phase-Two-Tracking-study.pdf.

"I call it a 'factory of voices.' That's all it is. Instead of assembling parts for the cars, you're just processing people or processing calls—a 'factory of voices.' Everybody is sitting there in their little stalls talking and producing customer service."

Source: Call-centre worker. Pupo, Norene J., and Andrea Noack. (2010). "Dialling for Service: Transforming the Public-Sector Workplace in Canada." In Norene J. Pupo and Mark P. Thomas, eds., *Interrogating the New Economy: Restructuring Work in the 21st Century.* Toronto: University of Toronto Press, p. 124.

"Retiring early if you call it that has not been good for me. I'm ok financially but I wasn't ready to retire. My wife goes to work every day and I've run out of projects around the house. Having me home all day while she works causes tension. I've got too much time on my hands and it's starting to get to me … and her. I've looked for a job, but no luck. I planned to work another five or six years before I retired. Being 56 and unemployed passes for early retirement these days. Not exactly how I saw it playing out."

Source: Former autoworker. Vrankulj, Sam. (2012). *Finding Their Way: Second Round Report on the CAW Worker Adjustment Tracking Project,* p. 23. http://www.caw.ca/assets/images/phase-Two-Tracking-study.pdf.

● INTRODUCTION

Pick up a copy of any Canadian newspaper and flip through it, looking for feature stories on work-related topics. You'll likely come across articles based on labour force statistics collected by Statistics Canada or by some other public- or private-sector data-collection agency. Most common are the unemployment rates, updated monthly. But the news media also carry stories on a wide array of themes, such as youth employment, part-time work, retirement patterns, education trends, and the growth of service jobs and the decline of the manufacturing sector.

Understanding these labour force statistics is important both for learning more about the Canadian labour market and for developing statistical literacy. In a society in which the media constantly bombard us with the latest figures on one social trend or another, it is helpful to have some understanding of the definition and source of these numbers, and even more important, to be able to interpret them critically. Hence, we will discuss these trends with reference to some of the broad theories of social and economic change discussed in Chapters 1 and 2. At the same time, this statistical overview will provide us with the background needed to evaluate some of the ideas discussed in later chapters about competing theories of labour markets.

We begin by outlining key demographic factors shaping the workforce, such as aging, immigration, and rising education levels. We then discuss labour force participation trends and Canada's occupational and industrial structures, emphasizing the rise of the service economy and the emergence of new occupations. As we will see, Canada has a dynamic, ever-changing labour market, shaped by the rise and fall of key industries, as well as specific regional forces. Our focus in this chapter is on Canadian workers and the types of jobs and industries in which they work. In Chapter 4, we delve into related issues of job quality, working hours, and unemployment. Throughout our discussions, we consider past and current labour market trends, exploring their implications and considering where trends may be headed.

● DATA SOURCES

Over the years a major data source used for this book has been the Canadian census, an enumeration of the entire population. Conducted every five years by Statistics Canada, the census gathered both basic (short-form) and detailed (long-form) information, providing the most complete and reliable picture of the Canadian labour market and allowing us to accurately examine historical changes. Unfortunately, in 2011, the Conservative government replaced the mandatory long-form census with a voluntary National Household Survey (NHS), raising concerns over the reliability and comparability of data (Chase and Grant 2013; Globe and Mail 2013a; Sheikh 2013). A key concern was the lower response rate in the National Household Survey, particularly among marginalized groups, leading to less accurate estimates of income, employment status, and other labour market measures.

A second useful source is the monthly Labour Force Survey, also conducted by Statistics Canada. Unlike the census, which attempts to cover a range of topics, this random sample survey is designed to collect only work-related information and so provides much more detail. Because the survey is done every month, information is always updated. In order to obtain precise estimates of the labour market activities of Canadians ages 15 and older, a large sample is needed. Approximately 56,000 households (most providing information on more than one individual) are included in the sample.[1] Households remain part of the sample for six months before being replaced.

The Labour Force Survey provides, for example, monthly estimates of unemployment and labour force participation rates, and descriptions of industries and occupations experiencing job growth or decline.[2] Frequently, more detailed surveys, designed to study specific work-related topics, are piggybacked onto the Labour Force Survey. Examples of such topics include student summer employment, self-employment, involuntary part-time work, and job search behaviour. Many of the statistics cited in this chapter are obtained from this useful source.[3]

■ THE DEMOGRAPHIC CONTEXT OF LABOUR MARKET CHANGE

Whether our focus is on the labour market today or 10 to 20 years in the future, there is no denying that *demographic shifts* (population changes) under way in Canadian society set some basic parameters. Of all the employment trends we will consider in this chapter, those related to the demographic composition of the labour force are perhaps the only ones we can confidently project into the future. So, while economists debate whether the unemployment rate may rise or decline next year, demographers (who specialize in studying the structure and dynamics of population) can quite accurately predict birthrates, life expectancy, population growth, age distributions of the population, and related trends. Three of these trends deserve particular attention: aging, cultural diversity, and educational attainment.

Workforce Aging

In his best-selling book, *Boom, Bust and Echo*, David Foot claims that "[d]emographics explain about two-thirds of everything." Although we might dispute that claim, we do agree that Canada's demographic trends influence many economic and social changes.[4] Foremost among these demographic factors is *population aging*, which has significant implications for job opportunities, pensions, work values, organizational structures, and economic growth (Gomez and Foot 2013).

The *baby-boom generation*, born between 1946 and 1964, is the largest generation in Canadian history. Writing about them in *Born at the Right Time*, historian Doug Owram observes, "Economics, politics, education, and family life would all have been considerably different without the vast demographic upsurge of births after the Second World War" (1996: xiv). As baby boomers have moved through the life course, they have left few institutions unchanged—from a revolution in popular music in the 1960s to the rapid expansion of postsecondary institutions in the 1970s to debates over mandatory retirement in the 2000s. Coupled with smaller birth cohorts following in their wake, due to sharply declining birthrates, the aging of the baby boom has fundamentally altered the demographic shape and social structure of Canada.

This huge and slowly aging bulge in the workforce has affected the career opportunities of many Canadian workers. The baby-boom generation entered the workforce when the economy was still expanding, and many obtained good jobs. Some of the smaller generations that followed boomers into the labour force have been less fortunate, since higher unemployment and global economic uncertainties have frequently led to layoffs, not hiring. Yet many baby boomers hit career plateaus, or worse, in the 1990s and 2000s.

Because most work organizations are pyramids, career success has been defined in terms of climbing a ladder that has room for fewer and fewer people on each higher rung. But with growing numbers of older workers, the competition for the few top jobs has intensified. For younger workers experiencing difficulty finding satisfactory entry-level jobs, this may not seem a serious problem. But for older, long-term employees who have learned to view personal success as upward movement, career blockages, as well as growing risk and insecurity, can be unsettling (Foot and Venne 1990; Cappelli 1999; Lippmann 2008).

Figure 3.1 documents the workforce aging process by profiling the *age distribution* of labour force participants in 1976 and 2012. Note the decline in the relative proportion of teenagers (15 to 19 years) and young adults (20 to 24 years) over the three decades. Compare this with the increased size of the 35-to-44-, 45-to-54-, and 55-to-64-year-old cohorts over this time. While we saw a marked trend toward early retirement in the 1980s and 1990s, due to labour market restructuring and downsizing in the 1990s, this trend reversed in the late 1990s. The proportion of 55- to 64-year-olds in the workforce has increased as growing numbers of boomers reach what is deemed retirement or near retirement age (Carrière and Galarneau 2011). According to the 2011 National Household Survey (which replaced the long-form census in 2011), there were just over 3 million people of age 55 and older in the workforce. This

FIGURE 3.1   Age Distribution of the Labour Force by Gender, Canada, 1976 and 2012

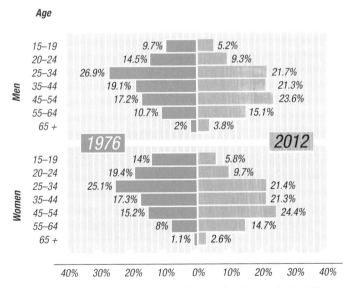

Source: Statistics Canada. CANSIM Table 282-0002 - Labour Force Survey estimates (LFS), by sex and detailed age group, Annual (persons x 1,000). <http://www5.statcan.gc.ca/cansim/a05?lang=eng&id=2820002>

result is equivalent to 18.7 percent of total employment, up from 15.5 percent in the 2006 Census (Statistics Canada 2013b).

Looking back over history we know from the Census that, in 1921, only 5 percent of Canadians were 65 years of age and older. Over the next 50 years, this figure grew slowly to 8 percent. Then the aging of the Canadian population began to accelerate, and by 2000, almost 13 percent of Canadians were senior citizens. Statistics Canada predicts that, by 2036, about one person in four will be 65 years of age or older.[5] The relative size of the working-age population that funds government old-age security programs through payroll contributions will shrink considerably during this period. The earliest baby boomers, now in their mid-60s, have begun or are soon planning to pursue retirement.

Pensions have become a prominent public concern, as have the issues of mandatory retirement and expected skill shortages. Will the Canada/Quebec Pension Plan, one of Canada's main *social safety nets*, be able to support all the retiring baby boomers? Will today's youth have to pay more to cover the added costs? Or, as an alternative solution, will Canadians have to wait until they are a few years older than 65 to begin collecting a government pension? Will employer-sponsored pension plans make up the difference? Probably not. Access to such plans has never been widespread. Indeed, according to the Pension Plans in Canada Survey, in 2010, just 38.8 percent of the labour force were covered by a registered retirement plan (RRP), down from 42.8 percent in 1995.[6] How to balance the needs of retiring baby boomers against the needs of people still in or joining the Canadian workforce is a big challenge.

It would seem reasonable to expect that workforce aging will open up opportunities for younger workers (Easterlin 1980). For example, in 2011, roughly one-third of senior managers in health, education, social and community services, construction, transportation, and production were 55 years of age or older. Bus drivers, farm managers, and realtors have even older age profiles, sparking concerns over skill shortages as older workers retire (Statistics Canada 2013b: 13). Who will fill these jobs, especially in blue-collar areas, when there is growing emphasis on gaining postsecondary education? Consider, as well, the relatively small size of the 15-to-19-year-old and 20-to-24-year-old cohorts in today's labour force (Figure 3.1). As more and more baby boomers retire, labour shortages in some sectors and regions may become a growing concern. Even so, we need to recognize that many in the generation in between have difficulty finding satisfactory jobs.

Immigration and Greater Workforce Diversity

Immigration is an important determinant of Canada's population mosaic. For centuries, Canada has been a country of immigrants. In the post–World War II era, Canadian governments attempted to tailor immigration policy to labour market trends, partly in anticipation of labour shortages in key areas. Immigration levels have been kept low when unemployment was high, but have been allowed to rise when economic expansion required more workers. In fact, there have been times when immigration levels were considerably higher than they are today (e.g., around 1910, when the western provinces were being settled). But, along with economic factors, immigration policies have been influenced by demographic trends. For more than four decades now, birthrates have been below replacement level, so low that our population would have declined unless supplemented by immigration.

Immigration is thus again taking on increasing importance. In 2011, Canada had the highest proportion of immigrants among G8 nations, with 20.6 percent of the population having been born outside the country (Statistics Canada 2013b). This increase reflects federal government quotas that are currently set around 240,000 to 265,000 immigrants per year (less than 1% of the total population) (Citizenship and Immigration Canada 2012).[7] Despite concerns by some that immigrants "take jobs away" from native-born Canadians, research shows that this is rarely the case. Immigrants frequently create their own jobs or take jobs that others do not wish to have. Or, they are selected to match shortages of workers in specific occupational categories. With anticipated labour shortages due to population aging in coming years, there is much interest by federal and provincial governments in ensuring that immigrants' skills and abilities are recognized and properly utilized.

Until quite recently, there was far less *visible* diversity among immigrants to Canada. For example, in 1981, two-thirds of all immigrants living in Canada (including those who had been here for many decades) were born in Europe. Today the source countries have dramatically changed. Between 1991 and 2001, 58 percent of immigrants came from Asia, with top countries including China, India, Pakistan, and the Philippines. Just 20 percent of immigrants came from Europe (Statistics Canada 2003). In the 2000s, this trend has continued. Between 2006 and 2011, for example, about 57 percent of immigrants came from Asia, including the Middle East (Statistics Canada

2013c). Why the shift? Canadian immigration policies no longer favour European immigrants but, more important, the demand to immigrate to Canada has declined in Europe, while it has increased dramatically elsewhere. Consequently, more immigrants are members of visible minority groups with distinctive cultural backgrounds.

According to the 2011 National Household Survey (NHS), 19.1 percent of the Canadian population identified themselves as a member of a *visible minority* group (excluding Aboriginal Canadians). In large urban centres, such as Toronto and Vancouver, visible minorities now comprise nearly half of the population (47.0% and 45.2%, respectively). Together, three main groups account for about two-thirds of all visible minorities in Canada: South Asian Canadians account for 25.0 percent of all visible minorities (and 4.8% of the Canadian population), while Chinese Canadians comprise about 21 percent of visible minorities (and 4.0% of the total Canadian population). Finally, just under a million people identify as Blacks, accounting for 15.1 percent of the visible minority population (and 2.9% of the Canadian population overall).

Recent estimates suggest that, with current immigration patterns, the proportion of visible minorities in Canada will increase to approximately 30 percent by 2031 (Statistics Canada 2010). Equally important for the diverse nature of the Canadian labour market, nearly 1.4 million (4.3%) of the nation's population is of Aboriginal origin. This figure will increase in the decades ahead, given the younger age profile of Aboriginal Canadians—a median age of 28 years compared to 41 years for the non-Aboriginal population (Statistics Canada 2013d: 4, 16). Immigrants are also younger, on average, so both Aboriginal Canadians and immigrants will make up a growing share of the workforce as older Canadians retire.[8] As discussed in later chapters, these demographic trends have prompted governments and employers to develop employment equity policies to facilitate greater workplace cultural diversity and reduce the potential for labour market discrimination.

A Better-Educated Workforce

On the whole, Canadians are becoming increasingly well educated, a trend that has also fundamentally changed the character of the labour force. Figure 3.2 shows the dramatic change in *educational attainment* of the labour

FIGURE 3.2   Educational Attainment of the Labour Force by Gender, Canada, 1975 and 2012

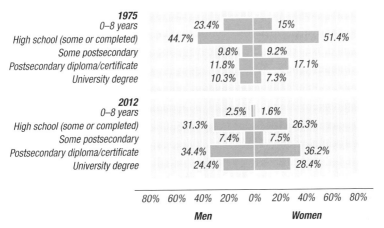

Source: Statistics Canada. CANSIM Table 282-0004 - Labour Force Survey estimates (LFS), by educational attainment, sex and age group, Annual. <http://www5.statcan.gc.ca/cansim/pick-choisir?lang=eng&p2=33&id=2820004>

force between 1975 and 2012. In 1975, 66 percent of females and 68 percent of males in the labour force had only a high-school education or less. Very few (only 7% percent and 10%, respectively) had a university degree. In the nearly 40 years since, large numbers of both women and men obtained postsecondary credentials. In 2012, well over 20 percent of labour force participants had a university degree (28.4% for women and 24.4% for men).

This rising educational attainment has been the backdrop for a debate on the role of education in a rapidly changing and increasingly global and technological economic environment. In fact, many analysts argue that a well-educated workforce is a nation's key resource in today's global marketplace. Business and government have argued that additional education and training, and an overhaul of the education system to make it more job relevant, will help Canada become more competitive internationally.[9] The latest variant of this perspective is found in the concepts of *lifelong learning* and *learning organizations* (see Chapter 9).[10] Essentially, these refer to continuous education, both formal and informal, in educational institutions and at work and home, throughout one's adult life. Educators, parents, and students have responded by raising concerns that closer links between education and the economy might mean too much business influence over what is taught at all levels of the education system.

By international standards, Canadians are well educated in terms of post-secondary credentials and enrollment levels.[11] Nonetheless, there is more to developing a nation's human resources than the acquisition of formal education. No doubt, there are educational reforms that could lead to the graduation of more skilled, flexible, and enterprising labour force participants. Basic literacy and numeracy, along with other essential skills, are lacking in small pockets of the workforce.[12] But work-related training is not the responsibility of the education system alone. Canada has a mediocre record of employer-sponsored workplace training. According to the 2008 Access and Support to Education and Training Survey (ASETS), the most current Statistics Canada report available on this topic, only 36 percent of adults 25 to 64 years old participated in employer-supported training (Knighton et al. 2009: 11). Although this figure represents an improvement from 30.0 percent in 2002, when compared to the United States and Western European countries, Canada's training record remains average at best (Conference Board of Canada 2005; OECD and Statistics Canada 2011: 284–85). Moreover, as we discuss in later chapters, the people who typically receive training are well-educated workers already in good jobs, something that further accentuates labour market inequalities.[13]

The assumption underlying the "education and training" solution to economic growth is that our workforce is not sufficiently educated and trained; yet the above discussion suggests that there is more to the problem. For one thing, while unemployment is higher among the less educated, a considerable number of Canada's unemployed are well educated. In addition, many Canadian workers are in jobs that require little education or training. For example, in 2006, 19.0 percent of Canadians 25 to 54 years old and nearly 25.0 percent of 15- to 24-year-olds who held a university degree reported being in jobs that did not require university-level education (Certified General Accountants Association of Canada 2012). In another study, 23 percent of Canadians reported their job and education were unrelated (Yuen 2010). This mismatch between education and job requirements is often referred to as "underemployment." Young Canadians are typically more likely to be underemployed, as are well-educated new immigrants.[14] Of note, and not surprisingly, those experiencing an education–job mismatch are more likely to earn lower wages (Yuen 2010). Underemployment highlights the need to go beyond the supply side of the education–job equation to examine how job content and skill requirements could be upgraded—in short, asking how the demand for educated labour can be improved. Clearly, there are deeper problems in the structure of our economy as well, and concerted efforts by government, the private sector, organized labour, and professional associations are needed to address them. As two American sociologists concluded about the United States: "The problem is a shortage of good jobs to a greater extent than it is inadequate training and development."[15]

● LABOUR FORCE PARTICIPATION TRENDS

Now that we have a better demographic understanding of the workforce, we can examine key labour market and employment trends that define where, how, and for whom Canadians work. *Labour force participation* (LFP) is the main indicator of a population's economic activity, at least from the perspective of paid employment. Whether relying on census or monthly Labour Force Survey data, calculations of labour force size or participation rates are based on the number of individuals 15 years of age or older who are working for pay (including self-employed individuals working on their own or employing others) and those who are looking for work. Hence, the *unemployed* (those out of work but who have actively looked for work in the past four weeks) are counted as part of the labour force. Individuals performing unpaid household and child-care work in their home, however, are not included in official labour force calculations, even though their labour makes essential economic and social contributions. We explore such work in Chapter 7.

Using this official LFP definition to look at work patterns at the beginning of the last century, only 53 percent of Canadians (15 years of age and older) were participating in the labour force in 1901. The rate increased to over 57 percent by 1911 but did not go much higher until the 1970s. By the mid-1970s, more than 60 percent of the eligible population was in a paid job or seeking one (Figure 3.3). Participation rates rose to 67 percent in 1989 and then fell slightly during the recession of the early 1990s. Since then they have hovered somewhere between 65 and 67 percent. The 2012 LFP rate was 66.7 percent, representing a total of 18,876,100 labour force participants.

FIGURE 3.3   Labour Force Participation Rates by Gender, Canada, 1976–2012

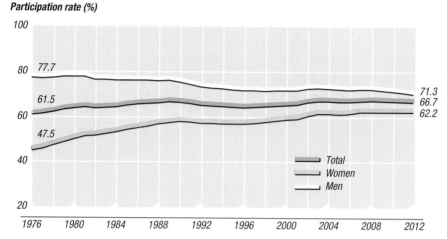

Source: Statistics Canada. CANSIM Table 282-0002 - Labour force survey estimates (LFS), by sex and detailed age group, Annual (persons x 1,000). <http://www5.statcan.gc.ca/cansim/a05?lang=eng&id=2820002>

Gender Differences in Labour Force Participation

Breaking down the LFP rate by gender, we find striking differences. In 1901, only 16 percent of females 15 years of age or older were in the paid labour force. However, this rate increased with each 10-year census. After World War II, the size of these increases was substantial. Between 1960 and 1976, female labour force participation jumped from 28 to 45 percent, and the following decade saw it rise steadily The landmark year was 1980, the first in which a majority of Canadian women were part of the labour force (which, as officially defined, leaves out unpaid family and household work).

By 1990 and 1991, the female LFP rate had risen to almost 59 percent; it then dropped slightly for a number of years before rising to a high of 62.7 percent in 2008 and then falling again slightly to 62.2 percent in 2012. Thus, over the course of a century, female labour force participation in Canada almost quadrupled, from 16 percent to over 62 percent. As we will see in Chapter 6, the impact of this long-term trend on workplaces, families, and society as a whole has been immense. During the 1960s and 1970s, much of the growth in female labour force participation was due to larger numbers of women returning to paid employment after their children were in school or had left home. In contrast, most of the female employment growth in the

1980s and 1990s occurred among mothers who were working for pay and raising young children at the same time. By 2009, over two-thirds of mothers worked for pay, compared to the mid-1970s when less than one-third of mothers with children under the age of six years were in the labour market (Ferrao 2010: 9).

While female participation rates have been climbing, male rates declined over most of the past century, although not as steeply. Between 1901 and 1931, the male LFP rate remained close to 90 percent, dropping in the decades before and after World War II to percentages in the mid-80s. In the 1970s and 1980s, the male rates fluctuated between 76 and 78 percent. More recently, the male LFP rate dropped quickly from 77 percent in 1989 to just over 72 percent in 1996, staying at this level until 2009 when it fell again slightly to the 71 percent range. Glancing back over the past two decades, we see a 4 percent increase in female labour force participation, compared to a 4 percent drop for men. Since the downturn of 2008, LFP rates have declined for both sexes, but more notably for men.

Thus, the long-term growth in total LFP rates in Canada has been the product of substantial increases for women and somewhat less dramatic declines for men. The latter change reflects two trends: men are living longer (with more men living past the conventional retirement age, the proportion of all men out of the labour force is increasing), and more men are retiring earlier than they have historically (that is, before the typical retirement age of 65). The causes of growing female labour force participation, which are more complex, are discussed in Chapter 6. A similar convergence of female and male rates has occurred in other industrialized countries (e.g., the United States, Britain, Germany, France, Italy, and Japan) but, over the past few decades, Canada has experienced the largest jump in female labour force participation.

It is important to note that these labour force participation rates are annual averages. Given the seasonal nature of some types of work in Canada (jobs in agriculture, fishing, forestry, construction, and tourism, for example), higher levels of labour force participation are typically recorded in the spring, summer, and autumn months. Furthermore, taking a full 12-month period, we observe higher proportions of Canadians reporting labour force participation at some point during the year. Thus, annual averages do not reveal the extent to which Canadians move in and out of different labour market statuses—for example, by changing employers or becoming unemployed. In recent years, concerns over *job stability* (average length of time in a job) in industrialized countries has been much debated (Hollister 2011; Fevre 2007). In Canada, job stability has not eroded as dramatically as some suggest; however, the Canadian labour market does reflect a considerable amount of individual mobility. During the recession of 2008–9, better-educated workers had the most stable employment, while immigrants, Aboriginal people, less-educated workers, and youth experienced the greatest labour market instability. Of note, industries such as manufacturing saw sharp declines in job stability, especially for longer-term workers, something that only worsened in the recession.[16]

In addition, there are a number of groups that continue to have much lower than average rates of labour force activity. Many Aboriginal Canadians are economically marginalized, facing huge barriers to paid employment. For instance, the 2011 National Household Survey (NHS) shows notable differences in unemployment rates between Aboriginal and non-Aboriginal workers—with a rate of 7.5 percent for non-Aboriginal, compared to 18.3 percent for First Nations, 10.4 percent for Métis, and 19.6 percent for Inuit populations. While the 2011 National Household Survey does not report differences between First Nations living on and off reserves, the 2006 Census suggests that unemployment rates are highest for those living on-reserve. Aboriginal Canadians also have much lower incomes, on average, and are much more likely to be living below the poverty line. In 2011, for instance, median employment income reported in the National Household Survey was $31,603 for the non-Aboriginal population, compared to $22,217 for First Nations, $28,075 for Métis, and $19,905 for Inuit populations.[17]

Similarly, research shows that Canadians with disabilities (who comprise 14.3% of the overall population) are much less likely to be in the paid labour force. In 2006, for example, employment for people with disabilities was 56 percent for men and 46 percent for women; for men and women generally, the rates were 75 percent and 65 percent, respectively. That said, employment rates for people with disabilities have risen in recent years. Yet people with disabilities work fewer hours and earn lower levels of income, something that cannot be accounted for by differences in work-interruption rates. Even after taking into account other demographic factors, women and men with disabilities earn up to 20 percent less than women and men without disabilities.[18]

Age Differences in Labour Force Participation

Younger Canadians

How does age shape labour force participation? How do participation rates and patterns differ for younger and older Canadians? With the exception of a small decline coinciding with the recession of the early 1980s, the labour force participation of Canadian youth (ages 15 to 24, females and males combined) rose more or less steadily from an annual average of 64 percent in 1976 to 71 percent in 1989. Figure 3.4 shows that the youth LFP rate then declined rapidly in the 1990s, dropping to 61 percent by 1997. Rebounding, it rose again to 67.3 percent in 2003, then wavered back and forth, falling sharply in the post-2008 context. Notably, in this period of time, female and male youth LFP rates have converged sharply, with nearly identical rates for males and females by 2012.

Over the past two or three decades, LFP rates for teenagers (ages 15 to 19) have always been considerably lower than LFP rates for young adults (ages 20 to 24), since a larger proportion of the latter group have left the education system. In 2012, female LFP rates for teenagers were higher than male rates (50.8% for girls and 48.3% for boys) but, among young adults, male rates (77.1%) were higher than female rates (75.0%).

FIGURE 3.4   Youth Labour Force Participation Rates by Gender, Canada, 1976–2012

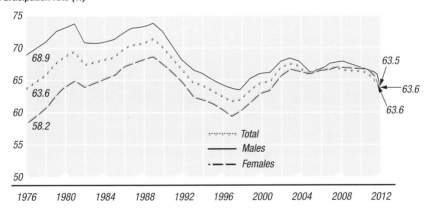

Source: Statistics Canada. CANSIM Table 282-0002 - Labour Force Survey estimates (LFS), by sex and detailed age group, Annual (persons x 1,000). <http://www5.statcan.gc.ca/cansim/a05?lang=eng&id=2820002>

Why did youth LFP rates decline so notably in the 1990s? The recession that lasted until mid-decade sharply reduced the number of "good" entry-level jobs for youth. In fact, during this period, youth wages declined more than for any other age group in the labour force. In turn, a larger proportion of youth decided to continue their education to improve their employment prospects. For example, between 1989 and 1998, the percentage of Canadian youth (ages 15 to 24) who were in school and not working rose from 29 to 40 percent. Furthermore, the size of the 20-to-24-year-old cohort declined, compared to the 15-to-19-year-old cohort. Since young adults have historically had higher LFP rates than teenagers, the overall youth LFP rate declined.[19]

What about trends since then? Certainly the stronger economy in the early 2000s, as well as more rapidly rising postsecondary tuition costs, may have led some Canadian youth to choose work over school. Since 2008, however, youth LFP rates again declined, likely reflecting narrowing job prospects as many other Canadians sought out work.

Labour Force Participation among Older Canadians

In recent decades, labour force participation among older Canadian men declined notably. From 1976 to 2012, for example, the LFP rate for men ages 60 to 64 fell from 66.5 to 58.0 percent. As we would expect, the older members of this cohort are most likely to leave the labour force. For example, in 2012, the LFP rate for men ages 55 to 59 was 78.9 percent, more than 20 points higher than for those ages 60 to 64 (58.0%). With somewhat better benefits provided to the elderly by government, compared with a generation or two earlier, and with a larger number of older men having employer-sponsored pensions as well as other personal savings (RRSPs, for example), income security among older men has increased. Consequently, men's average retirement age fell from 65 years in 1976 to 61 years in 1997, then hovered in the range of 62 to 63 years for many years.[20]

Recently, however, it appears that a larger proportion of Canadians may be delaying retirement. Data on "expected working life" (rather than on "average retirement age"), which better capture the likely behaviour of those *currently* in the labour market, show that from 1998 to 2009, the expected working life for a 50-year-old rose from 12.5 to 14.6 years for men, and from 11.6 to 14.2 years for women (Carrière and Galarneau 2012). Such changes may reflect growing economic insecurity, related to declining pension coverage and retirement investments. Alternatively, it may result from more positive developments, such as enhanced work opportunities for older workers in key sectors where labour shortages exist (Carrière and Galarneau 2011).

Indeed, many factors influence retirement plans and patterns. According to the 2007 General Social Survey, which last studied this issue, there is considerable uncertainty about retirement plans, with one-quarter of near-retirees (individuals of 45 to 59 years of age) either not knowing when they will retire or not planning to retire (Schellenberg and Ostrovsky 2008). Another half of near-retirees planned to retire between the ages of 60 and 65. Since the early 1990s, there has been a decline in those wishing to retire before age 60 and an increase in those planning to work beyond age 65. Two-thirds of near-retirees expected to have adequate retirement income, which was a major influence on retirement plans. Looking at retirees, one-third stopped work for health reasons (Schellenberg and Silver 2004); and another one-third retired for a range of reasons, having no wish to continue working. But the remaining third of retirees would continue working under different circumstances—for example, if they could work fewer days or hours, take more vacation, or work part time (Morissette, Schellenberg, and Silver 2004). Those who retire "involuntarily" are far more likely to have retired due to health or downsizing, to have low income, and to report low life satisfaction. These retirees were also more likely to lack pension benefits from a former employer and to return to work for financial reasons. Higher education and self-employment status also increase the odds of working as a senior (Duchesne 2004). These patterns challenge the traditional three-stage model of the work life—education, employment, then retirement. Instead, many researchers are now using a *life-course perspective* that views individuals' roles as more fluid and examines the choices and constraints underlying transitions across roles.[21]

Despite a small trend toward re-employment among retired men, the fact remains that older men who lose their jobs have more difficulty finding work, since many employers are reluctant to hire and retrain older workers. In addition, older men are more likely to be employed in industries where employment is declining (manufacturing and the resource-based industries, for example). As a rule, most unemployed older men decide to retire. Some are offered early retirement packages by employers trying to downsize their workforce, while others decide that "retired" would be an easier label to live with than "unemployed." Thus, while a shortage of jobs may have pushed some men over the age of 55 out of the labour force, an adequate pension encouraged others to retire voluntarily.

Among older women, we see different work and retirement patterns. Typically, women have retired at an earlier age, on average, than men. But LFP rates for older women have still increased because of their historically lower levels of participation. In 2012, for example, the LFP rate for women ages 55 to 59 was 69.4 percent, up dramatically from 38.2 percent in 1976. For women ages 60 to 64, the LFP rate increased from 24.4 percent in 1976 to 45.7 percent in 2012. Financial reasons may be a key motivator for women. Typically, they earn less than men and receive fewer benefits, including government and employer pensions (Marshall 2000), as discussed in Chapter 6. Compared with men of the same age, then, fewer older employed women have the financial resources needed to retire.

■ INDUSTRIAL CHANGES: THE EMERGENCE OF THE SERVICE ECONOMY

There are several ways to classify the work done by labour force participants. We begin below by discussing industrial shifts and then examine occupational changes in the following section. *Industry* classifications direct our attention to the major type of economic activity occurring within the workplace. In the broadest sense, we can distinguish the *primary sector*, including agriculture, mining, forestry, and other resource extraction industries, from the *secondary sector* (manufacturing and construction), where goods are produced from the raw materials supplied by the primary sector, and the *tertiary sector*, where services rather than products are provided. A *service*, simply defined, is the exchange of a commodity that has no tangible form. These general industrial categories can be further subdivided into more specific industries. The service sector, for example, includes, among others, the finance, education, retail trade, government (public administration), and health service industries.

Service-Sector Growth

In 1891, the primary industries accounted for 49 percent of the Canadian labour force; the secondary sector, for 20 percent; and the service sector, for the remaining 31 percent (Matthews 1985: 36). In the following half-century, the primary sector lost its dominance, while the manufacturing industries expanded. At the same time, the service industries were also increasing in size. By 1951, almost half (47%) of all employed Canadians were working in the service industries, while the secondary sector accounted for almost one-third (31%) of employment (Picot 1987: 11). The relative size of both the primary and secondary sectors has been declining steadily ever since. By 2012, 77.9 percent of employed Canadians held service-sector jobs, and 22.1 percent were working in the goods-producing sector. Agriculture and natural resources, once domi-nant industries more than a century ago, now account for just 1.8 percent and 2.1 percent of all employment in Canada. In contrast, the portion of workers in the service sector has more than doubled over this time. This sector has also come to represent a much larger share of the total value of goods and services produced in the Canadian economy.[22]

These statistics clearly demonstrate that we are now living in a service-dominated economy. A similar transition from a pre-industrial to an indus-trial to a service economy occurred in other capitalist countries such as the United States, the United Kingdom, Japan, Sweden, and Germany. But manufacturing continues to play a larger role in some of these countries. Using the U.S. definition of the service sector for accurate comparisons, in 2012, the United States, the United Kingdom, and the Netherlands were the leading service economies, with roughly 81 percent of all workers in that sector. Canada and Sweden followed closely with service-sector employment accounting for about 79 percent of the labour force. But even Japan and Germany, two leading exporters of manufactured goods, have service sectors accounting for about 71 percent of all employment (U.S. Bureau of Labor Statistics 2012).

The rise of the service sector can be attributed to a combination of fac-tors. Productivity gains due to new technologies and organizational forms in manufacturing, but also in the resource industries, have meant that fewer people can produce much more. In primary industries, the growing size and declining number of farms in Canada is perhaps the best indicator. Toward the end of the 19th and into the early 20th century, factory mechanization greatly enhanced workers' productivity, despite a reduction in hours worked. In more recent decades, automated production systems (robotics and informa-tion technology) have once again accelerated this trend. Thus, the expansion of production in the primary and secondary sectors has been accompanied by a relative decline in the need for employees.

Industrial expansion and productivity gains over the years have also led to higher incomes and increased leisure time. These factors, in turn, have fuelled the demand for a wider range of services, particularly in the last few decades when the recreation, accommodation, and food service industries have been growing rapidly. In addition, the expansion of the role of the state as a provider of educational and social services and as a funder of health services contributed significantly to the growth of the service sector. In the 1990s, governments' pursuit of deficit reduction resulted in reduced program funding, organizational downsizing, and privatization, thus slowing the trend toward public-sector employment. In the early 2000s, governments at all levels and public services, particularly education and health care, increased their hiring—in part, to replace the growing number of retiring baby boomers. With massive stimulus spending by governments in response to the 2008–9 recession, the hiring trend continued. With government deficits a constant public concern, however, there are ongoing pressures to reduce or minimize public-sector jobs and wages.

Employment Diversity within the Service Sector

The wide range of specific industries within the broad service sector can be usefully categorized into six broad groups: (1) distributive services (transportation, communication, and wholesale trade); (2) business services (finance, insurance, real estate, and other services to business); (3) the education, health, and welfare sector; (4) public administration; (5) retail trade; and (6) other consumer services. Distributive services differ from the others by being the final link in the process whereby raw materials are extracted, transformed, and then delivered to the ultimate consumer. Business services also provide support to the primary and secondary industries (the goods-producing sector), but in a less tangible way. Like public administration, the education, health, and welfare sector contains primarily non-commercial services provided by the state, while retail trade and other consumer services (e.g., food and beverage, accommodation, and the tourism industries) are commercial services aimed directly at consumers.[23]

It is useful to further combine the six service categories into an *upper tier* (distributive, business, education, health and welfare, and public administration) and a *lower tier* (retail trade and other consumer services) since, as we will demonstrate later, many more good jobs are located in the former. Table 3.1 uses these concepts to profile the industrial distribution of Canada's employed (other tables in this chapter also include only employed members of the labour force). In 2012, just over one-fifth (22.1%) of employed Canadians were working in the goods-producing sector while, as already noted, 77.9 percent were employed in the service industries. Just over half (51.9%) of the employed were located in the upper-tier services, while one-quarter (25.9%) had jobs in the lower-tier service industries.[24]

We have already observed that similar proportions of workers are employed in the service and goods-producing sectors in Canada and the United States. However, we find a very different industrial distribution in Mexico, the other major North American economy. Compared to Canada and the United States—where about four-fifths of workers hold service jobs—Mexico has a smaller service sector, employing just 63 percent of workers there. In contrast, the agricultural sector employs 13.6 percent of workers in Mexico, compared to just 1.5 percent in the United States and 2.2 percent in Canada. Likewise, the industrial sector is larger in Mexico (23.5%) than in the United States (17.3%) and Canada (19.2%), although the difference in the size of this sector is not as marked.[25]

Gender and Age Differences in Service-Sector Employment

Table 3.1 also reveals distinct gender differences in industrial locations. In 2012, almost 32.9 percent of employed Canadian men were working in the goods-producing sector, compared with 10.2 percent of employed women. Women were more likely to be employed in the lower-tier services (28.4%, compared with 23.7% of men—though this gap has narrowed notably in recent years). Within the upper-tier services, women were much more heavily concentrated in the health, education, and social services industries than were men. Men were considerably more likely to be employed in trade, transportation, and professional, scientific, and technical industries.

Age plays an important part in further stratifying the employed labour force across these industrial categories. Young workers (ages 15 to 24) are much less likely to be employed in the upper-tier services. Instead, young workers are more likely to hold jobs in the lower-tier retail trade and consumer service industries. Many of these young workers are students in part-time jobs. Thus, the expansion

TABLE 3.1   Industry by Gender, Employed Population, Canada, 2012

Industry	% of Total	% of Women	% of Men
Goods-producing sector (total)	22.1	10.2	32.9
Agriculture	1.8	1.1	2.3
Natural resource-based	2.1	0.8	3.3
Manufacturing	10.2	6.0	14.0
Utilities	0.8	0.4	1.2
Construction	7.2	1.8	12.2
Service-producing sector (total)	77.9	89.8	67.1
Upper-tier services (total)	51.9	61.4	43.4
Transportation and warehousing	4.9	2.4	7.1
Finance/insurance/real estate/leasing	6.2	7.5	5.1
Professional/scientific/technical services	7.4	6.6	8.2
Business/building/other support services	3.9	3.7	4.2
Educational services	7.4	10.2	4.8
Health care/social assistance	12.2	21.1	4.1
Information/culture/recreation	4.5	4.2	4.8
Public administration	5.5	5.7	5.2
Lower-tier services (total)	25.9	28.4	23.7
Retail trade	15.1	15.4	14.8
Accommodation/food services	6.3	7.8	4.9
Other consumer services	4.5	5.3	3.9
Total percent	100.0	100.0	100.0
Total (in 000s)	17,508	8,320	9,188

Source: Statistics Canada. CANSIM Table 282-0008 - Labour Force Survey estimates (LFS), by North American Industry Classification System (NAICS), sex and age group, Annual (persons x 1,000). <http://www5.statcan.gc.ca/cansim/pick-choisir?lang=eng&p2=33&id=2820008>

of the lower-tier service industries (for instance, shopping malls, fast-food restaurants, and tourism) since the 1970s has relied heavily on the recruitment of student workers, creating a distinct student-worker segment of the labour force. However, older female workers are also much more likely than older male workers to be employed in the retail trade and other consumer service industries.

● OCCUPATIONAL CHANGES

While the industrial classification system is based on what is being produced, we also can categorize workers according to their *occupation*. Occupational distinctions are determined by the work an individual typically performs: the actual tasks that she or he completes. Thus, secretaries, managers, office cleaners, and accountants (occupational titles) work in mining companies, automobile factories, and government bureaucracies—that is, in the primary, secondary, and tertiary (or service) sectors of the economy. Other occupations are typically found only within specific industrial sectors. For example, teachers, nurses, and retail clerks are occupational groups largely unique to the service sector. So the two classification systems parallel each other to an extent but also overlap considerably.

For many years, Statistics Canada used the Standard Occupational Classification (SOC) system to categorize occupations. But a basic limitation of the SOC system was that it did not adequately capture the skill content of jobs. From our earlier discussions of education and training, it is clear that developing human resources—the skills of the workforce—has become a public policy priority. Consequently, in the 1990s, Human Resources Development Canada (HRDC) teamed up with Statistics Canada to develop a new occupational typology: the National Occupational Classification (NOC). Essentially, this classification identifies two dimensions of *skill*, providing information on generic *skill type* (e.g., business, natural sciences, arts, trades) and *skill level* (e.g., manager, clerical) for each of the 40,000 detailed occupations in the Canadian labour market. Four basic skill levels, tied directly to the education and training required, are used. For example, occupations in skill level A include managers and the professions, and require a university education; occupations in skill level D require no formal education and only short demonstrations or some on-the-job training. Nine skill types, plus a separate category for managers, indicate the type of work performed. Generally, the highest-skill groups are concentrated mainly in what we earlier referred to as "upper-tier services," while skill-level-D occupations are in lower-tier services and goods production. The National Occupational Classification, now 20 years old, is revised and updated every five years by Statistics Canada and Employment and Social Development Canada to ensure that it reflects the changing nature of the labour market (Statistics Canada 2012).

Blue-Collar, White-Collar, and Pink-Collar Occupations

Many but not all of the people employed in the primary and secondary industries would be classified as blue-collar workers, while most of those working in the service industries would be identified as white-collar workers. The term *blue-collar* has traditionally been used to distinguish occupations with unclean and potentially hazardous working conditions (e.g., farming, mining, truck driving, construction work, and factory work) from *white-collar* occupations (clerical, sales, managerial, and professional). The explanation, of course, is that for the former jobs, wearing a white collar would be inappropriate, since it would not stay clean. In the past, white-collar occupations were viewed as having "higher status." But with the expansion of the service sector, especially lower-tier services where low-paying jobs are quite common, the white-collar occupational category has come to include the majority of the labour force, including many people in less desirable jobs.

As primary-sector industries became less important over the last century, there was a huge decline in the size of some occupational groups and a proportional increase in others. A few examples can make the point. The 1911 Census reported that 34 percent of the labour force worked in agricultural occupations, compared with only 4 percent in clerical occupations and a similarly small proportion in professional occupations. By 1951, agricultural occupations had declined to 16 percent of the labour force, compared with 11 percent in clerical occupations and 7 percent in professions (O'Neill 1991: 10). The 1996 Census revealed less than 5 percent of the labour force in occupations unique to primary industry, 9 percent in management, 19 percent in business, finance, and administrative occupations, and almost 20 percent in natural science, social science, government, and other white-collar occupations.[26] Thus, over the course of the past century, white-collar jobs have come to dominate the Canadian labour market.

Of note, many of the new white-collar positions have been filled by women, while the remaining blue-collar jobs in the primary and secondary sectors are still typically held by men. In fact, given the heavy concentration of women in clerical, sales, and service occupations, the term *pink collar* has been used to describe these occupational categories.

Using a revised occupational classification to ensure comparability with earlier data, Table 3.2 presents a gender breakdown of Canadian occupational distributions for 1987 and 2012.[27] Note that the total employed labour force increased from 12.3 million to 17.5 million workers. Hence, even though some occupational categories may have declined slightly in relative (percentage) size, they might still have increased in absolute size between 1987 and 2012.

Considering first the total distributions (female and male combined), we note stability as well as small changes. Managerial occupations have remained stable at 8.6 percent. In contrast, professional occupations have risen from 2.1 percent to 3.5 percent of all employed, while the other administrative and clerical category occupations (office jobs without major planning and supervisory roles) decreased marginally, from 17.3 to 14.3 percent. The remaining white-collar occupational categories—professional, and sales and service— have seen slight changes, with an overall upward trend.

However, in the blue-collar occupations, we see relative declines in primary occupations (from 5.1% to 3.1%) and in manufacturing occupations (from 7.7% to 4.6%). This pattern represents a continuation of long-term losses evident well before the 2008 crash. The decline in blue-collar occupations is a result of the massive restructuring in the goods-producing sector outlined in earlier chapters, while the changes in clerical occupations reflect a complex set of related changes, from advancing information technology to downsizing to the upgrading of some of these jobs to administrative categories.

Chapter 6 focuses on the unequal employment experiences and rewards of women and men, so we will comment only briefly at this point on the gender differences indicated in Table 3.2. The 2012 data show a more even distribution of men than women across the occupational structure, though not in blue-collar jobs. Overall, women are more heavily concentrated than men in pink-collar occupations, with 22.4 percent employed in administrative and clerical occupations, 8.6 percent in retail sales, and 20.1 percent in other sales and service occupations, totalling 51.1 percent. In contrast, just 26.8 percent of men are employed in these three occupational groups. Women are also relatively overrepresented in jobs in health (11.5%) and social science, education, and government (13.7%).

Nonetheless, it is important to note the changes over time in the gender composition of the occupational structure, however slowly they may be in taking place. In 1987, for instance, only 7.9 percent of employed women were in managerial or professional administrative occupations. Now 25 years later, 10.4 percent of women work in these higher-status white-collar occupations. Table 3.2 also shows a small increase over time in the proportion of women in other non-traditional areas, such as natural sciences, and a corresponding decline in the percentage of women in clerical jobs.

To conclude, there have been some significant shifts in the Canadian occupational structure, especially between white-collar, blue-collar, and pink-collar jobs. Although female–male differences have not disappeared, we

TABLE 3.2   Occupation by Gender, Employed Population, Canada, 1987 and 2012

	1987			2012		
	Women	Men	Total	Women	Men	Total
	%	%	%	%	%	%
Management occupations	6.0	10.5	8.6	6.6	10.4	8.6
Business, finance, and administration						
Professionals	1.9	2.3	2.1	3.8	3.2	3.5
Administrative and clerical	29.7	7.9	17.3	22.4	6.9	14.3
Natural and applied science	2.3	7.0	5.0	3.4	11.1	7.4
Health occupations	9.2	1.8	5.0	11.5	2.4	6.7
Social science, education, and government	8.2	4.7	6.2	13.7	5.5	9.4
Culture, recreation, and sport	2.7	2.1	2.4	3.9	2.7	3.2
Sales and services						
Retail sales	9.7	3.0	5.9	8.6	3.8	6.1
Other sales and services	20.3	15.4	17.5	20.1	16.1	18.0
Trades, transportation, and related	2.1	28.9	17.4	2.1	26.8	15.1
Occupations unique to primary industries	2.3	7.2	5.1	1.3	4.7	3.1
Occupations unique to manufacturing	5.8	9.1	7.7	2.8	6.3	4.6
Total percent	100.0	100.0	100.0	100.0	100.0	100.0
Total (in 000s)	5,308	7,025	12,333	8,320	9,188	17,508

Source: Statistics Canada. CANSIM Table 282-0010 - Labour Force Survey estimates (LFS), by National Occupational Classification for Statistics (NOC-S) and sex, Annual (persons x 1,000). <http://www5.statcan.gc.ca/cansim/pick-choisir?lang=eng&p2=33&id=2820010>

must keep in mind that Table 3.2 shows very broad occupational categories. Health occupations, for example, include doctors, nurses, orderlies, nursing assistants, and other support workers. Women are still more likely to be in the lower-status occupations within these broad categories and are still typically supervised by men. Hence, it is necessary to look in more detail at the specific occupations within which women and men typically are employed, as we do in Chapter 6.

● THE CANADIAN LABOUR MARKET: REGIONAL VARIATIONS

So far, we have treated Canada as a single economic entity, putting aside important regional differences. Yet anyone who has driven across Canada will have a strong sense of its regional diversity. The fishing boats and lumber mills of the West Coast are left behind as one begins to head east toward the Prairies, where there are oil wells and grain elevators. The flat landscape disappears a few hours after leaving Winnipeg, and one is faced by the rocks, forests, and water of the Canadian Shield. The smokestacks of Sudbury and other mining communities are reminders of the natural resource base of that region, but they eventually give way to the old grey barns of Ontario, symbols of an agricultural economy older than the one observed several days earlier.

But the barns are unlikely to be the only memory of the trip through Ontario and into Quebec. The huge Highway 401 pushing its way past miles of warehouses and suburban factories will also leave a strong impression as it takes one through the industrial heartland of the country. Then, repeating the pattern observed in the West (but in reverse, without the mountains, and on a smaller scale), the farming economies of Quebec and the Atlantic provinces begin to merge with a forest-based economy. Eventually, one returns to a region where fisheries are once again important. In short, regional diversity means economic diversity.

This description obviously over-generalizes. There are high-technology firms in the Fraser Valley, large factories in Calgary, and oil wells off the East Coast. And in the northern parts of Canada, energy development and mining compete uneasily with traditional Aboriginal hunting, fishing, and trapping. Still, it is essential to take into account the regional distribution of industries when considering work opportunities available to Canadians. Some regions are much more economically advantaged than others, as we point out below in our discussion of unemployment trends. Labour force participation rates also vary significantly across provinces. For example, in 2012, Alberta's LFP rate of 73.4 percent was much higher than the 61.6 percent rate in Newfoundland and Labrador.

A brief comparison of industrial patterns of employment in 2012 highlights these regional variations (Table 3.3). For example, 5.2 percent of the employed labour force in Manitoba and Saskatchewan had jobs in agriculture, compared with less than 2 percent in nearly every other region save Alberta (2.6%). Larger-than-average concentrations of workers in the resource-based industries reflect the presence of the fishing industry on the East Coast and in British Columbia; forest-based industries in the Atlantic provinces, Alberta, and British Columbia; and the oil and gas industry in Alberta. Meanwhile, approximately 12 percent of workers in both Quebec and Ontario had jobs in manufacturing, compared with less than 8 percent in other regions. Of note, Alberta, the province that has taken the lead in scaling back government since the early 1990s, has the lowest employment in publicly funded industries (education, health, and welfare, and public administration).

Canada is not unique in having some regions in which primary industries are most important and others in which manufacturing is concentrated. But its

TABLE 3.3   Industry by Region, Employed Population, Canada, 2012

Industry	Total %	Atlantic Provinces %	Quebec %	Ontario %	Manitoba/ Saskatchewan %	Alberta %	British Columbia %
Goods-producing sector							
Agriculture	1.8	1.4	1.4	1.4	5.2	2.6	1.1
Natural resource-based	2.1	3.7	0.9	0.5	2.8	8.3	2.0
Manufacturing	10.2	7.1	12.5	11.8	7.7	6.4	7.7
Utilities	0.8	1.0	0.6	0.8	1.2	1.0	0.6
Construction	7.2	7.3	6.1	6.4	7.6	10.5	8.3
Service sector							
Upper-tier services							
Wholesale trade	3.5	2.5	3.8	3.3	3.6	3.8	3.7
Business services	17.6	13.8	16.7	20.1	13.0	15.6	17.8
Education/health/ welfare	19.5	23.4	20.7	18.7	21.9	16.6	19.5
Public administration	5.5	7.3	5.8	5.6	5.9	4.1	4.4
Lower-tier services							
Retail trade	11.6	12.8	12.0	11.3	11.3	11.2	11.8
Other consumer services	20.2	19.8	19.4	20.0	19.8	19.9	22.9
Total percent	100.0	100.0	100.0	100.0	100.0	100.0	100.0
Total (in 000s)	17,508	1,110	3,984	6,784	1,167	2,150	2,313

Source: Statistics Canada. CANSIM Table 282-0008 - Labour Force Survey estimates (LFS), by North American Industry Classification System (NAICS), sex and age group, Annual (persons x 1,000). <http://www5.statcan.gc.ca/cansim/pick-choisir?lang=eng&p2=33&id=2820008>

economic history is marked by a reliance on exports of raw materials such as furs, fish, timber, wheat, coal, natural gas, and oil. Indeed, exporting raw materials was Canada's colonial role in the British empire, and even as an independent industrialized nation, Canada has continued to provide natural resources to the global economy. The *staple theory of economic growth*, developed by Harold Innis and others, documents the economic, political, and social consequences of this dependence on the export of unprocessed staple products. The theory argues that overcommitment to extraction and export of a single or few resources makes a nation or region vulnerable in world markets. The relative absence of manufacturing industries means that large portions of the workforce remain employed in lower-skill primary- and tertiary-sector jobs. In addition, a weak manufacturing sector does not encourage significant quantities of research and development and does not generate spin-off industrial activity. These factors create a "staples trap" in which there are few economic development alternatives (Watkins 1991).

Indicative of Canada's natural resource base is the number of single-industry communities scattered across the country. These towns and cities, often situated in relatively isolated areas, exist only because the extraction of some natural resource requires a resident labour force. While some of these communities have attempted to diversify their economies, few have been successful. Instead, their economic activity remains dominated by the primary resource extraction industry (oil in Fort McMurray, Alberta, for example, or nickel in Sudbury, Ontario). If the market for the staple declines or the resource is depleted, the economic base of the community will crumble. Examples since the 1980s include mine shutdowns in Saskatchewan, Quebec, and Ontario; the struggle for Newfoundland fishing communities to survive; and recent mill closures in forestry-dependent towns in British Columbia.[28] By contrast, a growing world market for oil and advances in extraction technologies have made it economically feasible to invest in northern Alberta and southeastern Saskatchewan.

Over the decades, the prospects of better jobs and higher incomes have led many thousands of people to "go down the road" to the industrial cities of central Canada. But many have also been attracted to the resource towns of the hinterland for the same reasons. Such communities have historically provided work for unemployed or underemployed migrants from other regions of the country. However, work opportunities for residents and migrants in resource towns, which move through fairly predictable stages of development, do not remain constant. Moreover, since mining, forestry, the railway, and other blue-collar industries traditionally have been male occupational preserves, women have had trouble finding satisfactory employment. Many single-industry towns are located in areas with sizable Aboriginal populations, yet these groups seldom benefit from the employment opportunities generated by the towns.

◼ CONCLUSION

Over the past century or so, there have been profound changes in how, where, and for whom Canadians work. The late 19th and early 20th centuries were times of rapid industrialization and workplace rationalization. Years that followed brought further growth in white-collar occupations, expansion of the service sector, and a decline in self-employment. By the 1960s, the Canadian work world had been largely transformed. But, as our examination of more recent trends has shown, the Canadian labour market has once again gone through a significant restructuring in the final decades of the 20th century and the early decades of the 21st.

The service sector has expanded enormously, producing both good and bad jobs, with many more of the latter in the lower-tier service industries. Meanwhile, manufacturing industries have continued to contribute less to employment growth in Canada. As we will discuss in the next chapter, we have also seen a substantial increase in part-time employment, while other forms of nonstandard work (temporary or contract work, for example) have become more prevalent, as well. Unemployment rates, as we discuss in Chapter 4, are also a concern for certain groups in the labour market—especially in the aftermath of the 2008 "Great Recession."

With respect to the trends discussed here, what lies ahead? We can be fairly certain that several of the trends we have documented will continue. Demographic factors are a given, especially workforce aging and the increasing diversity of the labour force. We can expect continued expansion of service-sector employment.

Currently, some of the most debated questions pertain to the quality and types of jobs the economy is producing, as well as employment levels and the likely trajectories of growth in the Canadian and global economies. In particular, the following questions will have to be addressed: Given concerns over the environment and sustainability, what levels of economic growth are sustainable? What are the limits posed by population aging and a shrinking workforce in many industrialized countries? And what types of jobs will be generated in an increasingly service-oriented context? We continue to explore these questions in the next chapter where we discuss trends, such as job quality, unemployment, working hours, and the rise of nonstandard work.

● DISCUSSION QUESTIONS

1. What are three of the most important demographic changes occurring in Canada? Explain what is involved in these trends, and how they will affect employers and workers in the next 10 to 15 years.

2. In your view, what, if anything, could federal or provincial governments do to help respond to demographic changes occurring in the next 10 to 15 years?

3. How and why does labour force participation vary by region, age, and gender?

4. What are the most important occupations and industries in the Canadian economy? How has the occupational and industrial structure changed over time, and why?

5. Work in Canada is strongly shaped by regional location. Discuss how region influences key aspects of the work experience, such as unemployment, participation, and industry location.

ADDITIONAL RESOURCES

WORK AT THE MOVIES

- *Boomer Revolution* (directed by Sue Ridout, 2013, 45 minutes). This film explores the impact of an aging population in Canada on trends in work, retirement, and consumption. It is available through CBC Doc Zone: http://www.cbc.ca/doczone/episodes/boomer-revolution.
- *About Schmidt* (directed by Alexander Payne, 2002, 125 minutes). After retiring from his long-held office job, Schmidt (Jack Nicholson) embarks on a road trip and experiences a journey of self-discovery and an awakening to life outside work.
- *A Better Life* (directed by Chris Weitz, 2011, 98 minutes). After illegally immigrating to the United States from Mexico and finding work as a gardener, a father struggles to provide better economic and social opportunities for his son.
- *Park Avenue: Money, Power and the American Dream* (directed by Alex Gibney, 2012, 59 minutes). This documentary film offers an analysis of growing income inequality in the United States and the difficulty of achieving upward mobility for the working poor.

SOUNDS OF WORK

- "Shiftwork" (Kenny Chesney). The country song describes the perils of nonstandard working arrangements. Chesney notes the presence of shiftwork in diverse workplaces.
- "Make and Break Harbour" (Stan Rogers). In this song, Rogers comments on the downslide of Atlantic Canada's fisheries and considers its effect on community and out-migration.

- "The Idiot" (Stan Rogers). Rogers addresses migrant work and regional employment opportunities in this song about an East Coaster working in Western Canada's oil industry.
- "Trouble in the Fields" (Nanci Griffith). Griffith sings about the challenges involved with rural work, particularly as they relate to shifts in the economy and changing expectations of family.

NOTES

1. Excluded are those residing on reserves or in other Aboriginal settlements; those living in institutions such as prisons or nursing homes; and full-time members of the Canadian Armed Forces. While both provinces and territories are included in the survey's coverage, data on the latter are not included in national estimates but are published separately (Statistics Canada 2013a). For additional information about this and other Statistics Canada data sources, visit the Statistics Canada website: http://www.statcan.gc.ca.

2. See Statistics Canada (1995, 2013a) for an overview of changes made to the Labour Force Survey (LFS) to reflect changing patterns of work in Canada.

3. Unless otherwise noted, the data (1976–2012) in this chapter come from annual averages compiled by Statistics Canada and made available through CANSIM (Canadian Socioeconomic Information Management system), the agency's key socioeconomic database. As estimates from the Labour Force Survey are regularly adjusted, the figures presented here are not comparable to data presented in earlier editions of this text. Access to CANSIM is at http://www5.statcan.gc.ca/cansim/a01?lang=eng.

4. Foot (2001). This author provides a fascinating account of how demographic trends, particularly the baby boom, influence all aspects of society. In our opinion, however, he underestimates the effects of the profound economic, political, ideological, and organizational changes that have also occurred in the past several decades. For additional discussion on demography, labour markets, and economic growth, see Sunter (2001) and Gomez and Foot (2013).

5. Statistics Canada (2010). This projection is based on population estimates as of July 1, 2009. Projections take into account trends in fertility, mortality, international migration (immigration and emigration), non-permanent residents (NPR), and internal migration. Various scenarios by age and sex are provided for 2009–36 for Canadian provinces, and for territories; and for 2009–61 for Canada. For a visual representation of Canada's aging population, see David Foot's website: http://www.footwork.com/pyramids.asp.

6. See Statistics Canada (2009a: 81) and summary statistics from the Pension Plans in Canada Survey at http://www.statcan.gc.ca/tables-tableaux/sum-som/l01/ cst01/labor26a-eng.htm. For recent discussions of pension trends, see Wannell (2007) in Canada and Wiatrowski (2012) in the United States.

7. Immigration and visible minority statistics in this section are taken from Statistics Canada's (2013c), *Immigration and Ethnocultural Diversity in Canada*. See Boyd and Vickers (2000) on historical Canadian immigration trends and Picot (2008) on economic outcomes in recent decades.

8. Aboriginal statistics are based on Statistics Canada's (2013d) *Aboriginal Peoples in Canada: First Nations People, Métis and Inuit*, which presents findings from the 2011 National Household Survey.

9. See Reich (1991, 2000), OECD and Statistics Canada (2011), Livingstone and Guile (2011), and Slowey and Schuetze (2012) on the role of education in a global knowledge economy.

10. On lifelong learning trends in Canada, see Statistics Canada (2009b). For a more global perspective, see Slowey and Schuetze (2012).

11. For a profile of educational attainment in Canada, see Statistics Canada (2008d) and Schuetze (2012). See also Clark (2000), who provides a long-term overview of the growth of the formal education system in Canada.

12. See Grenier et al. (2008). See also OECD and Statistics Canada (2011) and Krahn and Lowe (1999) on workplace literacy concerns.

13. On workplace training, see also Hurst (2008) and Cooke, Zeytinoglu, and Chowhan (2009).

14. See Livingstone (2005). For underemployment among immigrants, see Galarneau and Morisssette (2009). For additional discussions of underemployment, see Livingstone (2009) and Yuen (2010).

15. Bellin and Miller (1990: 187). For past discussions on presumed skill shortages, see Green and Ashton (1992) on the United Kingdom and Krahn (1997), Krahn and Lowe (1999), and Gingras and Roy (2000) on Canada. For recent discussions, see Burleton et al. (2013).

16. For past trends in job stability, see Statistics Canada (2002) and Heisz (2005). On specific sectors and the 2008–09 downturn, see Bernard (2009) and LaRochelle-Côté and Gilmore (2009). For youth trends, see LaRochelle-Côté (2013).

17. Data come from the 2011 National Household Survey (NHS) online data tables, specifically labour force and unemployment rates (Catalogue no. 99-012-X2011039) and income (Catalogue no. 99-014-X2011032). Usalcas (2011), Wilson and Macdonald (2010), and Perusse (2008) present useful analyses of the labour market activity and economic conditions of Aboriginal Canadians.

18. See Statistics Canada (2007b), *Participation and Activity Limitation Survey 2006: Analytical Report*, as well as Galarneau and Radulescu (2009). While Statistics Canada carried out the Canadian Survey on Disability in 2012, labour force results have not yet been released; see Statistics Canada, *The Daily* (December 3, 2013).

19. See Morissette (1997), Marquardt (1998), Clark (1999), Sunter (2001), and Labour Market Ministers (2000) on labour market difficulties faced by Canadian youth in the 1990s; Picot (1998) on declining youth wages; and Bowlby (2000) on school-to-work transition trends, including information on the number of youth attending school and not working.

20. LFP rates for older workers come from Statistics Canada (2004b), Sunter (2001: 31), and CANSIM (Tables 282-0002 and 282-0051). Gougeon (2009) discusses participation in pension plans. See also Stone (2008) on retirement transitions, Marshall (2011) on debt and retirement, and Powell and Cook (2009) for an international perspective on population aging.

21. Marshall and Mueller (2002) use a life-course perspective to discuss the aging workforce and social policy. Myles and Quadagno (2005) address population aging and retirement issues in a variety of countries.

22. Data on industrial sectors come from the Statistics Canada CANSIM database, Table 282-0008. Crompton and Vickers (2000) provide a century-long overview of labour force trends in Canada.

23. See Krahn (1992: 17–18) for further discussion of this classification system, which is quite similar to the industry typology developed by the Economic Council of Canada (1990) in its studies of the service sector. The Economic Council distinguished *dynamic services* (distributive and business services) from *non-market services* (education, health and welfare, public administration) and *traditional services* (retail trade and personal services).

24. Please note that comparisons of the percentages in Table 3.1 to similar industry distributions in earlier editions of this textbook are inappropriate, because of changes to Statistics Canada's industry classification system in 1999.

25. Data come from the United States Department of Labor (2013), *International Comparisons of Annual Labor Force Statistics, 1970–2012* (Full Series by Indicator and Underlying Levels, Tables 2-6, 2-7, 2-8, and 2-9). They are available at http://www.bls.gov/fls/#laborforce.

26. Statistics Canada, *The Daily* (March 17, 1998). As some occupations (e.g., agricultural) have declined in size, Statistics Canada has combined them with related occupations. Alternatively, as other occupations have grown in size, they have been subdivided and re-named.

27. As of 1999, Statistics Canada began to use a revised Standard Occupational Classification System (SOC91), rather than the SOC80, for presentations of Labour Force Survey and census data. The biggest impact of the change was on the management category, with some occupations formerly coded in this category now being placed in other categories. Statistics Canada revised its databases only back to 1987, so Table 3.2 begins with that year.

28. See Lucas (1971), Clemenson (1992), Angus and Griffin (1996), and Palmer and Sinclair (1997) on single-industry communities; Statistics Canada, *The Daily* (April 14, 2008), for a study of vulnerable communities that have experienced population decline; and Dorow and O'Shaughnessy's (2013) special issue of the *Canadian Journal of Sociology*, which provides a contemporary examination of the resource town of Fort McMurray.

GOOD JOBS, BAD JOBS, NO JOBS

"Last year, during his best three-month stretch, Jordan Golson sold about $750,000 worth of computers and gadgets at the Apple Store in Salem, N.H. It was a performance that might have called for a bottle of Champagne—if that were a luxury Mr. Golson could have afforded. 'I was earning $11.25 an hour,' he said. 'Part of me was thinking "This is great. I'm an Apple fan, the store is doing really well." But when you look at the amount of money the company is making and then you look at your paycheck, it's kind of tough.' Americans' love affair with the smartphone has helped create tens of thousands of jobs at places like Best Buy and Verizon Wireless and will this year pump billions into the economy. Within this world, the Apple Store is the undisputed king, a retail phenomenon renowned for impeccable design, deft service, and spectacular revenues. Last year, the company's 327 global stores ... sold $16 billion in merchandise. But most of Apple's employees enjoyed little of that wealth.... The Internet and advances in computing have created untold millionaires, but most of the jobs created by technology giants are service sector positions—sales employees and customer service representatives, repairmen and delivery drivers—that offer little of Silicon Valley's riches or glamour."

Source: David Segal, "Apple's Retail Army, Long on Loyalty but Short on Pay." *New York Times*, June 23, 2012. http://www.nytimes.com/2012/06/24/business/apple-store-workers-loyal-but-short-on-pay. html?_r=0.

● INTRODUCTION

More than two decades ago, the Economic Council of Canada's *Good Jobs, Bad Jobs* (1990) posed some important questions about the future of job quality in Canada's emerging "new economy." Highlighting shifts in new technologies and trade, the rise of the service sector, and the growing role of knowledge and education, the Council asked whether Canada might see growing polarization between those with "good jobs" and "bad jobs," as well as those with and without employment. Fast-forward to the present day, we see public attention fixed firmly again on such questions, in the aftermath of the 2007–8 financial collapse and the ensuing Great Recession. While some regions and industries in Canada boom, others are in decline. Globalization, layoffs, and downsizing continue to raise fears for many. Of note, the Economic Council of Canada no longer exists—a victim of government cuts and restructuring back in the early 1990s.

Amid this landscape, movements such as Occupy have given a public voice to concerns over growing disparities in wealth and income. Mass strikes by fast-food workers have drawn public attention to the struggles of those working for minimum wage. Best-selling books, such as *The Spirit Level* by Wilkinson and Pickett (2009), *Capital in the Twenty-First Century* by Piketty (2014), and *The Price of Inequality* by the Nobel Prize-winning economist Joseph Stiglitz (2012), have focused attention on the economic and social costs of inequality and polarization. Even YouTube has seen a dryly titled video, *Wealth Inequality in America*, go viral, attracting millions of views to date.

Clearly, economic inequality and labour market polarization are growing concerns for many, worthy of careful reflection and study. In this chapter, we draw together available empirical evidence to delve into this issue, exploring current trends in job quality, income, benefits, and occupational status. We also explore the emergence of "nonstandard," or "precarious," jobs, such as part-time, temporary, and self-employment, as well as trends in working hours. Moving beyond questions of good versus bad jobs, we also consider the question of no jobs, examining how access to employment has changed over time in Canada, and how unemployment varies today for workers in different regions, occupations, and social locations. As will become clear, an important question concerns the tradeoffs we may be seeing between the quantity and quantity of jobs. Related to this, we also touch on recent public policy initiatives that wrestle with questions about economic inequality and work.

■ WHAT IS JOB QUALITY?

Discussions about whether jobs are good or bad focus on job quality. For many Canadians, the ideal job is full time, full year, and permanent, providing steady income and security. But some individuals may prefer working in nonstandard jobs, such as part-time or temporary work, for educational, personal, or family reasons. Typically, however, nonstandard jobs are less likely to be considered good jobs. Certainly, some types of nonstandard work—for example, business consulting on a contract basis—pay very well. But as we will see, well-paying nonstandard work is the exception rather than the rule.

The criteria for deciding whether a particular job is good or bad are not universal.[1] Individuals compare the rewards a job provides against their own needs, preferences, and ambitions (see Chapter 13). Personal decisions are also shaped and constrained by the quality and quantity of jobs available in one's community. Since most workers are concerned about maintaining or improving their standard of living and quality of life, material or *extrinsic job rewards* are important. How much does the job pay? What kinds of benefits come with it? Is it full time and secure, or seasonal? In the following section, we examine some of the most important differences in job quality, with respect to pay, benefits, and full- or part-time status. We also look at *occupational status*, which refers to the prestige ranking of a particular job. Other factors, such as *intrinsic work rewards*, are discussed in Chapter 14.

Income Differences

Income is one of the most commonly considered job features for anyone seeking employment. But how do occupations in Canada compare? Statistics Canada collects information about income through several sources. For many years, the most reliable and detailed source of data came from the Census. As discussed in Chapter 3, however, in 2011, the long-form census was replaced by the voluntary National Household Survey (NHS). Given concerns about the reliability of NHS income data (Hulchanski et al. 2013), we draw on Labour Force Survey (LFS) data to highlight some of the most important factors influencing income differences in the Canadian labour market.

Considering only *paid employees* (that is, excluding the self-employed, discussed later in this chapter), incomes in the service industries are typically lower than in the goods-producing industries. For example, in 2012, measured as a median, annual average weekly earnings for full-time workers in the goods-producing sector were $958, compared to $854 for services. Looking more closely at the goods sector, we see further differences, with weekly earnings ranging from $1,320 in resource extraction (e.g., forestry, mining, and oil and gas) to $1,000 in construction to $847 in manufacturing. In contrast, weekly earnings in the service sector averaged just $481 in accommodation and food services, and $621 in retail and wholesale trade. But the large and growing service sector contains both lower-tier and upper-tier services, with many better-paying jobs in the latter. Hence, in 2012, we also observed higher weekly earnings in educational services ($1,153), public administration ($1,151), and professional, technical, and scientific services ($1,057).[2] As these comparisons suggest, there is more variation in employees' incomes within the service sector than within the goods-producing sector.

Moving from industry to occupation comparisons, again drawing on 2012 LFS data for individuals working full time, we also see notable differences. For instance, weekly median earnings are highest among senior managers ($1,912); professionals in business and finance ($1,153) and in health care ($1,288); workers in natural and applied sciences ($1,228); and teachers and professors ($1,307). But contractors and supervisors in the trades also earn relatively high incomes ($1,225). In contrast, the lowest weekly earnings are found in service-related occupations, including chefs and servers ($572), child-care and home support workers ($592), and retail sales and cashiers ($614).[3] Obviously, these broad groupings mask important differences within. For example, the category "professional occupations in health" includes everyone from specialist physicians to general practitioners (GPs), optometrists, dietitians, registered nurses (RNs), and more.

Higher earnings in some goods-producing and upper-tier services, and in managerial and professional occupations, can be traced, in part, to the presence of unions and professional associations that have bargained for higher incomes and full-time jobs. It is also apparent that workers with specific professional skills (e.g., teachers, doctors, and engineers) and more formal education are generally paid much more than those with less training. Thus, some of the industrial and occupational differences in earnings are due to supply and demand factors in a labour market that rewards educational investments. Important, too, are differences in the bargaining power of the various groups participating in the labour market, a subject to which we return in Chapters 5 and 11.

These occupational earning patterns also hide large gender differences. According to the 2012 Labour Force Survey, among Canadians working full time, women received 81.2 percent of men's median weekly earnings. Looking more closely, we learn that women employed in professional positions in natural and applied sciences reported median weekly earnings of $1,087, which translates to 86.3 percent of men's weekly pay ($1,260). Similarly, female teachers and professors earned 90.9 percent of the weekly earnings of their male counterparts ($1,250 and $1,375 respectively). In contrast, the gender wage gap is much wider in retail sales, with women receiving just 71.9 percent of men's median weekly pay ($460 and $640 respectively). The same pattern is observed in trades, transport, and equipment-related occupations, with women earning 75.0 percent of men's pay ($720 compared to $960). As these examples demonstrate, the *female–male earnings ratio* varies considerably across occupations, and, as already noted, these comparisons involve broad occupational groups, mixing distinct job types. It is most important to note that these figures are based on weekly earnings for full-time workers. Since women are more likely to work part time, as discussed in Chapter 3, the female–male earnings gap for all employed Canadians (full-time and part-time) is even wider than what we observed above, standing at 74.0 percent.[4]

While the *gender wage gap* has not declined significantly in the past few years, over the past several decades, it has been decreasing: women's earnings have been rising slowly while the earnings of men, on average, have stalled. Part of the reason for the long-term trend in rising female incomes is that more women have invested in higher education and, as a result, have gained access to better-paying jobs. However, if the explanation were this simple, we would expect female incomes to be higher than male incomes, since the proportion of female labour force participants with university degrees is now higher than the proportion for men (see Chapter 3). But that is not the case. Women, on average, still have less labour force experience and are more likely to enter fields of postsecondary study that lead to lower-paying jobs (Drolet 2002). Equally relevant, as discussed in Chapter 6, gender-biased hiring and promotion practices affect the female–male earnings ratio, too.

By restricting our discussion to these broad occupational categories, we also overlook the extreme ends of the *income distribution* in the Canadian labour market. At the top of the earnings hierarchy, chief executive officers (CEOs) of Canada's largest firms typically earn huge incomes (based on salaries, performance bonuses, and options to purchase stocks in their company at below-market value). In 2011, for instance, the CEOs of the top 100 companies listed on the Toronto Stock Exchange received an average compensation package of $7.7 million (Canadian Centre for Policy

Alternatives 2013). Looking at the top 50 CEOs, we see average earnings that are more than 235 times higher than the average income in Canada. Although executives have always been more highly compensated, current ratios are far higher than in the past. In 1995, for instance, the top 50 CEOs made 85 times more than the average income. It should be noted, as well, that the 2011 "average" includes a wide range of incomes. Among the top 10 earners are executives such as Frank Stronach, ex-chair of Magna, with combined earnings (base salary plus options) of over $40 million; and Gerald Schwartz of Onex, who earned $14.1 million. Certain industries also figure prominently. For instance, one-quarter of the top 20 earners come from Canada's five largest banks—Royal Bank of Canada, Toronto-Dominion Bank, Scotiabank, Bank of Montreal, and CIBC—with earnings ranging from $10.6 to $11.4 million. Of note, no one in the top 50 earned less than $6 million, and the lowest earner among the top 100 still earned $3.7 million overall.[5]

At the other end of the wealth scale are numerous workers with very low incomes. Legislated minimum wages in Canada have always been low, and in the past several decades, they have not kept up with inflation. Thus, in 2014, if a worker earning a minimum wage worked 40 hours a week for 52 weeks, she or he would earn anywhere from $20,696 annually in Alberta (the province with the lowest minimum wage of $9.95/hour) to $21,736 in Manitoba (with the highest provincial minimum wage in Canada of $10.45/hour).[6] However, few, if any, minimum wage workers would be employed year-round for 40 hours a week, so these estimates of annual income are likely too high for this group of workers.

Recognizing growing concern over minimum wage workers, the Ontario government appointed a Minimum Wage Advisory Panel in June 2013, which carried out extensive research and consultation. Its final report recommends regular reviews of minimum wage levels (adjusting annually for inflation) and in-depth tracking to understand the impact that minimum wages have on workers and families. As the report makes clear, there is growing concern about whether current minimum wage rates provide sufficient income to escape poverty; those most affected include youth, women, immigrants, and workers in fast-food, accommodation, and retail jobs (Ontario 2014).

Many, but certainly not all, of these lowest-paid workers are students in the lower-tier services (retail trade and consumer services), frequently part time. Some older, full-time workers also have minimum wage jobs, but many more are hired at pay rates only a few dollars above the minimum wage. As a second income in a household, such salesclerk, waitress, cashier, and service-station attendant jobs might help pay some bills. However, if a household relied only on this income, especially if it contained children, it would likely be living well below the official *low-income cutoff*, more commonly called the "poverty line."[7]

Hourly wage rates in blue-collar occupations, such as construction or manufacturing, are typically at least twice as high as the minimum wage. Yet even with a $20-per-hour wage and working full time and year-round, these earnings would still make it extremely difficult to raise a family in most major Canadian urban centres. Furthermore, many of these blue-collar jobs are seasonal and are subject to frequent layoffs. Service jobs are also prone to erratic and insufficient hours. Consequently, when we look closely at the characteristics of Canadian families living below the poverty line, we find that low wages, insufficient work (part time or part year), and periodic unemployment combined are usually the problem. Some of the *working poor* lack education or marketable skills, but many simply cannot find well-paid and secure employment.[8]

Other Employment Benefits

Additional *employment benefits*—a form of indirect pay and increased income security—are another important dimension of the quality of jobs. Canadian employers are legally required to contribute to Employment Insurance (EI), the Canada/Quebec Pension Plan, and Workers' Compensation. Many employers, particularly large firms and public-sector organizations, also spend large amounts on additional benefits, including paid vacation; sick leave; medical, dental, disability, and life insurance; private pension plans; and maternity/paternity leave. Over the second half of the last century (1953 to 1998), the costs of non-wage benefits doubled in Canada, from about 15 percent of total labour costs to more than one-third. Given how much employers spend on such non-wage forms of compensation, it is probably inappropriate to call them "fringe benefits," as has been the custom (Budd 2004: 597).[9]

Though we lack current national-level data on this issue, a Statistics Canada national survey in 2005 shows that between 50 percent and

60 percent of Canadian private-sector employees (government employees and the self-employed were excluded) had an employer-sponsored pension plan or group registered retirement savings plan (33% reported the former and 18% the latter), supplementary health insurance, a dental plan, and a life insurance/disability plan. But one in four (26%) received none of these five non-wage benefits (Statistics Canada 2008a: 50). Likewise, more recent provincial analysis for Ontario finds that about 55 percent of workers had access to an employer-sponsored pension plan from 1999 to 2009 (Noack and Vosko 2011). Much like income, access to benefits varies widely across occupation and work status. As shown in Figure 4.1, full-time private-sector employees are much more likely than part-time workers to receive various benefits. We also see that those in high-status professional occupations have far greater access to most non-wage benefits than those working in more routine work, such as marketing or sales. Unionized employees also have higher levels of coverage. In short, the distribution of benefits, like income, is highly polarized within the Canadian labour force.

Although these additional comparisons are not shown in Figure 4.1, the same 2005 survey revealed differences by age, education, and size of workplace. Specifically, older, and better educated, workers were more likely to receive each of these benefits, as were those working in larger workplaces and those who had been with the same employer for a longer time (Statistics Canada 2008a: 50–51). The 2005 survey did not provide information about temporary workers, but we know from other studies that they are much less likely than workers with permanent jobs to have pension, medical, dental, and life-insurance plans (Lowe and Schellenberg 2001). The same applies to the self-employed, particularly those who work alone, since it is expensive (and sometimes quite complicated) to purchase health and dental plans for oneself. Furthermore, higher-paid workers, as well as those employed in larger workplaces and in unionized settings, are more likely to receive formal job-related training (Jackson 2005: 47–50) which, in time, can translate into better jobs and higher income.[10] It is apparent, then, that pay differences within the Canadian labour market are accentuated by the uneven distribution of non-wage benefits. And, as the costs to employers of providing such benefits increase, we may continue to see relatively fewer workers receiving them (Waldie 2005).

FIGURE 4.1 Non-wage Benefits by Occupation, Full-Time/Part-Time, and Union Status, 2005

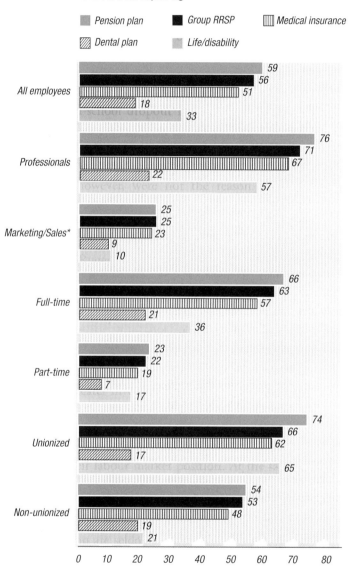

Source: Adapted from Statistics Canada (2008f: 50) *Workplace and Employee Survey Compendium 2005.* Cat. no. 71-585-X.

Occupational Status

We seldom find doctors, lawyers, scientists, or professors avoiding the question: "What do you do?" But for clerks, janitors, parking-lot attendants, and many others, the same question might elicit an apologetic "I'm just a ..." In short, there is considerable consensus in our society about which jobs have higher status. Although less important than income and benefits (which directly determine one's standard of living) and job security (which ensures continuity of that standard), *occupational status* (or prestige) is something we must also consider when comparing different jobs. To a great extent, our self-image and the respect of others are determined by our occupational status, although there is probably also a tendency for individuals situated higher within a stratification system to take occupational status more seriously (Ollivier 2000).

On average, individuals in higher-status occupations have higher incomes. It may seem that both higher pay and higher status are a direct result of the greater skill and responsibility required by certain jobs. Generally, higher-status jobs do require more education, cognitive ability, and skill (Hunter and Manley 1986). But it is also possible that some occupations have come to be seen as more prestigious because, over time, incomes in this line of work have risen. Higher incomes, in turn, might be the result of skill increases, but they may also reflect the ability of a powerful occupational group to limit entry into its field or to raise the prices for the services it provides. It is also clear that some occupations have traditionally had higher social status because they were viewed as men's work rather than as women's work (see Chapter 6). Thus, for a variety of reasons, jobs defined as "better" in terms of extrinsic rewards (e.g., pay, benefits, safety) typically also have higher status in society.

Researchers have developed two different basic types of occupational status scales to rank occupations and thus locate individuals or families within a social hierarchy or stratification system. In Canada, updated scales of both types have recently been made available.

Goyder and Frank (2007) used a national survey to ask Canadians to rank the 26 major broad occupational categories in the National Occupational Classification (NOC) system (discussed in Chapter 3) on their "social standing" or *occupational prestige*. This scale, ranging from a possible low value of 0 to a high value of 100, provides prestige scores as low as 52 for unskilled labourers in primary industries, as well as unskilled sales and service occupations, through, for example, 57 for clerical occupations, 67 for skilled occupations in primary industries, and 72 for professional occupations in business and finance, up to 81 for professional occupations in health (2007: 69).

Boyd (2008) took the alternative approach of ranking occupations according to the average income and education of Canadians currently in these occupations. Using 2001 national census data, she created a *socioeconomic status* (SES) scale, ranging from a possible low of 0 to a possible high of 100, that ranked more than 500 detailed NOC categories (as well as the smaller number of major categories). Examples of socioeconomic status scores, at the detailed occupational level, range from, for example, 9 for nannies, 29 for hairstylists, 38 for receptionists, 53 for radio announcers, and 75 for dental hygienists, up to 92 for psychologists and 100 for doctors. While the socioeconomic status scale has a much wider actual range than does the prestige scale, both scales help us to compare "good jobs" and "bad jobs" and the many in between.

■ NONSTANDARD WORK ARRANGEMENTS

Varieties of Nonstandard Work

While most employed Canadians have a full-time, year-round, permanent paid job, alternatives to this standard type of employment arrangement—referred to as either "nonstandard," "precarious," or "contingent" work—have been slowly increasing, not just in Canada, but in all industrialized societies.[11] *Part-time work* is the most common type of nonstandard work, but the number of *multiple-job holders* has also been expanding. The *self-employed* category, especially *own-account* (who work alone), has likewise grown. And there are also indications that *temporary* (or contract) work has become more widespread.

Why these changes? Nonstandard work may be mandated by employers or initiated by individual workers. Many employers, in both the private and public sectors, have responded to the economic difficulties of recent decades by replacing full-time with part-time workers (and sometimes part-year workers) and by eliminating permanent positions. The latter have sometimes been replaced with temporary (limited-term contract) positions or workers hired from a temporary help agency (a form of subcontracting). These employment strategies allow employers greater flexibility to respond to uneven demands for goods and services, and they clearly reduce labour costs (probably a more important factor, in many cases). This "flexible firm" model (see Pollert 1988) is discussed in Chapter 9. At the same time, a growing number of Canadians have chosen to set up business (the own-account self-employed) or to take on a second job. Finally, the rise of the service sector has driven some of these trends to the extent that workers may be needed only for a few hours at a time to cover peak periods, such as lunch- or dinner-time in restaurants and cafés.

Some workers choose alternative forms of employment (part-time work or self-employment, for example) because of personal preference. But for many others, such choices are a response to a difficult labour market. Workers may create their own jobs because few paid jobs are available; accept temporary or part-time work only when permanent, full-time jobs are scarce; or take on a second job because their first job pays poorly. Nonstandard jobs typically pay less, provide fewer benefits, are less likely to be covered by labour legislation, and have less employment security (Vosko 2005; Law Commission of Ontario 2012; Kalleberg 2011), so an increase in nonstandard employment means an increase in the precariousness of employment and income for many Canadian workers. Furthermore, there is evidence that a job history of nonstandard work carries a long-term cost: such workers have reduced access to workplace training and education, making it difficult to move into better paying, more stable, jobs. Given this, growing public and policy attention is being paid to this trend, as evidenced by the Law Commission of Ontario's (2012) recent report and recommendations, *Vulnerable Workers and Precarious Work*.

We mentioned above the increase in *own-account self-employment* in the past decades. Approximately 10.5 percent of employed working-age Canadians (15 to 64 years old) are in this category, which includes farmers, doctors, lawyers, and business consultants, as well as the small entrepreneurs we typically associate with self-employment. Multiple-job holding increased from 2 percent in 1977 to roughly 5 percent in 1993 and has held steady at this level ever since.[12] People take on a second job for a variety of reasons, including topping up an inadequate income, paying off debts, and saving for the future. However, since most are supplementing a full-time job, and since about 20 percent in 2012 had professional or managerial jobs, we should be cautious about assuming that all Canadians with more than one job are in a precarious financial or employment situation. In this regard, it is interesting to note that, in 2007, over 30 percent of multiple-job holders were self-employed in one of their two jobs, and another 10 percent were self-employed in both (Statistics Canada 2007a: 86).

Nonstandard jobs are much more common in some sectors of the economy. In terms of industry variations, agriculture has the highest rate of nonstandard work. A large proportion of these nonstandard workers are the own-account self-employed. Construction also has a high rate of nonstandard work, reflecting extensive self-employment and temporary contract work. But, given their relative size in the economy, the lower-tier service industries—retail and other consumer services—are the main source of nonstandard employment. A worker's demographic characteristics also influence her or his likelihood of being employed in a nonstandard job. Women are more likely to be in nonstandard jobs than are men. Nonstandard forms of employment also are concentrated among the youngest and oldest members of the workforce.

Part-Time Work

Half a century ago, in 1953, less than 4 percent of employed Canadians held part-time jobs, but that is far from the case now. During the 1960s and 1970s, part-time work became more common, and today it is the most prevalent type of nonstandard work. Until recently, full-time work was defined by Statistics Canada as working 30 or more hours per week in total. But the rise in multiple-job holding forced a rethinking of this definition, since some people holding several part-time jobs (totalling more than 30 hours) were being counted as full-time workers. Since 1996, part-time workers have been defined as those who work fewer than 30 hours per week in their *main* job.

Figure 4.2 displays part-time rates for the past several decades, calculated using the new definition. Back in 1976, the national part-time rate for all employed Canadians (ages 15 and older) was roughly 13 percent. The recession in the early 1980s pushed the part-time rate much higher, to 17 percent by 1983. The recession at the beginning of the 1990s led to another increase in part-time employment rates, to 19 percent in 1993. Since that time, the part-time rate has hovered between 18 and 19 percent. In 2012, 18.8 percent of all employed Canadians were working part time (nearly 3.3 million).

Part-time rates for adult women and men (ages 25 and older) are also plotted in Figure 4.2. It is apparent that few employed men 25 years of age

FIGURE 4.2   Part-Time Employment by Age and Gender, Canada, 1976–2012

Part-time employment rate (%)

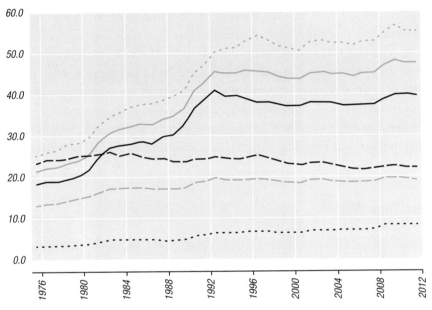

Source: Statistics Canada. CANSIM Table 282-0002 - Labour Force Survey estimates (LFS), by sex and detailed age group, Annual (persons x 1,000). <http://www5.statcan.gc.ca/cansim/a05?lang=eng&id=2820002>

and older are working part time, although the rate for this group climbed from 2 percent in the mid-1970s to 7.6 percent in 2012. As for adult women, their much higher part-time rates have fluctuated between 21 and 26 percent over the same period. In 2012, 21.7 percent of women 25 years of age and older worked part time. Overall, women comprise 67 percent of all part-time workers (ages 15 and older). The most prominent trend observed in Figure 4.2 is the increase in part-time employment among young people (ages 15 to 24). In 1976, the youth part-time employment rate was 21 percent. By 1983, the rate had soared to over 30 percent, then climbed further to 41 percent by 1991. By 1995, the youth part-time rate had risen to 45 percent, before dropping marginally to 43.5 percent in 2001 and then rising back to over 47 percent in 2012. Thus, in the first decade of the 21st century, nearly half of all employed 15- to 24-year-olds in Canada (47 percent, or nearly 1.2 million) were working part time. As with older workers, youth part-time rates vary by gender, with a male rate of 39.4 percent in 2012, compared to a part-time rate of 55.2 percent for 15- to 24-year-old females.

Some people choose part-time work because it allows them to balance work and family responsibilities, to continue their education while still holding a job, or simply to have more leisure time. Others, *involuntary part-time workers*, are forced to accept part-time jobs because they cannot find one that is full time. The monthly Labour Force Survey asks part-time workers why they are working part time, providing a range of answers. Figure 4.3 displays the reasons given by Canadian part-time workers in 1975 and 2012. Although these figures offer a glimpse of change over time, it is important to underline that the data are not strictly comparable because of changes in how "reasons for part-time work" have been measured (Statistics Canada 2011: 15). Still, they offer the best available information we have to assess how working patterns have changed over time.

FIGURE 4.3   Reasons for Part-Time Work, Canada, 1975 and 2012

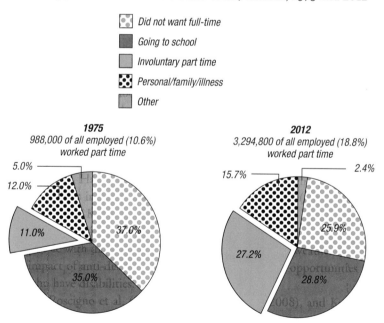

Source: Adapted from Statistics Canada. Labour Force Historical Review 2001. Cat. no. 71F0004XCB; and Statistics Canada. CANSIM Table 282-0002 - Labour Force Survey estimates (LFS), by sex and detailed age group, Annual (persons unless otherwise noted). <http://www5.statcan.gc.ca/cansim/a05?lang=eng&id=2820002>

As we can see, in 1975, 37 percent of less than 1 million part-time workers stated that they did not want a full-time job—that is, they had a personal preference for working part time. Another 35 percent chose part-time work because they were attending school. For a majority of youth, such jobs fit well alongside high school, college, or university. Another 11 percent of part-time workers indicated they were working part time "involuntarily"—that is, they were "only able to find part-time work," suggesting a lack of suitable alternatives. Finally, 12 percent of workers indicated personal reasons, such as illness or family matters, as well as "other" unspecified reasons' (5%). From the Labour Force Survey, we do know that adult women working part time, especially those with children, are likely to cite personal or family reasons, or simply state that they do not want full-time work. But had such workers been asked whether they would still prefer a part-time job if they had access to adequate and affordable childcare, it is likely that at least some would have expressed interest in full-time work. In other words, traditional assumptions about caregiving responsibilities, together with a shortage of affordable, quality childcare, may lead us to underestimate the real level of involuntary part-time work among adult women (Duffy and Pupo 1992).

Looking at the 2012 data, we see both similarities and change—though again, we should keep in mind that "reasons for part-time work" have been measured somewhat differently. Despite this, we again see a fairly sizable group (25.9%) who did not want full-time work, suggesting that for some Canadians, part-time work remains a preference and choice. Similar to 1975, another sizable group (28.8%) were working part time while also attending school. Personal, family illness, and other reasons together account for about 18 percent of workers. What is most notable, however, is the large size of the "involuntary" part-time group, which accounts for well over one-quarter of workers. These individuals indicated they were working part time due to "business conditions" or being "unable to find full-time work" (whether or not they have looked for full-time work in the last month). While the rise in involuntary part-time work may reflect measurement issues, in part, it also serves as a reminder that there is more to this trend than any change in worker "preferences." Part of the increase stems from employer practices as they seek to increase the flexibility of their staffing and hours, and reduce payroll and benefit costs.

Part-time rates vary considerably across industries and occupations. In 2012, the part-time rate in the goods-producing sector was still low (only 6.3%). Thus, most of the part-time jobs are in the service industries, in both the lower- and upper-tier services. For example, the part-time rate in the retail trade industry in 2012 was almost 35.2 percent. High rates are also found in accommodation and food services (41.0%), education (24.8%), and health care and social assistance (23.3%). However, many of the part-time jobs in the upper-tier services (nurses and teachers, for example) are better paid than the part-time jobs (often held by students) in the retail trade and other consumer services. As for occupational differences, only 6.5 percent of managers were working part time in 2012, compared to 17.4 percent of clerical workers, 47.9 percent of retail sales-clerks, and 40.0 percent of child-care and home-care workers. As we will see in Chapter 5, there is a strong correlation between occupational status, income, and the prevalence of nonstandard work arrangements, including part-time work.

Temporary Employment

Some forms of temporary employment, like seasonal employment in the tourism or construction industry, have been part of the Canadian labour market for many decades (Vosko 2000; Smith and Neuwirth 2008; Galarneau 2010). However, both private- and public-sector employers have begun to hire more employees on a limited-term contract basis (perhaps six months or a year), rather than offering permanent positions as was the custom a decade or two ago. In addition, temporary help agencies have been hiring more workers to be sent out on assignment to employers seeking to fill a temporary employment need. In terms of detailed statistical trends, though, we know less about the growth in *temporary employment*, since Statistics Canada only began monitoring this phenomenon on a regular basis in the late 1990s. Defining temporary jobs as those with a specific end date, the 2012 Labour Force Survey shows 13.6 percent of Canadians (2,020,000) in such positions, up from 11.3 percent in 1997 when Statistics Canada began tracking this trend. About one-quarter (22.3%) of all temporary workers were in seasonal jobs, and slightly more (24.3%) were in casual jobs (very short-term, with no specific contract). Most others (52.7%) held positions with a specific, contracted term. Of note, temporary jobs grew by 57 percent between 1997 and 2008, compared to a 27 percent growth rate for permanent jobs. More recently, during the 2008–9 downturn, growth rates declined somewhat (Galarneau 2010).[13]

Women of ages 25 and older are slightly more likely to be in temporary work than men (11.0% and 9.7% respectively). Once more, as in part-time work, young workers are heavily overrepresented in temporary jobs. In 2012, approximately 30.9 percent of 15-to-24-year-old employed Canadians were in a job with a specific end date, compared to 10.3 percent for those 25 years and older. Young student workers are more likely to be employed in the lower-tier consumer services, where low-paying temporary jobs are common. In the upper-tier services (the education and health and welfare industries, for example), it is much easier to offer a new (young) employee a contract position than to move someone already in a permanent position to a contractually limited job. Quite often, contract employees work along-side permanent employees, performing similar tasks and for comparable pay, but without the guarantee of continued employment beyond six months or a year. While some people, often those with highly marketable skills, find such arrangements quite satisfactory, others are frustrated and worried by their employment and income insecurity. Of note, temporary workers also experience a wage gap relative to permanent workers, even when taking other factors, such as age and education, into account (Galarneau 2010).

Finally, as noted in Chapter 2, another form of temporary work that has become increasingly common, and controversial, in Canada involves temporary foreign workers (TFWs) who migrate to fill jobs in a variety of low-paid sectors. As Thomas (2010) notes, the number of individuals admitted to Canada to work temporarily in recent years has grown rapidly, outpacing the growth of permanent immigrants. Typically, TFWs are restricted to specific occupations and locations, and to prescribed employers. This situation raises concerns about the potential for their exploitation as they lack mobility to leave unacceptable working conditions or to seek jobs that can improve their income, benefits, or opportunities. While we discuss this trend in greater detail in Chapter 5, we note here that most TFWs fill fairly routine, service jobs. In fact, just five occupations—nannies/babysitters, harvesting labourers, greenhouse workers, housekeepers, and farm workers—account for 46 percent of all such workers. Despite this, we also see polarization among TFWs, with a much smaller group holding professional jobs—the most common being postsecondary research and teaching assistants, scientists, and engineers (Thomas 2010: 43).

● SELF-EMPLOYMENT TRENDS

As in other industrialized capitalist economies, self-employment has dropped sharply over the past century. In 1946, for example, 33 percent of employed

Canadians were self-employed. By 1981 this figure had fallen to 10 percent (Riddell 1985: 9). This shift toward paid labour can be explained to a considerable extent by changes in the agricultural sector. Early in the 20th century, about three-quarters of those employed in agriculture were owner-managers, and most of the rest were unpaid family workers. Since the 1940s, however, the number of farms in Canada has undergone a huge decline, falling from a relative high of 733,000 farms in 1941 to just 229,373 in 2006, according to the 2006 Census. At the same time, the remaining farms have been getting larger, and the proportion of paid workers in agriculture has been increasing slowly. By 2012, the 309,200 Canadians employed in agriculture consisted of paid workers (39.4%), unpaid family workers (2.8%), and self-employed individuals (60.6%). Thus, while wage labour has become more common in agriculture, a major decline in the number of family farms has meant fewer self-employed individuals and unpaid family workers.[14]

Over the decades, self-employment in the secondary and service sectors also declined slowly; however, a reversal of this trend appeared about 25 years ago. As a result, in 2012, nearly 2.7 million (15.2%) of all employed Canadians (including those in agriculture) were self-employed, up from 12 percent in 1976 (but down from a high of 17.2% in 1998).[15] A similar increase has been observed in other industrialized capitalist economies, including that of the United States, but the trend has been especially notable in Canada. Thus, while self-employment in Canada rose in the 1990s, the self-employment rate in the United States has remained around 10 percent (Hipple 2010). In Canada, the number of *self-employed employers* (who hire others to work for them) has typically been smaller than the number of *own-account self-employed* (without employees), a group that has also been called "solo self-employed" (Hughes 2005). In recent decades, though, the size of this latter group has grown dramatically. Thus, while in the early 1980s, there were roughly 1.2 solo workers for every employer, by 2012, this ratio was 2.3 solo workers for every employer. Today, the solo self-employed make up nearly 70 percent of all self-employed and represent just over 1 in 10 employed Canadians. Yet, this figure is low compared to many less-industrialized countries: for example, about 25 percent of Mexico's workforce is in this category.[16]

Self-employment is still more prevalent among men than among women. In 2012, 11.4 percent of working women were self-employed, compared to 18.7 percent of working men. But the female self-employment rate has been rising steadily since the 1980s, and the rate of increase has been higher for women, especially as self-employed employers. By 2012, women made up almost 40 percent of all own-account self-employed in Canada and over one-quarter of all self-employed employers. Some women have moved into self-employment to better balance work and family, while others seek greater challenge and opportunity (Hughes 2005, 2010). Self-employment increases with age. In 2007, the self-employed were 46.5 years old on average, compared to just 37.7 years for private-sector employees and 42.1 years for those employed in the public sector (Statistics Canada 2009a: 47).

Historically, the recessions in Canada at the beginning of the 1980s and the 1990s may have contributed indirectly to the rise of self-employment, particularly own-account self-employment. Indeed, in 2000, about one-fifth of women and men reported being forced into self-employment by job loss or lack of other opportunities (Human Resources Development Canada and Statistics Canada 2002). But a direct relationship between economic downturns and growth in self-employment is weak at best (Arai 1997; Hughes 2005; Manser and Picot 1999: 43).

While many employers in both the private and public sectors reduced the size of their labour force during these recessions, leading to higher rates of unemployment, it was not necessarily those who lost their jobs who then set up their own businesses. Most of the self-employed typically come directly from the ranks of wage earners. Furthermore, managerial, professional, and technical workers are more likely to become self-employed than are clerical and manual workers (the groups typically most affected by unemployment). The self-employed are more highly educated than the rest of the labour force, suggesting that at least some of the growth in self-employment may have been a response by more advantaged workers to perceived job insecurity.

The self-employed are dispersed across a wide range of industries and occupations, with considerable variation in income and other rewards. According to the most recent data from Industry Canada (2009: 38), 19 percent are involved in management occupations; 17 percent, in trades and transport jobs; 16 percent, in sales and services; 11 percent, in blue-collar jobs in primary industries; and 11 percent, in business, finance, and administrative occupations. Given this wide dispersal of the self-employed across occupations and throughout the goods-producing and upper- and lower-tier services, it is not surprising that the income distribution of Canada's self-employed is bimodal. In 2005, 79 percent of the self-employed earned less than $20,000, compared to only 40 percent of paid workers. At the same time, 3 percent of the self-employed were among Canada's highest earners, reporting incomes in excess of $100,000, compared to 4 percent of paid workers (Statistics Canada 2009b: 80).

● HOURS OF WORK AND ALTERNATIVE WORK ARRANGEMENTS

In 1870, the standard number of hours in a workweek (the number beyond which overtime would typically be paid to full-time workers) in the Canadian manufacturing sector was 64. This number was subsequently reduced because of trade union pressures and the introduction of new manufacturing technologies that could produce more goods in a shorter time. By 1901, 59 hours per week was standard in manufacturing. Twenty years later, 50 hours per week was typical, but this average changed little until after World War II. Between 1946 and 1949, the manufacturing standard dropped quickly from 49 hours per week to 44 hours. It then fell to 40 hours by 1957, fluctuated slightly around this point for the next two decades, and dropped to 39 hours per week by 1976. Since then we have seen a small further decline. During most of the 2000s, the average time (usual hours) worked per week for the total employed labour force hovered around 36 and 37 hours. Thus, on average, Canadians spend far less time at work than they did a century ago.

A closer look at the decline in working time over the past two decades reveals an important change in Canadian work patterns. In particular, we witnessed a distinct polarization in hours worked—more people have been working long hours and more people have been working part time.[17] In 2012, only 60 percent of the Canadians employed worked between 35 and 40 hours per week in their main job, down from 66 percent in 1976. One in four (25%) worked fewer than 35 hours, and 14 percent worked more than 40 hours per week. Thus, while the average number of hours worked has declined slightly since the mid-1970s, the much bigger story concerns the proportion of Canadians working long hours, as well as the long-term rise of part-time work.

We have already discussed key trends in part-time work. But a few observations about long working hours are necessary. For some workers, particularly self-employed professionals, longer hours may provide higher incomes. For others, the added work may simply be an attempt to avoid a decline in standard of living when real incomes stagnate. But longer hours also cut into leisure and family time, and they have been shown to have detrimental effects on health and work–life balance. The Labour Force Survey documents a slight increase in workweeks in the 41-to-49-hour range since the early 1990s. What might be called extremely long hours—weeks averaging 50 or more hours—has seen a decline, however. Still, in 2012, 8.1 percent of employed Canadians worked 50 hours or more in their major job.

Overtime work is also relevant to consider. It is excluded from Statistics Canada's reporting of regular workweeks; however, the Labour Force Survey does ask respondents whether they have worked any paid or unpaid overtime in the week before the survey. Over the past decade, more than one in five workers reported putting in some overtime. What is particularly interesting is that about half of total overtime worked is unpaid. So, in 2012, for example, over 11 percent of all workers worked unpaid overtime in a typical month, usually giving about 8.3 hours, on average, to their employer without receiving any compensation in return. Unpaid overtime violates employment standards legislation; because of this, class-action lawsuits have been filed by employees at several Canadian banks, seeking compensation for their unpaid overtime hours.[18]

Shift work has long been common, but not always welcome, in some industries (e.g., health, consumer services), but there does seem to be some interest in alternative work schedules. *Flextime* (choosing the time to start and stop work) and *job sharing* (where two individuals share a full-time job) have been receiving more attention in the past decade, as has *teleworking* (working at home or in a remote site, often using computer technology), as noted in Chapter 2. These work options can help parents balance childcare with their jobs. But they can also have drawbacks, as they may hinder collaboration and satisfying interactions with coworkers.[19] Recently, Yahoo's CEO Marissa Mayer provoked debate and criticism when she suspended Yahoo's popular teleworking policy, just shortly after having her own baby and building a nursery right next door to her office (Kotkin 2013).

But how common are shift-work arrangements in Canada? Past data from the 2005 General Social Survey suggest that most workers (72%) had a regular day schedule, with another one-fifth of workers on either an irregular schedule (9%) or rotating shift (9%). Another 6 percent had a regular evening or night shift, and just 4 percent worked casual, on-call, or split shifts (Williams 2008). While some families use shift work as a way to create work–life balance (e.g., through tag-team parenting), in other cases, shift work—especially rotating shifts—can be a source of significant stress (Presser 2003). Likewise, a more recent, large-scale study of Canadian workers, by Duxbury and Higgins (2012), found that roughly two-thirds of workers had to adhere to a 9 to 5 work schedule—flexible work arrangements were not that common. For instance, just 15 percent reported use of flextime or a compressed work-week. Of note, less than 1 percent of workers had access to a formal telework policy, though many workers carried out telework informally. More than half reported regularly completing work in the evenings or on weekends, outside their normal business hours. In terms of satisfaction with working hours, Duxbury and Higgins found that, while a majority were content with their existing hours, one-quarter of employees would be happy to work fewer hours for less pay.

Shorter workweeks have been negotiated in several western European countries, in part, to reduce unemployment by sharing work among a larger number of workers. For example, in the mid-1990s, German autoworkers negotiated a new deal with Volkswagen in order to preserve jobs, achieving a reduced workweek with little pay loss. More significant, and contentious, was France's legislated introduction, in 2000, of a 35-hour workweek aimed at lowering unemployment. Although newer legislation allows overtime and higher maximum hours for some workers, the 35-hour week remains the standard for many public- and private-sector workers in France. Longer vacations also help spread work within a society—as well as contributing to the quality of life. Unlike workers in a number of European countries where vacations of four weeks or longer are required by law, many Canadian workers have just two weeks of paid vacation per year (in addition to statutory holidays). For most Canadian employees, vacation entitlements might rise to three or four weeks per year only after many years in the job.

■ UNEMPLOYMENT TRENDS

Counting the Unemployed

Labour Force Survey estimates indicate that, during 2012, there were 18,876,100 Canadians ages 15 and older in the labour force, with 17,507,700 of them employed (including self-employed). The unemployed, numbering

1,368,400, made up the difference. To put this in perspective, the number of unemployed people in 2012 was larger than the total population (children included) of Nova Scotia (780,300), Newfoundland and Labrador (427,700), and Prince Edward Island (120,500) combined. The official *unemployment rate* is calculated by dividing the number of individuals out of work and actively looking for work (the unemployed) by the total number of labour force participants (including the unemployed). In 2012, the national unemployment rate was 7.2 percent–down from 8.3 percent in 2009, following the 2008 U.S. economic crash, which had ripple effects in the Canadian economy. While higher than the historic low of 6.0 percent in 2007, current rates are still nowhere near the dramatically high levels (which peaked around 11%) of the recessions of the early 1980s and 1990s.

Such calculations reveal the percentage of labour force participants who are unemployed at a particular point (an annual average provides the average of 12 monthly estimates). But over the course of a year, many people find jobs while many others quit or lose them. Consequently, if we were to count the number of people who had been unemployed at some point during a year, this alternative unemployment rate would be higher. For example, in 1997, when the annual average unemployment rate was high (9.1%), over the course of the entire year, 17 percent of individuals and 28 percent of all families had experienced unemployment (Sussman 2000: 11).

The official definition of unemployment, whether we calculate rates for a single point in time or over the full year, identifies a state of being without paid work (including self-employment). It excludes students who do not wish to work while studying, individuals performing unpaid work in the home, people with disabilities who are not seeking work, and the retired, all of whom are considered to be outside the labour force. It also excludes potential labour force participants who have given up the search for work, believing there is no work available. Historically, economic downturns create a surge in *discouraged* workers. For instance, during the 1981–82 recession, the Labour Force Survey estimated there were 197,000 such workers (Akyeampong 1992: 1). While these numbers declined in the latter 1980s as the economy recovered, they peaked again in the early 1990s recession, at 99,000 in March 1992. Lower numbers of discouraged workers in the 1990s reflect other basic labour market changes already discussed: declining youth labour force participation, rising educational enrollments, and earlier retirement. In other words, rather than waiting for new jobs to materialize, a larger proportion of jobless Canadians may have stayed in or returned to school, or retired early, during the 1992–93 recession.[20] With record high employment levels in the 2000s, until early 2008—the year the financial crisis hit the global economy—the issue of discouraged workers received little attention. Yet, while long-term unemployment (defined as 52 or more weeks without a job) has fallen significantly since the 1990s, 6.7 percent of the unemployed in 2008 had not worked in at least a year (Statistics Canada 2008a). By 2012, the average duration of unemployment stood at 16 weeks, up 5 weeks from pre-2008 levels; nearly one in five unemployed Canadians had been without a job for more than six months (Tal 2012: 3–4).

Canadian Unemployment Rates over Time

Canadian unemployment rates reached their highest point in the last century (around 20%) during the Depression of the 1930s (Brown 1987). But these hard times were quickly replaced by labour shortages during World War II and in the immediate postwar years. The average national unemployment rate was only 2 percent during the 1940s. Since the end of World War II, unemployment has slowly climbed higher, responding to successive business cycles of recession and expansion. Unemployment rates peaked at over 11 percent during recessions at the beginning of the 1980s (11.9% in 1983) and the 1990s (11.4% in 1993).

In the first decade of the 2000s, the national jobless rate fell to around 7 percent, dropping to 6.0 percent in 2007. This development marked the reversal of a long-term upward trend in unemployment that had taken place in the last few decades of the 20th century. Comparing unemployment across time, Statistics Canada figures show that the 10-year average unemployment rate was 4 percent in the 1950s, 5 percent in the 1960s, 6.7 percent in the 1970s, and 9.5 percent in the 1980s and 1990s. The opening decade of the 21st century presented a boom–bust picture of the economy and, therefore, unemployment. After dipping below 7 percent in 2000, unemployment rates increased slightly in the early 2000s and then fell steadily, hitting a 33-year low in 2008. The "Great Recession" in late 2008 caused a spike in unemployment, but rates did not even reach 9 percent in 2009. Thus, despite pockets of high unemployment in the late 2000s, the decade resembles the 1970s more than the 1980s or 1990s, when high and persistent unemployment was a significant problem.[21]

Indeed, in the late 1980s and 1990s, as unemployment rates climbed upwards, the duration of unemployment also increased. Consider this: in 1976, the average spell of unemployment was just about 14 weeks. By 1983, the period rose to 21 weeks, falling and then rising to 26 weeks in 1994. By 1998, unemployment rates began to decline, but the average duration of unemployment was still over 20 weeks. More than one in five unemployed Canadians (22%) had unsuccessfully sought work for six months or longer, and 10 percent of the unemployed had been seeking work for a full year or longer (see Statistics Canada, CANSIM, Table 282-0048). Older workers laid off during the recessions of the early 1980s and 1990s were most likely to experience prolonged periods of unemployment. By contrast, the average duration of unemployment in 2012 was 16 weeks—a rate more in line with the mid-1970s than the 1980s or early 1990s (Tal 2012).

Regional Variations in Unemployment

National rates of unemployment conceal considerable variation across regions of the country. In 2012, Newfoundland and Labrador's unemployment rate averaged 12.5 percent, compared with 10.2 percent in New Brunswick, 9.0 percent in Nova Scotia, and 11.3 percent in Prince Edward Island. Ontario and Quebec—both 7.8 percent—were just above the national average of 7.2 percent. Moving through the Prairies, rates decline, from 5.3 percent in Manitoba, 4.7 percent in Saskatchewan, and 4.6 percent in Alberta, before notching up again to 6.7 percent in British Columbia.

The Atlantic provinces, particularly Newfoundland and Labrador, have had higher-than-average rates of unemployment for decades, while the provinces of Ontario and Quebec have typically had lower rates—despite recent shocks in the manufacturing sector. Alberta, with its oil-based economy, has recorded particularly low unemployment rates when high international oil prices have fuelled the provincial economy. But with this exception, the regions most dependent on a few natural resources have typically experienced the most severe unemployment.

Unemployment also tends to be concentrated within specific occupational groups and industrial sectors. Seasonal work such as fishing, logging, and construction carries a high risk of unemployment and helps account for some of the higher levels of unemployment in the natural resource–dependent regions of the country. Manufacturing jobs are also prone to unemployment because economic downturns often lead to layoffs and plant shutdowns. In the downturn of the late 2000s, the manufacturing sector in Canada was particularly hard hit. On the other hand, professional and technical services have been somewhat more protected, though this is changing.

Aboriginal people experience exceptionally high rates of unemployment. When this ongoing problem is combined with lower-than-average rates of labour force participation, it is clear that this group faces serious disadvantages in the labour market. According to estimates from the Labour Force Survey, for example, the unemployment rate for the Aboriginal population was 12.8 percent in 2012, with little difference in rates between women and men; at the same time, the unemployment rate for the general Canadian population age 15 and older was 7.2 percent (HRSDC 2013: 8). More detailed labour force information from the National Household Survey (NHS) is not yet available, but we do know from past census analysis that, while unemployment rates dropped over the long term for this population, rates are still far higher for those living on-reserve than off-reserve. Isolated Aboriginal communities in regions such as northern Manitoba, Saskatchewan, Alberta, and the territories offer few employment opportunities. In addition, low levels of education, limited work experience other than in short-term, low-skill jobs, minimal access to information about jobs and employers, and discrimination in hiring all contribute to high rates of Aboriginal unemployment. Past census data show that, in urban census metropolitan areas, unemployment rates are lower but still high relative to the rest of the Canadian population. For instance, according to the 2006 Census, the six Canadian cities with the largest Aboriginal populations—Winnipeg, Vancouver, Edmonton, Calgary, Toronto, and Saskatoon—had unemployment rates that were two to four times higher for Aboriginal people.[22]

Gender and Unemployment

A comparison of female and male unemployment rates since the end of World War II reveals some interesting shifts in relative position. Looking at adult workers (25 years and older), during the 1950s and early 1960s, male unemployment rates were generally about twice as high as those for females. The two rates converged in the mid-1960s, and by the 1970s, female rates were typically about 2 percent higher than male rates. This trend continued until the recession of the early 1980s when, for a second time, the two rates came together. For the rest of that decade, female rates of joblessness were again higher than male rates, but the difference was always less than 1–2 percent. During the 1990–92 recession and its aftermath, men were slightly more likely to be unemployed. Since the mid-1990s, however, there has been a third convergence, and in the past few years, women's unemployment has fallen slightly below that of men. In 2012, for example, unemployment rates for women and men (aged 25+) were 5.7 and 6.3 percent respectively.

We would need a much more detailed analysis than is possible here to explain these shifts in female and male unemployment rates. Nevertheless, a large part of the explanation would focus on women's locations in the labour market. Female labour force participation was much lower in the 1950s and 1960s, and women were employed in a limited number of traditionally female occupations. Unemployment then, as now, was considerably higher in the blue-collar occupations, in which few women were found. Since that time, women have made their way into the rapidly expanding service sector alongside men. But many women continue to be employed in lower-level, less secure positions and thus have become more vulnerable to unemployment in recent decades. For men, however, the recessions at the beginning of the 1980s and 1990s, as well as the downturn of 2008–9, have meant widespread layoffs in blue-collar industries (manufacturing, for example), thus leading to higher male rates when the economy weakens.

Youth Unemployment

Young Canadians (ages 15 to 24), particularly those with the least education (high-school dropouts, for example), have experienced high rates of unemployment for several decades (Lowe and Krahn 1999). Youth unemployment fluctuated between 9 and 14 percent in the 1970s. As Figure 4.4 shows, the 1981–82 recession pushed the rate to about 20 percent, but it had dropped to around 11 percent by 1989. The recession that began in 1990 reversed this decline; rates in the 15–17 percent range were reached in 1993 and 1994. By 2000, as the economy strengthened and the total unemployment rate dropped to 6.8 percent, the youth unemployment rate also declined, falling as low as 11.2 percent in 2007, before spiking up to 15.2 percent in 2009. By 2012, it had

FIGURE 4.4   Unemployment Rates by Age and Gender, Canada, 1976–2012

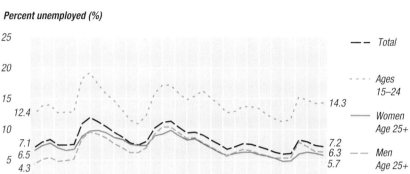

Source: Statistics Canada. CANSIM Table 282-0002 - Labour Force Survey estimates (LFS), by sex and detailed age group, Annual (persons x 1,000). <http://www5.statcan.gc.ca/cansim/a05?lang=eng&id=2820002>

declined slightly to 14.3 percent. Even though youth unemployment is affected by the same economic forces that determine the risk of joblessness for adults, young workers have fared much worse for several decades—the youth unemployment rate has not been below 10 percent since the early 1970s. And even though young people typically have shorter spells of unemployment, because more of their previous employment has been part time and part year, they are less eligible for Employment Insurance (Betcherman and Leckie 1997).

A closer look at Figure 4.4 suggests that the gap between the youth and adult unemployment rates was particularly high in the early 1980s. Why? The shifting age distribution of the population provides a partial explanation. Canada experienced an exceptionally large baby boom during the 1950s and 1960s. The last of the children born in that era of high birthrates were making their way into the labour force during the early 1980s, just as a severe recession was reducing employment opportunities. Subsequent cohorts of school leavers became smaller. By way of example, in 1982, people of ages 15 to 24 made up 24 percent of the total Canadian population, compared to only 14 percent in 2000. Thus, since the early 1980s, when youth unemployment rates peaked, smaller cohorts of youth have meant less competition for jobs typically held by young workers (Foot and Li 1986; Gunderson, Sharpe, and Wald 2000).

Throughout the past several decades, unemployment rates for teenagers (ages 15 to 19) have been higher than jobless rates among young adults (ages 20 to 24). Compared with teenagers, young adults are typically better educated and have more work experience. In 2012, for example, the unemployment rate for 15- to 19-year-olds was 20.1 percent, compared with 11.0 percent for 20- to 24-year-olds. While female and male adult (25 and older) unemployment rates have again converged (see Figure 4.4), we still see a gender difference in joblessness among youth. For teenagers, the female unemployment rate in 2008 was 18.2 percent, compared to 22.0 percent for males. Among young adults, the female unemployment rate (9.3%) was also lower than the male rate (12.5%). These differences reflect, in part, the higher proportion of young males who seek employment in blue-collar industries where unemployment rates remain higher than in service industries (where a larger proportion of young women look for work).

Causes of Unemployment

We have already hinted at some of the causes of rising unemployment over the past several decades. Obviously, there is a demographic factor to consider. The sizable increase in the birthrate in the years following World War II led to rapid growth in the labour force several decades later. In addition, the increased proportion of women entering the labour force generated greater demand for jobs. But people working for pay are also people with money to spend, so the growth in labour force participation led to substantial job creation. Thus, past econometric analyses conclude that these demographic shifts have had little impact on the overall increase in unemployment (Gera 1991: 3).

Another basic type of explanation focuses on the characteristics of the jobless. Such arguments are typically supported by anecdotal evidence and little else. One version suggests that many of the unemployed could be working if only they would accept the less attractive jobs available. In many communities, however, the number of jobless far exceeds the total number of available jobs (Hironimus-Wendt 2008). Furthermore, many of the jobs that may be available (and perhaps are even hard to fill) are part-time positions in the lower-tier services with pay rates so low that it would be impossible to support oneself, let alone a family. For many of the unemployed, accepting such work would be economically irrational because it would force them to try to survive on very little income and discontinue actively searching for a better job.

A different version of the blame-the-unemployed explanation argues that they have insufficient skills and so are unable to compete for the jobs available in the new knowledge-based economy. However, studies have concluded that there is little evidence of a "skills gap" in Canada that might explain high rates of unemployment (Gingras and Roy 2000; Burleton et al. 2013). In fact, there is at least as much evidence of widespread underemployment in Canada as there is evidence of a skills shortage (Krahn and Lowe 1999; Livingstone and Guile 2012).

Yet another version of this type of explanation of high unemployment is the presumed laziness of the unemployed, in combination with the generosity of the government (Swanson 2001). But it is hard to believe that more than a few Canadians would prefer the low level of government social assistance to a higher and more secure earned income.

Indeed, research on work values (Chapter 13) suggests that few Canadians would choose the economic hardship and the stigma of unemployment over a regular job. Thus, as experts have noted, we cannot blame unemployment rates on unemployment policies, labour laws, or tax policies (Betcherman 2000; Stanford 2005). Furthermore, since the mid-1990s, unemployment insurance has become increasingly more difficult to access. For instance, in 1996, the old Unemployment Insurance (UI) program was replaced by the Employment Insurance (EI) program. By the late 1990s, only 36 percent of unemployed individuals received EI support, down from 74 percent in 1989 (Jackson et al. 2000: 153). More recently, new changes to EI in 2013 require job seekers to accept work at lower rates of pay and at commuting distances of up to one hour from their home (Leonard 2013).

Economists often distinguish between *cyclical unemployment*, which rises during recessions and then declines as the economy recovers, and *frictional unemployment*. The latter results from the ongoing movement of workers in and out of jobs as they seek to match their skills and interests with the jobs offered by employers. Some unemployment, therefore, is normal, even in the strongest economy, since a perfect match between all jobs and workers is never possible. In the 1980s and 1990s, researchers were concerned that periods of high cyclical unemployment had increased the "natural rate of unemployment" to such a degree that it might be unlikely to go back down. Accordingly, some believed Canada had developed a serious problem of *structural unemployment*, one that would require new policy approaches because it was more deeply rooted and permanent than cyclical or frictional unemployment. Through the 2000s, however, record low unemployment levels and increased baby-boom retirements shifted the focus to addressing labour shortages within a highly competitive—and, in some industries, global—job market. As the economy recovers from the recession in 2014 and beyond, labour shortages are expected in some occupations and industries.[23]

Some of the industrial and employment trends discussed in Chapter 3 have contributed to unemployment. With industrial restructuring, many corporations have shifted their activities to countries and regions where labour costs are lower, and where government legislation regarding labour relations, worker safety, and environmental protection is less developed. Automation and information technologies have replaced workers in some sectors. In private and public firms, employers have responded to financial problems by downsizing, cutting full-time jobs, and relying increasingly on temporary workers (a trend discussed later in this chapter). In addition, parts of Canada's staple- and manufacturing-based economy have been hit hard by recent global economic shifts.

The impact of government policies on unemployment trends is equally important and must also be scrutinized. Periods of high unemployment in previous decades have been linked to the federal government's pursuit of low inflation via high interest rates (Fortin 1996). With a market-oriented approach to economic development that included a continental free trade agreement, the federal government may have also made it easier for large corporations to close Canadian factories and lay off workers.

International Comparisons

In 2009, the global economy experienced the worst recession since the 1930s. Even so, unemployment rates did not rise as much as during previous recessions. This change was partly due to massive government stimulus spending, which preserved jobs in some sectors, and the cushion provided by record high employment levels and low unemployment rates in most industrial nations heading into the recession. On one hand, Canada's 2012 unemployment rate of over 7 percent may seem high when compared to that of Australia (5.4%), Japan (4.6%), South Korea (3.3%), Germany (5.5%), or the Netherlands (5.3%).

On the other hand, jobless rates during 2012 were slightly higher across the 25-nation European Union (8.2%) and even higher within specific countries. Spain's unemployment rate reached 25.2 percent; Ireland's, 15.3 percent; and France's, 9.9 percent. The United States, being at the epicentre of the global financial crisis, experienced a much deeper downturn than Canada, and its 2012 unemployment rate of 8.2 percent reflects this.[24]

Given that these countries have struggled with economic challenges similar to those of Canada, why do some have high unemployment while others have nearly full employment? In terms of labour market policies, Canada lies between the laissez-faire, or free-market, approach of the United States and the more interventionist European approach. In countries such as the Netherlands and Japan, employers, organized labour, and governments frequently work together toward a common goal of full employment. And if it were not for proactive labour market programs, such as subsidized work sharing, in other European countries, the unemployment rates likely would have been higher in the recent recession. In Canada, while the government has relied on the private sector to create jobs and to train and retrain workers, there are suggestions (yet to be fully evaluated) that stimulus measures, such as infrastructure projects or the 2009 home renovation tax rebate, helped keep the unemployment rate from going higher. A wide range of other factors also influenced how employment was affected by the 2008–9 recession: these include a country's reliance on manufacturing exports, its role in global auto production, the stability of its banks and other financial institutions, and the extent to which there had been a "bubble" that inflated prices in the housing market.[25]

There are also interesting differences in what underlie unemployment trends within North America. Mexico's unemployment rate has been below that of Canada for decades (5.0% in 2012), according to the Organisation for Economic Co-operation and Development (OECD). Low rates in Mexico are, in large part, a function of the much larger informal economy and self-employed sector. Individuals seeking work are more likely to find jobs, albeit low-paying and insecure jobs, in the informal sector, or to support themselves with small-scale entrepreneurial activities (Martin 2000). Comparing unemployment levels in the United States and Canada, the rates were similar in the 1950s, 1960s, and 1970s; however, beginning with the early-1980s recession, Canada's jobless rate began to outstrip that of the United States, and the gap widened further in the 1990s. During this period, there was considerable research trying to explain this difference. For example, Canada's unemployed tended to stay in the labour market searching for work longer than their American counterparts. As a result, larger numbers of the jobless in the United States were not officially counted as unemployed. In addition, the United States imprisons many more of its citizens, which reduces the number of young men counted as unemployed.[26] During the 2008–9 recession, for the first time in many decades, the U.S. unemployment rate exceeded that of Canada. Canada has typically relied on the marketplace to reduce unemployment, while instituting Employment Insurance (EI) and social assistance programs to help deal with the social problems created by persistently high levels of unemployment. Recent changes to EI have further curtailed support to unemployed workers when, in fact, the present policy challenge is how to improve support and opportunities for unemployed job seekers (Mendelsohn 2012; Leonard 2013).

Although some other countries have devised more effective approaches to dealing with unemployment, we cannot simply import solutions. Canada has a unique economic history and industrial structure, a complicated political system where federal and provincial responsibilities are separate (and frequently disputed), and its own unique business and labour institutions. In short, we will have to fashion our own solutions. Nevertheless, the examples provided by other countries demonstrate that long-term high levels of unemployment need not be seen as inevitable and that employers, the government, and organized labour all have to be active participants in any efforts to solve our structural unemployment problem.

▮ CONCLUSION

As our examination of recent trends has shown, the Canadian labour market has undergone significant change in the final decades of the 20th century and into the early decades of the 21st. The service sector has expanded enormously, producing both "good" and "bad" jobs, with many more of the latter in the lower-tier service industries. Meanwhile, manufacturing industries contribute less to employment growth in Canada than once was the case. We have also seen a substantial increase in part-time employment, while other forms of nonstandard work (temporary or contract work, for example) are now much more prevalent. Though unemployment rates declined in the late 1990s and into the early to mid-2000s, they are still high enough to cause concern—especially in the aftermath of the 2007–8 financial collapse While general public concern about high unemployment abated in the strong economic climate of the early to mid-2000s, today it remains a pressing concern in certain regions and sectors. Most important, with respect to inequality and polarization, some populations (youth, Aboriginal, and immigrant, for example) have not experienced the same economic opportunities as others have. As a result, there are grounds for concern both with the *quantity* and *quality* of jobs, and the rising incidence of low-paying, vulnerable work.

What lies ahead? By posing this question, we enter the debates and controversies surrounding the future of work, which often set out a bewildering range of contradictory scenarios. Students of the sociology of work and industry are encouraged to critically appraise such writing. Reflecting on the trends presented in Chapters 3 and 4, it is clear that most evidence does not support a view of radical or extreme transformation. Still, changes are occurring, and we can be fairly certain that several of the trends we have documented will continue. Demographic factors (discussed in Chapter 3) are a given, especially workforce aging and the increasing diversity of the labour force. So, too, we can expect continued expansion of service-sector employment. Nonstandard work, as discussed in this chapter, is now a central feature of the labour market, but equally a growing source of concern given the precariousness experienced by many workers. In early 2014, the trajectory of recovery within the Canadian and global economies was uncertain. What level of economic growth is reasonable to expect? And what is sustainable, given growing concerns over the environment as well as the limits posed by population aging and a shrinking workforce in many industrialized countries? Finally, to what extent might current public interest and debate over economic disparities and inequality spark meaningful efforts to reduce labour market polarization? To our mind, this latter question is a central one as we move into the future.

DISCUSSION QUESTIONS

1. Discuss the concept of job quality. How would you define "good job" and "bad job"? How does job quality vary by industry and occupation? Thinking about the jobs you have had so far, where would they fit in the discussion of good jobs and bad jobs?

2. What is nonstandard employment, and how has it grown in Canada in recent years? What are some implications of these trends for workers, employers, and society in general?

3. Unemployment has been a significant worry for many Canadian workers and their families. What are recent trends in unemployment? How do they compare to longer-term trends? How does unemployment affect different segments of the workforce (e.g., older and younger workers, women and men)?

4. Based on your reading in Chapters 3 and 4, outline what you see as the most important challenges facing Canadian workers in the next 10 years.

ADDITIONAL RESOURCES

WORK AT THE MOVIES

- *Roger & Me* (directed by Michael Moore, 1989, 91 minutes). American filmmaker Michael Moore explores the economic and social impact of the demise of General Motors in Flint, Michigan.
- *The Full Monty* (directed by Petter Cattaneo, 1997, 91 minutes). In this British comedy set in Sheffield, England, six unemployed men decide to form a male striptease act. The film explores issues of unemployment, job retraining, working-class culture, restructuring, economic depression, and alienation.
- *Generation Jobless* (directed by Sharon Bartlett and Maria LeRose, 2013, 45:13 minutes). *Generation Jobless* explores the challenges facing Canadian youth in finding meaningful employment. It is available through CBC Doc Zone: http://www.cbc.ca/player/Shows/ID/2330990900/.
- *Inequality for All* (directed by Jacob Kornbluth, 2013, 89 minutes). This award-winning documentary examines growing economic disparities and inequality, weaving together analysis from economist and former U.S. Labor Secretary, Robert Reich, with personal stories from the lives of workers and families.

SOUNDS OF WORK

- "Little Man" (Alan Jackson). This country song considers how small independent businesses will struggle for survival when big-box stores and chains come to town.

- "Telephone Road" (Steve Earle). In this song, Earle writes of families being split up when members are forced to migrate to find work.
- "Atlantic City" (Bruce Springsteen). Springsteen highlights how individuals struggle for survival when well-paying work is hard to find.
- "Hallelujah, I'm a Bum" (Traditional). This song describes an individual who cannot find work and so lives as a hobo.

◾ NOTES

1. In 2007, Statistics Canada and other European government agencies set up a Task Force on Measurement of the Quality of Employment to try to reach agreement on how best to measure "employment quality" (Jin 2008: 7). For early discussions of job quality, see the Economic Council of Canada's (1990) *Good Jobs, Bad Jobs: Employment in the Service Economy.*

2. Income figures by industry are from Statistics Canada's Labour Force Survey, accessed through CANSIM (Table 282-0072—LFS Estimates, Annual Wages by NAICS).

3. Income figures by occupation are from Statistics Canada's Labour Force Survey, accessed through CANSIM (Table 282-0070—LFS Estimates by NOC).

4. Figures for the female–male earnings gap come from Statistics Canada's Labour Force Survey, accessed through CANSIM (Table 282-0070—LFS Estimates by NOC).

5. Data on executive pay come from the Globe and Mail's (2013b) annual report on executive compensation and analysis by the Canadian Centre for Policy Alternatives (2013).

6. Current and forthcoming provincial minimum wage rates come from the Government of Canada's (Labour Program) Minimum Wage Database: http://srv116.services.gc.ca/dimt-wid/sm-mw/menu.aspx?lang=eng.

7. Statistics Canada's low-income cutoff (LICO) is the measure most often used to index poverty in Canada. A family (of a given size) is considered to be in the low-income category if, compared to the average Canadian family of that size, it spends at least 20 percent more of its total income on food, clothing, and shelter. LICOs are calculated separately for communities of different sizes since the cost of living varies. See Statistics Canada (2013f) for more detail on this and other measures.

8. See Winson and Leach (2002) and Fleury (2008) on Canada's working poor; Ehrenreich (2001) and Duncan, Huston, and Weisner (2007) on the working poor in the United States; and LaRochelle-Côté and Dionne (2009) on international differences in low-paid work.

9. Marshall (2003) outlines the growing costs to Canadian employers of non-wage benefit packages. Waldie (2005) notes that in the mid-2000s General Motors spent more on health care for its employees than it spent on steel for automobile production.

10. The 2005 Workplace and Employee Survey (WES) (Statistics Canada 2008f) excluded public-sector employees, as well as the self-employed. Since the former typically receive more benefits than average while the latter receive fewer, the WES results are likely a reasonable estimate for the total Canadian labour force (including government employees and the self-employed). Zeytinoglu and Cooke (2005) document the disadvantaged position of nonstandard workers with respect to non-wage benefits, while Zeytinoglu et al. (2008) and Cooke, Zeytinoglu, and Chowhan (2009) demonstrate that higher-paid workers are more likely to receive on-the-job training. Jackson (2005: 47–50) shows that employees in larger work organizations as well as unionized organizations are more likely to receive training paid for by their employer. See Budd (2004) on similar patterns in the United States, and Lowen and Sicilian (2009) on the distribution of family-friendly non-wage benefits in the United States.

11. For discussions of nonstandard work, also referred to as "contingent" or "precarious" work, see Krahn (1995), Vosko, Zukewich, and Cranford (2003), Lowe and Schellenberg (2001), and Law Commission of Ontario (2012). Regarding such work in the United States, see Kalleberg (2011) and Osterman and Shulman (2011).

12. In 2012, Labour Force Survey data in CANSIM Table 282-0031 show a 4.8 percent rate of multiple-job holding, down from 5.2 percent in 1997 (as reported by Sussman 1998). For discussions of Canadian trends, see Statistics Canada (2009a). On U.S. trends and implications, see Stinson (1997) and Campbell (2011). For a comparison of Canadian and U.S. trends, see Kimmel and Powell (1999).

13. Statistics for temporary and permanent employment come Statistics Canada's Labour Force Survey, accessed through CANSIM (Table 282-0080—LFS Estimate, Employees by Job Permanency). Lowe and Schellenberg (2001: 12) suggest that, because some individuals working for temporary help agencies report themselves to be in permanent jobs, LFS estimates of temporary employment may be too low. In Canada, see Vosko (2000) and Galarneau (2005, 2010) for an analysis of temporary work. In the United States, see Smith and Neuwirth (2008) and Henson (1996).

14. Statistics Canada, *The Daily* (June 4, 1992; April 26, 1999; April 18, 2005; and May 16, 2007). See also Bowlby (2002) and Winson and Leach (2002). Ilg (1995) documents the same trend in the United States.

15. Statistics for self-employment come from Statistics Canada's Labour Force Survey, accessed through CANSIM (Table 282-0012—Labour Force Survey Estimates, Employment by Class of Worker). In the 1990s, self-employment grew rapidly, accounting for 58 percent of employment growth from 1989 to 1998 (Picot and Heisz 2000). Rates declined in 2000 for the first time since 1986 (Bowlby 2001) but have since rebounded.

16. Relative to other countries, Mexico has high levels of self-employment, accounting for 35 percent of employment overall in 2010 (see *OECD Factbook 2011–12*). See also Fairlie and Woodruff (2005) for an interesting comparison of self-employment in Mexico and among Mexican immigrants in the United States.

17. Data on usual hours worked come from CANSIM Table 282-0016. For discussions of the polarization of hours in Canada, see Usalcas (2008). For interesting discussions in the United States on changes to working time, see Jacobs and Gerson (2004) and Presser (2003).

18. For discussions of work hours, see Bunting (2004), Hochschild (1997), and Shields (2000). Long hours are discussed by Heisz and LaRochelle-Côté (2007) and Moen et al. (2013). On the class-action lawsuits, follow the employment law blog at http://blog.toronto-employmentlawyer.com/.

19. See Mirchandani (1999), Turcotte (2010), and Hilbrecht et al. (2013) on the benefits and costs of teleworking; Akyeampong (1993) on flextime work arrangements; and Marshall (1997) on job sharing. Teasdale (2013) discusses their impact on working relationships.

20. Akyeampong (1992) discusses the number of discouraged workers during the recessions in the 1980s and 1990s. For the 2000 estimate of discouraged workers, see *Perspectives on Labour and Income* (Spring 2001): 64.

21. For discussions of unemployment trends in previous decades, see MacLean and Osberg (1996). Recent trends are reported in Statistics Canada, *The Daily* (February 5, 2010), and Statistics Canada (2009a).

22. Unemployment rates come from Human Resources and Social Development Canada (HRSDC), *Aboriginal Labour Market Bulletin* (Spring 2013). Detailed labour force information for the Aboriginal population is not yet available from the 2011 National Household Survey. For past analysis and trends, see Statistics Canada (2009a) and (2008e).

23. See the July 2000 special issue of *Canadian Public Policy* on structural unemployment and policy responses. On the competitive job market of the 2000s, see Statistics Canada (2009a), Fang (2009), and Tal (2012).

24. OECD (2010). These OECD data are adjusted to ensure international comparability, so the Canadian rate may vary slightly from what Statistics Canada reports.

25. For discussions of the role of government in job creation, see Riddell and St-Hilaire (2000). For up-to-date assessments of how countries are responding to the global recession and supporting recovery, see the OECD website, especially the country reports, found under "Countries," at http://www.oecd.org.

26. Riddell and Sharpe (1998) and Campolieti (2012) discuss the Canada–U.S. unemployment rate gap. Sherman and Judkins (1995: 53) comment on the impact of high rates of imprisonment on unemployment figures.

LABOUR MARKETS: OPPORTUNITIES AND INEQUALITY

"Increasingly, private security is a preferred option among newcomers, who haven't been able to find work in their own field.... I have first-hand experience—for the last six months, I have been working as a security officer myself [in Toronto]. After two months of futile attempts to get a job in the media (my profession for two decades prior to immigrating to Canada from India in July 2008), I had little choice but to take up a job as a security officer.... Facing barriers to finding employment in their area of expertise because of a lack of Canadian experience and credentials, newcomers turn to survival jobs out of desperation. Some work as telemarketers at call centres, others as maintenance workers, still others as security officers. But working in security is often considered a better choice than doing pressure sales over the phone or cleaning toilets.... It seemed the better choice for me. Although wages are low (around $9–12 an hour in the first year), it's enough for survival and paying bills.... Every night when I leave for my site to begin my shift I ponder, 'Is this what I came to Canada for?' Every morning when I return home and see my son's face, I stay determined that I'll do what it takes to survive and succeed here—even if it means patrolling a damp and bitterly cold parking lot in the dead of night."

Source: *Canadian Immigrant* (May 29, 2011): http://canadianimmigrant.ca/immigrant-stories/nightshift-as-security-officer-a-survival-job-for-many-immigrants. Courtesy of Mayank Bhatt.

◗ INTRODUCTION

As we saw in Chapter 4, there are large differences in income and other employment benefits, as well as varying risks of unemployment, across occupations. Why do high-school teachers earn more than retail salesclerks, or engineers more than construction workers? Presumably it's because teachers and engineers have invested in extra years of education that, in turn, lead to more skilled and responsible jobs. Why do electricians make more money than child-care workers? Although wiring a house requires considerable skill and we don't want electricians to make mistakes, caring for and teaching young children is also a highly complex and responsible task. Why are the children of middle-class parents much more likely to go to university compared with the children of less affluent Canadians? Why are Aboriginal Canadians, immigrants, and members of visible minority groups overrepresented in less rewarding jobs, and why are younger workers and Canadians living in different regions more likely to be unemployed?

Such questions about variations in educational outcomes, job rewards, and career patterns are central to the sociological study of labour markets. We can define a *labour market* as the arena in which employers seek to purchase labour from potential employees who are seeking jobs suitable to their education, experience, and preferences. In the labour market, workers exchange their skills, knowledge, and loyalty in return for pay, status, career opportunities, and other job rewards.

A number of other institutions and organizations support or interact with the operation of the labour market. Among their other functions, schools and families prepare individuals for entry (or re-entry) into the labour market. Government legislation affects how labour markets operate—minimum wage laws and legislation regulating trade unions are examples. The government may also assist the unemployed with financial support or job-training programs. Unions and professional associations are active in the labour market, looking after the interests of their members by bargaining for additional job rewards and, sometimes, by limiting access of non-members to good jobs. Organizations representing employers also try to influence labour market operations, sometimes lobbying governments to change laws regarding unions or to maintain a low minimum wage, or encouraging schools to include more employment-related subject matter in their teaching.

Labour economists and sociologists study many of these institutions and how they influence labour market operations.[1] Of particular interest to sociologists are the distributive aspects of the labour market, that is, how the profits generated by workers are shared. In other words, does the labour market provide opportunities for hard-working individuals to improve their social position and quality of life, or, does it reinforce long-standing patterns of inequality in Canadian society? Is it possible it does both?

In this chapter, we address questions about who gets better jobs and why, and about whether and how patterns of social inequality are reinforced, by comparing two alternative theoretical perspectives and data that may or may not support them. According to *human capital theory*, jobs requiring more effort, training, and skill typically receive greater rewards. This theory assumes that labour market participants compete openly for the best jobs and that the most qualified people end up in the jobs requiring their particular skills. The outcome should be an efficient and productive economy and a fair allocation of job rewards. But in reviewing research on how the labour market really operates, we find considerable evidence that the open competition assumptions of human capital theory need to be seriously challenged. As *labour market segmentation theory* explains, many substantial barriers keep disadvantaged groups from gaining access to better jobs. Thus, the study of labour markets is not only about who gets better and worse jobs. It also addresses the much broader questions raised in Chapters 1 and 2 about how social inequality is created, reinforced, and intensified, and sometimes reduced.[2]

THE HUMAN CAPITAL MODEL OF LABOUR MARKET PROCESSES

Chapter 3 explained that many jobs today require specific skills and extensive training, while Chapter 4 showed how some jobs are clearly better than others. Ideally, jobs with specific requirements would be filled by individuals most suited for these positions. If that means having an advanced education, then it would be only reasonable that workers with more education should obtain the better jobs. Stripped to its essentials, these are the basic premises of *human capital theory*, a major economic explanation of how today's labour market operates.

This theoretical perspective assumes that a job's rewards are determined by its economic contribution to society. It also predicts that more dangerous and unhealthy jobs should be paid more, since workers would have to be compensated for greater risks. The model assumes that labour market participants are all competing for jobs in a single, open labour market. Information about available jobs is widely circulated. All potential employees with the necessary qualifications have equal access to job openings. When it comes to choosing whom to hire, employers make rational decisions, based on an assessment of an individual's ability.

In order to "get ahead" in the working world, people may decide to obtain more education and training. Doing so means delaying entry into the labour market and forgoing immediate earnings. Yet this loss is not permanent because by obtaining more education, one is investing in *human capital*, which can later be "cashed in" for a better job. In short, the human capital model emphasizes the *supply side* of labour markets and largely overlooks the behaviour and characteristics of employers and work organizations (the *demand side*). It also ignores unequal power relationships within the labour market. The human capital perspective on labour markets is premised on a *consensus* view of society, in contrast to the assumptions of *conflict* underlying class-based and labour market segmentation approaches.[3]

The basic logic of human capital theory is compelling, given the evidence that better-educated individuals generally are less likely to be unemployed and more likely to hold well-paying, high-status jobs (Davies and Guppy 2006).[4] But it is also difficult to ignore the contrary evidence. There are many examples of well-trained and highly motivated people working in poorly paid, low-skill jobs. For example, although most recent university graduates have managed to find reasonable jobs, compared to graduates a decade or two ago, a larger minority have had difficulty finding full-time, permanent work that matches their training.[5] The problem is clearly not one of insufficient education or effort. Instead, much of this youth underemployment can be traced directly to organizational downsizing and large-scale cutbacks in the hiring of entry-level workers by employers in both the public and private sectors (see Chapters 2 and 4).

To make the same point, while many of the wealthiest members of our society are no more educated than the rest of us, they frequently appear to have had a head start in the career race. We continue to see the powerful influence of huge family firms largely controlled by individuals who inherited their money. For example, in 2013, David Thomson and his family were estimated to be worth $20.3 billion as a result of their control of Thomson Reuters Corporation (a media and publishing conglomerate owning, among other firms, the company that publishes this textbook) (Forbes Magazine 2013). Thomson took over control of the company in 2002 from his father, who, in turn, had inherited it from his father, who started it in 1934. Thus, the social standing of one's parents and grandparents can strongly influence later labour market outcomes.

In addition, effort and competence do not always correlate neatly with labour market rewards. For example, a 2007 study showed that many CEOs of money-losing companies listed on the Toronto Stock Exchange still received huge performance or resignation bonuses, in some cases totalling in the millions of dollars (McFarland 2007).

Thus, the relationships among initiative and effort, education and training, on the one hand, and occupational attainment and income, on the other, are not nearly as consistent as the human capital model would suggest. In fact, research shows that some groups are systematically less likely than others to have benefited from their investments in human capital and that good returns on education and training are obtained only in certain industrial sectors or from some types of employers. Furthermore, much evidence shows that some groups in society are more likely to have access to higher education. Thus, to really understand who gets the good jobs, we must look beyond the labour market to families, schools, and other institutions that shape labour market outcomes.

Social Structure and Occupational Choice

The human capital model attempts to explain how people are sorted into different occupational positions by focusing on the characteristics of individual workers. People whose skills and abilities are more valued by society, and who have invested more in education and training, will be leading candidates for the better jobs, according to this model. Another assumption is that individuals choose among work options, eventually settling in the job that best suits them. But to what extent do individuals have a choice from among the wide range of occupations? Does everyone start the "career race" from the same position, or are some groups disadvantaged at the outset? Does chance play a role in matching individuals and jobs? We probably all know a few people who accidentally ended up in their present job with little planning or who landed a great position by being in the right place at the right time. We probably also know people who, as children, decided they wanted to be a teacher or a doctor and then carefully pursued the educational route to such a goal. Such behaviour and outcomes are consistent with human capital predictions, although the theory does not ask why these individuals had such high occupational goals.

We can easily imagine how socioeconomic origins might influence career patterns. It would be hard to picture a member of the wealthy Thomson family aspiring to be a bus driver. In contrast, many people who make their living as farmers would probably cite growing up on a farm as a major career influence, while growing up in a working-class family in a single-industry community would likely channel a young person into one of the local mills or mines. It is also clear that many women in today's labour force were constrained in their career choices by society's attitudes about appropriate gender roles. As Chapter 6 will show, until only a few decades ago, it was typically assumed that women could work as teachers and nurses, for example, but not in traditionally male occupations. Thus, while aptitudes and investments in education do play an important role, for many working Canadians, *family socio-economic status* (SES) and community of origin, along with personal attributes such as gender, race, and ethnicity, are important determinants of educational and occupational choices and outcomes.

Equality of Educational Opportunity

One core value underlying our education system is that of *equality of opportunity*. According to this belief, gender, ethnicity, family background, region of residence, or other individual characteristics should not be an impediment to obtaining a good education and, through this, access to good jobs and a decent standard of living. As we have already seen (Chapter 3), basic gender differences in educational attainment have disappeared (although, as Chapter 6 discusses, there are substantial gender differences in types of educational choices). But research continues to show large differences in educational attainment depending on one's family background (SES).

A recent analysis of data from Statistics Canada's longitudinal Youth in Transition Survey (YITS) revealed that, by the age of 19, 50 percent of Canadian youth from high-income families (the top 25%) were attending university, compared to only 31 percent of those from low-income (the bottom quartile) families (Frenette 2007a: 7). Studies that focus on parents' education, rather than their income, show even larger differences. For example, in 2009, for Canadians ages 25 to 39, a total of 31 percent had acquired a university degree. But among those from families where at least one parent had a degree, 56 percent had completed university, compared to only 23 percent of those from families where neither parent had a degree (Turcotte 2011a). Thus, coming from a family with a tradition of university attendance substantially increases the chances of completing university oneself.[6]

How do such patterns of *intergenerational transfer of advantage* develop? Over the past several decades, a number of different studies have highlighted how middle- and upper-class parents have higher expectations of their children, serve as role models for postsecondary educational participation and successful careers, and raise them in neighbourhoods and send them to schools where others also have high postsecondary expectations. These parents are also more able to financially support their children's postsecondary activities. For example, an Ontario study of the "class of 1973" tracked a large number of high-school graduates for several decades and conclusively demonstrated that a more advantaged background leads to higher *educational and occupational aspirations*, greater educational attainment, and, in time, higher-status occupations and higher incomes (Anisef et al. 2000). This study also noted that rural youth were less likely to aspire to and participate in higher education. The researchers speculated that the more "limited horizons" of rural youth might be due to their underexposure to beliefs about the value of higher education (p. 143). In addition, rural youth would have to leave their home communities to go to college or university, making the transition more difficult and costly. More recent studies in Nova Scotia and British Columbia (Looker and Dwyer 1998; Andres and Looker 2001) have reinforced conclusions about problems faced by rural youth wishing to continue their education.

But the world of postsecondary education has changed dramatically since the 1970s. The proportion of Canadian youth going on to college or university has risen sharply with the opening of new postsecondary educational institutions, continued demand by employers for people with higher qualifications, and the introduction of new student finance systems (Davies and Guppy 2006; Turcotte 2011a).

So, has inequality in access to higher education declined? Yes, to some extent. Gender differences in postsecondary educational aspirations (Andres et al. 1999) and participation (Association of Universities and Colleges of Canada 2007) have disappeared. In fact, young women today are more likely than young men to complete university (Turcotte 2011b), although women are still more likely to enroll in traditional "female" areas such as education, nursing, and the humanities (see Chapter 6). The construction of community colleges in smaller urban centres in some provinces has also reduced rural–urban differences in postsecondary educational participation (Frenette 2003; Krahn and Hudson 2006).

In addition, improved access to higher education has somewhat reduced the impact of family socioeconomic status (SES) on university participation. For example, in 1986, among Canadians between 25 and 39 years old, 12 percent of those from families where neither parent had a degree had completed university, compared to 45 percent of those with at least one parent with a degree. As already noted, in 2009, the comparable statistics were 23 percent and 56 percent (Turcotte 2011a). So the SES gap in access to higher education has narrowed but, even so, children from more affluent and better-educated families are still significantly overrepresented among university students (Frenette 2007a; Turcotte 2011a). And, as a comparison of Canadian *school–work transition studies* from the 1970s, 1980s, and 1990s demonstrated, children from more advantaged families have much higher occupational aspirations (Andres et al. 1999).

Such school–work transition studies are typically longitudinal, tracking study participants for a number of years, and show how higher aspirations translate into higher postsecondary participation and completion rates. For example, in 1985, we began a longitudinal study of high-school graduates in Edmonton. As in the 1970s Ontario studies, we found much higher educational aspirations among young people from higher-SES families. To be specific, 64 percent of high-school graduates from families where at least one parent had a supervisory, managerial, or professional occupation planned to obtain a university degree, compared with only 38 percent of those from lower-SES families. Four years later in 1989, we observed that 43 percent of sample members from higher-SES families had attended university during at least three of the four intervening years, compared with only 21 percent of those from lower-SES families (Krahn 2009).

Study participants were interviewed several more times over the next two decades. By 2010, 25 years after this cohort had left high school, SES differences in postsecondary educational attainment were highly pronounced. Sixty percent of study participants from families where at least one parent had completed university had themselves acquired a university degree, compared to only 28 percent of those from families without a university tradition.[7]

Economic Advantage and Cultural Capital

The fact that children of university-educated parents are more likely to graduate from university is not simply a function of their higher educational and occupational aspirations. More highly educated parents also have higher incomes, on average, and more money means access to more and better postsecondary education (Davies and Guppy 2006). The rapid expansion of Canada's postsecondary system three or four decades ago increased access to higher education, and the introduction of new student finance systems (student loans) allowed more children from lower-SES families to take advantage of the new universities, community colleges, and technical schools.[8] However, some of these gains have been lost over the past two decades, an era when postsecondary tuition fees tripled (Shaker and Macdonald 2013)[9] and student loan debts increased substantially (Luong 2010). Furthermore, higher tuition fees may also begin to affect postsecondary dropout rates[10] and are already creating additional stresses for low-income families juggling their other financial responsibilities with the growing costs of educating their children.

So parents' money continues to matter. But the process whereby advantaged backgrounds translate into educational success and better jobs begins long before high-school students begin to consider postsecondary education. Children in Canada's poorest families frequently go to school hungry. Parents with low incomes may have to work long hours to cover basic living costs and will have less time and money to invest in their children's education. Schools in poorer neighbourhoods tend to have fewer resources.[11] Not surprisingly, children in Canada's poorest families are three times more likely than children of the wealthy to be in remedial education classes at school. In contrast, the most advantaged children are twice as likely to be in classes for "gifted" students (Mitchell 1997). A long list of studies has also demonstrated that, even though the high-school dropout rate has been declining over the past few decades, teenagers from less affluent families are still much more likely to leave school without a diploma.[12]

These are among the more obvious explanations of the relationship between economic disadvantage and less successful educational outcomes. In his analysis of social stratification in contemporary society (see Chapter 2), Pierre Bourdieu (1986) introduced the concept of *cultural capital* to further explain why middle-class youth perform better in the education system. Schools encourage and reward the language, beliefs, behaviour, and competencies of the more powerful groups in society. Middle-class youth bring more of this cultural capital to school with them, and so have a distinct advantage. They are more likely to speak like their teachers, to be comfortable in a verbal and symbolic environment, to know something about the subjects being taught, to have additional skills (music training, for example), and to have access to learning resources at home.[13]

So, schools are not neutral institutions; rather, they are part of the process whereby structural inequalities and power differences within society are reproduced, within and across generations, because the culture of the more powerful classes is embedded within them. In fact, this process continues within universities as well. A recent study of the experiences of working-class youth in an Ontario university showed how their ambitions for, and chances of entry into, high-paying and high-status occupations were reduced over the course of their studies. *Extra-credential experiences*, such as spending a year studying abroad or interning in a prestigious law firm during the summer, can increase an undergraduate's chances of being admitted into law or medical school. Such experiences can be interpreted by selection committees as indicators of motivation and the willingness to take on challenges (Lehmann 2012). Working-class youth, however, are unlikely to have the money for foreign travel. Nor can they afford to take on unpaid internships, even if they had the social connections required to obtain them. Indeed, the use of unpaid internships has attracted growing concern in Canada and the United States (Levitt 2014).

Status Attainment Research

In its explanation of who gets the best jobs in society, the human capital model emphasizes the critical importance of educational attainment. Innate differences in aptitudes and skills, and how hard one works in acquiring an education and, later, in the workplace, determine occupational position in this theoretical perspective. But in assuming that only skill and effort matter, that our society is truly a *meritocracy*, the human capital model ignores evidence that family SES is linked to educational attainment and that schools are not neutral institutions.

Status attainment research extends the critique of human capital theory by explicitly highlighting the role that education and family SES play in determining occupational outcomes. Four national surveys (1973, 1986, 1994, 2001) focused on the education and occupations of adult Canadians, as well as on the education and occupations of their parents. Data from them reveal that the most important determinant of an individual's current job is the status of her or his first job; in turn, the status of that first job is heavily influenced by the amount of education obtained (Wanner 2009).[14]

Taken alone, these findings lend support to the human capital model—a higher education allows one to enter the labour market at a higher level, and, in turn, move up even higher. However, as we have already shown, children from families with well-educated parents in high-status occupations tend to get more education. Comparisons of status attainment results across the four national surveys show that the effects of family background declined some-what between the 1970s and 1980s (Wanner 1999), perhaps because of the expansion of Canada's postsecondary education system, but not in the 1990s. Even so, "Canada is still a stratified society characterized by a considerable amount of inheritance of privilege" (Wanner 2009: 129).

Status attainment studies do not explain how social origin affects labour market opportunities, but we have already mentioned some of the processes. Obviously, wealthier parents can afford more (and better) education for their children and can provide the cultural capital needed to succeed in school. They can have a strong influence on aspirations and can give their children more and better information about how to find good jobs. Being well situated in the labour market and in society, they can also provide their children with more *social capital*, that is, useful contacts and networks that will help them succeed (Lin 1999).

Turning to gender, despite being more likely than men to acquire a university degree, Canadian women today are still less able to translate academic credentials into jobs with higher pay and more career potential. As we will see in Chapter 6, this disparity is partly due to the different types of education acquired by women and men. If women typically choose to become nurses and men to become engineers, then perhaps the higher status (and pay) of men's jobs makes sense. But this line of reasoning simply raises other questions: What influences women's and men's occupational choices, and why do tradi-tionally female jobs have lower status and less pay? Are the contributions made by individuals in these occupations really less valuable to society?

A large part of the gender difference in career mobility is because women are more likely to be employed in industries and occupations where promotion opportunities are limited. Some of the difference is also a result of women's interrupted careers due to child-rearing responsibilities. Of course, the human capital model would predict that less career experience (as a result of interruptions) would translate into less upward mobility. But to fully understand the careers of women and men, we must also examine the societal values and institutions that put the biggest share of responsibility for child rearing on women (see Chapter 6).

Research also shows that, despite their higher education on average, foreign-born Canadians (immigrants) experience less upward movement in the course of their careers. Limited knowledge of the Canadian labour market and limited social capital, language difficulties, licensing requirements that keep some immigrants from practising in their area of training, and discrimination in hiring and promotion all can create substantial career barriers (Reitz 2007a, 2007b). In addition, we know that despite their greater investments in higher education, young Canadians today are facing a more difficult labour market than did earlier generations.[15]

▉ LABOUR MARKET SEGMENTATION

While the human capital model assumes a single, open labour market in which everyone competes equally, *labour market segmentation* researchers question this assumption, arguing instead that better and worse jobs tend to be found in very different settings and are usually obtained in distinctly different ways. Certain types of labour force participants (women, visible minorities, immigrants, and youth, for example) are concentrated in the poorer jobs.

Segmentation theories also highlight the slim chances of moving out of the *secondary labour market* into jobs in the *primary labour market*. This is a key proposition, since the human capital model does not deny that some jobs are better than others; it simply maintains that those individuals who have the most ability and initiative and who have made the largest investment in education and training will be more likely to obtain the highly skilled and rewarding jobs. The segmentation perspective emphasizes the barriers that limit access to the primary labour market for many qualified individuals, as well as the ability of primary labour market participants to maintain their more advantaged position.[16]

There are three varieties of labour market segmentation research, each outlined below. All share these basic propositions, but they differ in their explanations of the origins of segmentation and in their breadth of analysis.

Dual Economies

The *dual economy* perspective describes how capitalist economies changed in the 20th century, with a few large and powerful firms coming to dominate key industries such as automobile manufacturing, mining, oil and gas, railways and airlines (Edwards 1979; Hodson and Kaufman 1982). Similarly, the finance sector came to be controlled by a handful of large banks, investment firms, and insurance companies. These dominant firms can exert considerable control over suppliers and markets, and are also able to manipulate their political environment. For example, at various times automobile manufacturers have been able to limit foreign imports, and mining and oil companies have influenced government environmental policies.

These *core sector* firms operate in an economic environment very different from the *periphery sector*, where we find many much smaller companies. Because they are smaller and generally face more intense competition, these smaller businesses have a much greater chance of failure. Many lower-tier service-sector firms (e.g., small retail shops and restaurants) are found here, as are some smaller firms in the upper-tier services (e.g., small office-supply firms in the business services) and in the goods-producing sector (e.g., small manufacturing companies). Such enterprises are typically less profitable, have lower capital investments, are less technologically advanced, and are generally more labour intensive.

The dual economy perspective proposes that the core sector contains a *primary labour market* with better jobs, while the periphery sector contains a *secondary labour market*. Capital-intensive core enterprises, by definition, require fewer workers to equal or exceed the productivity of more labour-intensive firms, although they frequently require workers who are more highly trained and better educated than those hired in the periphery sector. In fact, replaceable unskilled or semiskilled workers are often preferred by employers in the secondary labour market. The large and bureaucratic nature of core-sector enterprises means that there are reasonably good opportunities for career mobility. The workers in these firms tend to be well paid and to have good benefit packages; they are also more likely to receive training and may have greater job security.[17]

Why would core-sector employers be willing to pay more than the going rates in the secondary labour market? Higher profit margins make it easier to do so, of course, but equally important are the strong labour unions and professional associations that have been much more active in the primary sector, demanding higher pay and better benefits (see Chapter 11). Further, it would be too costly for core-sector firms not to pay well. Such enterprises have sizable capital investments so would try to avoid costly shutdowns due to labour disputes. In addition, high labour turnover resulting from low wages would lead to the expense of training many new employees. It is simply good business practice to offer job security (negotiated with a union, if necessary), provide generous wage and benefit packages, and endeavour to improve working conditions.

In contrast, in the secondary labour market, smaller profit margins, more intense competition, difficulties in passing along increased labour costs to customers, and greater vulnerability to economic cycles keep wage levels down. In addition, labour turnover is less of a problem for periphery-sector employers: lower skill requirements and little on-the-job training make workers easily replaceable. Consequently, labour turnover is high, making union organizing more difficult. The term *job ghettos* has been used to describe work in such labour markets.

Barbara Ehrenreich (2001) describes how difficult it is to make a living in the secondary labour market. When researching the book *Nickel and Dimed: On (Not) Getting By in America*, she worked as a waitress, an assistant in a nursing home, an employee of a "cleaning maid" company, and a salesperson at Walmart. Her coworkers, who impressed her with how hard they worked, were often women, immigrants, members of visible minority groups, and students. The jobs they held were characterized by low pay, absent benefits, limited training, physically demanding work, limited authority, lack of respect (both from employers and members of the public), and lack of protection from exploitation and harassment. These difficult working conditions were matched by the equally difficult experiences her coworkers faced finding affordable housing and adequate transportation to get to work. Although the hard work and stress often led to health problems, her coworkers could not afford to be sick: they had no health benefits and a week without a paycheque could mean a missed rent payment.[18]

Internal Labour Markets

There are typically fewer chances for career mobility within firms in the periphery sector. A car-wash attendant, a cleaning maid, or a mechanic in an automobile repair shop would have few promotion prospects simply because the workplace would not have a bureaucratic hierarchy with well-defined career ladders. Conversely, many employees of Ford Canada, the Royal Bank, and other large private-sector firms do have such mobility opportunities, as do government employees and many health care workers. In contrast to the often dead-end jobs within the secondary labour market, most large corporations and public institutions have a well-developed internal training and promotion system, or what may be called an *internal labour market* (Althauser 1989). From the perspective of the work organization, such internal labour markets help retain skilled and valuable employees by providing career incentives. They also transmit important skills and knowledge among employees. From the perspective of employees, internal labour markets mean additional job security and career opportunities.

Researchers who study internal labour markets have usually sidestepped larger questions about the changing nature of capitalism, concentrating instead on specific features of these self-contained labour markets. Focus has been on *ports of entry*, specifically, the limited number of entry-level jobs that are typically the only way into such an internal labour market; *mobility chains*, or career ladders, through which employees make their way during their career within the organization; and training systems and seniority rules, which govern movement through the ranks.[19] Essentially, these concepts elaborate Max Weber's theory of bureaucracy (see Chapter 1).

Early segmentation researchers tended to assume that all core-sector firms contain well-developed internal labour markets open to all employees. However, while many major corporations have long career ladders, these are open to only some of their employees. Clerical workers (usually women) are often restricted from moving into higher ranks (Diprete and Soule 1988). Some large corporations, particularly in the fast-food industry, are built around small local franchises. These workplaces typically have all the characteristics of a secondary labour market. In addition, corporate and government downsizing and the increased use of temporary and other nonstandard workers mean that the number of advantaged workers in internal labour markets has declined dramatically.[20]

Labour Market Shelters: Unions and Professions

Internal labour markets are created by employers. In contrast, unions and professional associations have tried to improve job and income security for their members by setting up *labour market shelters*, sometimes within specific work organizations but more often spanning a large number of similar workplaces. Some occupational groups have restricted access to certain types of work since government legislation requires that such tasks be completed only by certified trades (e.g., electricians). Public safety is the rationale for this legislation, but it also serves to protect the jobs and (relatively high) incomes of members of these often-unionized trades.

Industrial unions bargain collectively with employers to determine the seniority rules, promotion procedures, and pay rates within manufacturing establishments (see Chapter 11). Such contracts shelter these industrial workers from the risk of job loss or pay cuts for a specified time. Negotiated staffing restrictions also restrict non-members from access to the better jobs by giving laid-off members priority if new jobs open up.

Professional associations using tactics different from those of unions also provide labour market shelters for their members. *Professions* have been distinguished from occupations in a variety of ways, but certain key features appear in most definitions. Professionals such as doctors, lawyers, engineers, and psychologists work with specialized knowledge acquired through extensive formal education in professional schools. They enjoy a high level of work autonomy and are frequently self-regulating, policing themselves through their own professional associations. Professionals also exercise considerable power over their clients and other lower-status occupational groups; they typically emphasize the altruistic nature of their work.[21]

For example, doctors spend many years training in medical schools, where they acquire knowledge specific to their profession. They go on to determine their own working conditions, whether they are employed in large health care institutions or work as self-employed professionals. In the past few decades, many doctors have increased their work autonomy by setting up professional corporations. Through their own professional associations, doctors can censure colleagues who have acted unprofessionally in the course of their work. Doctors have much power over their patients and those in helping occupations, such as nurses and medical laboratory technicians. Finally, members of this profession emphasize their code of ethics, by which they are committed to preserving human life above all other objectives.

In short, professions are much more powerful than occupations.[22] Randall Collins (1990) uses the term *market closure* to describe the ability of professionals to shape the labour market to their advantage, rather than simply responding to it as do most occupational groups. Like the craft guilds of an earlier era, professional groups in contemporary Western society can restrict others from doing their type of work by controlling entry into their profession. Professional associations have close relationships with their (typically university-based) professional schools and can strongly influence both course content and entrance quotas. Many professional groups have actively lobbied for and obtained legislation that both requires practitioners of their profession to be officially licensed and prohibits anyone else from performing certain tasks.

◙ BARRIERS TO PRIMARY LABOUR MARKET ENTRY

We can now see how internal labour markets and labour market shelters not only provide better work rewards to some groups but also help them maintain labour market closure. Generally, there are only a limited number of positions within the primary labour market, and entry is often restricted to those with the proper credentials—a degree, union membership, or professional certification (Kim 2013). As we explained earlier, a more advantaged family background gives one a substantial head start on obtaining such credentials. Furthermore, information about job vacancies is not always widely distributed. Often, it is passed only through small and informal networks (Marin 2012). Without "contacts" within the primary labour market, gained through family and friends—that is, without sufficient social capital—qualified applicants might never be aware of job openings (Petersen, Saporta, and Seidel 2000).

For some individuals, a history of employment in marginal jobs may act as a barrier. In Atlantic Canada, for example, the collapse of the fishing industry and the prevalence of seasonal work in resource industries in general have forced many people into an annual cycle where income is obtained from part-year jobs, Employment Insurance, and welfare assistance.[23] Thus, a work record showing frequent layoffs or job changes may simply be reflecting the nature of the local labour market. But it could also be interpreted by employers as an indication of unstable work habits. Similarly, a long sequence of temporary jobs and part-time jobs, a common career trajectory for many well-educated and highly motivated young Canadians in all regions of the country, could handicap them because employers might assume the problem originates with the job applicant rather than with the labour market.[24]

Historical Patterns of Racial and Ethnic Discrimination

Employer *discrimination* in hiring and promotion can also block movement into better jobs, leading to overrepresentation of disadvantaged groups in secondary labour markets. Before we discuss this, it would be useful to look back in Canadian history at examples of officially sanctioned racial and ethnic discrimination. After Canada was colonized, members of various Aboriginal nations frequently participated in the pre-industrial labour market, acting as guides, fighting for the French against the English (and vice versa), and providing the furs sought by the trading companies for their European markets.[25] But as central Canada began to industrialize, and later as western Canada was opened for settlement, the traditional economies of the Aboriginal nations in these regions were largely destroyed. Usually, the presence of Aboriginal groups was seen as an impediment to economic development. The most common solution was to place them on reserves, far out of sight.

Nevertheless, some Aboriginal workers were employed in the resource industries (forestry, mining, and commercial fishing and canning, for example), in railway construction, and in agriculture, particularly in western Canada. Not all of this paid employment was completely voluntary, though. For example, in the 1950s and 1960s, by cutting off social assistance benefits, the provincial and federal governments forced many Aboriginal people to migrate to southern Alberta to work in the sugar-beet industry (Laliberte and Satzewich 1999). The decline in demand for large numbers of unskilled and semiskilled workers in Canada's resource and transportation industries meant declining wage-labour opportunities for Aboriginal people. Even when jobs were available, racist attitudes and labour market discrimination were rampant (Knight 1978). In a society that clearly viewed members of First Nations as second-class citizens, these problems should not be surprising—First Nations people were not even allowed to vote until 1960.

During the 1880s, many Chinese men were recruited to work on railway construction in western Canada and in resource-based industries. They were generally paid much less than what others received for the same job and encountered much hostility from the white population (Anderson 1991: 35). Labour unions lobbied for legislation restricting Chinese workers from entering specific (better-paid) trades. Chinese workers were forced into marginal jobs in a racially split B.C. labour market. In addition, the B.C. government passed legislation that severely restricted the civil rights of Chinese residents of the province. For its part, the federal government required Chinese immigrants to pay a head tax on entering Canada, while other immigrants were not required to do so; later, it passed the Chinese Immigration Act which, for several decades, virtually stopped all potential Chinese immigrants from entering the country.[26]

Perhaps the discrimination faced by Chinese workers was simply the result of white workers' fears that they would lose their jobs to non-whites who were willing to work for lower wages. However, studies of this era suggest that racist attitudes—fears about the impact of too many Asian immigrants on a white, anglophone society—were frequently the underlying source of publicly expressed concerns about job loss and wage cuts. White workers seldom tried to bring Chinese workers into their unions (a tactic that would have reduced employers' ability to pay lower wages to non-whites), even though the latter frequently showed interest in collectively opposing the actions of employers.[27]

Peter Li (1982) has described how, early in the 20th century (1910 to 1947), Chinese Canadians living in the Prairie provinces encountered similar forms of racial discrimination. Barred from entry into many trades and professions, Chinese workers were mostly restricted to employment in *ethnic business enclaves* where, by supporting one another and working extremely hard, they could make a living. Chinese restaurants and laundries, for example, provided employment for many members of the Prairie Chinese community.

Similar experiences of racial discrimination were encountered by Black Canadians in pre-industrial and early industrial Canada. Some members of the Canadian Black community were descendents of slaves brought to Nova Scotia by Loyalists leaving the United States (Milan and Tran 2004). Others were former American slaves who had left the United States, often via the Underground Railroad (a network of sympathetic individuals and groups in the United States and Canada who assisted slaves fleeing north), and had settled in the area west of Toronto to the Detroit River. During the mid-19th century, white Canadians frequently lobbied to have Blacks sent back to their former owners in the United States (Pentland 1981: 1–6).

By the 1860s, officially sanctioned discrimination against Blacks had largely disappeared, but labour market discrimination continued. For example, many Blacks worked for railway companies but were restricted to a limited number of lower-paying jobs, such as sleeping-car porter. White workers had the better-paying, less menial jobs such as sleeping-car conductor or dining-car steward. Such patterns were embedded in the contracts between railway companies and their unions. The system was supported by societal values that took for granted that Blacks should work in menial jobs. Not until 1964 were the arrangements that legitimized this *racially split labour market* abolished (Calliste 1987).

Today, labour laws and human rights legislation make it considerably more difficult for employers to discriminate against specific groups of labour market participants. Nevertheless, some groups are still severely disadvantaged in the contemporary Canadian labour market for various reasons. The following three sections of this chapter focus on some of the most important of these groups. Chapter 6 is devoted to a discussion of the experiences of women in the paid labour market.

Immigrants and Visible Minorities

By 2011, visible minorities (not including Aboriginal Canadians) made up 19.1 percent of the Canadian population (more than 6 million people), up from 9.4 percent in 1991 (2.5 million people), and only 4.7 percent (1.1 million people) in 1981. Three out of four (78%) of all immigrants who arrived in Canada between 2006 and 2011 were members of visible minority groups.[28] Compared to the rest of the adult population, recent immigrants are more highly educated and more likely to be trained in science, technology, engineering, and math (STEM) specializations that are in high labour-market demand. In 2011, for example, 25 percent of Canada's total adult population were immigrants ages 25 to 64. However, immigrants made up 34 percent of the adult population holding university degrees. In fact, they held more than half (51%) of all STEM degrees in 2011.[29] Recent immigrants are also more likely to be in the labour force because of their higher level of education and their somewhat younger age profile. Since Canadian immigration policies favour better-educated immigrants, these higher education and labour force participation patterns are not surprising.

Nevertheless, university-educated immigrants, particularly recent ones, are much more likely than native-born Canadians with university degrees to be working in jobs in sales and services with low education requirements (Reitz 2007b). In 2006, about 10 percent of native-born Canadians with university degrees were working in such low-skill jobs, compared to 44 percent of recently immigrated women with degrees and 28 percent of recently immigrated men with degrees (Galarneau and Morissette 2009: 15).

It is not surprising, then, that immigrants earn far less than their native-born counterparts with equivalent education. For example, in 2000, male immigrants who had been in Canada for one year were earning 63 percent of the amount earned by their male Canadian-born counterparts. For those who had been in the country for 10 years, the comparable figure was 80 percent (similar patterns were observed for female immigrants). These statistics suggest that, in time, immigrants slowly catch up with Canadian-born workers; however, a three-decade comparison of the experiences of different cohorts of immigrants tells a different story. The 1991 Census showed that one-year male immigrants were making 63 percent of the amount earned by Canadian-born men in 1990 (the same percentage observed in the 2001 Census). In contrast, 10-year immigrants were earning 90 percent (compared to 80 percent in the 2001 Census). Going back another decade, in 1981, one-year male immigrants were earning 72 percent of what Canadian-born men were earning, while 10-year male immigrants had completely caught up. Similar over-time changes were seen among female immigrants. In short, over the past several decades, the average education of immigrants to Canada has been rising, but in terms of income, it is taking longer for immigrants to catch up to their Canadian-born counterparts.[30]

This gap is clearly a serious social and economic problem for both immigrants and society as a whole. The immigrants are having difficulty benefiting from their investments in human capital—that is, their educational attainment and prior work experience—and they report that finding an adequate job is the biggest problem they experience after arriving in Canada (Schellenberg and Maheux 2007: 7). As for society as a whole, the under-utilization of recent immigrants' skills and training comes at a significant cost to the larger economy.

It is important to note the "changing colour of poverty in Canada" (Kazemipur and Halli 2001). As already mentioned, more than three-quarters of recent immigrants to Canada have been members of visible minority groups, so, when discussing the difficult labour market experiences of recent immigrants, we are talking primarily about newcomers from South and East Asia, the Middle East, and, to a smaller extent, Africa, Central America, and South America. Related to this, evidence is beginning to accumulate that, with a few exceptions, Canadian-born visible minority group members earn as much as their white counterparts with similar amounts of education and training.[31] In other words, it is not visible minority status per se that is associated with labour market disadvantage, but the combination of visible minority and immigrant status. Thus, we find much higher-than-average proportions of non-white recent immigrants underemployed in the secondary labour market, earning less than they could and should. Taxi drivers, janitors, domestic workers, parking-lot attendants, security guards, and workers in ethnic restaurants are obvious examples (Krahn et al. 2000).[32] And as a Toronto study revealed, many recent immigrants also must rely on work in the informal economy, with all its risks and uncertainties, to make ends meet (Wellesley Institute 2013).

A substantial part of the problem lies in the non-recognition or undervaluing of non-Canadian educational credentials (Reitz 2007a). Canadian employers and professional licensing organizations (e.g., medical or engineering associations) often assume that university degrees or technical diplomas acquired outside Canada are inferior and use such assumptions to avoid hiring (or licensing) well-educated immigrants who were enticed to come to Canada with promises of finding good jobs in their areas of training. For example, a 1999 study of recent refugees who had settled in Alberta showed that, even though 39 percent had held management and professional positions in their home country, only 11 percent had found similar employment in Canada (Krahn et al. 2000). For many of the former professionals interviewed in this study, the problem lay in Canadian employers and educational institutions being unwilling to recognize their foreign credentials.[33]

Along with the undervaluing of their non-Canadian credentials, some recent immigrants may be held back by English or French language deficiencies (Fuller and Martin 2012) and by having less social capital, that is, fewer personal contacts within the primary labour market.[34] In addition, racial discrimination continues to handicap visible minority immigrants, as well as some Canadian-born visible minority groups, seeking to improve their employment situation. Statistics Canada's 2003 Ethnic Diversity Survey revealed that one in five visible minority labour force participants had experienced discrimination or unfair treatment in the previous five years based on ethnicity, language, accent, or religion, compared to only 5 percent of non–visible minority Canadians.[35]

Such treatment might involve *systemic discrimination*, which is subtle and hidden beneath the everyday practices within a workplace bureaucracy, as in situations where employers routinely pass over qualified visible minority candidates when making hiring or promotion decisions (Beck, Reitz, and Weiner 2002). Or it may be deliberate and blatant. A recent Toronto study of Filipino and West Indian women recruited to work in Canada as nannies and nurses provides some telling examples. The owner of a nanny agency explained her hiring and referral practices as follows: "If you're from Jamaica, I won't even interview you. I know this is discrimination but I don't have any time for this … Jamaican girls are just dumb. They are not qualified to be childcare workers." Black nurses told the researchers how their ward assignments typically required much heavier physical labour, involved considerably less skilled work, and offered few supervisory opportunities. The long-term impact of such employment experiences would be less upward career mobility.[36]

Aboriginal Canadians

In 2011, Canada had about 1.41 million Aboriginal citizens (4.3% of the total population), including about 850,000 self-identifying as members of a First Nation, 450,000 as Métis, and 60,000 as Inuit. About 41 percent of the Aboriginal population lived in the three Prairie provinces, along with 22 percent in Ontario and 17 percent in British Columbia.

The Aboriginal population is growing much faster than the rest of the population, and it is also considerably younger. Between 2006 and 2011, Canada's Aboriginal population increased by 20 percent, compared to only 5 percent for the rest of the Canadian population. The median age of Aboriginal Canadians in 2011 was 28 years, compared to 41 years for the rest of the population. Hence, a much higher proportion of Aboriginal people are of working age (25 to 64 years old) or will soon move into this age category.[37]

At the same time, Aboriginal Canadians have lower employment rates, face higher unemployment rates, and are much more likely to be living in low-income households. In 2011, the employment and unemployment rates for Aboriginal Canadians between the ages of 25 and 64 years were 63 percent and 13 percent, respectively. In sharp contrast, the employment and unemployment rates for working-age non-Aboriginal Canadians were 76 percent and 6 percent.[38] As a result, the median income (in 2006) for Aboriginal Canadians (ages 15 and older) was 30 percent lower than for non-Aboriginal Canadians ($18,962, compared to $27,097).[39]

What produces these very large differences? On average, Aboriginal Canadians are not nearly as likely as other Canadians to have acquired the educational credentials that translate into better jobs (Davies and Guppy 1998), although the proportions with postsecondary diplomas and degrees have been rising slowly. In 2011, 48 percent of working-age Aboriginal Canadians had some type of postsecondary credential compared to 65 percent of other Canadians of the same age. But only 10 percent of Aboriginal Canadians had acquired a university degree, compared to 26 percent of the rest of the population.[40] And it is university degrees that seem to matter. Over 10 years (1996 to 2006), the income gap between Aboriginal Canadians with degrees and non-Aboriginal Canadians with degrees shrank from $3,382 to only $648 (Wilson and Macdonald 2010). Clearly, access to good schooling has been a serious problem for Aboriginal Canadians for generations, as has racism and discrimination within the education system (Schissel and Wotherspoon 2003).

But lack of education does not fully explain the marginal labour market position of Aboriginal Canadians. In 2011, 49 percent of First Nations Canadians with Registered Indian status (about 315,000 people)[41] were living on reserves (Statistics Canada 2013d) where their great-grandparents were forced to settle when white settlers took over their ancestral lands, destroying their livelihood, and making them dependent on a far-from-charitable government (Shewell 2004). Employment opportunities are severely limited in many of these frequently isolated communities, as they also are in many of the smaller communities inhabited by Canada's Métis and Inuit. Large industrial megaprojects in Northern Canada (e.g., mines, mills, pipelines, and dams) have typically offered only limited employment to residents of local Aboriginal communities. At the same time, these projects have often damaged traditional hunting, trapping, and fishing economies, further undermined traditional culture (Stabler and Howe 1990; Niezen 1993), and caused environmental damage.[42]

The employment situation of urban Aboriginal Canadians is slowly improving (Luffman and Sussman 2007), but there is still a huge gap separating them from non-Aboriginal urban residents. The former may have a patchy employment record, which can seriously restrict entry into the primary labour market. They may also often encounter prejudice among employers, which, along with a lack of contacts and limited job-search resources (such as transportation), can further handicap them in their search for satisfactory employment. Thus, an explanation for the disadvantaged labour market position of Aboriginal Canadians must examine the many other factors beyond the acquisition of human capital that contribute to the segmenting of the Canadian labour market and to the generation of urban poverty.

Disability and Age

Canadians with disabilities are another group characterized by low labour force participation and high unemployment rates, fewer hours of work, and lower incomes. As with the Aboriginal population, the people with disabilities who obtain employment are frequently found working in low-skill, poorly paid jobs in the secondary labour market. A 2006 national study (Statistics Canada 2007c) estimated the number of working-age Canadians with disabilities at just under 2.5 million (17% of 15- to 64-year-olds). The labour force participation rate for this segment of the population was very low—just 42 percent, or about 1 million people—due to severe disabilities (Galarneau and Radulescu 2009: 33).[43]

Huge barriers keep people with disabilities from obtaining satisfactory employment. Many employers, and even some of those involved in assisting Canadians with disabilities, assume that all those with visual, hearing, cognitive, and movement handicaps are equally impaired, though many of these individuals could cope well in a variety of jobs, with limited assistance. Some employers are uncomfortable with or fearful of people who have disabilities. Although a significant number of employers say they would hire people with disabilities, few do so. In addition, many people with disabilities face serious transportation problems and are held back by buildings designed without their needs in mind.[44] Despite there being a little progress in improving their labour market position in recent years, Canadians with disabilities continue to be significantly overrepresented in the secondary labour market. In fact, many find work only in special institutional settings where pay rates are low and career opportunities are nonexistent.

Age discrimination occurs when older workers, laid off in a factory shutdown or a company or government department downsizing, for example, apply for another core-sector job and are rejected in favour of younger applicants because of the belief that older workers are harder to retrain and will have difficulty adapting to new technologies. It may also occur when qualified and hard-working older workers are passed over for promotions within companies in favour of younger workers, or when older workers are actively encouraged to retire to reduce payroll costs.[45]

Youth seeking their first permanent job also face age discrimination. Even if they have the educational qualifications, they find it far easier to gain employment in the part-time student labour market within the lower-tier services than to get an interview for a full-time career position in a major corporation or a government department. "Lack of experience" is a term heard all too frequently by unsuccessful young job applicants (Marquardt 1998).

■ CHANGING PATTERNS OF SOCIAL INEQUALITY

Questions about how labour markets work, about why some people get better jobs than others do, are really questions about social inequality. As we saw in Chapter 1, Karl Marx used the concept of social class to analyze inequality, focusing on economic and social relationships between capitalists and the proletariat and on what he believed to be a declining middle class (the petite bourgeoisie). He predicted growing class conflict that would eventually lead to the emergence of a new type of egalitarian society. While Marx's theories have been useful for explaining conflict within industrial capitalist societies and for helping us understand how people feel about work (see Chapter 10), they are unable to accurately map the complexities of employment structures (see Chapters 3 and 4) and patterns of social inequality in contemporary Western societies. Social scientists have taken two different approaches to going beyond Marx: the first involving descriptions of the class structures of postindustrial societies and the second focusing on how labour market segmentation has evolved over the past two centuries.

Postindustrial Class Structure

Erik Olin Wright (Wright et al. 1982) developed one of the most widely used updated versions of Marx's model of social class relationships. He took into account a number of different factors: ownership of the means of production; the employment of others; the supervision of others, and control over one's own work. He also distinguished between large business owners and small employers, two groups that have legal ownership and also employ others, and the petite bourgeoisie, who own their businesses (or farms) but do not have others working for them (the own-account self-employed). Large employers (the group most closely resembling Marx's class of capitalists) are in a different category from small employers with only a handful of employees, since the latter would typically be directly involved in the production process (working alongside employees).

The large class of paid employees was separated by Wright into managers, who, while not owning the enterprise, would be involved in decision making, along with (or in the absence of) the legal owners; supervisors, who are not involved in planning and decision making but who nevertheless exercise authority over others; and workers, who have no ownership rights, decision-making power, or authority over others. One final class grouping, *semi-autonomous workers* (for instance, social workers, university professors, and other salaried professionals), are identified by the relatively greater control they retain over their own work.

Unfortunately, the official data sources we have used in Chapters 3 and 4 to describe Canadian employment patterns and trends do not contain information on the planning, decision making, and exercise of authority over others that workers might do in their jobs. Consequently, we are unable to profile the contemporary Canadian class structure using Wright's typology of social class relations.[46]

Evolving Labour Market Segmentation in North America

Taking a labour market segmentation rather than a strictly social class approach to explaining contemporary patterns of social inequality in North America, Gordon, Edwards, and Reich (1982) separated the last two centuries into three major epochs. During the period of *initial proletarianization*, from about 1820 to 1890, a large, relatively homogeneous industrial working class emerged. While modern forms of capitalist management were still in their infancy, craftworkers were beginning to lose control over the labour process. This trend did not develop fully until the era of *homogenization of labour*, from the end of the 19th century until the start of World War II, however. This period saw extensive mechanization and deskilling of labour, the growth of large workplaces, and the rise of a new managerial class within American capitalism. The period from the end of World War II to the early 1980s was one of *segmentation of labour*—distinct primary and secondary labour markets emerged.

Canada began to industrialize later and has always remained a heavily resource-based economy. Thus, the same three stages do not precisely describe our economic history, although some similarities exist (see Chapter 1). However, the emphasis on change in this historical overview encourages us to ask: Have further changes in labour market segmentation been occurring as we have moved into the 21st century? The answer is yes. There is much evidence of fundamental realignments in the industrial and occupational structures, and in the nature of employment relationships, not only in Canada, but also in the United States and other Western industrialized countries.

Labour Market Polarization

The goods-producing industries have declined significantly over the past several decades. Factory closures due to increased overseas competition in the 1980s were followed by the movement of manufacturing bases to low-wage countries such as Mexico in the 1990s and, more recently, China, India, and other rapidly industrializing countries (see Chapter 2). The widespread introduction of microelectronic and robotic technologies allowed other manufacturing sectors to maintain production levels with fewer employees. A similar situation developed in Canada's resource industries, where unstable world markets, in combination with technological innovations that reduced the need for labour, led employers to substantially reduce their workforces.[47]

During the 1990s, downsizing and hiring cutbacks were extensive in many large corporations in the business and distributive service industries, and by the turn of the century, many white-collar jobs were being outsourced to countries such as India (Friedman 2005). As for the public sector, downsizing became the norm in the 1990s as governments (both federal and provincial) cut deficits by laying off employees or privatizing some of the services they had previously provided directly to the public. For example, a recent study of hospital support workers in Vancouver showed how privatization (contracting-out of jobs) led to workers receiving fewer benefits and having their wages cut in half (Zuberi 2011). While the economic expansion that took place in the first part of the 21st century slowed down some of these trends, the global recession that began in 2008 intensified them once again.[48]

Although a shrinking workforce has been observed in both the goods-producing and service sectors, there has still been employment growth over the past three decades. Most of it has been in the service industries. While new high-skill, well-paying jobs have been created, leading some observers to proclaim the emergence of a "knowledge economy" (Drucker 1993; Florida 2002), there has also been a significant increase in the proportion of jobs in the secondary labour market. As a result, others have written about a "new risk economy" (Mendenhall et al. 2008). Many of the new jobs created have been part time or temporary, paying less and offering fewer benefits and career opportunities than the full-time, permanent jobs that have disappeared. In other work settings, traditional employment relationships have been altered when workers retired—temporary positions and contract work have replaced the previously permanent positions. In addition, employers in some industries have come to rely on *temporary foreign workers* whose labour force situation is even more precarious because they do not have Canadian citizenship and are not as protected by labour legislation (Brickner and Straehle 2010). Thus, nonstandard jobs with less security have been increasing, leading to new forms of labour market segmentation (Hudson 2007).[49]

Industrial restructuring and the growth in nonstandard work have led to *labour market polarization.* Compared to the 1970s and 1980s, the 1990s saw more Canadians unemployed and relatively fewer people employed in the well-paying, full-time, permanent jobs that were once taken for granted. Put another way, the primary labour market shrank during the 1990s, leaving fewer workers with access to its good jobs, as defined by income, benefits, and job security. The economic recovery at the end of the last century and the beginning of the 21st century slowed, but did not reverse, this polarization trend as relatively fewer of the new jobs were "good jobs."

Within the broadly defined secondary labour market, three relatively distinct new segments have emerged. The first is a *student labour market*, consisting mainly of part-time jobs, most of them in the lower-tier consumer services and retail trade industries (Lowe and Krahn 1999; Tufts and Holmes 2010). Many young Canadians participate voluntarily in this labour market, using their low-wage, part-time jobs to earn discretionary income or to pay for their education. But this part-time workforce also contains non-students, women who cannot work full time because of their family responsibilities, and others who simply cannot find a full-time job (see Chapter 4).

The *temporary/contract labour market* exists in both the upper- and lower-tier service industries (Vosko, Zukewich, and Cranford 2003; Fuller 2008). As employers in both the private and public sectors have come to rely more heavily on temporary workers for both low- and high-skill jobs (Stinson 2010), a larger proportion of well-educated young adults are spending some years in such jobs before they are able to obtain more secure employment. Women, immigrants, and members of visible minority groups are also overrepresented in this labour market segment (Hudson 2007; Fuller and Vosko 2008). While some of these temporary and contract jobs require higher levels of skill and training, they nevertheless offer less job security, fewer benefits, fewer training and career opportunities (Hoque and Kirkpatrick 2003; Davis 2010), and less income (Galarneau 2005).

Temporary foreign workers, or TFWs, recruited to fill specific jobs in Canada (often with specific employers) for specified periods of time inhabit a third, somewhat different labour market segment that has emerged in the 21st century. By 2012, more than 200,000 TFWs were living and working in Canada, up from about 130,000 only three years earlier.[50] Some were filling low-paying jobs clearly in the secondary labour market, doing janitorial work (Foster and Barnetson 2011–12), taking part in seasonal agricultural work (Hennebry and McLaughlin 2012), or serving as live-in nannies (Brickner and Straehle 2010), for example. Others were recruited to work in typically higher-paying occupations like nursing (Taylor, Foster, and Cambre 2012). As reported by Thomas (2010), both higher- and lower-skill TFWs, but particularly the latter, were working in a precarious environment with limited job security, less legal protection against exploitation by employers than Canadian citizens have, and fewer opportunities for developing a rewarding and long-term career.

Rising Income Inequality

Although real earnings (taking inflation into account) rose systematically in Canada in the three or four decades following World War II, this trend stopped in the 1980s, for the reasons discussed above. For many workers, more often men, real incomes have declined since then. In contrast, on average, women's incomes have increased somewhat (Chung 2006). At the same time, incomes rose for the highest-paid groups in society. Thus, labour market polarization has contributed to a substantial increase in *income inequality* in Canada over the past several decades (Osberg 2008).[51] For example, in 1985, the top 10 percent (in terms of earnings) received 35 percent of all income, but by 2007, this figure had increased to 41 percent of all income. The top 1 percent did even better. In 1977, they received less than 8 percent of all income, but two decades later, members of this group (246,000 individuals) were earning almost 14 percent of all income in Canada (Yalnizyan 2010). Income inequality has been increasing, for the same reasons, in most other western industrialized countries. While income inequality today is somewhat lower in Canada than in the United States or the United Kingdom, it is higher than in Sweden, Norway, and Switzerland, for example (OECD 2011).[52]

Equally significant have been the growing income difference across age groups. Despite their high levels of education, on average, the relative earnings of young Canadians, particularly young men, have been dropping over the past several decades (Chung 2006: 32; Green et al. 2011). For example, the 2001 national census showed that, for full-time, full-year employed Canadians, men under 40 years of age were earning only marginally more (in relative terms) than their counterparts a decade earlier (in 1991) and considerably less than this age cohort in 1981. For women, the dividing line was age 30. In contrast, women older than 30 and men older than 40 were doing relatively better in 2001 compared to these age cohorts in earlier decades. In other words, as Statistics Canada concluded based on these analyses, "[t]here is a clear generational divide in the labour market."[53] Thus, it is apparent that industrial restructuring and new forms of labour market segmentation (that is, an increase in nonstandard jobs) have seriously disadvantaged younger workers.

We have also seen a significant change in the composition of low-income households. In the 1970s, the elderly made up a sizable portion of Canada's poor. Since then, improvements in income security for senior citizens have substantially reduced poverty among the elderly (Myles 2000), although low income rates among Canadian seniors did begin to rise again during the first decade of the 2000s (Murphy, Zhang, and Dionne 2012). The combined labour market trends noted above, however, point to an increase in problems of poverty among working-age Canadians. The *working poor* have become a larger group in the Canadian labour market (Sauvé 2006). Younger households, especially those headed by female single parents (Fleury 2008), have been particularly disadvantaged.

Some observers have used the term *declining middle class* to describe these trends toward greater inequality. Others have commented on the emergence of an *underclass* of citizens, individuals largely marginalized from the labour market. But neither concept has been precisely defined. As already noted, we prefer to use the broader term *labour market polarization* to refer to the interrelated trends we have described—industrial and occupational realignment, rising levels of nonstandard work, and growing individual income and wealth inequality. But whatever the term used, it is clear that social inequality in Canada has increased over the past several decades.

■ POLICY RESPONSES TO LABOUR MARKET BARRIERS AND GROWING INEQUALITY

What might be done to create better jobs and to counter the trend toward greater labour market polarization? Responses based on a human capital perspective would primarily emphasize access to education as the most important public policy goal. In fact, access was a central concern of Canadian governments throughout the second half of the last century, particularly during the 1960s and 1970s when many new postsecondary educational institutions were opened and student loan systems were introduced, and again, in the late 1990s and the start of this century, when provincial governments once more undertook to improve access to postsecondary education.

These policy efforts did have an effect. Over time, the average educational attainment of the Canadian population rose dramatically, and some of the systemic barriers to equal access to education were reduced. Even so, as we have seen in this chapter, not all groups in Canadian society have equal educational opportunities. Consequently, continued policy responses targeting this goal are needed. With rising postsecondary tuition costs, and with provincial governments struggling with deficits (leading them to reduce funding for post-secondary education), we might even see a reversal of the slow trend toward greater equality of educational opportunity that characterized the last part of the 20th century.

Over the past several decades, government education policies also began focusing on encouraging young Canadians to stay in school (thereby reducing high-school dropout rates) and promoting skill upgrading among older labour force participants, particularly the unemployed. At the same time, more emphasis was placed on policies promoting formal training and skill upgrading in the workplace.[54] Concerns about reducing labour market inequalities, however, were not the reason. Governments were becoming anxious about Canada's competitive position in the global economy. Without a heavier investment in human capital, along with more advantage taken of it, it was argued, Canada would fall behind in the global economy (Laroche, Merette, and Ruggeri 1999).

Clearly, greater investments in education and training are important (Lowe 2000), but they cannot resolve all problems. Some groups of Canadian labour force participants are still educationally disadvantaged, and some could benefit from improvements in their literacy skills (Finnie and Meng 2007). The Canadian record on workplace training is not very good, and there are many barriers to receiving needed training. Thus, if global competitiveness is our goal, greater investments in human capital are part of the longer-term solution. However, if reducing labour market inequalities is another equally important goal, human capital investments are only part of the solution. We know that additional education and training would assist some Canadians in improving their labour market position. At the same time, we are aware that a large minority of other working Canadians, including many with university degrees, believe they are overqualified for their jobs. Research on literacy requirements in the workplace, for example, documents large proportions of workers who are seldom required to use literacy skills in their jobs. Thus, *underemployment* is also a serious problem in the Canadian workplace.[55]

While the human capital explanation of labour market processes focuses our attention on education as the key policy variable, the labour market segmentation perspective encourages us to identify the barriers that keep large numbers of qualified individuals out of better jobs. Obviously, a shortage of good jobs is part of the problem. So, too, is labour legislation that still largely overlooks the rights and needs of the working poor, of nonstandard workers, a majority of whom are women (Fudge and Vosko 2001), and of temporary foreign workers (Brickner and Straehle 2010). Legislation that would significantly increase the minimum wage in all provinces would also make a difference, particularly for the working poor (Green et al. 2011).

In addition, we need strong legislation that discourages discrimination against disadvantaged groups in the Canadian labour market. Equity programs that help disadvantaged groups to catch up with mainstream labour market participants are part of a policy package that could help reduce labour market inequality. Improved school-to-work transition programs are needed to assist young people in their search for rewarding jobs and careers, given how young Canadians have been hurt by labour market polarization trends.

Finally, we believe that unions have a larger role to play in the Canadian labour market. If more Canadian workers were covered by union contracts, some of the inequality within the labour market could be reduced. If unions were involved on a more equal basis in decisions about national, regional, and firm-level industrial strategies, we might also move further toward the goal of global competitiveness. We will return to many of these topics in subsequent chapters.

● CONCLUSION

After examining the varying quality of jobs and the problems of unemployment and underemployment in previous chapters, in this chapter we discussed the human capital and labour market segmentation explanations of labour market processes in order to answer the critical question of why some people tend to get better jobs. While the human capital model highlights the central role of education in determining occupational outcomes, it fails to account for the many examples of qualified and highly motivated individuals working in unrewarding jobs; it also ignores intergenerational transfers of advantage. In contrast, the segmentation approach recognizes inequalities in labour market outcomes and provides a better account of how such power differences are created and maintained. Our analysis of the segmented nature of the Canadian labour market led us to conclude that it has become more polarized and that income inequality has increased over the past several decades. The following two chapters on gender in the paid workplace and on household, caring, and community work focus in detail on another critically important source of differentiation—between women and men—in work opportunities, experiences, and rewards.

DISCUSSION QUESTIONS

1. Many people would argue that, in Canadian society today, everyone has more or less the same chance to get ahead in life. Do you agree or disagree? Why?

2. Compared to several decades ago, does education play a larger or smaller role in determining labour market outcomes? Why?

3. Based on what you read in Chapters 3 and 4, and in this one, in your opinion, how effectively do human capital and labour market segmentation theories explain present and past patterns of social inequality in Canada?

4. In your opinion, which groups of Canadian workers are most disadvantaged? Have these patterns of labour market inequality changed over time?

5. Should the state—that is, the provincial and federal governments—get involved in trying to reduce labour market inequalities? If no, why not? If yes, what would be some of the most effective approaches?

ADDITIONAL RESOURCES

WORK AT THE MOVIES

- *The Road Taken* (directed by Selwyn Jacob, 1996, 52:00 minutes). This NFB documentary explores racism and the fight against discrimination by sleeping-car porters working on Canada's railways during the first six decades of the 20th century. It is available through the National Film Board of Canada: http://www.nfb.ca/film/road_taken.
- *High Steel* (directed by Don Owen, 1965, 13:47 minutes). This NFB documentary provides an interesting historical perspective on the experiences of Kahnawake Mohawks who migrated to do steelwork on Manhattan skyscrapers. It is available through the National Film Board of Canada: http://www.nfb.ca/film/high_steel.

- *Farmingville* (directed by Carlos Sandoval and Catherine Tambini, 2004, 79 minutes). In this documentary film on migrant and illegal workers in the United States, the story of the attempted murder of two Mexican labourers in Farmingville, New York, is told.
- *Chinese Cafés in Rural Saskatchewan* (directed by Tony Chan, 1985, 26: 25 minutes). This documentary profiles the lives of four Chinese café owners and their families in Saskatchewan, examining the contemporary and historical, social, and economic issues they faced.

SOUNDS OF WORK

- "Jack of All Trades" (Bruce Springsteen). Springsteen's song explores labour market inequality and the experiences of workers forced to take any jobs available in the context of the 2008 global downturn.
- "Allentown" (Billy Joel). Joel examines the impact of socioeconomic change during the 1970s and 1980s on the opportunities for blue-collar workers.
- "Tramp Miner" (The Rankin Family). These Cape Bretoners sing about migrant miners who find jobs in unhealthy work environments and dream about returning home.
- "Jobs" (Chris Tse). This spoken word piece addresses the intersections of work, race, and immigration by highlighting the work and education experiences of the Canadian poet's father.

NOTES

1. See Rubery (1996), Jones (1996), and van den Berg and Smucker (1997) on how economists and sociologists analyze labour markets.
2. See Clement and Myles (1994), Spilerman (2000), and Browne and Misra (2005) on labour markets and social inequality.
3. Becker (1975), with his book first published in 1964, is credited for developing human capital theory, although its basic premises originate in neoclassical economics. As we describe it here, the model is closely linked to the functionalist theory of stratification (Davis and Moore 1945).
4. See also Conference Board of Canada (2013) and Boudarbat, Lemieux, and Riddell (2010).

5. See Marquardt (1998), Livingstone (1999), Lowe (2000), Mills (2004), Côté and Bynner (2008), and Krahn, Howard, and Galambos (2012) on problems of underemployment among Canadian youth.

6. See Goldrick-Rab (2006), Alon (2009), Bowen, Chingos, and McPherson (2009), and Faas, Benson, and Kaestle (2013) for studies of the impacts of socioeconomic background on postsecondary education and career outcomes in the United States.

7. Unpublished analysis by the first author. Andres and Wyn (2010) also show strong SES effects on postsecondary educational outcomes, using longitudinal data from similar studies in British Columbia and Victoria, Australia. Their comparative study highlights interesting and important cultural and institutional differences across countries.

8. Government-provided student loans defer the costs of higher education, but scholarships can reduce them. Research in the United States (Titus 2006) shows that higher-status universities with larger endowments can provide more scholarships, but that lower-SES students are more likely to attend lower-status universities where scholarships are less available. The situation is likely the same in Canada.

9. Between 1981 and 2011, the proportion of Canadian universities' operating budget based on student tuition rose from 13 percent to 37 percent (Canadian Association of University Teachers 2013). Shaker and Macdonald (2013) report that average Canadian university tuition fees in 1990–91 were $1,464. By 2016–17, they are estimated to be $7,437. Taking inflation into account, average tuition will have tripled in 16 years.

10. Goldrick-Rab (2006) reports that young people from lower-SES backgrounds are more likely to interrupt their postsecondary studies rather than moving straight through as do most middle-class youth. Bernardi (2012) shows that, among students doing poorly in and dropping out of postsecondary studies, those from higher-SES families are more likely to have a "second chance" at earning a postsecondary degree. While these studies were completed in the United States and Spain, respectively, it is likely that the same patterns would be observed in Canada.

11. See Duncan, Hill, and Hoffman (1998), Corak (1998), and McMullin (2010) on the impact of family background on educational attainment, physical and mental health, and other outcomes.

12. Tanner, Krahn, and Hartnagel (1995) review Canadian research on high-school dropouts. Alexander, Entwisle, and Horsey (1998) present similar information for the United States.

13. See Frenette (2007a) and Davies and Maldonado (2009) on the impacts of cultural capital on educational outcomes.
14. See Hauser et al. (2000) for recent U.S. status attainment analyses.
15. See Marquardt (1998), Mills (2004), Côté and Bynner (2008), and Krahn, Howard, and Galambos (2012).
16. See Rubery (1996), Leontaridi (1998), and Bauder (2001a) on labour market segmentation theory.
17. See Lowe and Schellenberg (2001) for Canadian data on better jobs in large, capital-intensive firms, and Kalleberg and Van Buren (1996) for U.S. data. Park (2012: 34) reports higher levels of training in the public sector and in white-collar occupations.
18. Aguiar (2001) describes low-paid, low-skill work in the contract building-cleaning industry in Toronto; see Backett-Milburn et al. (2008) on British women working in the low-paid food-retailing sector.
19. Smith (1997), Camuffo (2002), and Osterman and Burton (2005) provide overviews of research on internal labour markets. Specific studies of internal labour markets include Barnett, Baron, and Stuart (2000) and Petersen, Saporta, and Seidel (2000).
20. See Vosko (2000, 2005), Vosko, Zukewich, and Cranford (2003), and Fuller and Vosko (2008) on precarious work in Canada; Kalleberg (2009) and Young (2010) discuss the same trends in the United States.
21. Macdonald (1995), Leicht and Fennell (2001), and Evetts (2003) discuss the sociology of professions; see Witz (1992) for an early feminist critique of research on professionals.
22. Over time some occupational groups have gained more autonomy and power, while others have experienced *de-professionalization*. See Drudy (2008), Randle (1996), Adams (2000, 2003), and Cant and Sharma (1995) for how these processes have affected, respectively, teachers, scientists, dentists and dental hygienists, and practitioners of non-traditional medicine.
23. See Osberg, Wein, and Grude (1995) and Palmer and Sinclair (1997).
24. See Ferber and Waldfogel (1998), Mills (2004), Worth (2005), Fuller (2008), and Krahn, Howard, and Galambos (2012) on the career liabilities of irregular work histories.
25. See Jenness (1977: 250–51) and Patterson (1972); Pentland (1981: 1–3) reports that some Aboriginal people were kept as slaves in Quebec, but this practice had largely disappeared by the early 1800s.
26. See Li (1982), Anderson (1991), and Chui, Tran, and Flanders (2005).
27. See Baureiss (1987), Creese (1988–89), Muszynski (1996), and Anderson (1991).
28. Statistics Canada, *The Daily* (May 8, 2013).

29. Statistics Canada, *The Daily* (June 26, 2013).
30. Statistics Canada, *The Daily* (March 11, 2003). See Reitz (2007a, 2007b) and Morissette and Sultan (2013) on changing patterns of immigrant employment success in Canada.
31. See Bauder (2001b), Tran (2004), Palameta (2004), and Maximova and Krahn (2005).
32. See Colic-Peisker and Tilbury (2006) for similar research from Australia.
33. See also Li (2001), Palameta (2004), and Galarneau and Morissette (2009).
34. See also Thomas (2009) and Creese and Kambere (2003) on immigrants' language disadvantages, and Lamba (2003) on how refugees with more extensive social networks tend to find better jobs.
35. Palameta (2004: 37); see also Das Gupta (1996), Satzewich (1998), and Creese (2007).
36. Stasiulis and Bakan (2003: 78, 128–36); see also Milan and Tran (2004) on the disadvantaged labour market situation of Blacks in Canada.
37. See Statistics Canada (2013d) for 2011 National Household Survey (NHS) data on Aboriginal Canadians.
38. Aboriginal Affairs and Northern Development Canada (2013).
39. Wilson and Macdonald (2010). Data on Aboriginal incomes from the 2011 National Household Survey (NHS) were not yet available when this chapter was written (October 2013).
40. Aboriginal Affairs and Northern Development Canada (2013); see also Statistics Canada (2013e).
41. In 2011, the 851,560 Aboriginal Canadians who said they were of First Nations (North American Indian) descent formed the membership of about 600 First Nations bands. About three-quarters of them (637,660) were also registered under the Indian Act of Canada (Statistics Canada 2013d).
42. Armitage (2005) and O'Faircheallaigh and Corbett (2005) discuss the involvement of Aboriginal groups in environmental assessment and management in Canada and Australia, respectively.
43. See Fogg, Harrington, and McMahon (2010) on the employment of people with disabilities in the United States, and Jones and Wass (2013) on the situation in the United Kingdom.
44. Prince (2004) comments on the inadequacy of Canadian public policy related to people with disabilities; Burkhauser, Schmeiser, and Weathers (2012) discuss the impact of anti-discrimination laws on employment opportunities for Americans who have disabilities.
45. See Roscigno et al. (2007), Mendenhall et al. (2008), and Kunze, Boehm, and Bruch (2011) on age discrimination.
46. Livingstone (1999: 158) describes Ontario's workforce in the mid-1990s using Wright's classification system. See Wright (2009: 14) for a concise description of

the class structure of the United States at the beginning of the 21st century and Wright (1997) for a more detailed discussion of social class and social mobility.

47. Clement's (1981) study of technological change at INCO documented the beginning of this trend. Osberg, Wein, and Grude (1995) and Russell (1999) discussed the continuing trend.

48. Zuberi (2013) shows how the contracting-out of hospital support staff jobs in Canada, the United States, and Europe has led to reductions in pay for workers and greater health risks for patients. Winson and Leach (2002) and Ehrenreich (2001) discuss the effects of industrial restructuring and downsizing during the 1990s on Canadian and U.S. families, respectively. See Harrison (2005), Shalla and Clement (2007), and Camfield (2011) for more studies of downsizing and layoffs in the Canadian private and public sectors.

49. See Vosko (2000), Vosko, Zukewich, and Cranford (2003), Galarneau (2005), Young (2010), and Fuller (2011) on trends in nonstandard work.

50. Employment and Social Development Canada: http://www.hrsdc.gc.ca/eng/jobs/foreign_workers/lmo_statistics/annual2012.shtml.

51. See also Murphy, Roberts, and Wolfson (2007) on growing income inequality and Morissette and Zhang (2007) on increases in wealth inequality. Along with labour market restructuring, changes to income tax policies that favour the very rich have also deepened income inequality (Yalnizyan 2010). Neckerman and Torche (2007) discuss similar trends in the United States.

52. Both Yalnizyan (2010) and OECD (2011) rely on tax data to calculate income inequality. In the past, Canadian census data were also a useful source for measuring trends in income inequality. However, the decision of the Canadian government to collect income data in 2011 with the voluntary (and hence, lower response rate) National Household Survey rather than the mandatory census (see Chapter 3) has made low-income (and income inequality) comparisons over time less valid: see Statistics Canada, *The Daily* (September 11, 2013).

53. Statistics Canada, *The Daily* (March 11, 2003); see also Bell and Blanchflower (2011) who show how in both the United States and the United Kingdom young people were most severely affected by the Great Recession of 2008–9.

54. On work-related training, see Jackson (2005: Chapter 3), Underhill (2006), and Hurst (2008). Muhlhausen (2005) describes the limited effectiveness of U.S. training programs for increasing the income of participants. McBride's (2011) U.K. case studies focus on the conditions under which gender inequalities in the workplace might be reduced by training programs.

55. See Livingstone (1999), Lowe (2000), Frenette (2001), and Yuen (2010) on self-reported underemployment in Canada; on literacy under-utilization, see Krahn (1997).

GENDER AND PAID EMPLOYMENT

"In the morning, I dropped my children off at the bus stop where there were three other children waiting with their mothers, all of whom had advanced degrees (the mothers, not the children) and who would then return home to wait for their children's day to end. The children's bus would take them to their middle school where together they would spend the day with fourteen different teachers, two of whom were men.... As I drove to my office, I passed a fire station. If I were to have stopped to look inside, I would likely find all men.... Nearby I passed a library, and if I had gone inside, I would have found all women, unless I was looking for the director, who is a man. Continuing my drive, I encountered road construction crews and, while slowly moving past ... I saw one woman who was directing traffic. For some reason the construction sites remind me that we have work that needs to be done at home, and if I were to have called a plumber, there is a ninety-nine percent chance that the plumber I reached would have been a male, and the same would be true for the electrician we also happen to need. If I were to call for someone to clean our home, however, I would have to look hard to find a man (unless I wanted our yard cleaned, in which case it would almost certainly be a man) ..."

Source: Michael Selmi and Sonia Weil. (2013). "Can All Women Be Pharmacists? A Critique of Hanna Rosins' The End of Men," *Boston University Law Review* 93(3): p. 851–852.

■ INTRODUCTION

In 2012, Hanna Rosin's book *The End of Men* sparked debate by suggesting that traditional gender patterns at work were being dramatically overturned. Women, she argued, were rapidly displacing men, proving themselves to be more talented, accomplished workers, better attuned to the needs of a knowledge-based, service economy. Certainly, women have made strong gains in the workplace. In Canada, for instance, the share of adult women in the paid workforce has jumped from one-third in 1970 to nearly two-thirds by 2010.[1] Traditional attitudes about women's economic roles have also shifted.

Rising education levels and job opportunities have made more women career minded. Economic realities and changing family forms have also meant that, for many women, there is no choice but to work for pay.

Yet, despite such change, traditional gender patterns in the workplace are still striking. So, too, is men's continued presence in more lucrative and prestigious jobs, and women's tendency to fit employment around family duties. Critiquing Rosin's arguments, Michael Selmi and Sonia Weil (quoted above) recount their own "mini experiment," tallying the gender of workers encountered in a typical day. Their discussion, worth reading in detail, confirms the persistence of fairly traditional gender patterns in the workplace, suggesting that change may not be quite as dramatic as Rosin claims.

Tackling this debate, this chapter examines the gendering of work in Canada. We discuss the rise of female labour force participation in recent decades, but also show how the labour market continues to be segmented into men's and women's jobs. We also explore two seemingly contradictory trends: on the one hand, significant gains in women's employment opportunities and rewards, and on the other, the persistence of major work-related gender inequities. A central theme is that despite gains by some women, a great deal of women's work continues to be undervalued and poorly rewarded. Consequently, gender remains a key determinant of inequality in our society.

To better grasp the causes and consequences of gender inequity in the work world, we examine historical and contemporary questions: What forces created a gender divide between the home and paid labour market? What factors have either pushed or pulled women into paid employment in recent decades? Why do women remain concentrated in a limited range of jobs at the bottom of the occupational ladder? How did these jobs come to be labelled "female"? Conversely, why do men still predominate in the most challenging and rewarding jobs that have come to be defined as "male"? Finally, what barriers prevent equality of opportunity, and how can greater gender equity in the workplace be achieved?

A word of clarification before we proceed. To avoid confusion, we should define how we use the terms *sex* and *gender*. Basically, sex is the biological distinction between men and women; gender is socially constructed in the sense that it refers to how a particular society defines masculine and feminine roles. Thus, one can observe the sex segregation of occupations. But to explain this, it is necessary to look at how jobs are *gendered*—that is, how they take on societal images of appropriate male or female behaviour. We tend to prefer the term *gender*, given that male–female differences in employment are almost solely a product of socially created gender roles and ideologies.

● GENDER AND WORK IN HISTORICAL CONTEXT

Although history has, for the most part, been written from the perspective of men, even a quick glance back to the past reveals that women have always performed a vital, if somewhat unacknowledged, economic role. Aboriginal women, for example, were indispensable to the fur trade, the major industry during much of Canada's colonial period (Van Kirk 1980). White male traders relied on Aboriginal women to act as interpreters, prepare food, clean pelts for market, and teach them wilderness survival skills. Little wonder that fur traders sought out Aboriginal women as wives. When an agrarian economy began to develop in Upper Canada (Ontario) during the 19th century, the family was the basic production unit, in which women played a key role. Men worked the fields, while women looked after all domestic work associated with child rearing, tending the livestock and garden, making clothes, and preparing food.[2] Similarly, in the Canadian West in the early 1900s, women contributed significantly to agricultural development by working on their family farms and by making the farm home "a haven of safety and healthfulness."[3]

Industrialization and Women's Work

In Chapter 1, we noted that one consequence of the rise of large-scale factory production was a growing separation between the work that men and women did. Men were drawn into the industrial wage-labour market; women were increasingly confined to the domestic sphere of the household. Marjorie Cohen's feminist analysis of economic development in 19th-century Ontario reveals that, prior to wide-scale industrialization, an integration of family and household existed within the emerging market economy (Cohen 1988). Traditional theories of industrialization, Cohen points out, tend to ignore the contribution of households to the economy. Ontario's early economy was primarily based on two staple exports, wheat and timber, which were subject to unstable international markets. Consequently, women's household labour had to fulfill two functions: generate family income by producing agricultural goods to sell in the local consumer market, and perform the domestic chores necessary for the family's survival. Cohen's research underlines the importance of examining how the public and private spheres of market and household have been intertwined in diverse ways during all phases of economic development, with women always performing pivotal roles, albeit quite different from those performed by men.

The absence of a wage-labour market and the necessity of contributing to the household economy meant that few women were formally employed outside the home before the rise of industrial capitalism. Even in late 19th-century Canada, only a fraction of women were engaged in paid employment. In 1891, for example, 11.4 percent of girls and women over the age of 10 were employed, accounting for 12.6 percent of the entire labour force (Lowe 1987: 47). But as factories sprang up in the late 19th century, they began to redefine women's economic role. Employers in some light industries, such as textiles, recruited women as cheap unskilled or semiskilled labourers who, according to prevailing stereotypes, would be less likely to unionize and more tolerant of boring tasks.

By focusing only on paid employment, we risk ignoring the work activities of most women during this era. The *unpaid domestic labour* of women—raising the future generation of workers and feeding, clothing, and caring for the present generation of workers—was an essential function within capitalism (also referred to as *social reproduction*). Out of these competing pressures on women emerged a gendered division of labour that persists today. As we discuss in more detail in Chapter 7, this now takes the form of the *double day* (or, in equally graphic terms, the *second shift*), whereby many women spend their days in paying jobs, yet still assume most of the responsibilities of childcare, eldercare, and domestic chores when they get home.

Early-20th-century attitudes about women's economic roles distinguished between single and married women. Expanding manufacturing and service industries had an almost insatiable demand for both blue- and white-collar workers. The employment of young, single women prior to marriage came to be tolerated and socially acceptable in domestic, clerical, sales, and some factory jobs. Once married, however, women were expected to retreat into the matrimonial home. Of course, some wished to remain in the labour force, and others were forced to stay through economic necessity. In these cases, married women laboured at the margins of the economy in domestic and other menial jobs that usually had been abandoned by single women.[4]

Industrialization accentuated age and gender divisions in the economy. Examining the work patterns of working-class women in Montreal, Canada's first large industrial city, Bettina Bradbury documents how age and sex determined who was drawn into wage-labour. Women made up about 35 percent of the city's industrial workforce during the 1870s. In certain industries, such as domestic work and the sewing and dressmaking trades, four out of five workers were women, and most of them were single. Given the scarcity of wage-labour for wives because of strong sanctions against their employment, such women could make a greater contribution to the family economy by being *household managers*. In this role, wives "stretched the wages" of male family members and single daughters as far as possible, occasionally supplementing this by taking in boarders or turning to neighbours or charities for help (Bradbury 1993).

The Family Wage Ideology

Powerful social values justified this division of labour. Especially influential in perpetuating women's subordinate role as unpaid family workers was the ideology of the *family wage*. As working-class men began organizing unions to achieve better wages and working conditions, one of the labour movement's demands was that wages should be high enough for a male breadwinner to support a wife and children. The labour movement's successes in this regard had the effect of drastically reducing women's presence, and the cheap labour they provided, in the workplace (a policy typical of unions until a serious male labour shortage arose in World War I). Middle-class reformers also lobbied for restrictions on female industrial employment due to its presumed harmful personal and social effects. In response, employers limited their hiring mainly to single women, further reinforcing this ideology. Despite its sexist tone, the family wage ideology may have helped raise the standard of living in working-class families. The price, of course, was female dependence and the restriction of women's labour market opportunities to areas where they did not compete directly with men—hence the endurance of the term *male breadwinner*.[5]

The family wage ideology tells only part of the story of women's lives during early industrialization, however. Joy Parr's (1990) study of two Ontario industrial towns, Paris and Hanover, between 1880 and 1950, clearly shows there was variation in the broad contours of gendered work patterns. On the surface, both Paris and Hanover appeared to be typical small, thriving manufacturing communities. But the knit-goods industry based in Paris relied on a largely female workforce, while in Hanover's large furniture factory, the workers were almost exclusively male. Consequently, different gender identities, attitudes, and behaviours arose to maintain each town's labour force. In Paris, employers organized production to fit around childbearing and child rearing, and it was common for women to work for pay throughout their lives. Certainly, Paris was the exception at the time in Ontario. Nonetheless, its flow of daily life during the 80 years covered by Parr's study forces us to reconsider a model of industrialization based on one dominant mode of production in which males are the breadwinners.

This brief historical sketch has identified a number of prominent themes. First, although their widespread participation in the paid labour force is a recent development, women have always made essential economic contributions. Second, women's entry into paid employment occurred in ways that reproduced their subordinate position in society relative to that of men, although the specific forms this took varied across time and place. Third, the changing interconnections among households, families, and the wage-labour market are crucial to understanding women's roles in the continuing evolution of 21st-century capitalism.

● GENDER AND LABOUR FORCE PARTICIPATION PATTERNS

Few changes in Canadian society since World War II have had as far-reaching consequences as women's influx into paid work. Virtually all industrialized nations have experienced rising *female labour force participation rates* since the end of World War II. This trend has been especially rapid in Canada. Figure 6.1 provides a comparison of labour force participation rates among adult women (ages 15 and older) for nine major industrial nations between 1975 and 2012. Note that rising female employment is a trend in virtually all countries. Canada experienced the largest change, followed closely by Australia and the United States. The tremendous expansion of white-collar service-sector jobs, coupled with rising education and a declining birthrate, drew millions of Canadian women into employment at an accelerated rate.

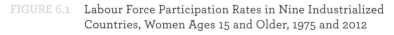

FIGURE 6.1   Labour Force Participation Rates in Nine Industrialized
Countries, Women Ages 15 and Older, 1975 and 2012

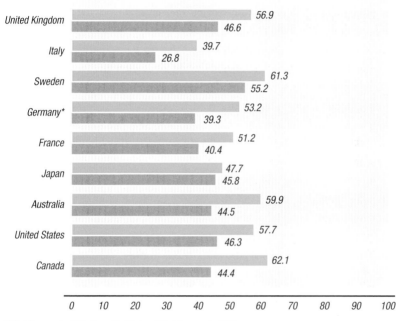

* West Germany in 1975; the unified East and West Germany in 2012.

Source: Adapted from U.S. Bureau of Labor Statistics, 2013. *International Comparisons of Labor Force Statistics, 1970–2012.*
Full Series by Indicator and Underlying Levels (Tables 3-4 and 3-5). http://www. bls.gov/fls/#laborforce.

By 1985, Canada's female labour force participation rate surpassed that of all
countries in Figure 6.1 except for Sweden. The latter is an interesting case,
given that it experienced far less change than nearly all other countries in the
1975–2012 period: women's employment outside the home has been actively
encouraged by state policies for decades.

Influences and Intersectionality in Women's and Men's Employment

What social and economic factors account for this remarkable increase in
Canada's female labour force participation? Clearly, there was no single

cause. The huge postwar baby-boom generation was completing its education and flooding into an expanding job market by the late 1960s. Young women were becoming much better educated, which raised their occupational aspirations and made them more competitive with men in the job market. Traditional stereotypes of women's work no longer fit reality. The massive expansion of white-collar service-sector jobs boosted the demand for female labour, and the growth of feminism contributed to more liberal social values regarding women's work roles. As we have seen, service-sector growth also fuelled a trend to part-time jobs, which are convenient for women with family responsibilities. Shrinking family size allowed married women to pursue employment more readily. Moreover, rising divorce rates forced a growing number of women to earn their own income. And in many families, the reality (or threat) of declining living standards made a second income essential.

The interaction of supply and demand factors underlay the sharp rise in female employment.[6] Interpreting the impact of these changes on women's lives, Charles Jones, Lorna Marsden, and Lorne Tepperman (1990: 58–59) argue that as more women have entered paid employment, their work patterns have not come to mirror those of men. Rather, because women are heavily concentrated in the secondary labour market and often juggle family responsibilities with a job, their lives have become increasingly individualized. Compared with their mothers' generation, younger women today combine work, education, and family in new ways. Hence, since the 1950s, there is now much greater diversity in women's lives. For Jones, Marsden, and Tepperman, the *individualization process* is defined by these elements: (1) variety, through greater opportunities for employment and education; (2) fluidity, in terms of increased movement among these roles and domestic/household roles; and (3) idiosyncrasy, in the sense that it is more difficult to predict whether, when, and where a woman will work for pay.

How women make choices and tradeoffs between paid employment, marriage, and child rearing has been the subject of much debate. Researchers such as Catherine Hakim (2002, 2006) argue that it is women's "preferences" that explain the growing diversity in female employment. Downplaying the role of gender segregation or discrimination, Hakim (2002: 436) contends women choose one of three patterns—"home-centered" (where family is the priority), "career-centered" (where work is the priority), or "adaptive" (where non-career jobs are blended with family responsibilities). Similar ideas inform an influential *New York Times* article by Lisa Belkin (2003) on the "opt out revolution," suggesting that highly educated women are choosing motherhood over paid work. Yet while work preferences play a role, so do many other factors, including workplace inflexibility, access to childcare, discrimination, and the availability of suitable work. Joan Williams and colleagues (2007, 2014) have critiqued the "opt out" thesis. They show that "maternal walls" and "glass ceilings" play an equal role in shaping women's work, while noting that for many women, work is a necessity, not a choice. Likewise, Stone's (2007) in-depth study of professional women shows they are more likely to be "shut out" than to "opt out" of the workplace. Thus, as McRae (2003: 317) argues, an adequate analysis of women's work "depends as much on understanding the constraints that differentially affect women as it does on understanding their personal preferences."

Indeed, there is no question that many factors have a bearing on the labour force participation of women and men. Figure 6.2 identifies important variations in 2012 participation rates by region, age, marital status, family status, and educational level. Provincially, women in Alberta have the highest participation rate (67.0%), followed by those in Manitoba (63.3%) and Ontario (62.1%). Newfoundland and Labrador has the lowest rate at 57.5 percent. Men's rates in all provinces are higher than women's, though the gender gap is more pronounced in provinces such as Alberta (a 12.6% difference) and lowest in Nova Scotia (a 6.6% difference). Local and regional job opportunities have a direct bearing on female and male participation rates, as do regional differences in age structure and educational attainment. For example, Alberta has had a booming economy through much of the 2000s, with a young and well-educated workforce—hence, its high rate of labour force participation for both women and men, but also a higher gender gap given a population in prime childbearing years. In contrast, Newfoundland and Labrador has far fewer employment opportunities for women (and men) with economic underdevelopment, the decline of the fisheries, and an older population explaining differences in formal labour force rates.

Personal characteristics, such as education and family status, also influence work patterns. For instance, women with higher levels of educational attainment are more active in the labour force—77.6 percent of women with

FIGURE 6.2   Female and Male Labour Force Participation Rates by Selected
Characteristics, Canada, 2012

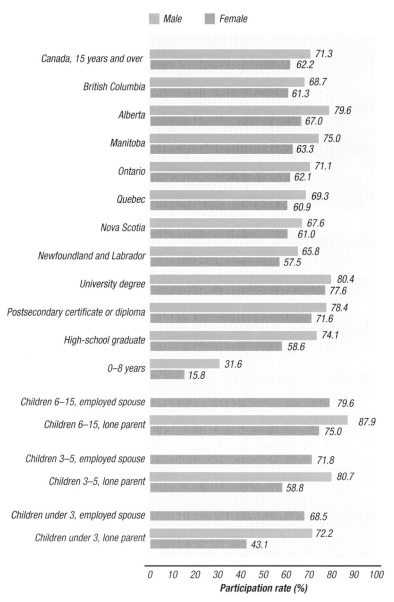

Source: Adapted from Statistics Canada. CANSIM Table 282-0004 - Labour Force Survey estimates (LFS), by educational attainment, sex and age group, Annual. <http://www5.statcan.gc.ca/cansim/a05?lang=eng&id=2820004> and CANSIM Table 282-0211 - Labour Force Survey estimates (LFS), by family type and family age composition, Annual. <http://www5.statcan.gc.ca/cansim/a05?lang=eng&id=2820211>

university degrees compared with 15.8 percent who do not complete high school. For men, we see the same pattern of rising labour force participation with education, though participation rates are higher for less-educated men than they are for comparable women. Family status situation also matters; however, because a high proportion of mothers with children under the age of 15 are relatively young and well educated, their labour force participation rates are also above average. For example, 79.6 percent of mothers with school-aged children (6–15 years) and an employed spouse participate in the labour force, either part time or full time. Indeed, this rise of "working mothers" is one of the most significant changes of the past several decades. Still, rates of labour force participation for mothers are lower when they have younger, preschool children, or are raising children alone. While labour force participation rates for fathers are typically higher than for mothers, they also decline when younger, preschool children are at home (full data are not available). Finally, though not shown in Figure 6.2, age is a key consideration. Among young people 15 to 24 years old, both women and men are less likely than adults of 25 to 54 years old to work for pay, largely because more of them are full-time students.

Financial necessity is often a major factor in the decision to work. Generally, wives in low-income families or women who are lone parents may be compelled to work to meet basic expenses. As Figure 6.2 shows, the participation rate for female lone parents with school-aged children (6–15 years old) was 75.0 percent in 2012, just below that of mothers with similarly aged children who had an employed spouse. Rates fall for lone mothers with preschool children, especially children under three years of age. For many single mothers, finding or keeping a job may be difficult, depending on level of educational attainment and availability of childcare. Low-paid, unstable work is a major reason for the high incidence of poverty in this group.[7] Growing concern about child poverty in Canada is clearly linked to the difficulties lone-parent females face in the labour market (Fleury 2008). In contrast, better-educated, urban, middle-class women who are married and whose spouse or partner is a professional or a manager have greater opportunities and the luxury of choice with regard to employment (Lowe and Krahn 1985: 4). Among families with the highest incomes in Canada, it is very likely that the female partner is a high-earning manager or professional.[8]

● GENDER SEGREGATION IN THE LABOUR MARKET

At the heart of gender inequality in the work world is the structuring of the labour market into male and female segments. *Occupational gender segregation* refers to the concentration of men and women in different occupations.[9] A potent combination of gender-role socialization, education, and labour market mechanisms continue to channel women into a limited number of occupations in which mainly other females are employed.

Female Job Ghettos

Female *job ghettos* typically offer little economic security and opportunities for advancement; furthermore, the work is often unpleasant, boring, and sometimes physically taxing. Women in job ghettos lack ready access to the more challenging and lucrative occupations dominated by men. These male segments of the labour market operate as *shelters*, conferring advantages on workers through entrance restrictions. The concepts of ghettos and shelters emphasize the unequal rewards and opportunities built into the job market on the basis of a worker's sex. It is especially important to recognize that job opportunities determine an individual's living standard, future prospects, and overall quality of life—in Max Weber's words, *life chances.*

One fundamental mechanism underlying segmentation is the *gender labelling* of jobs. Employers do not always make hiring decisions on strictly rational grounds, despite what economics textbooks would have us believe (Rivera 2012). If all hiring decisions were totally rational, women would have been recruited much earlier in the industrialization process and in far greater numbers, given their cost advantage as cheap labour. But, as discussed, men typically opposed female employment for fear of having their wages undercut. Traditional values also narrowly defined female roles to child rearing and homemaking. Women, therefore, were relegated to the poorer jobs that men did not want. Because these occupations came to be labelled "female," future employers would likely seek only women for them, and, regardless of the skills demanded, pay and status remained low.

Dominant social values about femininity and masculinity have long been used to define job requirements. For instance, by the late 19th century, teaching, social work, nursing, and domestic work were socially acceptable for women. Society could justify this on the ideological grounds that these occupations—caring for the sick, the old, and the unfortunate, transmitting culture to children, and performing domestic chores—demanded essentially "female" traits. Exclusive male rights to the better jobs and higher incomes thus went unchallenged, and the role of homemaker and wife was preserved for women. Once a job was labelled male or female, it was difficult for workers of the other sex to gain entry (Lowe 1987).

Trends in Labour Market Gender Segregation

In Chapter 3, we noted a number of gender differences in the occupational distribution of the labour force. Figures 6.3a and 6.3b explore this further, summarizing employment distribution and concentration in 2012. Figure 6.3a identifies the percentage of female and male employees in each occupation. Here we see that health occupations, such as nursing, continue to

FIGURE 6.3a   Employment Concentration of Women and Men, Canada, 2012

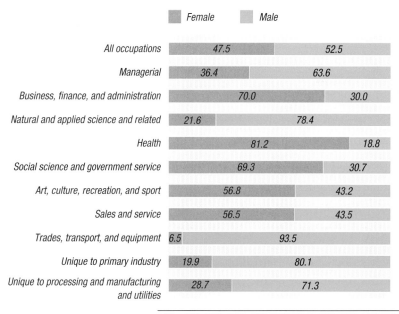

Source: Statistics Canada. CANSIM Table 282-0010 - Labour Force Survey estimates (LFS), by National Occupational Classification for Statistics (NOC-S) and sex, Annual (persons x 1,000). <http://www5.statcan.gc.ca/cansim/pick-choisir?lang=eng&p2=33&id=2820010>

FIGURE 6.3b   Occupational Distribution of Women and Men, Canada, 2012

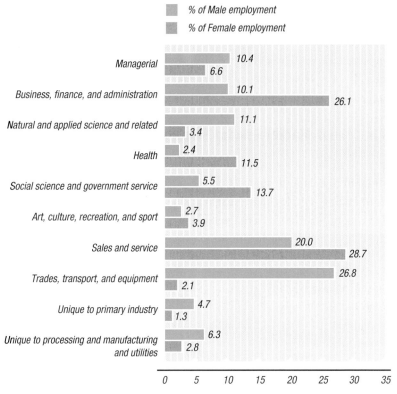

□ *% of Male employment*
□ *% of Female employment*

Managerial
10.4
6.6

Business, finance, and administration
10.1
26.1

Natural and applied science and related
11.1
3.4

Health
2.4
11.5

Social science and government service
5.5
13.7

Art, culture, recreation, and sport
2.7
3.9

Sales and service
20.0
28.7

Trades, transport, and equipment
26.8
2.1

Unique to primary industry
4.7
1.3

Unique to processing and manufacturing and utilities
6.3
2.8

0   5   10   15   20   25   30   35

Source: Statistics Canada. CANSIM Table 282-0010 - Labour Force Survey estimates (LFS), by National Occupational Classification for Statistics (NOC-S) and sex, Annual (persons x 1,000). <http://www5.statcan.gc.ca/cansim/pick-choisir?lang =eng&p2=33&id=2820010>

have high concentrations of women (over 80%). So do occupations in business, finance, and administration (70%), which include administrators, secretaries, and various professionals such as accountants and financial planners; and in social sciences and government services (69%), which include teachers, civil servants, social workers, and lawyers. Sales/service occupations (e.g., jobs in restaurants, bars, hotels, tourism, hairdressing, and child-care facilities, and as domestics and building cleaners) are more mixed, with just over 55 percent female. By contrast, women form a small minority of workers in the sciences, trades, primary industries, and manufacturing. Here men predominate, accounting for nearly 80 percent of jobs in natural and applied sciences (e.g., engineers, computer programmers), over 93 percent in trades, transport, and equipment operation, 80 percent in primary industries (e.g., forestry, mining, fishing, farming), and over 70 percent in processing and manufacturing.

Figure 6.3b shows the distribution of the female and male labour force across all occupations. Of note, two broad occupational groups account for more than half of the female labour force, attesting to women's continuing concentration and overrepresentation in key sectors. Sales and services jobs employed over one in four women workers, as did jobs in business, finance, and administration, which are largely clerical and secretarial. Health occupations, as well as social science and government service jobs, together employed another quarter of women. For men, there is somewhat more dispersion across occupations, although men likewise cluster in distinct realms. Trade, transport, and equipment-related occupations employ over one in four men, while sales and service jobs account for one in five workers. Three other broad groupings— management jobs; business, finance, and administration; and natural and applied science—are important, accounting for 3 in 10 male workers overall.

For a more complete understanding of where men and women are located in the labour market, we also need to investigate the industrial distribution of employment. Recall from Chapters 3 and 4 that Canada's service-based economy is generating polarization between good jobs and bad jobs. How then are men and women distributed within the upper and lower tiers of the service sector? Referring back to Table 3.1 (page 78) helps to answer this question. Here, we can see that nearly one-third of the male labour force are in the goods sector—a trend with potential downsides for men given dramatic restructuring and outsourcing in manufacturing areas such as the auto sector. Women's jobs are far more likely to be in services; indeed, nearly 90 percent of women worked there in 2012, with nearly 30 percent in lower-tier services such as retail and over 60 percent in upper-tier sectors. Women's greater likelihood to be in upper-tier services (61.4% of women compared to 43.4% of men) is a result of women's strong presence in the education, health, and social services sectors. Despite there being good jobs in these areas, however, we know from discussions in Chapters 3 and 4 that relatively more women than men are in nonstandard, low-quality jobs.

Indeed, there is a growing body of research on the gendered nature of nonstandard work (self-employment, part-time, temporary contract). The very notion of the "standard job" can be considered a masculine norm of employment—the husband as family breadwinner, working full time and in a permanent job with the same employer throughout his working life. These standard job assumptions underlay the postwar employment contract, which has changed dramatically with the spread of a range of nonstandard employment relationships (Vosko 2000, 2005, 2010; Fudge and Owens 2006). A major reason some women seek self-employment, for example, is to gain the independence and flexibility they need to balance work with family life. But there are costs, including considerably lower wages than employees receive and the lack of benefits and career supports, such as access to training or business networks (Hughes 2005).

Linked to gender is also a racial dimension of nonstandard work (Zeytinoglu and Muteshi 2000). Visible minority women are employed in economically marginal forms of work, family-run businesses, domestic labour, or the garment industry (Sassen 2002). Perhaps the most feminized form of nonstandard work is temporary employment (Vosko 2000; Fernandez-Mateo 2009). As Leah Vosko (2000) argues, the expanding temporary-help industry is based on traditional stereotypes of "women's work," even though the flexible and impermanent employment relationships it offers are seen as a hallmark of the "new economy."

With women's rising participation in the labour force, how has the segregation of women's work changed over the long term? Table 6.1 shows that, in 1901, 71 percent of all employed women were concentrated in five occupations. Within this small number of socially acceptable women's jobs, that of domestic servant employed the greatest portion of working women at 36 percent. Next in importance were those of seamstress and school teacher, each employing roughly 13 percent of the female labour force. These three occupations fit our description of a job ghetto, given that three-quarters or more of all workers in the job were female. In the early 20th century, outright exclusion was the prominent form of gender-based labour market segregation, with professions such as law and medicine barring women, while others, such as dentistry, allowed women to enter but under conditions that ensured their marginalization (Adams 1998).

This pattern was not the case, however, for the two other main female occupations. Clerical work at the turn of the century was still a man's job, although by the 1940s, the gender balance had shifted toward women. It is interesting to note that clerical work was one of the few traditionally male jobs to undergo this *feminization* process. Behind this change was the rapid expansion of office work accompanied by a more fragmented and routinized division of labour. As a result, a layer of new positions emerged at the bottom of office hierarchies, opening office doors to women (Lowe 1987). Finally, the fact that farmers and livestock raisers appear as one of the five prominent

TABLE 6.1   Five Leading Female Occupations in Canada, 1901, 1951, 2011

Occupation	Number of Employed Women	Percent of Total Female Employment in Occupation	Females as Percentage of Employment in Occupation
1901			
1. Domestic servants	84,984	35.7	87
2. Seamstresses	32,145	13.5	100
3. School teachers	30,870	13.0	78
4. Office clerks	12,569	5.3	21.4
5. Farmers and stock raisers	8,495	3.6	2
All five occupations		**71.1**	
1951*			
1. Stenographers and typists	133,485	11.5	96.4
2. Office clerks	118,025	10.1	42.7
3. Salesclerks	95,443	8.2	55.1
4. Hotel, café, and private household workers n.e.s†	88,775	7.6	89.1
5. School teachers	74,319	6.4	72.5
All five occupations		**43.8**	
2011			
1. Retail salespersons	371,345	4.7	56.6
2. Administrative assistants	316,565	4.0	96.3
3. Registered nurses	270,425	3.4	92.8
4. Cashiers	260,190	3.3	84.2
5. Elementary and Kindergarten teachers	227,810	2.9	84.0
All five occupations		**18.3**	

*1951 Census does not include the Yukon or the North West Territories.
†n.e.s.: Occupations not elsewhere specified.

Source: Adapted from *Occupational trends in Canada, 1891–1931*, Statistics Canada, Call Number 98-1931M-4 1939; *Occupation and Industry Trends in Canada Ninth Census of Canada, 1951*, Statistics Canada, Call Number 98-1951M-4 1954; and Statistics Canada *2011 National Household Survey*, Data Tables - Occupation - National Occupational Classification (NOC) 2011 (691), Class of Worker (5), Age Groups (13B) and Sex (3) for the Employed Labour Force Aged 15 Years and Over, in Private Households of Canada, Provinces, Territories, Census Metropolitan Areas and Census Agglomerations, Cat. no. 99-012-X2011033.

female occupations may seem peculiar. Considering that Canada was an agricultural economy in 1901, it is understandable that women would form a small part of the paid agricultural workforce.

The 20th-century march of industrialization saw a decline in some female jobs, such as those of domestic servant and seamstress, and the rise of new employment opportunities in booming service industries. By 1951, the two leading female occupations were in the clerical area. Along with salesclerks, hotel, café, and domestic workers, and teachers, stenographers and typists and office clerks made up 44 percent of the female workforce.

As we have seen, female job ghettos still exist. Office and sales jobs have topped the list since World War II. Still, while gender segregation remains a persistent problem in many countries (Charles and Bradley 2009), it is also important to note that women have entered a broader range of occupations and professions, and secretarial and support functions have diminished in importance with the proliferation of new mobile technologies and a "wired" younger generation adept at using them. By 2011, the top five female-dominated jobs accounted for just over 18 percent of the entire female labour force—a dramatic decline. This change is a positive sign of occupational diversification, but how far have women moved into non-traditional (in other words, male-dominated) occupations? Karen Hughes's analysis of the 484 detailed occupations in the 1971 Census shows that 86 percent of women worked in traditionally female occupations.[10] Over the next 15 years, the proportion of women in these traditional occupations declined to 79 percent, then changed little between 1986 and 1991. This pattern raises questions about the degree to which women can move out of gender-typed occupations over their working lives—"female" jobs can be seen as a way station through which some women pass on their way to better jobs that are not gender typed (Chan 2000). Having said this, however, some women did make gains into *non-traditional jobs*. By the early 1990s, women had achieved equal representation with men in optometry and financial management, and nearly equal representation in sales management and government administration (Hughes 1995, 2001). More recently, analysis in the United States suggests that women's influx into non-traditional areas has stalled (England 2010).

Additional insights about gender and work can be gleaned by focusing on professional occupations. Because professions are organized around specific bodies of knowledge and expertise, usually acquired through a university degree, access to these jobs is strongly shaped by changing gender patterns in education. Figure 6.4 shows the steady rise of women in university programs. From the early 1970s to 1990s, women's share of undergraduate registrations jumped from 43 to 53 percent, and then again to 58 percent in 2006–7. Gains are also notable at the master's and doctoral levels. Most programs saw rising female enrollments. Math, science, and engineering are the only fields in which women did not make up more than half of all students; in fact, women are significantly underrepresented in these areas, and female enrollment has declined or stabilized in recent years. More recent 2009–10 data from Statistics Canada (using different classifications than those in Figure 6.4) show women made up just 23.8 percent of students in math, computers, and

FIGURE 6.4 Women as a Proportion of Total Full-Time University Enrollment, by Degree and Program, Canada, 1972–73, 1992–93, and 2006–7

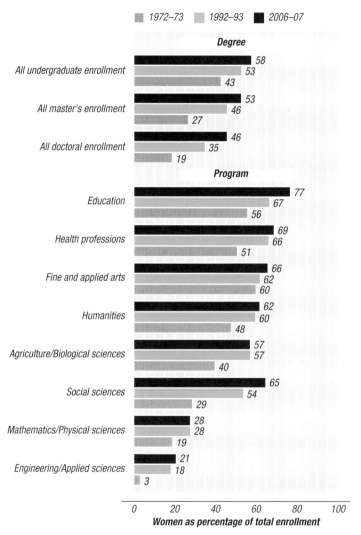

1972–73 *1992–93* *2006–07*

Degree

All undergraduate enrollment — 58 / 53 / 43

All master's enrollment — 53 / 46 / 27

All doctoral enrollment — 46 / 35 / 19

Program

Education — 77 / 67 / 56

Health professions — 69 / 66 / 51

Fine and applied arts — 66 / 62 / 60

Humanities — 62 / 60 / 48

Agriculture/Biological sciences — 57 / 57 / 40

Social sciences — 65 / 54 / 29

Mathematics/Physical sciences — 28 / 28 / 19

Engineering/Applied sciences — 21 / 18 / 3

0   20   40   60   80   100
Women as percentage of total enrollment

Source: Adapted from Statistics Canada (2005) *Women in Canada: A Gender-based Statistical Report*, Cat. no. 89-503XIE 2005001; and CANSIM Table 477-0013 - University enrolments, by registration status, program level, Classification of Instructional Programs, Primary Grouping (CIP_PG) and sex, Annual. <http://www5.statcan.gc.ca/cansim/a26?lang=eng& retrLang=eng&id=4770013&paSer=&pattern=&stByVal=1&p1=1&p2=-1&tabMode=dataTable&csid=>

information systems and 20.8 percent in architecture, engineering, and related areas (Statistics Canada, CANSIM, Table 477-0029).

Higher education has contributed to women's growing presence in several professions (Marshall 1989; Hughes, Lowe, and Schellenberg 2003). In 2010, for example, 58 percent of new graduating physicians, and roughly 40 percent of practising physicians and lawyers, in Canada were women (AFMC 2013; Statistics Canada 2013h; Kay and Gorman 2008). Pharmacy is also an interesting case, having become 50 percent female by the mid-1980s. Research by Tanner and colleagues (1999) on Ontario pharmacists sheds light on this feminization process, showing that despite gender parity, pharmacy remains segregated horizontally and vertically. Women pharmacists are more likely to work in chain stores or hospitals than in independent pharmacies and are more likely to be employees than owners or franchisees; what's more, their earnings are significantly lower. Yet women are more satisfied with their current job and careers than men are. Recent analyses in the United States comparing pharmacy to other professions suggest it is the leading profession in offering gender parity in pay (Goldin 2014).

Still, many traditional male professions present hurdles to female entry. Equally important, there has been little movement of men into female-dominated occupations. While increasing numbers of men have entered previously "female occupations," such as nursing, social work, librarianship, and elementary teaching, their presence remains relatively low (Williams 1989, 1992, 2011). Thus, to the extent that occupational gender segregation is breaking down, it has largely been due to women moving into male-dominated areas, not vice versa (England 2010; Hughes 1995).[11] Equally important, many occupations that have seen change are relatively small, thus muting their impact on the labour force as a whole. Indeed, when we look at the top 20 largest occupations for women and men, in Table 6.2, we still see fairly firm boundaries between "female" and "male" jobs. Nursing, administrative support, and childcare remain strongly female dominant. Conversely, truck driving, carpentry, auto mechanics, construction, and other trades such as welding are predominantly male. Of note, these 20 occupations account for nearly one-fifth of all male workers. For women, it is higher, at 30 percent of the female labour force.

Gender Stratification within Occupations

Thus far, we have traced broad historical patterns of *horizontal* occupational gender segregation—that is, segregation across different occupations. Now

TABLE 6.2   Top 20 Jobs for Women and Men, Canada, 2011

Women		Men	
Occupation	% F	Occupation	% M
Retail salespersons	56.6	Retail salespersons	43.4
Administrative assistants	96.3	Transport truck drivers	96.8
Registered nurses	92.8	Retail and wholesale trade managers	58.3
Cashiers	84.2	Carpenters	98.1
Elementary and kindergarten teachers	84.0	Janitors, caretakers, bldg. sup	74.4
Administrative officers	81.5	Material handlers	87.6
Food counter, kitchen helpers	64.2	Auto-service techs, truck and	
General office support	84.4	bus mechanics	98.4
Early childhood educators	96.8	Managers in agriculture	75.2
Nurse aides, orderlies, patient services	85.7	Construction trades helpers and	
Retail and wholesale trade managers	41.7	labourers	93.9
Light-duty cleaners	70.6	Food counter, kitchen helpers	35.8
Receptionists	94.0	Cooks	57.2
Food and beverage servers	78.8	Info systems analysts and consultants	72
Accounting and related clerks	85.1	Store shelf stockers, clerks, order	
Other customer and info services reps	64.2	fillers	66.5
Accounting technicians and bookkeepers	87.3	Financial auditors and accountants	44.8
Financial auditors and accountants	55.2	Shippers and receivers	77.6
Secondary school teachers	58.6	Sales and account reps—wholesale	
Social and community service workers	76.9	trade	66
		Welders and related machine	
		operators	96
		Electricians (except indus &	
		power system)	98.1
		Security guards and related security	76.9
		Delivery and courier service drivers	91.5
Percentage of Female Labour Force	**30.0**	**Percentage of Male Labour Force**	**19.6**
Number of Female Workers (millions)	**3.6 M**	**Number of Male Workers (millions)**	**2.6 M**

Source: Statistics Canada (2013) *Portrait of Canada's Labour Force.* Ottawa: Statistics Canada. Cat. no. 99-012-X2011002. http://www12.statcan.gc.ca/nhs-enm/2011/as-sa/99-012-x/ 99-012-x2011002-eng.pdf. Tables 2 and 3.

we will examine a related obstacle women face: *vertical* segregation, or the gendered division of status, responsibilities, and tasks within specific occupations. As a rule, men tend to have positions of greater authority in organizations and, consequently, usually receive better job rewards than women. Consider the teaching profession. Even though women made up 84.0 percent of elementary and kindergarten teachers, and 77.1 percent of educational counsellors in 2010, they occupied just 55.9 percent of school administrative and principal positions. While just 16 percent of elementary and kindergarten teachers are men, they make up 58 percent of secondary school teachers. Looking at the education profession overall, men are far more likely to be found in the higher-status, better-paying jobs in universities, colleges, high schools, and educational administrations (Statistics Canada 2008b; Statistics Canada 2013h).

The situation is much the same in other professions. Women have made significant inroads recently, particularly in law and medicine, but they predominate in lower-status specialties such as family law or general medical practice.[12] This pattern reinforces traditional assumptions about women being best suited to tasks involving their "natural skills" as caregivers and mothers.

In their probing investigation of the changes in legal careers in Canada, John Hagan and Fiona Kay portray a gender-stratified profession in which work environments are not family friendly. Large numbers of women entered law in the 1970s and 1980s, when the profession was expanding and reorganizing into larger firms. According to Hagan and Kay,

> women were recruited into the profession during a period when they were needed to fill entry- and intermediate-level positions and were perceived to be compliant employees.... It is possible that ... many partners in law firms were encouraged by the belief that as in the teaching profession of an earlier era, women would assume entry-level positions in the profession, work diligently for a number of years, and then abandon their early years of invested work to bear children and raise families, leaving partnership positions to men assumed to be more committed to their occupational careers.[13]

These assumptions were largely borne out in research findings. The changing professional climate in law firms restricted opportunities for both men and women to attain partnerships—a financial and management stake in the firm that results in much higher earnings. However, women lost out even more than men, mainly because of conflicts and compromises made in the interplay between professional demands and family responsibilities. Still, women who continue to practise law full time after having children have high work commitment and job satisfaction, despite lower earnings than men. As other researchers have noted, however, women are far less likely than men to have children once they become lawyers and far more likely to leave the profession due to work–family conflict, relatively low pay, and discrimination (Brockman 2001). They also face escalating disadvantage with respect to mentoring and promotion, making it more difficult to keep moving up the ranks relative to their male peers (Gorman and Kmec 2009; Kay and Gorman 2012).

Medicine, dentistry, and business are also areas where women have made breakthroughs. According to the 2011 National Household Survey (NHS), women made up 37.0 percent of general practitioners, 42.3 percent of specialist physicians, 31.0 percent of dentists, and 37.2 percent of all managers. However, in management, especially at the senior levels, women have lower representation, and there are distinct patterns of segregation. For instance, the 2011 National Household Survey shows that women accounted for just 13.1 percent of senior managers in construction and 24.0 percent in finance and communications. Likewise, few female managers are found in natural sciences and engineering or in the mining and oil sector. Instead, women are concentrated in 'female' enclaves, such as education and health (56.6%) or human resources (64.3%) where they make up the majority of managers.

Women still encounter a *glass ceiling*—barriers to advancement that persist despite formal policies designed to eliminate them. Looking at the 529 employers covered by the federal Employment Equity Act (discussed in more detail below) in 2011, women made up 41.2 percent of the 768,547 employees (7 percentage points below their representation in the labour market overall). While women's share of senior management posts increased somewhat, the level still fell well below levels for the labour force overall. Men had strong representation at senior management levels and in semiskilled and technical jobs. Women remain overrepresented in support and mid-level occupations, especially in clerical and administrative positions. In other words, gender segregation persists in this workforce, despite women's gains into professional and middle management jobs. It is interesting to note that women's success has occurred largely in the banking sector; in other sectors, especially transportation, their presence remains low, as does their likelihood of being hired and promoted. Comparing salaries, women are far less likely to be among top earners—for instance, just 13.6 percent of women earn $85,000 or more, compared to 24.2 percent of the full-time male workforce.[14]

At the executive and board levels, women continue to face many hurdles. Despite select appointments of women to top corporate jobs—such as president, chief executive officer (CEO), executive vice-president, or chief operating officer—Canadian women still held less than one in five (18.1%) senior officer positions in the Financial Post 500 firms in Canada in 2012

(Catalyst 2012). This trend is in line with many other industrialized countries (Burke and Mattis 2000; Hughes 2000; Hillman, Shropshire, and Cannella 2007). Striking differences also exist between firms in Canada. While one-third of firms have women in over 25 percent of their senior officer positions, another one-third have no women at all. Women's presence is highest in Crown corporations, which are covered by Employment Equity legislation, and lowest in public companies (Catalyst 2012).

In sum, although women now experience much wider employment horizons than was once the case, progress toward full gender equality in the workplace has been halting and uneven. Achieving full equality requires women and men to be more evenly distributed across the occupational structure, rather than segregated along gender lines as we now observe. We would also need to see more women at senior occupational levels. This requirement immediately raises the question of how such change might be achieved.

■ THE WAGE GAP

One obvious consequence of labour market segmentation is the *gender wage gap* (or female–male earnings ratio). Figure 6.5 shows that women who worked full time for the entire year earned an average of 72.0 percent of what similarly employed men earned in 2011. This approach is an accurate way to compare male–female earnings differences, because part-time or part-year workers, who have lower earnings and are disproportionately female, are not included. Despite women entering some of the higher-paying managerial and professional jobs, the wage gap narrowed by just 9 percentage points from 1980 to 1995, and has since plateaued at the low 70 percent range ever since. This pattern partly reflects the way in which employment growth trends often counteract each other. During the 1970s, the number of women in the 20 highest-paying occupations swelled more than fourfold, compared with a twofold increase for men (Boulet and Lavallée 1984: 19). But this trend was offset by an expansion of female employment at the lower end of the pay scale. While not used in our calculation of the wage gap, the big rise in the number of part-time jobs is important as it reduces the earning potential of many women. This distinction between full- and part-time earnings reflects the growing employment disparities among women and between the sexes in the service economy.

FIGURE 6.5   Average Earnings for Full-Time/Full-Year Workers, by Gender, Canada, 1976–2011 (in 2011 Constant Dollars)

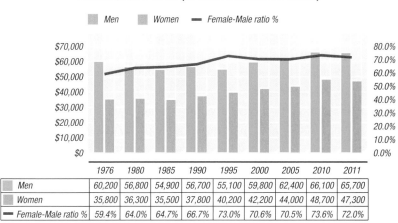

	1976	1980	1985	1990	1995	2000	2005	2010	2011
Men	60,200	56,800	54,900	56,700	55,100	59,800	62,400	66,100	65,700
Women	35,800	36,300	35,500	37,800	40,200	42,200	44,000	48,700	47,300
Female-Male ratio %	59.4%	64.0%	64.7%	66.7%	73.0%	70.6%	70.5%	73.6%	72.0%

Source: Statistics Canada. CANSIM Table 282-0102 - Average female and male earnings, and female-to-male earnings ratio, by work activity, 2011, constant dollars, Annual. < http://www5.statcan.gc.ca/cansim/a26?lang=eng&retrLang=eng&id =2020102&paSer=&pattern=&stByVal=1&p1=1&p2=-1&tabMode=dataTable&csid=>

Gender-Based Inequality of Earnings

Trends in earnings between 1976 and 2011 deserve brief comment. Figure 6.5 displays *real earnings*, which means that the effects of inflation have been eliminated by adjusting earnings. Looking at the 1976–2011 period (in 2011 constant dollars) illustrates the startling fact that male real earnings declined in the 1980s and 1990s, while women's earnings slowly nudged upwards. Quite different labour market and organizational processes underlie these divergent earnings profiles. While women were being recruited into intermediate-level professions and junior- and middle-level management, males were losing ground as traditionally well-paying (often unionized) manual occupations became less common and downsizing pushed older professionals and managers (mostly men) into early retirement. Within the labour market as a whole, some of men's loss was women's gain. A rising proportion of employed women, with incomes somewhat higher than the incomes of women a generation earlier, have kept family incomes from dropping as far as they otherwise might have. Without the wife's income, many husband–wife families now in the middle or working class would likely join the ranks of the poor.

Wages are a basic indicator of overall job quality. Recall from Chapters 4 and 5 that high wages also are part of a larger package of extrinsic and intrinsic job rewards. Stated simply, in addition to paying relatively well, "good jobs" usually offer other advantages: a range of benefits, job security, advancement opportunities, and interesting and challenging work. We can also recall from Figure 4.1 that access to various benefits, such as pensions and medical insurance, varies by occupation, union status, and full-time and part-time status. Access to benefits also varies by gender. Drawing on the same Statistics Canada data used for Figure 4.1 (data not shown here), we know that working women are less likely than men to receive a variety of non-wage benefits, such as a group RRSP, life and disability insurance, supplementary health insurance, or a dental plan (Statistics Canada 2005: 50). Low access to benefits is especially noticeable in part-time employment, where women are highly concentrated. Women are also more likely to report job quality deficits in terms of extrinsic rewards such as wages and non-wage benefits (Hughes, Lowe, and Schellenberg 2003). Jobs occupied by men tend to offer more decision-making authority, have higher skill requirements, and be less repetitive (Krahn 1992: 96). In short, the gender wage gap is part of a much more broadly based discrepancy between the quality of jobs performed by men and women.

Women's lower earnings also mean reduced living standards. Historically, women in Canada have been more likely than men to be poor. For example, in the late 1990s, 45.6 percent of all elderly unattached women lived in poverty, mainly due to inadequate pensions. Recent improvements in income support programs for elderly Canadians appear to have helped reduce this number. Yet, some groups of women are still at high risk of living in poverty. For example, one-fifth of female lone-parents with children under 18 had low income in 2008, compared to just 7 percent of male lone-parent families and 6 percent for two-parent families with children. Women 65 years and older are still twice as likely as elderly men to have low income (7.6% versus 3.6%, respectively), notwithstanding the improvements in living standards noted above.[15.]

Shifting our focus from the bottom to the top of the income distribution, average male and female earnings in the 20 highest-paying occupations are displayed in Table 6.3. We draw on data from the 2011 National Household Survey, which provide median employment income for full-time employees in 2010. Observe that, in many of these jobs, the female–male earnings gap is narrower than in other occupations. Specifically, the ratio is greater than 73.6 percent in most of these jobs (see comparable 2010 figure in Figure 6.5). Looking down the list, we see many jobs with ratios in the high 80 percent or low 90 percent range, including GPs and family physicians (88.4%),

TABLE 6.3 Median Employment Income of Full-Time, Full-Year Workers in the 20 Highest-Paying Occupations, Canada, 2010

	Median Income, Men ($)	Median Income, Women ($)	F–M Earnings Ratio	Men as % of Total Employees	Women as % of Total Employees
Judges	229,794	239,325	104.1	60.3	39.7
Specialist physicians	142,408	98,206	69.0	63.4	36.6
Petroleum engineers	133,254	102,887	77.2	86.6	13.4
GPs and family physicians	128,137	113,224	88.4	60.0	40.0
Dentists	125,388	93,235	74.4	67.6	32.4
Managers in natural resource production	120,491	84,967	70.5	90.3	9.7
Senior managers—Financial, communications	120,781	104,429	86.5	77.0	23.0
Mining engineers	116,072	98,156	84.6	86.7	13.3
Engineering managers	111,462	87,474	78.5	89.2	10.8
Lawyers and Quebec notaries	119,871	95,321	79.5	59.7	40.3
Utilities managers	107,849	99,374	92.1	84.4	15.6
Geoscientists and oceanographers	109,942	85,823	78.1	79.1	20.9
Contractors and supervisors, oil and gas drilling	102,219	63,252	61.9	94.5	5.5
Supervisors, mining and quarrying	101,443	79,691	78.6	95.0	5.0
Fire chiefs and senior firefighting officers	100,598	86,452	85.9	96.5	3.5
Commissioned police officers	105,445	91,853	87.1	80.4	19.6
Senior managers—construction	100,350	89,088	88.8	87.6	12.4
University professors	105,444	90,194	85.5	61.6	38.4
Pharmacists	101,629	94,899	93.4	41.3	58.7
Railway and locomotive engineers	98,138	65,770	67.0	96.9	3.1

Source: Statistics Canada *2011 National Household Survey*. Data Tables: Employment Income Statistics in 2010 by National Occupational Classification. Cat. no. 99-014-X2011042. <https://www12.statcan.gc.ca/ nhs-enm/2011/dp-pd/dt-td/Index-eng.cfm>

senior managers in finance (86.5%), utilities managers (92.1%), fire chiefs (85.9%), police officers (87.1%), and pharmacists (93.4%). In one case— judges—females earn more than their male peers (104.1%). Notwithstanding these narrowed gaps, however, even in these 20 highest-paying occupations, as elsewhere, women are still more likely to receive a lower salary. Granted, their salary is considerably more than the average female income. But we also need to note that, with just a few exceptions, the highest-paid occupations are male dominated. Only pharmacists have a majority of women. Elsewhere, women make up anywhere from 40 percent of employees (e.g., lawyers, family doctors) to a low of 5 percent of employees or less (e.g., fire chiefs, mining supervisors, railway engineers). Similarly, if we examine the list of Canada's 100 best-paid CEOs in 2011, we find just one woman.[16]

When interpreting such data, we must keep in mind that because of the quite recent entry of women into managerial and professional jobs, gender differences in age and experience will account for part of the earnings gap—but by no means all of it. Studies of women and men with comparable education, age, and work experience have found a wage gap (albeit a small one) immediately after graduation. Researchers have also noted a "motherhood penalty" in wages received by working mothers (Budig and England 2001; Budig and Hodges 2010), as well as evidence of gender bias in lower starting salaries for women (Moss-Racusin et al. 2012). Yet, while differences in experience, education, field of study, occupation, and industry help explain the wage gap, part of the gap remains unexplained (Drolet 2002, 2011).[17]

Accounting for Women's Lower Earnings

Two forms of discrimination affect female earnings. The first is *wage discrimination*, whereby an employer pays a woman less than a man for performing the same job. The second stems from the *gender-segregated structure* of the labour market, documented earlier. *Occupational gender segregation* results in lower female wages by channelling women into low-paying job ghettos which, in turn, provide few opportunities for mobility into more rewarding jobs.

To what extent does each form of discrimination contribute to the overall wage gap? To answer this question, one must look at an employee's education, training, and work experience, as well as at the occupation, industry, and geographic location of employment. All of these factors may influence a worker's productivity and thus earnings. Past research by Gunderson (1994) shows that when productivity factors were taken into account (or are statistically controlled), earnings ratios increase from 60 percent to between 75 and 85 percent. Differences in work experience, combined with the segmented structure of the labour market, emerge as key determinants of the pay gap. In short, there is little evidence of *direct* pay discrimination by employers; rather, the division of the labour market into male and female jobs, and an undervaluing of female areas of work, underlie pay inequities (Mandel 2013; Perales 2013; Doucet, Smith, and Durand 2012; Glauber 2012).[18]

Human capital theory emphasizes that education is the great equalizer in the job market. Ideally, people with identical educational credentials should

200

have the same amount of human capital and, therefore, be equally competitive in their earning power. But as Chapter 5 emphasized, human capital theory fails to explain why some individuals with equivalent education are much better paid. Nonetheless, education does matter. Ever since World War II, obtaining a good education has been a route to upward mobility for many young Canadians, particularly males from working-class families.

Does the same hold true for women? There is little doubt that women have become better educated. As noted previously (see Figure 6.4), women have entered a wider range of programs and increasing numbers go on to graduate studies. Dramatic gains have been made in male-dominated professional faculties, such as law, medicine, and business. But women also continue to be concentrated in traditional areas, such as education and nursing. By contrast, training in science and technology remains heavily male dominated. For instance, in university programs in 2011–12, there were 2.7 males for every female student in math, computing, and information sciences, and 3.5 males for every female student in architecture and engineering (see Statistics Canada, CANSIM, Table 477-0019). Referring back to the many high-paying science and engineering occupations in Table 6.3, we can easily see the impact this has on female earning potential.

The challenge of attracting more women into these areas has been a focus of many studies over the years.[19] In a 1992 report, the Canadian Committee on Women in Engineering highlighted the complex social and cultural barriers obstructing women's careers in engineering. More recently, the Canadian Coalition of Women in Engineering, Science, Trades and Technology (CCWESTT) has launched a national initiative to improve the representation of women in these fields. Women are not only underrepresented at the university level, but also in well-paying trades, where they make up only a fraction of apprentices, ranging from 2.0 percent in building construction and motor vehicles/heavy equipment; 1.5 percent in metal fabricating, and electrical, electronics and related; and just 1.0 percent in industrial and related mechanical trades (Turcotte 2011b; Skof 2010; Braundy 2011).

■ THEORETICAL PERSPECTIVES ON WORK AND GENDER INEQUALITY

How has occupational gender segregation become so deeply entrenched? Once we can answer this, we can better inform discussions about how to achieve greater equity in the workplace. However, a comprehensive theory that explains the origins, development, and perpetuation of work-related gender inequities has yet to be formulated.

Feminist analysis has provided a much-needed antidote to the long-standing male bias in much of the sociological research on work. Feldberg and Glenn (1979) characterized research in the 1970s in terms of *job* and *gender models* of the workplace. Studies of male workers focused on working conditions and organizational factors (the job model); explanations of women's employment discussed their personal characteristics and family roles (the gender model).[20] Since then, feminist analysts of work and political economy have probed the link between the private and public spheres of domestic work and paid employment, illuminating how the formal economy depends on unpaid caring work (largely done by women), while rewarding the "model" worker who is free of caregiving responsibilities. While gender remains a central consideration, research is increasingly "intersectional," exploring how factors such as motherhood, race, ethnicity, age, and sexuality work to create differences and similarities in women's and men's economic lives.[21]

Human Capital and Labour Market Segmentation Models

Two of the main competing theories of how labour markets operate are *human capital theory* and *labour market segmentation theory*, as discussed in Chapter 5. We have already criticized the human capital model for its inability to explain the persistence of gender segregation.[22] While the human capital model is concerned with worker characteristics—the supply side of the labour market—the segmentation model examines how employers organize work to generate a demand for specific types of workers. Labour market segmentation theory distinguishes between secondary and primary labour markets. Secondary labour markets are located in competitive industries that continually shave wages and operating costs. In contrast, corporations and state bureaucracies in the primary sector offer high wages, decent benefits, job security, and pleasant working conditions. They also have well-developed internal labour markets providing employees with good career opportunities and employers with a stable, committed workforce.

For the segmentation model to accurately explain why men and women hold different kinds of jobs, women would have to be concentrated in the secondary segment of the labour market. This idea holds true in some part since, it will be remembered, relatively more women than men are employed in lower-tier service industries. However, many women are also employed in the primary sector; thus, a segmentation perspective cannot account for gender differences within the same industry or establishment, or inequalities among women. It also does not explain how gender segregation developed in the first place.[23]

Additional factors need to be considered to explain why gender is a major source of inequality in the labour market. Some researchers, for instance, link women's labour market position to their traditional roles within the family. Women's family roles have centred on activities such as raising children and caring for dependents; cooking, cleaning, and other services essential to enabling family members to hold down jobs; and contributing a secondary income to the family budget—roughly in that order. Many employed women experience a conflict when forced to choose between work and family (Blair-Loy 2003). According to this view, women's loyalty usually goes to the latter, and employers consequently often view these women as lacking commitment to their work. Barriers to interesting and better-paying jobs therefore persist.

Gender-Role Socialization

But how are employers' stereotypes of women, women's expectations and restricted employment opportunities, and women's family roles linked to their employment patterns within the workplace? Are such patterns best explained with reference to women's early socialization, including awareness of family roles and feminine qualities, or as a response to their employment conditions? It is clear that both processes may be involved.

The socialization of girls and boys into traditional gender roles creates cultural norms and expectations that they will carry into the workplace as adults. For example, research conducted in the 1980s of children ages 6 to 14 in Ontario, Quebec, and Saskatchewan documented the effects of *gender-role socialization*. Although the girls recognized the expanding occupational horizons of women, at a personal level, they still held traditional aspirations. As the researchers conclude, "Many seem to be saying 'Yes, women can become doctors, but I expect to be a nurse'" (Labour Canada 1986: 55). Further discussions with these girls revealed that when they imagined themselves as adults, most saw women who were mothers with small children, supported by a husband.

By the middle of the 1990s, evidence suggested that attitudes were beginning to change, albeit slowly. Consider our 1996 survey of Albertan Grade 12 students. It showed that while gender-role attitudes were becoming more egalitarian among youth—the vast majority of female and male respondents agreed that a woman should have the same job opportunities as a man—more traditional work preferences continued to influence career choices. Nurse, social worker, and teacher were the popular career choices for females, compared with computer programmer/analyst, engineer, and auto mechanic for males.[24]

As Jane Gaskell's research illuminates, the choices young working-class women make while they are in school, and upon leaving it, prepare them for domestic labour and employment in female job ghettos. Gaskell explains that the young women whom she studied end up re-creating the world they are not happy with. They see what men are like; they see what jobs pay and how one gets trained for them; they see the lack of child-care options. Within the world as they experience and know it, they do their best. The young men take their gender privilege equally for granted. The result is the reproduction of gender divisions, not because they are desired, but because these young people don't believe the world can be otherwise (1992: 134–35).

More recently, studies suggest that while young women's occupational aspirations have widened, they are still shaped by fairly traditional messages, especially with respect to combining work and motherhood. Class and racial differences are also important in shaping young women's expectations about their future labour force attachment and what they see as desirable work (Massoni 2004; Damaske 2011).

Gendered Work and Organizations

Indispensable to an understanding of female work behaviour is how socialization patterns are built upon, strengthened and reproduced within the workplace. Rosabeth Moss Kanter's research suggests that the main sources of gender inequality are located within work organizations. Her core argument is that "the job makes the person." She elaborates:

Findings about typical behaviour of women in organizations that have been used to reflect either biologically based psychological attributes or characteristics developed through a long socialization to the female sex role turn out to reflect very reasonable and very universal responses to current organizational situations.[25]

In Kanter's view, men and women employed in similar jobs in an organization will react in similar ways to their job conditions. (We return to this subject in Chapters 13 and 14.) A good example is Donald Roy's (1959–60) study of male machine operators. These men escaped the drudgery and isolation of their work— "kept from 'going nuts,'" in Roy's words—by engaging in idle chatter, playing games, and fooling around. Female keypunch operators, file clerks, or assembly-line workers may seek similar relative satisfactions to cope with the numbing tedium of their work. In either case, management can use the coping behaviour as evidence that these workers are incapable of performing more demanding jobs. This perception creates a double bind for employees: the most effective ways of personally coping in jobs at the bottom of the organization are also indications to management that workers in these jobs deserve to be kept there.[26]

Kanter does not ignore possible gender differences in socialization or non-work roles. Rather, she underlines the pervasive influence of an individual's job content and organizational position on her or his attitudes and behaviour. This perspective is similar to what Pat and Hugh Armstrong (2010) call the *materialist* explanation of the gendered division of labour. These researchers document the strong connection between women's self-perceptions and the kinds of work they do. The historical fact that men and women have performed different tasks in the home and in the labour force creates gender differences in work orientations and expectations. For example, women may be aware of their subordinate role, but may rationalize it as an outcome of their domestic responsibilities, or else feel powerless to change it. Likewise, managers may draw on traditional ideas about women's and men's skills and abilities in hiring or deciding on promotions.

Kanter advances the analysis of gender in organizations by showing how management is a social process that relies heavily on trust and conformity.[27] To reduce uncertainty, managers recruit and promote people like themselves— a process referred to as *homophily*. This social cloning reproduces male dominance in management, creating enormous barriers for women. While "managers" thus become equated with "men," in sharp contrast, the role of secretary draws on female stereotypes. Kanter uses the term *office wife* to describe the subordinate, paternalistic, and almost feudal relationship secretaries usually have with their male employers. The job becomes a trap through the dependency of managers on their secretaries and the personal loyalties that result. Many competent secretaries are not promoted because their good performance makes them indispensable to the boss. Unlike other positions in modern bureaucracies, there are no safeguards in place that would curb or restrict the exercise of managerial authority and the expectation that personal services, such as fetching coffee, are part of the job.

Men who receive more opportunities take advantage of them, developing behaviours, values, and work attitudes that help them move ahead. Once young male management trainees are identified as "fast trackers," the resulting halo effect creates the impression that they do not make mistakes and gives their careers momentum. Conversely, women in dead-end jobs quite rationally decide to give up, losing both work commitment and motivation. Their supervisors will then determine that they do not deserve promotions or raises.

Women who do succeed in entering management face the problem of *tokenism.* Kanter argues that a goldfish bowl phenomenon, resulting from being an identifiable minority, means women or members of visible minorities must work harder to demonstrate their competence—the "prove it again" pattern (Williams and Dempsey 2014)—thus reinforcing the view that they are different and do not belong. Tokens also lack the support systems essential for surviving in the middle and upper ranks of organizations. According to Kanter, the problem is not sex or race per se; it is simply part of being a numerical minority. Other empirical research, however, suggests tokenism is specific to women in traditionally male occupations (Yoder 1991). Men in non-traditional jobs may actually benefit from their token status, depending on available opportunities (Williams 1989, 2011). Yet, Kanter's more general point still holds: the *structure of opportunities* in an organization—basically, who has access to which positions, resources, and rewards—tends to create self-fulfilling prophecies that serve only to reinforce the subordinate status of women.

Recent research continues to develop many of these ideas. Acker's (1990) influential writing shows how gender is firmly embedded in organizations at multiple levels, from organizational culture, to policies and procedures, to employee interactions, and worker identities (see Britton and Logan, 2008 for a valuable review). Cultural stereotypes of women as more oriented toward pleasing others and putting domestic responsibilities first may infuse organizational policies, job descriptions, managers' assessments of employees, and promotion opportunities. Likewise, the tendency to equate stereotypically male behaviours with leadership may rule women out as "natural leaders." Ridgeway (2011) contends that gender has a "master status" in organizations, operating through ingrained bias and assumptions to shape assessments of competency and suitability. Likewise, Ely, Ibarra, and Kolk (2013) suggest that "second generation bias" operates in subtle ways through stereotypes and organizational practices to position women and men unequally. Reflecting these processes, a growing number of studies show how bias operates in hiring and pay decisions (Moss-Racusin et al. 2012; Rivera 2012; Correll 2007). In a well-known study, Goldin and Rouse (2000) found the use of "blind auditions" by orchestras led to a significant increase in the hiring of female musicians from 1970 to 1996—a period when women were commonly described as "inferior" players. Having musicians audition behind blinds eliminated visual cues about gender, thus boosting women's evaluations and hiring. Likewise, Reskin and McBrier (2000) found that formalized hiring procedures overrode the power of informal networks in identifying candidates for management jobs.

Research has also increasingly explored the linkages between gender and sexuality. In her study of secretaries, Rosemary Pringle comments:

> Far from being marginal to the workplace, sexuality is everywhere. It is alluded to in dress and self-presentation, in jokes and gossip, looks and flirtations, secret affairs and dalliances, in fantasy, and in the range of coercive behaviours that we now call sexual harassment. Rather than being exceptional in its sexualization, the boss–secretary relation should be seen as an important nodal point for the organization of sexuality and pleasure.[28]

By focusing on sexuality, researchers are able to advance our understanding of how employment relations and work structures contribute to defining gender, both for men and for women. This research challenges us to rethink how masculinity, femininity, and heterosexuality are socially constructed categories reinforced by existing work institutions.[29]

On a larger scale, *sexual harassment* is the most draconian use of male power over women in the workplace. In one of the most comprehensive surveys ever conducted on this topic, the 1993 national Violence Against Women Survey found that 23 percent of Canadian women 18 years old and over had experienced some form of workplace sexual harassment, the most common being inappropriate comments about their bodies or sex lives. Other Canadian and U.S. surveys suggest higher rates, since there is likely underreporting of "poisoned environment" harassment—the display of a demeaning attitude toward women or unwanted sexual attention.[30] Some researchers consider harassment to be one form of the rising trend of aggression and violence in the workplace (DiGiacomo 1999). Harassment, or the fear of it, may lead women to quit jobs or avoid entering non-traditional occupations (Barling, Kelloway, and Frone 2005; Pringle 1989: 164). Of special note, sexual harassment is not limited to employers or coworkers; in a service economy, it may originate from customers as well (Hughes and Tadic 1998). New forms of harassment, such as, "textual harassment", have also been documented with mobile technologies being used to send inappropriate, offensive messages virtually (Mainiero and Jones 2013).

● ACHIEVING WORKPLACE EQUALITY

We have catalogued the inequities women face in terms of work opportunities and rewards. Some of the evidence leads to optimism that the stumbling blocks to equal labour market opportunities and rewards are slowly being pushed aside. But the agenda of equality in employment can be achieved more effectively and sooner through innovative policy and workplace initiatives. We conclude this chapter with a brief overview of some options that have been pursued to date. Unions and collective action can also play a decisive role in achieving gender equity at work, as discussed in Chapter 11.

Employment Equity

In 1984, the Royal Commission on Equality in Employment (chaired by Rosalie Abella, now a Supreme Court judge) introduced the concept of *employment equity* as a strategy to eliminate the effects of discrimination and fully open up competition for job opportunities to those who had been excluded and disadvantaged in employment historically. Four groups were identified as "equity groups": women, visible minorities, Aboriginal peoples, and persons with disabilities. With respect to women, the Abella Commission asserted that equality in employment required a revised approach to women's role in the workplace. It articulated the growing belief that all individuals, regardless of their personal characteristics, should be treated fairly in recruitment, hiring, promotions, training, dismissals, and any other employment decisions.

The commission provided the rationale for the federal 1986 Employment Equity Act by arguing that *systemic discrimination* creates work barriers that can be dismantled only through strong legislation. Systemic discrimination is the unintentional consequence of employment practices and policies that have a differential effect on specific groups. This form of discrimination is built into the system of employment, rather than reflecting the conscious intent of individuals to discriminate. For example, minimum height and weight requirements for entry into police or fire departments have used white males as the norm; they have thereby excluded women and members of certain visible minorities, even though that was not the intent.

The 1986 Employment Equity Act covers federal government employees, federally regulated employers and Crown corporations, and employers that have 100 or more employees and bid on government contracts worth more than $200,000. The thrust of the act is twofold. First, it requires these employers to identify and remove employment practices that act as barriers to the four *designated groups* (women, visible minorities, Aboriginal peoples, and persons with disabilities). Second, it establishes targets and timetables for achieving a more representative workforce that will reflect the proportion of qualified and eligible individuals from designated groups in the appropriate labour pool (not in the entire population).

Employment equity policy also recognizes a need for positive measures that will rectify historic imbalances in staff composition (e.g., special training programs for Aboriginal people) and the reasonable accommodation of differences (such as changing the RCMP dress code to permit Sikhs to wear turbans and Aboriginal officers to have braids) to make workplaces more accessible and hospitable for a greater diversity of individuals. In this way, organizations are able to become more representative of the increasingly varied composition of Canadian society.

The Employment Equity Act requires employers to file annual reports showing their progress in recruiting and promoting members of the four designated groups—generally, these reports show a slow pace of change. For the positive, some studies suggest a measure of success, with the increased access of designated groups to professional, supervisory, and upper-management positions contributing to reduced wage gaps, for example.[31] There has, however, been wide-ranging criticism of employment equity. The Special Committee of the House of Commons that reviewed the Act responded to criticism by recommending the following: stricter monitoring and enforcement; inclusion of more workplaces; greater employer commitment to the equity goals, timetables, and plans; and the establishment of a comprehensive national employment equity strategy.[32] Backlash and resistance to employment equity have also slowed change.[33]

In a detailed examination of women's progress under the Employment Equity Act, Leck (2002) highlights both positive and negative outcomes. On the plus side, evidence suggests that organizations with equity programs have generally improved their human resource practices, increased the presence and status of women, and narrowed the wage gap between women and men. On the downside, however, are complaints from employers about the administrative costs of equity programs, perceived declines in productivity, and evidence of a rising male backlash. In Leck's view, negative outcomes stem largely from a poor understanding of what equity programs seek to do. Even university students educated in human resource management hold the mistaken belief that these programs involve quotas set by government or are unnecessary because discrimination against women no longer occurs.

Stronger legislation may indeed speed progress toward equality. But business motives may be a more powerful influence. As discussed in Chapter 3, many employers realize they will face growing labour shortages as baby boomers retire. Employers are being confronted by the reality that women and members of the other three designated groups will make up a large majority of new labour force entrants in coming years. Thus, in the current language of employers, the "business case for diversity" has become a major human resource management challenge, which means that making workplaces welcoming for everyone is a priority.

In order for equity programs to thrive, Leck (2002) suggests organizations improve practices in a number of areas. First, effective communication is critical, ensuring that employment equity is understood not just by supervisors and managers responsible for human resource issues, but by employees throughout the organization. Employee forums to discuss equity and diversity issues, diversity booths at company events, equity councils, and written articles in internal company newsletters are just some ways, she believes, organizations can better educate employees about equity and diversity issues. Second, involving employees, unions, and other employee groups in formulating and reviewing employment practices is crucial for increasing acceptance, reducing backlash, and easing fears about myths and misinformation. Third, well-designed and well-delivered training is also critical for ensuring that human resource practices, such as performance appraisals, recruitment, and selection, are bias free and that diverse groups are made to feel welcome in organizations.

Pay Equity

Another important policy initiative is *pay equity*. Pay equity, or "comparable worth," as it is called in the United States, focuses specifically on the most glaring indicator of gender inequality in the labour market: the wage gap. Pay equity is a proactive policy, requiring employers to assess the extent of pay discrimination and then to adjust wages so that women are fairly compensated. Frequently a topic of heated public debate, pay equity recognizes that occupational gender segregation underlies the wage gap. It attempts to provide a gender-neutral methodology for comparing predominantly female jobs with predominantly male jobs in different occupational classifications under the same employer. For example, a secretarial job (female) would be compared with the job of maintenance technician (male) in the same organization. A standardized evaluation system assigns points to these jobs on the basis of their skill level, effort, responsibility, and working conditions.

Underpinning the process is the recognition that women's work is valuable but has been under-rewarded in the past. The objective is to pay employees on the basis of their contribution to the employer. Achieving this will establish *equal pay for work of equal value*, a more far-reaching concept than *equal pay for equal work* or *equal pay for similar work*, which only compares women and men in the same (or "substantially similar") jobs. However, developing and applying a truly gender-neutral system for evaluating jobs has proved exceedingly difficult because it challenges long-standing assumptions about the nature of skill (Steinberg 1990).

Pay equity legislation mainly covers the public sector, although in Ontario and Quebec, which have the most extensive legislation, parts of the private sector are also included (Cornish 2007).[34] Pay equity policies are explicit in their intent. As the Pay Equity Task Force noted in its 2004 report, pay equity begins from the premise that "differences in pay for comparable work which is based solely on differences in sex are discriminatory, and that steps should be taken to eliminate these differences" (Canada 2004). Opponents argue that the economy cannot afford wage adjustments; that businesses may be driven into bankruptcy; or that pay equity interferes with the operation of the labour market. But for millions of employed women, pay equity may provide long-overdue recognition of their economic contributions to society.

Pay equity legislation has gone some distance toward creating fairer, gender-neutral compensation schemes. For example, in Ontario, 100,000 women working in public-sector childcare and nursing homes received hundreds of million dollars in pay adjustments under provincial legislation. In Quebec, more than 300,000 women working in the public sector received substantial pay adjustments, as well as $1.5 billion in back pay, for a total settlement estimated at $4 billion.[35] Ontario pay equity legislation was once heralded as the most comprehensive in North America; however, the election of a Conservative government in the mid-1990s saw the weakening of legislation, funding cuts to tribunals, and growing noncompliance (Equal Pay Coalition 2008: 15–17). Loopholes, exclusions, and cumbersome procedures also muted its impact.[36] Thus, while pay equity policies have not eliminated the female–male wage gap, they have contributed to narrowing it. Furthermore, by increasing earnings at the bottom of the female earnings distribution, the policies have benefited more than just middle-class women.[37]

To date, one of the most publicized pay equity cases has involved the federal government, which after 14 years was forced to settle with its employees (librarians, clerks, and others) in 1999. Following this episode, the federal government established a Pay Equity Task Force to review existing legislation. Reporting in 2004, the Task Force made more than 100 recommendations for improving federal pay equity legislation. Central among these were moving away from complaint-based to proactive legislation; extending coverage to all employees (part-time, casual, seasonal, temporary); and extending pay equity to visible minorities, Aboriginal peoples, and persons with disabilities. In addition, the Task Force recommended the creation of a federal Pay Equity Commission, which would administer the pay equity law and conduct investigations and audits, and a Pay Equity Tribunal with expertise in pay equity and human rights to adjudicate disputes (Canada 2004).

Another policy instrument for achieving gender equality in employment is section 15 of the Canadian Charter of Rights and Freedoms. This section of the Charter became law in April 1985. It established for the first time in our history a constitutional entitlement to full equality for women in law, as well as in the effects of law. This latter point is crucial, for regardless of the wording or intent of a law, if, in practice, it results in discrimination against women, the courts can rule it to be unconstitutional. This legal process may gradually come to have an influence on gender inequality in the workplace.

● CONCLUSION

We began this chapter by discussing recent suggestions that traditional gender patterns of work were being dramatically overturned. On the basis of a comprehensive review of past and present trends in Canada, we can now conclude that while some changes have occurred for both women and men in the workplace, gender continues to be central to the organization of paid work. Certainly, we are beginning to rectify some of the most glaring problems women confront. Higher education and changing attitudes about women's capabilities and commitment as workers have played a key role, as our analysis shows. But gender segregation, inflexible workplaces, and subtle forms of "second generation" bias (Ely et al. 2013) continue to create barriers for women.

Employment equity and pay equity programs now operating in Canada are reform oriented, aiming to modify existing employment institutions, values, processes, and social relationships. But how effective will these work-place reforms be? And what impact will such policies have, if any, in altering women's traditional non-work roles—especially within the family—and the supporting socialization processes and ideologies? The limitations of such reforms prompt some to argue for greater recognition of women's unpaid caregiving work and greater involvement of men in such activities—issues we take up in Chapter 7. For them, equity can be achieved only when women and men begin to share this work, and employers begin to recognize that all workers have family responsibilities. Any successful strategy must recognize that employment inequities are firmly embedded in the very structure and values of our society. So, while we look for ways of reducing the effects of traditional gender practices within families, schools, and other institutions, we also need to continue to focus directly on the organizational barriers that stand in the way of gender equality in the workplace and labour market.

DISCUSSION QUESTIONS

1. Discuss women's and men's economic contributions in the early days of Canada's industrialization. To what extent did their work differ and why?

2. How does women's labour force participation vary internationally? Nationally? What are some of the key factors that shape Canadian women's labour force participation?

3. What is gender segregation, and why is it so important for understanding inequalities in work? When you compare the jobs women and men have done historically, and those they do today, what has changed most dramatically? What has stayed the same?

4. How do the wages of women and men compare? How has the wage gap changed over time, and how do we explain it?

5. Compare the processes and goals of employment equity and pay equity. How useful do you think these types of policies are for improving equity in the workplace? Discuss.

ADDITIONAL RESOURCES

WORK AT THE MOVIES

- *Albert Nobbs* (directed by Rodrigo Garcia, 2011, 113 minutes). This mainstream film focuses on gender and the history of work, limited job opportunities, and a woman who chooses to "pass" as a man to improve her economic security.
- *Rosies of the North* (directed by Kelly Saxberg, 1999, 46:40 minutes). The NFB documentary is based on oral histories of women's contributions during World War II to aircraft manufacturing in Thunder Bay. It is available through the National Film Board of Canada: http://www.nfb.ca/film/rosies_of_the_north.
- *Norma Rae* (directed by Martin Ritt, 1979, 110 minutes). Based on real events centred on a textile factory, this dramatic film explores gender and union activism in blue-collar America.
- *North Country* (directed by Niki Caro, 2005, 126 minutes). This film explores sexual harassment in mining work and is based on the true story of Lois Jenkins.

SOUNDS OF WORK

- "Tecumseh Valley" (Townes Van Zandt). In this song, a young woman leaves her coal-mining town in search of work as a manual labourer, only to become a bartender and then a sex worker.
- "Working Man" (Rita MacNeil). Rita MacNeil sings about the lives of men who work in the coal mines on Cape Breton Island in Nova Scotia.
- "She Works Hard for the Money" (Donna Summer). Purportedly based on an experience Summer had with a female bathroom attendant, this song highlights the struggles involved in low-wage service work.
- "Bread and Roses" (James Oppenheim/Judy Collins). Collins brings Oppenheim's poem to life with this song about women and men marching for fair wages and decent living conditions.

NOTES

1. The female labour force participation rate is the number of women in the paid labour force (employed, or unemployed and actively looking for work) divided by the female population ages 15 and older (14 and older, prior to 1975). This calculation undervalues women's economic contribution because it overlooks unpaid household work. See Statistics Canada, CANSIM, Table 282-002, for current and historical participation rates.
2. See Cohen (1988). Useful sources for women's history in Canada are Strong-Boag and Fellman (1997), Bradbury (1993), and the labour studies journal *Labour/Le Travail*.
3. Danysk (1995: 150) examines the gendered construction of work roles in western Canadian agriculture. The quotation is from a 1923 prairie farm publication. Rollings-Magnusson (2000) presents further useful information on the vital contribution of women to the development of the Canadian West.
4. For historical background on the transformation of women's work inside and outside the home during the rise of industrial capitalism, see Cohen (1988), Bradley (1989), and Armstrong and Armstrong (2010).
5. On the family wage, see Humphries (1977), Land (1980), and Bradbury (1993: 80, and Chapters 3 and 5). For more recent discussions of changing norms around breadwinning, see Livingstone and Luxton (1996), Coltrane (1996), and Marshall (2006, 2011).
6. These factors are discussed in Armstrong and Armstrong (2010) and Jones, Marsden, and Tepperman (1990). For an overview of trends related to gender and employment in Canada, see Ferrao (2010).

7. For recent analyses of lone parents and income, see Morissette and Ostrovky (2007) and Williams (2010).

8. Rashid's (1994: 48) analysis of the top percentile of all families shows that wives in these families had incomes four times greater than the average for all wives, and that without this income, 57 percent of these families would not reach the top income percentile.

9. For overviews and discussions of gender segregation in industrialized countries, see Charles and Grusky (2004) and Jarman, Blackburn, and Racko (2012). See Feuchtwang (1982: 251) for a definition of *job ghetto.*

10. Hughes (1995, 2001). Traditional occupations are those in which women constitute a greater proportion of employment than they do in the labour force as a whole.

11. Statistics Canada (2000: 128). On the health professions, see Armstrong, Choinière, and Day (1993) and Armstrong, Armstrong, and Scott-Dixon (2008). On men in non-traditional jobs, see Williams (1992, 1995, 2011), Synder and Green (2008), Lindsay (2007), and Lupton (2006).

12. On women in medicine, see Gorham (1994), Cassell (1998), and Ku (2011). On women's experiences in the legal profession, see Brockman (2001), Hagan and Kay (1995), and Kay and Gorman (2008, 2012).

13. Hagan, John, and Fiona Kay. (1995). *Gender in Practice: A Study of Lawyers' Lives.* New York: Oxford University Press, p. 182.

14. Data are from the *2012 Annual Report, Employment Equity Act,* produced by Human Resources and Skills Development Canada 2009, available at http://www.labour.gc.ca/eng/standards_equity/eq/pubs_eq/annual_reports/2012/docs/ee2012.pdf. Of note, the level of detail provided in the 2012 report is much less than in previous reports. The size of the workforce covered by employment equipment has also declined.

15. Data for lone parents and elderly families come from Williams (2010: 20–21).

16. Mackenzie (2012) analyzes Canada's CEO Elite 100, which includes the best-paid 100 CEOs of companies listed on the TSX Index. The total compensation packages of the top 100 ranged from $3.8 million to $61.8 million, including base salary, bonuses, shares, options, pensions, and other remuneration.

17. Davies, Mosher, and O'Grady (1996) and Drolet (2011) discuss the narrowing of the wage gap in Canada. Goldin (2014) discusses the wage gap in the United States, noting how it has narrowed differently within distinct occupations.

18. For valuable discussions of the gendered wage gap in Canada, see Drolet (2011) and Cool (2010); for the United States, see Blau and Kahn (2007) and Goldin (2014); for the United Kingdom, see Perales (2013).

19. Canadian Committee on Women in Engineering (1992: 1). For recent trends, see also Engineers Canada (2012). On the male culture of engineering, see Braundy

(2011), McIlwee and Robinson (1992), Miller (2004), and William, Muller, and Kilanski (2012).

20. See Feldberg and Glenn (1979), Acker (1990), and Britton and Logan (2008) for critical discussions of the male biases in the sociological study of work and organizations.

21. On feminist approaches to understanding gender and work, see Armstrong and Armstrong (2010), Reskin and Padavic (2002), Britton and Logan (2008), and Ridgeway (2011).

22. On human capital explanations of sex differences in occupations and earnings, see Blau and Ferber (1986: Chapter 7).

23. For critical discussions of occupational gender segregation, see Siltanen (1994) and Armstrong and Armstrong (1990: Chapter 1). Hagan and Kay (1995) critically utilize human capital theory and a more general version of labour market segmentation theory in their study of gender inequalities in the legal profession. Developments in the measurement of occupational gender segregation and the underlying factors are discussed in Rubery and Fagan (1995) and Blackburn, Jarman, and Siltanen (1993).

24. Unpublished data from the 1996 Alberta High School Graduate Survey. Virtually all females (97%) and 85 percent of males agreed or strongly agreed with the statement "a woman should have the same job opportunities as a man." Career choices and other study findings are presented in Lowe, Krahn, and Bowlby (1997).

25. Kanter, Rosabeth M. (1977). *Men and Women of the Corporation.* New York: Basic Books, p. 67.

26. For an interesting discussion of the significance of workplace conversations about household work, see Hessing (1991).

27. For a summary of related research on women and management, see Powell and Graves (2011) and Wirth (2004).

28. Pringle, Rosemary. (1989). "Bureaucracy, Rationality and Sexuality: The Case of Secretaries." In Jeff Hearn, Deborah L. Sheppard, Peta Tancred-Sheriff, and Gibson Burrell, eds., *The Sexuality of Organization.* London: Sage, p. 162.

29. The growing area of *men's studies* examines the social construction of masculinity in work and unemployment (Morgan 1997). On sexuality and power in organizational life, see Hearn et al. (1989).

30. See Johnson (1994: 11) for the 1993 survey, conducted by Statistics Canada. A survey reported by Crocker and Kalemba (1999) found, in contrast, that 56 percent of working women surveyed had experienced workplace sexual harassment in the year before the survey. See Sev'er (1999) and Bowes-Sperry and Tata (1999) for discussions of research evidence, theoretical interpretations, and measurement issues on this topic.

31. Leck (2002) discusses a number of studies documenting a narrowing of the wage gap.
32. Canada (1992). For critical discussions of employment equity, see Abu-Laban and Gabriel (2002) and Bakan and Kobayashi (2000). On affirmative action in the United States, see Reskin (1998). For Employment Equity Act Annual Reports in Canada, see http://www.labour.gc.ca/eng/standards_equity/eq/pubs_eq/annual_reports/2013/index.shtml.
33. Resistance to equity policies are discussed by Cockburn (1991) and Leck (2002).
34. For an overview of pay equity legislation in federal, provincial, and territorial jurisdictions, see the final report of the Pay Equity Task Force (Canada 2004). For an international perspective, see Gunderson (1994) and Cornish (2007). For a discussion of recent developments in Ontario, see the Equal Pay Coalition (2008) as well as updates on their website: http://www.equalpaycoalition.org/.
35. Cornish (2007) discusses various provincial settlements in the Canadian context. For more detail on the history and methodology of pay equity, see Armstrong and Cornish (1997) and the final report of the Pay Equity Task Force (Canada 2004).
36. Neale (1992). Under the former New Democratic government, Ontario extended pay equity into the private sector, but subsequent evaluations suggest that pay equity awards have been small and that there are considerable difficulties administering and gaining compliance with the act (McDonald and Thornton 1998; Cornish 2007). See also the Equal Pay Coalition—History website for discussions of noncompliance.
37. For critiques of pay equity and how it has been implemented, see Fudge and McDermott (1991) and Armstrong and Cornish (1997). Forrest (2000) discusses the large federal government pay equity settlement with female members of the Public Service Alliance of Canada in 1999. Simulations of the U.S. economy show that the wage gap would close 8 to 20 percent if comparable worth were nationally applied (Gunderson 1994: 111). Figart and Lapidus (1996) provide a positive evaluation, showing that such policies would generally contribute to reducing earnings inequality between the sexes and among women. However, other researchers suggest that the closing of the wage gap (at least in the United States) is, in large part, due to the increasing stagnation of white male earnings (Bernhardt, Morris, and Handcock 1995).

HOUSEHOLD, FAMILY, AND CARING WORK

"When I think about what I do every day—I cook meals for my family, I make cereal for breakfast and sandwiches for lunch and meat and potatoes for supper. Nothing unusual about that. But when I think about all those thousands of other women all doing the same thing, then I realize I'm not just making porridge. I'm part of a whole army of women who are feeding the country."

Source: Stay-at-home mother. Meg Luxton. (1980). *More than a Labour of Love*. Women's Press, p. 13.

"There are times when I go insane. There are times when I think the demands of the home are too much, the responsibilities and the constant nagging and the whining of the kids and the diapers and the crap.... Sometimes I think, By God, my life would be a lot less complicated if I just had a nine-to-five job.... But there are other times—just being with them in the summer, being in the backyard, colouring or doing puzzles or hanging out with them, just playing squirt-gun games for an entire hour—that are just great. There is nothing that can replace that."

Source: Tom, stay-at-home father. Andrea Doucet. (2006). *Do Men Mother? Fathering, Care and Domestic Responsibility*. University of Toronto Press, p. 3–4.

"You know the first question they always ask you is, 'Well, what do you do? Where do you work?' And I say, 'Well I'm not working now. I'm staying home with my children.' And it was like this wall of invisibility. You know, I remember reading *The Invisible Man* by Ralph Ellison.... And that was what came to mind. It was like all of a sudden I didn't exist. If I didn't have an identity in the working world, I didn't exist."

Source: Maeve Turner, stay-at-home mom and lawyer. Pamela Stone. (2007). *Opting Out? Why Women Really Quit Careers and Head Home*. University of California Press, p. 145.

● INTRODUCTION

In October 2012, Jessica Stilwell, a social worker and mother living in Calgary, made national and international headlines when she went on a "household strike," refusing to clean up after her two 12-year-old twin daughters and their younger 10-year-old sister. Frustrated by their unwillingness to pick up after themselves and pitch in with daily household chores, Stilwell reduced her housework to the bare minimum, cooking meals and packing school lunches. Everything else, from washing her children's dirty dishes, to picking up their toys, games, and clothes, to unpacking their school lunch bags, was left to her daughters. She did not remind or nag them about what needed to be done; in fact, she did not even tell them she was going on strike—she simply quit cleaning up after them. Six days later, her house in disarray, with dirty dishes overflowing from the dishwasher, unpacked lunch bags fermenting on the kitchen counter, and clothes, jackets, toys, and games strewn about, her children called a truce, apologizing for not doing more. They then spent two frenzied days cleaning and returning the house to its original pristine condition, serving coffee to their mother while she watched them work.[1]

Such examples highlight the important, but often taken-for-granted and "invisible" nature of household, family, and caring work. In this chapter, we examine this work, exploring the skills and demands involved, and how participation in and responsibility for such work is distributed among family members. We also consider how families accomplish household and caring work in a context where women have increased their attachment to paid work, but where traditional ideas about gender and household responsibility persist. What is striking, for instance, about media coverage on Jessica Stilwell's strike is the sole focus on her as a mother. Her husband and the father of her daughters, who lives in the same household, merits just a passing mention, and it seems to be assumed that the work of organizing the household naturally belongs to her. What gives rise to such assumptions? And to what extent are gendered patterns of household and caring work really shifting? Moreover, how does responsibility for household and caring work underlie or contribute to the broader gender inequalities we observe in the labour market and paid work? We examine these questions while considering how employers and governments are supporting women's and men's changing roles as earners and caregivers, and their efforts to balance work and family life.

● HOUSEHOLDS, FAMILIES, AND WORK

Conceptualizing Household and Family Work

Most early studies in the sociology of work paid scant, if any attention to *household work*, *unpaid work*, or *caregiving*. In her article "Invisible Work," sociologist Arlene Kaplan Daniels suggests several reasons for this. First, to the extent that caring and housework are done in the private realm, they are often seen as falling outside the formal economy, thus lacking economic value. Second, the fact that household work is unpaid—that it does not receive a salary or wage—reinforces common perspectives that it lacks value, as it is not readily thought of in dollar terms. Finally, according to Daniels, women's historical and ongoing responsibility for household work further contributes to its devaluation. Rather than being seen as skilled work requiring knowledge and ability, caring and cleaning are seen as something women "naturally" do. Illustrating this, Daniels asks how many people consider the following to be work: comforting a child, cooking meals, creating warm and caring family relations. Certainly, she contends, such activities are work, but traditional ideas about family and gender impede this recognition.

Today, while some Canadians continue to hold the views described by Daniels, there is also growing awareness of the importance of household and caring work. Sociologists, in particular, have increasingly focused on the household as an important site of research and study. Not only does such research help us build a more complete picture of work, but it also helps us understand the fluid boundary between the labour market and household. Equally important, given that women still carry much of the responsibility for families, a sharper picture of household work is key to understanding the nature of the gender inequality we observe in Canada and other countries. Typically, household responsibilities are far more likely to limit women's labour force participation, keeping women financially dependent on their partners.

Some experts argue that gender inequality is the result of two systems of domination: *capitalism* and *patriarchy*. Broadly speaking, *patriarchy* refers to male domination over women, but more specifically it describes forms of family organization in which fathers and husbands hold the power.[2] Capitalism incorporated earlier patriarchal social arrangements. Remnants of patriarchy still reinforce stereotypes of women as cheap, expendable labour.

Women's traditional roles as mothers and partners also restrict their economic opportunities and, for those who are employed, create a double day of paid and unpaid work.

In delving into the work of households, researchers have identified and shed light on a wide variety of work, including *housework* (e.g., cooking, cleaning, laundry), *caring and emotion work* (e.g., bearing and raising children, caring for the elderly and infirm), and *kin and community work* (e.g., communicating and coordinating with larger family networks and neighbours). Taken together, such activities have often been referred to as *domestic work, unpaid work*, or *social reproduction* (as opposed to *production* which occurs in the formal economy). Laslett and Brenner (1989: 382) define *social reproduction* as activities "involved in the maintenance of life on a daily basis, and intergenerationally." Such work is organized and accomplished through "family strategies" or decisions made by families about the nature of family life (e.g., size of family) and the division of labour in the home and labour market. As we will see, the work of households is also shaped both by economic realities and dominant cultural ideals about how family life should be.

Changing Family Forms

We have already outlined in previous chapters the important role of households and families in Canada's economic development. But the specific nature of that role has changed and shifted over time. Before the rise of capitalism and industrialization, the household operated as a primary site of economic production with men, women, and children working together to sustain family life (Cohen 1988). The emergence of factory production and a wage-labour economy shifted the role of the household again, as men (primarily) were drawn into paid jobs in the labour market, leaving women responsible for a wide range of work in the home—from cooking and cleaning, to caring for children, the elderly, and the infirm.

Although we tend to think of families and households as part of the private realm, standing apart from the market and economy, the household was a site for paid work, though often at the margins of the informal economy. In early industrializing Canada, for example, working-class women often took in laundry or boarders to earn extra money for their families (Bradbury 1993). Women also sewed piecework at home as part of factory-based "putting out" systems. At the other end of the economic spectrum, families with resources hired domestic servants to cook and clean, bringing employment relationships into the home. Boundaries between the *household* and *market*, and *private* and *public* realms, were therefore fluid and not always clearly demarcated—a situation that persists today.

Traditional gender ideologies, especially the idea of "separate spheres," also played an important role, ensuring that household work remained culturally and materially associated with women. Typically, married women and mothers did not work for pay, except in cases of dire economic need. At certain points in the 20th century, these gender norms relaxed—for example, during World War II when women were drawn into the war effort and formal economy (Pierson 1986). But such moments were fleeting. After World War II, a return to breadwinner norms meant that the most common pattern was for women to work briefly before having children, stay home to raise them, and then return to the labour force in middle age after the children had grown up.[3] Because most mothers in the 1950s responded to the demands of child rearing by leaving the labour force, employers tended to assume women had a weak attachment to paid work. Yet, while some women did leave voluntarily, others did not. Instead, they were forced out by marriage or pregnancy bars—formal policies and informal practices that required women to resign their jobs upon marriage or motherhood (Sangster 1995, 2010).[4]

Since the 1970s, there has been a pervasive trend in Canada and other industrialized nations for mothers to continue working while raising their children, and this group accounts for most of the increase in labour market participation in recent decades. Looking back to Figures 3.3 and 6.1 reminds us of how dramatic this change has been. Today, far fewer women leave the labour force when they have children, and those who "take time out" do so for a much shorter time. Growing numbers of women are now juggling paid work with family roles, and the traditional *single-earner family* has been eclipsed. In 2011, for instance, most Canadian families were *dual-earner*, accounting for nearly two-thirds (62.8%) of all families (see Statistics Canada, CANSIM, Table 111-0020). In comparison, single-earner families comprised just one-quarter of all families—with single female-earner and single male-earner families making up 7.9 percent and 17.2 percent of all families, respectively. *Lone-parent families* made up the remainder (12.2% of all families), and roughly 80 percent of these were headed by women (Milan et al. 2011: 12).[5]

In short, there is growing diversity in families, and the traditional breadwinner family (where a working male earns the sole wage) is no longer the norm.

● TRENDS IN HOUSEHOLD AND CARING WORK

Given these dramatic changes, especially women's growing role as earners, how has the work of households changed? Is there now more sharing of unpaid work among family members, or do traditional patterns persist? Evidence from early *time budget studies*, which ask people to detail their use of time, suggests that despite change, many working women are still responsible for what U.S. sociologist Arlie Hochschild calls a "second shift" in the home.[6] After working seven or eight hours on the job, they come home to cook, clean, shop, and look after children—the same domestic work their mothers and grandmothers did as full-time housewives. Hochschild's findings in her classic 1989 study, *The Second Shift*, echo those of earlier Canadian research: Martin Meissner and colleagues (1975) found that a job outside the home meant a double burden for working women and a decrease of 13.5 hours per week in leisure time.

But perhaps these early studies reflect a time period when families had not yet adjusted to the new realities of working women. If so, are new generations redefining how household work is done? Media stories and television often give the impression that men are doing more cooking and cleaning; however, do recent studies confirm this?[7]

Housework

To answer these questions we can draw on time-use data generated from self-reported responses to survey questions or diaries, as well as qualitative information from individual- or couple-level interviews or observation. Studies of housework typically distinguish between core/regular housework, such as meal preparation, meal cleanup, indoor cleaning, and laundry that are done daily; and non-core/infrequent housework, such as outdoor cleaning, interior or exterior maintenance, and repairs (Marshall 2006: 2). Note that housework is measured separately from childcare—even though both tasks may be done at the same time and the amount of housework is strongly shaped by the presence and age of children. An important distinction can also be made between the *time* spent on activities and who carries *responsibility*—that is, planning and anticipating household work, rather than simply carrying it out.

Concerning the extent of change, Kan, Sullivan, and Gershuny (2011) compare time-use trends in housework from the 1960s to the present for 16 different countries (including Canada). They find evidence of convergence in the time women and men spent on housework, but note that the gap is narrowing largely due to *reductions* in women's housework, with much smaller *increases* in the time contributions of men. Casting a glance over more detailed Canadian data confirms and helps to unpack this dynamic. Using Statistics Canada's General Social Survey (GSS), we can compare participation and time use in housework for Canadian households for 1986, 1992, 1998, and 2005. Trends for the 1990s[8] confirm that women in dual-earner families still hold primary responsibility for housework (defined in the GSS as meal preparation and cleanup, cleaning, and laundry). Comparing the mid-1980s to the mid-2000s, however, suggests change. More men participated in housework by the mid-2000s—three-quarters (71%) reported they had contributed to housework in 2005, compared to just over half (54%) in 1986. But they increased the time they spent on housework only slightly, from 1.1 hours in 1986 to 1.5 hours per day by 2005. In comparison, women reduced the time they spent on housework, from 3.3 hours per day in 1986 to 2.8 hours per day by 2005. Taken together, these studies suggest that men are becoming more involved, but in time-limited ways, while women continue to hold domestic responsibility.[9]

Of course, these figures reflect averages, whereas contributions may vary by family type, age/generation, ethnicity, sexuality, gender attitudes, and other factors. Indeed, in Canadian families with very young children, women spend significantly more time than men on housework. But this gap narrows dramatically as children grow older, suggesting a family life-cycle effect (Milan, Keown, and Urquijo 2011: 22). Generation and age also matter, with younger and university-educated couples favouring less traditional patterns (Marshall 2011). More egalitarian patterns in time use and domestic responsibility are also found in same-sex households according to studies in Canada, the United States, and the United Kingdom (Dunne 1996; Nelson 1996; Sullivan 1996). Single parenthood, gender ideologies, and women's relative earnings also influence time spent on household tasks and how these are divided. At a more institutional and societal level, research suggests that countries with high levels of female employment, and childhood exposure to maternal employment, have higher contributions to household work by men (Cunningham 2007; Hook 2006; Gupta 2006).

Family income and resources also play a critical role in shaping how household work is done. Trends in "assortative mating" (where people of similar class backgrounds partner) mean that households are increasingly advantaged or disadvantaged (England 2010). For working-class families, the challenge is juggling household work alongside the demands of precarious, low-paying work, which may have erratic schedules (Presser 2003). In contrast, professional dual-career families are often time strapped, as are those in two-person careers (e.g., elite CEOs who are expected to have the unpaid services of a wife who can put on dinner parties, plan social events and travel, and organize household moves). Such dynamics often see well-resourced families outsourcing family work—an issue we return to shortly.

Childcare, Mothering, and Fathering

Caring for children is one of the most important and time-intensive activities in family life, involving both *instrumental care* or *caring for* (e.g., feeding, dressing, bathing) and *expressive care* or *caring about* (e.g., love, support, encouragement). Studies suggest that fathers have taken on an increasingly active role as caregivers, though the extent and nature of this change is debated.[10] In a fascinating study, Andrea Doucet (2006) examines a seemingly simple question posed in the title of her book—*Do Men Mother?*—showing the complexity of mothering and fathering, and the challenges for stay-at-home fathers who engage in household and caring work that has strong cultural associations with women. Traditionally, women have carried the responsibility of caring for children, leading scholars to argue that they engage in an "ethic of care," specific maternal practices, and "maternal thinking," which is attuned to the needs of children and family life (Ruddick 1995; Tronto 1993; Held 2006). Even today, when women increasingly work for pay, caring for children largely remains their responsibility. Contemporary norms around intensive mothering, where women are expected to devote ever more of their attention, effort, and identity to their children, create sharp contradictions for working mothers who carry far more economic and workplace responsibilities than ever before (Hays 1996; Stone 2007). In her insightful study—*Competing Devotions*—Mary Blair-Loy (2003) suggests that competing moral schemas—"devotion to family" versus "devotion to work"—set up cultural expectations for professional working women that are impossible to fulfill.

What do recent studies show us with respect to involvement and responsibility for childcare? Studies typically define *childcare* as feeding, dressing, helping, reading to, talking or playing with, medical care, and related travel, such as taking children to school or sports activities (Marshall 2006: 2). Overall, time-use studies suggest a narrowing of the gap in the time spent by women and men in caring for children, as mothers have increased their hours in paid employment, and fathers in many countries have taken a more active role in their children's lives (Beaujot 2000; Beaujot, Liu, and Ravanera 2008; Bianchi and Milkie 2010; Hook 2006; Marshall 2006, 2011). Despite signs of change, however, there is still a significant, and persistent, gender gap, with mothers devoting more *time* to daily direct care and assuming the bulk of *responsibility* for planning and coordinating caring work. Indeed, the analysis of time use by Kan and colleagues (2011), which considered 16 countries (including Canada) from the 1960s to the present, suggests low levels of change in childcare patterns, with women still assuming the bulk of *time* involved in children's care.

In Canada, data gathered from Statistics Canada's Labour Force Survey (LFS) and the General Social Survey (GSS) offer further detail on the time spent caring for children (Marshall 2006). What is striking across all family types is the enduring, persistent link between women and childcare. On average, mothers spend roughly twice as much time caring for children than fathers: 2.05 hours for every hour by men. As shown in Figure 7.1, Canadian mothers spent, on average, 50.1 hours each week caring for children, compared to 24.4 hours reported by fathers (Milan et al. 2011: 20). Since this average mixes different family types, it is important to look at more specific employment and family situations. Comparing single-earner, dual-earner, and lone-parent families, for instance, we see the gender gap is largest in single-earner families, two hours for women for every hour by men. Yet, interestingly, the gender gap within dual-earner families is narrower when one partner works part time (1.47 hours for women for every hour by men) than it is for full-time, dual-earner families (1.83 hours). Not surprisingly, mothers of young children (four years old or less) devote the most time to care. Here, the gender gap is largest (2.23 hours for women for every hour by men), falling notably for older children. Amid

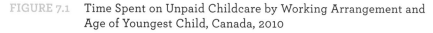

FIGURE 7.1   Time Spent on Unpaid Childcare by Working Arrangement and
Age of Youngest Child, Canada, 2010

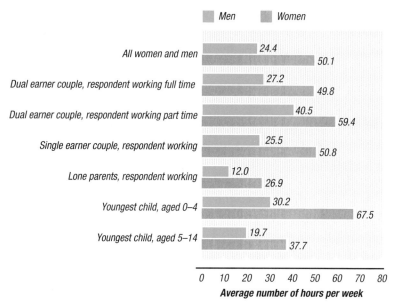

Source: Adapted from Milan, Anne, Leslie-Anne Keown, and Covadonga Robles Urquijo (2011). "Families, Living Arrangements, and Unpaid Work," *Women in Canada: A Gender-Based Statistical Report.* Ottawa: Statistics Canada. Catalogue No. 89-503-X, 2011, p. 20.

women's continued responsibility for children, especially at a young age, there is a growing trend toward more "involved fathering"—a pattern documented in qualitative studies, as well (Doucet 2006; Ball and Daly 2012).

Eldercare

Caring for elderly parents and relatives is another important part of household work. Population aging (discussed in Chapter 3) has significant implications for the future, especially for women who often carry responsibility for eldercare. From a policy standpoint, *eldercare* is seen as a pressing issue in Canada and many other industrialized countries, and there are predictions of a "caregiving crunch" as fewer women can meet such demands because of their own jobs.[11] The 2007 General Social Survey (GSS) showed that roughly 2.7 million—or one in five—Canadians 45 years old and over provided care to a senior, most typically a parent. Many of these caregivers were part of the "sandwich generation," juggling eldercare with caring for their own children. In 2007, three out of four caregivers were married, and nearly half were young enough (ages 45–54) to still be caring for their own children. Well over half (57%) also worked in a paid job.

What is involved in providing eldercare? According to the 2012 General Social Survey (GSS), those helping an elderly parent or in-law spent between three and four hours, on average, each week. Of note, a small minority (about 7%) put in the equivalent of a full-time job with 30 hours or more of care-giving each week. Typically, the main reason for providing care to a parent, parent-in-law, or grandparent was aging and frailty, followed by specific medical conditions, such as dementia, cancer, and cardiovascular disease. The most common forms of care involved phoning and visiting (reported by 99%) and offering emotional support (reported by 92%), followed by transportation (reported by 41%) and meals and cleaning (reported by 37%). Women were slightly more likely than men to provide care to aging family members and were also at greater risk of reporting psychological distress or health impacts as a result.[12] Overall, about 60 percent of those caring for parents felt worried or distressed by their responsibilities, and about one-third had an elevated level of psychological distress (Turcotte 2013: 6–12).

Recognizing the growing demands of eldercare, the federal government introduced *Compassionate Care* benefits in January 2004, which provides eight weeks of paid leave to care for a gravely ill family member. This develop-ment is important but, similar to other employment-related benefits, many individuals are ineligible due to the types of caregiver relationships involved or insufficient employment-related hours and earnings. Since introducing this leave, the federal government has expanded the eligibility criteria to recognize a wider range of situations and caregivers (HRSDC 2007). Recent evaluations, however, suggest additional changes are needed (see, for example, Williams et al. 2010).

Kin and Volunteer/Community Work

Two other important types of household work occur *across* and *beyond* households.

Kin work describes a wide range of work that goes into building and maintaining family ties, through communication, ritual celebrations, and the exchange of resources (di Leonardo 1987). Examples of kin work include regular or periodic phone calls, cards, and visits, as well as e-mails, texts, or Facebook posts, to share family news. Special celebrations—such as birthdays, Thanksgiving, or other seasonal, religious, and secular holidays—are also important, creating shared family bonds, traditions, and memories. Exchanging resources is also a part of kin work—for example, sharing children's clothing, toys, tools, recipes, photos, and family history.

Kin work, like domestic work, involves not only the doing but also the mental work of conceiving, initiating, and organizing such work. It may involve pleasant tasks, such as organizing a family reunion or birthday, or difficult work, such as helping family members patch up a dispute. Studies suggest kin work is important because it fulfills deeply held cultural expectations of a satisfying family life (di Leonardo 1987). Typically, it falls to women, even when it does not involve their side of the family (e.g., in-laws or distant relatives on their partner's side). In her study of kin work, di Leonardo (1987) found it involved extensive knowledge and skill, and thus was not easily "out-sourced" or passed along to others. Given this, women may often cut back on kin work during times of competing demands or stress.

Equally, *volunteer work* is an important form of work often overlooked if we rely only on official labour force statistics. According to the 2010 Canada Survey on Giving, Volunteering and Participation (CSGVP), 47 percent of Canadians ages 15 and over (or 13.2 million individuals) contributed time and energy to volunteer activities in 2010 (Vézina and Crompton 2012). This rate of volunteering was up just slightly, from 45 percent in 2004. Canadians volunteered about 2.1 billion hours in 2010, equivalent to nearly 1.1 million full-time jobs. Between 2004 and 2010, the average number of hours that each volunteer contributed declined slightly (168 hours to 156 hours, respectively). A minority of volunteers account for most of these volunteer hours, with the top 10 percent of volunteers contributing 53 percent of total hours. Participation in volunteer work rises with education and income level, and with the presence of children in the household.[13]

Volunteer workers are found in a wide variety of clubs and associations, as well as in religious and political organizations. However, a very large number work in the publicly funded service industries, assisting in the provision of health, social, recreational, educational, environmental, and other types of services. In recent years, as governments at all levels have cut costs, volunteers have increasingly replaced paid employees—in schools, for instance, where parent-volunteers play a growing role, helping in libraries, in classrooms, and on field trips. As this trend continues, volunteer work will become an ever greater part of the unpaid work performed by Canadians. In her study, *Opting Out?*, Pamela Stone (2007) found that women forced to exit demanding professions, in order to raise their families, often pursued volunteer work in order to maintain adult connections, overcome isolation at home, and retain a sense of professional identity.

● BALANCING WORK AND FAMILY

Over 25 years ago in her classic study, *The Second Shift*, U.S. sociologist Arlie Hochschild observed:

> Work has changed. Women have changed.... But most workplaces have remained inflexible in the face of the family demands of their workers and at home, most men have yet to really adapt to the changes in women. This strain between the change in women and the absence of change in much else leads me to speak of a "stalled revolution."[14]

Today researchers continue to puzzle over the "stalled revolution" (England 2010; Doucet 2006), trying to understand why there has been such a slow pace of change in efforts to reconcile work and family life (Correll et al. 2014; Pocock 2003; J. Williams 2010; Williams and Dempsey 2014).

Work–Family Conflict

One consequence of the stalled revolution is the rise of *work–family conflict* and *role overload*. *Work–family conflict* involves mutually incompatible demands arising from work and family domains (Greenhaus and Beutell 1985: 77). *Role overload* involves having more role demands than one can possibly fulfill (Coverman 1989). While some researchers use these terms interchangeably, others view them as distinct, noting that *overload* leads to *conflict* only when there are no mechanisms (e.g., resources or time flexibility) to help people meet their responsibilities. For example, having extra income allows families to buy in household help or time-saving conveniences.

Researchers also make distinctions based on the *directionality* of conflict.[15] *Work-to-family conflict* occurs when workplace demands interfere with family needs—for instance, a parent missing a family birthday because of a meeting or an evening shift. *Family-to-work conflict* occurs when family interferes with work—for example, a child's illness preventing a parent from being at work.

Distinctions can also be made by the perceived *nature* of conflict. *Time-based conflict* is by far the most commonly studied type of conflict, arising when it is physically impossible to meet the time demands of different roles (e.g., official work hours prevent a parent from dropping off or picking up a child at school). *Strain-based conflict* focuses on the physical, mental, and emotional fatigue attached to meeting competing work and family demands—for example, lacking the energy to play with one's children, or help with homework, when one gets home from work. Finally, *behaviour-based conflict* occurs when work and family behaviours are incompatible. For instance, managers and supervisors who act in an authoritarian, commanding manner at work may experience difficulties at home in caring for young children who need emotional warmth, connection, and flexibility.

How common is work–family conflict? Empirical studies suggest that it affects a significant proportion of the workforce in Canada, the United States, and other industrialized countries. Prevalence rates vary, however, depending on occupational roles, workplace demands, and family composition.[16] In Canada, three large-scale surveys conducted by Duxbury and Higgins—The National Study on Balancing Work and Caregiving in Canada—track trends in 1991, 2001, and 2011.[17] Overall, the Duxbury and Higgins studies confirm that *role overload* and *work–family conflict* are significant issues for the working population in Canada. In 1991, nearly one-half of respondents (47%) reported high levels of role overload, while over one-quarter (28%) reported high levels of work-to-family conflict. Rates of high family-to-work conflict were much lower, with just 5 percent of respondents reporting this (Duxbury and Higgins 2001: 14). In 2001, there was a notable jump in rates, with 59 percent of respondents reporting high role overload, 31 percent reporting high levels of work-to-family conflict, and 10 percent reporting high family-to-work conflict.

Duxbury and Higgins attribute rising levels of work–family conflict in 1991–2001 to changing work demands, in particular, downsizing and increased workloads; organizational norms requiring long hours; and the growing use of email, cellphones, and mobile technologies that blur boundaries between work and home (Duxbury and Higgins 2001: 14). With respect to rising family-to-work conflict, the authors point to population aging and the increased prevalence of juggling both child-care and elder-care responsibilities. More recent 2011 survey results suggest reduced, though still high, levels of conflict and overload. Overall, 40 percent of Canadians reported high role overload, and 30 percent reported high levels of work-to-family conflict. Of note, rising proportion of respondents (15%) reported high levels of family-to-work conflict up from 5 percent in 1991 (Duxbury and Higgins 2012: 13).

Consequences of Work–Family Conflict

Work–family conflict has many negative outcomes for individuals and their families.[18] In Canada, Duxbury and Higgins (2001) compared employees with high and low work-to-family conflict, finding a 40 percent gap in job satisfaction, with just 20 percent of those with high work-to-family conflict reporting high job satisfaction, compared to 60 percent of those where work-to family conflict was low. Outcomes for job stress were especially striking, with 57 percent of those with high work-to-family conflict reporting high job stress, compared to just 9 percent of employees where work-to-family conflict was low. Looking at a range of countries, Kossek and Ozeki (1998) reviewed 50 studies that examined job satisfaction and/or life satisfaction, concluding there was clear evidence of a "negative relationship between all types of work–family conflict and job and life satisfaction" (145). In their meta-analysis of 67 studies, Allen and colleagues (2000) also found strong links between high work–family conflict and reduced job satisfaction, reduced life satisfaction, and higher stress.

Pressures created by work–family imbalance have costs not only for employees and families, but for employers too. As Linda Duxbury and Higgins (2001) found, employees with high work–family conflict have lower levels of organizational commitment and higher rates of absenteeism. Indeed, absenteeism is a significant source of lost productivity for employers. According to Statistics Canada, female rates of absenteeism have risen steadily since the late 1970s, mainly due to family or personal obligations as growing numbers of mothers with preschool children sought employment. For example, in 2011, employed women lost an average of 11.4 days, compared to 7.7 for men, due to illness, disability, or personal and family responsibilities (Dabboussy and Uppal 2012). While some employers are working to support family-friendly work environments, firms in the most dynamic sectors of the economy are often defined by heavy workloads and long hours. This culture is not sustainable, however. It may suit younger, single workers who have no dependents, but lack of attention to work–life balance issues will cause problems (e.g., high turnover) as workers move into their 30s, find life partners, and begin raising children. Not surprisingly, studies are increasingly exploring the problems generated by "greedy organizations" (Coser 1967) and the culture of long work hours (Burke and Cooper 2008; Correll et al. 2014; J. Williams 2010).

Policies Supporting Work–Family Reconciliation

What types of policies and supports help individuals reconcile their work, family, and personal responsibilities? Research suggests that flexible work hours and schedules, generous personal and family-related leave, the ability to refuse overtime, and the presence of supportive managers are all important (Duxbury and Higgins 2001; Duxbury, Higgins, and Schroder 2009; Lowe 2007; Hill et al. 2006). Slowly, in part due to studies such as these, heightened awareness of the economic and individual costs of work–family conflict is challenging employers to reconsider some long-standing policies. Yet many employers remain locked into a traditional 9 to 5, five-days-a-week schedule (Correll et al. 2014). Many workers do not have flexibility in the hours and location of their work. Many also lack extended employer-sponsored coverage for paid parental or elder-care leave (beyond standard government-provisioned leaves), or may be unable to take full advantage of such policies due to insufficient earnings or hours.[19]

All in all, we have documented what Hochschild called a "stalled revolution." Well over two decades ago, the Conference Board predicted that more employers would respond to these needs as the drain on productivity became more visible and employee pressure for such policies mounted (Paris 1989). Unfortunately for many working parents, there is little tangible sign of this happening, something Duxbury and Higgins (2012) show in the key findings for their most recent study. As Figure 7.2 shows, many employees (both women and men) still have quite limited flexibility, finding it difficult to work from home for part of the day, or to be home to meet their children, or to pick them up after

FIGURE 7.2   Flexible Workplace Options, Canada, 2011

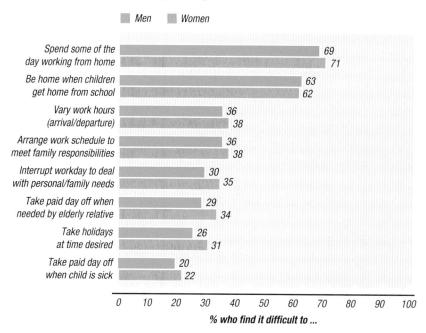

■ *Men*   ▥ *Women*

Spend some of the day working from home	69 / 71
Be home when children get home from school	63 / 62
Vary work hours (arrival/departure)	36 / 38
Arrange work schedule to meet family responsibilities	36 / 38
Interrupt workday to deal with personal/family needs	30 / 35
Take paid day off when needed by elderly relative	29 / 34
Take holidays at time desired	26 / 31
Take paid day off when child is sick	20 / 22

% who find it difficult to ...

Source: Adapted from Duxbury, Linda, and Christopher Higgins (2012) *Key Findings: Revisiting Work–Life Issues in Canada— The 2011–12 National Study on Balancing Work and Caregiving in Canada*, p. 17. <http://newsroom.carleton.ca/wp-content/ files/2012-National-Work-Key-Findings.pdf>

school. Roughly one-third of workers have little control over their work schedules, being unable to vary arrival and departure times, control the time of their specific shifts or overtime, interrupt and return to work in the case of family emergencies, or take a paid day off to help sick children or elderly relatives.

Moreover, employees who have flexible work arrangements, and make use of them, may still find these arrangements do not always help to reduce the stresses of balancing job and family. After examining a variety of alternative work arrangements, Janet Fast and Judith Frederick (1996) concluded that self-employment, flex-place (working some hours at home), and shift work had no effect on workers' perceived time stress. Both women and men in part-time jobs were less stressed about time than full-timers, however, although far more women than men chose part-time work for family-related reasons. Flextime (employees choosing when their work day starts and stops) helped to reduce time pressures, but was less available to women than to men.

Compressed workweeks (fewer days per week with longer hours each day) seemed to increase women's level of time stress, likely because they interfered with family routines. Job sharing was not examined by Fast and Frederick (1996), but other studies suggest it may contribute to reduced time pressure and better integration of work and family (Marshall 1997).

More recent research also confirms the benefits of limiting hours. For instance, in a study of the "60-hour dual-earner workweek" (where both partners limit employment to 30 hours), Hill and his colleagues (2006) found that individuals experienced lower levels of work–family conflict and enhanced family satisfaction and work–family fit.[20]

Barriers to achieving work–family balance, however, are numerous and complex. Arlie Hochschild's (1997) research suggests that even in organizations that provide family-friendly policies and programs, employees may experience difficulties finding enough time for their families. One of the largest barriers is the fact that society places great value, and confers rewards, on people who are successful in their careers. The result, especially among professionals and managers, is that employees spend more, not less, time at work. As Hochschild (1997: 198–99) suggests, "in a cultural contest between work and home, working parents are voting with their feet, and the workplace is winning." Research by Williams, Blair-Loy, and Berdahl (2013) suggests reasons why this may be the case. In taking advantage of flexible workplace arrangements, mothers and fathers appear to experience a "flexibility stigma" that has an impact on their careers and future opportunities. Given this, many are understandably reluctant to take advantage of such options.

Yet, emerging legal decisions on "family accommodation" in Canada and the United States suggest that employers may increasingly need to consider how their working hours and traditional practices affect working parents. In their article "Will Working Mothers Take Your Company to Court?" U.S. legal scholar Joan Williams and Amy Cuddy (2012) outline recent U.S. rulings that require companies to consider the impact of their work hours and location on parents, and make accommodations where possible. Likewise, in Canada, the case of *Johnstone v. Canadian Border Services Agency (CBSA)* saw the Canadian Human Rights Tribunal rule that the CBSA had engaged in "family status" discrimination when it refused Fiona Johnstone's request for a static schedule rather than an irregular day/night schedule that changed every six weeks, making it impossible for her to find reliable childcare.[21] Evidence presented showed the CBSA could have easily accommodated Johnstone's request, as they had done for other employees, and Johnstone was therefore awarded damages. If emerging legal decisions support this direction of change, then employers will need to ensure reasonable working hours, shifts, and schedules for working parents where feasible.

Early Childhood Education and Care

Of all types of support, quality childcare is perhaps the most pressing need. According to the 2008 report, *Early Childhood Education and Care in Canada* (Beach et al. 2009), child-care arrangements present an ongoing problem for many parents in Canada—although preferences for different forms of childcare (e.g., family, informal, formal) vary widely (Beaujot 1997; Statistics Canada 2004a). Despite past promises by Canadian governments to improve child-care availability, the number of licensed child-care spaces by no means fills the need. By 2008, for example, there were 876,194 regulated child-care spaces (for children up to 12 years old) across Canada, up from 373,741 in 1992 (Friendly and Beach 2005; Beach et al. 2009). This figure represents a near tripling of available spaces, a positive change given the historical heel dragging that has accompanied the promise of a national daycare program (Timpson 2001). But even with this increase, regulated child-care spaces still only accommodate a small fraction of what is needed.

Several challenges are commonly identified in empirical studies of child-care with respect to availability, cost, and quality. With respect to *availability*, in Canada the Childcare Resource and Research Unit (CRRU) has produced regular reports on provincial trends in childcare provision. Their most recent reports, analyzing trends to 2012, highlight ongoing shortages of child-care spots (Friendly et al. 2013). Nationally, in 2012, regulated full-time or part-time child-care spaces were available for just 22.5 percent of children five and under who required care because their parents were working. Though up from 14.9 percent in 2001, this percentage still falls well short of what is needed, given that nearly three-quarters of mothers with preschool children are employed. Care shortages are equally pronounced for older, school-aged children, with regulated spaces available for just 20.5 percent of children up to age 12. With respect to *cost*, average full-time fees vary widely, from a high in Ontario of $1,150/month (for infants) and $925/month (for toddlers), to a low of $152 per month for infant and toddler care in Quebec's publicly subsidized system.

So far, Quebec is the only jurisdiction in Canada to make a concerted effort to address these issues: in 1997, it introduced a comprehensive program of universal subsidized daycare and early childhood education (Albanese 2006). Despite further change to existing programs (including an increase in cost from $5 per day to $7 per day for childcare), Quebec remains a leader in child-care access, offering regulated spaces to over 37 percent of children up to age 12 (Friendly et al. 2013: 55).[22] Still, even with such changes, finding high-quality, accessible childcare remains a significant challenge for most working parents. Given the high costs and low availability of spaces, many children of working parents are looked after informally by sitters, neighbours, nannies, or relatives (Statistics Canada 2004a: 55).

● MARKETIZATION OF CARE AND THE "OUTSOURCED FAMILY"

Discussions of childcare illustrate how women's increased participation in the labour market has sparked a growing market for household and caring services in the formal economy. These services include childcare, house-cleaning, restaurant meals, and prepared deli and grocery food. Such developments respond to growing time pressures and "care deficits" within the home, which increasingly led families to buy in services and—in the words of Robert Reich (2000) and Arlie Hochschild (2012)—"outsource" family life. In a study on the rising marketization of caregiving in Canada, Nickela Anderson and Karen Hughes (2010) note estimates from Statistics Canada that value the domestic market for childcare at more than $3.5 billion in the early 2000s. Of note, nearly one-third of dual-earner families purchased childcare and one in 10 families purchased some type of house-cleaning service. Consumption was heavily tied to income, but even among low-income, female-headed households (typically the most financially strapped), more than one quarter purchased childcare.

Examining this phenomenon in a recent study—*The Outsourced Self*—Arlie Hochschild catalogues a wide array of family and household work that was once done in the home but is now being purchased in local, regional, and national markets in North America. Childcare is certainly common. But Hochschild also shows there is an ever-expanding range of services. Beyond basic domestic assistance, such as Molly Maid, other businesses—with names such as Rent-A-Husband and 1.877.99HUBBY—cover household repairs, outdoor work, snow shovelling, and lawn mowing. Special celebrations and "kin work" can also be purchased, with children's birthdays, anniversaries, and family reunions now falling under the purview of birthday planners. Other services, such as Kids in Motion and Driving Miss Daisy, Inc., help get children and elderly family members safely to school, activities, and medical and other appointments. Cooking services, which stockpile fridges and freezers with day-to-day and special meals, as well as personal shoppers, who purchase gifts or run time-consuming errands, are also increasingly in demand.

Developments such as these illustrate how some families are adapting to workplace demands and also highlight the fluid, ever-changing boundary between market and household work. At the same time, the marketization of household and caring work draws attention to the ways in which hierarchies based on class, race, and citizenship are reproduced. As Canadians increasingly outsource family life, they come to rely on systems of *transnational caregiving* and *stratified hierarchies of reproduction*—hiring working-class women and women from countries in the global south to provide paid care as nannies or as child- and elder-care workers, or to cook, clean, and work as housekeepers and domestic cleaners (Ehrenreich and Hochschild 2002; Duffy 2011).[23] Such arrangements may solve care deficits in their own homes, but they create new sets of problems, worsening inequalities and care deficits in the families of paid caregivers, both within and outside Canada.

CONCLUSION

We began this chapter by noting the often invisible nature of household and caring work, and the persistence of women's responsibility for family life. We also questioned whether gendered patterns of household caring work have shifted in recent decades as more women work as earners and breadwinners than ever before. Certainly, many people have expected to see men play a growing role in the household as women's labour force participation has soared since the 1970s. Yet, accumulating evidence shows small degrees of change—for example, greater sharing of household work among younger generations and in same-sex households. Overall, the pace of change is exceptionally slow. Reductions in the gender gap in family work stem as much, if not more, from women reducing the time they devote to certain tasks than to men dramatically expanding their contributions. Increasingly, one way North American families appear to be reconciling work and family life is through outsourcing—a trend that has fuelled the growth of low-paid caring work in the formal economy, and the reproduction of gender-, race-, and class-based inequalities, given that such work is typically done by women, immigrants, and those with little education. Another response has been to limit family size or simply not have children—thus fuelling trends toward population aging in Canada, as we discussed in Chapter 3.

With many employers offering still fairly limited options for effectively balancing work and family life—despite public concern about the need for more family-friendly workplaces—these patterns are perhaps not surprising. Further, they reflect Canada's failure to develop a system of affordable, accessible, quality childcare. Within this context, families struggle to juggle work and household demands, with high rates of work–family conflict the result. Those who can afford to do so may opt out of paid work to nurture young children (typically the mother, though stay-at-home dads are a growing trend). Such choices, however, carry high costs for individual caregivers, reducing future earnings and job prospects, and creating risks of poverty and financial insecurity in cases of family breakdown. Sociologists, especially feminist analysts, have long noted that the costs of raising families are borne largely by individuals (mainly women), while the wider benefits flow to the society as a whole. Shifting from a *universal breadwinner* model (which assumes that workers are endlessly available and free of caring responsibilities) to a *universal caregiver* model (which recognizes the caring responsibilities of all workers)[24] would go a long way to recognizing the economic value of care, while also reducing gender and other social inequalities, and resolving persistent social problems of work–family conflict.

◾ DISCUSSION QUESTIONS

1. Discuss the changing relationship between household work and market work in the course of Canada's economic development. How has the work in each domain changed in the transition from a pre-industrial, to an industrial, to a postindustrial society?

2. What is meant by the terms *household work* and *social reproduction*? What types of activities do these terms refer to?

3. Discuss key trends in women's and men's contributions to housework, childcare, and eldercare. How much change has taken place? How do we explain these patterns?

4. What is work–family conflict, and how does it affect working women and men? How might employers and governments assist in reducing work–family conflict?

ADDITIONAL RESOURCES

WORK AT THE MOVIES

- *No Time to Stop: Stories of Immigrant Women* (directed by Helene Klodawsky, 1990, 29.05 minutes). This NFB documentary tells the story of immigrant women of colour in Canada and their struggles at home and at work. It is available through the National Film Board of Canada: http://www3.nfb.ca/acrosscultures/theme_vis.php?id=2004& mediaid=660690&full.
- *The Motherload* (directed by Cornelia Principe, 2014, 45:10 minutes). Focusing on working women in Canada, this documentary examines the challenges they face as they struggle to balance work and family. It is available through CBC Doc Zone: http://www.cbc.ca/doczone/episodes/motherload.
- *When Strangers Re-Unite* (directed by Florchita Bautista and Marie Boti, 1999, 52 minutes). This NFB documentary explores the challenges faced by foreign domestic workers in Canada navigating through the immigration process, dealing with being separated from their families back home, and reuniting with family as they eventually come to Canada. It is available through the National Film Board of Canada: http://www3.nfb.ca/ acrosscultures/toutvoir_vis.php?mediaid=665737&mc=102&full.
- *Baby Mama* (directed by Michael McCullers, 2008, 99 minutes). A successful single businesswoman hires a working-class woman to be her surrogate child-bearer.

SOUNDS OF WORK

- "The Scaffolder's Wife" (Mark Knopfler). Knopfler's song describes the struggles of the wife of a scaffolder whose hard work, keeping company books, has helped their business stay afloat.

- "Nice Work If You Can Get It" (George Gershwin). The song champions care work, family, and human connections over paid work.
- "One's on the Way" (Loretta Lynn). Lynn describes the unpaid work that often falls to women. Her song highlights the various kinds of work women perform for the home and as caregivers.
- "Somebody's Hero" (Jamie O'Neal). Here is an ode to the women who forgo paid work to perform essential housework and carework. O'Neal's heroes work as cooks, waiters, and taxi drivers, only for no pay.

NOTES

1. Details of the strike were covered in articles in the *Globe and Mail* and the *National Post*. A personal account is provided by Stilwell at http://strikingmom. blogspot.ca/.
2. For discussions of patriarchy, see Hartmann (1976), Lerner (1986), and Walby (1990).
3. This post-WWII pattern is described in Ostry (1968). See also Canada, Department of Labour (1958). On the concept of breadwinning, see Warren (2007).
4. For a discussion of how married and pregnant women were expected to exit paid jobs, see Sangster (1995). For a personal account of a woman who transgressed cultural norms by working throughout her pregnancies, see *Rebel Daughter* by Doris Anderson (1996).
5. Calculations are from Statistics Canada, CANSIM, Table 111-0020, "Family Characteristics, Single-Earner and Dual-Earner Families by Number of Children." For additional information on families, living arrangements, and unpaid work in Canada, see Milan et al. (2011).
6. Hochschild (1989). See Pupo (1997), Marshall (2006b, 2009), and Beaujot and Anderson (2007) for recent trends in Canadian families. For studies of household divisions of labour, see Luxton (1980) and Duffy and Pupo (1992). For valuable conceptual discussions of household work, see Eichler and Albanese (2007), Luxton (1997), and Warren (2011). For poems on household work, see Treathaway (2000).
7. For Canadian and U.S. surveys of this literature, see Coltrane (2000), Bianchi and Milkie (2010), Doucet (2006), Beaujot (2000), and Kan et al. (2011). For recent studies of factors shaping fathers' contributions to housework and caring, see Cunningham (2007), Gupta (2006), Hook (2006), and Halrynjo (2009).

8. Marshall (1993: 12). Data are from the 1990 General Social Survey (GSS). A note of caution: There is some bias in how the survey measures housework because it is based on the perceptions of only one respondent per household (either male or female).

9. See Marshall (2006: 10–13) for more details. Doucet (2006), Coltrane (2000), and McFarlane, Beaujot, and Haddad (2000) provide excellent overviews of research in this area.

10. There are many insightful studies on this issue. On fathering, see Doucet (2006), Ball and Daly (2012), and Fox, Pascall, and Warren (2009). On mothering, see Blair-Loy (2003), Hays (1996), McMahon (2005), and Stone (2007). On parenting, see Ranson (2010), Nelson (1996), and Fox (1997).

11. For valuable discussions and overviews of recent trends in Canada, see Cranswick and Dosman (2008), Cranswick (2003), Turcotte (2013), Stonebridge (2013), and Sinha (2013).

12. While Turcotte (2013) does not examine gender patterns in detail, analysis of the 2010 General Social Survey by Milan et al. (2011: 24) shows that women typically provide more hours of care to seniors. While women and men are equally likely to provide care to a senior living in the same household, nearly half of the women (48.9%) report providing 10 hours or more of care, compared to just one-quarter of men. Women are also more likely to report longer hours of care (10 hours or more) for seniors not living in the same household.

13. For more information about the voluntary sector, visit the websites of the Voluntary Sector Initiative (http://www.vsi-isbc.org) and Imagine Canada, which represents voluntary and nonprofit organizations (http://www.imaginecanada. ca). For a more theoretical analysis of volunteer work, based on trends in the United States, see Wilson (2000). An interesting discussion of community work is provided by Uttal (2009).

14. Hochschild, Arlie. (1989). *The Second Shift: Working Parents and the Revolution at Home*. New York: Viking Penguin, p. 12.

15. Concepts and measurement are discussed in Bellavia and Frone (2005), Carlson and Grzywacz (2008), and Greenhaus and Beutell (1985).

16. For valuable reviews and discussions, see Bellavia and Frone (2005), Bianchi and Milkie (2010), Byron (2005), Kelly, Murphy, and Kaskubar (2008), and Korabik, Lero, and Whitehead (2008).

17. See Duxbury and Higgins (2001), Duxbury (2004), and Duxbury and Higgins (2012). The 1991 study surveyed 37,000 employees across Canada, while the 2001 study surveyed close to 33,000 employees in 100 medium to large Canadian organizations: for details, see Duxbury (2004: 1–2). The third survey,

conducted in 2011, surveyed more than 25,000 Canadians working in 71 public, private, and non-profit organizations (Duxbury and Higgins 2012).

18. For excellent reviews and meta-analysis on such outcomes, see Kossek and Ozeki (1998), Allen et al. (2000), Bellavia and Frone (2005), Dorio, Bryant, and Allen (2008), Mullen, Kelley, and Kelloway (2008), and Amstad (2011).

19. For a review of work and family policies in Canada, see Skrypnek and Fast (1996). For a discussion of U.S. policies, see Blau and Ehrenberg (2000) and Bianchi and Milkie (2010). For the United Kingdom, see Lewis (2009).

20. For valuable discussions of the impact of work–family policies on women's employment, see Hedgewisch and Gornick (2011) and Gornick and Meyers (2009).

21. For an overview and discussion of *Johnstone v. CBSA*, see the Legal Education and Action Fund (LEAF) website at http://leaf.ca/2014/02/leaf-intervening-in-johnstone-v-canada-border-services-agency-at-the-federal-court-of-appeal/.

22. For a comparison of family-related policies and programs in Canada and other countries, see Beach et al. (2009) and Mahon (2002). For a valuable discussion of childcare in Quebec, see Albanese (2006).

23. For additional discussions of global care deficits, see Isaksen, Devi, and Hochschild (2008), Spitzer et al. (2003), and Zimmerman, Litt, and Bose (2006).

24. These ideas have been developed in a wide body of writing by feminist scholars, but are well articulated by Nancy Fraser (1997) in her article "After the Family Wage: A Post-Industrial Thought Experiment."

ORGANIZING AND MANAGING WORK

8

"Pushing the tiny lightbulb into its holder four hundred times a night (two per van) and pushing in eight hundred clips (four per van) per night hurt my thumb and forefinger. These trim jobs waste your hands, I thought.... Some of the familiar tiredness returned. Once again I was falling behind on a job, working into the repairman's area, where he was supposed to inspect the Trim 2 jobs.... I was so slow that I was using my few short breaks to put putty in the lenses."

"The line went down for a few minutes, and I sat on the stool attached to the job station, next to my table full of red and yellow lenses, ropes of black putty, boxes of screws and light bulbs. Maybe it was because I had a few moments to think, maybe it was the sensory overload of the past few weeks, but for the first time an abrupt, raw hatred of the place rose in my craw, a loathing of the noise, the dirt. All the people are stupid, I thought. The work is meaningless and exhausting. There is no privacy. The line never stops. The last was a bit irrational, since I was thinking this during the instant that the line had stopped."

[Solange De Santis describing assembly-line work after several weeks on the job in the General Motors' assembly plant in Scarborough, Ontario]

Source: De Santis, Solange. (1999). *Life on the Line: One Woman's Tale of Work, Sweat, and Survival.* New York: Doubleday, p. 85.

● INTRODUCTION

The word "bureaucracy" almost always has a negative connotation when used in conversation. It is typically associated with inefficiency and with a lack of caring. While the word "management" does not elicit quite the same negative reaction, it is seldom used to make a positive statement. Cartoonists love to lampoon bureaucracies ("we need to strike a committee to study the problem of bureaucracy") and, as the popular comic strip Dilbert reveals, managers are also in their sights. Yet over a century ago when industrial capitalism was beginning to reshape Western societies, bureaucracies were seen by organizational analysts as both necessary and efficient. As for managers, the goal was, and remains as we will see in this chapter and the next, to make them more effective.

We begin by reviewing Max Weber's assessment of bureaucracy, a topic first introduced in Chapter 1. We then go beyond the theory to examine the reality of large contemporary bureaucratic work organizations, focusing on some of the key problems with this organization form, particularly when merged with assembly-line production technologies. Our attention then shifts to the role of managers within large workplace bureaucracies. The core of this chapter is a detailed discussion of two major approaches to management that emerged in the past century—scientific management and the human relations approach. We examine their assumptions about human nature, their prescriptions for how best to manage workers, and their failings. Chapter 9 will then assess some of the newer managerial paradigms that emerged in response to these failings in the latter half of the 20th century.

● UNDERSTANDING BUREAUCRACY

As industrialization progressed in the latter half of the 19th century, craftwork gave way to an extensive division of labour (see Chapter 1). Less skilled labourers could perform narrow tasks more cheaply. But once all the parts of a craftworker's job had been simplified and reassigned, coordinating and integrating these tasks became a problem, particularly within the large factories that were emerging. Questions about how best to integrate and coordinate the activities of large numbers of workers within a single enterprise gave rise to organizational studies and theories of management.

The organizational structure adopted by 19th-century businesses was the bureaucratic hierarchy. Max Weber (1946) considered *bureaucracy* to be the organizational form best able to efficiently coordinate and integrate the multitude of specialized tasks conducted in a big factory or office (see Chapter 1). He believed that capitalism could not be successful without bureaucracies. Weber's description of them has, however, become the model for a highly mechanistic type of work organization. Gareth Morgan defines bureaucracies as organizations "that emphasize precision, speed, clarity, reliability, and efficiency achieved through the creation of a fixed division of tasks, hierarchical supervision, and detailed rules and regulations."[1]

Bureaucracies were clearly an improvement over the tradition-bound and frequently disorganized methods used to run most 19th-century businesses. Their predictability greatly increased the productivity of industrial capitalism. Furthermore, a bureaucracy is a system of authority. Its hierarchical structure, formal lines of authority, and impartial rules and regulations are designed to elicit cooperation and obedience from employees. In fact, with an elaborate hierarchical division of labour, employers can gain employee commitment by offering the prospect of career advancement (the internal labour markets described in Chapter 5). It would seem that bureaucratic work organizations are ideal.

The Problems of Bureaucracy

Most sociologists, along with many people who work in bureaucracies, would agree that they have some serious flaws, however.[2] Organizational researchers have shown that bureaucracies are often overly complex and, therefore, difficult to manage, resistant to change, and unable to cope with uncertainties. Working conditions in bureaucracies are frequently unsatisfying, as we will argue in Chapter 14. A paradox of bureaucracy is that, far from achieving machinelike efficiency, it often unintentionally creates inefficiency, a problem Weber largely failed to see. Furthermore, sociologists have documented a "dark side of organizations," where things can go seriously wrong (Vaughan 1999). Examples of such mistakes, mishaps, or misconduct are plentiful: they include the meltdown of banks and other financial institutions that led to a global economic crisis in 2008, British Petroleum's *Deepwater Horizon* oil spill in the Gulf of Mexico in 2010, and the sudden collapse in 2013 of Research in Motion (RIM), the previously highly successful Canadian company that produced BlackBerry smart phones.

A number of classic sociological studies challenge the notions of bureaucratic rationality and efficiency. For example, Robert Merton (1952) described how employees who slavishly obey bureaucratic rules could undermine efficiency. For them, rules become ends in themselves, rather than the means of achieving organizational goals. Such employees can acquire a *bureaucratic personality*, compulsively following procedural manuals to the last detail. Alvin Gouldner (1954) demonstrated how events in work organizations (promotions or dismissals, for example) are far from predictable. Moreover, the rules that reduce uncertainty for management may be a major source of discontent among employees. In fact, Gouldner argued, bureaucracies in work organizations are often created not to increase efficiency so much as to give managers more power over workers.

The notion of bureaucratic efficiency rests, in part, on the assumption that employees will readily submit to *managerial authority*. In Weber's view, workers accept the legitimacy of the existing authority structure, abide by the rules, and obey their bosses because they believe the basis for such authority is impartial and fair. In other words, underlying capitalist bureaucracies is a *rational–legal value system*. However, the assumption that there is general acceptance of goals is contradicted by the realities of employee–employer relations, which are frequently punctuated by conflict and resistance (see Chapter 10). People in positions of power set organizational goals. These goals are, therefore, "rational" from management's perspective, but not necessarily from the perspective of workers. What is rational for workers is what reflects their own interests, such as higher pay, a safer and more comfortable work environment, or more scope for making work-related decisions. As we will see later in this chapter, managers have gone to great lengths to try to convince workers to accept organizational goals as their own personal goals, and to gain worker compliance.

The Informal Side of Organizations

Weber's description of bureaucracies focuses on their formal structure. But all work organizations, including bureaucracies, also have an *informal* side where employees reinterpret, resist, or adapt to work structures and management directives (Blau and Scott 1963). The organizational charts found in corporate annual reports present management's image of how things ought to operate. Employees further down the hierarchy often see things differently and act accordingly. Thus, to get a complete picture of a work organization, we must also examine employees' informal practices and social relations. Some classic sociological studies of work organizations are insightful.

Donald Roy (1952) studied *informal work groups* by working as a machinist in a Chicago factory that ran on a *piecework payment system* and carefully observed how workers responded to management. Productivity was regulated by management through bonus payments for output that was above established quotas. Machine operators constantly battled with managers over these quotas and payment rates. The machinists invented ingenious shortcuts to maximize their wages while minimizing effort. Their informal system of production involved what in shop-floor jargon was called "gold-bricking" on "stinker jobs." That is, on difficult jobs for which they could not possibly earn a bonus, workers relaxed and enjoyed some free time. On easy jobs, however, they could "make out" by exceeding the quota to receive a bonus. Any production beyond an unofficial quota was stored up in a "kitty" to be used to boost output figures on a slow day. Management rarely challenged the workers' system because production usually fluctuated within an acceptable range. What's ironic is that the workers had designed a more predictable and efficient production process.

Managers also participate in similar manipulations of informal work practices. With limited authority over workers, many middle- and lower-level managers and supervisors feel constrained in their roles. Consequently, they may not entirely follow the directives of top executives. Melville Dalton's classic study, *Men Who Manage* (1959), illustrated how managers bent rules and short-circuited bureaucracy in order to achieve their objectives. "Freewheeling," or following unofficial practices rather than formal rules, was rampant in these bureaucracies. For example, obtaining a promotion depended less on merit than it did on social characteristics such as, for example, being a member of the Masonic Order or the local yacht club. Furthermore, employees at all organizational levels regularly engaged in what, to the outside observer, was dishonest activity. Workers borrowed tools and equipment; managers had home improvements done at company expense. The company's resources were dispensed as personal rewards in order to keep the bureaucracy running, to acknowledge someone's special services, or to solidify social relationships in order to get a job done.

Bureaucracy and Fordism

As an organizing principle, the bureaucratic hierarchy was integrated with technology to create the huge factories that formed the backbone of industrial capitalism (Chapter 1). When Henry Ford introduced the moving assembly line in 1914, launching the era of mass-production manufacturing, the machine-like logic of bureaucratic organization was intensified. By the mid-20th century, *Fordism* dominated North American manufacturing as well as other industrial sectors. As Robert Reich observes:

America's corporate bureaucracies were organized like military bureaucracies, for the efficient implementation of preconceived plans. It is perhaps no accident that the war veterans who manned the core American corporations of the 1950s accommodated so naturally to the military like hierarchies inside them. They were described in much the same terms as military hierarchies—featuring chains of command, spans of control, job classifications, divisions and division heads, and standard operating procedures to guide every decision.... As in the military, great emphasis was placed upon the maintenance of control—upon a superior's ability to inspire loyalty, discipline, and unquestioning obedience, and upon a subordinate's capacity to be so inspired.[3]

In *The Work of Nations*, Reich (1991) describes how, in today's global economy, the distinction between the production of goods and services has blurred. While the key to prosperity used to be large volume production in giant factories by corporations that dominated world markets, today specialized expertise in finance, research, and development, as well as marketing, adds considerable value to products produced, and successful corporations are more flexible, responding quickly to market demands. With rapidly changing markets in the global economy, networked forms of business organization, including franchises, joint ventures, outsourcing, and strategic alliances, have become more common (Podolny and Page 1998). Thus, to a considerable extent, Fordist bureaucracies are an outmoded model of organization and management.

But bureaucracies, and the management systems used within them, have certainly not disappeared. And we continue to encounter examples of the "dark side of organizations" (Vaughan 1999). As organizational researchers Samuel Culbert and Scott Schroeder (2003: 105) observe, "When it comes to the conduct of hierarchical relationships and how those with organizational authority are expected to direct and account, the 20th century concluded the way it began—with a steady stream of abuses, scandals, and exposés of hierarchy gone awry." So, even though a range of new, and to some extent improved, management approaches emerged in the second half of the 20th century (Chapter 9), there is good reason to continue our analysis of bureaucratic organizations and their management systems.

Technology and Organizational Structure

As our review of a number of classical organizational studies has revealed, organizational researchers have long been aware of some of the core problems of bureaucracy. They have also recognized that the single organizational model described by Weber was not the only type of work organization that emerged in the 20th century. For example, in the 1950s, Burns and Stalker studied synthetic fibre, electronics, and engineering industries, proposing a continuum of organizational forms from the *mechanistic* (or highly bureaucratic) to the *organic*. More open and flexible organizational structures and management styles were required, they concluded, in industries with rapidly changing technologies and market conditions (Burns and Stalker 1961). The studies of Joan Woodward (1980) revealed a direct relationship between production technology, on one hand, and structural forms and management styles on the other. Woodward concluded that bureaucracy and tight management controls are more appropriate in industries with mass-production technology. When the workflow is varied and production processes are nonroutine and complex—as in craft or continuous-process technologies—more flexible, organic structures function best.

Woodward's research attests to the importance of technology as a key variable in organizational analysis. The concept of a *sociotechnical system*, introduced by researchers at London's Tavistock Institute of Human Relations, took this idea one step further. In their study of the mechanization of British coal mining, Trist and Bamforth (1951) documented how social relations in teams of miners were dependent on the technology used.[4] Replacing the traditional method of mining with mechanical conveyor belts reduced productivity by destroying the technical basis for the work teams and creating negative social–psychological consequences for workers. Consequently, optimizing the fit between social and technical aspects of production has become an important goal in work design. As we will see in Chapter 10, the information technology revolution continues to raise concerns about the impact of technological change on work organization, the quality of working life, workers' skills, and organizational performance (Green 2006).

Technology and Social Inequality

The studies reviewed above have examined the effects of technology on work organizations and the people employed in them. Some sociologists have asked broader questions about how technology might be linked with patterns of social inequality within societies. Gerhard Lenski (1966), for example, placed technology at the centre of his sweeping theory explaining differences over time in the level of social inequality. He proposed that a society's technological base largely determines its stratification system. In simple hunting and gathering societies, he argued, the few resources of the society were distributed primarily on the basis of need. But, as societies became more complex, *privilege*, or the control of the society's surplus resources, came to be based on power. In agrarian societies, there evolved a governing system that gave the ruling elites control of the political system and access to even more of the society's wealth. However, the arrival of the industrial era reversed this "age old evolutionary trend toward ever-increasing inequality" (Lenski 1966: 308).

Lenski's explanation hinged on the complex nature of industrial technology. Owners of the means of production could no longer have direct control over production. In the interests of efficiency, they had to delegate some authority to subordinates. A middle level of educated managerial and technical workers who expected greater compensation for their training grew as a result. Education broadened the horizons of this class of workers, introducing them to ideas of democracy, as well as making them more capable of using the political system to insist on a greater share of the profits they produced.

But why would employers give in to this demand? Lenski argued that elites in industrial societies needed educated workers; the productive system could not operate without them. Equally important, the much greater productivity of industrial societies meant that the "elite can make economic concessions in relative terms without necessarily suffering any loss in absolute terms" (Lenski 1966: 314). Because so much more wealth was being produced, everyone could have a larger share.

Lenski accurately described the social and economic changes accompanying industrialization. Twentieth-century capitalism had provided a higher standard of living for the working class. Compared to the era observed by Marx, workers were not as exploited and powerless. Social inequality was slowly declining in the decades of economic expansion and full employment after World War II. However, it is virtually impossible to prove that industrial technology was the primary cause. We should also look carefully at changing social relations of production. Workers had gained relatively more collective power, through unions, for example (Chapter 11). In addition, the state had legislated rules governing the labour market and provided a social safety net that reduced the level of poverty.

But, as we argued in Chapter 5, we are again seeing evidence of growing inequality in North American society. Industrial restructuring, organizational downsizing, outsourcing of work, the growth of nonstandard jobs, and a reduction in the social safety net are all part of the explanation. And is it possible that computers, robotics, and new information technologies have also contributed to the slow increase in social inequality? Again, we should not focus on technology alone; rather, we should view it as an outcome of decisions made by corporate leaders and the senior-level managers who work for them.

John Child (1985) identifies four goals that managers have when they introduce new technology: reducing costs and boosting efficiency; increasing flexibility; improving quality; and achieving greater control over operations. These goals, which often overlap, are "evolving," and the end results may not be predictable. They also depend on the type of technology, its application, and the nature of the business. For example, customer service jobs in call centres span a wide continuum, from the skilled and rewarding in financial services, to the unskilled, routinized, and low-paid in telemarketing (Frenkel et al. 1999).

Shoshana Zuboff's conclusion, drawn from her study of several high-tech firms, aptly expresses the contingent and often unpredictable quality of technological change:

> Even where control or deskilling has been the intent of managerial choices with respect to new information technology, managers themselves are also captive to a wide range of impulses and pressures. Only rarely is there a grand design concocted by an elite group ruthlessly grinding its way toward the fulfillment of some special and secret plan. Instead, there is a concentration of forces and consequences, which in turn develop their own momentum.[5]

● THE ROLE OF MANAGERS

Managers became a prominent new social group in the early 20th century. *Cost accounting* techniques for calculating how much each factor of production, including labour, contributes to profits was one way capitalists initially tackled the problems of running increasingly large and complex enterprises. Appointing trained managers, often factory engineers, was an equally important social innovation. As business historian Alfred D. Chandler Jr. suggests, the "visible hand" of the corporate manager replaced the "invisible hand" of market forces (Chandler 1977). Corporate boards of directors, representing the shareholders, delegated to managers the authority to operate the business profitably (see Chapter 2), giving them a great deal of power and responsibility.

But what exactly do managers do? In the most general sense, they try to obtain employee compliance and prevent opposition to authority. In this respect, the workplace is a microcosm of the larger society. Maintaining orderly and harmonious social relations among people who are not equals has always been a problem for those in power. Managers also try to motivate workers to achieve the quantity and quality of output considered necessary by those in charge of the organization. Ideally, they would like to generate employee engagement in the enterprise by convincing employees to work hard for the good of the organization (Macey and Schneider 2008). But employers in both the private and public sectors, and the managers who work for them, have far from complete control over the attitudes, beliefs, and effort expended by employees. Hence, conflict often erupts over different perceptions of what should be expected in return for a specific wage and work environment, a topic discussed in detail in Chapter 10.

In assessing the role of managers, it is important to distinguish between what they say they do and why, and what they may really do and for what reasons. Henry Mintzberg (1989: 9) argues that the goals that supposedly guide managers are often vaguely defined: "If you ask managers what they do they will most likely tell you that they plan, organize, coordinate, and control. Then watch what they do. Don't be surprised if you can't relate what you see to those four words." Mintzberg's advice underscores the importance of looking closely at how management theories are applied and at the results, something we will do in this chapter and the next. All too often, descriptions of new management approaches include overly optimistic assessments of their impact

(Pfeffer and Sutton 2000). On a related note, Reinhard Bendix criticizes *management ideology*, or the beliefs of managers that their higher incomes and the right to give orders to others are justified. "All economic enterprises have in common a basic social relation between the employers who exercise authority and the workers who obey, and all ideologies of management have in common the effort to interpret the exercise of authority in a favourable light" (Bendix 1974: 13).

No matter how they explain and justify their actions, managers nevertheless do try, to the extent possible, to achieve organizational goals by motivating employees, planning for and coordinating organizational change, making decisions about a variety of things, including technological change, and generally increasing productivity. During the past century, a variety of different theories of management emerged in North America. The two most influential were scientific management and the human relations approach, which we discuss below. In Chapter 9, we will examine some of the alternative managerial paradigms that later sought to take a different approach to motivating employees and increasing productivity.

● SCIENTIFIC MANAGEMENT (TAYLORISM)

Charlie Chaplin's classic 1936 movie *Modern Times* humorously depicts the life of a factory worker whose job consists of nothing more than tightening a bolt every few seconds as another identical piece of equipment speeds past him on an assembly line. He goes crazy. Once out on the street, he continues repeating the motions on anything that fits his two wrenches. We laugh when we see the movie, but Chaplin, playing the role of the super-stressed factory worker, was criticizing a real and widespread approach to managing work organization in industrialized societies.

Scientific management began in the United States as a set of production methods, tools, and organizational systems designed to increase the efficiency of factory production. The term itself was coined over a century ago by an engineer, Frederick W. Taylor. Given the extent to which he promoted his management approach and the frequency with which it was adopted in North America as well as in Europe, the approach soon also came to be known as *Taylorism*. Taylor's theory was at the cutting edge of the "thrust for efficiency" that contributed to the rise of 20th-century industrial capitalism (Palmer 1975). Taylor and other early management consultants advocated workplace reorganization, job redesign, and tighter administrative and employee controls, all in the name of efficiency and profits.

Taylor was convinced that workers deliberately restricted production by keeping their bosses ignorant of how fast a job could be done.[6] His solution was to determine "scientifically" the one best way of performing a job through *time and motion studies* of each step. Management consultants used stopwatches to record how long each job took and recorded in writing exactly how workers completed each task. They then subdivided complex tasks to gain maximum efficiency and issued instructions on how each new job was to be performed. They also sought ways of identifying potential employees who would be best able to perform each highly repetitive task and devised training strategies to ensure that new workers would follow the rules. Essentially, they removed most of the control and decision making regarding work tasks from employees and handed them over to managers. In addition, a base rate of pay was tied to a production quota. If workers exceeded the quota, they received a pay bonus. Workers unable to achieve the quota would be forced to quit because their base rate fell below a minimum level. In other words, scientific management was founded on the assumption that workers were motivated by economic gain alone.

Taylor's view of human nature was coloured by his preoccupation with technical efficiency. In his mind, the ideal worker was more like a machine than a human being. Taylor was also a leading spokesman for early 20th-century management consultants, articulating their strongly expressed concerns about the "labour problem."[7] Industrial cooperation would replace class conflict, he predicted, only once both management and labour began thinking differently. As he wrote in *Industrial Canada*, a prominent Canadian business magazine at the time:

> The new outlook that comes to both sides under scientific management is that both sides very soon realize that if they stop pulling apart and both push together as hard as possible in the same direction, they can make that surplus [i.e., profits] so large that there is no occasion for any quarrel over its division. Labour gets an immense increase in wages, and still leaves a large share for capital.[8]

Taylor believed his management techniques would benefit all parties involved: workers, managers, and the owners of the means of production. Yet their overriding effect was to give management tighter control over workers, allowing them to make virtually no major work decisions (Bendix 1974; Nelson 1980). As we will elaborate in Chapter 10, according to the *labour process perspective*, Taylorism deskilled and degraded work, minutely fragmenting tasks, reducing skill requirements, and eliminating workers' input about how their jobs should be done.[9] From the start, scientific management failed to provide a successful formula for labour–management cooperation.

Taylor's package of managerial reforms was seldom adopted completely. Yet various aspects of scientific management, those most useful for management, were quickly introduced into Canadian factories and, by the 1920s, were used to overhaul large corporate and government offices.[10]

The Legacy of Scientific Management

In many ways, Taylorism represented the practical application of bureaucratic principles to a manufacturing setting. Henry Ford's moving assembly line used technology to develop the logic inherent in scientific management and bureaucracy. But the increased monotony and speed of production sparked a huge increase in employee turnover. Only by doubling wages was Ford able to induce workers to accept the new production methods. As we will see in Chapter 9, a variety of alternative management approaches have tried to move beyond Taylorism. Even so, it is still very much alive in manufacturing. One case study of a Welsh appliance factory described efficiency gains obtained through time and motion studies, piece-rate payments, and reduced operator discretion—practices all favoured by mid-level managers (who were work-study engineers); yet it had been the desire of senior management to change these practices (Jones 2000). Elements of Fordism can also be found in *lean production*, a Japanese-inspired management system that has become widespread in vehicle production and now is being adapted to other sectors, such as health care (see Chapter 9).

The detailed job descriptions, planned workflows, and time and motion studies of scientific management also influence job design in the service sector (Davis 2010). For instance, Burger King attempts to maximize food sales and minimize labour costs by emphasizing SOS—"speed of service" (Reiter 1991: 85). Complying with this motto requires highly standardized work procedures and strict management controls in all Burger King outlets. Time and motion studies dictate how long it takes to prepare the fries, burgers, and drinks, exactly how workers should do these tasks, and where they should be positioned depending on the design of the kitchen. The cleaning of buildings is another type of service work that has been reorganized along scientific management lines. A study in Toronto found a shift away from a semi-autonomous and multi-skilled "zone cleaning" approach to "mono-task" assignments (Aguiar 2001). The latter resulted in simplified and repetitive tasks assigned to "cleaning specialists" who did only mopping, dusting, restroom duties, or other specific tasks. Software was used to analyze building cleaning needs and design efficient ways to do more cleaning with fewer workers. New technology, such as "backpack" vacuums, contributed to these efficiencies. While these changes were intended to improve quality and customer service, they also significantly reduced the decision making of employees.

History provides many examples of workers resisting scientific management. Frustrated by managerial rationalizations in the early 20th century, skilled workers responded by striking (Heron and Palmer 1977; Kealey 1986). Autoworkers were one occupational group that experienced a barrage of scientific management, along with extensive technological change. Chapter 14 will comment further on how Fordism combined scientific management techniques with mass-production, assembly-line technology to create some of the most alienating and stressful working conditions in modern industrial society.[11] Not surprisingly, in the early 1970s, when General Motors opened a Vega plant at Lordstown, Ohio, the relentless pace of the line, coupled with more restrictive management, led to massive labour unrest and sabotage (Aronowitz 1973).[12]

In short, major human costs often accompany increased efficiency, productivity, and profits. Other schools of management have tried to counteract the harshness that resulted from Taylorism and Fordism by developing more humane working conditions. As one organizational researcher aptly concludes, scientific management principles "make superb sense for organizing production when robots rather than human beings are the main productive force, when organizations can truly become machines" (Morgan 1997: 26).

● THE HUMAN RELATIONS MOVEMENT

Bureaucracy, scientific management, and mass-production technologies transformed work in the 20th century. Henry Ford, Taylor, and other "efficiency experts" sought to redesign production systems so that control would be firmly in the hands of management. Technical efficiency was paramount. Consequently, many jobs became routinized and monotonous, stripped of opportunities for workers to use their minds or develop their skills and abilities. Employee dissatisfaction, in the form of high turnover and absenteeism rates or industrial unrest, threatened to undermine the machine-like efficiency of the new industrial system.

Gaining the cooperation of workers within an increasingly bureaucratized, mechanized, and regimented labour process remained difficult. Some employers responded with programs, broadly known as *corporate welfare* or *industrial betterment*, which emphasized the need to treat workers as human beings. Well in place in major North American firms by the 1920s, corporate welfare programs were intended to reduce the alienating effects of bureaucracy and Fordist technologies (Barley and Kunda 1992). The goal was a loyal and productive workforce; the means were healthier work settings and improved job benefits. Recreation facilities, cafeterias, cleaner and more pleasant work environments, coherent personnel policies, medical care, and pensions are major examples of corporate welfare efforts.[13]

Taylor and other efficiency experts were quick to dismiss these ideas as a waste of money. Yet many firms committed to scientific management also used corporate welfare measures to gain greater cooperation from staff (Jacoby 1985). More than anything, the corporate welfare movement showed that the principles of bureaucracy and scientific management failed to address the key ingredient in modern industry: human beings. Not until the *human relations school of management* began to systematically examine some of the same concerns in the 1930s did the scientific management model face a serious challenge.

To operate effectively, large work organizations need employees to comply with management directives. Amitai Etzioni (1975) theorized that such *compliance* can be achieved in three different ways. *Coercive* management techniques rely on penalties and harsh discipline. *Utilitarian* methods emphasize pay and material benefits, for example, assuming that employees are motivated by economic self-interest. *Normative* approaches, however, assume that workers can and will align their own interests with organizational goals, thus becoming motivated to work hard for the greater good of the company or government department.

The human relations approach that emerged several decades after Taylor first promoted his ideas employs more of a normative approach; scientific management had combined coercive and utilitarian methods, with mixed results at best. The new approach endeavoured to cultivate a community of interests throughout the work organization, trying to get workers to identify with management goals and pursue them as their own. While the management consultants from the human relations school came to be more popular than the scientific management advocates, in practice, scientific management and human relations often operated side by side.[14]

The Hawthorne Studies

The human relations school of management originated in the *Hawthorne Studies*, a series of experiments conducted by Harvard Business School researchers between 1927 and 1932 at Western Electric's Hawthorne Works on the outskirts of Chicago.[15] Western Electric management was initially concerned with the effects of fatigue and monotony on production levels. At the time, these were central concerns of industrial psychologists, who were experimenting with industrial betterment (corporate welfare) techniques. Various studies examining the effect of rest pauses, hours of work, and lighting levels on productivity led researchers to unexpected findings.

In the Relay Assembly Test Room study, workers were placed in two separate rooms. Researchers then recorded production while varying light intensity for one group but not the other. To their surprise, productivity in both groups increased, regardless of lighting level. Only when light intensity was reduced to that of bright moonlight did productivity decline. Several variations on this study came up with the same puzzling findings. Searching for possible explanations, the researchers speculated that a fundamental change had occurred in the workplace. Involving workers in the study had the unintended effect of raising their morale. They now felt that management cared about them as individuals. Productivity, concluded the researchers, increased as a result.[16] A central premise of human relations management was established: if workers are treated as human beings working toward a collective goal, their motivation to cooperate will improve and their productivity will increase. Because of the Hawthorne Studies, workplaces came to be viewed more as social systems than in purely technical terms.

Later interviews with employees revealed the extent to which work groups were governed by informal behavioural codes (Wilensky and Wilensky 1951). The Bank Wiring Observation Room study further probed work-group behaviour. For seven months, 14 employees were observed as they wired telephone switching banks. Researchers documented how *informal group norms* replaced formal directives from management. The work team set its own production quotas, making sure that no member worked too quickly or too slowly. Infractions of the group's rules, such as reporting violations of company policy to management, were punished. Generally, strong pressures to conform to the group norms prevailed (Homans 1950: Chapter 3). This particular study was one of the first to highlight the informal side of work organizations (discussed earlier in this chapter) where workers sometimes consciously engage in practices to oppose or subvert established authority.

Assumptions Underlying Human Relations Theory

The human relations perspective on management assumes that workers want to cooperate, in contrast to the utilitarian assumptions of human nature underlying scientific management. Human relations theory emphasizes how workers' attitudes, values, emotions, psychological needs, and interpersonal relationships all shape their work behaviour. Thus, this approach to management seeks the best match between the worker, given her or his personal background and psychological makeup, and the job. Careful recruitment and effective training of employees, as well as good supervision and communication, are therefore essential.

Elton Mayo (1945), a leading early proponent of the human relations approach, saw modern workplaces as a microcosm of larger society. In the same way that productive capitalist enterprises required workers to be aligned with the goals of management, he believed that the survival of society depended on cooperation. So, he advocated a new industrial order run by an administrative elite. These leaders would encourage the development of work environments that would bring out the cooperative "instincts" and productive potential of employees (Mayo 1945). In short, Mayo and other human relations advocates believed that workers needed to be trained and led by managers and corporate leaders, but in a kind and friendly fashion. Human relationships had to be taken into account by managers, and the human needs of workers had to be met within work organizations.

Critics of human relations theory point out how, in general, it assumes that industrial harmony is healthy and that conflict is abnormal and destructive (Burawoy 1979). The approach advocates the close regulation of workers by management and has nothing to say about excessive inequality in power and pay within work organizations, both of which can often lead to conflict (see Chapter 10). Such inconsistency has led some to label human relations theory as an elaborate justification for management's exploitation and manipulation of workers (Rinehart 2006).

The human relations perspective dominated managerial thinking well into the middle of the 20th century. A few proponents pushed the boundaries of the theory by focusing on workers' potential for personal development and growth, in contrast to Elton Mayo's belief that workers simply needed to be treated well by managers and recognized for their contributions to the good of the organization. For example, Douglas McGregor (1960) drew on psychologist Abraham Maslow's concept of a hierarchy of human needs in his discussion of Theory X and Theory Y. He identified Taylorism as a classic example of Theory X because of its mechanistic approach to managing and motivating people, thereby stifling human potential. He contrasted it with Theory Y, which views a manager's main task as creating an environment that allows workers to develop their skills and become more fully involved in the work organization. Unfortunately, the more humanistic Theory Y did little to influence day-to-day management practice when McGregor's book was published more than 50 years ago.

Today, McGregor's ideas are reflected in a number of alternative managerial paradigms that we discuss in Chapter 9. Compared to the mechanistic and authoritarian approach of scientific management, and the paternalistic assumptions of the human relations perspective, these *human resource development* approaches place more emphasis on skill development and, to some extent, decision making by workers (Heil, Bennis, and Stephens 2000). Yet the structures and cultures of most large work organizations still pose major barriers to putting these ideas into practice. In this sense, McGregor's thinking remains futuristic.

■ CONCLUSION

The large hierarchical work organizations that evolved with industrial capitalism were initially considered to be both necessary and efficient. The combination of mass-production factory technology with bureaucratic organizational structures (Fordism) led to huge increases in productivity. But it did not take long for organizational analysts to begin outlining the problems of bureaucracy and, in particular, Fordism. Rigid, mechanistic organizations are slow to change. They can create workplace management cultures in which rules are more important than the larger goals of the organization, as well as informal workgroup norms that encourage workers to act in counterproductive ways. Bureaucratic rules and excessive hierarchies can leave frontline workers feeling relatively powerless and exploited, generating widespread worker dissatisfaction and, sometimes, open conflict.

During the first half of the 20th century, several "modern" management approaches evolved to try to address these problems. Scientific management (Taylorism) was clearly not successful in this regard. Instead, with the excessive division of labour it encouraged, along with the belief that managers (rather than workers) should do all the decision making, it essentially provided the theoretical justification for Fordism. The human relations approach offered an alternative, encouraging managers to think about a work organization as both a social and a technological system, to improve their communication skills, and to treat workers more humanely. But neither perspective had anything to say about reducing workplace inequalities (in material rewards and in power) or about providing workers with opportunities to develop their skills and become involved in decision making.

Scientific management and the human relations approach had different assumptions about what motivates workers (money and feeling part of a group, respectively), but both approaches assumed that workers and management could come to recognize their shared interests and the need to cooperate. The goal was to eliminate conflict, which was considered abnormal. Thus, both approaches can be seen as part of the consensus perspective within sociology (see Chapter 1). In the next chapter, we will examine a variety of newer managerial paradigms that gained popularity in Western industrial economies in the latter part of the 20th century. These approaches also have a consensus (versus a conflict) orientation, but place additional emphasis on encouraging workers to develop their skills and to become more involved in workplace decision-making (Lawler and Mohrman 2003; Becker, Huselid, and Ulrich 2001). Key questions we will be asking include these: Are these newer management approaches effective in solving the problems of bureaucracy? And how well do they address the material and power inequalities that are part of industrial capitalist economies?

DISCUSSION QUESTIONS

1. Organizational analysts have identified many problems with bureaucratic work organizations. In your opinion, which are the most serious problems? Do bureaucracies have any value? Support your view.

2. Universities are workplaces for professors, support staff, and students. Can you point to examples of some of the problems of bureaucracy within universities?

3. Scientific management and human relations theory have been seriously criticized for a variety of different reasons. Outline these criticisms. Are there aspects of these two approaches that are nevertheless useful?

4. Think back to some of the jobs you have held. Can you remember interactions with managers or other experiences that remind you of either scientific management or the human relations approach?

5. What do you thinks motivates people to work hard? Assuming that people differ, at least to some extent, in their work motivations, what might account for these differences?

ADDITIONAL RESOURCES

WORK AT THE MOVIES

- *Modern Times* (directed by Charlie Chaplin, 1936, 87 minutes). In this silent comedy, Chaplin depicts his character, the Little Tramp, struggling to deal with the assembly line and routinized work in a modern factory.
- *The Informant!* (directed by Steven Soderbergh, 2009, 108 minutes). The vice-president of a large agro-business blows the whistle on the company's price-fixing tactics. This film is based on a true story.

- *The Apartment* (directed by Billy Wilder, 1960, 125 minutes). An office worker at a big insurance company is eager to climb the corporate ladder. He does a favour for four company managers in exchange for positive performance reports and the opportunity for a promotion.
- *Working Girl* (directed by Kevin Wade, 1988, 113 minutes). A secretary pretends to be her boss in order to get back at the boss for stealing one of her ideas.

SOUNDS OF WORK

- "9 to 5" (Dolly Parton). Written for the movie *9 to 5*, this song provides a commentary on women's experiences of working in corporate America, including barriers and unfair treatment they face.
- "Boiled Frogs" (Alexisonfire). Apparently inspired by singer George Pettit's observations of his father experiencing no company loyalty in the workplace, this song speaks to the control and coercion that workers in bureaucratic organizations can experience.
- "Takin' Care of Business" (Bachman-Turner Overdrive). The song compares the routinization of white-collar office work with the flexibility that comes with self-employment.

NOTES

1. Morgan (1997: 15–17). This book provides an excellent overview of the multiple images, or metaphors, of organizations found in the literature.
2. See Juillerat (2010) for a carefully argued defence of *formalization* (written rules and procedures) which, she argues, has considerable value in large modern organizations and which need not be accompanied by an excessive division of labour (*specialization*) nor limited decision making by workers (*centralization*). Adler and Borys (1996) distinguish between *enabling formalization*, which assists workers in completing their tasks, and *coercive formalization*, used by management to force workers to act in specific ways.
3. Reich, Robert B. (1991). *The Work of Nations: Preparing Ourselves for 21st-Century Capitalism.* New York: Alfred A. Knopf, p. 51.
4. The work of Trist and the Tavistock Institute is summarized in Pugh, Hickson, and Hinings (1985: 84–91). See also Rankin (1990: Chapter 1).

5. Zuboff, Shoshana. (1988). *In the Age of the Smart Machine: The Future of Work and Power.* New York: Basic Books, p. 389.
6. Four decades after Taylor wrote his highly influential (1911) book, Roy (1952) documented how factory workers were still concealing their real productivity potential from their managers.
7. Another management consultant at the time was W. L. Mackenzie King, who later became Canada's longest-serving prime minister (in office for a total of 22 years in the 1920s, 1930s, and 1940s). In his book *Industry and Humanity*, King (1918) also expressed strong concerns about labour unrest. Unlike some other management consultants at the time, King advocated a central role for government in mediating disputes between employers and unions (see Chapter 11).
8. Taylor, Frederick W. *Industrial Canada,* April 1913, pp. 1224–25.
9. See Locke (1982) for a systematic defence of Taylor's prescriptions for how management techniques could be improved. In contrast, Wrege and Hodgetts (2000) question Taylor's claims of efficiency gains resulting from his scientific management techniques.
10. See Lowe (1987: Chapter 2), Palmer (1979: 216–22), and Craven (1980: 90–110).
11. Classic studies of auto assembly-line workers include Walker and Guest (1952), Beynon (1984), Linhart (1981), and Meyer (1981). Hamper (1986) and De Santis (1999) offer more personal accounts of this type of work.
12. Yet in the 1990s, management at the same Lordstown factory secured workers' consent to reduce the workforce from 12,000 to 3,000 through outsourcing, in the interests of keeping the factory competitive (Sallaz 2004).
13. Jacoby (1997) examines the historical roots of modern human resource management practices in the early-20th-century management ideology of welfare capitalism.
14. Barley and Kunda (1992) provide an excellent description of how managerial ideologies shifted over the course of the 20th century.
15. The research was originally described in Whitehead (1936) and Roethlisberger and Dickson (1939), and has been vigorously debated since then (Franke and Kaul 1978; Sonnenfeld 1985; Jones 1990; Gillespie 1991).
16. This study is the source of the well-known *Hawthorne effect* which concerns psychologists who try to ensure that results of experiments are not confounded by subjects' awareness of being part of a study.

IN SEARCH OF NEW MANAGERIAL PARADIGMS

"I feel fortunate to have the opportunity to work at [*my workplace*] because it is a place where all employees grow, learn, and network amongst co-workers and clients.... The experience ... is so much more than a job, it's an environment to learn valuable business techniques, network with other[s] ... and create family-like relationships with the staff and employers. There are so many skills learnt ... that cannot be taught through a book. Staff receive invaluable training on how to negotiate, perform a sales pitch, and conduct excellent customer service. All of these skills are necessities to be successful.... Because [*my employer*] has been in business since 1918, we get a lot of ... customers that you end up seeing around the city at various events. It's a fantastic opportunity to network and get to know professionals in the city, and hopefully have the opportunity to work with again!"

"The sense of family is a quality that is so unique about [*this*] workplace. You work with the same individuals daily which allows you to create strong bonds that will last a life-time. People stay at [*this workplace*] for a professional lifetime with our longest standing employee.... Having an enjoyable job can be difficult to find, but [*my employer*] creates a comfortable environment for personal and professional growth for years to come!"

Source: Online blog. (August 2013). Courtesy of Michelle McLennan.

● INTRODUCTION

Scientific management and the human relations approach were dominant management strategies for at least the first two-thirds of the 20th century in North America, and even now are still in use. Over the past four decades, however, scores of books about improving management practices have been written, many leaving the impression that large corporations and government departments are in constant upheaval. The large bureaucracies that came to dominate the economic landscape are often portrayed as dinosaurs: cumber-some, slow to respond and adapt, and, according to some critics, a dying breed. Globalization, with increased competition, rapid technological change, and heightened economic uncertainty, has prompted even the most vocal champions of bureaucracy to search for better ways to manage organizations.

Consultants, practising managers, and business school academics have created a growth industry writing books and delivering workshops on changing organizations and management approaches. Together, they have been seeking a new managerial *paradigm*, a different approach to coordinating workplace tasks and gaining compliance from workers, that will assist managers in meeting the challenges of an increasingly global, customer-focused, knowledge-based, technology-dependent economy (Pirson and Lawrence 2010).[1] Tom Peters and Bob Waterman Jr. set the tone in their enormously influential 1982 book, *In Search of Excellence*, in which they documented how rigid, inflexible organizations are less able to survive, let alone grow and profit, in today's rapidly changing economy (Peters and Waterman 1982). Despite the fact that many of Peters and Waterman's "excellent" firms later experienced problems, these writers fuelled debates about the need to rethink old ways of organizing and managing derived from the legacies of Weber, Taylor, and Ford. In this respect, the *new management literature* corresponds with the sociological critique of bureaucracy, outlined in Chapter 8. While some of the many management self-help books are not all that original or useful,[2] several quite different approaches to organizing workplaces and managing workers have nevertheless emerged. In this chapter, we will review them in turn, while also highlighting some of the criticisms these approaches have received.

▉ RECONSTRUCTING BUREAUCRACY

We will see several central themes in the discussion of new managerial paradigms in this chapter. The first is *decentralization of authority*. For example, Canadian management expert Henry Mintzberg (1989: Chapter 11) is a proponent of *adhocracy*, an organizational form with a fluid and decentralized operating structure. This approach contrasts with the inflexibility of what Mintzberg calls the "machine organization," or traditional bureaucracy, and even with the "entrepreneurial organization," which is too performance oriented. The work of an adhocracy is performed by multidisciplinary teams. Hierarchical top-down control, rigid lines of authority, and narrow job functions are replaced by a *matrix structure*, which enables experts to move between functional units for specialized administrative tasks and multidisciplinary project teams.

This description of an alternative organizational form reflects a second, but related core theme, the *flattening of organizational structures*, or the removal of some of the many layers of a traditional bureaucracy. In contrast, Max Weber's ideal bureaucracy was a highly hierarchical vertical structure, which critics claim cannot easily meet today's needs for product and service quality.

Mintzberg's analysis also highlights a third core theme—*flexibility*—the ability to adapt quickly to changing economic and social environments. Peter F. Drucker (1993: 59), the dean of management gurus, develops the same idea by arguing that, in a knowledge- and technology-based economy, successful organizations continuously change and renew themselves.

Frank Ostroff (1999) makes some of the same points but also suggests a fourth key theme: the *emphasis on customers or clients*. Ostroff is an advocate of horizontal organizations in which "the emphasis shifts from top down to focusing across at customers, from compliance with executive orders to meaningful participation in the production of customer satisfaction, quality, and team excellence"—all of which is essential in "today's radically different business world" (Ostroff 1999: 74).

In *Thriving on Chaos: Handbook for a Management Revolution*, Tom Peters (1987) refers to the same core themes but also draws attention to two more: the *empowerment of workers* (not just managers) and the *embracing* (not avoidance) *of change* by corporate leaders and managers. His model of what he calls a "winner" is based on five sets of characteristics: (1) an obsession with responsiveness to customers; (2) constant innovation in all areas; (3) the full participation and empowerment of all people connected with the organization; (4) leadership that loves change and promotes an inspiring vision; and (5) non-bureaucratic control by simple support systems.

In Chapter 8, we noted the importance of listening to what managers say they do, while also watching what they really do. In the same way, while reading about new managerial paradigms in this chapter, we need to continue to ask ourselves whether management practices have changed all that much, a point clearly made by management professor Gary Hamel (2007) in *The Future of Management*. Like some other critics, Hamel points to the persistence of bureaucracy and a preoccupation with reinventing business processes, such as logistics and customer support, rather than how things are actually managed. Hamel identifies Google, however, as an innovative organization that has gone considerably further:

> What makes Google unique, though, is less its Web-centric business model than its brink-of-chaos management model. Key components include a wafer-thin hierarchy, a dense network of lateral communication, a policy of giving outsized rewards to people who come up with outsized ideas, a team-focused approach to product development, and a corporate credo that challenges every employee to put the user first.[3]

But we need to recognize that Google may be an "outlier," rather than an example of a trend toward post-bureaucratic organizations.

In the remainder of this chapter, we will highlight the strengths and advantages of new approaches to organizing workplaces and managing workers, while also retaining a critical stance, asking why managers have implemented changes and if they have really made a significant difference. We will discuss the different approaches chronologically, that is, in the order that they were developed and became well known. As will become apparent, the history of new management paradigms has not necessarily been one of steady forward progress. Some of the more recent "innovations" might, in fact, be seen as steps back toward Taylorism.

JAPANESE MANAGEMENT

To better understand the social origins of the new managerial paradigms, we need to go back almost 70 years and leave North America. By the end of World War II, the Japanese military had been crushed by the Allied forces and the country's economy was a disaster. But over the next four decades, Japan grew to become a global economic powerhouse, developing a technology-driven, export-focused manufacturing industry that produced high-quality products.[4] The competition from Japan caused North American manufacturers to rethink their traditional ways of producing automobiles, appliances, and electronic goods, and the global success of Japanese corporations led many to conclude that their management systems, industrial organization, and technology were superior. Sociologists have asked whether the Japanese industrial system can be best explained by theories of social and economic organization, facilitating its adoption elsewhere, or whether the explanation lies in Japanese culture and history, in which case, application outside Japan would be difficult (Lincoln and McBride 1987; Jacoby 2005; Morita 2001). It is generally concluded that Japanese culture and history are less important than principles of industrial organization and management (Lincoln 1990).

The Japanese Employment System

The four basic elements of the Japanese management approach, which typically are found only in the major corporations, include (1) highly evolved internal labour markets (discussed in Chapter 5), with features such as lifetime employment (*nenko*), seniority-based wages and promotions, and extensive training; (2) a division of labour built around workgroups rather than specific positions, a feature that is the basis for the well-known quality circles; (3) a consensual, participative style of decision making involving all organizational levels (*ringi*); and (4) high levels of employee commitment and loyalty. As we will see later in this chapter, some but not all of these elements were adopted by management approaches that emerged closer to the end of the 20th century.

The core of the Japanese work organization is the *internal labour market*. Japanese employers strive to maintain a well-functioning internal labour market and to obtain a high level of employee commitment to the firm over the long term (Lincoln and McBride 1987). Teams share responsibility and accountability. When this is coupled with the consensus-building networking process used to make decisions, it is easy to see how individual workers are typically well integrated in their workplace. Japanese corporate decision-making combines centralized authority in the hands of executives who bear final responsibility for decisions with consultations that ensure everyone has some input. On the shop floor, participation commonly takes the form of *quality circles* (QCs). Made famous by Toyota, quality circles are now common in Japanese industry. Some, such as those at Toyota, are essential to maintaining and improving high levels of quality. Yet, others "may be little more than collective suggestion-making exercises, imposed by management, for which workers receive little training" (Lincoln and McBride 1987: 300).

Even so, quality circles represent a potentially useful approach to worker participation. As Stephen Wood (1989a) explains, workers' *tacit skills*, or intuitive expertise about how to do their job, are being utilized. Workers' informal expertise is crucial for overcoming the bugs in many new information technology systems. Quality circles and other forms of worker participation enlarge workers' overall knowledge of the business, sharpen their analytical and diagnostic skills, and can keep them more engaged with company goals. What is innovative about Japanese organization, then, is how it harnesses the tacit skills and latent talents of workers.

Probably the peak performance of this Japanese model of management occurred in the 1970s. Even then, the model was subject to criticism, for example, for the stifling of individual creativity through *nenko* and groupism; discrimination against non-permanent employees, particularly women; labour market rigidities that made the horizontal movement of workers among firms difficult; and long hours of work often at an intense pace (Kamata 1983). Japanese industry faced a barrage of new challenges in the 1980s and 1990s, including a prolonged recession, which altered its employment system (Whittaker 1990). In the decades following, the adoption of quality-enhancing work practices was inconsistent among the dozens of suppliers that manufacture components for Japan's major exporting firms—as became evident with the massive Toyota recall of defective automobiles in 2010. Additional stimuli for change included an aging workforce, changing attitudes of young workers influenced by Western culture, and the growing number of women workers. The seniority principle has given way to other means of rewarding and motivating workers. And the mobility of workers during their careers and across firms is increasing. It will be interesting to see whether this restructuring signals a growing convergence of Japanese and North American approaches to organizing and managing work.

The Japanese Approach in North America

How far have these Japanese management and organizational innovations infiltrated North America? Some organizational design concepts, particularly Toyota's *just-in-time* (JIT) system of parts delivery, have been readily adapted for use outside Japan. The JIT system reduces inventory overhead costs, forges a stronger alliance between a firm and its suppliers, makes it easier to change production specifications, and does not require major changes in job design. However, JIT parts delivery assumes a smoothly operating transportation system. For example, in the wake of the September 2001 terrorist attacks in the United States, a number of manufacturing firms, including auto plants in Canada, had to shut down for days because they quickly ran out of parts when the border closed and trucks were held up.

Quality circles, or QCs, have become fairly popular among North American firms facing global competition. Nevertheless, they do not go as far as delegating authority to autonomous work teams, a Swedish approach to management that we discuss later in this chapter. Quality circles generally place responsibility for monitoring quality and troubleshooting problems on production workers without a parallel expansion of their authority or increased rewards.[5]

The obvious place to look for the successful adaptation of Japanese employment techniques is in *Japanese transplants* (local plants owned and operated by Japanese firms) or in Japanese joint ventures with North American firms. We find mixed results. At one end of the continuum is the NUMMI plant in California, a unionized joint venture between Toyota and General Motors. Using methods imported by Toyota, employees work in teams and contribute ideas, although the daily management style is distinctly American (Kanter 1989: 274). However, the norm in transplants or joint ventures may be much closer to what Ruth Milkman (1991) observed in Japanese transplants in California. These workplaces closely resembled American firms employing nonunion labour. Few had introduced quality circles, and many local managers were unfamiliar with the principles of Japanese work organization or management approaches (Milkman 1991). These firms' employment strategies mainly emphasized cost reduction, leading them to take full advantage of low-wage immigrant labour.

Canada has numerous Japanese-owned plants, most notably the Honda and Toyota factories in Ontario. Managers at these plants have had to develop a hybrid system, modifying aspects of the Japanese approach in a way acceptable to Canadian workers (Walmsley 1992). The major success story among Japanese transplants is Toyota's Cambridge, Ontario, plant, which produces award-winning Corollas. From the Toyota workers' point of view, benefits include job flexibility, free uniforms, consensus decision-making, teamwork, good pay, and job security. However, there are drawbacks, including regular required overtime, open offices for managers, no replacement workers for absent team members, health problems, close scrutiny of absenteeism and lateness, and only selective implementation of employee suggestions. Despite efforts by the Canadian Auto Workers (CAW) to organize this Toyota facility, it remains nonunion.

● SWEDISH WORK REFORMS

With quality circles and some input by workers into decision making about their immediate job tasks, Japanese management approaches moved beyond the human relations approach that focused primarily on treating workers humanely and providing them with good working conditions (see Chapter 8). So, too, did North American quality-of-working-life initiatives (discussed below), which focused on job enlargement, job enrichment, and autonomous work teams. However, neither Japanese management systems nor quality-of-working-life programs went as far toward redistributing power relationships within work organizations and reducing bureaucratic hierarchies as did Swedish work reforms.

It is generally agreed that the potential of work humanization has been most fully realized in Sweden, which pioneered work reforms more than 40 years ago. Decades of social democratic government, a strong organized labour movement, and legislation giving individuals the right to meaningful jobs provide fertile ground for the humanistic work reforms that have taken place in Sweden.

The widely publicized Volvo Kalmar plant, which opened in the early 1970s, is based on a *sociotechnical work design* (a concept discussed in Chapter 8). The Volvo assembly line was replaced by battery-powered robot carriers, which automatically move car bodies to different work teams, each of which is responsible for a phase of assembly. Productivity and quality improved, but a major limitation of the Kalmar plant's sociotechnical design was that a computer (not teams) controlled the movement of the carriers and short task cycles. Most jobs provided little scope for personal development or for the use of skills and initiative. Workers still complained that their jobs were boring.

Volvo's Uddevalla factory, which opened in 1989 and shut in 1993 due to a market downturn, resolved some of these problems by pushing sociotechnical design much further. Small work teams were able to build entire cars at ergonomically designed stationary work locations. By comparison with other

Volvo facilities, this plant achieved high levels of quality, productivity, and worker satisfaction.

Another solution to the alienating monotony of assembly-line work can be found in Saab's main auto plant at Trollhattan. The body-assembly shop faced problems typical in mass production—high turnover and absenteeism, low quality, widespread dissatisfaction, and a numbingly fast work pace. Reforms initiated in the early 1970s sought to improve the work environment, make jobs intrinsically more satisfying, and boost productivity. As at Volvo, the local union played an active role.

Some remarkable changes were observed. The assembly line was eliminated. *Autonomous work teams* were created to devote about 45 minutes at a time to completing an integrated cycle of tasks. Robots took over arduous, repetitive welding jobs. In the welding area, groups of 12 workers controlled the entire production process, which involved programming the computers and maintaining the robots, ensuring quality control, performing related administrative work, and cleaning up their workspace. Buffer zones allowed teams to build up an inventory of completed bodies, giving them greater flexibility over how they used their time. Skill development, new learning opportunities, and a broader approach to job design provided the teams with what Saab calls "control and ownership" of their contribution to the production process. Far from being victims of work degradation and deskilling through robotics, these Saab employees were the beneficiaries of upgraded job content and greater decision-making autonomy.[6] Since productivity also increased with these work reforms, both employees and employers benefited (Kochan and Osterman 1994).

■ NORTH AMERICAN QUALITY-OF-WORKING-LIFE PROGRAMS

Quality of working life (QWL) became a buzzword among North American managers, academics, and consultants during the 1970s. *Quality of working life* is an umbrella term covering many different strategies for humanizing work, improving employee–employer cooperation, redesigning jobs, and giving employees somewhat greater participation in management. The underlying goal has been to improve employee satisfaction, motivation, and commitment. The expected payoffs are higher productivity, better quality products, and bigger profits. Proponents have argued that employers and employees alike will benefit (Levine 1995). However, as we will see, QWL programs have seldom gone as far toward sharing power within work organizations as did the Swedish work reforms.

Quality of working life has diverse intellectual roots. Its core ideas came from Japanese management systems, Swedish studies on work reform, the Tavistock Institute's sociotechnical systems approach to job design, and Norwegian Einar Thorsrud's experiments on self-managing groups. In addition, psychologist Frederick Herzberg's theory that work is satisfying only if it meets employees' psychological growth needs and Douglas McGregor's "Theory Y" (see Chapter 8) were influential in shaping this *human resource management* perspective that went quite far beyond human relations theory, discussed in the previous chapter (Oldham and Hackman 2010).[7]

QWL Techniques

A quick overview of some of the major QWL techniques, some directly borrowed from Japanese and Swedish approaches, would be useful. *Job enlargement* is meant to expand a job horizontally, adding related tasks to put more variety into the work done by an individual worker. *Job enrichment* goes further by combining operations before and after a task to create a more complex and unified job. For example, in the case of a machine operator in a clothing factory, job enrichment might mean that the operator is now responsible for obtaining necessary materials, doing the administrative work associated with different production runs, and maintaining the machines. This change might not be enormous, but it would lead to a somewhat more varied, demanding, and responsible job. *Job rotation* involves workers moving through a series of work stations, usually at levels of skill and responsibility similar to their original task. This tactic is frequently used to inject variety into highly repetitive, monotonous jobs. When job rotation is combined with more fundamental redesign strategies (especially the use of work teams), an employee can develop a considerable range of new skills.

An *autonomous work team* consists of about a dozen employees who are delegated collective authority to decide on work methods, scheduling, inventory, and quality control. They might also perform what previously would have been supervisory tasks, such as administration, discipline, and even hiring. *Quality circles*, or QCs, with a narrower mandate of having workers monitor and correct defects in products or services, are perhaps the best-known application of the team concept. But quality circles often fall short of redistributing authority to rank-and-file workers.

By the late 1980s, the team concept had become quite common in some industries, and Canadian auto production plants were embracing quality or "employee involvement" schemes to varying degrees (Robertson and Wareham 1987). Interest in QWL techniques continued into the 1990s (Leckie et al. 2001).

The flagship of the North American QWL movement, however, was Shell's chemical plant in Sarnia, Ontario (Rankin 1990). When the plant was built in the late 1970s, it was unique in North America: union and management had actively collaborated in its sociotechnical planning and design (Reimer 1979). Furthermore, it was a "greenfield site," a completely new facility that offered greater scope for innovative work arrangements. Shell's goal was a "post-bureaucratic organization"—suitable for the continuous-process technology used in the petrochemical industry—that would facilitate employee control, learning, and participation.

Six teams of 20 workers ran the plant around the clock, 365 days a year. Along with two coordinators, a single team operated the entire plant during a shift and was even responsible for hiring new team members when vacancies occurred. Teams were supported by technical, engineering, and managerial personnel, along with a group of maintenance workers, who also taught team members craft skills. The organizational structure was flat, having only three authority levels from top to bottom. Team members had no job titles, and they rotated tasks. Pay was based on knowledge and skills obtained through job training. It took about six years of training for an operator to reach the maximum pay level.

Compared to traditional bureaucracies, this innovative organizational design empowered workers and allowed them to apply and develop their skills. Continuous-process technology may lend itself more readily to this approach because of the huge capital investment per worker and the enormous losses to the firm should the system malfunction (Blauner 1964). Thus, management has a strong economic incentive to obtain a high level of employee commitment. Summing up, this sociotechnical organizational design seemed to have achieved its objectives: a high level of production efficiency, smoothly functioning teams, and mutually beneficial collaboration between union and management (Halpern 1984: 58–59).

QWL Critiques

The Shell experience, however, appears to be atypical. The union's involvement came only after guarantees that it would be a full partner in the QWL process and that its ability to represent the interests of employees would not be undermined. It is noteworthy that members of the same union at an adjacent, older refinery wanted nothing to do with QWL techniques. But the story of innovation at Shell's Sarnia plant is now history, because a change in management ushered in more traditional work organization and management systems. It is not unusual for work redesign initiatives to be abandoned when top management changes, especially if the new managers are mainly concerned about costs.

Overall, efforts to reform workplaces with QWL techniques generated heated debate between advocates—usually managers and consultants—and critics, who were often trade unionists. Research revealed that not all team-based production and employee participation initiatives necessarily led to improved working conditions (Milkman 1997). Frequently, changes in workers' job tasks were minimal. They did not gain the opportunity to influence decisions on larger workplace changes (the introduction of new technology, for example), and management imposed the programs rather than involving the workers in the decision (Robertson and Wareham 1987; Rinehart 2006: Chapter 6). Some critics have charged that QWL and other new management approaches are simply ways of encouraging workers to work harder and faster.

In the United States, some researchers have linked an increase in occupational injuries and illnesses (carpal tunnel syndrome, for example) to the increased prevalence of quality circles and JIT delivery systems (Askenazy 2001; Brenner, Farris, and Ruser 2004).

In Canada, the smorgasbord of QWL programs introduced by employers has resulted in both successes and failures (Lowe 2000). On the negative side, some QWL experiments resulted in declining work performance, heightened union–management tensions, employee dissatisfaction, and a breakdown in communication. Alternatively, in Canada, as well as in other Western industrial democracies, positive effects have included higher employee satisfaction and commitment (Gallie 2013), higher earnings, improved labour relations, and sometimes productivity gains. As the example of Shell's Sarnia plant demonstrates, the context into which changes are introduced, the level of management commitment to fundamental reform, and the involvement (or not) of organized labour will all strongly influence outcomes.

On the whole, autonomous work teams appear to have the greatest potential for significantly reallocating decision-making power, as well as for creating more interesting, challenging, socially integrated, and skilled work. Why, then, has the Canadian labour movement often been a vocal critic of QWL techniques? The drawback for unions is that management frequently has used the QWL approach cynically, to circumvent collective agreements, rationalize work processes, and co-opt workers into solving problems of quality and productivity. The QWL approach has often been used to undermine union bargaining power and spearhead labour relations schemes intended to keep firms union-free. Thus, from organized labour's perspective, gains in the quality of working life are best achieved through collective bargaining (see Chapter 11).

◼ TOTAL QUALITY MANAGEMENT

Total quality management (TQM) followed on the heels of the QWL movement, adopting some of its techniques but placing most of its emphasis on quality control and customer satisfaction. In one way, this approach was North American management's response to the competitive edge Japanese firms had gained in the 1980s through an obsession with product quality. However, its roots lie in the U.S. government's efforts to set quality standards for suppliers to the Defense Department during World War II and the pioneering work of American statistician W. Edwards Deming on quality control systems, which Japanese firms readily adopted (Aguayo 1990).

Total quality management advocates a customer-based emphasis on quality. "Customers" can be external consumers; citizens, in the case of public-sector organizations; or other units or individuals within the organization (internal customers). With its emphasis on continuous improvement, the TQM approach focuses on involving employees in identifying and quickly resolving problems, or anticipating future problems. Like other management schools, there is no unifying model. Some perspectives on total quality management complement ideas on organizational learning, reviewed below, because quality depends on more learning and creativity among employees (Argyris 1999). In addition to quality control systems, typical TQM elements include performance measures, improved communications and feedback systems, problem-solving work teams, employee involvement, and a culture of trust and cooperation (Clarke and Clegg 1998: 254–65). TQM champions claim that the model reduces costs and increases productivity, customer satisfaction, quality of working life, and firm competitiveness.

Six Sigma, pioneered by General Electric (GE), the giant manufacturing and financial services conglomerate, is an example of a TQM-influenced production system. Since the 1980s, GE has focused on developing a workplace culture that looks at all business processes from the customers' perspective (more on this later in the chapter). Addressing this required reducing bureaucracy, breaking down rigid boundaries, and encouraging workers to bring forward ideas about what needed improving. As the GE website explains: Six Sigma "is not a secret society, a slogan or a cliché. Six Sigma is a highly disciplined process that helps us focus on developing and delivering near-perfect products and services."[8] Six Sigma is a statistical concept describing the goal of 3.4 defects per million opportunities for each product or service: it means striving for virtual perfection. As at Toyota, at GE, quality is the responsibility of every employee. It is achieved, in part, by extensive measurement of all work processes, guided by "Black Belt" team leaders who relentlessly seek opportunities to improve processes that will increase customer satisfaction and strengthen productivity (Devane 2004).

Total quality management has also been adopted by some employers in the service industries, retail and hospitality, in particular. For example, the luxury hotel and resort chain Four Seasons focuses on creating the highest-quality guest experience by training and enabling all employees to do whatever they can to provide exceptional service (Sharp 2009). Best Buy, a consumer electronics chain, introduced what it calls a Results Only Work Environment, or ROWE. While not described as a TQM experiment, the organizational changes implemented nevertheless fit the model. The ROWE premise is that work performance should be measured by results, not by hours and "face-time." Employees working in teams are given responsibility for delivering results and figuring out the best ways to do so. Doing this may involve changing working hours and locations, without management's permission. A study conducted at Best Buy's U.S. head office showed that individuals in ROWE teams reported improved health and well-being, and increased job satisfaction (Moen, Kelly, and Chermack 2008). A second retailer, Gap Inc., implemented ROWE and documented reduced employee turnover and modest improvements in productivity and production quality, engagement, and quality of working life (Conlin 2009).

Assessing the TQM Approach

TQM programs have been heralded by proponents as a "win-win" approach to labour–management relations: workers benefit through improved working conditions, and productivity increases (Pfeffer 1994: Chapter 9). As with other management trends, however, it is sometimes difficult to sort out real change from the rhetoric. Some skeptics view total quality management, or TQM, as just a catchy label applied to a particular set of customer service initiatives with the help of computers (Micklethwait and Wooldridge 1996: 26). Nevertheless, it does seem that, if a quality-improvement strategy is part of a comprehensive set of high-performance work practices (discussed below), then there is a higher likelihood of tangible movement toward less bureaucracy, greater customer responsiveness, organizational flexibility, and employee participation (Rosenthal, Hill, and Peccei 1997). For example, two of the winners of a national U.S. quality award, Xerox Corporation and Milliken & Company (a textile manufacturer), invest heavily in employee training and use teams extensively; however, systematic analysis is needed to determine how specific changes contribute to measurable improvements in quality.

One example of this kind of analysis can be found in the health care sector, where, in some hospitals, patients are treated as "customers," and quality committees rethink processes and procedures in order to improve the quality of patient care and to cut costs. A study of the introduction of total quality management at an Edmonton hospital found much of the program counterproductive: it was linked in employees' minds with the downsizing of the organization, which was happening at the same time. Increased workloads, reduced competence resulting from multi-skilling, and the overall impact of doing more with less created "role ambiguity, conflicts and demoralization"— with potentially negative effects on health care costs and quality (Lam and Reshef 1999: 741).

Thus, as with other major shifts in management approaches, there is often resistance at various levels within an organization to the introduction of TQM practices, largely because they may be perceived as disrupting the existing power structure. Middle managers balk at the idea of empowering employees, knowing that it is their own power that will be redistributed downward. Employees and unions may resist, viewing total quality management as yet another attempt by management to co-opt and control workers (Sewell 1998), and to avoid unions. Employees may also have trouble with such vague goals as "continuous improvement," which suggests that their best efforts today may not be good enough tomorrow. As we noted with respect to QWL initiatives, workers in organizations employing TQM approaches are seldom invited to participate in decisions about whether to introduce new technologies, or to restructure or downsize organizations. Instead of being truly empowered, critics point out, workers have been invited to find ways to work harder, often in an atmosphere of anxiety about possible job loss (Zbaracki 1998). Consequently, promises of improved working conditions have frequently translated into only superficial changes (McCabe 1999).

◼ MANAGING VIA ORGANIZATIONAL CULTURE

During the 1980s when TQM techniques were being adopted in a range of large North American workplaces both in the private and public sectors, a parallel management literature emphasizing *organizational culture* also emerged (Martin 2002; Schein 2004). It drew on one aspect of the Japanese management literature, namely, the assumption (that we questioned earlier) that Japan's unique culture and history led to workers being more engaged with company goals.[9] Compared to Japanese teamwork approaches, Swedish work reforms, and QWL initiatives, though, it placed relatively little emphasis on redesigning jobs to get workers more involved and on giving them more decision-making opportunities. Instead, the organizational culture approach focused primarily on finding ways to align the values of workers with the goals of management, thus hoping to get them to motivate themselves and work harder (Barley and Kunda 1992). Thus, in many ways, it more closely resembled the human relations approach to management (see Chapter 8). In Amitai Etzioni's (1975) typology, it would be seen as an attempt to gain normative control over workers.

Large workplaces can be viewed as mini-societies in which organizational culture—shared beliefs, customs, rituals, languages, and myths—serves as "social glue," binding together the diverse elements of the organization. *Culture*, then, refers to a system of shared meanings about how organizational life ought to be conducted. It can also reflect how things get done at an informal level (Morgan 1997: Chapter 5). Shaping the *dominant culture* of an organization—that is, encouraging employees to identify strongly with the goals of the corporation—is central to the organizational culture approach to management. So, too, is keeping workplace *countercultures*, with dissenting norms and values, from gaining strength (the informal side of organizations is discussed in Chapter 8).

Senior managers may seek to "brand" their organization by marketing their company's core values. Toyota's commitment to quality (Liker 2004), the Body Shop's emphasis on social responsibility, and Benetton's focus on cultural diversity and environmental protection are examples. By so doing, these companies are trying to recruit customers who presumably share these values. They are also trying to shape the values of current employees and to recruit employees with shared values. Companies may also try to reinforce corporate identity by maintaining a mythology about organizational founders and legendary past leaders: the Dave Thomas ads used by the Wendy's burger chain are an example. Baseball hats, coffee mugs, and other items with company logos distributed to employees can be used for the same purpose. Rituals such as award dinners, where employees' achievements are recognized, and the giving of "employee of the month" citations, such as McDonald's does, also promote organizational culture.

Some management experts strongly believe that it is possible for workplaces to become "collaborative communities," grounded on a shared ethic of interdependent contributions (Adler and Heckscher 2006). However, the belief that a workplace could have a single unitary corporate culture, fashioned by management to gain employee commitment to goals they had little say in setting, greatly oversimplifies the nature of organizational life. In fact, most organizations have a variety of cultures—dominant and alternative—depending on the degree to which particular groups within them share similar work experiences and similar values. This cultural fragmentation can result in organizations saying one thing in their philosophy or mission statement, while their day-to-day operations reflect something quite different. In some cases, it has led to managers trying to stifle dissent and the expression of legitimate concerns by employees (Ray 1986).

Research suggests that more successful companies will promote "core values" while still encouraging smaller workgroup cultures that support performance in ways that overall corporate values or codes of conduct cannot (Collins and Porras 1994). A study of Xerox photocopier repair technicians found, for example, that this group devised their own elaborate oral culture that efficiently circulated stories with vital information on how to fix these idiosyncratic machines (Orr 1996). The oral culture was invisible to senior managers, who planned technicians' work on the incorrect assumption that corporate standards of design excellence ensured predictable machine operations.

Overall, when assessing management via organizational culture alongside the other new managerial paradigms that have been promoted over the past four decades, it is difficult to accept the strong claims by organizational culture consultants that their approach is the primary explanation for successful work organization (Collins and Porras 1994; Stubblefield 2005). Promoting a unified core culture and incorporating smaller workgroup cultures is part of the solution to the problems of bureaucracy but, as suggested earlier, this approach does not take us far past the human relations approach to management. Redesigning jobs to add rather than remove skills, and involving workers in decision making at various levels within the organization, are also critically important.

● LEARNING ORGANIZATIONS

In his discussions of *learning organizations*, Peter Senge (1990) brings this emphasis back into the managerial equation. He argues that, in order to gain and keep a competitive advantage in the rapidly changing global economy, companies need to develop a learning culture that takes advantage of and enhances employees' knowledge and skills. Better-trained workers will make an organization more adaptable, innovative, and flexible. Thus, unlike organizational culture proponents who hope to get everyone in an organization committed to its success, Senge's ideal workplace is one in which learning for its own sake becomes a valued and rewarded process that employees have the autonomy to pursue.[10] In a sense, from Senge's perspective, learning comes before earning (or productivity).

Senge proposes that both employees and organizations follow five "learning disciplines": (1) expanding your personal abilities and enabling others to do so; (2) breaking out of old ways of thinking; (3) developing a shared vision of the future; (4) team learning; and (5) holistic or systems thinking. These abstract principles are understandable, more or less, with respect to individual employees or work teams engaged in "personal mastery" through skill development and knowledge acquisition. As Senge argues, such workers or teams are better able to "embrace change" and, hence, increase productivity. It is less clear, however, what exactly it takes for a traditional work organization to become a learning organization (Popper and Lipshitz 2000), one that is "skilled at creating, acquiring, interpreting, transferring, and retaining knowledge, and at purposefully modifying its behavior to reflect new knowledge and insights" (Garvin 2000: 11).

Some firms claim to have developed a learning culture. For example, at Harley-Davidson Motorcycles, "intellectual curiosity" is a core value, "Harley University" offers extensive training programs, and the president promotes learning at every opportunity (Gephart et al. 1996: 39). Even so, it could be argued that Harley-Davidson simply has made greater investments in training, communicating this as a new value commitment. Training-intensive organizations, where skills are increased by regular on-site programs or through support for off-site courses, are clearly an improvement over Taylorist workplaces, where jobs are deskilled, but they go only part way to ensuring that individuals regularly engage in learning as they do their job and can apply and share that learning (Betcherman, McMullen, and Davidman 1998). Thus, creating a learning organization remains an ideal, perhaps because the concept is overly abstract (Argote 1999). Even so, Senge and other champions of organizational learning promote a humanistic vision of self-development and self-learning in organizations, quite the opposite to the mechanistic organizational models described by Weber and created by Taylor and Henry Ford.

● FLEXIBLE WORK ORGANIZATIONS

Standardized mass-production techniques were the hallmark of industrial capitalism for much of the past century. However, assembly-line mass production of standardized goods has become much less economically viable, and *flexible specialization* has become a preferred production model in some industries. Flexible production systems use computers to link all aspects of production into a coordinated whole. Much smaller product runs are possible than with assembly-line systems, and because sales trends and consumer tastes are closely monitored, changes in design or product lines can readily be made. Computers also reduce stock-control costs (zero inventory) and improve product quality (zero defects).

Describing the early success of northern Italian consumer goods firms employing this type of production system, Piore and Sabel sketched out a positive view of the future of manufacturing:

> Flexible specialization is a strategy of permanent innovation: accommodation to ceaseless change, rather than an effort to control it. This strategy is based on flexible (multi-use) equipment; skilled workers; and the creation, through politics, of an industrial community that restricts the forms of competition to those favouring innovation.[11]

Piore and Sabel also predicted that, as flexible specialization came to replace traditional assembly-line manufacturing, small firms would gain an advantage over huge companies. They believed that skilled workers employed in flexible specialization systems would gain more power relative to managers and employers. In a sense, they envisioned a return to craft forms of production (Chapter 1), with highly skilled, autonomous workers involved in all aspects of the production process.

There is evidence of an increase in flexible, computerized manufacturing systems, but it is unlikely that the full range of manufacturing industries can and will move in this direction. For example, in the late 1990s, Internet and multimedia firms began to spring up throughout North America and Europe, usually run by young, anti-bureaucratic entrepreneurs. These employers encouraged their creative employees to work in project-based teams, ignore conventional organizational structure, as in working regular hours, avoid workplace hierarchies, and essentially, "be their own bosses." While the term *flexible specialization* was not applied to these "blue jean companies," the model of management reflected the same values. However, in time, many of these small firms were bought by multinational information technology companies and folded into larger, more traditionally bureaucratic organizations. The limited research on the companies that stayed relatively small suggests that, in a short time, they too began to evolve into more hierarchical workplaces (Mayer-Ahuja and Wolf 2007).

Thus, Piore and Sabel's predictions of a shifting balance of power between workers and management, and between small firms and huge multinationals, appear to have been more in the realm of hope than of reality.[12] As Stephen Wood notes in a detailed assessment of the flexible specialization model, this part of the theory is really "an intellectual manifesto," a description of the type of workplace that Piore and Sabel believe would be preferable (Wood 1989b: 13). In a way, Piore and Sabel's optimistic predictions are reminiscent of the postindustrial society theorists, such as Daniel Bell, who were convinced that general skill levels would increase while inequality declined (Chapter 2) and of Gerhard Lenski's argument that modern technologies are associated with a decline in inequality (Chapter 8).

While evidence of a significant shift toward flexible specialization in manufacturing is limited, many employers in both the manufacturing and service sectors have reorganized their workforces to gain greater flexibility and to reduce payroll costs, building what some have called a *flexible firm* (Pollert 1988; Kalleberg 2001). Frequently, these employer initiatives have involved greater reliance on part-time or part-year workers, and temporary or contract employees. In Canada, over the past decade, we have also seen a significant shift toward employment of temporary foreign workers, as governments have sought ways of allowing private-sector firms to become more flexible (Arai 2007). Thus, the economic uncertainties experienced by employers in the past several decades have also meant an increase in *nonstandard jobs* for their employees (Chapter 4). Flexibility is also one of the goals of corporate outsourcing and off-shoring of jobs in the global labour market. All of these trends are associated with greater employment insecurity and increased work-place inequality (Chapter 5).

This more flexible type of work organization, with a core of full-time workers and a periphery of low-cost nonstandard workers whose numbers and functions vary with business conditions, gives companies a competitive advantage in an environment of quickly changing markets and technologies. This adaptability could be achieved three ways: *functional flexibility* (training workers to perform a variety of different tasks, thus making them more interchangeable); *numerical flexibility* (being able to quickly alter the size of the workforce, or the number of hours worked, through hiring of part-time, temporary, subcontracted, and other types of nonstandard workers); and *pay flexibility* (the ability to reduce pay and benefit costs by using alternative wage rates for nonstandard workers and by avoiding traditional collective agreements). Research suggests that

Canadian employers have pursued numerical flexibility and pay flexibility more so than functional flexibility (Macdonald 1991).

● LEAN PRODUCTION

While flexible specialization in manufacturing has not become widespread, *lean production* (LP) has certainly taken hold in North America, particularly in automobile manufacturing.[13] LP manufacturing is an evolution of earlier Japanese management innovations and also total quality management (TQM), in some respects; it is well established in Japanese transplant factories in North America. Lean production uses a team-based approach and advanced production technology to obtain the highest amount of productivity possible. *Re-engineering*, the radical redesign of a firm's entire business process, is used to achieve maximum output and quality with the least labour input (Hammer and Champy 1993: 65–66). A number of specific elements, some discussed earlier in this chapter, characterize lean production: these include continuous improvement (*kaizen*), continuous innovation, flexible production, work teams, zero downtime, zero defects, just-in-time inventories and production, and employment security, at least when unions are involved (Drache 1994).

Lean production is presented by its advocates as a major improvement over mass-production manufacturing and traditional bureaucracy, as a *post-Fordist* approach to organizing work. Case studies of GM's former Saturn plant in Tennessee and the GM–Toyota NUMMI factory in California have assessed these claims. Both factories were victims of GM's bankruptcy in 2009: the Saturn brand was terminated, and GM pulled out of the NUMMI joint venture before Toyota closed the factory in 2010. Still, the assessments of these LP examples remain relevant.

At Saturn, workers and the United Auto Workers union played an active role in all phases of designing the plant (Appelbaum and Batt 1994: Chapter 8), much like what occurred with the Shell chemical plant in Sarnia, discussed earlier. A sociotechnical approach was adopted, integrating technology and the social organization of production. Work teams of 6 to 15 members were self-managed, with responsibility for deciding important issues such as workflow and quality. Teams also managed human resources, including hiring, absenteeism policies, and replacement of absent workers. Saturn employees were paid 80 percent of the industry wage in an annual salary (as opposed to hourly), but they could receive up to an additional 40 percent if production and customer satisfaction goals were met or exceeded. A unique feature was the partnership approach to strategic planning, operating, and problem-solving decisions, whereby managers were "partnered" with elected union representatives. In short, in the Saturn plant, lean production appeared to be acceptable to both management and workers, and productivity and quality appeared to be high.

NUMMI differed from Saturn in that it was an old GM factory plagued with production problems and suffering from labour–management disputes. When it reopened as a GM–Toyota joint venture, a new approach to work organization and human resource management was applied (Pfeffer 1994: Chapter 3). The NUMMI system included extensive employee training, promised job security, teams of multi-skilled workers, reduced status distinctions, an elaborate suggestion system, and extensive sharing of what used to be exclusively management's information. Compared with the old GM factory, this new work system resulted in impressive reductions in absenteeism and grievances, and significantly improved quality and productivity. An employee survey showed 90 percent satisfied or very satisfied with work at NUMMI.

Assessing Lean Production

Both the Saturn and the NUMMI cases demonstrate the potential for lean production to positively alter the worker–management relationship. Lean production goes well beyond the rigid and standardized mass production of Fordism by encouraging a flexible approach to product redesign and maintaining an emphasis on quality and continuous improvement. Like the QWL and TQM approaches, lean production claims to rely on highly skilled and thinking workers, and promises a reduction in workplace conflicts through its teamwork model of decision making. With all of these features, it is little wonder that lean production has been portrayed by its advocates as the final solution to Taylorism and Fordism (Womack, Jones, and Roos 1990).

But the Saturn and NUMMI examples may be outliers. As with previous new management models that arrived with great promise, implementation of lean production in other locations has often omitted some of the most important positive features and exacerbated some of the most problematic. Some critics have been harsh in their assessments of LP's impact on workers' lives (Rinehart, Huxley, and Robertson 1997; Russell 1999).[14] They point out that re-engineering of all the tasks involved in production is reminiscent of Taylorism and that multi-tasking (requiring one person to do several jobs) is not the same as multi-skilling (training them to complete a variety of different tasks). Instead, multi-tasking is one of the ways in which management has squeezed more work out of a smaller number of workers. The elimination of replacement workers, a cost-saving decision, has also had this effect, as has *kaizen*, the consensus-based approach to continuous improvement. By emphasizing how workers in a particular factory need to outperform their competition elsewhere, management essentially harnesses peer pressure to speed up production.

By way of example, James Rinehart describes a California automobile factory that, before lean production, managed to keep its workers busy for 45 out of every 60 seconds they were on the job. Lean production brought this up to 57 out of 60 seconds. As Rinehart puts it, "[t]o call kaizen a democratization of Taylorism is to demean the concept of democracy" (2006: 162). Other critics agree, noting that management continues to tightly control the topics discussed in *kaizen* sessions (Graham 1995). Essentially, lean production has generally not led to significant skill enhancement or to worker empowerment (Yates, Lewchuk, and Stewart 2001) or to increased worker satisfaction (Vidal 2007). But it has meant a faster pace of still repetitive work (Schouteten and Benders 2004), higher stress for employees (Anderson-Connolly et al. 2002; Carter et al. 2013), higher injury rates (Brenner, Farris, and Ruser 2004), and increased concerns about worker health and safety (Landsbergis, Cahill, and Schnall 1999; Spencer and Carlan 2008). Hence, lean production has also led to resistance by workers—the 1992 strike at the CAMI plant in Ingersoll, Ontario, is an example. Thus, as Rinehart (2006: 200) concludes, "lean production constitutes an evolution of rather than a transcendence of Fordism." It therefore can be called "neo-Fordism."

● HIGH-PERFORMANCE WORKPLACES

One of the latest additions to the long list of alternative managerial paradigms hoping to solve the problems of bureaucracy and improve worker–management relationships is the attempt to construct *high-performance workplaces* (Godard 2001, 2004). A high-performance workplace (HPW) is characterized by employee involvement in decision making, team organization and flexible work design, extensive training and learning opportunities, open information sharing and communication, financial incentives for improved performance (including profit sharing), support for family responsibilities, and a work environment that improves health and reduces stress (Kalleberg et al. 2006). In other words, this model of an ideal organization appears to draw on most of the best features of the various other approaches described earlier in this chapter. The HPW approach goes further, however, by advocating human resource management programs that are family friendly and emphasizing the importance of a healthy, non-stressful work environment.[15] But the HPW approach emerged late in the 20th century when many or most large employers were already trying to divest themselves of commitments to lifetime employment for workers. Consequently, the HPW model assumes that employment security can no longer be guaranteed (Betcherman et al. 1994). Furthermore, profit sharing also means risk sharing—if the company loses money, so do the workers. In some respects, the HPW approach is an updated version of the QWL approach in an internal labour market system (see Chapter 5), but with even greater emphasis on employee participation and human resource development for the core of advantaged workers.

Unlike lean production, which has been largely restricted to manufacturing, HPW practices are also adaptable to a range of service industries, as one study of personal care workers suggests (Harley, Allen, and Sargent 2007). A major study of human resource practices in Canadian private-sector workplaces in the early 1990s concluded that, while a high-performance workplace may cost an employer more than traditionally run firms initially, economic performance and worker productivity improved over time (Betcherman et al. 1994). The study also showed that there is no single HPW model. One typical approach emphasizes QWL-style employee participation and enhanced job quality; another focuses more on providing employee incentives through improved performance-based compensation. According to Statistics Canada's Workplace and Employee Survey (WES), in 2005, only 28 percent of Canadian businesses had implemented one or more employee involvement systems associated with high-performance workplaces (Leckie et al. 2001). More specifically, 8 percent of firms were using self-directed teams; 14 percent, some kind of flexible job design; and 17 percent, problem-solving teams. The survey also indicated that the presence of employee involvement systems in companies was associated with higher job satisfaction among employees. Furthermore, firms using an integrated approach to human resource management—combining training, performance-based pay incentives, and employee involvement in decision making—also tended to be more innovative in their products or services (Therrien and Léonard 2003; Mohr and Zoghi 2008).

Assessing High-Performance Workplaces

Like flexible specialization, the high-performance workplace is more a model of a desirable future than a description of current practice. Only a minority of work organizations have moved in this direction, and among those that have, a majority have adopted only some of its core features (Osterman 2000; Koski and Järvensivu 2010). Furthermore, as studies evaluating the effectiveness of the HPW approach accumulate, it is becoming apparent that, in many situations, there are only negligible payoffs.[16] On balance, research points to some productivity gains when "bundles" of HPW practices are introduced, especially if these changes increase employee involvement and skill levels (Appelbaum et al. 2000). As for improved quality of working life, there are clearly potential benefits for the advantaged workers in a high-performance workplace, skill upgrading, decision-making opportunities, profit sharing, and improved working conditions among them. But there are also risks, since employment security can no longer be guaranteed, and profit sharing is only a benefit so long as the company is making a profit.

Critics of the HPW approach are skeptical of the level of commitment asked of workers (Godard 2001; Danford et al. 2004), pointing to previous examples of companies using QWL, TQM, and LP approaches to speed up work and sideline unions. Nevertheless, there are some examples of unions and management working together to build high-performance organizations. Clarke and Haiven (1999) describe how, in Saskatchewan in the 1990s, the Communications, Energy and Paperworkers Union participated in redesigning the Saskatoon Chemicals work organization, including profit sharing and payment for skills. As in other successful union–management projects, what made the difference was a strong union centrally involved in all aspects of the change process. In addition, both parties agreed to a process of *continuous bargaining*, in contrast to the traditional approach of seeking a collective agreement that would remain unchanged for several years.

There have been few efforts to introduce HPW practices in the lower-tier service industries. However, a study of large U.S. retail companies that have attempted this (e.g., Wal-Mart and Home Depot) concludes that workers have not really benefited (Bailey and Bernhard 1997). Wages did not rise appreciably, skill sets were not significantly enhanced, and only a few workers found new career opportunities. HPW organizations, while not widespread, are more likely to be found in the upper-tier services and in some of the goods-producing industries. Thus, the advent of this form of work organization may signal greater labour market segmentation. In fact, downsizing and layoffs have frequently accompanied the implementation of HPW systems (Osterman 2000; Danford et al. 2004). Thus, with more high-performance workplaces, we may also be seeing a further shift toward a society in which a small, privileged elite of highly skilled, relatively autonomous workers are well rewarded while the majority of workers face greater risk of low-skill, less rewarding work with greater employment insecurity (Kashefi 2011). In short, the HPW model does not offer a solution to the larger social problem of growing labour market inequality.

■ CONCLUSION

We began this chapter by commenting on the decades-long search for a new managerial paradigm that will help address the problems of bureaucracy and the dilemmas of managers who are seeking to gain compliance from the workers they supervise. Japanese management approaches and Swedish work reforms provided some significant improvements over scientific management and the human relations approach, as did quality-of-working-life programs that drew on many of the management innovations developed in Japan and Sweden. Most important, they emphasized enhancing the skills of workers and building complexity back into jobs—in contrast to scientific management (Taylorism), which took exactly the opposite approach—and recommended involving workers in decision making in a variety of different ways, something that the human relations approach felt was largely unnecessary.

However, the history of new management approaches has not been one of steady forward progress (Barley and Kunda 1992). Total quality management

(TQM) added a focus on customer satisfaction and on continuous improvement to the recipe for effective modern organizations, and proponents of the learning organization put particular emphasis on enhancing the skills and knowledge of workers. In contrast, the organizational culture approach to gaining compliance from workers and increasing productivity seemed to be taking us back to the human relations model that was so popular in the mid-20th century. Lean production aggressively promoted the skill enhancement and worker involvement central to the QWL and also Japanese and Swedish approaches to management, but also relied on Taylorist re-engineering of all the job tasks in a production system to speed up production and force workers to work harder and faster. The high-performance workplace (HPW) model of management added reducing workplace and work–family stress, along with profit sharing, to the checklist of criteria for effective modern workplaces, but also reminded workers that they should no longer count on job and income security. In addition, like the flexible firm model, it conceded that only a minority of workers could expect to have secure and satisfying employment and that higher social inequality might have to be accepted as the norm in contemporary Western capitalist societies.

So, a century after Taylor promoted scientific management as a solution to the dilemmas of organizing work and motivating workers in large modern workplaces, we have made some progress but not as much as management experts have promised. To some extent, this discrepancy may be a function of what Pfeffer and Sutton (2000) call the "knowing–doing gap." Managers may believe that "employees are their most valuable asset" but face many barriers to acting on this understanding. Furthermore, fads launched by "management-knowledge entrepreneurs" have a short life cycle and are difficult for senior managers to successfully implement (Carson et al. 2000). Workers faced with a succession of "new" approaches to being managed that frequently involve more talk than action might quickly become cynical and reluctant to "buy into" the latest attempt to improve productivity and service (Carter and Mueller 2002).

An alternative explanation of the relatively slow movement forward takes us back to our discussion in Chapter 1 of the *consensus* and *conflict* perspectives used by sociologists when analyzing society. All of the new management approaches we have reviewed in this chapter begin with the assumption that a consensus in the workplace is possible, if we can simply find the right workplace structures and best managerial formulae. In contrast, the more critical assessments of workplace social relationships presented in Chapter 10 are influenced by the conflict approach, which assumes that, in capitalist societies, there are inherent conflicts of interest between employees, on the one hand, and corporate owners and the managers who work for them, on the other. If so, we should perhaps not expect to find ultimate solutions to the problems of bureaucracy and the dilemmas of managing workers in them.

DISCUSSION QUESTIONS

1. Think back to some of the jobs you have held. Describe any interactions with managers or other job experiences that relate to managerial approaches discussed in this chapter.

2. Critically discuss the following statement: "Worker participation in decision making is neither desirable from the point of view of management nor desired by workers."

3. Which of the many approaches to management discussed in this chapter would be most effective at motivating younger workers? Why?

4. Assume that, five years after graduating, you are promoted into a management position with responsibility for 50 employees. Discuss what you have learned from this chapter that could help you be an effective manager.

5. Which of the new managerial paradigms discussed in this chapter have the greatest potential to improve both productivity *and* the quality of working life?

ADDITIONAL RESOURCES

WORK AT THE MOVIES

- *The Internship* (directed by Shawn Levy, 2013, 119 minutes). Made redundant due to technological advancements, two salesmen take internships with Google and cooperate and compete with other younger, tech-savvy interns for a chance at a paying job.
- *Officeland* (directed by Marcy Cuttler, 2014, 45:04 minutes). This documentary addresses the rise of open concept offices and assesses the benefits

and negative aspects of this movement. It is available through CBC Doc Zone: http://www.cbc.ca/doczone/episodes/officeland.

- *The Social Network* (directed by David Fincher, 2010, 120 minutes). The film focuses on Mark Zuckerberg and the development of Facebook and its unique organizational culture.

- *Gung Ho* (directed by Ron Howard, 1986, 111 minutes). Michael Keaton plays a manager who is tasked with helping the workers at his U.S. auto plant incorporate Japanese management techniques after the car manufacturer is taken over by a Japanese corporation.

SOUNDS OF WORK

- "Factory" (Bruce Springsteen). Springsteen highlights the daily drudgery of blue-collar factory work.

- "Working Man Blues" (Merle Haggard). In Haggard's song, a hard-working family man visits a tavern and sings about his experiences to escape the daily grind.

- "Why Work Doesn't Happen at Work" (Jason Fried, 2010). In this Ted Talk, Fried discusses the challenges for collaboration and productivity in the workplace. His talk is available through Ted.com at http://www.ted.com/talks/jason_fried_why_work_doesn_t_happen_at_work.html.

NOTES

1. Kuhn (1970) described scientific revolutions as shifts from old to new paradigms. A *paradigm* is a set of assumptions, principles, and guides to action. For useful overviews of shifting paradigms of management knowledge, see Clarke and Clegg (1998) and Osterman (2010).

2. Micklethwait and Wooldridge (1996) are highly critical of management consultants, calling them "witch doctors." See also Carson et al. (2000) and Miller and Hartwick (2002) on management fads, and Krause-Jensen (2010) for an anthropological analysis of the role of management consultants within large work organizations.

3. Hamel, Gary. (2007). *The Future of Management.* Boston: Harvard Business School Press, p. 102.

4. The Japanese "economic miracle" following World War II is most often attributed to the combination of extensive government intervention in the economy, resulting

in manufacturers, unions, and banks working together, and large-scale foreign investment by the United States, which, during the Cold War years, was concerned about promoting Western ideas of democracy (Johnson 1982; Pyle 1996).

5. See Knights, Willmott, and Collison (1985) and Rinehart's (1984) Canadian case study. Hampson (1999) suggests that key features of Toyota's production system are not easily transplanted.

6. On Volvo Kalmar, see Jonsson (1980) and Aguren et al. (1985). On Saab's work reorganization, see Logue (1981). These accounts of the Volvo and Saab factories are also based on Graham Lowe's personal observations and discussions with union officials, management, and shop-floor workers during visits to both plants in late 1985. The specific situation in each factory could be different now. For a critical view, see Van Houten (1990).

7. See Emery and Thorsrud (1969), Herzberg (1966), Cherns (1976), and Gardell (1977). On the development of the QWL approach in Canada, see Rankin (1990), Long (1989), and Jain (1990).

8. http://www.ge.com/en/company/companyinfo/quality/whatis.htm [retrieved November 5, 2013].

9. Ouchi (1981) argued that successful North American corporations adopting Japanese management techniques had created strong, clan-like internal cultures that led to workers aligning with the goals of the company.

10. See Shieh (1992: Chapter 18) on "learning cultures," and Lipshitz (2000) and Garvin (2000) on organizational learning.

11. Piore, Michael J., and Charles F. Sabel. (1984). *The Second Industrial Divide: Possibilities for Prosperity.* New York: Basic Books, p. 17.

12. See Jenson (1989), (Macdonald (1991), and Fox and Sugiman (1999) for critiques of flexible specialization.

13. On lean production in manufacturing, particularly in the auto sector, see Womack, Jones, and Roos (1990), Rinehart, Huxley, and Robertson (1997), Yates, Lewchuk, and Stewart (2001), Kochan, Lansbury, and MacDuffle (1997), and Green and Yanarella (1996). For applications of lean production, see Nilsson (1996) for a white-collar setting and Beata, Jens, and Per-Olaf (2007) for a health care setting.

14. Nilsson (1996) offers a somewhat more positive assessment of lean production.

15. The term *high commitment management* has been used to describe supervisory systems in telephone call centres that combine "fun and surveillance"; see Kinnie, Hutchinson, and Purcell (2000). In other words, while monitoring their work closely, managers also try to keep employees amused and distracted with a variety of minor benefits, including non-traditional and trendy workspaces (Baldry and Hallier 2010). Research suggests that this approach seldom leads to job

enlargement or employee involvement in significant decision-making (Godard 2004; Fleming and Sturdy 2011; D'Cruz and Noronha 2011); indeed, it may be resented by some workers (Baldry and Hallier 2010).

16. White et al. (2003), Leckie et al. (2001), and Kashefi (2012) assess the quality of work life in high-performance workplaces. Bowen and Ostroff (2004) and Godard (2004) examine productivity gains.

CONFLICT AND CONTROL IN THE WORKPLACE

"Our philosophy is that engineers can't possibly know as much about the jobs as the people that are doing them. And the people are going to feel a lot better and they're going to be much more inclined to implement a change that they have proposed that works for them than having some time and motion engineers come in and tell them, 'This is what we're going to do' and have people sitting here saying, 'Well, that's dumb, but we'll do it.'"

[Manager talking about work teams making decisions in a "lean production" Ontario automobile factory]

"We pretty well have an outline of how many people are supposed to be at each station and how many people are supposed to be on the team. Sometimes we might try and reduce steps in a particular job ... because over an entire day production will be higher if your steps are less and in some cases the production associate won't have to go through so much, they won't get as tired in a full day. Everybody in the team is interested in that. If they create less steps and make the job easier, then your time is more productive. Let's say they were to speed the line up or speed the process up, if you had fewer steps it's going to even out."

[Team leader in the same factory talking about types of decisions made]

Source: David Robertson, James Rinehart, Christopher Huxley, and the CAW Research Group on CAMI. (1992). "Team Concept and Kaizen: Japanese Production Management in a Unionized Canadian Auto Plant." *Studies in Political Economy* 39 (Autumn): 77–107, pp. 88, 91.

■ INTRODUCTION

Over the past century, employers sought new ways of managing workers in order to increase efficiency and productivity and to reduce workers' resistance to authority. Scientific management, with its emphasis on complete managerial control and an extreme division of labour, gave way to the softer human relations approach, which tried to motivate workers by making them feel that they were an integral part of the larger work organization. By the

1970s, North American management consultants were busy advocating changes to organizational structures and job design, drawing on principles of sociotechnical design developed in the United Kingdom, ideas about employee involvement in decision making from Sweden, and particularly, Japanese-style management strategies (Chapter 9). The Japanese influence could be seen in QWL programs, TQM management models, organizational culture initiatives, and later, lean production.

Proponents of the new managerial paradigms might argue that many of the problems of bureaucracy, as well as the dilemmas faced by managers trying to motivate workers, have been solved. Some might go so far as to propose that the outcome has been a less conflict-ridden and more egalitarian society, that we are getting closer to Émile Durkheim's vision of modern society in which employers, managers, and workers recognize that pulling together is in everyone's best interest (see Chapter 1). But if we take a more critical look at employment and managerial trends over the past decades through a conflict, rather than a consensus, lens, it can lead us to a different conclusion.

As we noted in Chapter 9, some of the new management strategies involved few real changes to employees' jobs. The organizational culture approach would be an example. In contrast, attempts to develop high-performance workplaces (HPW) put much more effort into reducing the negative effects of bureaucracy, increasing job skills, enhancing worker decision-making, and improving work–life balance. Even so, few work organizations introduced the full HPW package, and furthermore, the benefits to workers of this approach were counterbalanced by increased risk of job loss or pay reductions. Thus, responses to employees' desires for more autonomy and responsibility and their needs for more family-friendly workplace benefits and policies continue to be the exception rather than the rule (Lowe 2000; Jackson 2005; Duxbury, Higgins, and Lyons 2008).

Furthermore, as we note later in this chapter, while some North American managers were experimenting with new approaches to organizational design and employee motivation, others were busy downsizing organizations and outsourcing jobs. There has also been a parallel trend toward replacing full-time permanent workers with part-time and temporary employees (Fuller and Vosko 2008; Kalleberg 2009) and the contracting-out of work previously done by better-paid permanent employees (Shalla 2002; Zuberi 2013). As a result, we have seen an increase in income inequality and labour market polarization (see Chapters 4 and 5). Not surprisingly, then, organized labour continues to challenge the status quo. Despite their decline in some sectors, unions still frequently oppose management policies (Collinson and Ackroyd 2005) and sometimes engage in strikes or threaten to do so (see Chapter 11).

We begin this chapter by reviewing Karl Marx's critique of work in capitalist society, since his arguments shaped the conflict perspective. We then discuss the *labour process* approach to analyzing the workplace, an effort to update Marx's ideas to explain contemporary worker–management relationships. This alternative approach begins with the assumption that conflict is to be expected in work settings, where the interests of owners and managers are in opposition to those of workers. It focuses directly on attempts by management to control workers, and on how workers resist such efforts, trying to gain more control over their own labour. While the labour process approach has been criticized on various grounds, it does provide a much more critical assessment of the new managerial paradigms, as well as the introduction of new information technologies in the workplace and trends toward workplace downsizing and job outsourcing. In Chapter 11, we continue the discussion by examining the origins, functions, and future of trade unions, another vehicle through which workers have tried to look after their interests.

◼ MARX ON EMPLOYMENT RELATIONSHIPS WITHIN CAPITALISM

As we have observed in Chapters 1 and 5, class conflict was central to Marx's perspective on social change. Looking back in history, he argued that feudalism had been transformed into a new mode of production—capitalism, characterized by wage-labour relations of production—because of conflict between different class groupings. Looking forward, he predicted that capitalism would eventually give way to socialism because of the inherently conflictual and exploitative relationships between owners and workers.

Central to Marx's arguments was a specific economic theory of the capitalist labour market. Beginning with the premise that the value of a product was a direct function of the labour needed to produce it, Marx observed that wage-labourers produced more than the amount needed to pay their wages. *Surplus value* was being created, and employers were exploiting workers by keeping the profits from their labour. By purchasing labour, capitalists gained control over the labour process itself. Factory forms of organization and mechanization of production further increased employer control. Thus, the craftsmen forced into the industrial mills of Marx's time were, according to one commentator, "subjected to inflexible regulations, and driven like gear-wheels by the pitiless movement of a mechanism without a soul. Entering a mill was like entering a barracks or prison."[1]

These relationships of production led, according to Marx, to feelings of *alienation* among workers in a capitalist economy.[2] Marx identified a number of different sources of alienation. Products did not belong to those who produced them, but rather to those who owned the enterprise and who purchased the labour of workers. Decisions about what to produce and how to sell the finished products were not made by the workers, and profits generated in the exchange remained with the owners of the enterprise. In fact, given an extensive division of labour, many of the workers involved might never see the finished product. Thus, workers were alienated from the product of their own work.

Marx also emphasized alienation from the very activity of work. Transfer of control over the labour process from individual workers to capitalists or managers meant that individual workers lost the chance to make decisions about how the work should be done. In addition, extensive fragmentation of the work process had taken away most intrinsic work rewards. Alienation also involved the separation of individual workers from others around them. Obviously, bureaucratic hierarchies could have this effect. But more important, because capitalist employment relationships involve the exchange of labour for a wage, work was transformed from a creative and collective activity to an individualistic, monetary activity. Work itself had become a commodity. As a consequence, Marx argued, workers were even alienated from themselves.[3]

Marx believed, of course, that eventually members of the working class would overcome their alienation and rise up in revolt against their exploitation. This revolt has not happened in Western industrial and postindustrial societies, in part, because the extremely harsh, dangerous, and exploitative working conditions of early industrialization have been largely eliminated. Looking back over the past century, we can see that the combination of labour legislation, unions and professional associations, and more sophisticated employers has led to higher incomes and standards of living, safer working conditions, and more responsibility and autonomy for workers, at least in relative terms.

However, in earlier chapters we have documented the growing number of working poor in Canada, a polarization of work rewards, and the rise in involuntary nonstandard employment. Unions continue to resist management attempts to reduce wages and cut jobs (Chapter 11), while most nonunion workers have little choice but to accept what they are offered. Hundreds of workers are still killed on the job each year, and thousands suffer workplace injuries (Chapter 12). Despite the calls for new management approaches to empower workers, some employers continue to act as if control over work belongs to them and must never be shared. So, while Marx's descriptions of working conditions in early capitalist society may no longer be applicable, the core themes in his writings can still help us to gain a better understanding of work in today's economy. These themes—power relationships in the workplace, attempts by owners and managers to control the labour process, resistance to these attempts by workers, and conflict between class groups—are central to the labour process perspective on worker–management relationships.

THE LABOUR PROCESS PERSPECTIVE

Harry Braverman on the "Degradation of Work"

Writing 40 years ago in *Labor and Monopoly Capital*, Harry Braverman (1974) argued that 20th-century capitalism had changed a great deal from the mode of production examined by Karl Marx. A relatively small number of huge, powerful corporations now controlled the national and international economies. The role of the state in the production process had expanded. New technologies had evolved, workplace bureaucracies had become larger, and the labour process itself had become increasingly standardized.

Braverman, focusing on the transformation of office work in large bureaucracies, observed that, at the beginning of the 20th century, (male) clerks and bookkeepers had exercised considerable control over their work and had been responsible for a wide variety of tasks. But this was no longer the case. An extensive division of labour in offices had narrowed the scope of the work done by one clerk. Clerks essentially processed an endless stream of paper on a white-collar assembly line, their routinized tasks devoid of much mental activity. In short, clerical work had been degraded and deskilled.

Braverman attributed these changes to management strategies designed to improve efficiency and gain more control over the office labour process, the same strategies employed in factories many decades earlier. Thus, Braverman saw Taylorist tendencies at the heart of all modern management approaches, even those used to organize the work of technicians, professionals, and middle-level managers. He believed that both lower- and higher-status, white-collar workers were becoming part of the same working class. The deskilling and degradation of work in general was setting the scene for future class conflict.

Braverman's provocative book was highly influential, but it was also criticized by researchers sympathetic to its general thesis.[4] First, Braverman over-generalized from scattered evidence in North America to assert that deskilling was a universal pattern present in all occupations within all industrial capitalist societies. Important cultural differences in the labour process were ignored, as were situations in which automation, work reorganization, and management strategies provided more autonomy and responsibility to workers. Furthermore, while focusing on declining skills in some occupations, Braverman overlooked new skills required in industrial and postindustrial economies. For example, the management of large numbers of employees required the development of a wider range of leadership skills, office work in service industries required sophisticated "people skills," and efficient use of new manufacturing and information technologies required computer skills.[5]

Second, Braverman ignored the gendered nature of workplace skills, as have many other researchers (see Chapter 6). Technical skills, frequently more central to "male" jobs, have been valued more highly than people skills, which figure more prominently in jobs typically held by women.[6] Hence, Braverman probably underrated the skill requirements of clerical work. In addition, he overlooked how race and ethnicity have played a major part in determining access to better jobs in North American labour markets (Creese 2007; see also Chapter 5).

Third, Braverman implied that workers passively accepted management assaults on their job skills and autonomy. Seldom in *Labor and Monopoly Capital* does one find mention of workers resisting management, even though power struggles have always been part of the informal side of bureaucracy (Chapter 8). Furthermore, as we will argue in Chapter 11, Canadian workers have formed unions for well over a century to collectively oppose their employers. The main flaw in Braverman's theory of the degradation of work is its determinism, the belief that an inner logic of 20th-century capitalism compelled capitalists to devise Taylorism, Fordism, and the many managerial strategies that followed them.

Why, then, was Braverman's book so influential? The answer is that he challenged work researchers to ask new questions about changes in the labour process in contemporary capitalist societies. Braverman brought the sociology of work and organizations back to issues of class and inequality, power and control, resistance and conflict (Smith 1994). Even in his failings—over-generalizing about deskilling, not taking account of gender, and overlooking worker resistance—he motivated other researchers to ask critical questions about shifting methods of managerial control and about trends in the deskilling or enskilling of work.

Models of Managerial Control

Richard Edwards (1979) extended labour market segmentation theory (see Chapter 5) to describe the evolution of workplace control systems, distinguishing between three basic types of managerial control. With *simple control*, most common in secondary labour markets, employers regulate the labour process with coercive or paternalistic methods, or, in larger organizations, through a bureaucratic hierarchy of authority. *Technical control* is achieved by machine pacing of work and can, in part, replace the direct supervision of simple control methods. For example, Henry Ford's assembly line gave managers a powerful means of controlling the pace of work. *Bureaucratic control* has evolved in large corporations in the core sector of the economy. Good salaries, generous benefits, and pleasant work settings are the inducements provided, usually to middle- and upper-level, white-collar employees and some groups of skilled manual workers. The internal labour market (see Chapter 5) and the prospects of an interesting and rewarding career are part of an employment package designed to win employees' commitment.

Gordon, Edwards, and Reich (1982) argued that the evolution of segmented labour markets resulted in a socially fragmented and politically weak working class. Employers gained the upper hand over workers in the "contested terrain" of the workplace by continually developing new and more effective means of control (Nolan and Edwards 1984). However, critics have argued that this theory portrays workers as largely passive, without any *agency*, not recognizing how they might resist, reshape, or even actively participate in management control strategies. Andrew Friedman (1977: 82–85), for instance, describes a shifting *frontier of control*, which is influenced alternately by conflict and accommodation between employers and employees. At issue is who sets the hours, pace, and sequence of work tasks, and what constitutes fair treatment and just rewards. Sometimes, workers gain a say in these matters through union bargaining. Or, rather than using *direct control* (like the simple control described by Edwards), management may initiate some work reforms, giving workers what Friedman calls *responsible autonomy*. Examples would be the quality-of-working-life (QWL) programs and other participative management schemes, described in Chapter 9.

Both types of control have been observed in the Canadian mining industry. In his early study of the International Nickel Company (Inco), Wallace Clement (1981: 204) described the introduction of sophisticated "people technology" at the modern Copper Cliff Nickel refinery. Inco's emphasis on a "one big happy family" feeling, a flatter job hierarchy, and a new on-the-job training system looked progressive. However, these changes led to a breakdown of traditional job autonomy and erosion of the bargaining power of unionized workers. As a result, the level of direct control by management increased. In contrast, Inco's teams of underground miners possessed considerable responsible autonomy. These small, closely knit groups made their own decisions about how and when to complete various tasks.

A more recent study of potash mining in Saskatchewan (Russell 1999: 193–94) revealed that managers in post-Fordist work settings were less likely to employ a "rough" style of management (direct control in Friedman's terms). However, it was also apparent that management could not afford to act in this manner, since doing so might jeopardize the cooperation of workers who were expected to maintain high levels of productivity in a lean-production environment. Ultimately, Russell (1999) concluded that, despite the rhetoric, workers had not really been empowered.

Turning to the service sector, a nightclub in a western Canadian city provides an interesting example of the shifting frontier of control. Mike Sosteric (1996) describes the strong informal workplace culture that had emerged in the club and the great degree of job autonomy enjoyed by workers. As a result, workers were loyal and committed, and customers received high-quality, personalized service. But new management saw some of the norms of the informal workplace culture as problematic. It tried to take charge by implementing what might be seen as a system of responsible autonomy.

The workers were put off by the training seminars, disliked the new system of job enlargement, and found that elimination of supervisors made their work more difficult. Consequently, they actively resisted the changes. In turn, management adopted a direct and coercive control strategy that led, ultimately, to workers quitting and the quality of service in the nightclub deteriorating.

While Friedman describes responsible autonomy being offered to selected groups of workers in return for their cooperation, Michael Burawoy (1979, 1984) goes even further. Burawoy suggests that, in many work settings, employees actively choose to cooperate. In his study of machine shop workers, he described how an unspoken agreement with company goals emerged. Some employees adapted to management's control system by treating wage bonuses as a game they tried to win, thus exhibiting an individualistic response or adaptation to an otherwise boring job. As long as each worker had a fair chance of "winning" bonuses, management's rules went unchallenged. For these workers, coercion (Burawoy called this the *despotic organization of work*) was unnecessary since, by accepting workplace rules, they basically motivated and managed themselves.

Burawoy describes the *hegemonic organization of work* in much the same way that Richard Edwards presents bureaucratic control. In large corporations and government departments, employees often see their own futures linked with the success of the organization. Hence, management's goals and values are dominant, or hegemonic. The presence of internal labour markets and responsible autonomy helps to maintain management control. Individual workers are subtly encouraged to adopt the value system or organizational culture of the company or department, and good job conditions foster long-term commitment to the organization (Courpasson and Clegg 2012).

A study of how the Klein government in Alberta restructured the department responsible for museums and cultural heritage sites in the 1990s is a good example (Oakes, Townley, and Cooper 1998). By requiring all government departments to develop standardized business plans, an apparently neutral strategy from which everyone would benefit, senior management shifted the department's emphasis from public education and cultural preservation to the logic of business while, at the same time, gaining greater control over professionals who adopted the language and values of business planning.

Electronic Control

The rapid growth of computer-based information technologies has given rise to yet another type of management control system: *electronic control* (Sewell 1998). Such surveillance may be relatively passive, as when workplaces are monitored by security cameras, or highly active, as when supervisors keep track of work performance electronically and send warning messages to workers who are not producing as much as others (Davis 2010: 303). Electronic control is typically intrusive, particularly in the case of supervisors listening to telephone calls, reading e-mail messages, and monitoring Internet searches. Some even use Global Positioning Systems (GPS) to track the physical movements of their employees (Richards 2008: 95). Consequently, it is not surprising that most workers resent the implementation of such control systems. Nevertheless, most are affected by one of them. It is estimated that close to 80 percent of U.S. workers may be experiencing some kind of electronic control (Hansen 2004).

Managers in charge of teleworkers (people working from their homes) frequently use electronic control to monitor off-site employees. However, this tactic may not always be effective. A U.K. study showed how managers had difficulty distinguishing between productive and unproductive work being completed by teleworkers (Felstead, Jewson, and Walters 2003). They were also unable to get a sense of the employees' frame of mind and general level of commitment to the work organization. As a result, some managers relied on long, chatty phone calls with their employees. Or they resorted to regular home visits, essentially reverting to traditional methods of direct control. But home visits created their own complications since "the boss" now had to fit into the role of being a guest in a worker's home where others (children, spouses) might not always be welcoming.

The rapid growth of *call centres* within which telephone and computer systems are linked to generate large numbers of outgoing calls (e.g., for telephone sales or market research) or to handle many incoming calls (typically regarding customer service) has led to extensive electronic control of workers. Computers are used to assign calls to individual workers who may handle hundreds of calls a day. They are also often used to monitor worker performance, both quantitatively (How long did each call take?) and qualitatively (Was the client's problem solved? Did the salesperson try hard enough to make a sale?). Supervisors may or may not listen in on individual calls, but the possibility that someone is listening has the same effect. If work teams are part of the management strategy, electronic performance monitoring can be used to push teams to compete with each other against high-performance targets.

Some researchers (Fernie and Metcalf 1998) have described these new workplaces from the perspective of the French social theorist Michel Foucault (1977), who wrote about the all-encompassing power of surveillance in modern society (Chapter 2). They see call centres as "electronic sweatshops" in which workers have virtually no decision-making opportunities. In fact, because they know they can be monitored at any time, workers essentially become their own taskmasters. However, a wide range of subsequent studies have documented considerable resistance by workers to management moni-toring and surveillance, and have described the varying amounts of control that call-centre workers have, depending on the types of services they provide (Taylor and Bain 2001).[7] For example, customer service agents providing complex financial information to clients have considerably more decision-making authority and are much less likely to be working in a computer-paced environment (Batt 2000). Similarly, nurse advisers working in call centres in the United Kingdom report having some autonomy in deciding how to provide health care advice to callers, despite being expected to work from a software-driven script that is meant to ensure that only "safe advice" is pro-vided (Mueller et al. 2008).

Summing up, managers use a variety of approaches to try to control the labour process in contemporary workplaces. Direct, technical, bureaucratic, hegemonic, and electronic control, along with responsible autonomy, are all possibilities, alone or in some combination. The balance of power and control in any given workplace can range from strictly coercive, with management fully in control, to situations where workers have considerable responsibility for regulating their own work, essentially controlling themselves. As John Jermier (1998: 241) observes, regimes of control range from those "anchored in the iron fist of power [to] those that rely on the velvet glove." In turn, workers continue to find ways to resist many management control efforts. As Friedman would say, the labour process remains a shifting "frontier of control" and conflict.

The Deskilling Debate

According to Braverman, the application of Taylorist-style management, along with the adoption of new technologies, was systematically deskilling both blue-collar and white-collar work in capitalist society. In contrast, Daniel Bell and other postindustrial society theorists argued that a new economy relying heavily on highly skilled "knowledge workers" was taking shape (see Chapter 2). More recently, other writers have put forward a similar *enskilling* argument about the growing number of multi-skilled workers required by flexible specialization, lean production, and other postindustrial modes of production (Chapter 9), as well as by the proliferation of computers, robotics, and new information technologies in the workplace.

Policy makers also frequently warn that additional investments in education and training are needed to increase the skill levels of Canadian workers and make our economy more competitive (Smith 2001). At the same time, we see that rising levels of educational attainment among Canadians, in the absence of enough jobs requiring higher education and training, can lead to significant problems of underemployment (Chapter 4). In short, it is unclear whether we are seeing primarily deskilling or enskilling. As Wallace Clement and John Myles (1994: 72) graphically asked, are we faced by "a postindustrial Nirvana of knowledge where everyone will be a brain surgeon, artist, or philosopher (Bell) or, alternatively, a postindustrial Hades where we shall be doomed to labour mindlessly in the service of capital (Braverman)"?

Before answering, we need to define "skill" and ask whether we can measure it accurately.[8] A first basic question is this: Is deskilling something that happens to individual workers or to the jobs they occupy? The answer is "both," since jobs can be redesigned to increase or decrease skill content, and workers can lose skills if they do not have the opportunity to use them regularly (Krahn 1997). Second, are skills such as the ability to use advanced computer software, drive a semitrailer, or teach children to read completely objective job requirements that can be reliably measured and ranked in terms of their importance and complexity? The answer is "not necessarily." We have already noted (see Chapter 9) how *tacit skills*—the informal knowledge that workers have gained through experience or from coworkers about how to do their job—are seldom part of job descriptions and, thus, often go unrewarded. Furthermore, research has shown how skills are, to some extent, socially constructed, reflecting the social status, power, and traditions of a particular occupation. For example, we have seen how much more value has been placed on traditionally "male skills" while "female skills" have frequently been devalued (Chapters 6 and 7).

Despite these definitional difficulties and measurement concerns, there is considerable consensus among researchers that, in general terms, work-related skills have two components: *substantive complexity* (the level and scope of intellectually, interpersonally, and manually challenging tasks performed in a job), and *decision-making autonomy* (the opportunity for individual workers to decide how, when, and at what speed to complete a task). Large-scale studies using multiple measures to explore these two dimensions of skill, and covering several decades, reach a fairly definitive conclusion about Braverman's deskilling hypothesis. On average, the long-term trend in North America and Western Europe has been in the direction of increased skill requirements in the workplace. Although Daniel Bell's overly optimistic predictions of an emerging knowledge society have not been fulfilled, "the net result of the shift to services has been to increase the requirements for people to think on the job" (Clement and Myles 1994: 72).

This conclusion, however, comes with several important caveats. First, Myles and Clement comment on the "net result," acknowledging that deskilling has occurred in some specific occupations and work settings. An example would be the secondary labour market jobs in the contract building-cleaning industry described by Luís Aguiar (2001). In his Toronto-based study, Aguiar observed how, in the traditional "zone cleaning" approach, a single individual was responsible for a range of cleaning tasks. But in order to increase efficiency (and profits), supervisors subdivided the tasks into "restroom specialists," "dusting specialists," and "mopping specialists," essentially creating a "mobile assembly line" within which workers had to work harder and faster on a more limited number of tasks.

Second, we also need to recognize that an overall increase in skill requirements may not be accompanied by other improvements in the quality of working life. For example, total quality management, lean production, and other recent management innovations may require workers to learn additional skills, but in downsized organizations, workers also have to work harder and faster, under more stressful conditions (Russell 1999; Carter et al. 2013). Some of the critical assessments of these management strategies (see Chapter 9) distinguish between *multi-tasking* (simply adding more tasks to a worker's job description) and *multi-skilling* (adding to the skill repertoire of workers), arguing that the former merely makes employees work harder, not smarter (Rinehart, Huxley, and Robertson 1997).

Third, the studies showing increased skill requirements over time included data only up until the late 1980s. Until then, growth in higher-skill jobs, most in the upper-tier services and the goods-producing industries, outstripped the expansion of less skilled positions, many in the lower-tier services. But we have continued to see substantial industrial restructuring and organizational down-sizing, and widespread introduction of automated technologies, the sum of which might have slowed or stopped the enskilling trend. These trends might account for Michael Smith's (2001: 17) conclusion that "recent technological change has not distinctly raised average skill levels" in Canada.

Finally, we have also witnessed increased polarization between skilled workers and those with less skill over the past several decades (Chapter 5). In the United States, writers such as Robert Reich (2000) and Richard Florida (2005) worry about this growing inequality and its consequences for social cohesion and the future of American society. In Canada, Clement and Myles (1994: 76) discuss the skill polarization issue in terms of social class, noting that almost all executives and a majority of the new middle class are in skilled jobs, compared to less than a quarter of the working class. Thus, the polariza-tion of skills may be accentuating the already pronounced class differences in income, status, and power in the Canadian labour market.

▮ TECHNOLOGY AND THE LABOUR PROCESS

Technology figured prominently in debates about industrialization and postin-dustrial society where it has typically been seen as contributing to increased productivity, greater societal prosperity, and as Daniel Bell (Chapter 2) and Gerhard Lenski (Chapter 8) predicted, reduced social inequality. Labour process researchers, including Harry Braverman, have, instead, focused on how employers have at times used new technologies to deskill work and increase control over employees.

The new technologies of the industrial age increased productivity largely by reducing the amount of physical labour required in the goods-producing industries. In contrast, today's computer-based information and automated production technologies are reshaping the physical and mental require-ments of work in both the goods-producing and service sectors (Aoyama and Castells 2002). Factory robots and 3-D printers, globally linked office com-puter networks, e-commerce and social media marketing in the retail sector, automated materials-handling systems in transportation, computer-assisted design in engineering firms, computer-assisted diagnostics in health care, and cellphones, the Internet, and Skype in workers' homes are all part of a rapidly changing technological context for work (Baldry 2011). Thirty-five years ago, only a small minority of Canadian workers used computers, in any form, in their jobs, but by 2000, well over half (57%) were doing so (Marshall 2001). By 2007, close to 90 percent of Canadian private companies were using the Internet, and 41 percent had a website (Statistics Canada 2008h: 245). Smart phones, a technology barely a decade old, were already being used by over half of the employees surveyed in a 2012 Canadian study (Battams 2013).

The number of Canadians working in information and communications technology (ICT) industries (e.g., manufacturing computer equipment or providing computer or telecommunications services) increased rapidly from 411,000 to 546,000 between 1997 and 2001. Employment in the ICT sector then dropped back down to 529,000 workers by 2003 (Beckstead and Brown 2005), and a bit further to 522,000 (3% of total employment) by 2011,[9] as ICT industries suffered setbacks, and some of the largest companies outsourced many jobs. Globally, more than 17 million people were working in ICT manufacturing alone in 2004 (Ferus-Comelo 2008: 148). The economic recession of 2008, however, led to a substantial decline (up to 7%) in this figure.[10]

Information technology (IT) innovations have clearly contributed to increased productivity (Harchaoui et al. 2002). At the same time, the potential for electronic control of workers has been enhanced by new forms of information technology, as we noted earlier in this chapter. But have these new technologies also led to improvements in other aspects of job quality? Automation's potential to eliminate dirty, dangerous, and boring factory jobs has been partly realized through robotics.[11] Robots are ideal for work in cramped spaces, in extreme temperatures, or in otherwise hazardous situations, and have been used to eliminate dangerous jobs in many factories (e.g., welding and painting automobiles). It is also possible to organize automated production systems in ways that offer workers much opportunity for skill improvement and job autonomy. The Saab factory, described in Chapter 9, is an example.

But what is possible is not always what happens. For example, computer numerical control (CNC) machines, used to make metal parts and tools, could lead to enskilling; instead, they have often led to an erosion of workers' knowledge requirements and responsibilities. CNC machines, run by semiskilled operators, have replaced tool and die makers, who traditionally were among the most skilled manufacturing workers. As one skilled Canadian machinist described the impact of CNC machines on his job:

> You don't even need a man to monitor, the [CNC] machines will monitor themselves. They've got all these electronic scans that tell when the tool edge is wearing, what horsepower the machine is using. They've got all these tool change systems, so they even can change tools whenever they want, so you don't even need a man there.[12]

As for white-collar office employees, the impact of information technology has generally been more positive than negative.[13] Many of the dreary filing and typing chores of office work have disappeared, and opportunities to acquire advanced computer skills have produced more challenging and interesting jobs. But the full potential of information technology for enhancing the quality of work has seldom been realized. On the basis of her early case studies of computer use in the workplace, Shoshana Zuboff (1988: 57) concluded that information technology "creates pressure for a profound *reskilling.*" Yet, as her studies showed, old-style management control and bureaucracy often prevented workers from learning how to effectively employ technology. Fearing loss of power, many middle managers were reluctant to give workers the training and responsibility they needed to make the leap to *informated* (as opposed to simply *automated*) work.

Twenty-five years later, can we say we have made progress? Probably in some workplaces, but not in all. Consider a Swedish study of the introduction of hand-held computers for work teams providing home-care services (Hjalmarsson 2009). The study documents how the new technology was used not to enhance the services provided or to allow the caregivers to make better decisions, but to monitor more accurately the types of services provided and how long it took workers to complete each task. Further, a 2012 Canadian survey reported 44 percent of employees saying that, during the past year, they had received work-related phone calls or e-mail messages from their employer while on vacation or during time off (Battams 2013). In short, the technology is 21st century, while some of the purposes for which it is being used would please Frederick Taylor.

The widespread adoption of information technology may also have led to greater polarization of skills and increased income inequality. Workers who already are highly skilled (professionals, managers, and technicians) are more likely to have the opportunity to work with information technology and to receive the necessary training (Marshall 2001). As Thomas Idle and Arthur Cordell (1994: 69) concluded: "We are beginning to see the creation of a workforce with a bi-modal set of skills. Highly trained people design and implement the technology, and unskilled workers carry out the remaining jobs." In addition, the outsourcing (or "off-shoring," as some call it) of what were well-paying IT jobs to developing countries has led to a higher proportion of relatively low-paying jobs in Canada (Green et al. 2011).

And what about job creation and job loss? Have new technologies created more jobs than they have eliminated? Or will the further spread of information technology result in the "end of work" as Jeremy Rifkin predicted two decades ago:

> Within less than a century, "mass" work in the market sector is likely to be phased out in virtually all of the industrialized nations of the world. A new generation of sophisticated information and communication technologies is being hurried into a wide variety of work situations. Intelligent machines are replacing human beings in countless tasks, forcing millions of blue and white collar workers into unemployment lines, or worse still, breadlines.[14]

New automated technologies have frequently led to workforce reductions within specific organizations and industries, but the rise of the ICT industry has also led to some new job creation (Frenette 2007b). Hence, on balance, there appears to be little evidence that IT adoption led directly to increased unemployment in Canada (Sargent 2000). Instead, to the extent that job losses have occurred in different industries and regions, and social inequality has increased in Canada, corporate downsizing, the shrinking of the government sector, and the outsourcing of jobs have been much more directly responsible.[15]

Technological, Economic, or Social Determinism?

Historically, technology has been used to create jobs and to improve the quality of life. It has also been used to eliminate jobs, to destroy the natural environment, and to kill people. The new information technology is no different—it can have both positive and negative outcomes for society.[16] Our challenge is to find ways to use technology to provide rewarding employment for as many people as possible.

Writing in the 1960s, Gerhard Lenski viewed industrial technology positively, arguing that it had led to reduced inequality (Chapter 8). At the same time, Marshall McLuhan presented a far more pessimistic analysis of the impact of technology on social life. He concluded that human beings were at risk of becoming the servants of technology. His actual words were much stronger: he suggested that if trends continued, we might become "the sex organs of the machine world ... enabling it to fecundate and to evolve ever new forms." Half a century later, in early 2014 at the annual meeting of the world's political and business elite in Davos, Switzerland, Eric Schmidt, the executive chairman of Google, provided another example of technology being given superhuman status when he stated, "It's a race between computers and people—and people need to win."[17]

We do not agree with either of these positions since they attribute too much independent power to technology. *Technological determinism*, the belief that the developmental pattern and effects of a given technology are universal and unalterable, removes the possibility of human agency, the potential for people to shape technology for the greater social good. Furthermore, this position ignores the strong evidence that new technologies have been used in very different ways, with different outcomes, in different work settings and societies.

We also reject *economic determinism*, the belief that the "market knows best" how to choose and implement new technologies. Such a perspective would argue that, despite current problems with underemployment, deskilling, and loss of worker autonomy, new technologies will in time naturally lead to more positive than negative outcomes. But behind the "free hand of the market" are real people, making decisions about how to implement the new technologies. These decisions typically have been made by only a tiny minority of citizens—owners and managers guided by the profit motive. As Charley Richardson (1996) wrote some years ago, "Computers don't kill jobs, people do."

Instead, we prefer a *social determinism* perspective, advocating education, wide-ranging discussion, and open decision making about how technologies will be used, by whom, and for whose benefit. We believe that technology should be used to serve individual, community, and societal needs, not merely the needs of a particular company or work organization. Consequently, workers need to be able to participate in decisions about the choice and implementation of new workplace technologies that affect them directly, and citizens need a voice in shaping broader industrial technology strategies.

Because the quest for increased competitiveness through technology has frequently meant job loss or job downgrading for workers, labour movements in North America and Europe have often opposed the introduction of new technology. But this does not mean that unions oppose technological change on principle. Rather, they have insisted that employees be consulted so that the negative effects can be minimized and opportunities for upgrading jobs and improving working conditions maximized. Unions also have argued that any productivity gains should be shared equitably. While European unions have been successful in achieving some of these goals,[18] similar gains for organized labour have yet to be made in Canada (see Chapter 11).

● WHEN IN DOUBT, DOWNSIZE

The four-decade search for new managerial paradigms in North America (Chapter 8) has frequently been accompanied by large-scale organizational *downsizing*, typically driven by economic downturns in the private sector and deficit-cutting agendas in the public sector. Job cuts, accompanied by organizational restructuring, occurred in close to half of Canadian firms with 100 or more employees between 1991 and 1996 (McKay 1996). Job losses in the public sector were even greater (Lowe 2001). In the United States, the 100 largest firms on the *Fortune 500* list downsized an average of 15 times between the early 1980s and mid-1990s, eliminating 2.5 million workers from their payrolls (McKay 1996: 56).

Extensive downsizing has continued in the 21st century (Davis-Blake and Broschak 2009). Some of this has been a result of "off-shoring," the reloca-tion of jobs by multinational companies to developing economies such as India and China where labour costs are much cheaper. Downsizing may also follow company mergers and subsequent large-scale reorganization of produc-tion. An example is the closing, in 2014, of the Heinz ketchup factory in Leamington, Ontario, after the Heinz company was sold to new owners. More than 700 jobs were lost. Other companies have downsized to deal with serious economic difficulties. The most prominent recent Canadian example involved BlackBerry, the Waterloo-based smart-phone company, laying off 4,500 workers globally in September 2013 as it struggled to compete with Apple and Samsung products. About the same time, Canadian Pacific Railways was laying off between 4,500 and 6,000 workers in an effort to increase profits to the level of those being made by other North American railway companies.

The short-term cost savings associated with downsizing often do not translate into long-term improved profits (Baumol, Blinder, and Wolff 2003). Expenses may increase as managers realize they need to re-hire workers or contract-out work that otherwise would not get done. Large-scale staff cuts may weaken the social networks that are vital for the organization's capacity to learn and share knowledge (Fisher and White 2000), and departing employees may take "organizational memory" and vital skills with them (Littler and Innes 2003).

Downsizing negatively affects workers who lose their jobs and become unemployed. Medical researchers have tracked individuals who have been downsized, documenting damage to their health. For example, a study in four Finnish municipalities followed workers over 7.5 years, comparing those who experienced no downsizing, minor downsizing, and major downsizing (Vahtera et al. 2004). Those who experienced major downsizing were absent from work due to sickness at far higher rates than people in the other two groups, and they also died from cardiovascular causes at higher rates.

The term *survivor syndrome* describes the negative psychological effects of downsizing on employees who remain behind (Mishra and Spreitzer 1998). Workers may experience elevated levels of stress, and generally become demoralized and dissatisfied (Elmuti, Grunewald, and Abebe 2010). Motivation, loyalty, and productivity can suffer as employees avoid taking risks in their jobs and become absorbed in protecting their own interests. This problem is exacerbated by increased workloads as the organization tries to "do more with less." People may be reassigned to new duties without adequate training.[19] So it is not surprising that a national survey of Canadian employees, conducted in 2000, found that those who experienced downsizing and restructuring in the year prior to the survey had much lower levels of trust in and commitment to their employer, and reported poor communication and less influence on decision making, compared with employees who had not undergone such changes (Lowe and Schellenberg 2001).

Some organizations have reduced staff numbers more humanely. In the mid-1990s, Nova Corporation of Calgary, for example, established the Employment, Transition and Continuity Program to achieve a 10 percent staff reduction. The objective, according to the vice-president of human resources, was "to ensure that those who leave feel good about how they were treated and that those who stay feel energized and ready to move Nova forward."[20] The program underscores the importance of the process by which downsizing is carried out so that morale is not destroyed (Cascio 2002). It provides employees whose jobs are affected with more options and support, including alternative work arrangements (job sharing, reduced workweek, seasonal employment), financial support for education or working in nonprofit community organizations, small business start-up advice and grants, skills upgrading, leaves of absence, and help with relocation costs.

Staff reductions achieved by employees volunteering to leave can create new problems for work organizations, though. If the most experienced and productive employees are among those who leave, the knowledge assets of the organization are depleted. For example, extensive downsizing through voluntary departures at NASA deprived the U.S. space program of the scientific and engineering knowledge it needed to send astronauts on another mission to the moon (DeLong 2004). A more recent and close-to-home example for the authors resulted from large-scale cuts by the provincial government to the University of Alberta budget in 2013. To reduce operating costs, the university put in place a Voluntary Severance Package (VSP), inviting professors to resign in return for a year's salary. A significant number accepted the package, and not just those close to retirement, leaving some departments struggling to offer required courses and students dealing with larger classes and fewer course options.

NEW MANAGERIAL PARADIGMS: AN IMPROVED LABOUR PROCESS?

The new managerial paradigms, discussed in Chapter 9, use labels such as *participative management* and *employee empowerment*. More critical observers have described them as *neo-Fordist* or *post-Fordist*, implying that the positive changes have not been nearly as significant as their proponents claim (Vidal 2007). By offering some small concessions to workers, the new approaches have maintained the basic production framework and power structure of industrial capitalist society. Some critics go even further, using a term such as *hyper-Taylorism* (Russell 1997: 28) or *neo-Taylorism* (Pruijt 2003). They argue that work intensification signals a new era of "management by stress" in which workers push themselves and each other to make more profits for their employers (Kunda and Ailon-Souday 2005: 209). An excellent example is provided by Vivian Shalla (2004, 2007b), who documents how Air Canada has required its flight attendants to work longer hours in order to help the company through a financial crisis and make it a more flexible and competitive global airline.

But labels are not as important as real outcomes. What do we see when we look back at four decades of new management approaches in North America? All of them offer some potential for skill upgrading, increasing worker participation in decision making, and reducing bureaucracy. In some cases (Shell's Sarnia refinery and the Saskatoon Chemicals workplace, for example), these approaches helped to improve the quality of working life for employees. None of these new managerial paradigms, however, really provides permanent and effective avenues for workers to have ongoing input into larger organizational decisions, such as the introduction of new technologies or a decision to restructure or downsize a work organization.

Approaches that go the furthest to counter Taylorism and Fordism—high-performance workplaces, for example—have not been implemented often (Koski and Järvensivu 2010). Other approaches typically deliver less than they promise. We sometimes find that they have also been used to increase control over workers and to speed up work (Burchell, Ladipo, and Wilkinson 2002). In addition, as already explained, the advent of the new management approaches has been accompanied by widespread organizational restructuring, downsizing, and outsourcing of work. The outcome, for society as a whole, has been a polarization of the labour force in terms of skill, income, work intensification, and job security, leading to greater social inequality (see Chapter 5).

As we concluded about the impacts of new technologies on the labour process, the problem does not lie in the management system so much as in how it is implemented, by whom, and for what purposes. Overall, new management paradigms—we might call them *social technologies*—have almost always been introduced with productivity and profit as the main goals. For example, an in-depth study of four U.S. manufacturing plants that introduced a wide range of teamwork and other management approaches in the 1990s confirms this. Steven Vallas (2003) concluded that the overriding emphasis on increasing profit margins led managers and corporate executives to maintain or re-introduce standardized, or Taylorist, production methods, which clearly stood in the way of job enrichment and increased worker involvement in decision making. A more recent U.S. study concludes that one outcome of wide-scale organizational restructuring between 1984 and 2001 was an increase in managers' incomes relative to those of other workers (Goldstein 2012). In short, improvements in quality of working life and worker empowerment have been secondary motivations, while reductions in social inequality have seldom figured in the decision and have not occurred. What's more, workers have rarely been involved in the decision to implement new technologies, either directly or through their unions.

■ CONCLUSION

In this chapter, we have presented a more critical analysis of the new managerial approaches that have tried to solve the problems of bureaucracy, engage and motivate workers, and reduce conflict in the workplace. Our starting point was Harry Braverman's analysis of the labour process in modern societies, which was framed by a Marxist understanding of social relations of production in capitalist societies. Braverman's critique led us to focus on questions about deskilling trends, shifts in methods of controlling workers, and how technology is used in the workplace.

Our review of the evidence indicates that, over the long term and on average, skill requirements have increased in the workplace, contrary to what Braverman predicted. Nevertheless, there is evidence that deskilling has clearly occurred in some specific occupations. New (hard) technologies have been involved in both deskilling and enskilling processes. Braverman's deterministic view of owners and managers tightly controlling workers who have little or no agency is also an inadequate description of the contemporary labour process. Managers use a wide variety of approaches (soft technologies), some clearly coercive and others more participatory, to control and motivate workers. But workers also frequently resist in the shifting "frontier of control" (Friedman 1977), which characterizes the labour process today.

Even so, we concluded that the new managerial paradigms have frequently not lived up to their promises. In fact, in some cases, the rhetoric of new management models has been used to gain additional control over workers and speed up work processes. And none of the new management approaches go so far as to directly involve workers in decisions about the choice of new hard technologies or plans to restructure or downsize organizations. Thus, with respect to new technologies, both "hard" and "soft," our central point is that they are a result of human choices. We believe it is our responsibility to try to use these technologies, not simply to increase profits, but also to improve working conditions, empower workers, create jobs, and reduce social inequality.

In the next chapter, we examine the primary collective vehicle for worker resistance in North America over the past century, namely, the organized labour movement. We will explore the history of unions, how they are evolving, and the problems they are facing. In Chapter 12, we move beyond the new managerial paradigms discussed in Chapter 9 and the organized labour movement (Chapter 11), to explore some interesting alternative approaches to traditional employment relations that offer much potential for worker empowerment and conflict reduction.

● DISCUSSION QUESTIONS

1. Some years ago, a U.S. executive told a Stanford University MBA class that "all organizations are prisons. It's just that the food is better in some than in others." What point was the executive making, and do you agree? Why or why not?

2. Discuss how technology shapes work, work organizations, and social relations of production, and speculate about the future impacts of technology.

3. Some social theorists have argued that conflict is inevitable in the workplace; others believe that some kind of consensus might be possible. Critically discuss these two positions.

4. Outline the "labour process" perspective on work in industrial capitalist societies. Does this perspective have any relevance in 21st-century Canada? Explain your answer.

5. Managers use different approaches to try to control workers. In your opinion, which types of control would be most effective for workers in general? Which type of control would be most likely to make you work hard? Why?

ADDITIONAL RESOURCES

WORK AT THE MOVIES

- *Chicken Run* (directed by Peter Lord and Nick Park, 2000, 84 minutes). Having been hopelessly repressed and facing eventual certain death at the chicken farm where they are held, Rocky the rooster and Ginger the chicken decide to rebel against the evil Mr. and Mrs. Tweedy, the farm's owners.
- *Up in the Air* (directed by Jason Reitman, 2009, 109 minutes). George Clooney plays a consultant who travels around the United States firing people on behalf of his corporate clients.
- *Outsourced* (directed by John Jeffcoat, 2006, 103 minutes). This American romantic comedy is focused on the Seattle manager of a call centre who is outsourced to India and charged with motivating employees to improve call response times.
- *The Company Men* (directed by John Wells, 2010, 104 minutes). Set in the aftermath of the 2008 recession, this drama explores the varying impacts of corporate downsizing on the employees and CEO of a large, publicly held corporation.

SOUNDS OF WORK

- "Maggie's Farm" (Bob Dylan). A literal reading of this song suggests it is about a disgruntled worker ready to quit his or her job.
- "Take This Hammer" (Traditional/Lead Belly). This song on a work camp, prison, or forced labour theme is about defying authority and escaping work.
- "Fire in the Hole" (Hazel Dickens). Dickens sings about workers refusing to go down into a mine considered unsafe for work until the union has been consulted.
- "Will a Computer Decide Whether You Get Your Next Job?" (Planet Money podcast, NPR, January 15, 2014). This podcast examines the practice of companies preferring to use data, more than resumés, to hire new employees. It is available at http://www.npr.org/blogs/money/2014/01/15/262789258/episode-509-will-a-computer-decide-whether-you-get-your-next-job.

NOTES

1. Paul Mantoux, quoted by Beaud (1983: 66).
2. The verb "alienate" refers to an act of separation or to the transfer of something to a new owner. Marx used the term in the latter sense and referred to the overall experience of working in a capitalist economy with the noun "alienation."
3. See Hodson (2001: 23–25), Grabb (2002: 19–21), and Rinehart (2006: 11–20) for further discussion of Marx's writings on alienation.
4. See Shalla (2007a) and Heisig (2009) on Braverman's contributions to the sociology of work.
5. See de Witte and Steijn (2000), Handel (2003), and Carey (2007) for contributions to the deskilling debate. Canadian studies include Myles (1988), Clement and Myles (1994: Chapter 4), Russell (1999), Hughes and Lowe (2000), and Livingstone and Scholtz (2007).
6. See Hughes (1996), Brynin (2006), Corman and Luxton (2007), Kelan (2008), and Payne (2009) on the gendered nature of occupational skills.
7. Lund and Wright (2009) describe how unions have set up call centres to advise their members and to potentially assist with recruitment and organizing of workers. For additional call-centre research, see Taylor and Bain (2003), Beirne, Riach, and Wilson (2004), Wood, Holman, and Stride (2006), Schalk and van Rijckevorsel (2007), D'Cruz and Noronha (2011), and Fleming and Sturdy (2011).
8. See Spenner (1983), Form (1987), Handel (2003), and Payne (2009) on the definition and measurement of skill.
9. Industry Canada: http://www.ic.gc.ca/eic/site/ict-tic.nsf/eng/h_it07229.html [retrieved November 14, 2013].
10. Organisation for Economic Co-operation and Development (OECD): http://www.oecd.org/sti/ieconomy/43969700.pdf [retrieved November 14, 2013].
11. On robotics, see Block (1990: 100–103) and Suplee (1997).
12. Robertson, David and Jeff Wareham. (1987). *Technological Change in the Auto Industry*. Willowdale, ON: Canadian Auto Workers (CAW), p. 28. See also Noble (1995).
13. See Zuboff (1988), Hughes (1996), and Brynin (2006).
14. Rifkin, Jeremy. (1995). *The End of Work: The Decline of the Global Labor Force and the Dawn of the Post-market Era*. New York: Putnam, p. 3. See Noble (1995) for a critical but less pessimistic view and Smith (2006) for a critique of Rifkin's apocalyptic view of the future.
15. Kristal (2013) links growing income inequality in the United States to the greater profits employers have received from computerization compared to income increases for employees.

16. See Rubery and Grimshaw (2001), Mishel and Bernstein (2003), and Dolton and Pelkonen (2008).

17. McLuhan (1964: 56), as quoted by Menzies (1996: 44). It is interesting that, in 2013, Spike Jonze produced and directed the movie *Her* in which the lead (Joaquin Phoenix) falls in love with his smart-phone's operating system. Erik Schmidt's quotation is from http://www.bbc.co.uk/news/business-25872006 [retrieved January 26, 2014].

18. Mahon (1987). Canadian studies have also demonstrated how a strong union (Clarke and Haiven 1999) and a positive labour relations climate (Smith 1999) can influence workers' willingness to accept change.

19. Gandolfi (2009) discusses the stress experienced by a third group (alongside victims and survivors) involved in downsizing: the "executioners," who must implement the layoffs.

20. *Globe and Mail* (1995, March 21: B12); *Nova Now* [monthly employee publication] (July–August 1995).

UNIONS AND INDUSTRIAL RELATIONS

"He is 26 and worked at U.S. Steel for just over five months before getting locked out. He sits with his friends—five others, also junior employees at U.S. Steel—all leery of the media and reluctant to give their names. They range in age from 26 to 45. They have gathered around on camp chairs and an old wooden box that they use as a bench. On a grassy lot to the right of the main gates of U.S. Steel at Burlington and Wilcox streets, their conversation quickly turns to their frustration, anger and rage about being locked out. Talking over each other, one of them says that picket duty is 'boring as hell.'"

"It's hard to avoid politics. Stan, 54, who has worked at the plant for 33 years, says the workers have been 'good soldiers' while U.S. Steel has 'reneged on everything' and 'raised unemployment levels.' They are angry with people, allegedly scabs from other unions, crossing their picket line. They criticize politicians for showing up for 'photo-ops' during the federal election campaign and they are angry that they haven't heard from them since...."

"They are worried about their employment insurance running out at the end of August. Currently, they receive $400 a week in EI, plus $200 a week in strike pay for picketing eight hours a week.... One of the younger workers who chose to remain anonymous said that above all else: 'I don't want pity. I just want my job back.'"

[Interview with some of the more than 600 Hamilton workers locked out by their employer in July 2011]

Source: Vidya Kauri. "Life on the picket line." *The Spectator*, July 7, 2011. http://www.thespec.com/news-story/2213930-life-on-the-picket-line/. Reprinted with permission of *The Hamilton Spectator*.

● INTRODUCTION

The members of the United Steelworkers union were locked out, or not allowed to work, by their Hamilton employer, who thus hoped to force their union to accept the company's wage and benefits offer. Eventually, in mid-October 2011, members voted to accept essentially the same offer they had received before the lockout began. They did not get the salary increase they had hoped for, and they had to accept the fact that new employees would not get the kind of pension plan that older workers already had.[1]

In contrast, in July 2013, after a three-week strike against Coca-Cola, 700 members of the Canadian Auto Workers union voted to accept an offer their union leaders had negotiated with the company. Union leaders announced that their concerns about pensions and about the outsourcing of jobs had been resolved through collective bargaining, while company officials stated they felt the deal was fair for everyone.[2]

Three months later, in early October 2013, more than 80 percent of 8,500 members of the United Food and Commercial Workers voted to accept the new offer their company had made. They had been on strike against Real Canadian Superstores in Alberta for only three days. While there was one key worker demand that the company did not meet—guaranteed minimum weekly hours for part-time workers—it did agree to higher hourly wages and improved benefits, including health care coverage.[3]

Meanwhile, in mid-2013, young baristas in a Halifax coffee shop voted to join the Service Employees International Union, while their counterparts in two other local coffee shops were organizing to do the same.[4] Labour analysts were somewhat surprised by this development, assuming that because many workers in this industry are employed part time while attending school, they would not be so interested in joining a union.

A month later, in Weyburn, Saskatchewan, the results of a vote by Wal-Mart employees to decertify a union were released—51 of 56 employees voted to get rid of the union already in their workplace. This left Wal-Mart union-free at all its locations across Canada, and the United Food and Commercial Workers (UFCW) vowing to renew its efforts to unionize Wal-Mart's Canadian outlets, something it has been trying to do since 1977.[5]

These brief accounts highlight a number of points we will make in this chapter. The ongoing battle between Wal-Mart and UFCW Canada highlights the rights of workers to join a union, widely considered a basic human right. As we will see, a large minority of Canadian workers are already union members, but the majority are not, some because they do not have the opportunity and others because they are unaware of or ambivalent about unions' goals and methods. We will also learn that the union movement is not limited to blue-collar manufacturing and resource-extraction industries. Unions have become very active in the upper-tier services (particularly in the public sector) and are also trying to organize lower-tier service workers in the retail and food and accommodation sectors.

These examples remind us that when labour negotiations reach an impasse and a strike or lockout occurs, we are not simply looking at a "union problem." There are two parties involved. Both employers and workers (through their unions) are trying to get a better deal for themselves, and both typically think that their own position is fair. Furthermore, when unions resort to strike action, the outcome is not always beneficial to workers. What is not evident from these examples, though, nor from media accounts of strikes and lock-outs, is that the vast majority of contracts between Canadian employers and unions are settled without any work disruptions. The data we will examine clearly demonstrate this.

We have already noted the ambivalence of many Canadian workers regarding unions. The Canadian public, as a whole, is similarly uncertain about its response to organized labour. For example, a 2012 EKOS Research national public opinion survey found that only 40 percent of Canadian adults agreed that "all in all, unions are a positive force in society."[6] Another survey, conducted by the Public Response Group in 2012, revealed that 61 percent of Canadians felt that unions "do a good job of protecting their members' jobs," but only 46 percent agreed that "gains made by unions for their members also improve the lives of other Canadians."[7] And, in 2011, a poll conducted by Abacus Research showed that 60 percent of Canadians supported the federal government when it passed legislation to force striking unionized Canada Post and Air Canada employees back to work.[8]

These polling results frame several other questions asked in this chapter. Just how beneficial are unions for their members but also for society as a whole? Should unions be rethinking their goals and strategies? What is the role of government in regulating industrial relations? As we will see, public-sector unions are now the largest and fastest-growing unions in Canada. This development raises a unique and difficult dilemma since, for these unions, the government is both the employer and the institution that makes and enforces the rules governing what unions can do. When is it justifiable for "the public good" to take precedence over the rights and interests of employees? But before tackling these contentious subjects, we will review some relevant theoretical perspectives and provide a brief history of organized labour in Canada.

■ THEORETICAL PERSPECTIVES ON ORGANIZED LABOUR

Mainstream industrial relations theory views the *system of job regulation* as the core of worker–management relations (Bain and Clegg 1974).[9] The rules and regulations that form the basis of collective agreements are assumed to inject stability into employment relations by tilting the balance of power slightly away from management and toward workers. However, this perspective over-plays the importance of predictable and harmonious industrial relations. By focusing on the formal system of rules and institutions governing industrial relations, the mainstream perspective does not question the existing distribution of power between workers and management. It also overlooks much of the daily informal interaction between workers and employers, as "the rules of the game" are constantly being negotiated. It is important to recognize that work is a power relationship in which conflict is always a possibility (Chapter 10) and in which unions are frequently involved.

Conflict and Cooperation in Union–Management Relations

Collective bargaining is the process by which a union, on behalf of its members, and an employer reach a negotiated agreement (called a *collective agreement* or a contract), which defines for a specific time period wages, work hours and schedules, benefits, and other working conditions, and procedures for resolving grievances. Collective agreements are negotiated and administered under provincial and federal labour laws and are designed to reduce conflict. Indeed, the main thrust of modern industrial relations practice is the avoidance of conflict. Thus, for the system to operate with some degree of fairness and equity for workers, who, on the whole, are in the weaker bargaining position, there must be the threat of conflict that could disrupt the employer's business. While critics often insist that the Canadian industrial relations scene is too adversarial, a federal government task force on labour relations responded to these concerns decades ago, explaining that

> [p]aradoxical as it may appear, collective bargaining is designed to resolve conflict through conflict, or at least through the threat of conflict. It is an adversary system in which two basic issues must be resolved: how available revenue is to be divided, and how the clash between management's

drive for productive efficiency and the workers' quest for job, income and psychic security are to be reconciled.[10]

As noted frequently in Chapters 8 through 10, managers of work organizations must balance the profit-seeking goals of owners (and shareholders) and the resulting need to control employees with the necessity of achieving a workable level of cooperation and commitment from them. Workers aim for higher wages, better working conditions, and more autonomy in their jobs. Employers pursue higher profits, lower costs, and increased productivity. The chronic tension between these opposing interests forces tradeoffs on both sides, and may also generate open conflict. However, not all union–management negotiations are a *zero-sum game*, or a situation in which one side can gain something only if the other gives up something. Indeed, on some issues, such as improved health and safety conditions (see Chapter 12), negotiations can produce a win-win situation in which both workers and management benefit. This approach to negotiations is called "mutual gains bargaining" (Weiss 2003).

Unions as "Managers of Discontent"

Having observed the oppressive conditions experienced by mid-19th-century factory workers, Marx concluded that eventually their misery and poverty would ignite a revolution (Chapter 1). But, as Stephen Hill (1981: Chapter 7) pointed out, even Marxists, committed to the belief that capitalism pits workers and bosses against each other in constant struggle, acknowledge that collective bargaining integrates workers into the existing capitalist system. In fact, Vladimir Lenin, leader of the Russian Revolution, dismissed trade unions as capable only of reform, not revolution.

In some respects, contemporary unions function as *managers of discontent* (Mills 1948). They channel the frustrations and complaints of workers into a carefully regulated dispute-resolution system. Unions help their members to articulate specific work problems or needs, and solutions are then sought through collective bargaining, or through grievance procedures. For example, labour legislation prohibiting strikes during the term of a collective agreement puts pressure on union leaders to contain any actions by their members that could disrupt the truce with management. Thus, most unions today operate in ways that contribute to the maintenance of capitalism, seeking reforms that reduce power imbalances favouring owners and managers.

Generally speaking, unions are democratic organizations whose constitutions allow members to elect their leaders. Theoretically, then, union leaders are responsive and accountable to the union members who elected them, translating their wishes into tangible collective bargaining goals. But this has not always been the case. Robert Michels (1959) was the first to investigate the issue of *union democracy*. His study of German trade unions prior to World War I concluded that leaders in working-class organizations always dominate members. Michels's famous *iron law of oligarchy* draws on technical, organizational, and psychological explanations. According to this theory, leaders develop expert knowledge, which gives them power. Once in office, leaders can control the organization to maintain their power. Finally, the masses tend to identify with leaders and expect them to exercise power on their behalf.

But in Canada and elsewhere, over a number of decades, we have witnessed the emergence of strong grassroots movements challenging entrenched union leadership cliques and, in effect, opposing oligarchic rule. Most unions today espouse democratic principles, but some have been more successful in putting these into practice than others. In fact, union officials seem to be constantly trying to increase the participation of members in union activities (Freeman 1982). Images of corrupt and autocratic leaders, while headlined by the media and reinforced by the history of a few unions, are far from typical. Thus, what Michels (1959) discovered was not a universal trait of unions, but a potential problem faced by all large bureaucratic organizations.

Business versus Social Unionism

Typically, the daily activities of unions focus on two types of goals: gaining more control over the labour process (Chapter 10) and increasing work rewards for members. There are frequently compromises between these two goals. Because of their immediate economic needs or because they are not all that involved in their work (Marx would have called this "alienation"), workers may want their unions to focus primarily on economic rewards. In addition, employers are sometimes willing to give up more of their profits rather than concede to workers' greater decision-making authority. This emphasis by unions on material gain rather than job control, known as *business unionism*, has become a hallmark of the North American labour movement.

In the last few decades, however, we have also seen the emergence in some unions of *social unionism*. While still engaging in collective bargaining with employers over wages, benefits, and other work rewards, some public-sector unions, such as the Canadian Union of Public Employees (CUPE), along with some large private-sector unions, such as the Canadian Auto Workers (CAW; now renamed Unifor), have taken on a much broader agenda of societal reform, entering public debates about issues such as globalization, international human rights, and health care reform (Gindin 1995). And, in a few cases, some union locals (rather than the complete union) have actively collaborated with social justice organizations to implement social reforms in their communities, across the country, or even globally. David Camfield (2011) describes such involvement by unions in networks of organizations that are trying to benefit others, not just union members, as *social movement unionism*. In a similar manner, some U.S. and Mexican unions have collaborated to resist the negative effects of globalization on workers in both countries (Kay 2011).

The Economic Impact of Unions

Unions benefit their members financially. On average, Canadian unionized workers earn about 10 percent more than nonunion workers do, with the impact being greater for women than for men. However, in recent years, this *union wage premium* has declined, or even reversed in firms with 500 or more employees (Statistics Canada 2008i: 41). Union members also are more likely than comparable nonunion workers to receive additional non-wage benefits. For example, a study of Canadian child-care workers found that unions raised wages by 15 percent, had a positive impact on benefits, and provided financial incentives for workers to improve their qualifications and skills (Cleveland, Gunderson, and Hyatt 2003). Unions also contribute to reducing overall wage inequality in a nation's labour market, although less so than in the past. The union impact on wages is greatest for workers in the lower and middle ranges of the income, education, and skill distributions. In other words, without unions, income inequality in Canada would likely be even higher (Chapter 5). Indeed, in Canada, the United States, and the United Kingdom, growing income inequality has been linked, in part, to declining union membership.[11]

Access to these economic advantages of union membership obviously depends on where one works. Unionization is significantly higher in large workplaces in the core sector of the economy (Chapter 5), where employers are in a better competitive position to provide decent wages and working conditions. In turn, nonstandard jobs, with their lower wages, fewer non-wage benefits, and less job security (Chapter 4), are typically nonunionized (Kalleberg, Reskin, and Hudson 2000). Barriers to unionization of part-time and temporary workers include restrictive legislation and, until recently, lack of interest among unions. However, some unions have begun to recognize the need for and importance of organizing workers in nonstandard jobs (Vosko 2000).

The most thorough analysis of what trade unions do continues to be a study by two Harvard economists, Richard Freeman and James Medoff (1984: 5–19), who make a useful distinction between the two "faces" of unionism. The *monopoly* face represents unions' power to raise members' wages at the expense of employers and of nonunionized workers. The *collective voice* face shifts attention to how unions democratize authoritarian workplaces, giving workers a collective voice in dealing with management. Freeman and Medoff admit that unions do impose some social and economic costs, but think that these are far outweighed by their positive contributions. Unions significantly advance workers' economic and political rights and freedoms. And, to the chagrin of their opponents, unions also typically boost productivity through lower employee turnover, better management performance, reduced hiring and training costs, and greater labour–management communication and cooperation (Lee 2007; Gunderson and Hyatt 2009). But because of higher wage costs, productivity gains do not necessarily make unionized firms more profitable. On balance, unionization appears to improve rather than to harm the social and economic systems (Walsworth and Long 2012).

HISTORY OF THE CANADIAN LABOUR MOVEMENT

Craft Unionism

Skilled craftworkers—carpenters, bricklayers, masons, cabinetmakers, blacksmiths, shoemakers, and tailors—were the first to unionize in Canada. A strike by Toronto printers in 1872 resulted in the Trade

Unions Act, which, for the first time, legalized union activity. Prior to that, unions had been considered a conspiracy against the normal operations of business. Other significant events that laid the foundations for trade unionism in Canada were the Nine-Hour Movement in the 1870s, involving working-class agitation for shorter working hours; and the creation of the Trades and Labour Congress (TLC) in 1883 as the first central labour body.[12]

Craft pride based on the special skills acquired through a long apprenticeship, solidarity with fellow artisans, and a close integration of work and communities were the hallmarks of these early *craft unions.* Craftsmen (there were no women among them) were the aristocrats of the working class. Printers, for example, reinforced their status by referring to their work as a "profession." As other craftsmen have done, shoemakers bolstered craft pride by going back into history to identify St. Crispin as their patron saint (Kealey 1980: 292).

Craft unions served as benevolent societies, providing members with a form of social insurance years before the rise of the welfare state. They also protected their members' position in the labour market by regulating access to the craft, thus monopolizing its unique skills. Today, this practice would be referred to as a *labour market shelter* (see Chapter 5). And as small local enterprises of the 19th century gave way to the factories and large corporations of the 20th, unions provided craftsmen with a defence against the erosion of their way of life. Through their unions, artisans vigorously opposed scientific management and the mechanization and reorganization of craft production in factories.

Craft unions dominated the young Canadian labour movement well into the 20th century, a time when the labour market for many skilled trades spanned both sides of the Canada–U.S. border. Hence, these *international unions* were American based and affiliated with the conservative American Federation of Labor (AFL). The internationals quickly came to control the Canadian labour scene. At the 1902 convention of the Trades and Labour Congress, the AFL unions purged their Canadian-based rivals by successfully moving that no organization duplicating one already in the American federation could be a member of the Trades and Labour Congress. They thus stole power from more radical Canadian labour leaders (Babcock 1974).

Industrial Unionism

The craft principle underlying the early AFL unions contrasts with *industrial unionism*, where all workers in an industry are represented by the same union, regardless of their occupation. The Knights of Labour, the earliest industrial union in Canada, organized their first local assembly in Hamilton, Ontario, in 1875. For a brief period in the 1880s, they challenged the dominance of the AFL craft unions. Driven by an idealistic radicalism, the Knights' immediate goal was to organize all workers into a single union, regardless of sex, skill level, craft, or industry, in order to eventually abolish the capitalist wage system and create a new society. Their membership peaked in 1887, with more than 200 local assemblies representing workers in 75 occupations. But rapid membership growth made it difficult to maintain an idealistic philosophy, and political rivalries both internal and external (with the AFL craft unions) led to the demise of the Knights. By the early years of the 20th century, they had all but disappeared in Canada (Kealey 1981) and the United States (Voss 1994).

Only a handful of industrial unions emerged in the early 20th century. Several were part of the rising tide of labour radicalism that reached a crest with the 1919 Winnipeg General Strike. There was a distinctive regional flavour to these working-class protests, as most were rooted in western Canada (McCormack 1978). For example, the radical ideology of the Chicago-based Industrial Workers of the World (the "Wobblies") attracted unskilled immigrants employed in lumbering, mining, agriculture, and railways in the West prior to World War I. One Big Union (OBU), a revolutionary industrial union, received widespread support in the western provinces, particularly among miners, loggers, and transportation workers. One Big Union called for secession from the conservative AFL and its Canadian arm, the Trades and Labour Congress. Its support for the Russian Revolution brought vigorous counterattacks from employers, governments, and craft unions, and caused the union's eventual defeat in the 1920s.

Not until the 1940s did industrial unionism become firmly established in Canada. The breakthrough was the UAW's milestone victory in 1937 against General Motors in Oshawa, Ontario. The United Auto Workers sprang up under the banner of the left-leaning Congress of Industrial Organizations (CIO) in the 1930s to organize unskilled and semiskilled workers in mass-production industries. Many of the initial forays into the auto, electrical, rubber, and chemical factories of corporate North America were led by communist organizers. Craft union leaders opposed the CIO largely on political grounds, despite the fact that Canadian workers embraced the CIO form of industrial unionism (Abella 1974).

In 1956, Canadian craft and industrial unions buried their differences, uniting skilled and unskilled workers within a single central labour organization: the Canadian Labour Congress (CLC). A similar merger of the AFL and the CIO had occurred one year earlier in the United States. The CLC remains Canada's "house of labour." Its affiliated unions represented 3.2 million workers in 2013, almost 70 percent of all Canadian union members.[13] The CLC promotes the economic, political, and organizational interests of affiliated unions by providing research, education, and organizational and collective bargaining services, as well as by eliminating jurisdictional conflicts. It sometimes becomes embroiled in inter-union disputes over jurisdictions and complaints about unions *raiding* other unions for members. One prominent example was the Canadian Auto Workers' (CAW) recruitment in 1987 of Newfoundland fishery workers who were at that time represented by the United Food and Commercial Workers International Union. At times, the CLC has become active on the national political stage, for example, by forming coalitions with other community-based groups to oppose free trade in the 1980s. The CLC also has had strong ties to the New Democratic Party (NDP), taking a leading role in founding the party in 1961. In the last several elections, though, CLC leaders have been slower to encourage CLC members to vote NDP, although they have almost always opposed the Conservative government in Ottawa.

Quebec Labour

The history and present character of the labour movement in Quebec contribute to the distinctiveness of social and economic life in that province (Déom, Grenier, and Beaumont 2009). Quebec labour's history is a fascinating topic in its own right and deserves more than the brief treatment we can afford to give it here. Many of the issues central to Canada's ongoing constitutional debates are amplified in the arena of labour relations. For example, industrial relations have been shaped by a different legal framework in Quebec (its laws are derived from the Civil Code of France, rather than British-based common law). A more interventionist state role has created a higher degree of centralized bargaining than in other provinces, as well as resulting in some innovative legislation, such as the 1977 anti-strikebreaking law. Nationalist politics have left an indelible mark on union policies and priorities, too. Indeed, the question of special representation for Quebec on the executive of the Canadian Labour Congress at the congress's 1992 convention raised the spectre of a split between the national umbrella group and the Quebec Federation of Labour, which represents CLC affiliates in that province.

The development of unions in Quebec followed a different path from that of the rest of Canada. For example, in the early 20th century, the Roman Catholic Church organized conservative unions that, unlike their counterparts elsewhere, emphasized the common interests of employers and employees. During the years that Premier Maurice Duplessis and the ultraconservative Union Nationale held power (from 1936 to 1960), the state took repressive actions to stifle more independent union development. Worker militancy flared up in response, the most violent manifestations being the 1949 miners' strike at Asbestos and the 1957 Murdochville copper miners' strike. Some analysts view these strikes as major catalysts in Quebec's Quiet Revolution, which ushered in sweeping social, economic, and political reforms in the 1960s.

During this period, the old Roman Catholic unions cut their ties with the church, becoming one of the main central labour organizations in the province (the CNTU, or Confederation of National Trade Unions) and adopting an increasingly radical stance. Hence, the Quebec Federation of Labour, made up of CLC-affiliated unions, differs from its counterparts in other provinces; it represents a minority of union members in the province and operates in a more independent manner. Another influential union organization is the Fédération des syndicats de l'enseignement, the organization representing about 60,000 teachers in French school boards across the province. Thus, there is no unified Quebec labour movement, although these central organizations have banded together on occasion, the most notable example being the 1972 Common Front strike by some 200,000 public-sector workers against government policies.

The Role of the Canadian State in Industrial Relations

In Canada, there has developed a legislative and administrative framework that casts the state as *impartial umpire*, mediating between labour and capital in an effort to establish and maintain industrial peace. The architect of this system was William Lyon Mackenzie King, the first federal minister of labour and later a Liberal prime minister. King's 1907 Industrial Disputes Investigation Act (IDIA) became the cornerstone of Canada's modern industrial relations policy that strives to *institutionalize conflict* through the control of law. The Act provided for compulsory *conciliation* (fact finding) in disputes during a "cooling off" period, a tripartite board of *arbitration*, and special treatment of public interest disputes involving public services. It also banned strikes or lockouts during the term of a collective agreement. At first, the Act was applied to disputes in coal mines and railways. Its scope was extended during World War I, and in the 1950s, its principles were incorporated into provincial legislation. In some instances, the state used the powers of the Act to legislate an end to strikes. This type of state intervention has shaped the pattern of industrial conflict in Canada—some would argue, in the interests of employers (Craven 1980; Huxley 1979).

In 1944, the National War Labour Order, regulation P.C. 1003, brought Canadian industrial relations into its modern phase. Modelled on the 1935 U.S. National Labor Relations Act (Wagner Act), P.C. 1003 granted employees in the private sector collective bargaining rights, set down union certification procedures, spelled out a code of unfair labour practices, and established a labour relations board to administer the law. These measures paved the way for a postwar labour–management pact designed to maintain industrial peace. This truce was enshrined in federal legislation in 1948 and in subsequent provincial legislation.

Another milestone in the legal entrenchment of *collective bargaining rights* came out of a 1945 strike by the United Auto Workers at the Ford Motor Company in Windsor, Ontario. The *Rand Formula*, named after Justice Ivan Rand of the Supreme Court, whose ruling was instrumental in settling the strike, provided for union security through a *union shop* and *union dues checkoff*. According to the Rand Formula, even though no one should be required to join a union, it is justifiable to automatically deduct union dues from the paycheques of all employees in a workplace because a union must act for the benefit of all employees. It does not matter whether or not the employees belong to the union.

The emergence of public-sector unions in the second half of the 20th century changed the industrial relations scene yet again. The movement toward full-fledged public-sector unionism began in Saskatchewan in 1944.

The real push, however, started when Quebec public employees were granted collective bargaining rights in 1964. Another major breakthrough was the 1967 Public Service Staff Relations Act, which opened the door to unions in the federal civil service.

Some analysts argue that industrial relations entered a coercive phase during the 1980s. Leo Panitch and Donald Swartz (1993) view government imposition of wage controls, more restrictive trade union legislation, and the use of courts to end strikes as signals of the end of "free collective bargaining," as established by the industrial relations system set out in earlier federal legislation. Panitch and Swartz characterize this new era as *permanent exceptionalism*, reflecting how the suspension of labour's rights and more heavy-handed state intervention became the rule rather than the exception.[14] As we shall see later, there is now considerable debate over whether Canadian industrial relations are being destabilized.

"Canadianizing" Unions

The rise of public-sector unions has also helped to *Canadianize* the labour movement. At the beginning of the 20th century, U.S.-based international unions represented about 95 percent of all unionized workers in Canada. By 1969, this proportion had dropped to 65 percent, and it has continued to decline rapidly since then.[15] The vulnerability of Canada's branch-plant economy, particularly during the 1980s, taught growing numbers of workers the need for greater local control of union activities. Different bargaining agendas also tended to arise in the two countries, reflecting their distinctive industrial relations environments. Canadian autoworkers, for instance, roundly rejected the concessions made to employers by the U.S. wing of their union. The issue of national autonomy came to a head in the 1984 strike against General Motors by the Canadian division of the United Auto Workers. These Canadian autoworkers found themselves pitted against not only General Motors, but also the UAW leadership in Detroit, which wanted Canadian workers to accept the concessions agreed to by their American counterparts. While autonomy was not the goal of the Canadian workers going into the strike, it became an inevitable result.[16]

Beyond having different bargaining priorities and strategies, some Canadian branches of international unions felt that their dues were flowing into the U.S. headquarters with few services flowing back. These and other factors prompted a growing number of separations. In addition to the Canadian Auto Workers, the Communications, Energy and Paperworkers Union grew out of a Canada-U.S. split in an international union.[17] However, even after they split, good working relations were maintained between Canadianized unions and their former U.S. parents. What will be interesting to watch in the future is how unions create new forms of international cooperation—beyond Canada and the United States—to address the impact of economic globalization on workers. For example, the United Steelworkers recently joined with Unite, the biggest union in the United Kingdom, to create the first global union: Workers Uniting (Workers Uniting 2010).

A strong argument in support of international unions has been that they are organized labour's best defence against the global strategies of multinational corporations (Garver et al. 2007). Yet the international unions have not always been effective in dealing with the sorts of problems multinational corporations created for Canadian employees. For example, in response to the global recession in 2008, U.S.-based unions supported protectionist trade policies in an effort to preserve members' jobs within the United States, thus putting Canadian workers' jobs at risk.

◼ UNION MEMBERSHIP TRENDS

Figure 11.1 traces union membership growth in Canada since 1911, when there were only 133,000 union members in the country (5% of all non-agricultural paid workers). In 2012, there were approximately 4.66 million union members in the Canadian workforce (30% of non-agricultural paid workers). These percentages measure the unionization rate—or *union density*—and reflect the proportion of actual union members to potential members. The exclusion of agriculture, where most workers are self-employed and are, therefore, ineligible for union membership, allows for more accurate comparisons with earlier periods when agriculture was a much larger sector, and with other countries at different levels of industrialization.

It is important to note that *collective bargaining coverage* is typically about two percentage points higher than the unionization rate (Statistics Canada 2008i: 73). This difference is a result of some non-members in unionized workplaces being entitled to the wages and benefits negotiated by the union

FIGURE 11.1   Union Membership in Canada, 1911–2012

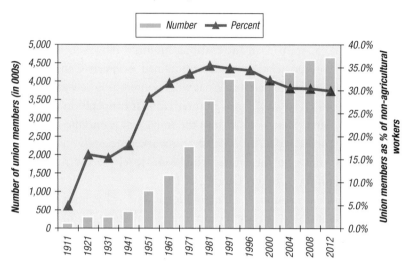

Source: Source: 1911–1975, Statistics Canada. *Historical Statistics of Canada.* Table E175-177 – Union membership in Canada, in total and as a percentage of non-agricultural paid workers and union members with international affiliation, 1911 to 1975. <http://www.statcan.gc.ca/pub/11-516-x/sectione/4147438-eng.htm#6>; 1976–1996, Statistics Canada. CANSIM Table 279-0025 - Number of unionized workers, employees and union density, by sex and province, annual (persons unless otherwise noted). <http://www5.statcan.gc.ca/cansim/a26?lang=eng&retrLang=eng&id=2790025&paSer=&pattern=&stByVal= 1&p1=1&p2=-1&tabMode=dataTable&csid=>; 1997-2012, Statistics Canada. CANSIM Table 282-0078 - Labour force survey estimates (LFS), employees by union coverage, North American Industry Classification System (NAICS), sex and age group, annual (persons). <http://www5.statcan.gc.ca/cansim/a05?lang=eng&id=2820078&pattern=2820078&searchTypeByValue=1&p2=35>

in a collective agreement. Among them are supervisory employees who are excluded because of their management role, new hires on probation, and individuals who, perhaps because of their religious or other personal beliefs, opt not to join. In 2011, there were 295,000 nonunion members in this category (Uppal 2011). Furthermore, Canadian labour law permits nonunion forms of collective representation, such as staff associations, which represent 5 percent of all employees. Another 9 percent of employees belong to professional associations, and some of these set wages and working conditions for members.[18]

Three major surges in Canadian union membership growth can be seen in Figure 11.1. The first two coincided with the two world wars (1914–18 and 1939–45). This pattern is not surprising because national mobilization for these wars resulted in economic growth, labour shortages, and the need for a high level of cooperation between employers and employees, all of which are key ingredients for successful union recruitment. As already noted, in the years during and immediately following World War II, Canada's contemporary industrial relations system took shape. The third growth surge, largely facilitated by supportive legislation, took place in the 1970s. The rise of *public-sector unions* in that decade brought many civil servants, teachers, nurses, and other public employees into the organized labour movement.

Canadian union density peaked at 37 percent in 1984. The decline over the next three decades can be traced to a number of recessions and to industrial restructuring, which both cut deeply into the traditional membership strength of unions in manufacturing and other blue-collar occupations. Similarly, periodic budget cuts and downsizing in the public sector, beginning in the 1990s, have led to lower union density. Employer pressures for concessions and the whittling away of collective bargaining rights by governments and the courts have contributed to a more hostile climate for labour relations, a topic to which we return below.

The labour movement has also undergone organizational changes. A notable trend is consolidation, resulting from mergers and membership growth since the 1960s (Chaison 2004). In 1968, there were 14 large unions (30,000 or more members), accounting for just under half of total union membership. By 2012, 42 unions had memberships of 30,000 or more, comprising over 75 percent of total union membership in the country.[19] Nevertheless, a defining feature of the Canadian labour movement is the large number of *locals*. In 2008, the 213 national and international unions contained 14,691 locals, the basic self-governing unit of the labour movement and the legal entity for collective bargaining. Membership in locals ranged from just a few members to more than 45,000. In short, despite consolidations, Canadian labour remains fragmented and, consequently, collective bargaining is decentralized. Unlike the situation in some European nations, where industry-wide national bargaining is the norm, the Canadian pattern of single-establishment, single-union bargaining results in thousands of collective agreements in effect at any one time.

A Comparative Perspective on Unionization

Figure 11.2 provides two key measures for 18 countries—recent rates of union membership[20] and the change in union density since 1970. In terms of current union density, Canada is higher than the United States, several European countries, the United Kingdom, Australia and New Zealand, and Japan and South Korea. But it is lower than the Scandinavian countries (Finland,

FIGURE 11.2   Unionization Rates in 18 Countries, 2010, and Absolute
Change, 1970–2010

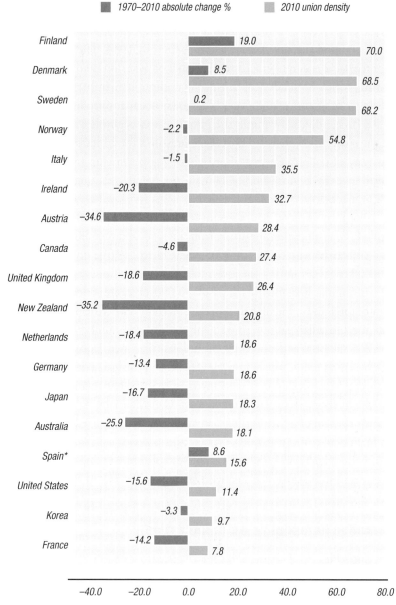

■ *1970–2010 absolute change %*　　■ *2010 union density*

Finland	19.0 / 70.0
Denmark	8.5 / 68.5
Sweden	0.2 / 68.2
Norway	–2.2 / 54.8
Italy	–1.5 / 35.5
Ireland	–20.3 / 32.7
Austria	–34.6 / 28.4
Canada	–4.6 / 27.4
United Kingdom	–18.6 / 26.4
New Zealand	–35.2 / 20.8
Netherlands	–18.4 / 18.6
Germany	–13.4 / 18.6
Japan	–16.7 / 18.3
Australia	–25.9 / 18.1
Spain*	8.6 / 15.6
United States	–15.6 / 11.4
Korea	–3.3 / 9.7
France	–14.2 / 7.8

–40.0   –20.0   0.0   20.0   40.0   60.0   80.0

*Absolute change 1980–2010, since 1970 data are not available.

Source: 1970, *OECD Employment Outlook 2004*. Table 3.3 – Trade union density and collective bargaining coverage in OECD countries, 1970–2000, p. 145. <http://www.oecd.org/employment/emp/oecdemploymentoutlook2004.htm>; 2010, OECD *StatExtracts*. Trade Union Density. <http://stats.oecd.org/Index.aspx?QueryId=20167>

Denmark, Sweden, and Norway), Austria, Ireland, and Italy. Union density reveals only part of the strength of unions, however; collective bargaining coverage also must be considered. In Europe, it is more common than in Canada, the United States, or Japan for workers who are not union members to have terms and conditions of employment set by collective agreements. For example, in France, the Netherlands, and Germany, where relatively few wage and salary earners are union members, between 80 and 90 percent are covered by the provisions of collective agreements that these unions negotiate (International Labour Office 1997).

What accounts for these cross-national differences? In North America, key factors are management's traditional opposition to unions, labour laws that make the certification process for new bargaining units difficult, and a decentralized industrial relations system based in local workplaces (Lipsig-Mummé 2009). In Japan, where density and coverage are similar, collective bargaining also is decentralized and firm based. But, unlike in North America and Japan, in many western European countries there is much greater coordination within each industrial sector. This pattern is a result of highly centralized collective bargaining systems, supported by law, in which national unions negotiate with large employers' federations. Pay and other basic working conditions are set nationally or by industrial sector, greatly reducing competition among individual workplaces on these issues (unlike in Canada, where a firm may resist union pay demands because it would increase its wage costs relative to local competitors). So, in France, for example, despite a union density of less than 10 percent (Figure 11.2), employer associations are legally required to regularly negotiate broad agreements with unions, the benefits of which are extended to virtually all employers and employees.

We noted earlier that Canadian union density has been in slow decline over the last several decades. This fact is reflected in Figure 11.2, which also indicates ongoing declines in union membership density in 13 of the other 17 countries listed. Declines in both density and coverage were more common in nations with employer-centred, decentralized industrial relations systems—notably the United States and Japan. Drops in coverage were less likely in countries with strong sectoral or national bargaining regulated by the state to balance employers' and employees' interests. The United Kingdom and New Zealand, two countries with previously centralized systems, stand out with declining density and coverage. In each case, market-oriented governments deregulated and decentralized industrial relations systems in efforts to weaken the power of unions—basically, a shift to a more American model of industrial relations (Freeman 1995). There are also signs in other European countries, Australia, and New Zealand of a shift in collective bargaining from national or sectoral levels down to firms, largely due to the introduction of more flexible forms of work organization, although the extent and implications of this decentralization process vary considerably (International Labour Office 1997).

In the field of *comparative industrial relations* there is growing interest in the transformation of labour relations in countries with economic and political histories quite different from the countries featured in Figure 11.2 (Bamber, Lansbury, and Wailes 2011). Researchers are interested in unionization trends in Asia, the former Soviet Union, and Central and South America. At issue are how different patterns of economic development and political change affect workers' freedom to join unions and, equally important, the efficacy of unions. In Mexico, union density has declined in the face of increasing employer resistance to unions and the growing use of what are called "protection contracts," whereby employers pay unions not to represent their members' interests in a workplace (Fairris and Levine 2004). In India, public-sector unions, traditionally aligned with specific political parties, have been unsure of how to respond to these same parties freezing public-sector wages or cutting jobs (Roychowdhury 2003). And in former socialist countries such as China and Russia, unions are struggling to find a new role (Clarke 2005). In China economic reforms have reduced direct state regulation of labour relations, but because unions remain integrated with management, they are unable to consult or negotiate on behalf of workers (Clarke, Chang-Hee, and Qi 2004). In Russia, former communist trade unions have pursued social partnerships to reduce industrial conflict and protect members' interests during the transition to a market economy, but these initiatives have been largely ineffective because of the history of union collaboration with government and employers during the Soviet era (Ashwin 2004).

An interesting new development, in response to the growth of *globalized production networks* that link smaller producers, manufacturers, and distribution companies in one part of the world with massive distribution and retail companies in another, is the emergence of *transnational union networks* that allow unions in different parts of the world to cooperate in pursuing common goals of safer and less exploitative working conditions and improved human rights (Helfen and Fichter 2013).[21] For example, unions representing seafarers and port workers have formed a global alliance through the International

Transport Workers' Federation, with its Flags of Convenience campaign (Lillie 2005). Based in London, England, the federation coordinates actions to maintain minimum pay standards, negotiate collective agreements with shipowners, and prevent union-busting at ports around the world.

The Decline of U.S. Unions

While it has declined somewhat, Canadian union membership has remained relatively stable compared to the United States and Japan which also have employer-centred industrial relations (Lowe 1998). In fact, U.S. unions appear to be in a struggle for survival (Devinatz 2013).[22] Membership has plunged from 20.1 percent of the workforce in 1983 to 11.4 percent in 2010 (Figure 11.2). Observers attribute this decline to a number of factors, but, in particular, to fierce anti-union campaigns launched by some private-sector employers and labour laws that permit these coercive tactics. In addition, management innovations offering workers some form of decision-making participation (see Chapter 9) have been used to keep unions out of many workplaces, and public-sector downsizing and the privatizing of government services have led to many fewer unionized jobs (Goldfield and Bromsen 2013). Where unions still exist, *concession bargaining* (unions agreeing to roll-backs in wages, benefits, and collective rights) has frequently weakened them. Significant, too, is the shift of employment away from the union strongholds of the northeastern industrial regions to southern states, where *right-to-work laws* undermine union security; under such laws, neither union membership nor payment of union dues may be required as a condition of employment, even if the workplace is unionized (Dixon 2008).[23]

Another perspective is offered by Seymour Martin Lipset (1990) who argues that a core difference between Canada and the United States is the historically stronger commitment among Americans to individualistic values, and Canadians' greater sense of collective rights, which are more amenable to unionization. However, a recent study found that American workers were slightly more approving of unions than were Canadian workers, and considerably more nonunion workers in the United States would vote for a union if they had the opportunity (Lipset and Meltz 1997). Yet the actual level of union membership in the United States, as we have seen, is about one-third that of Canada. This paradox reflects the difference between deep-rooted *values*, which underlie the institutions of labour relations, and more immediate *attitudes* toward unions, which reflect current labour market conditions and union strength. So, in the United States, unions are so weak today that workers believe they should be stronger, while, in Canada, the greater power of unions ends up being a source of criticism among many.

The U.S. experience shows the decisive role of legislation and management opposition in encouraging or inhibiting free collective bargaining. Some analysts argue, pessimistically, that unions lack the resources and supportive public policies required for the massive new organizing successes needed to grow their membership. However, other scholars detect a few signs of union revival in the United States, which may reverse or at least slow down the trends described above.[24] Some local unions have developed innovative organizing strategies that have appealed to low-wage workers, women, and racial and ethnic minorities.

The Justice for Janitors campaign in Los Angeles is an example. As in many North American cities, janitorial work in Los Angeles is done under short-term contracts by companies who employ immigrant workers. Trying to counter many years of industrial restructuring and de-unionization, in the 1990s the Service Employees International Union launched a successful public campaign to reunionize the industry and improve the lot of Central American immigrants. Many of these workers were women, and many had entered the United States without documentation. The campaign focused on getting building owners to help provide health and welfare benefits to janitors and their families (Cranford 2004). Justice for Janitors shows how some U.S. unions are trying to build broad coalitions with other community groups to address social justice issues (Krinsky and Reese 2006), a strategy we earlier labelled as social movement unionism. This strategy has also been effective in Canada, as in 2010 when the same union organized temporary foreign workers employed as janitors at the University of Alberta and helped them negotiate a better wage and overtime settlement with their private-sector employer to whom the university had outsourced its janitorial work (Foster and Barnetson 2012).

Canadian Union Membership Patterns

Because of the large industrial and labour force changes that have occurred over the past half century (see Chapters 3 and 6), the much higher rate of union representation for men compared to women that once existed in Canada has largely disappeared (Morissette, Schellenberg, and Johnson 2005). In fact, in 2011, 31 percent of female employees (excluding the unemployed and self-employed) belonged to a union, compared to 28 percent of men, reflecting the large number of women employed in the public sector, which is much more highly unionized.[25] However, age remains a major source of variation in union membership rates. While 30 percent of all Canadian employees were unionized in 2011, only 14 percent of young workers (ages 15 to 24 years) belonged to unions, compared with 30 percent of 25- to 44-year-olds, 36 percent of those ages 45 to 54 years, and 34 percent of employees 55 years of age and older. Again, the explanation can be traced back to industry differences—young workers are much more likely to be employed in the retail and food and accommodation industries, which have low unionization rates (14% and 7%, respectively, in 2011).

Looking further at industry differences, education and public administration had the highest unionization rates in 2011 (68% and 67%, respectively). The rate in the utilities sector was almost as high (64%), since many utility companies are or were government owned and, hence, more highly unionized. Health care's unionization rate was somewhat lower (53 percent); although almost all nurses are unionized, doctors are not, and neither are some other health care support workers. In the transportation sector (e.g., railways, airlines, trucking), 41 percent of employees were unionized, as were 30 percent in construction, and 25 percent in manufacturing. In sharp contrast, only 9 percent of employees in finance, insurance, and real estate were union members. The unionization rate in agriculture was even lower (5%).

Provincial differences in labour legislation, industrial mix, and economic performance also influence union membership. Newfoundland and Labrador had the highest rate of unionization in 2011 (38%) because of the disproportionately large size of the unionized public sector in a historically weak economy and the strength of unions in the fishing industry. Quebec (36%), Manitoba (35%), and Saskatchewan (34%) are next, for reasons that largely reflect the political contexts more supportive of collective bargaining rights. In 2011, Ontario's union density was 27 percent, while Alberta's was the lowest in the country at only 22 percent. Alberta's industrial relations have moved closer to the American model, given this province's more restrictive labour legislation and American-style nonunion human resource policies found in key industries such as oil and gas (Noël and Gardner 1990; Block and Roberts 2000).

Other employment characteristics are also associated with union membership, with workplace size being one of the strongest predictors. In 2011, 54 percent of employees in workplaces with more than 500 employees were unionized, compared with 41 percent in workplaces with between 100 and 500 employees, 30 percent in 20 to 99 person workplaces, and only 13 percent in even smaller establishments. Full-time workers (33%) were more likely to be unionized than part-time employees (25%), and permanent employees had somewhat higher unionization rates than did temporary workers (30% compared to 26%).

In short, the composition of the labour movement has been transformed since the 1960s. The typical unionist today is a white-collar worker employed in one of the service industries, quite likely in the public sector. Women have joined the ranks of organized labour faster than men, and some experts claim that even more women could become members if union recruitment practices were less gender biased (Yates 2006). There also is the potential for growing union representation among immigrants and racial minorities. Wages for immigrants and visible minorities (often the same people) tend to be lower than average (Chapter 5). With the exception of Black immigrant women, immigrants and racial minorities are less likely to be union members than the white majority (Reitz and Verma 2004). This gap in unionization is somewhat reduced the longer that immigrants are in Canada. Union campaigns targeting meatpacking, building services, and other sectors with high concentrations of immigrants could speed up this process.

Canada's Largest Unions

As already noted, total union density has declined somewhat in Canada over the past three decades, in part, because of significantly reduced employment in traditionally unionized sectors like manufacturing. In marked contrast, union membership has continued to grow in the public sector and in some other service industries. This trend began back in 1967 when the federal government passed the Public Service Staff Relations Act, thus allowing collective bargaining for federal civil servants. Provincial government employees were already moving in this direction; Quebec public employees had received collective bargaining rights in 1965. Unionism soon spread into municipal governments, hospitals, schools, prisons, social services, and other expanding publicly funded institutions.

Canada's largest union is the Canadian Union of Public Employees (CUPE) with members employed in a wide spectrum of jobs in municipalities, social services, schools, libraries, colleges and universities, hospitals and nursing homes, and many other public institutions. Because it had diversified far beyond its core membership in public administration, CUPE had become the largest union of any kind in Canada by the early 1980s. By the beginning of this century, it already had close to half a million members, and by 2013, its membership had grown to 612,000.[26] The National Union of Public and General Employees (NUPGE), the second-largest union in the country (440,000 members in 2013), is also a public-sector union, as is the Public Service Alliance of Canada (PSAC), the sixth-largest Canadian union, with 188,000 members. NUPGE is an umbrella organization for various federal and provincial government unions while PSAC has members employed only in federal government departments.

Three industrial unions are in third, fourth, and fifth place on the list of Canada's six largest unions. In mid-2013, the Canadian Auto Workers (CAW), with close to 200,000 members, merged with the Communications, Energy and Paperworkers Union of Canada (CEP), which was about half this size, to form Unifor, a powerful Canadian-based industrial union with 309,000 members spread across the manufacturing, transportation, utilities, and many service industries. The CAW had already been aggressively diversifying into other sectors, including food services and casinos before the merger. The merger made the new union the third-largest in Canada. The United Food and Commercial Workers Union (UFCW Canada), with 245,000 members in 2013, is the Canadian wing of a U.S.-based union. The fourth-largest Canadian union, it has been actively trying to recruit workers in service industries outside the food-processing sector, where it has been dominant. In fifth place is the United Steelworkers union (231,000 members), also an international union with its home base in the United States. It, too, has been organizing workers in a wide range of manufacturing as well as service industries, including security guards, call-centre employees, and taxi drivers.

WOMEN AND UNIONS

While the unionization rate among female employees in Canada today is higher than the male rate, historically the pattern was reversed. A frequent explanation was that women would be less interested in unions because of their family responsibilities and presumed lower commitment to paid employment. Hence, work problems that might prompt unionization among men would be of secondary concern to women. Whether these assumptions were ever supported by fact is difficult to determine, but they certainly have not held true for the past four decades when women have been joining unions at a much faster rate than men. During union-organizing campaigns in Ontario during the 1980s and 1990s, for example, female-dominated workplaces were far more likely to vote in favour of union representation than were male-dominated workplaces (Yates 2000: 662–64).[27] Women today may be more pro-union than men because of their generally lower-paid and lower-status positions in workplaces (Chapter 6). Historical differences in unionism across industries are also important; men and women alike join unions and engage in militant action according to the established patterns of their industries or occupations (Briskin 2010). Thus, gender segregation in the labour market is the key factor in gendered unionization patterns.

In addition, in the past, male-dominated unions have acted to keep women out of certain jobs and, therefore, out of unions. In the early 20th century, for example, craft unions lobbied with middle-class reformers to keep women out of the industrial labour force, allegedly to protect them, but also because of fears that their wages would be undercut. In Canada, for example, the failure of the 1907 strike by female Bell Telephone operators in Toronto was partly due to the lack of support their unionization campaign received from the International Brotherhood of Electrical Workers, an exclusively male craft union (Sangster 1978).

Consequently, for many women the option of joining a union has not existed. Only in the last three or four decades, for example, were major organizing efforts launched in the largely female retail and financial industries, with massive counterattacks by management in banks and in retail stores. Despite a huge investment of organizing resources since the late 1970s, the Canadian Labour Congress has achieved only limited success in unionizing banks (Lowe 1981). Thus, while some areas of the retail industry, such as grocery stores, have achieved moderate levels of unionization, vast areas of the service sector are still not organized.

Feminist scholars have cast new light on the collective struggles of women to achieve fairness and equality through unions. In predominantly female occupations, women have a long tradition of collective action. As professionals, female teachers have been organized for many decades, although sometimes in professional associations rather than unions (Strong-Boag 1988). A history of union activism also exists among women in the garment and textile industries, particularly in unions such as the International Ladies' Garment Workers (Gannagé 1995; Frager 1992). Women also have exerted pressure on the male-dominated unions to which they belong to have their concerns addressed. As Pamela Sugiman shows in her study of women's struggle for gender equality within the Canadian wing of the United Auto Workers during the 1960s, feminists active in the union used "gendered strategies of coping and resistance," drawing on women's combined experiences as autoworkers, unionists, wives, and mothers. Even so, male UAW members had difficulty getting beyond their patriarchal ideology (Sugiman 1992: 24).

Because of such pressure from feminists within the organized labour movement, *pay equity* (discussed in Chapter 6) has become a major workplace objective for many unions. Perhaps the most prominent example was the 1991 strike on this issue by the Public Service Alliance of Canada (PSAC), which represents federal civil servants. However, it took until the end of that decade to reach a pay equity settlement with the government for these clerical and administrative workers. Gillian Creese's (1999) case study of the white-collar workers' union at BC Hydro shows how public-sector unions' quest for pay equity in the 1990s was made more difficult by the fact that it coincided with employers downsizing, restructuring, and contracting-out work. Even though the job hierarchy at BC Hydro did become more open to women and members of racial minorities, union traditions and culture continued to reflect the values and interests of white males.

Overall, however, women's demands for equality of opportunities and rewards in the workplace have had a major impact on Canadian unions. The CLC elected its first female president in 1986, and CUPE, the largest union in Canada, did the same in 1991. Women are making up a growing share of elected union officers and paid staff, especially in public-sector unions, many of which have developed policies and processes to ensure that women have equal representation in leadership positions (Parker and Foley 2010). Gradually, "women's issues"—which really are issues for all workers—have come to have higher stature in labour's collective bargaining and social action. Important bargaining items, at least for large unions, now include gender-neutral contract language and clauses dealing with discrimination, sexual harassment, family-related leave, childcare, and rights for part-time workers. Organized labour's success in achieving this bargaining agenda is obviously crucial to its future.

■ MANAGEMENT OPPOSITION TO UNIONS

Despite laws giving each employee the right to join a union and to participate in free collective bargaining, employer opposition to unionism has historically been a major obstacle to putting these rights into practice. Before the introduction of a legal framework for union certification and collective bargaining procedures during World War II, many industrial disputes occurred over an employer's outright refusal to recognize the workers' union. Surveying the historical record, Pentland (1979: 19) observes, "It is sad but true that Canadian employers as a group and Canadian governments have never taken a forward step in industrial relations by intelligent choice, but have had to be battered into it." Interestingly, a contemporary study of the attitudes of managers toward unions showed that Canadian managers were more hostile toward unions than were managers in the United States. The researchers attribute this unexpected difference to the fact that, compared to the Canadian situation, U.S. unions are very weak and hence not seen as much of a threat by managers (Campolieti, Gomez, and Gunderson 2013).

Even though disputes over union recognition are less common in Canada today than they were in the past, there are still many reasons why the climate for union organizing remains inhospitable (Bain 1978: 23). White-collar employees, who form the majority of the workforce today, often have direct contact with management and, therefore, may identify more closely with a company's anti-union position than do blue-collar workers. During union-organizing drives, management usually prefers to deal with each employee individually. This tactic creates a highly uneven playing field, pitting individual employees against the power of a corporation. Workers join unions for the benefits, such as better working conditions, higher wages, job security, or access to a grievance procedure. Concrete proof that unions can "deliver the goods" is obviously lacking in workplaces and industries that have never had high levels of unionization. In some cases, a *company union* or employee association supported by the employer creates the appearance of democratic employee representation. The difficulty of overcoming such obstacles can discourage unions from launching recruitment drives. Consequently, the option of joining a union has not been available to many private-sector, white-collar workers.

New managerial strategies such as lean production and high-performance workplace models that encourage employee participation and commitment (Chapter 9) have also been used by large companies to maintain a union-free workplace. The basic assumption, derived from the human relations management tradition, is that if management treats employees well and listens to their concerns, a union will be unnecessary. IBM is a good example of this approach in action. In Scotland in the late 1970s, the corporation's employees were balloted at the request of the government's industrial relations board to find out whether they desired union recognition. Over 90 percent voted against unionization (Dickson et al. 1988). This vote was not the result of corporate coercion or intimidation. Rather, it reflected the attention and resources that the company had devoted to employee relations. These human resource management policies produce a corporate culture based on strong employee loyalty and identification with management's goals (Keenoy 1985: 98–102). Some Canadian firms, most notably the Hamilton steel producer Dofasco, have developed their own unique brand of nonunion labour relations to obtain the cooperation of employees (Storey 1983). They thus remain union-free.

Pradeep Kumar explains why innovative managerial strategies pose difficulties for unions:

> ... unions and management have different views of the goals of workplace innovations. Management goals are primarily efficiency-oriented. The general mission of HRM [human resource management] is to improve organizational effectiveness and achieve competitive advantage through a more efficient utilization and development of human resources.... Unions, on the other hand, are voluntary organizations of workers that serve as their collective voice in order to improve their physical, economic, social, and political well-being. The underlying values of the unions are inherently pluralistic and collective.[28]

Even so, as Kumar (1995: 148) observes, some of the more successful innovations of this kind suggest that union involvement may be a prerequisite. The examples of Saturn, Shell, and NUMMI (see Chapter 9) make this point. But in most cases, unions have tended to respond with either passive acceptance of such new managerial initiatives or active rejection (Downie and Coates

1995). The CAW, after extensive experience with lean production, adopted a policy of carefully assessing the benefits and costs of participation (CAW 1993: 12). Only if workers' interests could be advanced and the union as an organization strengthened would the CAW enter into such change programs with management. Crucial ingredients are worker education and openness on management's part to share information (Martin 1995: 118–21).

An insightful study of a union's experience with new management systems (Rinehart, Huxley, and Robertson 1997) focused on CAMI, a joint venture between General Motors and Suzuki involving a new automobile factory in Ingersoll, Ontario. The CAW represented the workers, making CAMI one of the few North American "Japanese transplants" to be unionized. While the company's position was that lean production had empowered workers and, thus, made the enterprise highly competitive, the researchers concluded that CAMI was just fine-tuning Fordism. Chronic understaffing to reduce costs put intense pressure on workers who, despite the rhetoric of involvement, were still doing largely low-skill and repetitive work with a high risk of injury. "CAMI values" declined as worker discontent rose, and the reality of conflict replaced the promise of "win-win." Workers eventually went on strike for five weeks in 1992. As a result of the strike, the union gained more voice in setting production standards, in addition to negotiating higher wages.

■ ORGANIZED LABOUR AND COLLECTIVE ACTION

How do workers come to act collectively through unions in a capitalist society where individualism is strongly valued and where employers may actively oppose unions? There are two dilemmas that a worker must resolve if she or he is to seriously consider joining a union or, if already a member, becoming an activist.

The first is the *free-rider problem*. Just like social movements concerned with environmental, peace, or feminist issues, unions provide collective goods. In other words, all potential members have access to the organization's achievements—a sustainable environment, a world with fewer weapons, employment equity programs, or a grievance procedure and negotiated regular wage increases—whether or not they have assisted in achieving these objectives

(Crouch 1982: 51–67). Mancur Olson (1965) asserts that individuals will not naturally organize to further their collective interest. "The rational worker," explains Olson (1965: 88), "will not voluntarily contribute to a union providing a collective benefit since [s]he alone would not perceptibly strengthen the union, and since [s]he would get the benefits of any union achievements whether or not [s]he supported the union." This insight provides one reason for low unionization levels in European countries such as France and Germany. Given that the centralized, state-regulated industrial relations systems in these countries guarantee many non-members the full benefits of union-negotiated wage agreements, the incentive to join is considerably reduced. In contrast, in the United States where such legislation is absent, right-to-work laws weaken unions by taking advantage of the free-rider dilemma.

Albert Hirschman's (1970) comparison of *exit* and *voice* methods of expressing discontent highlights the second dilemma. According to Hirschman, a dissatisfied employee can either leave the employer or stay and push for changes. The presence of a union increases the chances that the employee will pursue the latter strategy. But in nonunion workplaces, the poor employment conditions that could spark an organizing drive also increase the chances of an individual opting to quit the job and look for another one. This kind of response is a major obstacle to unionization in low-wage job ghettos in the service industries today.

Joining and Becoming Active in a Union

The process of mobilizing initial support for a union requires obtaining signed union cards from the majority of employees in a workplace. This effort seldom succeeds without the financial assistance and organizational expertise of an established union. Once organized, a union faces the problem of rallying members in support of collective bargaining goals. According to Charles Tilly's (1979) research on the causes of social protest, what is essential is a sense of shared identity with the group. Collective action in the workplace will be easier when the work group is an important part of each employee's life. Strong social ties inside and outside the workplace integrate employees into the group. Individual interests become synonymous with group interests, acting as a springboard to collective action. Good examples of groups possessing this *solidarity* are miners and members of other blue-collar occupations, in which an occupational culture encompasses much of a worker's life. Levels of unionization and industrial militancy tend to be higher under such conditions (Conley 1988).

Strong leadership is also critical. Especially important are *organic leaders* who, by virtue of being part of the group, understand the experiences of group members and can gain their trust better than an outsider could. As in any formal organization, effective leaders will build up group solidarity, create an awareness of common interests, map out a realistic program of action, and seize opportunities to launch the plan. Also important is the environmental context—a supportive community, a hostile employer, or fair labour legislation, for example—factors that can either nurture or dampen union activity. Even if such conditions are favourable, a majority of employees may not sign union cards, or unionized workers facing a deadlock in negotiations with management over a new collective agreement may not strike. Often missing is one or more precipitating factors: an arbitrary change in work practices; the denial of a long-awaited salary increase; the dismissal of coworkers; or a pent-up sense of being treated unfairly by management. Such perceived injustices could be the catalysts that mobilize workers to take collective action (Buttigieg, Deery, and Iverson 2008).

Research on the inner workings of two Canadian unions gives us glimpses of how some of these factors contribute to *militancy*. Julie White's (1990: 147) study of the Canadian Union of Postal Workers (CUPW) quotes a worker in a Saint John post office: "We're a militant union, and I really believe that Canada Post has made us that way." This view is typical of CUPW members, White argues. The union has developed a "culture of struggle," based on the belief that management does not have the interests of workers at heart and, further, that any past improvements have been extracted from management by militant action (Langford 1996). Against a background of unsuccessful efforts to resolve disputes through negotiation, mediation, and conciliation, this culture of struggle within CUPW has been cultivated by an openly democratic structure based on rank-and-file involvement. Similarly, Charlotte Yates (1990) attributes the CAW's success at resisting concessions demanded by North American auto firms in the 1980s to its greater membership solidarity, compared with the United Auto Workers union in the United States, which agreed to concessions. Some of the key features of union organization that contributed to CAW militancy were members' influence over union decision making and effective communication channels linking all levels in the union (Yates 1990: 77).

Going on Strike

Strikes are high drama on the stage of industrial relations. Members of the public typically view strikes as an inconvenience or even as a major social problem. Many politicians and business leaders argue that strikes harm the economy. The participants seldom want strikes, least of all the union members, who will seldom recoup the wages lost should the dispute drag on. But if conflict has been largely *institutionalized*, as described earlier in this chapter, why do strikes occur at all? What motivates workers to strike, and what are the larger social and economic implications of their actions?

Workers go on *strike*, that is, they deliberately stop working in order to try to force their employer to agree to some set of demands. Since workers are selling their labour power to an employer in return for wages, their ultimate bargaining lever is to withdraw that labour. Similarly, employers may initiate a *lockout*—refusing to let workers come to work and, hence, be paid—to get workers to agree to some demand. Overall, strikes are infrequent events, as we will see in the next section, and lockouts occur even less often. So, contrary to what the media sometimes suggest, settlement of union–management disputes without recourse to work stoppages is clearly the norm in Canada today.

But strikes are only one possible form of workplace conflict. Richard Hyman distinguishes between *unorganized* and *organized conflict* (1978: Chapter 3). The former is not a calculated group action and typically involves workers responding to oppressive situations by individual absenteeism, quitting, or sabotage. The latter is a planned collective strategy, the aim of which is to change the source of the discontent. Canadian labour legislation insists that strikes are legal only after the collective agreement has expired and specific conditions, such as a strike vote, have been met. Unauthorized strikes during the term of an agreement, often spontaneous responses by ordinary workers to an immediate problem in the workplace, are known as *wildcat strikes.*[29] For example, in April 2013, two Edmonton jail guards were suspended for writing e-mails to management about poor working conditions. Within hours the next shift of guards was picketing the jail, and within several days, guards at 10 jails across Alberta had joined the wildcat strike. In addition, many court workers, sheriffs, and parole officers, members of the Alberta Union of Public Employees, left work to take part in a *sympathy strike* (Wingrove and Walton 2013). Strikes do not necessarily entail all members of the union leaving the work site as a group. Under certain situations, *rotating strikes* across a number of work sites, *working-to-rule* (doing the minimum required or refusing overtime work), or staging work stoppages by "sitting down" on the job are variants of strike activity that can also communicate workers' demands to management.

Research by Eric Batstone and his colleagues in a British automobile factory highlights the day-to-day processes that may culminate in a strike (Batstone, Boraston, and Frenkel 1978). Strikes, argue these researchers, do not just happen. Rather, as a form of collective action, they require a high degree of *mobilization*. A crucial factor is how the social relations within the union allow some individuals or groups to rhetorically frame the course of events leading up to a strike and identify potential strike issues. Typically, most workers are reluctant to strike, so there will not be much support for a strike until a vocabulary has developed to justify such action. This undertaking involves the translation of specific grievances into the language of broad principles and rights such as fairness and equality.

Nevertheless, sometimes strikes erupt because of grassroots protest by workers who don't need union organizers to frame the issues for them. Jerry White (1990) provides an example in his analysis of the 1981 illegal strike in Ontario hospitals by nonprofessional service workers, such as orderlies, housekeepers, food handlers, lab technicians, and maintenance workers. While the union leadership was generally not in support, the workers went on strike anyway. Interestingly, the motivations to strike were different for women and men involved. Male workers wanted higher pay, a reduced workload, and guaranteed benefits. Women, in contrast, were far more concerned with how cutbacks had led to deteriorating relationships with patients. In the end, the workers won slight wage improvements, but at a price: thousands of strikers were suspended, 34 were fired, and 3 union leaders were jailed.

Canadian Strike Trends

On an annual basis for more than the past two decades, work stoppages have typically accounted for less than one-tenth of one percent of all working time in Canada (Table 11.1). This pattern indicates that the seriousness of the strike "problem" often gets blown far out of proportion. Historically, though, we can identify eras when strikes were much more common and widespread. There have been four particularly stormy periods of industrial conflict in Canada during the 20th century, gauged by the percentage of total working time lost due to strikes and lockouts.

A number of issues were at stake in early-20th-century strikes. Skilled artisans in the 19th century had been able to retain much of their craft status, pride, and economic security through their control of the production process. This privileged position was eroded by industrialization after 1900, as advancing technology and scientific management techniques undermined craftworkers' autonomy. Thus, craftworkers angrily resisted rationalization of their work, sparking many of the 421 strikes and lockouts that occurred between 1901 and 1914 in southwestern Ontario manufacturing cities (Heron and Palmer 1977).

Before union recognition and compulsory collective bargaining became encoded in law during World War II, many strikes were precipitated by an employer's refusal to recognize the existence of a union, much less bargain with it. The historic peak in labour militancy occurred at the end of World War I. Workers across the country were protesting against oppressive

TABLE 11.1 Work Stoppages (Strikes or Lockouts) Involving One or More Workers, Canada, 1976–2012, Multi-year Averages

	Work Stoppages during Year	Workers Involved	Average Number of Workers per Stoppage	Person Days Not Worked	Average Days Lost per Worker Involved	Days Lost: % of Estimated Working Time
1976–79	988	666,622	654	7,510,188	14.5	0.33
1980–84	823	293,677	445	6,401,314	18.5	0.26
1985–89	684	376,852	562	3,974,936	14.4	0.17
1990–94	338	171,986	375	2,110,056	12.8	0.09
1995–99	347	212,933	635	2,666,832	12.7	0.09
2000–04	323	153,480	538	2,349,609	14.8	0.07
2005–9	192	83,103	350	1,949,830	24.0	0.05
2010–12	201	95,121	478	1,157,335	14.1	0.03

Source: Adapted from data provided by Government of Canada, Labour Program. <http://www24.hrsdc.gc.ca/dr-ir/default.aspx?lang=eng>

working conditions, low wages, and declining living standards due to soaring wartime inflation. Most of all, they wanted recognition of their unions. Western Canadian unions were far more militant and inclined toward radical politics than those in the rest of the country. Thus, in 1919, when Winnipeg building and metal trades employers refused to recognize and negotiate with unions over wage increases, the Winnipeg Trades and Labour Council called a *general strike.*

A massive display of working-class solidarity erupted, bringing the local economy to a halt. Sympathy strikes spread to other cities across Canada and even into the United States. The battle lines of open class warfare (one of the few instances of this in Canadian history) were drawn when, fearing a revolution, Winnipeg's upper class fought back with the help of the state. For several days, strikers squared off against police and employer-sponsored armed vigilantes. The confrontation ended in violence after the Royal Northwest Mounted Police, sent in by the federal government, charged a crowd of demonstrators. Strike leaders were arrested and jailed, while the workers' demands were still unmet (Bercuson 1974; Jamieson 1971).

Strike activity declined with rising unemployment during the Depression of the 1930s. As a rule, unions are less likely to strike in tough economic times. Conversely, when industry is booming and there is a relative shortage of labour, reflected in low unemployment rates, a strike becomes a more potent bargaining lever. The World War II era marked the rise of industrial unionism in manufacturing industries. Organizing drives accelerated as military production demands helped to restore the ailing economy. Again, union recognition was a dominant issue, driving workers in automobile factories, steel plants, and mines onto the picket line. As mentioned earlier in the chapter, the 1945 Ford strike led to the introduction of the Rand Formula to protect union security and ensure orderly collective bargaining (Russell 1990).

Canada experienced a series of strikes in the mid-1960s. The fact that about one-third of these work stoppages involved wildcat strikes (mainly over wages) led the government to perceive a serious crisis in industrial relations. A task force, chaired by Professor H. D. Woods of McGill University, was set up to investigate the causes of industrial unrest and to recommend ways of achieving labour peace. Yet rampant inflation during the 1970s, and an increasingly militant mood among public-sector workers, escalated labour–management confrontations.

The most recent strike wave reached its apex in 1976. The Trudeau government's imposition of wage and price controls in 1975 as part of its anti-inflation program made strikes over higher wages a futile exercise (Reid 1982). But in the 20 years following 1976, lost time due to work stoppages dropped to post–World War II lows. The recession-plagued 1980s and 1990s dampened strike activity, a trend also evident in the recession that began in 2008.

Table 11.1 profiles the labour relations patterns of the past three decades by highlighting four ways to look at strike activity: *frequency* (number of work stoppages), *size* (number of workers involved), *duration* (days lost), and overall *volume* (days lost as a percentage of total working time). A series of multi-year averages clearly demonstrates how strike activity in terms of frequency, size, and overall volume has declined, although strike duration has not. For example, in the late 1970s, an average of 988 work stoppages per year involved almost 700,000 workers. Comparable figures for 2010–12 were an average of 201 work stoppages annually involving about 95,000 workers. What is most striking about these trends is that, even in the late 1970s, strikes and lockouts resulted in only one-third of one percent of estimated annual working time. By 2010–12, this figure was 10 times smaller. In short, while strikes and lockouts get a great deal of media attention, they no longer have much of a cumulative effect on economic productivity.

A Comparative Perspective on Strikes

How does Canada's strike record compare with that of other industrial nations? Even though there are some cross-national differences in how strikes are defined and measured (Ross, Bamber, and Whitehouse 1998), we can, nonetheless, get a rough idea of where Canada stands in this regard. Based on the annual averages of working days lost in nine industrialized countries between 1970 and 1992, Canada's rate was the second highest, with Italy first (Adams 1995: 512). But as we have seen in Table 11.1, the earlier years in this period were historically high for Canada, inflating the overall average. By the mid-1990s, Canada was reporting significantly lower strike volume than Italy, France, or Australia, but considerably higher than other countries, in particular, the United States and the Netherlands (International Labour Office 1997: 249–50). It is also important to note that the strike volume in highly industrialized countries had declined in general, in large part, because of difficult economic times and high unemployment through much of the 1990s. Some experts suggest that while strikes are less frequent, when they do happen they are now more intense confrontations (Aligisakis 1997).

There are major institutional differences that account for international variations in strikes. For instance, in Italy, disputes, while short, are frequent and involve many workers. By contrast, the Swedish system of centralized bargaining, along with the country's powerful unions and their huge strike funds, means that a work stoppage could quickly cripple the economy. This awareness imposes much pressure to peacefully resolve potential disputes. In Japan, unions are closely integrated into corporations in what really amounts to a type of company unionism. Strikes are infrequent; workers voice their grievances by wearing black armbands or by making other symbolic gestures calculated to embarrass management. German union–management collective bargaining is centrally coordinated but, at the individual workplace, employee-elected works councils frequently negotiate employment conditions (see Chapter 12). German laws require these participatory councils; the same laws also make it very difficult to strike. Even though the strike rate in Canada is relatively low now, the fact that employees in this country have to confront employers when seeking collective bargaining has created a far more adversarial system.

Thus, legislation governing the structure of collective bargaining is vitally important. The North American system of bargaining is highly decentralized and fragmented, involving thousands of separate negotiations between a local union and a single employer, each of which could result in a strike. Low-strike nations such as Austria, Germany, the Netherlands, and Sweden avoid these problems by having national or industry-wide agreements, and by legislating many of the quality-of-working-life issues that Canadian unions must negotiate with employers on a piecemeal basis.

There are also major industrial and regional variations in strikes within Canada, which may be the result of how industries are organized. The least strike-prone industries are finance, trade, and services, which makes sense given their low unionization levels. Of the highly unionized industries, mining has historically been the most strife ridden. Similarly, Newfoundland and Labrador and British Columbia have had significantly higher-than-average strike rates because of their high concentration of primary and other strike-prone industries.[30] With their *isolation hypothesis*, Kerr and Siegel (1954) provide one explanation of these differences, writing that isolated workers "live in their own separate communities: the coal patch, the ship, the water-front district, the logging camp, the textile town. These communities have their own codes, myths, heroes, and social standards."[31] Canada has always had large numbers of remote, resource-based, single-employer towns (Lucas 1971), where a combination of social isolation and a limited occupational hierarchy is more likely to mould workers into a cohesive group in opposition to management.

■ CONCLUSION

Canada's labour force has been growing steadily over the past several decades (Chapter 3). Union membership has also been growing, although not as quickly. There were more than 4.5 million Canadian union members in 2012. As for union density, it has remained around 30 percent since the beginning of this century (Figure 11.1). Compared to some other Western industrialized countries, however, organized labour in Canada remains relatively strong (Figure 11.2), at least in terms of numbers. But strike activity has clearly declined in Canada over the past 35 years (Table 11.1). Does this decline signify that the Canadian industrial relations system has reached some kind of equilibrium, with all three parties involved—employers, unions, and the state—being relatively satisfied with the outcomes?

Our assessment is that it does not. As we observed in Chapter 10, the labour process can be conceptualized as a shifting *frontier of control* (Friedman 1977) in which, at different times, employers and employees gain or lose power. The last several decades have been a time in which employers have been gaining the upper hand. As we have noted, union density has increased significantly in the public sector—CUPE and NUPGE are the two largest unions in the country. However, for public-sector workers, their employer (typically the federal or a provincial government) is also the rule maker, and the Canadian state has not always been the "impartial umpire" that William Lyon Mackenzie King envisioned a century ago.

During the 1990s, Canadians began to see nurses, teachers, librarians, social workers, government clerks and, in some cases where they were unionized, even university professors going on strike for higher wages and improved working conditions, and to maintain the quality of public services. In response, governments frequently resorted to legislated restrictions on strike action. Furthermore, the deficit-cutting strategies of both provincial and federal governments often involved imposing wage rollbacks through legislation, effectively suspending the collective bargaining rights of government employees (Reshef and Rastin 2003).

This trend has continued. In late 2013, for example, the federal Conservative government included in its budget implementation act (Bill C-4) a number of proposals that would restrict the rights of federal government workers. Included in the list was a planned change to the Public Service Labour Relations Act (PSLRA) that would give the government the right to decide, without any neutral third party involved as had been the case for many years, which of its employees were providing *essential services*. Once declared as essential, these workers would lose their right to strike.[32] About the same time, Canada Post (a Crown corporation) signalled that it intended to demand large cuts to the pension plan previously negotiated with CUPW (McKenna 2013). In late 2013, as well, the Alberta government introduced Bill 46, the Public Services Salary Restraint Act, which would force the Alberta Union of Provincial Employees (AUPE) to accept whatever wage rates the government proposed if a negotiated settlement was not reached by January 31, 2014 (Ibrahim 2013). In the past, if the union and the employer (the Alberta government) could not reach a satisfactory settlement, the law required binding arbitration whereby a neutral third party would decide what was fair.

In the private sector, the Canadian labour relations environment has also generally become more restrictive. Concession bargaining, or employers trying to force unions into accepting wage rollbacks, reduced benefits packages and pensions, and greater flexibility in hiring practices, has been widespread for the past several decades. Many large employers have reduced their costs and also the need to deal with unions by outsourcing much of their activity to nonunionized suppliers, in Canada or outside the country. Some employers with unionized workforces have moved quickly to lock out their workers, hoping to force them into accepting an offer. Applications for court injunctions and legislation to end strikes have been another employer strategy. In other cases, rather than trying to negotiate a settlement, employers have quickly brought in nonunionized workers, hoping to eventually force unions into accepting offers they considered to be unsatisfactory.

So, the declining strike rates in Table 11.1 clearly do not signify that organized labour in Canada is satisfied with changes in the industrial relations climate which some analysts see as having placed severe restrictions on free collective bargaining.[33] It remains to be seen whether and where the huge unions in the public sector begin to push back more aggressively to protect the job security and economic well-being of their members.[34] As for the private sector, it will be interesting to see whether unions' current organizing efforts in the service industries are effective, and whether the 2013 merger of the Canadian Auto Workers union and the Communications, Energy and Paperworkers (CEP) union into Unifor will shift the balance of power in the labour relations "frontier of control."[35] The involvement of Canadian unions in transnational union networks may also give them some new ideas and increased energy. In both sectors, it remains possible that a shift in tactics from business unionism to social or social mobilization unionism will have positive outcomes for organized labour.

In Chapter 12, we turn our attention to alternative approaches to economic organization that might move us beyond the adversarial nature of contemporary labour–management relations toward institutional structures that more fully recognize the rights and potential of workers and more effectively address the social problems of conflict and inequality.

DISCUSSION QUESTIONS

1. Public opinion in Canada is divided over the role of unions in the economy and society. Do you think that unions have outlived their usefulness? Why or why not?

2. What are the greatest challenges Canadian unions face today, and what strategies will most likely help them meet these challenges?

3. Do unions contribute to more or less income inequality in society? Could they have a larger effect?

4. In the typical strike or lockout, who are most often the winners and the losers? Why?

5. Would you join a union if one existed in your workplace? Why or why not?

ADDITIONAL RESOURCES

WORK AT THE MOVIES

- *On Strike: The Winnipeg General Strike, 1919* (directed by Joe MacDonald and Clare Johnstone Gilsig, 1991, 19:46 minutes). This NFB documentary focuses on the Winnipeg General Strike, which began with the building and metal trades and culminated with over 30,000 workers walking off their jobs. It is available through the National Film Board of Canada: http://www3.nfb.ca/objectifdocumentaire/index.php?mode=view&language=english&filmId=33.
- *Matewan* (directed by John Sayles, 1987, 135 minutes). This historical film is based on the Battle of Matewan, a deadly confrontation between coal miners struggling to form a union and company operators in West Virginia.
- *24 Days in Brooks* (directed by Dana Inkster, 2007, 42:03 minutes). Set in Brooks, Alberta, this NFB documentary tracks the transformation of a socially conservative, white town. As immigrants and refugees migrate to Brooks for work in a slaughterhouse, the town experiences its first-ever strike. The documentary is available through the National Film Board of Canada: http://www.nfb.ca/film/24_days_in_brooks.
- *Bread & Roses* (directed by Ken Loach, 2000, 110 minutes). Two Latina cleaners fight for the right to unionize in this film based on the Justice for Janitors campaign of the Service Employees International Union.

SOUNDS OF WORK

- "There Is Power in a Union" (Billy Bragg). This pro-union song asserts the potential power of collective action.
- "General Strike" (D.O.A.). Canadian punk rockers put forth a straightforward message about collective action, encouraging listeners to stand up and unite.
- "Horses" (Rheostatics). After going on strike, workers watch from the outside as replacement workers are brought in. Some say this song was inspired by the long and violent 1986 strike by the United Food and Commercial Workers against the Gainers meat-packing company in Edmonton, owned by Peter Pocklington.

• "Solidarity Forever" (Ralph Chaplin). Written in 1915 for the Industrial Workers of the World, this song carries a strong message of the power of worker solidarity. It retains relevance with many unions today.

NOTES

1. http://www.thespec.com/news-story/2222372-u-s-steel-lockout-over/ [retrieved December 8, 2013].
2. http://www.thestar.com/business/2013/07/18/caw_reaches_tentative_deal_with_cocacola_over_strike_in_brampton.html [retrieved December 8, 2013].
3. http://www.cbc.ca/news/canada/calgary/superstore-strike-ends-as-union-members-agree-to-new-deal-1.1930881 [retrieved December 8, 2013].
4. http://www.cbc.ca/news/canada/nova-scotia/halifax-coffee-shop-workers-in-unique-drive-to-unionize-1.1361776 [retrieved December 8, 2013].
5. http://www.huffingtonpost.ca/2013/08/16/walmart-canada-union-decertifies_n_3769807.html [retrieved December 8, 2013]
6. Cited with permission from EKOS Research Associates; all rights reserved.
7. http://www.cbc.ca/news/canada/unions-on-decline-in-private-sector-1.1150562 [retrieved December 8, 2013].
8. http://www.torontosun.com/2011/06/29/striking-unions-offside-with-public [retrieved December 8, 2013].
9. This systems approach to industrial relations is contrasted with a political economy approach by Taras, Ponak, and Gunderson (2005).
10. Canada. (1969). *Canadian Industrial Relations: The Report of the Task Force on Labour Relations*. Ottawa: Queen's Printer, p. 19.
11. Card, Lemieux, and Riddell (2004) and Gustafsson and Johansson (1999) provide a cross-national analysis. Brady, Baker, and Finnigan (2013) present U.S. data showing that higher levels of unionization are associated with lower rates of working poverty.
12. For historical accounts of the rise of the Canadian labour movement, see Heron (1989), Smucker (1980: Chapters 7 and 8), and Godard (1994: Chapter 4).
13. http://www.labour.gc.ca/eng/resources/info/tools/directory_labour_organizations/organizations.shtml [retrieved December 15, 2013].
14. See also Briskin (2010), Bartkiw (2008), Russell (1990), and Kettler, Struthers, and Huxley (1990). Similar concerns about collective bargaining in the United States and the United Kingdom are discussed in Freeman (1995).
15. See endnote 13 for an online source showing unions' Canadian or U.S. affiliations.

16. See Gindin (1995) and Wells (1997) for discussions of the CAW's shift away from principled militancy to more pragmatic cooperation with management. Yates (1998) and Eaton and Verma (2006) examine how the CAW has met the challenges of renewal and growing membership diversity.
17. See Roberts (1990). The Communications Workers, the Energy and Chemical Workers, and the Canadian Paperworkers Union later merged to form the Communications, Energy and Paperworkers Union of Canada.
18. On nonunion forms of representation, see Taras (2002) and Lowe and Schellenberg (2001: 25–29).
19. See endnote 13.
20. These union membership rates are based on all wage and salary earners (including agricultural workers and managers) so the Canadian rate is lower than the rate reported in Figure 11.1.
21. Dehnen (2013) refers to such networks as *global union federations*, an indication that this new field of study is still developing a common vocabulary. See also Lévesque and Murray (2010) and Youngdahl (2008).
22. Kimeldorf (2013) provides a useful historical account of the growth of the U.S. union movement a century earlier.
23. Bernhardt, Spiller, and Polson (2013) discuss violations of labour legislation in the United States. See Ponak and Taras (1995) on right-to-work legislation from a Canadian perspective.
24. On union renewal, see Voss and Sherman (2000) and Rose and Chaison (2001). Kay (2011) argues that the legal frameworks established by the North American Free Trade Agreement (NAFTA) allowed collaborating U.S. and Mexican unions to gain strength and resist globalization trends.
25. All 2011 unionization rates discussed in this section are from Uppal (2011). For additional data on unionization rates from 1981 through 2012, by occupation, industry, province, gender, and detailed age groups, see Galarneau and Sohn (2013).
26. Union membership data from Government of Canada Labour Program (2013): http://www.labour.gc.ca/eng/resources/info/tools/directory_labour_organizations/organizations.shtml [retrieved December 16, 2013].
27. On women in unions, see also Yates (2006), Briskin and McDermott (1993), Creese (1999), and Gannagé (1995).
28. Kumar, Pradeep. (1995). *Unions and Workplace Change in Canada*. Kingston, ON: IRC Press, pp. 148–49.
29. See Gouldner (1955) for a classic study of a wildcat strike. Jamieson (1971: Chapter 4) and Zetka (1992) discuss wildcat strikes during the decades after World War II in Canada and the United States, respectively.

30. Gunderson, Hyatt, and Ponak (1995); see also Craven (1980: Chapter 8).
31. Kerr and Siegel (1954: 191). For critiques, see Shorter and Tilly (1974: 287–305) and Stern (1976).
32. http://www.huffingtonpost.ca/larry-rousseau/turning-back-the-clock-50_b_4325416.html.
33. See Panitch and Swartz (1993), Russell (1990), and Godard (1997).
34. Cunningham and James (2010) discuss strategies used by public-sector unions in the United Kingdom to counter outsourcing of jobs.
35. Lorinc (2013) describes the union politics leading to the formation of Unifor and argues that the most vulnerable workers in Canada are not really the concern of Canada's largest unions.

ALTERNATIVE APPROACHES TO ECONOMIC ORGANIZATION

"At 7:30, on a cold December morning, you might find Neil Shaw at the car wash cleaning the salt and ice off his 1994 Ford. By noon, you can usually find him in the office reviewing the financial projections. In the evening, he might be meeting with city officials to discuss rezoning or cab stands. Like most cab drivers, Neil also puts in many hours a week behind the wheel of his car. A day for Neil and others can involve these activities, which all seem quite different, but once he explains that he is president of a taxi Co-op the pieces begin to fall into place."

"First and foremost, Neil is a cab driver, sometimes working 12 hours a day. At the same time, he is an owner of the Co-op Taxi Line Ltd. which has grown from three members when it was incorporated in 1992, to the most professional cab company in Prince Edward Island's capital city with 27 cabs and 11 members. As president, Neil works more than 40 volunteer hours a month for the Co-op. 'We have no manager so therefore we are a very hands-on board,' says Neil. He also noted that the directors must look after the interests of the Co-op by lobbying government for changes in regulations when necessary and by negotiating with suppliers for discounts on bulk purchases of gasoline."

Source: http://www.canadianworker.coop/worker-co-op/success-stories/co-op-taxi-line-ltd. Courtesy of Maureen MacLean and Brenda MacKinnon.

● INTRODUCTION

In Chapter 11, we discussed the history, changing function, and future of unions, a formal and institutionalized vehicle via which workers have collectively participated in the labour process. We concluded by examining strike patterns over time in Canada, comparing them to data from other countries, and then asked about the effectiveness of this adversarial form of workers' resistance to employers' profit-driven goals. In this chapter on alternative approaches to economic organization, we begin by asking whether unions and strikes—that is, labour militancy—might translate into class politics that could change the way societies are organized and, in turn, how power and profits are shared in work organizations. We conclude that this has not occurred, but also ask whether contemporary social movements in conjunction with organized labour offer a more effective way forward.

We then turn our attention to one specific area—the critical issue of how to improve workplace health and safety—where labour and management have come somewhat closer to reaching a consensus in Canada and other Western industrial democracies. This discussion leads us into an analysis of other alternative approaches to economic organization such as the different types of industrial democracy that have been institutionalized in Germany and Sweden, for example. The chapter concludes with a discussion of how, within capitalist industrial democracies, worker ownership of the means of production may offer the most far-reaching approach to reducing conflict and providing workers with more control over the labour process and their work organizations.

● WORKER MILITANCY AND CLASS POLITICS

As noted in Chapter 11, strikes are sometimes interpreted as a measure of worker *militancy*. But is this perception accurate? Are strikes deeply rooted in class antagonisms and signs of heightened *class consciousness*? Or do unionized workers merely act out of economic self-interest, using strikes as pressure tactics to force changes in specific government or employer policies?

Comparative Perspectives on Working-Class Radicalism

More than four decades ago, Michael Mann's (1970) comparative study of industrial conflict directly addressed this issue. At the time, workers in France and Italy were more politically radical than those in Britain or the United States. But the political potential of the French and Italian working classes was frequently limited by their failure to envision and articulate an alternative social system to capitalism. Furthermore, according to Mann, most workers possess a *dual consciousness*. Instead of having a unified understanding of how their work dissatisfactions are organically linked to the operations of capitalism—real class consciousness in the Marxist sense—workers tend to compartmentalize their work experiences from the rest of their lives.

They develop a "pragmatic acceptance" of the alienation and subordinate status they endure at work. Satisfactions in life are found in family, friends, and community, but not in the quest for a new society. Mann argued that strikes can lead to short-term *explosions of consciousness*, but the solidarity they generate rarely gathers momentum beyond the immediate event. A more recent Canadian test of this hypothesis among Hamilton, Ontario, postal workers who had participated in a strike found increased positive identification with fellow workers and the union, but little impact on class consciousness (Langford 1996). Ultimately, then, strikes by even politically radical workers are typically transformed into tactical manoeuvres to obtain concessions from employers.

Duncan Gallie (1983) compared the more radical attitudes and behaviour of the French working class with the more moderate British working class. Why is it, he asked, that British workers accepted major social inequities as inevitable while, for the French, they were a source of resentment and a catalyst for industrial militancy and political radicalism? Gallie observed that workers in both countries recognized class-based inequities in opportunity, wealth, and privilege. They differed, however, in their attitudes toward these inequities. For French workers, class position was an important part of personal identity. They identified with the larger working class, resented the system that put them at the bottom, and believed that political action could improve their situation. British workers, in contrast, were more concerned about changing things in the workplace rather than in society as a whole. Gallie's explanation of these differences hinges on the role of left-wing political parties in translating workplace experiences into a radical critique of society. France has a revolutionary political tradition going back to the late 18th century. Hence, French workers' grievances with their employers were more readily carried outside the workplace, where they could be moulded into a broad counter-ideology by exposure to trade unions and radical politics (especially the Communist Party).[1]

Unions and Politics in Canada

Have Canadian unions helped channel general working-class discontent into collective political action? The Canadian Labour Congress (CLC) helped to found the New Democratic Party (NDP) in 1961 and remains closely affiliated with it. However, the CLC has often been unable to convince a large majority of union members to vote for the NDP, particularly at the federal level. When the NDP became the Official Opposition in Ottawa in 2011, this breakthrough had more to do with party leader Jack Layton's charismatic appeal to Quebec voters than the appeal of the party's policies to union members across the country. Union members have, no doubt, helped elect NDP provincial governments in Manitoba (currently) and in British Columbia, Saskatchewan, Nova Scotia, Ontario, and the Yukon Territory in the past. Although reformist rather than socialist in governing approach, these NDP provincial governments have nevertheless made policy changes that improved working conditions (minimum wage increases, for example) and protected unions' rights to organize workers. But organized labour has not really pushed NDP provincial governments to significantly restructure either workplaces or society in general. In fact, when the 1990–95 Ontario NDP government, led by Bob Rae, tried to impose a "social contract" on unionized public-sector workers to reduce the government deficit, the public-sector unions fought back vigorously and ultimately helped defeat the government (Rose 2001: 73–74).

As for strikes making unionized workers more radical, we have already suggested that this is seldom the case (Langford 1996). Furthermore, some argue that in North America strikes can divide, rather than unify, the working class (Smith 1978). If unionized workers benefit from going on strike, the more disadvantaged, unorganized workers may blame their disadvantaged position on unions rather than on the way workplaces are structured in capitalist societies (Baer, Grabb, and Johnston 1991). This tendency is likely because Canadian workers have had limited encounters with alternative political ideologies, unlike workers in countries with a longer and stronger socialist history and culture. In short, Canadian workers do not have a particularly coherent and integrated set of political views (Tanner and Cockerill 1986).

Even if non-organized workers believe that corporate profits should be more equally distributed (a left-wing position), they may also agree that trade unions are part of the problem (Tanner 1984). And while individuals personally affected by unemployment during a recession may be somewhat more critical of the distribution of wealth in society (Krahn and Harrison 1992), we have not seen evidence in Canada of rising unemployment leading to significantly heightened class consciousness (Baer, Grabb, and Johnston 1991).

Unions, Social Movements, and Social Change

Despite the absence of a strong working-class radical ideology among Canadian workers and, moreover, a long-term decline in strike activity in Canada (Chapter 11), over the past decades, there have been instances of widespread worker militancy.[2] One example was the British Columbia Solidarity movement, which sprang up in opposition to the Social Credit government's 1983 public-sector restraint program. Proposed legislation would have limited the scope of public-sector bargaining, allowed the firing of employees at will, cut back on social services, ended rent controls, and abolished the B.C. Human Rights Commission. The movement began with grassroots community action organized by the Lower Mainland Budget Coalition, with the B.C. Federation of Labour becoming involved somewhat later. The protest marches, public rallies, picket lines, and community-based resistance that took place during the summer of 1983 were labelled "class warfare" by Bryan Palmer (1986) who suggested that these actions might signal that class conflict was on the rise in Canada.

In retrospect, Palmer's conclusion was inaccurate, but this example does suggest that, when organized labour gets involved with broader social movements, some social change can occur. In the 1980s B.C. example, negotiations between the government and mainstream union leaders eventually resulted in some revisions to the legislation. More recently, in the same province, a strike in 2004 by 40,000 members of the Hospital Employees Union became a flashpoint for public opposition to the Liberal government's policy of privatizing and contracting-out, but it did not lead to change in the government's policy (Camfield 2006).

In contrast, in the United States, the Living Wage movement has successfully brought together coalitions of citizens and community groups, including unions, to push municipal governments to enact city bylaws that ensure that all city workers (and also workers hired by contractors working for the city) receive a wage high enough to live on (Luce 2004; Adams and Neumark 2005). Similarly, the Clean Clothes Campaign (CCC) links trade unions and non-governmental organizations (NGOs) in Europe, North America, and Australia with a network of several hundred similar organizations in developing countries (Egels-Zandén 2011). Together, they have worked on educating consumers, lobbying governments, and putting pressure on retail companies in Western societies in order to improve the working conditions of factory workers producing clothing and sportswear in developing countries.[3] The involvement of North American unions in networks of other organizations with social justice goals yields examples of *social movement unionism* (Chapter 11), which can lead to social reforms, although not likely complete societal change. But examples of social movement unionism are rare in Canada, including among public-sector unions (Camfield 2011).[4]

■ PROMOTING WORKPLACE HEALTH AND SAFETY

History proves that dangerous machinery, unsafe work sites, polluted air, and exposure to carcinogenic substances and other risks have taken their toll on the working class in terms of shorter life expectancies and higher illness and disease rates. Most of the progress made over the past century in reducing workplace health and safety risks has been the result of workers fighting for improvements, typically through their unions, and often against the strong opposition of employers. Workplace health and safety continues to be a contentious issue in union–management contract disputes today and in the larger political arena. Even so, this issue is an example, at least to some extent, of workers and their employers managing to identify and work together toward common goals. Before examining how institutionalized processes designed to further these goals have evolved, we present an overview of the risks to personal health and safety experienced by Canadian workers.

Risks to Personal Health and Safety

Every year hundreds of Canadian workers die from work-related injuries or illnesses. To be precise, between 1993 and 2011, a total of 17,062 Canadian workers—an average of almost four per working day—died as a result of their job. While work-related deaths may receive less attention, the fact remains that the chances of being killed on the job are still greater than those of being killed on the road by a drunk driver. From the mid-1980s until the mid-1990s, *industrial fatality rates* declined to 5.2 deaths per 100,000 workers in 1996 (or 703 industrial fatalities). The number of fatalities then began to rise, going to 835 in 1999, 934 in 2002, and 1,098 in 2005 when the work-related fatality rate was 6.8 deaths per 100,000 employed Canadians (Sharpe and Hardt 2006). Since then, the annual number of work-related deaths has shifted up and down around 1,000, although the latest annual fatality count was 977 in 2012 (down from 1,014 in 2010). This count translates into a 2012 rate of 5.6 deaths per 100,000 workers, about the same as in the mid-1990s.[5]

Industrial fatality rates are generally much lower in the service industries than in the goods-producing sector (Sharpe and Hardt 2006). For example, in 2012, the fatality rates in the transportation, manufacturing, and construction industries were 11.7, 10.2, and 16.7 deaths per 100,000 workers, respectively. But these rates were still much lower than those found in the resource-extraction industries: the work-related fatality rate in mining was 23.2 deaths per 100,000 workers in 2012; in logging and forestry, it was even higher (34.3). Certain occupations within these industries carry extremely high risks. The most dangerous are those involving cutting, handling, and loading of materials in the mining industry, and working with insulation in the construction industry (Marshall 1996). However, since relatively small numbers of people work in these and other high-risk jobs, the four leading general causes of work-related death are exposure to harmful substances and environments (41% of all fatalities between 1996 and 2005), accidents involving transportation vehicles (23%), being struck by an object or piece of equipment (14%), and falls (8%). And since high-risk jobs are typically filled by men, almost all workplace fatalities are men. In Alberta in 2011, for example, 119 of the 123 people who died as a result of their work were men.[6]

The incidence of *work-related injury and illness* rose in Canada during the 1980s. In 1982, Workers' Compensation boards and commissions across the country compensated 479,558 individuals for work-related injuries and illnesses resulting in time loss or permanent disability. This number increased to 620,979 in 1989, but then began to decline steeply, to 410,464 in 1995. While the rate of decline then slowed, the number continued to drop, to 337,930 in 2005 and 249,511 in 2011.[7] Thus, over the past two decades, we have seen a steady decline in workplace injuries and illnesses. Some of this is likely due to the further shift away from goods-producing to service industries (Chapter 3), but changes in Workers' Compensation legislation and enforcement may also have had an effect (Breslin et al. 2006).[8] Even so, work-related injuries and illnesses remain a serious problem; in 2010, for every 68 Canadian workers, one received Workers' Compensation at some point during the year.[9] The compensation costs for workplace injuries are huge—in 2008, for example, they totalled $7.67 billion.[10] This figure does not include indirect costs resulting from production losses, damage to equipment, lower efficiency, decreased employee morale, and lost supervisory time. Although such indirect costs are notoriously hard to calculate precisely, estimates of total costs are typically about twice as high as the direct costs of compensation.[11]

As with work-related fatalities, rates of *time-loss work injuries* are higher in some of the resource-extraction and goods-producing industries (Figure 12.1). However, the distributive services (transportation and wholesale trade) also have high time-loss injury rates. Interestingly, time-loss injury rates are also quite high in health and government services, but low in financial services, perhaps because the former industrial sectors are heavily unionized (see Chapter 11). The presence of unions probably leads to a higher reporting of injuries by workers.

Time-loss work injury rates for men are 50 percent higher than the rates for women (Figure 12.1). The youngest labour force participants (ages 15 to 19) have the lowest injury rates, in part, because many are part-time workers and, hence, at lower risk of injury, but also because few are employed in unionized sectors. Injury rates are also somewhat lower among workers approaching retirement since, by this age, fewer workers would still be in physically demanding jobs with higher risks of injury.

Evolving Politics of Workplace Health and Safety

In the early years of Canada's industrialization (Chapter 1), workers had little protection from what were often extremely unsafe working conditions. Work in the resource industries, in construction of canals and railways, and in factories was hazardous, and the risk of injury and death was extremely high. As in other industrializing countries, an *administrative model of regulation*, in which the government set standards for health and safety and tried to enforce them, slowly developed (Lewchuk, Robb, and Walters 1996). Employers frequently opposed these efforts, arguing that their profits were threatened and that the state had no right to interfere in worker–employer relationships. In turn, unions fought for change, and the public was mobilized behind some causes, including restrictions on the employment of women and children in factories. Thus, the Factory Acts of the 1880s led to improvements such as fencing around dangerous machines, ventilation standards for factories, and

FIGURE 12.1 Time-Loss Work Injuries by Selected Industries, Age, and Gender, Canada, 2011

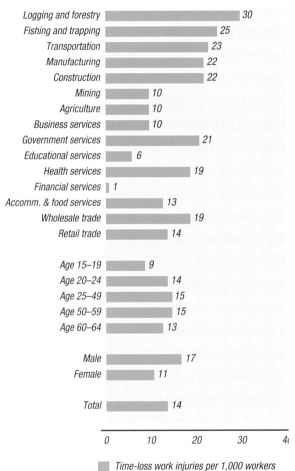

Time-loss work injuries per 1,000 workers

Sources: Work injury data, Association of Workers' Compensation Boards of Canada, *Injury Statistics*. <http://awcbc.org/?
page_id=14>; <http://www.awcbc.org/en/statistics.asp>; number of employees; Statistics Canada, CANSIM
Table 282-008 - Labour Force Survey estimates (LFS), by North American Industry Classification System (NAICS), sex and age
group, Annual (persons × 1,000). < http://www5.statcan.gc.ca/cansim/a26? lang=eng&retrLang=eng&id=2820008&paSer=&
pattern=&stByVal=1&p1=1&p2=-1&tabMode=dataTable&csid=>

lunchrooms and lavatories in large workplaces. The employment of women and children was also curbed on the grounds of protecting their health.

Over the years, additional safety standards were introduced. In unionized workplaces and industries, *collective bargaining* also made a difference as unions negotiated for better working conditions and the elimination of specific health and safety hazards (Chapter 11). By the second decade of the 20th century, provincial Workers' Compensation boards had put in place *no-fault compensation systems*, which still exist today. Injured workers are provided with some money, the amount depending on the severity of their injury, and with partial compensation for lost wages, no matter whose fault the accident. In return, they give up their right to sue for compensation if the employer was at fault. The system is funded by contributions from employers, with the amount based, in part, on their safety record. Thus, there is a monetary incentive for employers to reduce workplace health and safety hazards and to encourage safe working practices among employees. This system has been effective in reducing the incidence of workplace injuries and in compensating injured workers. Even so, women have benefited less than have men. In the first part of the 20th century, many "female" occupations were excluded from what was then called "Workmen's Compensation" legislation. This exclusion is no longer the case, but women continue to be over-represented in precarious forms of employment (see Chapter 4), where workplace hazards may not be recognized and health and safety legislation is less likely to be effective (Storey 2009a; Kosny and MacEachen 2010).

All of these approaches to dealing with health and safety issues—standards setting and enforcement by the state, collective bargaining between unions and employers, and the no-fault compensation system—offer little room for direct involvement on the part of workers. But the introduction of the *internal responsibility system* (IRS) changed this. A core IRS principle is that workers' personal experience and knowledge of work practices and hazards are an integral part of any solution to health and safety problems. In addition, the system calls for workers to participate in identifying and eliminating workplace hazards. Furthermore, health and safety is also management's responsibility. Overall health and safety is a workplace issue—an internal responsibility—too important to be left to government alone. In the internal responsibility system, employees are directly involved with management in monitoring and inspection, and in education and health promotion in their workplaces.

Direct worker involvement in health protection and promotion in the workplace increased dramatically in Europe in the 1970s. This trend grew out of demands for greater industrial democracy (discussed later in this chapter) and government reviews of traditional and unsatisfactory approaches to occupational health and safety (Tucker 1992). In Canada, the first major IRS initiative was the 1972 Saskatchewan Occupational Health Act. It broke new ground by broadly defining occupational health as "the promotion and maintenance of the highest degree of physical, mental, and social well-being of workers" (Clark 1982: 200) and by making *joint health and safety committees*, or JHSCs, mandatory. Other provinces and the federal government (about 10% of Canadian workers are covered by federal labour legislation) followed. Today the internal responsibility system, built around JHSCs, is part of the legislated workplace health and safety system across the country, although there are significant differences in the extent to which it has been implemented and promoted by provincial governments (Tucker 2003).

JHSCs range in size from 2 to 12 members, half of whom must be non-managerial employees (either elected or appointed by a union if one exists); they are required in any workplace employing 20 or more. In most provinces, workplaces with at least 5 but fewer than 20 employees must also have at least one non-managerial safety representative. The committees keep records of injuries, participate in safety inspections, make recommendations to management about health and safety concerns, inform employees about their rights with respect to such concerns, and develop safety enhancement and educational programs (Gordon 1994: 542–43).

Along with giving JHSCs the *right to be involved* in health and safety issues, legislation also allows workers the *right to refuse unsafe work*, based on the individual employee's belief that a particular task presents a genuine risk. If subsequent inspections determine otherwise, the legislation protects workers from reprisals from employers. Workers also have the *right to be informed* about potentially hazardous materials with which they might be working.

The internal responsibility system appears to be effective. Research has shown that the recommendations of JHSCs to management are usually heeded (Gordon 1994). An Ontario study examining data on claims for lost time due to accidents between 1976 and 1989 concluded that when both employers and unions were committed to the idea of working together in joint committees to improve workplace safety, the number of lost-time accidents declined (Lewchuk, Robb, and Walters 1996: 225). The success of JHSCs in Canada has led to recommendations that the Canadian system be copied in the United States. The more traditional U.S. system, which still relies primarily on legislation and, where unions are present, on collective bargaining, is less effective (Gordon 1994). However, as in Canada, U.S. research has shown that joint health and safety committees can be effective (Eaton and Nocerino 2000).

The Labour Process and Workplace Health and Safety

How has the IRS approach to reducing workplace health and safety risks affected the labour process, that is, the contest for power between employers/managers and employees within capitalist workplaces? Does the relative effectiveness of joint health and safety committees indicate that workers and management are no longer in conflict over health and safety issues: that this is a win-win situation? We would argue that, in Canada, workers and management have moved further in this direction on health and safety issues than on others. In part, this movement is due to the economic incentives built into the system for employers—a better safety record means lower costs of production. More important, legislation has reduced some of the power differences between management and workers, and directly involved each in addressing health and safety issues.

Even so, workplace health and safety remains a contested terrain, and there have been some backward movements over the past decades (Tucker 2003). For example, during the early 1990s the Klein government in Alberta shifted to more of a "voluntary compliance" approach to worker health and safety issues, and also reduced its expenditures on occupational health and safety programs.[12] As a result, many fewer employers were prosecuted for noncompliance with health and safety legislation during this era. But the number of government inspections and prosecutions rose again in the late 1990s, suggesting that, despite its ideological appeal, the *employer self-regulation* approach may have been found lacking by the provincial government.[13]

Critics of the internal responsibility system have pointed out that, in many JHSCs, non-management members continue to have much less influence, particularly in nonunionized workplaces. Some employers largely ignore the joint committees, despite legislation (Lewchuk, Robb, and Walters 1996: 228). Rather than seeking ways to make their workplace safer and healthier (and by so doing, reducing their costs), some employers instead focus on challenging workers' claims of injuries and pushing them to return to work sooner (Thomason and Pozzebon 2002; Storey 2009b). Research has also shown that workers are often unaware of their rights and lack the knowledge needed to address complex health hazards; further, scientific and medical experts give the appearance of impartiality to a system that continues to be dominated by employers for whom profits come first (Sass 1995). In some tragic cases, notably the Westray mine explosion in 1992 in Nova Scotia, the system failed completely (Comish 1993; McCormick 1998). Local miners had warned that the mine site was unstable, and the initial mining plan was rejected for safety reasons. But the mine still opened and remained open even after repeated problems with methane gas, coal dust, and roof falls. Eventually, 26 miners died in an explosion.

While Canadian unions have fought for safer workplaces for well over a century, they have sometimes found themselves balancing concerns about their members' health and well-being with equally strong concerns about potential job loss. Robert Storey and Wayne Lewchuk (2000) describe how, in the early 1980s, the United Automobile Workers of America tried to force Bendix Automotive in Windsor, Ontario, to deal with the deadly problem of asbestos dust in its brake shoe factory. Having already closed one of its plants because of this problem, the company announced that it now planned to close the remaining factory. Some of the workers wanted their union to insist that the workplace be made safer, whatever the cost. Others, fearful that the company would close the factory and they would lose their jobs, wanted the union to back down. The factory was eventually closed anyway.

Along with disputes over the rights of management and workers, the definitions and sources of work-related health problems continue to be contested. For example, there is mounting evidence that job-related stress takes a toll on employees' health. Stress-induced health problems can range from headaches to chronic depression and heart disease. But even though some new management systems (lean production, for example) are creating particularly stressful work conditions (Carter et al. 2013), stress is still frequently rejected as a legitimate concern by Workers' Compensation boards, which administer claims.[14] They tend to use a narrow definition of health and illness, focusing mainly on physical injuries and fatalities. Employers and compensation boards sometimes try to place the blame for workers' health problems on their lifestyles or family situations rather than on their jobs. Such a "blaming the victim" ideology assumes that workers are careless, accident-prone, or susceptible to illness.

Rather than accepting a narrow definition of workplace health and safety issues, Bob Sass has argued that we need to

> "stretch" the present legal concept of risk, which covers dust, chemicals, lighting, and other quantifiable and measurable aspects of the workplace to cover all work environment matters: how the work is organized, the design of the job, pace of work, monotony, scheduling, sexual harassment, job cycle, and similar work environment matters of concern to workers.[15]

Sass wrote this almost three decades ago, and since then others have made the same arguments (Sullivan 2000). Sass himself has gone even further to argue that the "weak rights" workers now have within the internal responsibility system need to be extended. "Strong rights," as he sees it, go beyond co-management and would involve "worker control in the area of the work environment" (Sass 1995: 123). In such a democratized work environment, workers would not have to accept the constant tradeoff between health risks to themselves and the efficiency and profit demanded by employers. Sass sees unions as the only vehicle for such change since they are worker controlled, even though most unions work within the current internal responsibility system and accept its basic premises and goals.

However, with some exceptions, it has not been unions that have been pushing for a broader and more inclusive definition of worker health and well-being. Corporate health promotion, or "workplace wellness" programs, emerged in the 1980s as yet another human resource management policy that would help to motivate workers and raise productivity (Conrad 1987). The orientation of these wellness programs has typically been to change workers' lifestyles or health-related behaviours (exercising more and quitting smoking, for example). Some have gone considerably further to promote family-friendly and less stressful employment policies and practices.[16]

Workplace wellness programs have good intentions and can benefit employees who participate in them. But they have not addressed issues of job redesign and have not had an impact on the unequal distribution of power within work organizations which contributes to health and safety problems.[17] Furthermore, because such programs are typically available only in larger work organizations, many workers are unable to participate. Thus, while offering assistance to some workers, corporate wellness programs do not improve working conditions for the working class as a whole.

◼ INDUSTRIAL DEMOCRACY: RETHINKING WORKERS' RIGHTS

Our evaluation of new management paradigms (Chapter 9) concluded that none really offered workers input into decisions beyond their own jobs. Decisions about organizational restructuring, introduction of new technologies, replacement of permanent with temporary workers, or company downsizing are rarely negotiated with employees or their unions (Chapter 10). The internal responsibility system acknowledges the need to involve workers in the co-management of health and safety risks, but still does not give workers and employers equal control over the work environment. In short, within capitalism, ownership carries with it the ultimate right to control how work is organized and performed.

Industrial democracy attempts to involve workers in a much wider range of decisions within the organization, applying the principles of *representative democracy* found in the political arena to the workplace. Workers have a voice at the work-group level, as well as indirectly through elected representatives on corporate boards and other key policy-making bodies. Even so, as we will argue below, industrial democracy in its various forms has not eliminated workplace power differences. Furthermore, industrial democracy does not guarantee less bureaucracy, reduced income inequality, skill upgrading, or even more task-related autonomy for workers. Even if workers are involved extensively in decision making through elected representatives, the debates might not be around these issues. Job security, for example, or health and safety might be the major concern. Thus, in some settings, industrial democracy has led to job redesign and profit sharing. In others, the results may have been fewer layoffs or more consultation about technological change.

Industrial Democracy in North America

Attempts to involve workers in management, at least to some extent, have a long history in North America. Following World War I, *works councils*, including elected workers and management representatives, were set up in large workplaces in a number of industries in both Canada and the United States. The councils met to discuss health and safety, workers' grievances, efficiency, and sometimes even wages. In a number of settings, particularly the coal industry, the impetus for these initiatives was a series of long and violent strikes.[18]

William Lyon Mackenzie King, who later became prime minister of Canada, was a labour consultant to some of these companies at the time. He was a strong advocate of the principles of industrial democracy, believing that works councils and related initiatives would reduce industrial conflict and help usher in a new era of social harmony (King 1918). Critics argued that mechanisms to encourage more cooperation between workers and management continued to favour the latter and that works councils were just a way to deter workers from joining unions. Clearly, in many companies this was the case. With the onset of the Depression at the end of the 1920s, interest in these earlier forms of industrial democracy waned, perhaps because unemployment led to fewer strikes.

Since then, calls have periodically been made for a revival of such worker–management decision-making systems. Not coincidentally, industrial democracy has attracted more interest during periods of labour unrest— immediately after World War II, for example, and again in the 1970s. During those strike-filled eras, employers and politicians looked to Germany and other European countries where industrial democracy had been implemented more widely. North American unions have generally opposed the idea, believing that works councils and other similar forms of industrial democracy undermine collective bargaining, the more traditional means by which workers have negotiated with management for improved working conditions (Guzda 1993: 67). Thus, overall, the spread of industrial democracy in North America has been slow (Frege 2005). Most employers have been more interested in avoiding strikes than in sharing power, and unions have not been supportive.

Institutionalized Industrial Democracy in Germany

North American experiments in industrial democracy have usually been introduced by management, occasionally with some pressure from unions. In contrast, principles of industrial democracy have been institutionalized via legislation in many northern European countries. Workers are given the right to elect representatives to sit on works councils or corporate boards, the right to consultation regarding technological changes, and more grassroots control over health and safety matters.[19]

The German model of *codetermination* has a century-long history. In the 1890s, concerns about widespread labour–management conflict motivated

Chancellor Bismarck to bring in legislation giving works councils the right to advise management on workplace regulations. This legislation was broadened in the 1920s as the Weimar government sought ways to counter the threat of the Russian Revolution spreading into Germany. After World War II, concerned that labour strife would hold back the reconstruction of Germany's devastated economy, the British, American, and French administrators of occupied Germany extended the codetermination legislative framework. A number of additional changes were made in the 1970s and 1980s.

In its current form, German legislation makes works councils mandatory in any workplace with more than five employees. Elected representatives of the workforce (their number proportional to the size of the firm) share decision making with management representatives. The legislation stipulates that, in larger work organizations where unions are present, a proportion of the elected members must be from the union. But nonunionized white-collar workers must also be represented. In larger companies, there are several layers of shared decision making. The most powerful management board, a group of three or four individuals, has only one worker representative.

The codetermination legislation requires employers to advise and consult with works councils about plans to introduce new technologies, restructure work, reallocate workers to different tasks or locations, or lay off workers. Works councils can demand compensation for workers negatively affected by new technologies or organizational restructuring. Consequently, the North American strategy of downsizing has been much less common in Germany. Elected representatives are jointly involved with management in determining hours of work, pay procedures (bonus rates, for example), training systems, health and safety rules, and working conditions. However, collective bargaining between employers and unions about overall pay rates takes place outside the works councils on an industry-wide level. Consequently, the right to strike remains with the larger unions, not with the local works councils. The unions, however, have much less influence in the joint decision-making process at the local level.

The German *dual representation system* of industrial democracy—industry-wide unions and local works councils—is viewed relatively positively by both employers and workers. There are some concerns that unions may be weakened by the dual system of representation, but union members still constitute a majority of elected representatives on the works councils. Overall, joint decision making has meant better communication between workers and management, greater protection of workers' rights, improved working conditions, and a reduction in labour–management conflict. The latter was, of course, an original goal of the codetermination legislation, and it has frequently impressed North American observers concerned about strikes and reduced productivity.

During the 1990s, the German economy began to lose some of its momentum, in part, because of the costs of reuniting West and East Germany. Employers began to call for changes in the dual system of representation. In particular, there were pressures to reform the industry-wide collective bargaining system that had meant similar pay rates and conditions of employment in different-sized firms throughout the country. Employers argued that they needed more flexibility to remain competitive (Beaumont 1995). But so far, major changes have not been made to Germany's labour legislation. Works councils continue to protect workers' rights, companies with works councils are more productive than those without them (Mueller 2012), and the German economy remains among the strongest in Europe.

Sweden: Industrial Democracy as a National Goal

In Sweden, the motivation to implement industrial democracy was somewhat different than in Germany, where concerns about strikes and social unrest led to codetermination legislation. An exceptionally strong union movement and the governing Social Democratic Party worked together to improve employment conditions and give Swedish workers more rights. During the 1970s and 1980s, industrial democracy was elevated to a national goal within a much broader policy of commitment to reduced inequality and full employment.[20]

As in Germany, Swedish law mandates employee representation on corporate boards of directors in all but the smallest firms. But the 1977 Act on Employee Participation in Decision Making extended Swedish employees' rights beyond the rights of German workers. Specifically, in addition to the obligation to inform and consult with workers on major decisions such as factory closures or introducing new technologies, Swedish employers must negotiate with unions prior to such decisions. Unions must also be given complete access to information on the economic status of the firm and its personnel policies. In 1984, Sweden went further by setting up Wage Earner Funds, which redirected corporate taxes into share purchases on behalf of employees in manufacturing and related industries (Whyman 2004).

The 1978 Work Environment Act goes beyond the goal of industrial democracy—joint decision making throughout a work organization—to address problems of worker satisfaction and personal fulfillment (see Chapter 14). The Act aims to achieve "working conditions where the individual can regard work as a meaningful and enriching part of existence." It is not enough for work to be free of physical and psychological hazards; it must also provide opportunities for satisfaction and personal growth, and for employees to assume greater responsibility. Thus, unlike recent management approaches, such as QWL, that view improved productivity and less conflict as desirable outcomes of worker satisfaction (see Chapter 9), this legislation makes worker satisfaction and individual growth the highest priority.

During the 1970s and 1980s, Sweden's impressive economic performance, low unemployment, and reduction of wage inequalities were seen as strong evidence of the success of its model of society-wide industrial democracy. But the following two decades brought changes. Some of the government's policies directed at maintaining full employment were eliminated, and unemployment was allowed to rise. Employers sought more flexibility in the allocation of labour in the production process and were able, as in Germany, to reduce the extent of nationwide centralized wage bargaining. Lean production made its appearance in Swedish factories, some of the most progressive factories (in terms of workers' autonomy and skill enhancement) closed, and employers introduced new technologies to cut jobs.[21] But the framework legislation that supports the Swedish system of industrial democracy is still in place, and the Swedish version of codetermination continues to be successful (Levinson 2000). Overall, compared to Canada and the United States, social inequality in Sweden is not as pronounced, because of its labour market policies (Olsen 2008).

● WORKERS TAKING OVER OWNERSHIP

A basic capitalist principle is that ownership carries with it the right to control how work is performed and how the organization is run. By offering some degree of co-management or codetermination, the various forms of industrial democracy have given workers a few of the rights traditionally attached to ownership. However, in some settings, workers have gone much further, taking over partial or complete ownership of the means of production. How economically viable is worker ownership within a global capitalist economy? And does worker ownership provide more opportunity for control over the labour process?

Employee Share Ownership Plans

In North America, *employee share ownership plans* (ESOPs) have been widely promoted as a way for workers to share in the profits of production and as a means of generating more consensus in the workplace. If workers are part-owners, the reasoning goes, they should be more likely to identify with the company, work harder, and cooperate with management (Wheeler 2008). In the past few decades, ESOPs have been part of the package offered to employees in many private-sector, high-performance workplaces.

In some companies with employee share ownership plans, shares in the company are purchased for employees and provided as part of a benefits package. In other workplaces, employees are allowed to purchase shares at reduced rates, or their employer pays for a portion of the cost if workers choose to buy shares (Luffman 2003). Depending on the details of the plan, employees in some categories might receive (or be allowed to buy) more shares than employees in other categories. Typically, higher-paid employees receive or can buy the most shares. Thus, employees receive some of the company profits, in the same way as would other shareholders. However, when shares available through the plan are provided as benefits in lieu of wages, employees will also lose when the company is losing money.

The presence of employee share ownership plans and participation in them varies in different countries. Wheeler (2008: 165) suggests that there are more than 9,000 employee share ownership plans in the United States, in firms representing over 10 million employees (not all of these employees would take advantage of the plan). In Canada, about two-thirds of the firms listed on the Toronto Stock Exchange have ESOPs. About half of these plans are available to all employees, with the company paying at least some of the cost. However, when we focus on the full Canadian labour force, we find that only 7 percent of all private-sector workers owned shares in their company in 2005, down from just under 10 percent in 1999 (Statistics Canada 2008f: 54–55).

Managers and professionals are much more likely to own shares, as are those working in very large companies. Similar plans exist in a number of European countries, although they are not nearly as widespread as various forms of institutionalized industrial democracy. A survey of large workplaces in 10 European Union (EU) countries showed ESOPs present in about one in 10 private companies. Employee share ownership plans were somewhat more common in the United Kingdom than in other EU countries with histories of industrial democracy (Poutsma, Hendrickx, and Huijgen 2003).

In North America, employee share ownership plans have been set up primarily to provide additional benefits to workers or to allow them to purchase shares, but not to promote joint decision-making. In workplaces where employees participate in an ESOP as well as in some form of joint decision-making, it is usually because some other managerial model (QWL, for example) has also been implemented. However, in these types of situations typically, the predicted productivity gains associated with the plans are found. In other words, the combination of both employee ownership and worker decision-making makes the difference (Pendleton and Robinson 2010).

An example of a company offering profit sharing, but going much further in terms of worker participation, is the fascinating Brazilian company SEMCO (Largacha-Martinez 2011). The company has grown steadily for several decades and now has annual sales of over $210 million. The 3,000 employees in its various businesses set their own production quotas, redesign products, develop marketing plans, and determine salary ranges. Employees even choose and evaluate their own managers. For big decisions, such as buying another company or relocating a factory, every worker gets a vote. Thus, SEMCO appears to have gone far beyond the basic principles of industrial democracy and also the ESOP model to give workers rights and obligations normally reserved for owners.

Worker Buyouts

Economic restructuring and factory and mill closures over the past several decades have led to interesting examples of worker ownership of a different kind (Long 1995). Workers have bought out their employers in an effort to save their jobs when the company was about to close. Unlike the situation with ESOPs, the majority ownership that comes with *worker buyouts* allows them to manage their own job security (to decide whether the business closes or not). Majority ownership also allows workers to change the management system, if they want to.[22]

One prominent example of a worker buyout in Canada was the purchase of Algoma Steel in Sault Ste. Marie in 1992. The company had been operating in the community since 1901 and employed about 5,000 workers at the beginning of the 1990s. If the company had folded, the community would have been decimated. Through their union (the United Steel Workers of America), and with the assistance of loan guarantees from the New Democratic provincial government, workers negotiated the purchase of a majority of shares in the company. Cost savings were obtained by a voluntary pay reduction and through a plan to eliminate several thousand jobs through attrition. A decade after the buyout, Algoma Steel ran into severe financial difficulties but, with the participation of the union, refinanced and restructured itself once more. As a result of the public sale of shares to finance the upgrading of the steel mill, workers now owned only about one-quarter of Algoma's shares. However, they still appointed 5 of the company's 13 board members, and the participative management structure set up years earlier continued to operate effectively. More recently, in 2007, Algoma Steel was bought by a multinational steel company with its home base in India. Today, the company still has an employee share ownership plan, but the bold experiment in industrial democracy and worker ownership is over.

New worker-owners do not typically implement some form of industrial democracy (Varghese et al. 2006). For example, when forestry workers and managers bought the mills in which they had been employed for many years in Kapuskasing, Ontario (1991), and Pine Falls, Manitoba (1994), they initially experimented with forms of worker participation in decision making. But within a year or two, the traditional system of management had been reinstated at TEMBEC (Krogman and Beckley 2002). By 2010, the worker-owners had sold their shares to private investors operating a series of mills across Ontario and Quebec, and today TEMBEC presents itself to potential employees, not as a firm that offers worker-ownership possibilities, but as a "lean company."[23]

Algoma Steel and TEMBEC were successful examples of employee buyouts that eventually failed, but probably not because of the ownership structure. Instead, they were the major employer in single-industry communities, which have generally not fared well in the contemporary global economy. In contrast, most ailing companies bought by workers become successful once again. An interesting case is the Great Western Brewing Company in Saskatoon. It has operated successfully as a worker-owned business for 25 years, since 1989 when 16 workers bought a brewery that Carling Molson was planning to shut down because it was not profitable (Lopez-Pacheco 2014). A meta-analysis of 43 published studies (Doucouliagos 1995) showed that profit sharing, worker ownership, and institutionalized industrial democracy are all associated with higher levels of productivity, with the largest impact occurring in worker-owned firms.

The chances of a worker buyout being successful are increased when all the participants, including the union if one is present, support the buyout plan. In addition, workers typically need expert advice to assist them in deciding how to restructure the organization, since major changes (often in wage rates and staffing) are usually needed. An example would be the unique working and financing arrangement developed by unionized workers and three different investor groups with various types of expertise who bought and revitalized the bankrupt Harmac pulp mill in Nanaimo in 2008 (Spalding 2010). Government support is also critical, particularly with respect to financing, since many lenders are reluctant to gamble on worker buyouts, despite their better-than-average track record.

Producer Co-operatives

Producer (employee-owned) co-operatives have a long history in North America and Europe. The first appeared in Britain more than 150 years ago as workers looked for alternatives to the exploitative excesses of early capitalism (Estrin and Pérotin 1987). However, the producer co-operative movement was overshadowed by another form of collective response by workers: the formation of trade unions (Chapter 11). Even so, the co-operative alternative continues.

In 2012, more than 600 employee-owned (producer) co-operatives were functioning in Canada, with more than 13,000 members.[24] A majority of these organizations are in Quebec, in large part, because the provincial government has put in place programs that provide financing for producer co-operatives. While producer co-operatives are not a widespread phenomenon, and those that exist are typically quite small, they nonetheless offer another alternative to conventional employer–employee relationships. Examples in Canada include everything from construction companies and daycare centres to taxi firms, recycling companies, coffee roasters, and fish farms, as well as small manufacturing companies, consulting firms, restaurants, and forestry management firms.

Producer co-operatives must be distinguished from other collective enterprises, including consumer co-operatives (such as co-op food stores) or housing co-ops, in which a number of individuals or families jointly own and maintain a dwelling or housing complex. They are also different from marketing co-ops (the wheat pools set up early last century by Prairie farmers are the best example) and financial services co-ops, such as credit unions. While sharing with these other organizations a general commitment to collective ownership and shared risk taking, *producer co-operatives* are distinguished by their function as collective producers of goods or services.[25]

Producer co-operatives are also different from other types of worker-owned enterprises in several important respects. First, central to the philosophy of producer co-operatives is a commitment to the democratic principle of "one person—one vote." This defining characteristic would eliminate companies with employee share ownership plans and many employee buyouts. Second, and related to the first point, producer co-operatives typically do not allow non-members to own shares. As a result, members cannot benefit financially from the success of the co-operative by selling their own shares. Instead, some arrangements are usually made to reimburse members for their previous contributions when they leave the organization.

Although generally quite small, producer co-operatives can nevertheless survive in a capitalist economy. A study of producer co-operatives in Atlantic Canada revealed an estimated median lifespan of 17 years for rural producer co-operatives and 25 years for those in urban settings (Staber 1993: 140). But producer co-operatives face many challenges. It is difficult to finance such enterprises, since banks are often skeptical of their ability to survive. This problem is also faced by other small businesses and by employees wanting to buy out their company. In situations where producer co-operatives are set up as a solution to high unemployment caused by economic downturns, the new worker-owned enterprises are at a disadvantage from the outset. And, as with any efforts to democratize workplaces, participants in producer co-operatives have to learn how to work collectively toward common goals, something not taught or encouraged in a competitive capitalist society.

Given their small size and collective ownership, it is not surprising that producer co-operatives tend to offer workers greater control over the labour process. Leslie Brown (1997) argues that producer co-operatives incorporate many of the democratizing and work-humanizing features of workplace reform that have been promised, but not always delivered, by the many new management approaches of the past decades (Chapter 9). She also concludes that producer co-operatives are a viable solution to problems of community economic development that have not been solved by efforts to encourage traditional forms of capitalist enterprise in underdeveloped regions of the country.

Worldwide, the most successful producer co-operative is found in and around Mondragon, a city in the Basque region of Spain. There, over 80,000 worker-owners (in 2013; up from about 20,000 25 years earlier) run several hundred diverse manufacturing and service companies with annual sales (in 2012) of almost 13 billion Euros.[26] Each worker has an economic stake in the enterprise where she or he works, and as a member of the firm's general assembly, helps establish policies, approves financial plans, and elects members to a supervisory board, which, in turn, appoints managers. Mondragon co-ops have replaced the private ownership of industry in this region with a system of collective ownership and control. By all accounts, these co-ops have achieved high levels of growth, productivity, and employment creation, strong links with the community, harmonious labour relations, a satisfying and non-alienating work environment, and a close integration between workplace and community (Whyte and Whyte 1988; Forcadell 2005).

Mondragon's success is linked to, among other things, the Basque region's decades-long struggle for greater autonomy from Spain, the destruction of the area's industrial base during the Spanish Civil War in the 1930s, and support from the local Roman Catholic church and unions. This unique historical mix of political, cultural, and economic circumstances has sometimes been used as an argument that producer co-operatives could not thrive in other settings such as North America. Granted, it is never easy to transplant production systems from one cultural and political context to another. But, if we are willing to accept that Japanese management techniques or German codetermination, for example, offer alternatives to the North American approach to organizing workplaces, we should not ignore the Mondragon-style producer co-operative alternative (Macleod 1997).

◘ CONCLUSION

In Chapter 9, we explored a range of new managerial models that, in contrast to Taylorism and the human relations approach (discussed in Chapter 8), promised to empower workers and enhance their skills. Chapter 10, with its critical assessment of the labour process in capitalist workplaces, reminded us of the power differences and inherent conflicts between owners and managers, on one hand, and employees on the other. In Chapter 11, we examined the role of unions in giving workers a voice and some organizational power in capitalist economies. In this chapter we shifted our focus to alternative ways of organizing work, workplaces, and society as a whole that might reduce industrial conflict and provide workers with more control over the labour process and their work organizations.

We began by asking whether union militancy might evolve into class politics that, in turn, could lead to capitalism being reformed, but concluded that there has been little evidence of this in Canada. Even so, we wondered whether broad-scale contemporary social movements, in conjunction with the trade union movement, might generate progressive social change. As our review of statistics on workplace injuries and fatalities revealed, workplace health and safety continues to be a contested issue in the workplace. However, the systems put in place to address health and safety concerns provide some evidence of workers and management finding common ground. Our discussion of the different forms of industrial democracy in Germany and Sweden also revealed alternative approaches to economic organization that can empower workers and provide them with a greater collective voice while, at the same time, reducing labour–management conflict. Finally, our examination of different forms of worker ownership highlighted once again that there are alternatives to traditional employment relationships within capitalism that deserve serious consideration.

◘ DISCUSSION QUESTIONS

1. Based on what you have read in Chapters 9 through 12, what do you consider to be the most effective ways to give workers a "voice" in their workplace today?

2. Based on information in Chapter 11 and this chapter, discuss whether you think unions have the potential to both transform workplaces and address broader social problems.

3. The way workplace health and safety issues are handled in Canadian workplaces today is an example of employers and employees identifying and working together to meet common goals. Do you agree with this proposition? Why or why not?

4. Workplaces are organized differently, workers are managed differently, and industrial relations have different rules in some European countries. What can we learn from these societies that would lead to higher productivity and less conflict in North American workplaces?

5. Critically discuss the following statement: "Producer co-operatives have been successful in places such as Mondragon, Spain, and in some isolated, small Canadian communities, but they are irrelevant for modern, urban Canada."

ADDITIONAL RESOURCES

WORK AT THE MOVIES

- *Wal-Town* (directed by Sergeo Kirby, 2006, 66:09 minutes). This NFB documentary concerns the work of student activists in raising awareness about the practices of Wal-Mart. It is available through the National Film Board of Canada: www.nfb.ca/film/wal_town.
- *Occupy: The Movie* (directed by Corey Ogilvie, 2013, 121 minutes). The documentary traces the rise and development of the Occupy movement following the 2008 global crash. It is available through the Hot Docs Library: http://www.hotdocs.ca/film/title/occupy_the_movie.
- *Erin Brockovich* (directed by Steven Soderbergh, 2000, 131 minutes). An unemployed single mother becomes a legal assistant and almost single-handedly brings down a California power company accused of polluting a city's water supply.
- *The Take* (directed by Avi Lewis, 2004, 87 minutes). Set in Argentina after its 2001 economic collapse, the Canadian documentary tells the story of a group of unemployed auto-parts workers who form a co-operative and strive to reopen their closed factory.

SOUNDS OF WORK

- "Join a Co-op" (Emily Erhardt). Written for the International Co-operative Alliance's Coop'Art competition in recognition of the International Year of Co-ops (2012), this song by a young Canadian rapper outlines the benefits of co-operative organizations.
- "Talkin' 'Bout a Revolution" (Tracy Chapman). Chapman sings about the need for poor people to stand up and fight for reshaping income distribution.
- "The Internationale" (Eugène Pottier). The 19th-century worker's song about the Paris Commune later became the first national anthem of the Soviet Union.
- "Chemical Worker's Song (Process Man)" (Great Big Sea). This band from Newfoundland and Labrador writes about men working in a chemical plant and suffering dire health consequences.

◼ NOTES

1. See Lash (1984) for a comparison of U.S. and French workers that reaches similar conclusions about how ideological and cultural factors shape worker militancy.
2. Briskin (2010: 217–19) distinguishes between labour militancy (unionized workers going on strike), worker militancy (nonunionized workers taking collective action), and union militancy (unions increasing involvement in broader social justice issues, rather than focusing only on benefits for their members).
3. http://www.cleanclothes.org/ [retrieved November 21, 2013]; Egels-Zandén and Hyllman (2006) discuss the conditions under which unions involved in the Clean Clothes Campaign are more likely to have an effect on corporations.
4. Roberts (2012) argues that the Occupy Wall Street movement that was highly visible several years ago was generally not successful because, despite the social justice goals of its participants, it failed to work with established institutions, such as unions, which have the organizational structure and resources required to maintain sustained pressure on corporations and governments.
5. Marshall (1996) provides work-related fatality data from 1976 to 1993. Sharpe and Hardt (2006) discuss trends in fatality and injury rates from 1993 to 2005. More recent data come from the Association of Workers' Compensation Boards of Canada: http://www.awcbc.org/en/nationalworkinjuriesstatisticsprogramwisp.aps [retrieved April 27, 2014].

6. http://work.alberta.ca/documents/2011-OHS-Data.pdf [retrieved April 27, 2014].

7. Association of Workers' Compensation Boards of Canada: http://www.awcbc .org/en/nationalworkinjuriesstatisticsprogramwisp.aps [retrieved April 27, 2014].

8. Conway and Svenson (1998) report a similar decline in occupational injury and illness rates in the United States.

9. Employment and Social Development Canada: http://www4.hrsdc.gc.ca/ .3ndic.1t.4r@-eng.jsp?iid=20 [retrieved April 27, 2014].

10. Government of Canada, Labour Program, Occupational Injuries and Diseases in Canada, 1996–2008: http://www.labour.gc.ca/eng/health_safety/pubs_hs/ oidc.shtml [retrieved November 23, 2013].

11. Human Resources Development Canada (2000b).

12. Barnetson (2013) describes how most farm workers in Alberta are still not covered by basic labour legislation, including Workers' Compensation, and how politicians insist that self-regulation is appropriate, despite high injury and fatality rates in agriculture.

13. See Walters (2006) for a discussion of how the U.K. government has preferred voluntary compliance approaches over strengthening workplace health and safety legislation and promoting further employee involvement.

14. Kompier et al. (1994) note that Sweden, the United Kingdom, and the Netherlands recognize work-related stress in their health and safety legislation, while Germany and France do not.

15. Sass, Robert. (1986). "Workplace Health and Safety: Report from Canada." *International Journal of Health Services* 16:565–82.

16. For information on workplace wellness programs, see the Canadian Centre for Occupational Health and Safety: http://www.ccohs.ca/oshanswers/psychosocial/ wellness_program.html [retrieved November 24, 2013].

17. Hansen (2004) is more critical, labelling employee assistance programs as the "caring cousin" of workplace surveillance strategies, since employers can use such programs to identify workers who may potentially become less productive.

18. See Russell (1990: Chapter 3) and Rinehart (2006: 48–49) on early works councils in Canada, and Guzda (1993) on the U.S. situation.

19. See Beaumont (1995), Poutsma, Hendrickx, and Huijgen (2003), Looise and Drucker (2003), Whittal, Knudson, and Huijgen (2007), and van den Berg, Grift, and van Witteloostuijn (2011) on industrial democracy in Europe.

20. This discussion of Sweden draws on Milner (1989), Smucker et al. (1998), Levinson (2000), Whyman (2004), and Olsen (2008).

21. See Sandberg (1994), Smucker et al. (1998), and Nilsson (1996).

22. This discussion of worker buyouts is based on Gunderson et al. (1995), Long (1995), and Nishman (1995).
23. http://jobs.tembec.com/what-expect/tembec-wants-people-who-want-make-difference [retrieved November 26, 2013].
24. http://www.canada2012.coop/en/cooperatives_in_canada/by-the-numbers [retrieved November 26, 2013].
25. See Lindenfeld and Wynn (1997) and Brown (1997) on producer co-operatives.
26. http://www.mondragon-corporation.com/language/en-US/ENG/Economic-Data/Most-relevant-data.aspx [retrieved November 26, 2013].

WORK VALUES AND WORK ORIENTATIONS

● INTRODUCTION

In previous chapters, we presented a structural analysis of work in Canada, discussing, among other topics, labour markets, the occupational structure, work organizations, management systems, labour unions, and gender, racial, and other forms of stratification. Some of this material addressed individual reactions to work—workers' problems in balancing work and family responsibilities, and resistance and conflict in the workplace, for example. But in this chapter and the next, we get to the very core of the individual–job relationship by examining the meaning of work in our society and workers' subjective response to their work.

We begin with a broad overview of work values. What does "work" really mean in our society today? Have work values changed over time, and are there cultural differences in work values? We then focus our analysis on the work orientations, or preferences, held by individual Canadians. How are these preferences shaped? Are alternative work orientations emerging in response to changing employment relationships and demographic shifts in Canadian society? Then, in Chapter 14, we turn our attention to job satisfaction and work-related stress. Overall, how satisfied are Canadian workers with their employment situation? Is this changing? What factors influence job satisfaction and dissatisfaction, and what are the underlying causes of work-related stress? Does satisfaction with or stress resulting from one's job have further consequences?

■ DEFINING WORK VALUES AND WORK ORIENTATIONS

Values, as sociologists use the term, are the benchmarks or standards by which members of a society assess their own and others' behaviour. We could talk about how personal attributes such as honesty and industriousness are valued in our society, about how we value freedom of speech, or about the value placed on getting a good education. We might also ask how work is valued, or, in other words, what the meaning of work is in a particular society.

Having identified work values as societal standards, we can define *work orientations* more narrowly as the meaning attached to work by particular individuals within a society. Blackburn and Mann (1979: 141) define an orientation as "a central organizing principle which underlies people's attempts to make sense of their lives." Thus, studying work orientations involves determining what people consider important in their lives. Does someone continue to work primarily for material reasons (either a desire to become wealthy or because of economic necessity), for income that will allow him or her to enjoy life away from work, or for the enjoyment and personal fulfillment that can come from work? Even more specifically, what types of work and work arrangements do individuals prefer?

The distinction between work values and work orientations is not always clear, since it hinges on the extent to which the latter are broadly shared within a society. As we will argue below, several different sets of work values can coexist within a society, influencing the work orientations of individuals within that society. In fact, as our earlier discussion of managerial ideologies and practices showed (see Chapter 9), particular work values have often been promoted by employers to gain compliance from workers.

An individual's work orientations are also shaped by specific experiences on the job. Indeed, a worker whose job or career is dissatisfying may begin to challenge dominant work values. Thus, over the long term, shifting work orientations on the part of many workers might also influence societal work values. *Job satisfaction* (or dissatisfaction), discussed in Chapter 14, is the most individualized and subjective response of a person to the material and psychological rewards offered by a job.[1]

● WORK VALUES ACROSS TIME AND SPACE

The meaning attached to work has changed dramatically over the centuries.[2] The ancient Greeks and Romans viewed most forms of work negatively, considering it brutalizing and uncivilized. In fact, the Greek word for "work," *ponos*, comes from the root word for "sorrow." According to Greek mythology, the gods had cursed the human race by giving them the need to work. Given these dominant work values, the ruling classes turned their attention to politics, warfare, the arts, and philosophy, leaving the physical work to slaves.

Early Hebrew religious values placed a different but no more positive emphasis on work. Hard work was seen as divine punishment for the "original sin" of the first humans who ate from the "tree of the knowledge of good and evil." According to Hebrew and Christian scriptures, God banished Eve and Adam from the Garden of Eden, where all of creation was at their easy disposal, to a life of hard labour, telling them that "[i]n the sweat of thy face shalt thou eat bread, till thou return unto the ground."[3] This perspective on work remained part of the early Christian worldview for many centuries.

A more positive view of work was promoted by Saint Thomas Aquinas in the 13th century. In ranking occupations according to their value to society, Aquinas rejected the notion that all work is a curse or a necessary evil. Instead, he argued that some forms of work were better than others. Priests were assigned the highest ranks, followed by those working in agriculture, and then craftworkers. Because they produced food or products useful to society, these groups were ranked higher than merchants and shopkeepers. A comparison of this scheme to contemporary occupational status scales (see Chapter 4) reveals some interesting reversals. The status of those involved in commercial activity—bankers, corporate owners, and managers, for example—has increased, while farmers and craftworkers have experienced substantial declines in occupational status.

During the 16th-century Protestant Reformation in Europe, Martin Luther's ideas marked a significant change in dominant work values. Luther argued that work was a central component of human life. Although he still had a negative opinion of work for profit, he went beyond the belief that hard work was atonement for original sin. When he wrote, "There is just one best way to serve God—to do most perfectly the work of one's profession" (Burstein et al. 1975: 10), he was articulating the idea of a "calling," that is, industriousness and hard work within one's station in life, however lowly that might be, as the fulfillment of God's will. Whether or not peasants or the urban working class shared these values is difficult to determine. However, to the extent that the ruling classes could convince their subordinates that hard work was a moral obligation, power and privilege could be more easily maintained.

The Protestant Work Ethic

The Industrial Revolution transformed the social and economic landscape of Europe and also generated a new set of work values. In his famous book, *The Protestant Ethic and the Spirit of Capitalism*, Max Weber (1958) emphasized how Calvinists, one of the early Protestant groups that had broken away from the Roman Catholic Church, embraced hard work, rejected worldly pleasures, and extolled the virtues of frugality. Weber argued that such religious beliefs encouraged people to make and reinvest profits and, in turn, gave rise to work values conducive to the growth of capitalism. Other scholars have questioned whether these early Protestant entrepreneurs really acted solely on religious beliefs and whether other groups not sharing these beliefs might have been equally successful (Dickson and McLachlan 1989).[4] Nonetheless, Weber did draw our attention to the role of work values in capitalist societies. He also recognized that such an *ideology of work*, while justifying the profit-seeking behaviour of capitalists, might also help control their employees who, for religious reasons, would be motivated to work hard.

Freedom and equality are additional secular values that fit into the belief system of capitalist democracies. A central assumption is that workers are participants in a labour market where they can freely choose a job. If this is so, the fact that some people are wealthier and more powerful than others must be because of their hard work and smart choices, most specifically, investments in higher education. Hence, within this ideology of work, equality does not refer to the distribution of wealth and power, but to access to the same opportunities for upward mobility in a competitive labour market. But, as explained in Chapter 5, some workers are advantaged by birth, and some occupational groups are more protected in the labour market. Consequently, for many workers, the daily realities of the labour market often contradict the dominant set of work values.

Work as Self-Fulfillment: The Humanist Tradition

The importance of hard work and wealth accumulation are only one perspective on work in a capitalist society. The belief that work is virtuous in itself gave rise to another set of values in the 17th and 18th centuries. The *humanist tradition* grew out of Renaissance philosophies that distinguished humans from other species on the basis of our ability to consciously direct our labour. A view of human beings as creators led to the belief that work should be a fulfilling and liberating activity, and that it constituted the very essence of humanity.

Karl Marx fashioned these ideas into a radical critique of capitalism and a formula for social revolution (Chapter 1). He agreed that the essence of humanity was expressed through work, but argued that this potential was stifled by capitalist relations of production. Because they had little control over their labour and its products, workers were engaged in alienating work. For Marx, capitalist economic relations limited human independence and creativity. Only when capitalism was replaced by socialism, he argued, would work be truly liberating.

Marx's theory of alienation has had a major impact on the sociology of work (Chapter 10); ironically, a similar set of beliefs about the centrality of work to an individual's sense of personal well-being underlies a number of contemporary management approaches, which are decidedly non-Marxist in their assumptions (see Chapter 9). It is frequently argued, for example, that workers would be more satisfied if they were allowed to use more of their skills and make more decisions in their jobs. But these management perspectives do not see capitalism as the problem. Rather, they advocate improved organizational and job design within capitalism. Humanistic beliefs about the essential importance of work in people's lives are also espoused by many contemporary sociologists of work.[5] Indeed, they underlie our own perspective (Lowe 2000). Such work values have also been promoted by various 20th- and 21st-century theologians, including the Roman Catholic priest who founded the system of Mondragon producer co-operatives in the 1950s (Chapter 12), as well as the current pope, who spoke about the dignity of work in his 2013 May Day sermon in St. Peter's Square in Rome.[6] The pope also expressed his concern for unemployed workers around the world, noting that this social problem was often the result of greater emphasis in society on profit-seeking rather than social justice.

Manifest and Latent Functions of Work

Many sociological and psychological studies tell us that unemployment is extremely traumatic for jobless individuals and their families.[7] Lost income leads to a lower standard of living, personal and family stress, and health problems. And, as the humanist perspective on work reminds us, the centrality of work to people's self-worth and identity means that unemployment has even deeper personal and social costs.

Based on her research among the unemployed during the Depression of the 1930s, Marie Jahoda (1982) identified some of the *latent functions* of work that people miss if they lose their jobs. While the *manifest function* of work is, primarily, maintaining or improving one's standard of living, the latent (less obvious) functions contribute to an individual's personal well-being. Work can provide experiences of creativity and mastery, and can foster a sense of purpose. It can be self-fulfilling, although clearly, some jobs offer much less fulfillment than others. When hit by unemployment, an individual loses these personal rewards, as illustrated by the following comments by a nutritionist about her 14 months of unemployment:

I feel like I'm wasting time. I feel like I'm not accomplishing anything. I don't really feel like I'm contributing to the marriage, to society, or anything like that.[8]

Work also provides regularly shared experiences and often enjoyable interactions with coworkers (Hodson 2004). When the job is gone, so are such personally satisfying routines. An unemployed person quickly comes to miss these social rewards and may also find that relationships away from work are no longer the same. Such feelings are expressed in the following way by an unemployed teacher:

> The whole feeling that I had ... [was] that nobody really understood where I was, what I was going through, what I cared about, what was important to me. Because I was no longer talking about my job as a teacher, in fact I wasn't talking about my job as anything. I had a strong sense of not fitting in.

In addition, work structures time. Individuals who have lost their job frequently find that their days seem not only empty, but disorienting. A divorced mother of a four-year-old, living with her own mother to make ends meet, explains:

> If you went to work, at least you're coming home in the evening. When I'm home all day ... I get confused. My whole metabolism's gone crazy, because it's, like, I'm coming back from ... where I have been. Or I've gone and I'm still waiting to come home.

Being unemployed often requires that one seek financial assistance, sometimes from family members, but more often through government agencies. Dealing with the bureaucracy can be frustrating. Even more problematic, receiving social assistance carries a great deal of *stigma*. As a former factory worker, the mother of two small children, explains:

> When I went down there, I felt that I just stuck right out. I thought, "Oh, my God, people think I'm on welfare...." You used to think "It's those people who are on welfare," and now you discover you're one of those people.

The same value system that rewards individuals for their personal success also leads to what Jean Swanson (2001) calls "poor-bashing," the perpetuation in the media, in our legislation and social programs, and in our everyday discourse, of myths and stereotypes about the poor and the unemployed being lazy, unmotivated, and undeserving of assistance. These myths and stereotypes, in turn, can lead unemployed people to blame themselves for their own problems, even if they recognize the structural barriers they are facing. Swanson quotes an unemployed former bank employee who exemplifies such contradictory feelings:

I never chose to be poor. I'm ashamed of what I am now, but it's beyond my ability to change things. I'm still alive. I haven't committed suicide. I'm living with hope. Although I know with all my heart that it's not my fault, the system makes you feel guilty. Society makes you feel guilty.[9]

These glimpses into the lives of unemployed Canadians reflect the value placed on work in our society as a potential source of self-fulfillment and social integration. Studies of recently retired workers similarly reveal the frequent loss of personal identity tied to an occupation or profession, the loss of status in families and communities, and the loss of fulfilling workplace relationships (Barnes and Parry 2004).[10] At the same time, a set of more materialistic work values is highlighted through the stigma and self-blame that can result from joblessness, seen by some unemployed people as a mark of their own labour market failure. Thus, while career success and wealth accumulation are central to the value systems in capitalist society, the humanist perspective on work as a source of self-identity and personal satisfaction reflects an equally important alternative set of work values.

Cultural Variations in Work Values?

More than a century ago, Max Weber argued that the Protestant work ethic provided a set of work values that ushered in a new capitalist mode of production in northern Europe. Over the past several decades, the remarkable economic performance of a number of emerging countries in the global economy has led some observers to make similar "cultural differences" arguments. Did Japan in the 1980s and the Southeast Asian tiger economies in the 1990s really owe some of their success to a different set of work values? What about China, India, and Brazil today?

Japan's economy clearly outperformed the rest of the world in the 1980s. A common explanation was that Japanese workers had a much stronger work ethic and a higher level of commitment to their employers. Underlying such explanations was an assumption of powerful cultural differences. The Japanese, it was argued, had always exhibited strong patterns of conformity and social integration. In modern times, the corporation had come to assume the once-central roles of the family and the community. From the vantage point of North America, the presumably stronger work ethic of Japanese employees appeared to be a key ingredient in the Japanese "economic miracle."

As the economies of Singapore, South Korea, Taiwan, and Hong Kong expanded rapidly in the 1990s, similar cultural explanations about different underlying work values were proposed. Like descriptions of the presumably more motivated Japanese workers, this "Confucian work ethic" argument attributed the economic success of these economies to traditional habits of hard work, greater willingness to work toward a common social goal, and employees' ready compliance with authority. While this argument might also be used to explain China's remarkable economic growth in the 21st century,[11] it would not account for the cases of India and Brazil, two of the most recent rapid-growth economies, since the dominant religion in India is Hinduism, and the vast majority of Brazilians are Roman Catholics.

Undoubtedly, there are cross-national differences in the way people respond to work in general, to new technologies, and to employers' demands for compliance. North American workers, for example, may be somewhat less accepting of Japanese-style management approaches that expect workers to show unwavering loyalty to company goals (Graham 1995). Workers in some Asian countries may think of their work organization in less individualistic and more family-like terms (Jiang et al. 1995), and managers' understandings of corporate social responsibility may be somewhat different in Japan compared to Western industrialized countries (Todeschini 2011). That said, it is overstating such differences to argue that a Confucian work ethic explains the rapid growth of the East Asian economies. If it does, why did the economic growth in these countries not begin decades earlier? As for China, after more than six decades of Communist dictatorship, it is unlikely that Confucianism is still the psychological fuel for its economy (*Economist* 1996).

Conceding that there are some cultural differences in work values (Super and Šverko 1995; Chen and Aryee 2007), we argue that they are not central to explanations of national differences in economic growth in today's global economy. Far more crucial are the production decisions of firms regarding technology, employment practices, and research and development, and the extent to which governments actively participate in economic development strategies. In fact, research suggests that the cause-and-effect relationship may frequently operate in the opposite direction—work values and, in turn, employee behaviour can be influenced by employment practices and labour market institutions (Schooler 1996).

Japan is a good example. Its labour market is highly segmented, even more so than in Canada. Only a minority of Japanese workers are employed in the country's huge, profitable, high-technology corporations. Most people work in smaller businesses that subcontract to make parts or provide services for the giant firms. The major advantages of this arrangement for the large corporations are the flexibility of being able to expand and contract their labour force without hiring permanent employees and the reduction in inventory costs through just-in-time delivery of component parts from the subcontracting businesses.

Until the 1990s, major Japanese firms generated worker loyalty by offering lifetime employment guarantees and opportunities for upward advancement within the corporation, along with higher wages and good benefits packages (Hill 1988). Critics argued that company loyalty was built on fears of job loss and that the economic benefits provided to workers in major firms simply made it easier for their employers to demand compliance and hard work (Kamata 1983). However, job security and access to internal labour markets were severely eroded in the 1990s as major Japanese corporations struggled to adapt to a changing global economy. By contrast, in small firms and family businesses, low pay, little job security, and long working hours had long been the norm. Thus, for both core- and periphery-sector Japanese employees, the "willingness" to work long and hard may always have had much more to do with organizational and economic factors than with unique cultural values (Lincoln and Kalleberg 1990).

Time for New Work Values?

During the 1980s and 1990s, unemployment rates rose steeply. They declined again for about a decade, then rose again sharply at the end of the first decade of the 21st century, before coming down again. In contrast, the growth in non-standard jobs that began several decades ago has continued steadily, placing more workers in precarious employment and financial situations. At the same time, a growing minority of workers have chosen or been required to work longer hours per week (Chapter 4). Given this polarization of employment experiences—not enough work for some and too much for others—perhaps we need to promote a new set of work values? Specifically, if more citizens would "get a life" beyond the workplace, perhaps our society could get back on track toward a better future.

This idea is not new. Three decades ago, in his provocative book, *Farewell to the Working Class*, Andre Gorz (1982) argued that higher levels of unemployment also meant more free time for individuals to participate in non-paid work and leisure activities. Recognizing that people still need to work to make a living, he argued that new technologies have reduced the time it takes to produce what is needed for a decent standard of living. Consequently, Gorz called for a new set of values that would replace hard work, labour market competition, and consumption of material goods with more emphasis on the personal fulfillment that comes from non-paid work activities and leisure pursuits.

Similar ideas have been promoted in more recent books about employment patterns and the future of work in Western societies. Jeremy Rifkin (1995) argued that contemporary industrial transformations would be more traumatic for workers than were previous industrial revolutions. While manufacturing jobs replaced agricultural jobs and, in turn, service jobs replaced manufacturing jobs, new technologies and global production patterns essentially meant the "end of work" as we know it for many people. Rifkin advocated the promotion of new work values that would encourage more people to participate in the voluntary sector of the economy where they could find personal fulfillment in caring for others, improving the environment, and making other contributions to society.

Jamie Swift's (1995) concerns were less about the "end of work" than about growing labour market inequality in Canada. He observed that, along with a growing number of working poor, many well-paid labour force participants were also overworked and stressed from the long hours they put into their jobs. Swift reflected on "the lunacy of lives driven by the compulsions of work, speed, and consumption" and called for more attention to "the good life" rather than "the goods life" (Swift 1995: 221, 224). Like Gorz and Rifkin, Swift also recommended a new set of work values that emphasize working less, consuming less, and seeking self-fulfillment not only in paid work but also in healthy leisure pursuits and in (non-paid) caring for others.

The "end of work" predicted by Rifkin has not occurred (Smith 2006), although unemployment rates in some industrialized countries are much higher than they are in Canada (OECD 2010). However, in Canada and elsewhere, labour market polarization and growing social inequality are serious social problems that need to be addressed (Chapter 5). Emphasizing the value of non-paid work and reducing inequities in access to paid work are part of the solution. So, too, are stressing the importance of caring for others and the environment and emphasizing that there is more to a good life than merely acquiring and consuming material goods.[12] But writers such as Gorz, Swift, and Rifkin failed to tell us how such a transformation of social values can be achieved. Nor did they explain how high levels of inequality between those with paid jobs and those without could be avoided.[13] In a society where women have traditionally been expected to do most of the "caring work" (see Chapter 7), would non-paid voluntary work continue to be seen as "women's work"? And since older workers are often more economically secure, is it fair to tell young Canadians to change their values, reduce their career aspirations, and accept less paid work?

While it is necessary to critically examine dominant work values, an overemphasis on the value of unpaid work (see Chapter 7) as *the* solution to labour market polarization diverts our attention from the sources of growing inequality within the labour market. Today's more precarious economy is not simply the product of natural market forces. Real people in positions of power make decisions to change technologies, to move factories, to reduce employment insurance, and to push workers to accept less income, fewer hours of work, and less job security. Consequently, there is also a need for individuals, unions, and the government either to resist these trends or to reshape them (Noble 1995). In fact, the work values of employers need to be reshaped as well, with commitments to profits at all costs being balanced with greater *corporate social responsibility.*[14]

In her description of "how the overwork culture is ruling our lives," Madeline Bunting (2004) continues the debate about the need for new work values. Like other observers of contemporary labour market trends, Bunting recognizes how industrial restructuring and organization re-engineering have deprived some people of jobs and forced others to work longer and harder to make a living. But she also documents how managers, professionals, and other advantaged workers are willingly taking part in the new culture of overwork. While leisure used to be a sign of status for the middle and upper classes, today overwork has become a status symbol as professionals take pride in the many hours they work, how they "multitask" while on the job, and how they continue to work (using laptop computers and sophisticated communication technologies) while on vacation.[15]

Bunting argues that a consumer-focused culture and economy (work hard to spend more) and new managerial ideologies (work hard to show how committed you are to the company) make many of us into "willing slaves" in an era where "narcissism and capitalism are mutually reinforcing" (Bunting 2004: xxiv). What is required, she concludes, is a return to a traditional work ethic that respects human dignity and autonomy, the promotion of a "care ethic" that places high value on looking after the needs of others and that adequately compensates the women and men in "caring" occupations, and the emergence of a new "wisdom ethic" that recognizes that building a better society is more important than heating up the economy by working harder and spending more (Bunting 2004: 312–24). Thus, while reinforcing many of the points made by the other writers discussed above, Bunting places more emphasis on the need to retool our work values, in contrast to replacing them with non-work values.

■ WORK ORIENTATIONS

Having discussed how societal work values have changed over time, might vary across cultures, and need to be re-examined in light of today's economic realities, we now shift our analysis to individuals' job expectations—the types of work orientations they bring to their jobs. Are most Canadians motivated primarily by a desire to be successful and become wealthy? Do they seek to work as hard as possible, whatever the costs? Or is their work a source of personal satisfaction and fulfillment? Do women and men have similar orientations to work? Are specific groups of labour force participants beginning to exhibit different types of work orientations, and if so, why?

Instrumental Work Orientations

Almost fifty years ago, David Lockwood (1966) discussed the differences he observed in how British working-class men perceived social inequality. *Proletarian workers*, argued Lockwood, saw the world in much the way Marx had predicted, seeing themselves in an "us against them" conflict with their employers. Lockwood noted that this worldview was more pronounced in industries such as shipbuilding and mining where large differences between management and workers in terms of income, power, and opportunities for upward mobility had produced heightened class consciousness.[16] *Deferential workers* also recognized class differences, but accepted the status quo, believing that wealth and power inequities were justified. Provided they were treated decently, deferential workers were unlikely to engage in militant actions against their employers who typically treated them paternalistically in the traditional service industries and family firms where they were employed.

Both of these traditional orientations to work were found primarily in declining industries. The third type, *instrumental work orientations*, was more typical of the work attitudes of the contemporary (1960s) working class, according to Lockwood; he labelled them *privatized workers*. Rather than expressing opposition or attachment to their employers, the dominant feeling of these workers was one of indifference. Work was simply a way to obtain a better standard of living, an "instrument" used to achieve other non-work goals.

Lockwood and his colleagues went on to study the work orientations of male autoworkers in Luton, a manufacturing town north of London, England. These "affluent workers" had chosen to move to this new industrial town because the jobs available would provide them with the money and security needed to enjoy a middle-class standard of living. The fact that work in the Vauxhall factory was boring and repetitive did not seem to matter. The research team again concluded that these workers exemplified the typical modern worker in Western industrialized economies (Goldthorpe et al. 1969).

In response, critics argued that British workers in the 1960s appeared to be instrumental only in comparison with an idealized proletarian worker of the past and that the conclusions drawn from this study were over-generalizations, at the very least applicable only to men. Based on their study of the male labour market in another British city, Robert M. Blackburn and Michael Mann found that most workers reported a variety of work orientations. In addition, there was often little congruence between an individual's expressed work preferences and the characteristics of the job. The major flaw in an *orientations model* of labour market processes, according to Blackburn and Mann (1979: 155), was that many people have few job choices, taking whatever work they can get, even if it is not what they would prefer.

Individuals' work preferences can also be modified in the workplace. If a job offers few chances to make decisions or develop skills, workers may adjust their priorities accordingly. This idea might explain why studies have shown instrumental work orientations to be more common among workers in monotonous, assembly-line jobs (Rinehart 1978) or low-skill, low-pay service-sector jobs (Berg and Frost 2005). Richard Sennett and Jonathan Cobb (1972) examined this theme in their book, *The Hidden Injuries of Class.* Their discussions with American blue-collar workers revealed a tendency to downplay *intrinsic work rewards*, few of which were available to them, while emphasizing *extrinsic work rewards*, such as pay and job security. Workers interviewed by Sennett and Cobb also redefined the meaning of personal success, frequently talking about how hard they were working in order to provide their children with the chance to go to college.[17] Thus, we should not be surprised if some workers do have instrumental work orientations, given the strong emphasis on material success in our society and widespread fears about job security.

But most employed Canadians today are not motivated primarily by work orientations that are instrumental, or extrinsic, as they are typically called in the North American research literature.[18] Instead, along with a desire for good pay, extensive benefits, and job security, workers also want intrinsically satisfying work, as the humanistic perspective on work as self-fulfillment suggests. For example, a 2012 survey of more than 1,800 Canadian workers revealed that 80 percent or more felt that good pay, good benefits, and job security were "important" or "very important" to them (Figure 13.1).[19] Almost as many placed importance on "good opportunities for career advancement." However, 9 out of 10 study participants stated that "work that gives a feeling of pride and accomplishment" and "challenging and interesting work" was "important" or "very important" to them. And about three-quarters of them placed importance on receiving recognition for doing a good job and on being able to make decisions about how to do their job. In short, Canadian workers are strongly motivated by both intrinsic and extrinsic work rewards.[20]

Gender and Work Orientations

The early British studies of work orientations focused only on men. When the work orientations of women were mentioned, it was often assumed that their interests were directed primarily toward the home. The argument

FIGURE 13.1 Intrinsic and Extrinsic Work Orientations, Canadian Workforce, 2012*

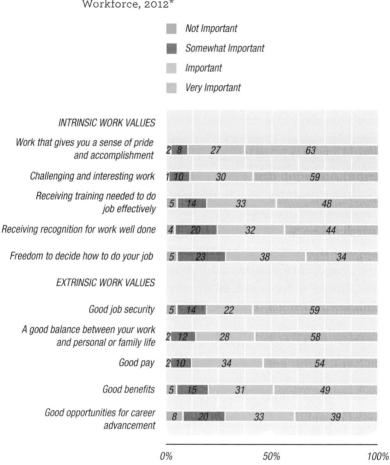

■ Not Important

■ Somewhat Important

▨ Important

▥ Very Important

INTRINSIC WORK VALUES

	Not Important	Somewhat Important	Important	Very Important
Work that gives you a sense of pride and accomplishment	2	8	27	63
Challenging and interesting work	1	10	30	59
Receiving training needed to do job effectively	5	14	33	48
Receiving recognition for work well done	4	20	32	44
Freedom to decide how to do your job	5	23	38	34

EXTRINSIC WORK VALUES

	Not Important	Somewhat Important	Important	Very Important
Good job security	5	14	22	59
A good balance between your work and personal or family life	2	12	28	58
Good pay	2	10	34	54
Good benefits	5	15	31	49
Good opportunities for career advancement	8	20	33	39

0%   50%   100%

*Item N's vary between 1,847 and 1,854.

Source: Used with permission of EKOS Research Associates, Inc. Copyright © 2013. All rights reserved.

that *gender-role socialization* might encourage women to place less value on intrinsic and extrinsic job rewards and more on social relationships in the family, in the community, and on the job seemed plausible in the 1960s and early 1970s when many of these studies were completed. However, there is another more compelling structural explanation. Women and men work in very different labour market locations, and women typically receive fewer job rewards. Hence, observed gender differences in work orientations might have reflected women's adaptations to their subordinate employment situation (Rowe and Snizek 1995: 226).

The rapid increase in female postsecondary participation in recent decades (Chapter 3), along with movement, albeit more slowly, of more women into higher-status occupations and professions (see Chapter 5) has altered gendered patterns of work orientations. For example, recent studies of both Canadian (Krahn and Galambos 2014) and U.S. youth (Johnson and Mortimer 2011) have shown somewhat higher intrinsic work orientations among women, but negligible differences in extrinsic work orientations. As for adults, a 2000 national survey of 2,100 paid employees (the self-employed were excluded), conducted by Canadian Policy Research Networks (CPRN), showed no gender differences in either intrinsic or extrinsic work preferences.[21]

Even so, the domestic and child-care responsibilities that many women continue to carry, even if they hold higher-status jobs, force some to readjust their work and career goals. As a part-time Canadian nurse explained:

> My career is important to me. I don't want to give that up. But my main concern is the children.... So I give about 100 percent to the children and maintain a career at the same time.[22]

Similarly, in her study of young university-educated women living in Alberta, Ranson (1998) observed that, particularly for those who had chosen non-traditional careers in science and engineering, the pressures of balancing family and job demands required a reassessment of either their parenthood or career aspirations, or both. As one young woman explained when asked about her parenthood plans:

> Actually I've thought, would I work or would I stay home? ... I've spent a lot of time going to school. I've worked my way up. Like, do I want to give all that up? [Because] if you come back to the work force in five years you're not going to work where you left off. Then the other part of me thinks, well, you have to make that choice, it's one or the other.[23]

Once again, these examples point to structural determinants—the gendered household division of labour and the frequent absence of family-friendly employment policies—rather than to female personality characteristics as the source of gender differences in work orientations.

The Work Orientations of Youth

Socrates is reputed to have said that "[c]hildren today are tyrants. They contradict their parents, gobble their food, and terrorize their teachers." If he had lived today, he might also have added that "they don't want to work hard" since such concerns about deficient work orientations have frequently been part of the public stereotype of youth. In the 1960s and 1970s, for example, the counterculture activities of some North American youth led to fears that the work ethic of this generation was declining. Most members of that cohort, the "baby boomers," are now getting close to the end of successful careers, thus demonstrating that these fears were largely unfounded. It seems that each generation, when observing the next generation, sees lifestyle experimentation, forgets its own similar experiences, and concludes that values are slipping.

What are the concerns about the work orientations of today's youth? At first glance, debates about the possibly inadequate *employability skills* of young Canadians seem to have little to do with the subject. The Conference Board of Canada, an organization representing large public- and private-sector employers, published an *Employability Skills Profile* (ESP) in 1993. This pamphlet listed a set of "critical skills required for the Canadian workplace" as identified by employers, including *academic skills* (communication, thinking, ability to learn), *personal management skills* (positive attitudes and behaviours, responsibility, adaptability), and *teamwork skills* (the ability to work with others). The Profile focused debate on the types of skills that schools should be developing in students and led some critics to argue that schools should have more of an employment focus. However, careful scrutiny of the public education system suggests that, with respect to teaching academic and employability skills, Canadian schools continue to perform well (Taylor 2001: 23; Krahn, Lowe, and Lehmann 2002). Furthermore, research indicates that when hiring young people for entry-level positions, many employers focus mainly on motivation, perceived work ethic, and the personality of the applicant—in other words, on work orientations rather than on skills. Young job seekers are told that "proper attitude earns a job" (Holzer 1996).

So, are today's youth less willing to "work hard" and to make a commitment to an employer? We lack reliable data documenting shifts in the "soft" employability skills of youth. But a majority of high-school students work part time at some point while completing school, suggesting that there is a strong desire to work, even if only for the money. Continued high rates of participation in postsecondary education (see Chapter 3) indicate that youth are willing to work hard to obtain the credentials needed for better jobs. And studies of youth continue to show high levels of general work commitment. For example, in 1985, we conducted a survey of about 1,000 Edmonton Grade 12 students about their work and education plans and experiences. In 1996, we repeated the study. Only 9 percent of the first cohort agreed that "I'd rather collect welfare than work at a job I don't like," compared to 7 percent of the 1996 cohort. Similarly, only one in eight respondents in both surveys agreed that "I would not mind being unemployed for a while" (Lowe and Krahn 2000). Such facts leave us skeptical about the supposed "work attitude" problem of today's youth.

The employment difficulties faced by Canadian youth are real, as we have demonstrated in Chapters 3 through 5. Corporate and public-sector downsizing, along with an increase in nonstandard jobs, has made it much more difficult for young people to cash in their educational investments for good jobs (Tomlinson 2007). It may also have led to a prolonged entry into adult roles, such as living on one's own, marriage or cohabitation, and parenthood.[24] Recognizing these trends, in 1993, Douglas Coupland published a fictional account of the experiences of today's youth moving between jobs and relationships. *Generation X: Tales for an Accelerated Culture* was a bestseller. Its portrayal of the post-baby-boom generation as cynical and alienated, with few career goals and largely instrumental work orientations, became part of popular culture.

The Generation X view of changing work orientations differs from public concerns about employability skills. It focuses on somewhat older, more educated youth rather than on recent high-school graduates and diagnoses "the problem" more specifically, pointing to a devaluing of careers and intrinsic work rewards, rather than simply a reluctance to work hard. It points to structural changes in the labour market—a lack of satisfactory employment opportunities—as the source of the problem, rather than to schools and their presumed failure to socialize appropriate work attitudes in youth.

So, again, is there evidence of the emergence of Generation X work orientations? The answer appears to be no. A majority of young Canadians continue to invest in higher education, despite rising tuition fees, hoping to get good jobs (see Chapters 3 and 5). Many continue to pursue additional work-related training after obtaining formal qualifications (Jackson 2005: 47). Surveys of youth fail to reveal a decline in commitment to work or a reduced interest in intrinsic work rewards. For example, in 1985, we surveyed graduates of the five largest faculties at the University of Alberta, asking them about their work goals and career ambitions. In 1996, we repeated the study, asking identical questions of graduates from the same faculties. In response to the question "How important would the following be to you when looking for a full-time job after leaving school?" 92 percent of the class of 1985 agreed that "work that is interesting" would be important to them, compared to 96 percent of the class of 1996. Similarly, over 90 percent of both cohorts agreed that "work that gives a feeling of accomplishment" would be important to them (Rollings-Magnusson, Krahn, and Lowe 1999). Other findings from these studies lead to the same conclusion: young Canadians continue to aspire to good jobs and satisfying careers.

The 1996 survey also showed 74 percent of the university graduates agreeing that "it will be harder for people in my generation to live as comfortably as previous generations," a sentiment echoed by 65 percent of Alberta Grade 12 students (Rollings-Magnusson, Krahn, and Lowe 1999). Thus, while the basic work orientations of youth may not have changed, and while their work ethic has not declined, there is considerably more anxiety about future employment prospects. More recent cohorts of Canadian youth also appear to have a stronger sense of job entitlement, the belief that if a person has invested in a higher education, that person should be able to get a good job (Krahn and Galambos 2014). A generation or two ago, an expanding economy allowed a larger proportion of youth to launch satisfying careers. Today, labour market restructuring has made career entry more difficult for Canadian youth and heightened their employment anxiety.

At the same time, reduced loyalty and commitment by many employers to their workers, as reflected in greater reliance on part-time and temporary workers, may also translate into less commitment and loyalty to the work organization by employees, both young and old. For example, the 2000 CPRN survey mentioned earlier showed 50 percent of paid employees agreeing that "I feel very little loyalty to this organization." Another 23 percent agreed strongly with the statement (Lowe and Schellenberg 2001). However, rather than indicating a decline in the work ethic, this finding points to a possible change in the relationship between workers and their employers. It also indicates a problem that employers, not schools, need to address. How do you motivate workers without offering them some degree of employment security and satisfaction in return? As nonstandard work becomes more common, employers will be forced to face this issue more directly.[25]

Welfare Dependency and an Emerging Underclass?

The poor also have been the frequent target of public concern about a "declining work ethic," since it is often easier to blame them for their plight than to try to understand the structural conditions that create poverty (Swanson 2001). During the 1970s, growing awareness of extensive poverty, particularly among Black Americans, prompted fears that fewer people were willing to work. By way of example, in 1972, U.S. president Richard Nixon stated that American society was threatened by the "new welfare ethic that could cause the American character to weaken."[26] However, in both Canada and the United States, national surveys conducted in the 1970s failed to reveal a declining work ethic. Few Canadian respondents agreed that they would rather collect unemployment insurance than hold a job. Most stated that, given the choice, they would prefer working to not having a job, and that work was a central aspect of their lives (Burstein et al. 1975). A national survey of Canadian workers conducted almost two decades later (in 2000) led to the same conclusion: Canadians have a strong work ethic (Lowe and Schellenberg 2001: 40).

Although the work ethic of low-income Canadians has not changed, social assistance programs have been substantially altered (Weaver, Habibov, and Fan 2010), to reduce government spending but also, in part, because of long-standing beliefs that the poor are reluctant to work. For example, during the 1990s, the Unemployment Insurance program (now called "Employment Insurance") was restructured, making it more difficult for seasonal workers to obtain benefits. In several provinces, social assistance benefits have been cut back for "able-bodied" recipients, including single mothers (Gazso 2007), and *workfare* programs that require recipients to work in public projects have been introduced.[27]

With the number of long-term unemployed increasing in many Western industrialized countries, and with income inequality rising, some observers have begun to label the most marginalized members of society as an *underclass*, even though the term has been used very imprecisely (see Chapter 5). Some discussions of this new underclass are sympathetic, arguing that this level of social inequality is unacceptable. Other commentators treat the trend toward greater inequality as largely inevitable, worrying instead about *welfare dependency*. Their argument, simply put, is that prolonged receipt of social assistance and unemployment insurance benefits leads to changed work orientations: both the stigma of receiving assistance and the desire to seek paid employment decline. Even more troubling, such accounts suggest, these welfare dependency orientations can be passed on to the children of the poor (Buckingham 1999).

Is there any basis for such fears about a declining work ethic within the poorest members of society, or are we simply seeing ideological justifications for reducing social assistance benefits to the poor and unemployed? The best test would be to determine whether the presumed weak work ethic of the poor translates into little effort to seek paid work or other sources of income. Research that has taken this approach invariably leads to a different conclusion—a weak work ethic and a lack of effort are seldom the problem. Much more often, the problem is one of not enough good jobs and inadequate social and labour market policies (Shildrick et al. 2013).[28]

In fact, a large minority of Canada's poor are not welfare dependent but "working poor," seeking to maintain their standard of living on low-paying jobs. In 2011, for example, 44 percent of all low-income Canadians were being primarily supported by someone holding a job (HRSDC 2012). There is considerable movement in and out of poverty as individuals lose jobs, move from social assistance to a low-paying job, become divorced, or enter retirement without an adequate pension.[29] In regions or cities where unemployment is high, much productive work takes place in the informal economy (Felt and Sinclair 1992), including subsistence work performed by street people and the homeless. Such widespread initiative is hardly evidence of a failing work ethic. As for the argument that welfare dependency attitudes are passed from one generation to the next, research shows little of this happening (Duncan, Hill, and Hoffman 1988).[30] Thus, while we are concerned about rising social inequality, we are not convinced by accounts of welfare dependency and a declining work ethic among the poor and unemployed.

CONCLUSION

In this chapter, we shifted from a largely structural analysis of work organizations, labour markets, and management systems to a more individually focused discussion of work values and work orientations. We commented on how work values in Western societies have changed over the centuries and speculated about the extent to which cultural differences in work values might explain different patterns of economic growth. Focusing further on North America today, we described how individuals are exposed to at least two competing work-value systems, the first suggesting that monetary rewards are paramount and the second emphasizing how work can be personally fulfilling. An examination of what unemployed people find lacking in their lives highlighted the extent to which work provides us with much more than a way of paying our bills.

Turning our attention to work orientations (or preferences), we argued that even though some workers are primarily instrumentally oriented—that is, motivated by the material rewards that work provides—most Canadians also desire work that is intrinsically satisfying as the humanist perspective on work as self-fulfillment would predict. We also observed that instrumental work orientations may be an adaptation on the part of some workers to low-skill or routinized work that has little but a paycheque to offer. We concluded our discussion of work orientations by critically examining arguments that young people today are less motivated to work than were previous generations and that poverty is the outcome of a weak work ethic. In both cases, we essentially reversed the causal argument, suggesting, instead, that labour markets and social policies have changed, making it more difficult for young people to get good jobs and for poor people to escape poverty.

In Chapter 14, we continue our examination of the personal experience of work, focusing specifically on job satisfaction and work-related stress. Work orientations will be part of that discussion since, to an extent, they affect how an individual feels about a job. Once again, however, we will argue that the nature of the work is likely to have a stronger impact, both on an individual's feelings of satisfaction and stress, and on his or her work orientations.

DISCUSSION QUESTIONS

1. Discuss the differences between work values, work orientations, and job satisfaction.

2. Do you think that, compared to their parents and grandparents, young people today have significantly different work orientations? How might you design a study to determine whether your opinion is correct?

3. Critically discuss the following statement: "The majority of Canadians go to work just to earn money. If they won a lottery, most would quit their jobs."

4. "Most poor people are not really all that motivated to work hard." Do you agree or disagree with this statement? What is your evidence?

5. Do cultural differences in work values explain why some countries have much higher economic growth rates than other countries? Justify your opinion.

ADDITIONAL RESOURCES

WORK AT THE MOVIES

- *Clerks* (directed by Kevin Smith, 1994, 92 minutes). This film presents a day in the lives of two convenience-store clerks as they annoy customers, discuss movies, and play hockey on the store roof.
- *Waiting* (directed by Rob McKittrick, 2005, 94 minutes). In this comedy, the young employees of an American chain restaurant find creative ways to stave off boredom in the workplace.
- *Empire Records* (directed by Allan Moyle, 1995, 90 minutes). A group of workers at an independent record store come together to help the store avoid being taken over by a massive chain.
- *Apollo 13* (directed by Ron Howard, 1995, 140 minutes). Based on the 1970 Apollo 13 mission, Howard's film chronicles how flight controllers at NASA (National Aeronautics and Space Administration) and the mission's astronauts worked together to bring the astronauts home safely after they experienced technical difficulties.

SOUNDS OF WORK

- "Rich Man's War" (Steve Earle). This song highlights the variety of reasons that prompt individuals from both sides of a conflict to go to war, financial reasons, national pride, boredom, tradition, and family among them.

- "Working Class Hero" (John Lennon). The song notes the loss of individuality and how people undergo processes to conform and accept control as they enter the workforce.
- "Working Man" (Rush). This Canadian band sings about the lack of ambition that develops after working a dead-end 9 to 5 job.

NOTES

1. See George and Jones (1997) for a somewhat different classification of work values, attitudes, and moods.
2. Bernstein (1997); see also Byrne (1990: Chapter 3).
3. Genesis 2:17, 3:19 (text as it appears in the King James Version of the Bible).
4. In a contemporary U.S. study, Keister (2007) argues that Catholic work values lead to upward wealth mobility.
5. Examples include Hodson (2001), Rayman (2001), and Bunting (2004).
6. http://www.vatican.va/holy_father/francesco/audiences/2013/documents/papa-francesco_20130501_udienza-generale_en.html.
7. See Burman (1988) and Winson and Leach (2002: Chapter 6) for Canadian studies of the social and psychological consequences of unemployment. Gabriel, Gray, and Goregaokar (2013) and Weller (2012) provide U.K. and Australian studies, respectively. Grün, Hauser, and Rhein (2010) report results from a German survey showing that even workers employed in "bad jobs" (defined both objectively and subjectively) typically report higher life satisfaction than their unemployed counterparts.
8. For this quotation and the next three: Burman, Patrick. (1988). *Killing Time, Losing Ground: Experiences of Unemployment.* Toronto: Wall & Thompson, pp. 161, 113, 144, 86.
9. Swanson, Jean. 2001. *Poor-Bashing: The Politics of Exclusion.* Toronto: Between the Lines, p. 10.
10. Because women and men have very different career pathways (Chapter 6), retirement expectations (Radl 2012) and experiences, including feelings of loss of identity (Price 2000), are highly gendered. See Fineman (2009) for a fascinating account of how the "retirement industry" tries to reshape the personal identifies of retired workers while marketing services and products to them.
11. Lin, Ho, and Lin (2013) go further, distinguishing between Confucian and Taoist work values. A parallel literature on Islamic, Arab, and Egyptian work values has emerged, although the distinction between religious (Mohamed, Karim, and

Hussein 2010), cultural (Sidani and Thornberry 2009), and national (Sidani and Jamali 2010) work values is unclear.

12. A recent Edmonton study (Huddart Kennedy, Krahn, and Krogman 2013) reports that members of households in which someone had "downshifted" (chosen to work fewer hours to increase leisure time) were more likely to exhibit sustainable household practices such as recycling. However, they were no more likely to exhibit sustainable transportation practices (e.g., driving less) since, where they lived (in central or suburban settings) rather than their environmental attitudes, largely determined their transportation practices.

13. Lautsch and Scully (2007) show that lower-paid workers both need and want more hours, not fewer. To reduce income inequality, Gorz (1999) proposed a guaranteed annual income and recommended cooperative economic organizations; Hayden (1999) emphasized job sharing.

14. Corporate social responsibility (CSR) has become a popular theme for a growing number of large corporations hoping to improve their business position (Vogel 2005). Examples include coffee retailers selling "fair trade" coffee, clothing and sportswear distributors trying to monitor working conditions in the Asian factories producing their products, and oil and gas companies promising to reduce greenhouse gas emissions. For useful discussions of CSR, see Berger, Cunningham, and Drumwright (2007), MacPhail and Bowles (2009), and Weyzig (2009). Banerjee (2008) is much more critical, arguing that CSR and other initiatives are simply ideological rhetoric used to increase corporate power and profits.

15. Schor (1991, 1998), Hochschild (1997), and Rayman (2001) criticize overwork and over-consumption in the United States. Green (2001) documents the extent of overwork in Britain. A 1995 Statistics Canada study revealed that 31 percent of employed Canadians considered themselves to be "workaholics" (*The Daily*, May 15, 2007).

16. Kerr and Siegel (1954) used a similar argument to explain high strike rates in single-industry communities (see Chapter 11).

17. Visible minority Canadian immigrants, faced with having to work in lower-tier, service-sector jobs, despite being well educated (see Chapter 5), also frequently put their efforts into ensuring that their children will get a good education and a rewarding middle-class career (Taylor and Krahn 2013).

18. Many North American researchers (e.g., Johnson, Sage, and Mortimer 2012; Wray-Lake et al. 2011) use the concept "work values" to describe what we call "work orientations" in this chapter. We prefer to use *values* to describe societal standards and *orientation*s to describe individual preferences, even though when engaging with the North American research literature, we also use their

terminology (Krahn, Howard, and Galambos 2012; Chow, Krahn, and Galambos 2013).

19. Unpublished data from a 2012 national survey of a random sample of Canadian workers conducted by EKOS Research Inc. and the Graham Lowe Group Inc.

20. A recent study reports that, between 1992 and 2006, intrinsic work orientations increased among British workers (Gallie, Felstead, and Green 2012).

21. http://www.jobquality.ca/indicators/rewards/rew1.shtml [retrieved December 28, 2013].

22. Duffy, Ann, and Norene Pupo. (1992). *Part-Time Paradox: Connecting Gender, Work and Family*. Toronto: McClelland & Stewart, p. 116.

23. Ranson, Gillian. (1998). "Education, Work and Family Decision-Making: Finding the 'Right Time' to Have a Baby." *Canadian Review of Sociology and Anthropology* 35(4): 517–33, p. 529.

24. See Shanahan (2000), Mitchell (2006), Côté and Bynner (2008), and Andres and Wyn (2010) on delayed transitions to adulthood.

25. See Sennett (1998), de Gilder (2003), and Coverdill and Oulevey (2007) on the dilemmas of managing contingent workers.

26. Nixon's comment was quoted in *Time* (September 7, 1987: 42).

27. See Burman (1996: 42–45) and Broad and Antony (1999) on welfare state restructuring in Canada, Swanson (2001) on stereotypes about the poor, Black and Stanford (2005) and Gazso and Krahn (2008) on "welfare reform" in Alberta, and Gazso (2012) on "welfare-to-work" programs in Ontario. Riddell and St-Hilaire (2000) discuss more progressive public policies for dealing with unemployment and poverty.

28. In a British study, Dunn (2010) reported that more educated individuals, who could afford to wait for a better job, were more likely to say they would not mind being on the "dole" (accepting unemployment insurance), compared to less educated (and poorer) people who were much more concerned about finding a job, no matter what it was.

29. See Winson and Leach (2002) and Morissette and Zhang (2005) on movement in and out of poverty in Canada.

30. In contrast, Page (2004) presents a U.S. study showing that children of parents who received welfare are more likely, as adults, to receive social assistance themselves. Even so, this researcher is reluctant to conclude that a culture of dependency is being passed from one generation to the next, and points out that a majority of children of welfare recipients did not become recipients themselves (Page 2004: 242).

JOB SATISFACTION, ALIENATION, AND WORK-RELATED STRESS

14

"... Wayne Brown, 52, describes [his] job as intense. 'As a rig manager, I have to guide and look after both crews, night and day.... We're usually on location for 80 to 90 days. I work two weeks in and have one week home.' The satisfying challenges come from dealing with complications like broken motors, he says. 'Every day is different.'"

[Oil and gas drilling supervisor: no. 1 "top job in Canada" in 2013, according to *Canadian Business* magazine]

"'I never know what my day will bring,' says Jennifer Zurba, principal of William Burgess Public School in Toronto. 'A kid with a broken arm, an angry parent, a teacher.' The lengthy screening process and high applicant rate means it can take a while to advance, so networking is key: 'Try to get out there and sit on different committees. The more superintendents who know your name, the better your chance of them placing you.'"

[School principal and administrator: no. 5 top job]

"Simon Farbrother, the city manager in Edmonton, says civil service is no longer a nine-to-five world. 'I'm at my desk by 7:30 in the morning. I don't have lunches and coffee breaks. ... And I have evening work as well.' The reward for all that work is a chance to build a great city. The downside, however, is that everything you do is in the public eye. 'Our decision-making is not behind closed doors.' That means everyone is your boss—and not everyone is nice about it."

[Senior government manager: no. 8 top job]

Source: Extracts from "Canada's Top 50 Jobs 2013 Edition," *Canadian Business*, April 12, 2013. http://www.canadianbusiness.com/companies-and-industries/canadas-top-50-jobs-2013-edition.

◼ INTRODUCTION

With its discussion of work values and work orientations, Chapter 13 shifted our attention from the structural perspective presented in earlier chapters to a more individually focused analysis of the meanings attached to work. In this chapter we continue by examining how work is personally experienced. We begin by discussing *job satisfaction* and *dissatisfaction*, defined as the subjective reactions of individual workers to the particular set of rewards, intrinsic or extrinsic, provided by their job (Blackburn and Mann 1979: 167). We then comment on a parallel line of research that uses the concept of *alienation* in a social–psychological framework, in contrast to the more structural Marxist analysis of alienation presented in Chapter 10. The third section of this chapter reviews the research literature on *work-related stress*, a complex phenomenon—with job dissatisfaction as one component—that can lead to serious health problems.

● JOB SATISFACTION AND DISSATISFACTION

What do Canadians find most and least satisfying about their jobs? Are most of them satisfied? Which subgroups of workers are most or least satisfied, and why? Do people's work orientations influence what they find satisfying in a job? Can job satisfaction or dissatisfaction affect workers off the job? Some researchers assume that productivity is a function of job satisfaction. Their goal has been to discover how to organize work and manage employees in a way that leads to increased satisfaction and, hence, higher productivity and profits. Others, adopting the humanistic view that work is an essential part of being human, view satisfying and self-fulfilling work for as many people as possible as a desirable societal goal in itself.

The Prevalence of Job Satisfaction

The standard measure of job satisfaction in North American survey research is some variation of "All in all, how satisfied are you with your job?" In response, a very large majority of workers typically report some degree of satisfaction. Just how large that majority is depends on the response categories offered to survey participants. If they cannot choose a neutral midpoint, a larger proportion indicate that they are satisfied. For example, according to a 2005 Statistics Canada national survey, 91 percent of private-sector employees said they were satisfied with their job; 34 percent reported being "very satisfied" (Statistics Canada 2008f: 36). But when provided with a neutral midpoint on a five-point job satisfaction scale, a significant minority choose this response, leading to a somewhat lower estimate of job satisfaction. Using such a scale, an EKOS Research national survey in 2012 found that 70 percent of Canadian workers were satisfied with their job (27%, very satisfied), 17 percent were neither satisfied nor dissatisfied, while only 13 percent expressed dissatisfaction (see Figure 14.1).[1]

These results, and many similar findings over the past few decades (Firebaugh and Harley 1995), imply that job dissatisfaction is not a serious

FIGURE 14.1   Job Satisfaction by Age, Gender, and Education, Canada, 2012*

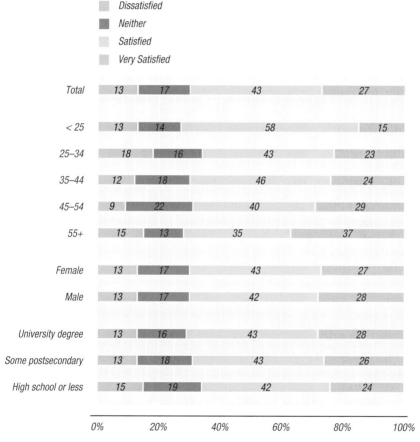

*Responses of "Very Dissatisfied" and "Dissatisfied" have been combined. N's range between 1,811 and 1,866.

Source: Used with permission of EKOS Research Associates, Inc. Copyright © 2013. All rights reserved.

problem. However, there are several reasons why we could question such a conclusion.

First, as James Rinehart (1978) observed, workers' behaviours—strikes, absenteeism, and quitting—all indicate considerably more dissatisfaction with working conditions than do attitude surveys. Rinehart (1978: 7) proposed that answers to general questions about job satisfaction are "pragmatic judgements of one's position vis-à-vis the narrow range of available jobs." Most workers look at their limited alternatives and conclude, from this frame of reference, they are relatively satisfied with their work.

Second, responses to general job satisfaction questions may be similar to replies to this question, "How are you today?" Most of us would say "fine," whether or not this is the case. Hence, more probing questions may be needed to uncover specific feelings of job dissatisfaction. We should also recognize that, in a society with highly individualistic work values (see Chapter 13), people may be unwilling to express dissatisfaction with their jobs because it could reflect negatively on their own ability and efforts.

These reasons point to why more indirect measures of job satisfaction are useful. For example, a national survey in 2000 revealed that 73 percent of paid employees feel little loyalty to their work organization (Lowe and Schellenberg 2001). *Behavioural intention* measures also typically reveal more widespread job dissatisfaction. A 1996 Angus Reid poll, for example, showed 32 percent of employed Canadians agreeing that they "would take a comparable job at another company if it were offered."[2] As Sandy Stewart and Bob Blackburn (1975: 503) wrote some decades ago, "while satisfaction is expressed within a framework of what is possible, liking is expressed within a framework of what is desirable."

Age and Job Satisfaction

A consistent finding in job satisfaction research is that older workers generally report greater satisfaction (Firebaugh and Harley 1995; Brisbois 2003: 58). Figure 14.1 documents this pattern clearly, with the proportion answering "very satisfied" increasing from 15 percent for the youngest respondents in this 2012 study to 37 percent for the oldest survey participants. Typical of the research on differences in job satisfaction, explanations for this age-related pattern take two basic forms. Some are individualistic, focusing on motivations and work orientations, while others are more structural, pointing to characteristics of the job and the workplace (Ospina 1996: 181).

The following five explanations cover the range of explanations. Perhaps older workers have reduced their expectations, becoming more accepting of relatively unrewarding work—an *aging* effect. Alternatively, a *cohort* explanation emphasizes lower expectations (and consequently higher satisfaction) on the part of a generation of older workers: it assumes that older workers grew up in an era when it was enough to have a secure job and when little self-fulfillment at work was expected. Third, a *life-cycle* effect argues that older workers are more likely to have family and community interests that might compensate for dissatisfying work. A fourth explanation emphasizes the nature of the work performed (a *job* effect), suggesting that older people have been promoted into more rewarding and satisfying jobs, or have changed jobs until they found one they liked. A final explanation points to *self-selection*, arguing that less satisfied workers will drop out of the labour force as they get older, leaving behind more satisfied workers.

Which is the best explanation? No clear answer emerges from the many studies on this topic, indicating that all of these processes may be involved. Regardless, we know that older workers are more likely to report satisfaction with their work and that this evaluation is due mainly to the better jobs they have obtained over time and to their cumulative social experiences and adaptations in the workplace and society.[3]

Returning to Figure 14.1, if we combine the percentage saying they are "satisfied" and "very satisfied," the data also tend to support several studies that have suggested that the relationship between age and job satisfaction is U-shaped (Clark, Oswald, and Warr 1996: 75; Birdi, Warr, and Oswald 1995). Specifically, satisfaction (both categories combined) is high among the youngest workers (73%), lower in the next cohort (66%), and then higher again (70% to 72%) in the older three cohorts. The explanation is that the youngest workers are usually reasonably satisfied with their entry-level jobs, perhaps because many are still attending school. But if they remain in the student labour market after completing their formal education, the mismatch between low-level jobs and higher aspirations begins to have an effect. Hence, job satisfaction is lower among workers in their late twenties and early thirties. With time, however, the combination of better jobs and declining expectations again leads to higher levels of job satisfaction. This argument points to both individualistic and structural determinants of job satisfaction. It also raises an interesting question for future research. Because today's youth are facing many more barriers to entry into good jobs (Chapter 5), will we continue to observe the overall strong positive relationship between age and job satisfaction in the future?

Gender and Job Satisfaction

Given that women are more likely to work part time and in the secondary labour market, are they less satisfied with their jobs? The research evidence offers a clear answer. Despite large differences in work rewards, there is typically little difference between men and women in self-reported job satisfaction (de Vaus and McAllister 1991; Brisbois 2003: 58). Figure 14.1 tells the same story—in 2012, job satisfaction rates for women and men were virtually identical. Again, as with age differences in job satisfaction, an explanation of this non-difference brings us back to the subject of work orientations. Some researchers suggest that women have been socialized to expect fewer intrinsic and extrinsic work rewards. Hence, the argument goes, women are more likely to be satisfied with lower-quality jobs, focusing instead perhaps on satisfying social relationships within the workplace (Phelan 1994).

However, we should not explain the job satisfaction of women with a *gender model* (differences due to prior socialization) while employing a *job model* (differences due to the nature of the job) to account for the satisfaction of men (de Vaus and McAllister 1991). In fact, it makes more theoretical sense to explain the satisfaction of both women and men with reference to the types of jobs they hold and their roles outside the workplace. While, on average, men might report high satisfaction with their relatively good jobs, women might be equally satisfied with less rewarding jobs, having modified their expectations because of the time spent in these same jobs. And as Chapter 7 discussed, the involvement of men and women in family roles differs greatly. This reality also needs to be taken into account when explaining the non-differences in job satisfaction between women and men.

The critical test would compare women and men doing similar work, as in a study of post office employees in Edmonton where men and women performed identical tasks (Northcott and Lowe 1987). The researchers found few gender differences in job satisfaction or in work orientations after accounting for both job content and family roles. Thus, while gender differences in work orientations may exist, characteristics of the jobs women typically hold and family responsibilities, rather than prior socialization, are probably responsible (Hodson 2004).

Educational Attainment and Job Satisfaction

Educational attainment and job satisfaction might be linked in several different ways. Following human capital theory (see Chapter 5), we might hypothesize that higher education should lead to a better job and, in turn, more job satisfaction. A second, more complex hypothesis begins with the assumption that better-educated workers have higher expectations regarding their careers but recognizes that not all well-educated workers will have good jobs. Hence, well-educated workers in less rewarding jobs would be expected to report low job satisfaction. As one commentator wrote several decades ago, "the placing of intelligent and highly qualified workers in dull and unchallenging jobs is a prescription for pathology—for the worker, the employer, the society" (O'Toole 1977: 60).

Job satisfaction studies completed in the 1970s and 1980s (Martin and Shehan 1989) typically found that education had little effect on job satisfaction, perhaps because the two hypothesized effects cancelled each other out. Even when comparing well-educated and less educated workers in the same blue-collar jobs, few differences in job satisfaction were observed. Perhaps the more educated workers anticipated future upward mobility and so were willing to tolerate less rewarding work for a time. The 2012 data featured in Figure 14.1 show that job satisfaction (the percent "satisfied" and "very satisfied") is somewhat higher among more highly educated Canadian workers—71 percent of those with university degrees said they were satisfied, compared to 66 percent of those with high school only or less education. This pattern may signal a shift in the education–job satisfaction pattern, but we will need future studies to confirm this.

In previous chapters, we have speculated that, as education levels have been rising, the mismatch between workers' skills, credentials, and aspirations, on one hand, and their job content, on the other, may be worsening. Again, our single-point-in-time analysis (of 2012 survey data) cannot answer this question, but we might hypothesize that overall levels of job dissatisfaction may slowly increase in the future as more well-educated young workers discover they cannot find jobs that meet their aspirations.[4] Researchers have yet to compare the relationships among age, education, and job satisfaction today with the situation several decades ago. However, one study from the 1990s did show that workers who felt underemployed in terms of their education and skills were much more likely to be dissatisfied with their jobs. In addition, several more recent studies have linked perceptions of job insecurity to reduced job satisfaction.[5] Given the extent to which young people, including well-educated young workers, have been negatively affected by increased labour market polarization and reduced employment security (Chapter 5), this is a trend to be monitored.

Work Rewards, Work Orientations, and Job Satisfaction

Our review of the effects of age, gender, and education on job satisfaction indicates that work orientations are frequently part of the explanation. Nevertheless, as we have also argued, differences in job characteristics and rewards are typically more directly linked to job satisfaction and dissatisfaction. In fact, hundreds of studies have sought to identify the specific job conditions that workers are most likely to find satisfying. Such studies have focused on pay, benefits, promotion opportunities, job security and other *extrinsic work rewards*; autonomy, challenge, skill-use, and a range of additional *intrinsic work rewards*; satisfying (or not) *social relationships* in the workplace; *work organization features* (e.g., bureaucracy, health and safety programs, and the presence of a union); and *job task design* characteristics, including the use of new technologies.

A popular theory developed decades ago by Frederick Herzberg drew on all of these traditions, emphasizing both the extrinsic and intrinsic rewards of work. *Hygiene factors*, such as pay, supervisory style, and physical surroundings in the workplace, could reduce job dissatisfaction, Herzberg argued. But only *motivators*, such as opportunities to develop one's skills and to make decisions about one's own work, could increase job satisfaction (Herzberg 1966). Herzberg also insisted that the presence of such motivators would lead, by way of increased job satisfaction, to greater productivity on the part of workers. (We will return to that issue below.)

Influenced by Herzberg's *two-factor theory*, most job satisfaction researchers now use multidimensional explanatory frameworks incorporating both intrinsic and extrinsic work rewards, as well as organizational and task characteristics. Although researchers categorize the specific features of work in somewhat different ways, there is considerable consensus at a broader level. Arne Kalleberg (1977), for example, identified six major dimensions of work. The first, an intrinsic reward dimension, emphasizes interesting, challenging, and self-directed work that allows personal growth and development. Career opportunities form a second dimension, and financial rewards (pay, job security, and fringe benefits) a third. Relationships with coworkers, convenience (the comfort and ease of work), and resource adequacy (availability of information, tools, and materials necessary to do a job) complete Kalleberg's list.

It is also clear from the research we have reviewed that work orientations, or preferences, must remain part of the job satisfaction equation. Indeed, Kalleberg argues that it is the specific fit or mismatch between work rewards (characteristics of the job) and work orientations that determines one's degree of job satisfaction. This equation would apply, he suggests, to both extrinsic and intrinsic dimensions of work. In his classic study, Kalleberg (1977) found that job rewards had positive effects on expressions of job satisfaction in the U.S. labour force, as predicted. But he also observed that, other things being equal, work preferences (orientations) had negative effects on satisfaction. In other words, the more one values some particular feature of work (the chance to make decisions, for example), the less likely it is that one's desires can be satisfied. However, job rewards had substantially greater effects on satisfaction than did work preferences. In addition, Kalleberg concluded that intrinsic job rewards were more important determinants of job satisfaction than were extrinsic rewards.[6]

Canadian Research on Intrinsic Job Rewards

What does Canadian research tell us about intrinsic and extrinsic work rewards and their fit or mismatch with the work orientations of workers? Respondents in a 1973 national Job Satisfaction Survey were given a list of more than 30 specific job characteristics and asked to assess, first, how important each was to them and, second, how their own job rated on these characteristics. The analysts then compared the average "importance" and "evaluation" scores, and examined the gap between them. The largest discrepancies appeared in the areas of "opportunities for promotion" and "potential for challenge and growth" (Burstein et al. 1975: 31–34). These findings are not unusual since most workers seek intrinsic rewards from their work and wish to "get ahead" in their careers.

But has labour market restructuring, particularly downsizing, outsourcing, and greater reliance on part-time and temporary workers, changed this pattern? Figure 14.2 presents selected findings from a 2000 national survey conducted by Canadian Policy Research Networks (CPRN). For each of five intrinsic and five extrinsic work rewards, sample members were asked to indicate how important it was to them personally (their own work orientation) and how much their job provided this particular work reward.[7] Thus, these "job quality deficit" comparisons replicate the contrasting of "importance" and "evaluation" scores in the 1973 study. They are, in a sense, the ingredients for the contemporary patterns of job satisfaction and dissatisfaction that we have described above.

It is clear that there still are sizable gaps between what Canadian workers desire and what they get from their jobs, in both the intrinsic and extrinsic dimensions, with the largest gap (34 percentage points) for "good chances for career advancement." Thus, with respect to this specific finding, little has changed since 1973 when "opportunities for promotion" was one of the two areas in which workers' desires far exceeded what their jobs provided. But unlike the situation in 1973, the work orientation–work reward gap for all of the extrinsic dimensions considered in this analysis (pay, benefits, job security, balancing of work and family) is larger than the gap for the five intrinsic dimensions (interesting work, feeling of accomplishment, freedom to decide how work will be done, chance to develop skills and abilities, recognition for work well done). Perhaps what we are seeing here reflects the growth in non-standard employment and, more generally, the labour market restructuring and polarization that have occurred over the past several decades in Canada.

That said, we still see that there are sizable gaps between workers' orientations and their job rewards on the five intrinsic dimensions of work featured in Figure 14.2. For example, 94 percent of Canadian workers report that having the freedom to decide how their job will be done is important to them, but only 76 percent feel that their job provides such freedom. Almost all (95%) value opportunities to develop their skills and abilities, but only 81 percent are in jobs that provide such opportunities. Similarly, 95 percent want an interesting job, but only 83 percent consider their current job to be interesting.

FIGURE 14.2   Work Orientations and Work Rewards, Canada, 2000

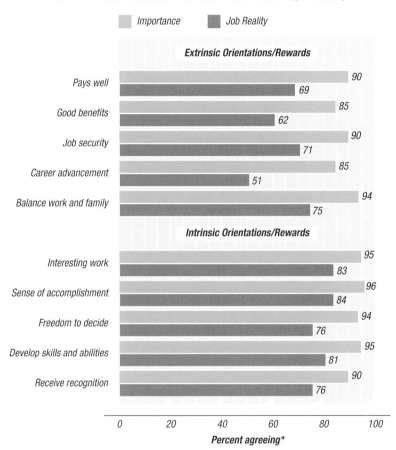

*For both work orientations ("how important is ... ?") and work rewards ("to what extent does your job provide ... ?"), survey respondents were asked to agree or disagree on a five-point scale. The percentage "agreeing" or "strongly agreeing" with each statement is presented in this chart.

Source: Used with permission of Carleton University on behalf of Canadian Policy Research Networks (CPRN).

Researchers agree that, for most workers, jobs that provide considerable autonomy, complexity, and variety are more personally fulfilling. Opportunities to make decisions about how a job should be done, develop and use a wide range of skills, and do interesting work can also increase a worker's satisfaction with a job. This set of relationships would help explain the very large differences in job satisfaction reported by self-employed women (86% satisfied) and women who were paid employees (68%) in a 2000 national survey of Canadian workers (Hughes 2005: 86). In this study, the self-employed women were much more likely than paid employees to indicate that their jobs were interesting and provided decision-making and skill-development opportunities.

In contrast, repetitive jobs with little variety often have the opposite effect. Compare the variety and challenge that are so satisfying for the male oil-field service company manager and the sense of accomplishment reported by the male professional engineer (the first two quotations below) with the comments on repetitive, low-skill work by a female food-processing factory worker and by a male assembly-line worker.[8]

> Every morning even now, I'm happy to come to work; I look forward to it. I think it's because this business is, well, you never know when you come in here in the morning what's going to be asked of you. It could be different every day; generally it is.
>
> ***
>
> I love it. I think I have one of the best jobs I know of.... I enjoy working on projects from start to finish as opposed to just having a small piece of them.... I have found over the years that I am very easily bored and in this field and this environment you don't get bored very often.
>
> ***
>
> Basically, I stand there all day and slash the necks of the chickens.... The chickens go in front of you on the line and you do every other chicken or whatever. And you stand there for eight hours on one spot and do it.
>
> ***
>
> Your brain gets slow. It doesn't function the way it should. You do the same thing day in and day out and your brain goes. I'm like a robot. I walk straight to my job and do what I have to do.

Fortunately, the jobs held by the majority of Canadians appear to be more challenging than those described in these last two quotations. The 2000 CPRN survey reveals, for example, that about three-quarters or more of Canadian workers report that their jobs are interesting, provide them with a sense of accomplishment, and offer some decision-making opportunities as well as chances to enhance skills and abilities (Figure 14.2). In addition, 77 percent of the respondents in this survey reported that their job required high skill levels, while a similar proportion (75%) agreed that "you get the training needed to do your job well" (results not shown in Figure 14.2).

Nevertheless, when asked to agree or disagree that "your job requires that you do the same tasks over and over," 59 percent of the 2000 survey respondents agreed or agreed strongly. These findings suggest that repetitive work (a lack of variety) is more common than non-challenging, low-skill work, or work with little autonomy. The 2000 survey also asked workers to respond with a "yes" or "no" to the question "Considering your experience, education, and training, do you feel that you are overqualified for your job?" One in four workers (27%) said "yes."[9] An earlier (1994) national survey of literacy skills also indicated that about 20 percent of employed Canadian workers are underemployed with respect to their reading and writing skills (Krahn 1997). As we also have noted, there is strong evidence that underemployment may lead to job dissatisfaction.[10]

Consequences of Job Satisfaction and Dissatisfaction

"If the job's so bad, why don't you quit?" Many of us may have thought this about an unsatisfying job, but fewer have acted on the idea. There may be some features of the job—pay, hours, location, friendly coworkers—that make it palatable, despite the absence of other work rewards. In addition, unless other jobs are available, most employees cannot afford to quit. Even during a period of relatively low unemployment, in 2000, the CPRN national survey found 41 percent of Canadian workers agreeing that it would be difficult to find another job as good as their current job. Two-thirds (67%) agreed that it would be difficult to cope financially if they lost their job. Thus, job dissatisfaction will not necessarily translate into quitting behaviour (Hammer and Avgar 2005), although it may be more strongly associated with intentions of quitting (Singh and Loncar 2010).

Feelings of job dissatisfaction may also allow workers to rationalize coming in late, calling in sick, or generally not working as hard as they could (Hausknecht, Hiller, and Vance 2008). Studies have also shown a relationship between job dissatisfaction and overt acts of employee deviance, such as theft of company property, or the use of drugs and alcohol on the job and away from work (Martin and Roman 1996). Dissatisfaction with work is also correlated with the number of complaints and grievances filed in unionized work settings. As for nonunion workers, surveys have shown that those dissatisfied with their work are more likely to view unions positively and are more likely to join a union, if given the chance.[11]

From an employer's perspective, however, the critical issue is whether increases in job satisfaction will boost productivity. If dissatisfaction can lead to tardiness, absenteeism, deviance, and, in some situations, quitting, surely improvements in the quality of working life will lead to a more satisfied and, hence, more productive workforce. This relationship would seem to be obvious (Fisher 2003). But although one can find studies showing such a pattern, there are also many studies that reject this hypothesis. Overviews of research on the topic typically show that the relationship between satisfaction and productivity is weak, or is present only in some work settings.

There are several possible explanations. One is that productivity is more often a function of technology and workers' skills than of their attitudes. Thus, even if high levels of satisfaction are evident, low skill levels, inadequate on-the-job training, or obsolete technology will limit opportunities for productivity increases. Another explanation is that work-group norms and expectations must be taken into consideration. Managers and consultants who have introduced job enrichment programs or high-performance work practices (see Chapter 9), and have perhaps even found higher levels of satisfaction as a consequence (Berg 1999), have frequently been disappointed when productivity increases did not follow. They failed to realize that workers might view an improved quality of working life as their just reward, or that informal work norms and long-standing patterns of behaviour are difficult to alter (Macarov 1982).

It may be that productivity can be influenced by job satisfaction, but only under certain conditions (Iaffaldano and Muchinsky 1985). For example, our earlier discussion suggested that workers in low-level jobs might report job satisfaction because they were assessing their work with a limited set of alternatives in mind. Workers in higher-status jobs might, on the other hand, report satisfaction because of tangible work rewards. If so, perhaps productivity increases due to job satisfaction might be expected only in the latter group. In fact, the most extensive overview of research on this topic—a meta-analysis of findings from 254 previous studies—concludes that the relationship is much stronger in high-complexity jobs (Judge et al. 2001: 388).[12]

● WORK AND ALIENATION

William Faulkner once wrote: "You can't eat for eight hours a day nor drink for eight hours a day nor make love for eight hours a day—all you can do for eight hours is work. Which is the reason why man makes himself and everybody else so miserable and unhappy."[13] Faulkner didn't use the term *alienation*, but he might have since his cynical observation about the misery of work captures some of the meaning of the term as used by social philosophers. Referring back to our discussion of the meaning of work (Chapter 13), we can define alienation as the human condition resulting from an absence of fulfilling work.

In his critique of capitalism, Karl Marx presented a structural analysis of how capitalist relations of production led to workers being separated—alienated—from the products they produced, from others involved in the labour process, from the very activity of work, and ultimately, from themselves as creative human beings (Chapter 10). Marx's argument rests on several key assumptions. First, alienation occurs because workers have little or no control over the conditions of their work, and few chances to develop to their fullest potential as creative human beings. Second, the source of alienation can be traced to the organization of work under capitalism. Third, given that alienation is characteristic of capitalism, it exists even if workers do not consciously recognize it.

Alienation, according to Marx, is a "condition of objective powerlessness" (Rinehart 2006: 11–20). Whether individual workers become aware of the cause of their discontent with work depends on a variety of factors. In the absence of a well-defined and legitimate alternative to the capitalist economic system (Chapter 12), we would not expect most North American workers to be able to clearly articulate their alienation, or to act on it.

A Social–Psychological Perspective on Alienation

Writing more than a century after Karl Marx, and in a decidedly capitalist era and country (the United States), Melvin Seeman (1967, 1975) outlined a narrower social–psychological theory of alienation that emphasized workers' feelings of powerlessness, meaninglessness, social isolation, self-estrangement, and normlessness. In a sense, Seeman focused primarily on the consequences for workers' self-identity and mental health of the absence of intrinsic job rewards. Nevertheless, his social–psychological perspective on alienation shares with Marx's structural perspective an emphasis on the powerlessness of workers and the conclusion that many jobs offer limited opportunities for personal growth and self-fulfillment.

Social–psychological studies of alienation, moreover, are unlikely to lay all or much of the blame on capitalism itself. Instead, technologies that allow workers few opportunities for self-direction, bureaucratic work organizations, and modern mass society in general are identified as the sources of alienation. This perspective also differs from the structural approach in its emphasis on feelings of alienation. Researchers within this approach have relied primarily on workers' self-reports, in contrast with the Marxist focus on the organization and content of work (see Chapter 10).

Consequently, social–psychological accounts of alienation resemble job dissatisfaction, although their explanations of the sources of alienation have pointed more explicitly to the negative consequences of work fragmentation and powerlessness. The general job satisfaction literature examines a broader array of causal variables (work orientations, for example). But since some social–psychological studies of alienation define the phenomenon as an "extrinsic orientation to work" (Seeman 1967: 273), there is really more congruence between the two research traditions than first impressions would suggest. Hence, it is not surprising to find studies that examine alienation and job dissatisfaction simultaneously, or writers who use the terms interchangeably.

Robert Blauner on Alienation and Freedom

Robert Blauner published *Alienation and Freedom*, a classic study of industrial differences in workers' responses to their jobs, in 1964. Following the social–psychological tradition, he defined *alienation* in terms of powerlessness, meaninglessness, isolation (or social alienation), and self-estrangement. The centrality of powerlessness in Blauner's theory of alienation is clear from his use of the word *freedom* to refer to the ability to choose how one does one's work.

Blauner compared work in four different industries to test his theory that technology (and the attendant division of labour) is a major determinant of the degree of alienation experienced at work. He argued that the traditional printing industry, which, at the time, still operated largely in a craftwork mode, produced low levels of alienation because of the considerable autonomy of workers and the high levels of skill required. The textile manufacturing industry represented an intermediate step in the process of technological development, while the culmination occurred with the assembly lines of the automobile industry. Here, alienation was most acute because of low-skilled, repetitive tasks that deprived workers of control over their actions.

For his fourth industry setting, Blauner argued that new automated technologies reversed this trend. In work settings such as oil refineries, skill levels were higher, tasks were varied, and individuals could make a number of decisions about how they would do their work. Since this industry was providing us with a glimpse of the future of industrialized societies, he reasoned, the prospects for individual freedom were good. By predicting that alienation would decline as fewer workers were employed in mass-production settings, Blauner was rejecting Marx's argument that work in a capitalist society was always alienating.

Alienation and Freedom was both influential and controversial. Blauner was undoubtedly correct about the negative consequences of continued exposure to low-skill, routinized work. But critics argued that a social–psychological definition does not address alienation in the broader way that Marx had defined it. Furthermore, Duncan Gallie's (1978) comparative study of refinery workers in France and England highlighted cross-cultural differences in workers' responses to technology, an important point Blauner overlooked. And as we have argued earlier, effects of technology are not predetermined (Chapter 10). A position of *technological determinism* conveniently overlooks why different technologies are designed or chosen by those who control an enterprise, and how these technologies are built into the organizational structure of the workplace.

Richard Sennett on the Corrosion of Character

Richard Sennett's views stand in sharp contrast to those of Robert Blauner. Writing in the middle of the 20th century, before the era of industrial restructuring, privatization, downsizing, and outsourcing began, and before the advent of widespread nonstandard employment, Blauner was optimistic in his assessment of the future of work in Western industrialized economies. Alienation would decline and freedom (to decide how to do work) would increase. In contrast, Sennett's more recent book on the "corrosion of character" in the 21st-century economy is extremely pessimistic in its predictions. While Sennett (1998) does not reference the social–psychological research literature on alienation, his analysis of the negative impact of contemporary work organizations and relationships on the minds and souls of American workers is firmly rooted in this tradition.

Sennett describes how today's labour market is characterized by the constant restructuring of work organizations, an emphasis on flexibility in production and the delivery of services, a greater reliance on nonstandard workers, and a glorification of risk taking. Together, these new values and practices have combined to get rid of the order and routine that traditionally defined the lives of workers. Why is this a problem? Because, Sennett argues, order, routine, and stability lead to the formation of personal and occupational identities which give meaning to our lives. In a working world where constant change is glorified and the positive aspects of structure and routine are lost, individual identities are also lost or fail to take shape. Even the teamwork that is central to so many new management approaches is criticized by Sennett, since he sees it as merely a way of gaining compliance from workers, as "the group practice of demeaning superficiality" (1998: 99). He concludes:

> The contradictions of time in the new capitalism have created a conflict between character and experience, the experience of disjointed time threatening the ability of people to form their characters into sustained narratives.[14]

Sennett recognizes that these fleeting personal identities and the resulting concerns about "who in society needs me?" (1998: 146) are shaped in a capitalist economy. But he does not blame the capitalist relations of production that separate workers from owners and that leave control of the labour process with the latter. Instead, the postmodern alienation that he describes is attributed to the forms of work organization and the much less stable divisions of labour that characterize the 21st-century workplace. In this sense, Sennett's critique of the meaninglessness, social isolation, and normlessness of work today fits centrally within the social–psychological tradition of alienation research.

But where it fits is ultimately less important than whether Sennett is correct in his analysis—perspectives differ. The management theorists, discussed in Chapter 9, see the changes taking place in today's workplace as largely positive, empowering workers and increasing their job satisfaction. Sennett is almost uniformly negative in his assessment of the alienating impact of contemporary work. These divergent perspectives on work experiences raise fundamental questions about whether, compared to earlier generations of workers, today's workers, individually and through their own organizations, are in a better or worse position to negotiate greater control over the labour process. However, as we have concluded a number of times in earlier chapters, there is not a single answer. Instead, increased labour market polarization may mean greater control (and less alienation) among well-paid and empowered "knowledge workers" and professionals, and less control (and more alienation) among poorly paid workers in low-complexity jobs and precarious employment situations.

■ WORK AND STRESS

If we take a broader *work and well-being* approach to the subject of how workers experience and react to their jobs, both physical and psychological reactions to work become part of our subject matter. This approach also encourages us to consider how paid work might affect an individual's life in the family and the community. Consequently, workplace health and safety issues, discussed in Chapter 12, are also relevant to discussions of work and well-being, as are concerns about balancing work and family responsibilities (Chapter 7). Here, we look more specifically at work and stress.

Defining Work-Related Stress

Defining *work-related stress* independent of job dissatisfaction is not easy. In fact, some researchers studying stress and its consequences rely on measures that might, in a different context, be considered indicators of job dissatisfaction. But there are important distinctions to be made between job dissatisfaction, anxiety and tension about work, job stress, and job burnout (Humphrey 1998: 4–9). It is possible to feel dissatisfied with work, perhaps even a little anxious about some aspects of a job, without experiencing a great deal of stress. But work-related stress, with its physical and mental symptoms, can also accumulate to the point of *burnout*, where an individual is unable to cope in the job (Maslach and Leiter 1997). It is useful, then, to conceive of work-related stress as a many-sided problem—with job dissatisfaction as one component—that can lead to serious mental and physical health problems.

It is also helpful to distinguish stressors, or strains, from an individual worker's reactions to them. *Stressors* are objective situations (e.g., noisy work environments or competing job demands) or events (a dispute with a supervisor or news that some workers are about to be laid off) that have the potential to produce a negative subjective or physical response. Thus, work-related stress is an individually experienced negative reaction to a job or work environment. Obviously, the absence of stress does not imply the presence of job satisfaction. What distinguishes stress reactions are the wide range of ill health symptoms, both physical and psychological.

The Incidence of Work-Related Stress

In 2000, Statistics Canada's national General Social Survey revealed that one-third (34%) of Canadian workers had experienced stress in the previous year due to "too many demands or too many hours." Fifteen percent of the employed survey participants reported stress from "poor interpersonal relations" (with supervisors or coworkers), and 13 percent had felt stressed because of the risk of accident or injury. The same proportion (13%) reported stress over possible job loss (Williams 2003: 24).

A decade later, in 2010, the General Social Survey included a somewhat different question about stress. The study showed 27 percent of working adults (ages 20 to 64) stating that, on most days, their lives were "quite stressful" or "extremely stressful." Sixty-two percent of these highly stressed adults said that work was their main source of stress. In other words, 17 percent of working adults (about 2.3 million people) typically felt highly stressed because of their job on an almost-daily basis (Crompton 2011). Clearly, work-related stress is not an isolated phenomenon.

Causes and Consequences of Work-Related Stress

In their study of workers who had lost well-paying manufacturing and resource-sector jobs in five rural Ontario communities, and who were now struggling with unemployment or low-paying, part-time service-sector jobs,

Anthony Winson and Belinda Leach (2002: 127–30) provided graphic examples of work-related stress. These workers and their families worried constantly about paying bills, making do with less, losing the family home, having to rely on food banks, and dealing with medical expenses that used to be covered by benefits packages.

Work-related stress, however, is not experienced only by low-income earners. The 2010 national survey discussed earlier revealed that more than half of the working Canadians feeling highly stressed on an almost-daily basis because of their work were in management, professional, or technical occupations, and almost three-quarters were college or university educated (Crompton 2011).

A vast amount of research has drawn our attention to the many different kinds of stressors in the work environment (Barling, Kelloway, and Frone 2005; Davis et al. 2008). We have already mentioned stress resulting from concerns about job insecurity. In addition, continual exposure to health and safety hazards, working in a physically uncomfortable setting, shift work, or long hours can all be stressors. Similarly, fast-paced work (especially when the pace is set by a machine), performance-based pay systems that link output to the amount earned (Ganster et al. 2011), lean production management approaches that continually push workers to increase output (Carter et al. 2013), and inadequate resources to complete a task can generate much stress for workers. The experience of constant organizational restructuring or increased productivity expectations from managers also causes stress.[15] In a recent study of Ontario nurses, for example, perceptions of work intensification resulting from organizational restructuring led to significantly increased stress and, in turn, reduced job satisfaction (Zeytinoglu et al. 2007). Working at tasks that under-utilize one's skills and abilities, that do not meet one's expectations for the job, or that allow little latitude for decision making are also stressful for many workers. An unreasonable and overly demanding supervisor can create a great deal of stress, as can bullying by coworkers or a supervisor.[16] Finally, workers might experience stress as a result of sexual harassment or from discrimination in the workplace based on gender, race, sexual orientation, religion, or disability.

As Chapter 7 documented, equally stressful for some workers, especially women, are the pressures of meeting family responsibilities while trying to devote oneself to a job or career (Ergeneli, Ilsev, and Karapinar 2010).[17]

As one of the young, university-educated women interviewed by Gillian Ranson lamented:

> In this job, in this particular job, I don't think I could do justice to the child and I've made the decision that ... either after maternity leave or in the near future, I'm quitting, because it's not fair. I come home, I can't even talk to my husband because I'm so wound up, stressed out.[18]

Research in many different settings has shown that physical reactions to stress can include fatigue, insomnia, muscular aches and pains, ulcers, high blood pressure, and even heart disease. Depression, anxiety, irritation, low self-esteem, and other mental health problems are among the documented psychological reactions to stressful work.[19] Given these widespread and serious physical and mental health consequences, work-related stress is also costly for employers and the economy, since it is associated with reduced productivity, absenteeism, and disability claims (Crompton 2011).

The "Demand–Control" Model of Work-Related Stress

A useful perspective for understanding workplace stress is the *demand–control model*, which redefines stressors as *job demands* but also introduces the concept of worker control (Karasek 1979).[20] It distinguishes between active jobs, where individual decision-making potential is high, and passive jobs, where it is largely absent. If psychological demands on a worker are high, but a worker can do something about them, stress is less likely to result. If demands are high and control is low, stress, along with the health problems that can follow, is far more often the outcome.

From this perspective, we can understand why researchers have repeatedly demonstrated that highly routinized, machine-paced work is extremely stressful. Assembly-line jobs are often considered to be among the most stressful. Demand is never-ending, the physical work can be extremely taxing, and worker control is virtually absent (Landsbergis, Cahill, and Schnall 1999). Earlier, we suggested that instrumental work attitudes may be a coping mechanism—the paycheque becomes the only relevant work reward. Some assembly-line workers rely on alcohol or drugs to get through a shift (De Santis 1999: 111–14). Others adapt to assembly-line work by "tuning out" the boredom and waiting for the chance to get away from the job.

Ben Hamper, better known as "Rivethead," describes how he was introduced to his new job on a truck-assembly line in Flint, Michigan:

"Until you get it down, your hands will ache, your feet will throb and your back will feel like it's been steamrolled ..."

"Are there any advantages to working down here?" I asked pitifully.

The guy scratched at his beard. "Well, the exit to the time clocks and the parking lot is just down these stairs. Come lunchtime or quittin' time, you can usually get a good jump on the rest of the pack."[21]

But psychological problems can also arise. Three decades ago, Robert Linhart described an extreme reaction to the assembly line in a French automobile factory:

He was fixing parts of a dashboard into place with a screwdriver. Five screws to fix on each car. That Friday afternoon he must have been on his five hundredth screw of the day. All at once he began to yell and rushed at the fenders of the cars brandishing his screwdriver like a dagger. He lacerated a good ten or so car bodies before a troop of white and blue coats rushed up and overcame him, dragging him, panting and gesticulating, to the sick bay.[22]

Highly routinized, monotonous, mechanized, and closely supervised jobs are also found in the service industries. A 1980s study of Canada Post mail sorters and letter carriers in Edmonton revealed that the most stressful job in the organization involved "keying" postal codes using automated machinery. The relentless pace of the machinery, conflicting demands imposed by management, constant repetition, and lack of challenges and job autonomy were associated with diminished mental and physical health among coders. The use of pain relievers and tranquillizers was significantly higher among the coders using automated technology compared with those sorting mail by hand (Lowe and Northcott 1986).

The widespread adoption of electronic communications systems in the contemporary workplace has created some highly rewarding and complex jobs, but also some new types of work that can be extremely routinized and, hence, very stressful. Most prominent here are jobs in call centres that require workers to repeatedly try to contact members of the public, either to sell products or services or to solicit their opinions on various topics (Chapter 10). The same technologies have also increased the scope for electronic surveillance, yet another new source of stress. This practice might involve monitoring the conversations of teleworkers and others who deal with the public by telephone, keeping track of Internet searches made by employees, recording output in settings where workers use computers or electronic communications systems, and even delivering electronic warnings to those performing below certain levels.[23]

Frederick Taylor would have applauded such high levels of work routinization and worker control, but employees do not. A data entry clerk whose work group had been told that they had not met management productivity goals the previous week comments:

> I feel so pressured, my stomach is in knots. I take tons of aspirin, my jaws are sore from clenching my teeth, I'm so tired I can't get up in the morning, and my arm hurts from entering, entering, entering.[24]

A Canadian call-centre employee describes the workplace in similar terms:

> They count on high turnover because of the way this business is run, there is a very high burnout level. People burn out quickly because of the stress, because of the pressure, because of the way people are treated, because of the degrading nature of the work.[25]

It is not difficult to see how such working conditions—high demands and virtually no worker control—can be stressful, and can lead to physical and psychological ill health.

The "Person–Environment Fit" Model

A different theoretical model of work-related stress emphasizes the *person–environment fit*. According to this model, stress results when there is a significant gap between an individual's needs and abilities and what the job offers, allows, or demands (Johnson 1989). To take a specific example, reports of stress and burnout among social workers, teachers, and nurses are common. Individuals in these helping professions have work orientations and expectations (the desire to solve problems and help people) and useful skills (training in their profession) that are frequently thwarted by the need to deal with an excessive number of clients, limited resources, and administrative policies that make it difficult to be effective.[26]

We might also use this perspective to help us understand the stress many workers feel when they try to juggle their work and family roles. A paid job requires one to be present and involved; at the same time, family responsibilities demand time and attention. Because women continue to carry a large share of domestic and child-care responsibilities, they are much more likely to experience role conflict and stress, as this individual interviewed by Duffy and Pupo reported:

> When I worked full-time, I felt very guilty about the children. If they were sick and I went to work, I felt guilty. If I stayed home with them, I felt guilty about work. Part-time work could offer the flexibility that full-time work cannot.[27]

This woman chose part-time work to try to handle her problem, but gave up additional income and career options (which are limited in most part-time jobs). From a person–environment fit perspective, she was attempting to improve the fit between demands of her family and her job (or the financial need to work). But that fit could also have been improved if structural, rather than just individual, changes were implemented.

Thus, while the person–environment fit model of stress broadens our explanatory framework by bringing in work orientations, its individualistic focus advocates primarily personal solutions. From the demand–control perspective, we are more inclined to seek solutions to the lack of worker control. In this case, if more men accepted an equal share of the responsibilities in their homes, if more employers offered flexible work schedules to their workers, and if affordable, quality childcare were more accessible, would the woman quoted above have been forced to make these choices? With respect to professional burnout, how could organizational structures and administrative policies be changed to allow social workers and nurses to be more effective? How can we use new technologies to reduce stress and increase job satisfaction, rather than merely to control workers and increase the speed and intensity of work?

CONCLUSION: THE "LONG ARM OF THE JOB"

In Chapter 13, we described how North Americans today are exposed to competing work-value systems: one that views work as merely a means to an end and another that insists work can be personally fulfilling. As a result, because of different socialization experiences, some workers may be primarily instrumentally oriented while others are more motivated by the intrinsic rewards of a job. In short, it could be argued that work orientations, or preferences, are typically shaped in society and brought to the job where they influence feelings of satisfaction or alienation and experiences of stress.

But a lot of research supports an alternative explanation, namely, that participation in low-skill or routinized work can produce instrumental work attitudes. For many workers, such attitudes may be a means of adapting to employment that has little but a paycheque to offer. Although it is important to recognize that work orientations affect how an individual feels about his or her job, the nature of the work itself is likely to have a stronger impact, both on an individual's feelings of satisfaction, alienation, and stress and on that person's work orientations.

We have suggested that work-related stress does not get left behind at the end of the workday. Chronic work pressures, as well as anxiety about potential job or income loss, can undermine an individual's overall quality of life. At the same time, it is apparent that satisfaction with work translates into a broader sense of well-being. But are there any other more long-term, perhaps even permanent, psychological effects a job can have on an individual? The answer appears to be yes—continued exposure to some kinds of work can have long-lasting effects on non-work behaviours and on one's personality.

In a study conducted more than four decades ago, Martin Meissner argued that the "long arm of the job" has an impact on one's life away from work. He studied male sawmill workers in British Columbia to test rival hypotheses about how the nature of work might affect after-work behaviours. The *compensatory leisure* hypothesis proposes that people will look for activities away from work that will compensate for what is absent in their jobs. Thus, workers who have little opportunity to develop their skills and abilities on the job might seek these opportunities away from work. The *spillover* hypothesis suggests that the effects of work will influence one's choice of after-work activities. Meissner concluded that there is more of a spillover effect. Workers who had little chance to make decisions about how their work should be done were considerably less likely to engage in free-time activities that required or allowed this kind of individual discretion. Similarly, those who had few opportunities for social interactions at work were more inclined toward solitary leisure-time activities (Meissner 1971: 260).

One could still argue that the subjects in Meissner's study had chosen their jobs in order to satisfy their personal preferences. Such an emphasis on work orientations would explain, for example, that individuals with a preference for solitary activities would choose both their jobs and their leisure activities with this in mind. While plausible, this explanation is not convincing for several reasons. First, it suggests that individuals have a much greater range of job choices than is typically the case. Second, subsequent studies comparing these two hypotheses have agreed with Meissner (Martin and Roman 1996). Third, other research has demonstrated even more conclusively that extensive exposure to work with limited scope has a negative effect on one's personality.

Melvin Kohn and his associates (1983) have examined this relationship for many years using the concept of *occupational self-direction*. Kohn argues that work that is free from close supervision, that involves considerable complexity and independent judgment, and that is non-routine will have a lasting positive effect on one's personality and psychological functioning. To be specific, individuals whose work allows self-direction are more likely to develop a personality that values such opportunities and an approach to life that is more self-confident, less fatalistic, and less conformist. They also will exhibit greater flexibility in dealing with ideas. Alternatively, jobs allowing little self-direction are more likely to lead to psychological distress, a finding we have already documented from stress research.

Kohn presents a convincing case, since he used longitudinal data in his studies. By comparing the jobs and personalities of workers at two points in time (up to 10 years apart), he clearly demonstrated the personality changes in those who had and those who did not have the opportunity to work in jobs allowing self-direction. Hence, he has also been able to demonstrate that "both ideational flexibility and a self-directed orientation lead, in time, to more responsible jobs that allow greater latitude for occupational self-direction."[28] The overall conclusion of Kohn's studies and a number of more recent studies[29] is that intrinsically rewarding work, particularly work that allows self-direction, can have important positive long-term consequences for the personalities and careers of those fortunate enough to participate in it.

But the "long arm of the job" extends even further, beyond feelings of satisfaction, dissatisfaction, and alienation; experiences of stress; difficulties balancing work and family; and actual personality change. A growing number of population health studies have documented that poor jobs and problematic working conditions are bad for your health. We have already seen how frequently workers are injured or killed on the job, or become ill because of hazardous working conditions (Chapter 12). But strong evidence linking heart and other diseases, as well as mental illness, to work settings is also accumulating. In fact, several excellent longitudinal studies have demonstrated that, other things being equal, workers in low-skill and poor-paying jobs don't live as long.[30] That, surely, must be a sufficiently convincing argument for increasing our efforts to improve the quality of working life for as many working Canadians as possible.

◼ DISCUSSION QUESTIONS

1. When asked, a large majority of workers say they are satisfied with their jobs. So, is there any need to change working conditions, management approaches, or organizational structures? Why or why not?

2. Older workers tend to be more satisfied with their jobs. What might explain this phenomenon? Do you think this long-standing research finding will continue to be observed in the future? Explain your opinion.

3. Discuss the difference between Marx's structural theory of alienation and the social–psychological perspective on alienation.

4. What kinds of jobs generate the most stress for workers? Why? What might be done to reduce the stress created by such jobs?

5. What is meant by the phrase "the long arm of the job"? Are you convinced by the argument presented? Why or why not?

◼ ADDITIONAL RESOURCES

WORK AT THE MOVIES

- *The Devil Wears Prada* (directed by David Frankel, 2006, 109 minutes). A naïve young woman comes to New York and scores a job as the assistant to one of the city's biggest magazine editors, the ruthless and cynical Miranda Priestly.
- *Nine to Five* (directed by Colin Higgins, 1980, 110 minutes). Three female employees find a way to deal with their sexist, egotistical, lying, hypocritical bigot of a boss.
- *American Beauty* (directed by Sam Mendes, 1999, 122 minutes). This drama centres on the life of Lester Burnham (played by Kevin Spacey),

a middle-aged man who becomes discontented with his office job and experiences a mid-life crisis.

- *Office Space* (directed by Mike Judge, 1999, 89 minutes). In this comedic tale, company workers who hate their jobs decide to rebel against their greedy boss.

SOUNDS OF WORK

- "Career Opportunities" (The Clash). British punk rockers offer a feisty commentary on the lack of jobs and meaningful work opportunities in the United Kingdom during the economic downturn of the 1970s.
- "Cleaning Windows" (Van Morrison). When he was a part-time musician, singer-songwriter Van Morrison spent his days cleaning windows. This song is purportedly autobiographical.
- "Bud the Spud" (Stompin' Tom Connors). A trucker from Prince Edward Island proudly hauls potatoes across the country.
- "Take This Job and Shove It" (David Allan Coe). This classic country song is about worker disillusionment and the fantasy of quitting a dead-end job.

NOTES

1. Unpublished data from a 2012 national survey of a random sample of Canadian workers conducted by EKOS Research Associates and the Graham Lowe Group Inc.
2. The *Edmonton Journal* (October 8, 1996: F1). See also Burstein et al. (1975: 29) on indirect measures of job satisfaction.
3. Kalleberg and Loscocco (1983) conclude that all of the explanations have some relevance, while Firebaugh and Harley (1995: 97) believe that "aging" and "life-cycle" explanations fit the data best.
4. Gjerustad and von Soest (2012) report an association between unmet occupational aspirations and negative mental health outcomes in their Norwegian study. Reynolds and Baird (2010) fail to find a negative relationship between unmet post-secondary educational aspirations and mental health outcomes in their U.S. study.
5. See Maynard, Joseph, and Maynard (2006) on underemployment and job dissatisfaction; Zeytinoglu et al. (2007) on work intensification and job satisfaction; and De Witte and Näswall (2003) on employment insecurity and job dissatisfaction.

6. Gallie (2013) reports that opportunities to make decisions about one's own job have stronger positive effects on job satisfaction than does participation in work teams. Busck, Knudsen, and Lind (2010) also question whether employee participation has positive effects on workers' well-being.

7. Figure 13.1, in Chapter 13, presents 2012 data on Canadians' work orientations, but this national survey did not ask about job rewards. The 2000 and 2012 data on work orientations cannot be directly compared since the two surveys used different measurement scales.

8. In order, the quotations are from House, J. D. (1980). *The Last of the Free Enterprisers: The Oilmen of Calgary*. Toronto: Macmillan, p. 335; Bailyn, Lotte, and John T. Lynch. (1983). "Engineering as a Life-Long Career: Its Meaning, Its Satisfactions, Its Difficulties." *Journal of Occupational Behaviour* 4:263–83, p. 281; Armstrong, Pat, and Hugh Armstrong. (1983). *A Working Majority: What Women Must Do for Pay*. Ottawa: Canadian Advisory Council on the Status of Women, p. 129; and Robertson, David, and Jeff Wareham. (1987). *Technological Change in the Auto Industry*. Willowdale, ON: Canadian Auto Workers (CAW), p. 29. For additional graphic "tales from the assembly line," see Hamper (1986) and De Santis (1999). Hodson (2001) provides an excellent content analysis of workers' reactions to their jobs as reported in 149 published workplace ethnographies.

9. See Kalleberg (2008) on the extent of over-qualification among U.S. workers.

10. See Maynard, Joseph, and Maynard (2006), Vaisey (2006), and Green and Zhu (2010) on the link between underemployment (or over-qualification) and job dissatisfaction.

11. See Bender and Sloane (1998) on job dissatisfaction and filing grievances. Kochan (1979) links dissatisfaction to willingness to join a union. Hammer and Avgar (2005) reverse the question by asking about the effects of union membership on job satisfaction.

12. An interesting recent study (Edmans 2012) identified the "100 Best Companies to Work For in America" based on employee satisfaction surveys and showed that these companies had higher annual stock returns between 1984 and 2011. This finding would fit with this explanation: workplaces in the secondary labour market are unlikely to be included in this annual corporate survey.

13. Faulkner is quoted by Studs Terkel (1971: xi).

14. Sennett, Richard. (1998). *The Corrosion of Character: The Personal Consequences of Work in the New Capitalism*. New York: W.W. Norton, p. 31.

15. A recent study (Johnston and Lee 2013) reports the interesting finding that even being promoted can generate stress, despite the increased extrinsic rewards and greater job satisfaction than can accompany a promotion.

16. On workplace bullying, see Einarsen (1999), Agervold and Mikkelsen (2004), and Tehrani (2004). The rapid increase in research on this topic in the last 15 years might leave the impression that workplace bullying is a recent phenomenon. It is likely, however, that the label is new, but the phenomenon is not. In earlier eras, bullying by coworkers might have been described by researchers studying the "informal side of organizations" (Chapter 8), while bullying by management might have been addressed by labour process researchers (Chapter 10).

17. Bass and Grzywacz (2011) look at the work–family balance relationship from the opposite direction, showing how individuals with better jobs (based on both extrinsic and intrinsic rewards) are better able to handle work–family conflict.

18. Ranson, Gillian. (1998). "Education, Work and Family Decision-Making: Finding the 'Right Time' to Have a Baby." *Canadian Review of Sociology and Anthropology* 35(4): 517–33, p. 527.

19. Research has also shown that the effects of work-based stressors can be conditioned by individuals' psychological coping mechanisms (Kinnunen, Mauno, and Siltaloppi 2010; Otto, Hoffmann-Biencourt, and Mohr 2010), as can the effects of stress resulting from work–family conflicts (Higgins, Duxbury, and Lyons 2010). Social support received from family, friends, and coworkers is also an important moderating variable (Jex 1998; Viswesvaran, Sanchez, and Fisher 1999).

20. See also Karasek and Theorell (1990); de Lange et al. (2003) and Bakker and Demerouti (2007) provide multi-study assessments of research based on the demand–control model.

21. Hamper, Ben. (1986). *Rivethead: Tales from the Assembly Line*. New York: Warner Books, p. 88.

22. Linhart, Robert. (1981). *The Assembly Line*. London, England: John Calder, p. 57.

23. See also Sewell (1998), Fernie and Metcalf (1998), and Felstead, Jewson, and Walters (2003) on workplace electronic surveillance. Mann and Holdsworth (2003) describe the stress generated among teleworkers, as well as the negative physical health symptoms they report as a result of their working conditions.

24. Nussbaum, Karen, and Virginia duRivage. (1986). "Computer Monitoring: Mismanagement by Remote Control." *Business and Society Review* 56(Winter): 16–20, p. 18.

25. Buchanan, Ruth, and Sarah Koch-Schulte. (2000). *Gender on the Line: Technology, Restructuring and the Reorganization of Work in the Call-Centre Industry*. Ottawa: Status of Women Canada. Catalogue no. SW21-44/2000E. http://www.swc-cfc.gc.ca.

26. See Maslach and Leiter (1997) and Hakanen, Schaufeli, and Ahola (2008) on burnout.

27. Duffy, Ann, and Norene Pupo. (1992). *Part-Time Paradox: Connecting Gender, Work and Family*. Toronto: McClelland & Stewart, p. 134.

28. Kohn and Schooler (1983: 152); see also Miller, Kohn, and Schooler (1985). Schooler (1984) develops a more general theory of "psychological effects of complex environments," which has applicability beyond the workplace.

29. Krahn (1997) describes how under-use of literacy skills at work can lead to decline in these skills. Ilies, Wilson, and Wagner (2009) show how job satisfaction can "spillover" to affect marital satisfaction. Brand and Burgard (2008) report that job loss early in a career can affect social participation later in life.

30. See Mustard, Lavis, and Ostry (2005) for a useful summary of the linkages between work and health outcomes, and Stansfeld and Candy (2006) for a multi-study assessment.

CONCLUSIONS

Our discussion of work, industry, and Canadian society has ranged widely over many different topics. We have reviewed and dissected key theoretical debates and have documented emerging industrial, labour market, and workplace trends. Instead of summarizing the many issues we have covered, we conclude by highlighting some of the major themes in current debates about changing labour markets and workplaces.

Debates about the emerging postindustrial society and global economy have been part of sociological discourse for several decades, and will no doubt continue. But it is clear that, like all major industrialized nations, Canada has become a service-based society with a globally linked economy. Natural resource, construction, and manufacturing industries will continue to play an important, if diminished, role in the Canadian economy, but the service sector, and the wide range of jobs it provides, now dominates. Three out of four employed Canadians depend on the service sector for their livelihood. Some service industry jobs are highly skilled, well paying, and intrinsically rewarding, yet a substantial number are relatively unskilled and less rewarding, both financially and psychologically. One of the most clearly defined characteristics of this postindustrial economy is the distinction between "good jobs" and "bad jobs." In particular, while most working Canadians are still employed in permanent, full-time jobs that have a Monday-to-Friday daytime schedule, a growing proportion of the millions of jobs in the Canadian labour market no longer fit this post-WWII definition of a "standard" job. Employment relationships and work arrangements have become much more varied and, in some key ways, less secure and more precarious.

Equally important demographic changes have been systematically transforming the Canadian workforce. The population is slowly aging, because of declining birthrates over the past half century and also because people are living longer. Consequently, over the last several decades, immigration has accounted for most of the growth in Canada's labour force. As a result, some of Canada's urban centres—Toronto and Vancouver, for example—are among the most ethnically diverse in the world, and Canada's workforce is becoming more multicultural.

The oldest members of the baby-boom generation have transitioned into retirement. Having lived through the mid-20th-century decades of economic expansion and rising personal incomes, the turbulent labour market restructuring of the 1990s, and also the uncertain first decade of the 21st century, this large cohort is looking ahead with mixed feelings. Some baby boomers eagerly anticipate retirement, planning to enjoy a leisurely lifestyle, while others love their job and can't imagine life without it. Both groups are no longer as certain that their pensions and savings will be sufficient—they have seen the results of the unanticipated financial crisis in 2008–9 and know that both governments and private-sector employers are thinking about ways to reduce pension liabilities. There is yet a third group, those who cannot even think of retirement given their current low-pay, no-pension, precarious employment situation. It remains to be seen how these trends play out.

At the other end of the age distribution, for the past three decades, successive cohorts of younger workers have experienced considerable difficulty finding good jobs, despite their increased investments in higher education. At the same time, postsecondary tuition rates have increased dramatically. As we have seen, the number of well-paying, full-time, secure jobs awaiting university- and college-educated youth has not kept pace with the number of postsecondary graduates in some fields. What are the long-term implications of this kind of intergenerational inequality for Canadian society; for worker–employer relationships; and for individual feelings of job satisfaction?

This three-pronged question highlights the issue of growing social inequality in Canadian society, clearly the most disturbing trend we have observed. While unemployment rates today are not nearly as high as they were during the recessions of the 1980s and 1990s, we still have more than 1.5 million people seeking jobs in our society. Nonstandard jobs have become much more common, and the ranks of the working poor have been growing. The causes of the observed increase in social inequality are complex and intertwined, but involve transformation of the global economy, including outsourcing of jobs, the desire for greater hiring flexibility, continued downsizing in both the private and public sectors, the use of new technologies as labour replacements, shrinking employment in the goods-producing sector, polarization within the growing service sector, a decline in the strength of labour unions, and governments backing away from their traditional role of labour market regulators. Together, these trends are creating a more distinctly segmented labour market in terms of income, benefits, job security, and skill requirements.

As we have noted throughout this book, there are clear patterns to the inequalities within this more polarized labour market. Some regions of the country, largely bypassed by the economic growth experienced by others, continue to have higher-than-average unemployment rates. Compared to the generations following them into the labour market, baby boomers have enjoyed more labour market advantages. The lack of opportunities and employment barriers faced by women, people with disabilities, racial and ethnic minority individuals, Aboriginal Canadians, and recent immigrants are still evident in Canadian society.

When we look back at the long and difficult battles fought by organized labour to obtain the employment rights and benefits and the standard of living that we have for so long taken for granted, we are reminded that social inequities such as these are not easily eliminated. As we have argued throughout this book, there is clearly a need for focused action by governments to tighten and improve employment standards (e.g., minimum wages, working hours, health and safety issues) and to revamp Employment Insurance, pension, child-care, and other work-related policies and programs so that more Canadian workers benefit. The Canadian economy would benefit as well, since workers who are healthy and secure in decent jobs are likely to be more productive. Equally important, there is a continued need for a strong organized labour movement and for socially and environmentally responsible corporate leaders. In *Good Jobs America*, Paul Osterman and Beth Shulman (2011) make the same argument about the U.S. economy.

There are a few signs of positive change. Some employers are taking their social and environmental responsibilities more seriously. For example, a larger number of employers have begun to address work–life balance problems faced by workers, to support workplace wellness initiatives, and to give employees time to volunteer for community causes. Even so, we need to remember the segmented nature of the Canadian labour market and acknowledge that some workers are much more likely than others to enjoy these benefits. Some Canadian unions have continued to play a strong role in promoting workers' rights and in seeking ways to improve the quality of jobs. In addition, some unions have become more involved in society-wide society justice issues in Canada and in other countries. And a few more politicians are beginning to recognize the vital role of caregiving in our society, and the negative consequences, for the economy and society as a whole, of growing social inequality.

Over the past few decades, we have made some progress in the struggle for gender equality in the labour market and in work organizations. While we acknowledge the present flaws of employment equity, pay equity, and work–family policies, their very existence has begun a slow process of institutional change that has benefited some, but not all, women. Although members of visible minorities continue to encounter labour market barriers, there is evidence that discrimination against them is becoming less acceptable. Unfortunately, there is also evidence that recent immigrants to Canada, most of whom are non-white, are not faring as well in the labour market as did immigrants several decades earlier. Even more troubling is the continued disadvantaged situation of Canada's First Nations. The levels of unemployment and underemployment in Aboriginal communities are unacceptably high.

Our examination of shifts in management strategies within North American work organizations also identifies conflicting trends. On one hand, we have seen how downsizing, outsourcing, and increasing reliance on nonstandard workers have frequently been the substitute for innovative approaches to increasing productivity. Similarly, despite their promise for humanizing work and empowering workers, new management schemes have frequently been used to push workers harder with no compensation in terms of autonomy, skill enhancement, or improved incomes. Yet, on the other hand, some of the management literature advocates significant workplace reforms, and there are some positive examples of their implementation. Furthermore, important alternatives, including legislated industrial democracy and incentives to encourage worker ownership, could lead to more worker autonomy, increased job security, and reduced social inequality. The challenge will be to convince employers of the benefits of real workplace reform, to assist workers in their efforts to obtain reform, and to encourage governments to remove legislative and other barriers to improvements.

Most Canadian unions have reacted to new management schemes with skepticism. Some have strongly resisted change while others have been willing to accept it, so long as job and income security have been maintained. A few have insisted on being active partners in the change process in return for their cooperation. Where equal-partner status has been obtained, and where real consultation took place, the outcomes have often been positive. Recognizing that unions have been responsible for many of the gains made by working Canadians over the past century, it is extremely important, in our opinion, to maintain and strengthen the labour legislation that has allowed this to happen, rather than to weaken it as some recent federal and provincial government initiatives have done.

The issues we have been raising here are ultimately about our societal goals. Is economic competitiveness at any social and environmental cost our objective? Or would we prefer that the primary goal be a better quality of life, achieved through a reasonable standard of living, employment security, and more opportunities for personally rewarding work for as many Canadians as possible within an environmentally sustainable economy? If it is the latter, and we strongly believe it should be, then a political response is also needed. Governments, at various levels, need to consider raising minimum wages, improving labour legislation in a way that benefits workers and not just employers, and implementing tax and other policies that might encourage employers to create more and better jobs rather than cutting jobs (Amable and Mayhew 2011; Osterman and Shulman 2011; Warhurst et al. 2012).

As we have argued throughout this book, a "let the market decide" approach (the position taken by most provincial and federal governments during the past several decades) is unlikely to assist us in reaching these social and environmental goals. We need to remind ourselves that ideally, "the market" is a mechanism for improving society (Levitt 2013). Robert Reich, commenting on American society 25 years ago but with observations equally relevant to Canada today, alerted us to the connection between economic globalization and polarization within national economies. In his view, left as things are, we will see further inequality between nations and within industrialized capitalist nations. In his words:

> The choice is ours to make. We are no more slaves to present trends than to vestiges of the past. We can, if we choose, assert that our mutual obligations as citizens extend beyond our economic usefulness to one another, and act accordingly (Reich 1991: 313).

We agree.

REFERENCES

Abella, Irving 1974 "Oshawa 1937." In Irving Abella, ed., *On Strike: Six Key Labour Struggles in Canada, 1919–1949*. Toronto: James Lewis and Samuel.

Aboriginal Affairs and Northern Development Canada 2013 *Fact Sheet— 2011 National Household Survey Aboriginal Demographics, Educational Attainment and Labour Market Outcomes*. Ottawa: Aboriginal Affairs and Northern Development Canada. http://www.aadnc-aandc.gc.ca/eng/ 1376329205785/1376329233875.

Abu-Laban, Yasmeen, and Christina Gabriel 2002 *Selling Diversity: Immigration, Multiculturalism, Employment Equity, and Globalization*. Peterborough, ON: Broadview Press.

Acker, Joan 1990 "Hierarchies, Jobs, Bodies: A Theory of Gendered Organizations." *Gender & Society* 4(2): 139–58.

Adams, Roy J. 1995 "Canadian Industrial Relations in Comparative Perspective." In Morley Gunderson and Allen Ponak, eds., *Union–Management Relations in Canada*. 3rd ed. Don Mills, ON: Addison-Wesley Publishers.

——— 2006 "The Campaign to Organize Wal-Mart in Canada." *Social Policy* 36(3): 12–15.

Adams, Roy J., and Parbudyal Singh 1997 "Worker Rights under NAFTA: Experience with the North American Agreement on Labor Cooperation." In Rick Chaykowski, Paul-André Lapointe, Guylaine Vallée, and Anil Verma, eds., *Worker Representation in the Era of Trade and Deregulation*. Selected Papers from the 33rd Annual Canadian Industrial Relations Association Conference, Brock University, St. Catharines, ON. CIRA.

Adams, Scott, and David Neumark 2005 "The Effects of Living Wage Laws: Evidence from Failed and Derailed Living Wage Campaigns." *Journal of Urban Economics* 58:177–202.

Adams, Tracy L. 1998 "Gender and Women's Employment in the Male-Dominated Profession of Dentistry: 1867–1917." *Canadian Review of Sociology and Anthropology* 35(1): 21–42.

——— 2000 *A Dentist and a Gentleman: Gender and the Rise of Dentistry in Ontario*. Toronto: University of Toronto Press.

——— 2003 "Professionalization, Gender and Female-Dominated Professions in Ontario." *The Canadian Review of Sociology and Anthropology* 40(3): 267–89.

Adler, Paul S. 2007 "The Future of Critical Management Studies: A Paleo-Marxist Critique of Labour Process Theory." *Organization Studies* 28(9): 1313–45.

Adler, Paul S., and Bryan Borys 1996 "Two Types of Bureaucracy: Enabling and Coercive." *Administrative Science Quarterly* 41(1): 61–89.

Adler, Paul S., and Charles Heckscher 2006 "Towards Collaborative Community." In Charles Heckscher and Paul. S. Adler, eds., *The Firm as a Collaborative Community*. Oxford: Oxford University Press.

AFMC [Association of Faculties of Medicine of Canada] 2013 *Trends in Graduates of Canadian Faculties of Medicine, 1940–2010*. http://www.afmc.ca/pdf/gradssection2011cmes .pdf.

Agervold, Mogens, and Eva Gemzoe Mikkelsen 2004 "Relationships between Bullying, Psychosocial Work Environment and Individual Stress Reactions." *Work & Stress: An International Journal of Work, Health & Organisations* 18(4): 336–51.

Aguayo, Rafael 1990 *Dr. Deming: The American Who Taught the Japanese about Quality*. New York: Simon & Schuster.

Aguiar, Luís L. M. 2001 "Doing Cleaning Work 'Scientifically': The Reorganization of Work in the Contract Building Cleaning Industry." *Economic and Industrial Democracy* 22(2): 239–69.

Aguren, Stefan, Christer Bredbacka, Reine Hansson, Kurt Ihregren, and K. G. Karlson 1985 *Volvo Kalmar Revisited: Ten Years of Experience*. Stockholm: Efficiency and Participation Development Council.

Akyeampong, Ernest B. 1992 "Discouraged Workers—Where Have They Gone?" *Perspectives on Labour and Income* (Winter): 38–44.

——— 1993 "Flextime Work Arrangements." *Perspectives on Labour and Income* (Autumn): 17–30.

Albanese, Patrizia 2006 "Small Town, Big Benefits: The Ripple Effect of $7/day Childcare." *Canadian Review of Sociology and Anthroplogy* 43(2): 125–40.

Alexander, Karl L., Doris R. Entwisle, and Carrie S. Horsey 1998 "From First Grade Forward: Early Foundations of High School Dropout." *Sociology of Education* 70(2): 87–107.

Alexandroff, Alan S., Gary Clyde Hufbauer, and Krista Lucenti 2008 *Still Amigos: A Fresh Canada–U.S. Approach to Reviving NAFTA.* Toronto: C.D. Howe Institute.

Aligisakis, Maximos 1997 "Labour Disputes in Western Europe: Typology and Tendencies." *International Labour Review* 136(1): 73–94.

Allen, Tammy D., David E. L. Herst, Carly S. Bruck, and Martha Sutton 2000 "Consequences Associated with Work-to-Family Conflict: A Review and Agenda for Future Research." *Journal of Occupational Health Psychology* 5(2): 278–308.

Alon, Sigal 2009 "The Evolution of Class Inequality in Higher Education: Competition, Exclusion, and Adaptation." *American Sociological Review* 74(5): 731–55.

Althauser, Robert P. 1989 "Internal Labor Markets." *Annual Review of Sociology* 15:143–61.

Amable, Bruno, and Ken Mayhew 2011 "Unemployment in the OECD." *Oxford Review of Economics* 27(2): 207–20.

Amstad, Fabienne T., Laurenz L. Meier, Ursula Fasel, Achim Elfering, and Norbert K. Semmer 2011 "A Meta-analysis of Work–Family Conflict and Various Outcomes with a Special Emphasis on Cross-Domain versus Matching Domain Relations." *Journal of Occupational Health Psychology* 16(2): 151–69.

Anderson, Doris 1996 *Rebel Daughter.* Toronto: Key Porter Books.

Anderson, Kay J. 1991 *Vancouver's Chinatown: Racial Discourse in Canada, 1875–1980.* Montreal and Kingston: McGill–Queen's University Press.

Anderson, Nickela, and Karen D. Hughes 2010 "The Business of Caring: Women's Self-Employment and the Marketization of Care." *Gender, Work & Organization* 17(4): 381–405.

Anderson-Connolly, Richard, L. Grunberg, E. S. Greenberg, and S. Moore 2002 "Is Lean Mean? Workplace Transformation and Employee Well-Being." *Work, Employment & Society* 16(3): 389–413.

Andres, Lesley, Paul Anisef, Harvey Krahn, Dianne Looker, and Victor Thiessen 1999 "The Persistence of Social Structure: Cohort, Class and Gender Effects on the Occupational Aspirations and Expectations of Canadian Youth." *Journal of Youth Studies* 2(3): 261–82.

Andres, Lesley, and E. Dianne Looker 2001 "Rurality and Capital: Educational Expectations and Attainments of Rural, Urban/Rural and Metropolitan Youth." *Canadian Journal of Higher Education* 31(2): 1–46.

Andres, Lesley, and Johanna Wyn 2010 *The Making of a Generation: The Children of the 1970s in Adulthood.* Toronto: University of Toronto Press.

Angus, Charlie, and Brit Griffin 1996 *We Lived a Life and Then Some: The Life, Death, and Life of a Mining Town.* Toronto: Between the Lines.

Anisef, Paul, Paul Axelrod, Etta Baichman-Anisef, Carl James, and Anton Turrittin 2000 *Opportunity and Uncertainty: Life Course Experiences of the Class of '73.* Toronto: University of Toronto Press.

Aoyama, Yuko, and Manuel Castells 2002 "An Empirical Assessment of the Informational Society: Employment and Occupational Structures in G-7 Countries." *International Labor Review* 141(1/2): 123–59.

Appelbaum, Eileen, Thomas Bailey, Peter Berg, and Arne L. Kalleberg 2000 *Manufacturing Advantage: Why High-Performance Work Systems Pay Off.* Ithaca, NY: ILR Press.

Appelbaum, Eileen, and Rosemary Batt 1994 *The New American Workplace: Transforming Work Systems in the United States.* Ithaca, NY: ILR Press.

Arai, Bruce A. 1997 "The Road Not Taken: The Transition from Unemployment to Self-Employment in Canada, 1961–1994." *Canadian Journal of Sociology* 22(3): 365–82.

Arai, Bruce 2007 "Re-organizing Flexibility and the Employment Standards Act in Ontario." *Journal of Change Management* 7(1): 89–102.

Argote, Linda 1999 *Organizational Learning: Creating, Retaining, and Transferring Knowledge.* Boston: Kluwer Academic.

Argyris, Chris 1999 "The Next Challenge for TQM—Taking the Offensive on Defensive Reasoning." *Journal for Quality and Participation* 22(6): 41–43.

Armitage, Derek R. 2005 "Collaborative Environmental Assessment in the Northwest Territories, Canada." *Environmental Impact Assessment Review* 25(3): 239–58.

Armstrong, Pat, and Hugh Armstrong 1983 *A Working Majority: What Women Must Do for Pay.* Ottawa: Canadian Advisory Council on the Status of Women.

———— **1990** *Theorizing Women's Work.* Toronto: Garamond Press.

———— **2010** *The Double Ghetto: Canadian Women and Their Segregated Work.* Revised 3rd ed. Don Mills, ON: Oxford University Press.

Armstrong, Pat, Hugh Armstrong, and Krista Scott-Dixon 2008 *Critical to Care: The Invisible Women of Health Services.* Toronto: University of Toronto Press.

Armstrong, Pat, Jacqueline Choinière, and Elaine Day 1993 *Vital Signs: Nursing in Transition.* Toronto: Garamond Press.

Armstrong, Pat, and Mary Cornish 1997 "Restructuring Pay Equity for a Restructured Work Force: Canadian Perspectives." *Gender, Work & Organization* 4(2): 67–85.

Aronowitz, S. 1973 *False Promises: The Shaping of American Working Class Consciousness.* New York: McGraw-Hill.

Arsen, David D., Mark I. Wilson, and Jonas Zoninsein 1996 "Trends in Manufacturing Employment in the NAFTA Region: Evidence of a Giant Sucking Sound?" In Karen Roberts and Mark I. Wilson, eds., *Policy Choices: Free Trade among NAFTA Nations.* East Lansing, MI: Michigan State University Press.

Ashwin, Sarah 2004 "Social Partnership or a Complete Sellout? Russian Trade Unions' Responses to Conflict." *British Journal of Industrial Relations* 42(1): 23–46.

Askenazy, Philippe 2001 "Innovative Workplace Practices and Occupational Injuries and Illnesses in the United States." *Economic and Industrial Democracy* 22(4): 485–516.

Association of Universities and Colleges of Canada 2007 *Trends in Higher Education.*

Vol. 1, *Enrolment.* Ottawa: AUCC. http://www.aucc.ca/_pdf/english/publications/trends_2007_vol1_e.pdf.

Aston, T. H., and C. H. E. Philpin, eds. 1985 *The Brenner Debate: Agrarian Class Structure and Economic Development in Pre-industrial Europe.* Cambridge, England: Cambridge University Press.

Avery, Donald H. 1995 *Reluctant Host: Canada's Response to Immigrant Workers, 1896–1994.* Toronto: McClelland & Stewart.

Babcock, Robert H. 1974 *Gompers in Canada: A Study in American Continentalism before the First World War.* Toronto: University of Toronto Press.

Backett-Milburn, Kathryn, Laura Airey, Linda McKie, and Gillian Hogg 2008 "Family Comes First or Open All Hours? How Low Paid Women Working in Food Retailing Manage Webs of Obligation at Home and Work." *The Sociological Review* 56(3): 474–96.

Baer, Douglas E., Edward Grabb, and William A. Johnston 1991 "Class, Crisis and Political Ideology in Canada: Recent Trends." *Canadian Review of Sociology and Anthropology* 24: 1–22.

Bailey, Thomas, and Annette D. Bernhard 1997 "In Search of the High Road in a Low-Wage Industry." *Politics and Society* 25(2): 179–201.

Bailyn, Lotte, and John T. Lynch 1983 "Engineering as a Life-Long Career: Its Meaning, Its Satisfactions, Its Difficulties." *Journal of Occupational Behaviour* 4: 263–83.

Bain, George S. 1978 *Union Growth and Public Policy in Canada.* Ottawa: Labour Canada.

Bain, George S., and H. A. Clegg 1974 "A Strategy for Industrial Relations Research in Britain." *British Journal of Industrial Relations* 12: 91–113.

Bakan, Abigail, and Audrey Kobayashi 2000 *Employment Equity Policy in Canada: An Interprovincial Comparison.* Ottawa: Status of Women Canada.

Bakker, Arnold B., and Evangelia Demerouti 2007 "The Job Demands-Resources Model: State of the Art." *Journal of Managerial Psychology* 22(3): 309–28.

Baldry, Chris 2011 "Editorial: Chronicling the Information Revolution." *New Technology, Work and Employment* 26(3): 175–182.

Baldry, Chris, and Jerry Hallier 2010 "Welcome to the House of Fun: Work Space and Social Identity." *Economic and Industrial Democracy* 31(1): 150–172.

Ball, Jessica, and Kerry Daly 2012 *Father Involvement in Canada: Diversity, Renewal and Transformation.* Vancouver, BC: University of British Columbia Press.

Bamber, Greg J., Russell D. Lansbury, and Nick Wailes, eds. 2011 *International and Comparative Employment Relations: Globalisation and Change.* 5th ed. London: Sage.

Banerjee, Subhabrata Bobby. 2008 "Corporate Social Responsibility: The Good, the Bad and the Ugly." *Critical Sociology* 34(1): 51–79.

Barley, Stephen, Debra Meyerson, and Stine Grodal 2011 "Email as a Source and Symbol of Stress." *Organization Science* 22(4): 887–906.

Barley, Stephen R., and Gideon Kunda 1992 "Design and Devotion: Surges of Rational and Normative Ideologies of Control in Managerial Discourse." *Administrative Science Quarterly* 37: 363–399.

Barling, Julian, Clive Fullagar, and E. K. Kelloway 1992 *The Union and Its Members: A Psychological Approach.* New York: Oxford University Press.

Barling, Julian, E. Kevin Kelloway, and Michael Frone, eds. 2005 *Handbook of Work Stress.* Thousand Oaks, CA: Sage.

Barnes, Helen, and Jane Parry 2004 "Renegotiating Identity and Relationships: Men and Women's Adjustments to Retirement." *Ageing & Society* 24: 213–33.

Barnetson, Bob 2013 "Alberta's Most Vulnerable Workplace." *Alberta Views* 16(4): 28–32.

Barnett, William P., James N. Baron, and Toby E. Stuart 2000 "Avenues of Attainment: Occupational Demography and Organizational Careers in the California Civil Service." *American Journal of Sociology* 106: 88–144.

Bartkiw, Timothy J. 2008 "Manufacturing Descent? Labour Law and Union Organizing in the Province of Ontario." *Canadian Public Policy* 34(1): 111–32.

Bass, Brenda L., and Joseph G. Grzywacz 2011 "Job Adequacy and Work-Family Balance: Looking at Jobs as a Whole." *Journal of Family Issues* 32(3): 317–45.

Basu, Kaushik, ed. 2004 *India's Emerging Economy: Performance and Prospects in the 1990s and Beyond.* Cambridge, MA: MIT Press.

Batstone, Eric, Ian Boraston, and Stephen Frenkel 1978 *The Social Organization of Strikes.* Oxford, England: Basil Blackwell.

Batt, Rosemary 2000 "Strategic Segmentation in Front-Line Services: Matching Customers, Employees and Human Resource Systems." *International Journal of Human Resource Management* 11(3): 540–61.

Battams, Nathan 2013 "Out of the Office: Workshifting and Remote Work in Canada." *Fascinating Families* [A Vanier Institute of the Family Publication], Issue 56 (August): 1–2.

Bauder, Harold 2001a "Culture in the Labor Market: Segmentation Theory and Perspectives of Place." *Human Geography* 25(1): 37–52.

———— **2001b** "Employment, Ethnicity and Metropolitan Context: The Case of Young Canadian Immigrants." *Journal of International Migration and Integration* 2(3): 315–41.

Bauder, Harold 2003 "Brain Abuse, or the Devaluation of Immigrant Labour in Canada." *Antipode* 35(4): 699–717.

Bauman, Zygmunt 2000 *Liquid Modernity.* Cambridge: Polity Press.

Baumol, William J., Alan S. Blinder, and Edward N. Wolff 2003 *Downsizing in America: Reality, Causes, and Consequences.* New York: Russell Sage Foundation.

Baureiss, Gunter 1987 "Chinese Immigration, Chinese Stereotypes, and Chinese Labour." *Canadian Ethnic Studies* 19: 15–34.

Beach, Jane, Martha Friendly, Carolyn Ferns, Nina Prabhu, and Barry Forer 2009 *Early Childhood Education and Care in Canada 2008.* Toronto: Childcare Resources and Research Unit. http://www.childcarecanada.org/ECEC2008/index.html.

Beata, K., J. D. Jens, and B. Per-Olaf 2007 "Measuring Lean Initiatives in Health Care Services: Issues and Findings." *International Journal of Productivity and Performance Management* 56: 7–24.

Beaud, Michel 1983 *A History of Capitalism 1500–1980.* New York: Monthly Review.

Beaujot, Roderic 1997 "Parental Preferences for Work and Childcare." *Canadian Public Policy* 23(3): 275–88.

———— **2000** *Earning and Caring in Canadian Families.* Toronto: Broadview Press.

Beaujot, Roderic, and Robert Anderson 2007 "Time-Crunch: Impact of Time Spent in Paid and Unpaid Work, and Its Division in Families." *Canadian Journal of Sociology* 32(3): 295–315.

Beaujot, Roderic, Jianye Liu, and Zenaida Ravanera 2008 "Models of Earning and Caring: Trends in Time-Use." *PSC Discussion Papers Series* 22(2). http://ir.lib.uwo.ca/pscpapers/vol22/iss2/1.

Beaumont, P. B. 1995 *The Future of Employment Relations.* London: Sage.

Beck, J. Helen, Jeffrey G. Reitz, and Nan Weiner 2002 "Addressing Systemic Racial Discrimination in Employment: The Health Canada Case and Implications of Legislative Change." *Canadian Public Policy* 28(3): 373–94.

Beck, Ulrich 1992 *Risk Society: Towards a New Modernity.* London: Sage Publications.

—— **2000** *The Brave New World of Work.* Cambridge: Polity Press.

Becker, Brian E., Mark A. Huselid, and Dave Ulrich 2001 *The HR Scorecard: Linking People, Strategy, and Performance.* Boston: Harvard Business School Press.

Becker, Gary S. 1975 *Human Capital: A Theoretical and Empirical Analysis with Special Reference to Education.* 2nd ed. Chicago: University of Chicago Press.

Beckstead, Desmond, and W. Mark Brown 2005 *An Anatomy of Growth and Decline: High-Tech Industries through the Boom and Bust Years, 1997–2003.* Ottawa: Statistics Canada. Cat. no. 11-624-MIE–No. 010.

Beirne, Martin, Kathleen Riach, and Fiona Wilson 2004 "Controlling Business? Agency and Constraint in Call Centre Working." *New Technology, Work and Employment* 19(2): 96–109.

Bélanger, Jacques, and Paul Edwards 2013 "The Nature of Front-Line Service Work: Distinctive Features and Continuity in the Employment Relationship." *Work, Employment and Society* 27(3): 433–50.

Belkin, Lisa 2003 "The Opt-Out Revolution." *New York Times,* October 26.

Bell, Daniel 1973 *The Coming of Post-industrial Society.* New York: Basic Books.

Bell, David N. F., and David G. Blanchflower 2011 "Young People and the Great Recession." *Oxford Review of Economics* 27(2): 241–67.

Bellavia, Gina M., and Michael R. Frone 2005 "Work–Family Conflict." In Julian Barling, E. Kevin Kelloway, and Michael R. Frone, eds., *Handbook of Work Stress* (Chapter 6). Thousand Oaks, CA: Sage Publications.

Bellin, Seymour S., and S. M. Miller 1990 "The Split Society." In Kai Erikson and Steven Peter Vallas, eds., *The Nature of Work: Sociological Perspectives.* New Haven, CT: American Sociological Association and Yale University Press.

Bender, Keith A., and Peter J. Sloane 1998 "Job Satisfaction, Trade Unions, and Exit-Voice Revisited." *Industrial and Labor Relations Review* 51(2): 222–40.

Bendix, Reinhard 1974 *Work and Authority in Industry.* Berkeley, CA: University of California Press.

Bercuson, David J. 1974 *Confrontation at Winnipeg: Labour, Industrial Relations, and the General Strike.* Montreal and Kingston: McGill–Queen's University Press.

Berg, Maxine 1988 "Women's Work, Mechanization and the Early Phases of Industrialization in England." In R. E. Pahl, ed., *On Work: Historical, Comparative and Theoretical Approaches.* Oxford, England: Basil Blackwell.

Berg, Peter 1999 "The Effects of High Performance Work Practices on Job Satisfaction in the United States Steel Industry." *Relations industrielles/Industrial Relations* 54(1): 111–34.

Berg, Peter, and Ann C. Frost 2005 "Dignity at Work for Low Wage, Low Skill Service Workers." *Relations Industrielles/Industrial Relations* 60(4): 657–82.

Berger, Ida E., Peggy Cunningham, and Minette E. Drumwright 2007 "Mainstreaming Corporate Social Responsibility: Developing Markets for Virtue." *California Management Review* 49(4): 132–57.

Berle, Adolf A., and Gardiner C. Means 1968 *The Modern Corporation and Private Property.* Rev. ed. New York: Harcourt, Brace and World. (Orig. pub. 1932.)

Bernard, Andre 2009 "Job Stability and Employment Duration in Manufacturing." *Perspectives on Labour and Income* (November): 5–14.

Bernardi, Fabrizio 2012 "Unequal Transitions: Selection Bias and the Compensatory Effect of Social Background in Educational

Careers." *Research in Social Stratification and Mobility* 30: 159–74.

Bernhardt, Annette, Michael W. Spiller, and Diana Polson 2013 "All Work and No Pay: Violations of Employment and Labor Laws in Chicago, Los Angeles and New York City." *Social Forces* 91(3): 725–46.

Bernstein, Paul 1997 *American Work Values: Their Origin and Development.* Albany: State University of New York Press.

Betcherman, Gordon 2000 "Structural Unemployment: How Important Are Labour Market Policies and Institutions?" *Canadian Public Policy* (July Supplement): S131–40.

Betcherman, Gordon, and Norm Leckie 1997 *Youth Employment and Education Trends in the 1980s and 1990s.* Working Paper No. W/03. Ottawa: Canadian Policy Research Networks.

Betcherman, Gordon, Kathryn McMullen, and Katie Davidman 1998 *Training for the New Economy: A Synthesis Report.* Ottawa: Canadian Policy Research Networks.

Betcherman, Gordon, Kathryn McMullen, Norm Leckie, and Christina Caron 1994 *The Canadian Workplace in Transition.* Kingston, ON: IRC Press.

Beynon, H. 1984 *Working for Ford.* 2nd ed. Harmondsworth, England: Penguin.

Bianchi, Suzanne M., and Melissa A. Milkie 2010 "Work and Family Research in the First Decade of the 21st Century." *Journal of Marriage & Family* 72(3): 705–25.

Birdi, Kamal, Peter Warr, and Andrew Oswald 1995 "Age Differences in Three Components of Employee Well-Being." *Applied Psychology: An International Review* 44: 345–73.

Black, Julie, and Yvonne Stanford 2005 "When Martha and Henry Are Poor: The Poverty of Alberta's Social Assistance Programs." In Trevor Harrison, ed., *The Return of the Trojan Horse: Alberta and the New World (Dis)Order* Montreal: Black Rose Books.

Blackburn, Robert M., Jennifer Jarman, and Janet Siltanen 1993 "The Analysis of Occupational Gender Segregation over Time and Place: Considerations of Measurement and Some New Evidence." *Work, Employment & Society* 7: 335–62.

Blackburn, R. M., and Michael Mann 1979 *The Working Class in the Labour Market.* London: Macmillan.

Blair-Loy, Mary 2003 *Competing Devotions: Career and Family among Women Executives.* Cambridge, MA: Harvard University Press.

Blau, Francine, and Ronald G. Ehrenberg 2000 *Gender and Family Issues in the Workplace.* New York: Russell Sage Foundation.

Blau, Francine D., and Lawrence M. Kahn 2007 "The Gender Pay Gap: Have Women Gone as Far as They Can?" *Academy of Management Perspectives* 21(1): 7–23.

Blau, Peter M., and W. Richard Scott 1963 *Formal Organizations: A Comparative Approach.* London: Routledge and Kegan Paul.

Blauner, Robert 1964 *Alienation and Freedom: The Factory Worker and His Industry.* Chicago: University of Chicago Press.

Bleasdale, Ruth 1981 "Class Conflict on the Canals of Upper Canada in the 1840s." *Labour/Le Travail* 7: 9–39.

Block, Fred 1990 *Postindustrial Possibilities: A Critique of Economic Discourse.* Berkeley, CA: University of California Press.

Block, Richard N., and Karen Roberts 2000 "A Comparison of Labour Standards in the United States and Canada." *Relations industrielles/Industrial Relations* 55(2): 273–306.

Bluestone, Barry, and Bennett Harrison 1982 *The Deindustrialization of America.* New York: Basic Books.

Bognanno, Mario F., and Kathryn J. Ready, eds. 1993 *The North American Free Trade Agreement: Labor, Industry, and Government Perspectives.* Westport, CT: Praeger.

Bolton, Sharon 2005 *Emotional Management in the Workplace.* London: Palgrave.

——— 2009 "Getting to the Heart of the Emotional Labor Process: A Reply to Brook." *Work Employment and Society* 23(3): 549–60.

Bolton, Sharon, and Carol Boyd 2003 "Trolley Dolly or Skilled Emotion Manager? Moving on from Hochschild's Managed Heart." *Work, Employment and Society* 17(2): 289–308.

Bolton, Sharon, and Maeve Houlihan 2010 "Bermuda Revisited: Management Power and Powerlessness in the Worker-Manager-Customer Triangle." *Work and Occupations* 37: 378–403.

Boudarbat, Brahim, Thomas Lemieux, and W. Craig Riddell 2010 *The Evolution of the Returns to Human Capital in Canada,*

1980–2005. Working Paper No. 53. Vancouver: Canadian Labour Market and Skills Researcher Network (CLSRN). http://www.clsrn.econ.ubc.ca/ home.php.

Boulet, Jac-André, and Laval Lavallée 1984 *The Changing Economic Status of Women.* Ottawa: Supply and Services Canada (Economic Council of Canada).

Bourdieu, Pierre 1986 "The Forms of Capital." In J. C. Richardson, ed., *Handbook of Theory and Research for the Sociology of Education.* New York: Greenwood Press.

Bowen, William G., Matthew M. Chingos, and Michael S. McPherson 2009 *Crossing the Finish Line: Completing College at America's Public Universities.* Princeton, NJ: Princeton University Press.

Bowes-Sperry, Lynn, and Jasmine Tata 1999 "A Multiperspective Framework of Sexual Harassment." In Gary Powell, ed., *Handbook of Gender and Work.* Thousand Oaks, CA: Sage.

Bowlby, Geoff 2000 "The School-to-Work Transition." *Perspectives on Labour and Income* 12(Spring): 43–48.

——— **2001** "The Labour Market: Year-End Review." *Perspectives on Labour and Income* 13(Spring): 9–19.

——— **2002** "Farmers Leaving the Field." *Perspectives on Labour and Income* 14(Spring): 23–28.

Boyd, Monica 2008 "A Socioeconomic Scale for Canada: Measuring Occupational Status from the Census." *Canadian Review of Sociology* 45(1): 51–91.

Boyd, Monica, and Michael Vickers 2000 "100 Years of Immigration in Canada." *Canadian Social Trends* (Autumn): 2–12.

Boyer, Robert, and Daniel Drache, eds. 1996 *States against Markets: The Limits of Globalization.* London: Routledge.

Bradbury, Bettina 1993 *Working Families: Age, Gender, and Daily Survival in Industrializing Montreal.* Toronto: McClelland & Stewart.

Bradley, Harriet 1989 *Men's Work, Women's Work: A Sociological History of the Sexual Division of Labour in Employment.* Cambridge: Polity Press.

Bradwin, Edmund 1972 *The Bunkhouse Man: A Study of Work and Pay in the Camps of Canada.* Toronto: University of Toronto Press. (Orig. pub. 1928.)

Brady, David, Regina S. Baker, and Ryan Finnigan 2013 "When Unionization Disappears: State-Level Unionization and Working Poverty in the United States." *American Sociological Review* 78(5): 872–96.

Brand, Jennie E., and Sarah H. Burgard 2008 "Effects of Job Displacement on Social Participation: Findings over the Life Course of a Cohort of Joiners." *Social Forces* 87(1): 211–42.

Braundy, Marcia 2011 *Men and Women and Tools: Bridging the Divide.* Halifax and Winnipeg: Fernwood Books.

Braverman, Harry 1974 *Labor and Monopoly Capital: The Degradation of Work in the Twentieth Century.* New York: Monthly Review Press.

Brenner, Mark D., David Farris, and John Ruser 2004 "'Flexible' Work Practices and Occupational Safety and Health: Exploring the Relationship between Cumulative Trauma Disorders and Workplace Transformation." *Industrial Relations* 43(1): 232–66.

Breslin, F. Curtis, Peter Smith, Mieke Koeboorn, and Hyunmi Lee 2006 "Is the Workplace Becoming Safer?" *Perspectives on Labour and Income* 20(Autumn): 36–41.

Brickner, Rachel K., and Christine Straehle 2010 "The Missing Link: Gender, Immigration Policy and the Live-in Caregiver Program in Canada." *Policy and Society* (2010): 309–20.

Brisbois, Richard 2003 *How Canada Stacks Up: The Quality of Work—An International Perspective.* Research Paper No. W/23. Ottawa: Canadian Policy Research Networks. http://www.cprn .org/doc.cfm?doc=499&l=en.

Briskin, Linda 2010 "Militancy and Resistance in the New Economy." In Norene J. Pupo and Mark P. Thomas, eds., *Interrogating the New Economy: Restructuring Work in the 21st Century* (pp. 217–34). Toronto: University of Toronto Press.

Briskin, Linda, and Patricia McDermott 1993 *Women Challenging Unions: Feminism, Democracy, and Militancy.* Toronto: University of Toronto Press.

Britton, Dana M., and Laura Logan 2008 "Gendered Organizations: Progress and Prospects." *Sociology Compass* 2(1): 107–21.

Broad, Dave, and Wayne Antony 1999 *Citizens or Consumers? Social Policy in a Market Society.* Halifax: Fernwood Publishing.

Brockman, Joan 2001 *Gender in the Legal Profession: Fitting or Breaking the Mould.* Vancouver: University of British Columbia Press.

Brohawn, Dawn K., ed. 1997 *Journey to an Ownership Culture: Insights from the ESOP Community.* Washington, DC: The ESOP Association and Scarecrow Press.

Brook, Paul 2009 "In Critical Defense of 'Emotional Labour': Refuting Bolton's Critique of Hochschild's Concept." *Work Employment and Society* 23(3): 531–48.

Brown, Leslie H. 1997 "Organizations for the 21st Century? Co-operatives and 'New' Forms of Organization." *Canadian Journal of Sociology* 22: 65–93.

Brown, Lorne 1987 *When Freedom Was Lost: The Unemployed, the Agitator, and the State.* Montreal: Black Rose Books.

Browne, Irene, and Joya Misra 2005 "Labor-Market Inequality: Intersections of Gender, Race, and Class." In Mary Romero and Eric Margolis, eds., *The Blackwell Companion to Social Inequalities.* Malden, MA: Blackwell.

Brym, Robert 1996 "The Third Rome and the End of History: Notes on Russia's Second Communist Revolution." *Canadian Review of Sociology and Anthropology* 33: 391–406.

Brynin, Malcolm 2006 "Gender, Technology and Jobs." *The British Journal of Sociology* 57(3): 437–53.

Buchanan, Ruth, and Sarah Koch-Schulte 2000 *Gender on the Line: Technology, Restructuring and the Reorganization of Work in the Call-Centre Industry.* Ottawa: Status of Women Canada. Catalogue no. SW21-44/2000E. http://www.swc-cfc.gc.ca.

Buckingham, Alan 1999 "Is There an Underclass in Britain?" *British Journal of Sociology* 50(1): 49–75.

Budd, John W. 2004 "Non-wage Forms of Compensation." *Journal of Labor Research* 25(4): 597–622.

Budig, Michelle, and Paula England 2001 "The Wage Penalty for Motherhood." *American Sociological Review* 66(April): 204–25.

Budig, Michelle, and Melissa Hodges 2010 "Differences in Disadvantage: Variation in the Motherhood Penalty across White Women's Earnings Distributions." *American Sociological Review* 75(5): 705–28.

Bunting, Madeline 2004 *Willing Slaves: How the Overwork Culture Is Ruling Our Lives.* London: HarperCollins.

Burawoy, Michael 1979 *Manufacturing Consent: Changes in the Labor Process under Monopoly Capitalism.* Chicago: University of Chicago Press.

——— **1984** "Karl Marx and the Satanic Mills: Factory Politics under Early Capitalism in England, the United States, and Russia." *American Journal of Sociology* 90: 247–82.

Burchell, Brendan, David Ladipo, and Frank Wilkinson, eds. 2002 *Job Insecurity and Work Intensification.* London and New York: Routledge.

Burke, Ronald, and Cary L. Cooper 2008 *The Long Work Hours Culture: Causes, Consequences, and Choices.* Bingley, England: Emerald Group Publishing.

Burke, Ronald J., and Mary C. Mattis 2000 *Women on Corporate Boards of Directors: International Challenges and Opportunities.* London, England: Kluwer Academic Publishers.

Burkhauser, Richard V, Maximillian D. Schmeiser, and Robert R. Weathers II 2012 "The Importance of Anti-discrimination and Workers' Compensation Laws on the Provision of Workplace Accommodations Following the Onset of a Disability." *Industrial and Labor Relations Review* 65(1): 161–80.

Burleton, Derek, Sonya Gulati, Connor McDonald, and Sonny Scarfone 2013 *Jobs in Canada: Where, What, and for Whom?* Toronto: TD Economics. http://www .td.com/document/PDF/economics/special/ JobsInCanada.pdf.

Burman, Patrick 1988 *Killing Time, Losing Ground: Experiences of Unemployment.* Toronto: Wall & Thompson.

——— **1996** *Poverty's Bonds: Power and Agency in the Social Relations of Welfare.* Toronto: Thompson Educational Publishing.

Burnham, J. 1941 *The Managerial Revolution.* Harmondsworth, England: Penguin.

Burns, T., and G. M. Stalker 1961 *The Management of Innovation.* London: Tavistock Publications.

Burrell, Gibson 2006 "Foucaldian and Postmodern Thought and the Analysis of Work." In Marek Korczynski, Randy Hodson, and Paul Edwards, eds., *Social Theory at Work.* Oxford, England: Oxford University Press.

Burstein, M., N. Tienharra, P. Hewson, and B. Warrander 1975 *Canadian Work Values: Findings of a Work Ethic Survey and a Job Satisfaction Survey.* Ottawa: Information Canada.

Busck, Ole, Herman Knudsen, and Jens Lind 2010 "The Transformation of Employee Participation: Consequences for the Work Environment." *Economic and Industrial Democracy* 31(3): 285–305.

Buttigieg, Donna M., Stephen J. Deery, and Roderick D. Iverson 2008 "Union Mobilization: A Consideration of the Factors Affecting the Willingness of Union Members to Take Industrial Action." *British Journal of Industrial Relations* 46(2): 248–67.

Byrne, Edmund F. 1990 *Work, Inc.: A Philosophical Inquiry.* Philadelphia: Temple University Press.

Byron, Kristin 2005 "A Meta-analytic Review of Work–Family Conflict and Its Antecedents." *Journal of Vocational Behavior* 67: 169–98.

Calliste, Agnes 1987 "Sleeping Car Porters in Canada: An Ethnically Submerged Split Labour Market." *Canadian Ethnic Studies* 19: 1–20.

Camfield, David 2006 "Neoliberalism and Working-Class Resistance in British Columbia: The Hospital Employees' Union Struggle, 2002–2004." *Labour/Le Travail* 57: 9–41.

——— **2011** "The 'Great Recession,' the Employers' Offensive and Canadian Public Sector Unions." *Socialist Studies* 7(1/2): 95–115.

Campbell, Jim 2011 "Multiple Job Holding in States in 2010." *Monthly Labor Review* (September): 32–33.

Campolieti, Michele 2012 "The Canada-U.S. Unemployment Rate Gap: A New Look with a New Decomposition for Cross-Country Differences in Unemployment Rates." *Canadian Public Policy* 38(3): 411–35.

Campolieti, Michele, Rafael Gomez, and Morley Gunderson 2013 "Managerial Hostility and Attitudes towards Unions: A Canada–U.S. Comparison." *Journal of Labor Research* 34: 99–119.

Camuffo, Arnaldo 2002 "The Changing Nature of Internal Labor Markets." *Journal of Management and Governance* 6(4): 281–94.

Canada 1969 *Canadian Industrial Relations: The Report of the Task Force on Labour Relations.* Ottawa: Queen's Printer.

——— **1984** *Report of the Commission on Equality in Employment* [The Abella Report]. Ottawa: Supply and Services.

——— **1985** *Employment Equity Act.* Chapter 23, 2nd Supplement, Revised Statutes of Canada.

——— **1992** *A Matter of Fairness. Report of the Social Committee on the Review of the Employment Equity Act.* Ottawa: House of Commons.

——— **2004** *Pay Equity: A New Approach to a Fundamental Right. Final Report, Pay Equity Task Force.* Ottawa: Department of Justice.

Canada, Department of Labour 1958 *Survey of Married Women Working for Pay in Eight Canadian Cities.* Ottawa: Queen's Printer.

Canadian Association of University Teachers (CAUT) 2013 *CAUT Almanac of Post-Secondary Education in Canada 2013–14.* Ottawa: CAUT.

Canadian Business 2013 "Canada's Top 50 Jobs 2013." April 12. http://www.canadianbusiness.com/companies-and-industries/canadas-top-50-jobs-2013-edition/.

Canadian Centre for Policy Alternatives (CCPA) 2013 *Overcompensating: A Fact Sheet on Executive Pay in Canada.* http://www.policyalternatives.ca/publications/facts-infographics/overcompensating.

Canadian Committee on Women in Engineering 1992 *More Than Just Numbers: Report of the Canadian Committee on Women in Engineering.* Fredericton: Faculty of Engineering, University of New Brunswick.

Canadian Immigrant 2011 "Night Shift as Security Officer, a Survival Job for Many Immigrants." (May 29). http://canadianimmigrant.ca/immigrant-stories/night-shift-as-security-officer-a-survival-job-for-many-immigrants.

Cant, Sarah, and Ursula Sharma 1995 "The Reluctant Profession: Homeopathy and the Search for Legitimacy." *Work, Employment & Society* 9: 743–62.

Cappelli, Peter 1999 The New Deal at Work: Managing the Market-Driven Workforce. Boston: Harvard Business School Press.

Caragata, Warren 1979 *Alberta Labour: A Heritage Untold.* Toronto: James Lorimer.

Card, David, Thomas Lemieux, and W. Craig Riddell 2004 "Unions and Wage Inequality." *Journal of Labor Research* 25(4): 519–62.

Carey, Malcolm 2007 "White-Collar Proletariat: Braverman, the Deskilling/ Upskilling of Social Work and the Paradoxical Life of the Agency Care Manager." *Journal of Social Work* 7(1): 93–114.

Carlson, Dawn S., and Joseph G. Grzywacz 2008 "Reflection and Future Directions on Measurement in Work–Family Research." In Karen Korabik, Donna S. Lero, and Denise L. Whitehead, eds., *Handbook of Work–Family Integration*. London: Elsevier.

Carrière, Yves, and Diane Galarneau 2011 "Delayed Retirement: A New Trend?" *Perspectives on Labour and Income* 23(4): 17–29.

—— **2012** "How Many Years to Retirement?" *Insights on Canadian Society* (December): 1–8. Ottawa: Statistics Canada. Cat. no. 75-006-X. http://www.statcan.gc.ca/pub/75-006-x/2012001/article/11750-eng.pdf.

Carroll, William K. 2004 *Corporate Power in a Globalizing World: A Study of Elite Social Organizations*. Toronto: Oxford University Press.

Carson, Paula P., Patricia A. Lanier, Kerry D. Carson, and Brandi N. Guidry 2000 "Clearing a Path through the Management Fashion Jungle: Some Preliminary Trailblazing." *Academy of Management Journal* 43(6): 1143–58.

Carter, Bob, Andy Dunford, Debra Howcroft, Helen Richardson, Andrew Smith, and Phil Taylor 2013 " 'Stressed out of My Box': Employee Experience of Lean Working and Occupational Ill-Health in Clerical Work in the U.K. Public Sector." *Work, Employment & Society* 27(5): 747–67.

Carter, Chris, and Frank Mueller 2002 "The 'Long March' of the Management Modernizers." *Human Relations* 55(11): 1325–54.

Cascio, Wayne F. 2002 *Responsible Restructuring: Creative and Profitable Alternatives to Layoffs*. San Francisco: Berrett-Koehler Publishers.

Cassell, Joan 1998 *The Woman in the Surgeon's Body*. Cambridge, MA: Harvard University Press.

Castells, Manuel 1996 *The Information Age: Economy, Society and Culture*. Vol. 1, *The Rise of the Network Society*. Oxford, England: Blackwell.

—— **1998** *The Information Age: Economy, Society and Culture*. Vol. 3, *End of Millennium*. Oxford, England: Blackwell.

Catalyst Canada 2012 *Financial Post 500 Senior Officers and Top Earners*. Toronto: Catalyst Canada.

CAW–Canada Research Group on CAMI 1993 *The CAMI Report: Lean Production in a Unionized Auto Plant*. Willowdale, ON: Canadian Auto Workers Research Department.

CBC News 2013 "Bangladesh Probes Garment Factory Fire That Killed 10." *CBC News World*, October 9.

Certified General Accountants Association of Canada 2012 *Youth Unemployment in Canada: Challenging Conventional Thinking?* www.cga.org/canada.

Chaison, Gary 2004 "Union Mergers in the U.S. and Abroad." *Journal of Labor Research* 25(1): 97–115.

Chan, Tak Wing 2000 "Revolving Doors Reexamined: Occupational Sex Segregation over the Life Course." *American Sociological Review* 64: 86–96.

Chandler, Alfred D. Jr. 1977 *The Visible Hand: The Managerial Revolution in American Business*. Cambridge, MA: Harvard University Press.

Charles, Maria 2011 "A World of Difference: International Trends in Women's Economic Status." *Annual Review of Sociology* 37: 355–71.

Charles, Maria, and David B. Grusky 2004. *Occupational Ghettos: The Worldwide Segregation of Women and Men*. Stanford, CA: Stanford University Press.

Charles, Maria, and Karen Bradley 2009 "Indulging Our Gendered Selves? Sex Segregation by Field of Study in 44 Countries." *American Journal of Sociology* 114(4): 924–76.

Chase, Steven, and Tavia Grant 2013 "Experts Debate How Much National Household Survey Statistics Count." *Globe and Mail*, May 6.

Chen, Zhen Xiong, and Samuel Aryee 2007 "Delegation and Employee Work Outcomes: An Examination of the Cultural Context of Mediating Processes in China." *Academy of Management Journal* 50(1): 226–38.

Cherns, A. 1976 "The Principles of Socio-Technical Design." *Human Relations* 29: 783–92.

Child, John 1985 "Managerial Strategies, New Technology and the Labour Process." In David Knights, Hugh Willmott, and David Collison, eds., *Job Redesign: Critical Perspectives on the Labour Process*. Aldershot, England: Gower.

Chow, Angela, Harvey Krahn, and Nancy Galambos 2013 "Developmental Trajectories of Work Values and Job Entitlement Beliefs in the Transition to Adulthood." *Developmental Psychology* [advance online publication: doi: 10.1037/a0035].

Chui, Tina, Kelly Tran, and John Flanders 2005 "Chinese Canadians: Enriching the Cultural Mosaic." *Canadian Social Trends* (Spring): 24–32.

Chung, Lucy 2006 "Education and Earnings." *Perspectives on Labour and Income* 18(3): 28–35.

Citizenship and Immigration Canada 2009 *Annual Report to Parliament on Immigration*. Ottawa: Citizenship and Immigration Canada. http:// www.cic.gc.ca/english/pdf/ pub/ immigration2009_e.pdf.

Citizenship and Immigration Canada 2012 *Annual Report to Parliament on Immigration, 2012*. http://www.cic.gc.ca/ENGLISH/ RESOURCES/publications/annual-report-2012/index.asp

Clark, Andrew, Andrew Oswald, and Peter Warr 1996 "Is Job Satisfaction U-Shaped in Age?" *Journal of Occupational and Organizational Psychology* 69: 57–81.

Clark, R. D. 1982 "Worker Participation in Health and Safety in Canada." *International Labour Review* 121: 199–206.

Clark, Warren 1999 "Search for Success: Finding Work after Graduation." *Canadian Social Trends* (Summer): 10–15.

———— **2000** "100 Years of Education." *Canadian Social Trends* (Winter): 3–7.

Clarke, Louise, and Larry Haiven 1999 "Workplace Change and Continuous Bargaining: Saskatoon Chemicals Then and Now." *Relations industrielles/Industrial Relations* 54(1): 168–91.

Clarke, Simon 2005 "Post-socialist Trade Unions: China and Russia." *Industrial Relations Journal* 36(1): 2–18.

Clarke, Simon, Lee Chang-Hee, and Li Qi 2004 "Collective Consultation and Industrial Relations in China." *British Journal of Industrial Relations* 42(2): 235–54.

Clarke, Thomas, and Stewart Clegg 1998 *Changing Paradigms: The Transformation of Management Knowledge for the 21st Century*. London: HarperCollins Business.

Clegg, Stewart, and Carmen Baumeler 2010 "Essai: From Iron Cages to Liquid Modernity." *Organization Studies* 31(12): 1713–33.

Clemenson, Heather A. 1992 "Are Single Industry Towns Diversifying? A Look at Fishing, Mining and Wood-Based Communities." *Perspectives on Labour and Income* (Spring): 31–43.

Clement, Wallace 1981 *Hardrock Mining: Industrial Relations and Technological Changes at Inco*. Toronto: McClelland & Stewart.

Clement, Wallace, and John Myles 1994 *Relations of Ruling: Class and Gender in Postindustrial Societies*. Montreal and Kingston: McGill–Queen's University Press.

Cleveland, Gordon, Morley Gunderson, and Douglas Hyatt 2003 "Union Effects in Low-Wage Services: Evidence from Canadian Childcare." *Industrial and Labor Relations Review* 56(2): 295–305.

Cobb, Clifford, Ted Halstead, and Jonathan Rowe 1995 "If the GDP Is Up, Why Is America Down?" *Atlantic Monthly* (October): 60–74.

Cockburn, Cynthia 1991 *In the Way of Women: Men's Resistance to Sex Equality in Organizations*. Ithaca, NY: ILR Press.

Cohen, Marjorie Griffen 1988 *Women's Work, Markets and Economic Development in Nineteenth-Century Ontario*. Toronto: University of Toronto Press.

Cohen, Ronald 2010 *Work and Sing: The History of Occupational and Labor Songs in the United States*. Champaign IL: University of Illinois Press.

Colic-Peisker, Val, and Farida Tilbury 2006 "Employment Niches for Recent Refugees: Segmented Labour Markets in Twenty-First Century Australia." *Journal of Refugee Studies* 19(2): 203–29.

Collins, J. C., and J. I. Porras 1994 *Built to Last: Successful Habits of Visionary Companies*. New York: HarperCollins.

Collins, Randall 1990 "Market Closure and the Conflict Theory of Professions." In Michael Burrage and Rolf Torstendahl, eds., *Professions in Theory and History: Rethinking the Study of the Professions*. London, England: Sage.

Collinson, David, and Stephen Ackroyd
2005 "Resistance, Misbehaviour, and
Dissent." In Stephen Ackroyd, R. Batt,
P. Thompson, and P. S. Tolbert, eds., *The
Oxford Handbook of Work and Organization.*
Oxford, England: Oxford University Press.

Coltrane, Scott 1996 *Family Man: Fatherhood,
Housework, and Gender Equity.* New York:
Oxford University Press.

———— **2000** "Research on Household
Labor: Modeling and Measuring the Social
Embeddedness of Routine Family Work."
Journal of Marriage and the Family 62(4):
1208–33.

Comish, Shaun 1993 *The Westray Tragedy: A
Miner's Story.* Halifax: Fernwood Publishing.

Commission for Labor Cooperation 2003
*North American Labor Markets: Main Changes
since NAFTA.* Washington, DC: Secretariat of
the Commission for Labor Cooperation.

Conference Board of Canada 2005 *Learning
and Development Outlook: Moving beyond
the Plateau—Time to Leverage Learning
Investment.* Ottawa: Conference Board of
Canada.

———— **2013** *Return on Investment in Tertiary
Education.* Ottawa: Conference Board.
http://www.conferenceboard.ca/hcp/details/
education/tertiary.aspx.

Conley, James R. 1988 "More Theory, Less
Fact? Social Reproduction and Class Conflict
in a Sociological Approach to Working-
Class History." *Canadian Journal of Sociology*
13:73–102.

Conlin, M. 2009 "Gap to Employees:
Work Wherever, Whenever You Want."
BusinessWeek.com, September 17. http://www.
businessweek.com/careers/ managementiq/
archives/2009/09/ gap_to_employee.html.

Conrad, Peter 1987 "Wellness in the
Workplace: Potentials and Pitfalls of Work-
Site Health Promotion." *Milbank Quarterly*
65:255–75.

Conway, Hugh, and Jens Svenson 1998
"Occupational Injury and Illness Rates,
1992–96: Why They Fell." *Monthly Labor
Review* (November): 36–58.

**Cooke, Gordon B., Isik U. Zeytinoglu, and
James Chowhan 2009** "Barriers to Training
Access." *Perspectives on Labour and Income*
21(Autumn): 45–56.

Cool, Julie 2010 *Wage Gap between Women
and Men.* Ottawa: Library of Parliament
Research Paper.

Copp, Terry 1974 *The Anatomy of Poverty: The
Condition of the Working Class in Montreal,
1897–1929.* Toronto: McClelland & Stewart.

Corak, Miles, ed. 1998 *Labour Markets,
Social Institutions, and the Future of Canada's
Children.* Ottawa: Statistics Canada and
Human Resources Development Canada.

Corman, June, and Meg Luxton 2007 "Social
Reproduction and the Changing Dynamics
of Unpaid Household and Caregiving Work."
In Vivian Shalla and Wallace Clement, eds.,
Work in Tumultuous Times: Critical Perspectives
(pp. 262–88). Montreal and Kingston:
McGill–Queen's University Press.

Cornish, Mary 2007 "Closing the Global
Gender Pay Gap: Securing Justice for
Women's Work." *Comparative Labor Law
and Policy Journal* 28(2): 219–49.

Correll, Shelley J. 2007 "Getting a Job: Is
There a Motherhood Penalty?" *American
Journal of Sociology* 112(5): 1297–1338.

**Correll, Shelley J., Erin L. Kelly, Lindsey
Trimble O'Connor, and Joan C. Williams
2014** "Redesigning, Redefining Work."
Work and Occupations 41(1): 3–17.

Coser, Lewis A. 1967 "Greedy Organisations."
European Journal of Sociology 8(2).

———— **1971** *Masters of Sociological Thought:
Ideas in Historical and Social Context.*
New York: Harcourt Brace Jovanovich.

Côté, James, and John M. Bynner 2008
"Changes in the Transition to Adulthood in
the U.K. and Canada: The Role of Structure
and Agency in Emerging Adulthood." *Journal
of Youth Studies* 11(3): 251–68.

Coupland, Douglas 1993 *Generation X:
Tales for an Accelerated Culture.* New York:
St. Martin's Press.

Courpasson, David, and Stewart Clegg 2012
"The Polyarchic Bureaucracy: Cooperative
Resistance in the Workplace and the
Construction of a New Political Structure of
Organizations." *Research in the Sociology of
Organizations* 34:55–79.

**Coverdill, James E., and Pierre Oulevey
2007** "Getting Contingent Work: Insights
into On-Call Work, Matching Processes,
and Staffing Technology from a Study
of Substitute Teachers." *The Sociological
Quarterly* 48(3): 533–57.

Coverman, Shelley 1989 "Role Overload,
Role Conflict, and Stress: Addressing
Consequences of Multiple Role Demands."
Social Forces 67(4): 965–82.

Cranford, Cynthia J. 2004 "Gendered Resistance: Organizing Justice for Janitors in Los Angeles." In Jim Stanford and Leah F. Vosko, eds., *Challenging the Market: Struggles to Regulate Work and Income* (pp. 309–29). Montreal and Kingston: McGill–Queen's University Press.

Cranford, Cynthia, and Dianna Miller 2013 "Emotion Management from the Client's Perspective: The Case of Personal Home Care." *Work Employment & Society* 27(5): 785–801.

Cranswick, Kelly 2003 *General Social Survey Cycle 16: Caring for an Aging Society.* Ottawa: Statistics Canada. Cat. no. 89-582-XIE.

Cranswick, Kelly, and Donna Dosman 2008 "Eldercare: What We Know Today." *Canadian Social Trends* (October): 48–56.

Craven, Paul 1980 *An Impartial Umpire: Industrial Relations and the Canadian State, 1900–1911.* Toronto: University of Toronto Press.

Creese, Gillian 1988–89 "Exclusion or Solidarity? Vancouver Workers Confront the Oriental Problem." *B.C. Studies* 80: 24–51.

——— 1999 *Contracting Masculinity: Gender, Class, and Race in a White-Collar Union, 1944–1994.* Don Mills, ON: Oxford University Press.

——— 2007 "Racializing Work/Reproducing White Privilege." In Vivian Shalla and Wallace Clement, eds., *Work in Tumultuous Times: Critical Perspectives* (pp. 192–226). Montreal and Kingston: McGill–Queen's University Press.

Creese, Gillian, and Edith Ngene Kambere 2003 "What Colour Is Your English?" *Canadian Review of Sociology and Anthropology* 40(5): 565–73.

Crocker, Diane, and Valery Kalemba 1999 "The Incidence and Impact of Women's Experiences of Sexual Harassment in Canadian Workplaces." *Canadian Review of Sociology and Anthropology* 36(4): 541–55.

Crompton, Susan 2011 "What's Stressing the Stressed? Main Sources of Stress among Workers." *Canadian Social Trends* (Winter): 46–53.

Crompton, Susan, and Michael Vickers 2000 "One Hundred Years of Labour Force." *Canadian Social Trends* (Summer): 2–14.

Crouch, Colin 1982 *Trade Unions: The Logic of Collective Action.* Glasgow: Fontana.

Culbert, Samuel A., and Scott J. Schroeder 2003 "Getting Hierarchy to Work." In Subir Chowdhury, ed., *Organization 21C:*

Someday All Organizations Will Lead This Way (pp. 105–23). Upper Saddle River, NJ: Financial Times Prentice Hall.

Cunningham, Ian, and Philip James 2010 "Strategies for Union Renewal in the Context of Public Sector Outsourcing." *Economic and Industrial Democracy* 31(1): 34–61.

Cunningham, Mick 2007 "Influences of Women's Employment on the Gendered Division of Household Labor over the Life Course: Evidence from a 31-Year Panel Study." *Journal of Family Issues* 28(3): 422–44.

Dabboussy, Maria, and Sharanjit Uppal 2012 "Work Absences in 2011." *Perspectives on Labour and Income* (Summer): 3–11.

Dalton, Melville 1959 *Men Who Manage: Fusions of Feeling and Theory in Administration.* New York: John Wiley & Sons.

Damaske, Sarah 2011 "A 'MAJOR CAREER WOMEN'? How Women Develop Early Expectations about Work." *Gender and Society* 25(4): 409–30.

Danford, Andy, M. Richardson, P. Stewart, S. Tailby, and M. Upchurch 2004 "High Performance Work Systems and Workplace Partnership: A Case Study of Aerospace Workers." *New Technology, Work and Employment* 19(3): 14–29.

Daniels, Arlene Kaplan 1987 "Invisible Work." *Social Problems* 34(5): 403–15.

Danysk, Cecilia 1995 *Hired Hands: Labour and the Development of Prairie Agriculture, 1880 to 1930.* Don Mills, ON: Oxford University Press.

Das Gupta, Tania 1996 *Racism and Paid Work.* Toronto: Garamond Press.

Davies, Lorraine, and Patricia J. Carrier 1999 "The Importance of Power Relations for the Division of Household Labour." *Canadian Journal of Sociology* 24(1): 35–51.

Davies, Scott, and Neil Guppy 1998 "Race and Canadian Education." In Vic Satzewich, ed., *Racism and Social Inequality in Canada: Concepts, Controversies and Strategies of Resistance* (pp. 131–56). Toronto: Thompson Educational Publishing.

——— 2006 *The Schooled Society: An Introduction to the Sociology of Education.* Don Mills, ON: Oxford University Press.

Davies, Scott, and Vicky Maldonado 2009 "Changing Times, Stubborn Disparities: Explaining Socio-economic Stratification in Canadian Schooling." In Edward Grabb and Neil Guppy, eds., *Social Inequality in Canada:*

Patterns, Problems, and Policies. 5th ed. Toronto: Pearson/Prentice Hall.

Davies, Scott, Clayton Mosher, and Bill O'Grady 1996 "Educating Women: Gender Inequalities among Canadian University Graduates." *Canadian Review of Sociology and Anthropology* 33: 125–42.

Davis, Gerald F. 2010 "Job Design Meets Organizational Sociology." *Journal of Organizational Behavior* 31: 302–8.

Davis, Kelly D., W. Benjamin Goodman, Amy E. Pirretti, and David M. Almeida 2008 "Nonstandard Work Schedules, Perceived Family Well-Being, and Daily Stressors." *Journal of Marriage and the Family* 70(4): 991–1003.

Davis, Kingsley, and Wilbert E. Moore 1945 "Some Principles of Stratification." *American Sociological Review* 10: 242–49.

Davis-Blake, Alison, and Joseph P. Broschak 2009 "Outsourcing and the Changing Nature of Work." *The Annual Review of Sociology* 35: 321–40.

D'Cruz, Premilla, and Ernesto Noronha 2011 "High Commitment Management Practices Re-examined: The Case of Indian Call Centres." *Economic and Industrial Democracy* 33(2): 185–205.

de Gilder, Dick 2003 "Commitment, Trust and Work Behaviour: The Case of Contingent Workers." *Personnel Review* 32(5): 588–604.

Dehnen, Veronika 2013 "Transnational Alliances for Negotiating International Framework Agreements: Power Relations and Bargaining Processes between Global Union Federations and European Works Councils." *British Journal of Industrial Relations* 51(3): 577–600.

de Lange, Annet H., Toon W. Taris, Michael A.J. Kompier, Irene L.D. Houtman, and Paulien M. Bongers 2003 " 'The *Very* Best of the Millennium': Longitudinal Research and the Demand-Control-(Support) Model." *Journal of Occupational Health Psychology* 8(4): 282–305.

DeLong, David W. 2004 *Lost Knowledge: Confronting the Threat of an Aging Workforce.* New York: Oxford University Press.

Déom, Esther, Jean-Noël Grenier, and Marie-Pierre Beaumont 2009 "Union–Management Relations in Quebec." In Morley Gunderson and Daphne Taras, eds. *Canadian Labour and Employment Relations.* 6th ed. Toronto: Pearson Addison Wesley.

De Santis, Solange 1999 *Life on the Line: One Woman's Tale of Work, Sweat, and Survival.* New York: Doubleday.

Devane, Tom 2004 *Integrating Lean Six Sigma and High-Performance Organizations: Leading the Charge toward Dramatic, Rapid and Sustainable Improvement.* San Francisco: Pfeiffer.

de Vaus, David, and Ian McAllister 1991 "Gender and Work Orientation: Values and Satisfaction in Western Europe." *Work and Occupations* 18: 72–93.

Devinatz, Victor G. 2013 " 'The Crisis of U.S. Trade Unionism and What Needs to Be Done." *Labor Law Journal* 64(1): 5–19.

De Witte, Hans, and Katharina Näswall 2003 " 'Objective' vs 'Subjective' Job Insecurity: Consequences of Temporary Work for Job Satisfaction and Organizational Commitment in Four European Countries." *Economic and Industrial Democracy* 24(2): 149–88.

de Witte, Marco, and Bram Steijn 2000 "Automation, Job Content, and Underemployment." *Work, Employment & Society* 14(2): 245–64.

Dickson, Tony, and Hugh V. McLachlan 1989 "In Search of the Spirit of Capitalism: Weber's Misinterpretation of Franklin." *Sociology* 23: 81–89.

Dickson, Tony, Hugh V. McLachlan, Phil Prior, and Kim Swales 1988 "Big Blue and the Unions: IBM, Individualism and Trade Union Strategy." *Work, Employment & Society* 2: 506–20.

DiGiacomo, Gordon 1999 "Aggression and Violence in the Workplace." *Workplace Gazette: An Industrial Relations Quarterly* 2(2): 72–85.

di Leonardo, Micaela 1987 "The Female World of Cards and Holidays: Women, Families, and the Work of Kinship." *Signs* 12(3): 440–53.

Diprete, Thomas A., and Whitman T. Soule 1988 "Gender and Promotion in Segmented Job Ladder Systems." *American Sociological Review* 53: 26–40.

Dixon, Marc 2008 "Movements, Countermovements and Policy Adoption: The Case of Right-to-Work Activism." *Social Forces* 87(1): 473–500.

Dolton, Peter, and Panu Pelkonen 2008 "The Wage Effects of Computer Use: Evidence from WERS 2004." *British Journal of Industrial Relations* 46(4): 587–630.

Dorow, Sara, and Sara O'Shaughnessy 2013
"Fort McMurray, Wood Buffalo and the
Oil/Tar Sands: Revising the Sociology of
Community. Introduction to the Special Issue."
Canadian Journal of Sociology 38(2): 121–40.

Doucet, Andrea 2001 "You See the Need
Perhaps More Clearly Than I Have:
Exploring Gendered Processes of Domestic
Responsibility." *Journal of Family Issues* 22(3):
328–57.

———— **2006** *Do Men Mother? Fathering,
Care and Domestic Responsibility.* Toronto:
University of Toronto Press.

**Doucet, Christine, Michael Smith, and
Claire Durand 2012** "Pay Structure, Female
Representation and the Gender Pay Gap
Among University Professors." *Relations
Industrielles/Industrial Relations* 67(1): 51–75.

Doucouliagos, Chris 1995 "Worker
Participation and Productivity in Labor-
Managed and Participatory Capitalist
Firms: A Meta-analysis." *Industrial and
Labor Relations Review* 49(1): 58–77.

Downie, Bryan, and Mary L. Coates 1995
"Barriers, Challenges, and Future Directions."
In Bryan Downie and Mary L. Coates, eds.,
*Managing Human Resources in the 1990s and
Beyond: Is the Workplace Being Transformed?*
Kingston, ON: IRC Press.

Doyle, Joyce 1980 Our Family History.
Unpublished family history.

Drache, Daniel 1994 "Lean Production
in Japanese Auto Transplants in Canada."
Canadian Business Economics (Spring): 45–59.

Drache, Daniel, and Meric S. Gertler 1991
"The World Economy and the Nation-State:
The New International Order." In D. Drache
and M. S. Gertler, eds., *The New Era of
Global Competition: State Policy and Market
Power.* Montreal and Kingston: McGill–
Queen's University Press.

Drolet, Marie 2002 "The Male–Female Wage
Gap." *Perspectives on Labour and Income*
14(Spring): 29–37.

———— **2011** "Why Has the Gender Wage
Gap Narrowed?" *Perspectives on Labour and
Income* (Spring): 3–13.

Drucker, Peter F. 1993 *Post-capitalist Society.*
New York: HarperBusiness.

Drudy, Sheelagh 2008 "Gender Balance/
Gender Bias: The Teaching Profession and
the Impact of Feminization." *Gender and
Education* 20(4): 309–23.

Duchesne, Doreen 2004 "More Seniors at
Work." *Perspectives on Labour and Income*
16(Spring): 55–67.

Duffy, Ann, and Norene Pupo 1992 *Part-
Time Paradox: Connecting Gender, Work and
Family.* Toronto: McClelland & Stewart.

Duffy, Mignon 2011 *Making Care Count: A
Century of Gender, Race and Paid Care Work.*
New Brunswick, NJ: Rutgers University Press.

**Duncan, Greg J., Martha S. Hill, and Saul
D. Hoffman 1988** "Welfare Dependence
Within and Across Generations." *Science*
(January): 467–71.

**Duncan, Greg J., Aletha C. Huston, and
Thomas S. Weisner 2007** *Higher Ground:
New Hope for the Working Poor and Their
Children.* New York: Russell Sage.

**Duncan, Greg. J., W. Jean Yeung, Jeanne
Brooks-Gunn, and Judith R. Smith 1998**
"How Much Does Childhood Poverty Affect
the Life Chances of Children?" *American
Sociological Review* 63: 406–23.

Dunn, Andrew 2010 "The 'Dole or
Drudgery' Dilemma: Education, the Work
Ethic and Unemployment." *Social Policy &
Administration* 44(1): 1–19.

Dunne, Gillian 1996 *Lesbian Lifestyles:
Women's Work and the Politics of Sexuality.*
Toronto: University of Toronto Press.

Durkheim, Émile 1960 *The Division of Labour
in Society.* New York: Free Press. (Orig. pub.
1897.)

Duxbury, Linda 2004 *Dealing with
Work-Life Issues in the Workplace: Standing
Still is Not an Option.* Don Wood Lecture
in Industrial Relations, Queen's University.
http://irc.queensu.ca/gallery/1/
dwls-linda-duxbury-on-work-life-conflict.pdf.

**Duxbury, Linda, and Christopher Higgins
2001** *Work–Life Balance in the New
Millennium.* Ottawa: Canadian Policy
Research Networks.

**Duxbury, Linda, and Christopher Higgins
2012** *Key Findings: Revisiting Work–Life
Issues in Canada—The 2011–12 National
Study on Balancing Work and Caregiving
in Canada.* http://newsroom.carleton.ca/
wp-content/files/2012-National-Work-Key-
Findings.pdf.

**Duxbury, Linda, Christopher Higgins,
and Sean Lyons 2008** *Reducing Work–Life
Conflict: What Works? What Doesn't—
Executive Summary.* Ottawa: Health Canada.

http://www.hc-sc.gc.ca/ewh-semt/pubs/occup-travail/balancing-equilibre/sum-res-eng.php.

Duxbury, Linda, Christopher Higgins, and Bonnie Schroder 2009 *Balancing Paid Work and Caregiving Responsibilities: A Closer Look at Family Caregivers in Canada.* Ottawa: CPRN.

Easterlin, Richard 1980 *Birth and Fortune: The Impact of Numbers on Personal Welfare.* New York: Basic Books.

Eaton, Adrienne E., and Thomas Nocerino 2000 "The Effectiveness of Health and Safety Committees: Results of a Survey of Public-Sector Workplaces." *Industrial Relations: A Journal of Economy and Society* 39: 265–90.

Eaton, Jonathan, and Anil Verma 2006 "Does 'Fighting Back' Make a Difference? The Case of the Canadian Auto Workers Union." *Journal of Labor Research* 27(2): 187–212.

Economic Council of Canada 1990 *Good Jobs, Bad Jobs: Employment in the Service Economy.* Ottawa: Supply and Services Canada.

——— 1992 *Pulling Together: Productivity, Innovation, and Trade.* Ottawa: Supply and Services Canada.

Economist 1996 "Cultural Explanations: The Man in the Baghdad Café." November 9, 23–26.

——— 2005 "The Tiger in Front—India." March 3, 3–5.

——— 2009 *Country Profiles—China, India, Russia.* Economist Intelligence Unit. http://www.eiu.com.

——— 2013 "Coming Home: Reshoring Manufacturing." January 19.

Edmans, Alex 2012 "The Link between Job Satisfaction and Firm Value, with Implications for Corporate Social Responsibility." *Academy of Management Perspectives* 26(4): 1–19.

Edwards, Richard C. 1979 *Contested Terrain: The Transformation of the Workplace in the Twentieth Century.* New York: Basic Books.

Egels-Zandén, Niklas 2011 "Clean Clothes Campaign." In Thomas Hale and David Held, eds., *Handbook of Transnational Governance: Institutions and Innovations.* Cambridge: Polity Press.

Egels-Zandén, Niklas, and Peter Hyllman 2006 "Exploring the Effects of Union-NGO Relationships on Corporate Responsibility: The Case of the Swedish Clean Clothes Campaign." *Journal of Business Ethics* 64: 303–16.

Ehrenreich, Barbara 2001 *Nickel and Dimed: On (Not) Getting By in America.* New York: Henry Holt and Company.

Ehrenreich, Barbara, and Arlie Russell Hochschild, eds. 2002 *Global Woman: Nannies, Maids, and Sex Workers in the New Economy.* New York: Metropolitan Books.

Eichler, Margrit, and Patricia Albanese 2007 "What Is Household Work? A Critique of Assumptions Underlying Empirical Studies of Housework and an Alternative Approach." *Canadian Journal of Sociology* 32(2): 227-58.

Einarsen, Ståle 1999 "The Nature and Causes of Bullying at Work." *International Journal of Manpower* 20(1/2): 16–27.

Elliott, Anthony, and John Urry 2010 *Mobile Lives.* New York: Routledge.

Elmuti, Dean, Julian Grunewald, and Dereje Abebe 2010 "Consequences of Outsourcing Strategies on Employee Quality of Work Life, Attitudes, and Performance." *Journal of Business Strategies* 27(2): 177–203.

Ely, Robin, Hermina Ibarra, and Deborah Kolk 2013 "Women Rising: The Unseen Barriers." *Harvard Business Review* (September): 61–66.

Emery, F. E., and Einar Thorsrud 1969 *Form and Content in Industrial Democracy.* London, England: Tavistock Publications.

Engels, Friedrich 1971 *The Condition of the Working Class in England.* Oxford: Basil Blackwell. (Orig. pub. 1845.)

Engineers Canada 2012 *Canadian Engineers for Tomorrow: Trends in Engineering Enrollment and Degrees Awarded, 2007–11.* Ottawa: Engineers Canada.

England, Paula 2010 "The Gender Revolution: Uneven and Stalled." *Gender and Society* 24(2): 149–66.

Equal Pay Coalition 2008 *A Framework for Action on Pay Equity in Ontario: A Special 20th Anniversary Report Contributing to Ontario's Future.* Toronto: Equal Pay Coalition.

Ergeneli, Azize, Arzu Ilsev, and Pinar Bayhan Karapinar 2010 "Work–Family Conflict and Job Satisfaction Relationship: The Roles of Gender and Interpretive Habits." *Gender, Work & Organization* 17(6): 679–95.

Estrin, Saul, and Virginie Pérotin 1987 "Producer Cooperatives: The British Experience." *International Review of Applied Economics* 1(2): 152–75.

Etzioni, Amitai 1975 *A Comparative Analysis of Complex Organizations.* 2nd ed. New York: Free Press.

Evans, Peter, and James E. Rauch 1999 "Bureaucracy and Growth: A Cross-National Analysis of the Efforts of 'Weberian' State Structures on Economic Growth." *American Sociological Review* 64:748–65.

Everett, Jeffery 2002 "Organizational Research and the Praxeology of Pierre Bourdieu." *Organizational Research Methods* 5:56–80.

Evetts, Julia 2003 "The Sociological Analysis of Professionalism: Occupational Change in the Modern World." *International Sociology* 18(2): 395–415.

Faas, Caitlin, Mark J. Benson, and Christine E. Kaestle 2013 "Parent Resources during Adolescence: Effects on Education and Careers in Young Adulthood." *Journal of Youth Studies* 16(2): 151–71.

Fairlie, Robert, and Christopher Woodruff 2005 *Mexican Entrepreneurship: A Comparison of Self-Employment in Mexico and the United States.* Working Paper no. 11527. Cambridge, MA: National Bureau of Economic Research.

Fairris, David, and Edward Levine 2004 "Declining Union Density in Mexico, 1984–2000." *Monthly Labor Review* 127(9): 10–17.

Fang, Tony 2009 "Workplace Responses to Vacancies and Skill Shortages in Canada." *International Journal of Manpower* 30(4): 326–48.

Fast, Janet E., and Judith A. Frederick 1996 "Working Arrangements and Time Stress." *Canadian Social Trends* (Winter): 14–19.

Feldberg, Roslyn, and Evelyn Nakano Glenn 1979 "Male and Female: Job versus Gender Models in the Sociology of Work." *Social Problems* 26:524–38.

Felstead, Alan, Nick Jewson, and Sally Walters 2003 "Managerial Control of Employees Working at Home." *British Journal of Industrial Relations* 41(2): 241–64.

Felt, Lawrence, and Peter Sinclair 1992 "Everybody Does It: Unpaid Work in a Rural Peripheral Region." *Work, Employment & Society* 6:43–64.

Feng, Wang 2008 *Boundaries and Categories: Rising Inequality in Post-socialist Urban China.* Redwood City, CA: Stanford University Press.

Ferber, Marianne A., and Jane Waldfogel 1998 "The Long-Term Consequences of Nontraditional Employment." *Monthly Labor Review* (May): 3–12.

Fernandez-Mateo, Isabel 2009 "Cumulative Gender Disadvantage in Contract Employment." *American Journal of Sociology* 114(1): 871–923.

Fernie, Sue, and David Metcalf 1998 *(Not) Hanging on the Telephone: Payment Systems in the New Sweatshop.* London, England: Centre for Economic Performance, London School of Economics.

Ferrao, Vincent 2010 "Paid Work." In *Women in Canada: A Gender-Based Statistical Report.* 6th ed. Ottawa: Statistics Canada. Catalogue No. 89-503-X.

Ferus-Comelo, Anibel 2008 "Mission Impossible? Raising Labor Standards in the ICT Sector." *Labor Studies Journal* 33(2): 141–62.

Feuchtwang, Stephen 1982 "Occupational Ghettos." *Economy and Society* 11:251–91.

Fevre, Ralph 2007 "Employment Insecurity and Social Theory: The Power of Nightmares." *Work, Employment & Society* 21(3): 517–35.

Figart, Deborah M., and June Lapidus 1996 "The Impact of Comparable Worth on Earnings Inequality." *Work and Occupations* 23:297–318.

Fineman, Stephen 2009 " 'When I'm Sixty Five': The Shaping and Shapers of Retirement Identity and Experience." In Philip Hancock and Melissa Tyler, eds., *The Management of Everyday Life.* New York: Palgrave Macmillan.

Finnie, Ross, and Ronald Meng 2007 "Literacy and Employability." *Perspectives on Labour and Income* 19(2): 44–52.

Firebaugh, Glenn, and Brian Harley 1995 "Trends in Job Satisfaction in the United States by Race, Gender, and Type of Occupation." *Research in Sociology of Work* 5:87–104.

Fisher, Cynthia D. 2003 "Why Do Lay People Believe That Satisfaction and Performance Are Correlated? Possible Sources of a Commonsense Theory." *Journal of Organizational Behavior* 24(6): 753–77.

Fisher, Susan R., and Margaret A. White 2000 "Downsizing in a Learning Organization: Are There Hidden Costs?" *Academy of Management Review* 25(1): 244–51.

Fleming, Peter, and Andrew Sturdy 2011 " 'Being Yourself' in the Electronic Sweatshop: New Forms of Normative Control." *Human Relations* 64(2): 177–200.

Fleury, Dominique 2008 "Low-Income Children." *Perspectives on Labour and Income* 20(Summer): 51–60.

Florida, Richard 2002 *The Rise of the Creative Class: And How It's Transforming Work, Leisure, Community and Everyday Life.* New York: Basic Books.

———— **2005** *The Flight of the Creative Class: The New Global Competition for Talent.* New York: HarperCollins.

Fogg, Neeta P., Paul E. Harrington, and Brian T. Mcmahon 2010 "The Impact of the Great Recession upon the Unemployment of Americans with Disabilities." *Journal of Vocational Rehabilitation* 33: 193–202.

Foot, David K. 2001 *Boom, Bust & Echo 2000: Profiting from the Demographic Shift in the 21st Century.* Toronto: Stoddart Publishing.

Foot, David K., and Jeanne C. Li 1986 "Youth Employment in Canada: A Misplaced Priority?" *Canadian Public Policy* 12(3): 499–506.

Foot, David K., and Rosemary A. Venne 1990 "Population Pyramids and Promotional Prospects." *Canadian Public Policy* 16: 387–98.

Forbes Magazine 2013 "The World's Billionaires." http://www.forbes.com/billionaires/.

Forcadell, Francisco Javier 2005 "Democracy, Cooperation and Business Success: The Case of Mondragon Corporacion Cooperativa." *Journal of Business Ethics* 56(3): 255–74.

Form, William 1987 "On the Degradation of Skills." *Annual Review of Sociology* 13: 29–47.

Forrest, Anne 2000 "Pay Equity: The State of the Debate." In Yonatan Reshef, Colette Bernier, Denis Harrison, and Terry H. Wagar, eds., *Industrial Relations in a New Millennium.* Selected Papers from the 37th Annual Canadian Industrial Relations Association Conference, May 25–27, 2000, Edmonton, Alberta.

Fortin, Pierre 1996 "The Unbearable Lightness of Zero-Inflation Optimism." In Brian K. MacLean and Lars Osberg, eds., *The Unemployment Crisis: All for Nought?* Montreal and Kingston: McGill–Queen's University Press.

Foster, Jason, and Bob Barnetson 2012 "Justice for Janitors in Alberta: The Impact of Temporary Foreign Workers on an Organizing Campaign." *Journal of Workplace Rights* 16(1): 3–29.

Foucault, Michel 1977 *Discipline and Punish: The Birth of the Prison.* Harmondsworth, England: Penguin.

Fox, Bonnie 1997 "Reproducing Differences: Changes in the Lives of Partners Becoming Parents." In Meg Luxton, ed., *Feminism and Families.* Halifax: Fernwood Publishing.

Fox, Bonnie, and Pamela Sugiman 1999 "Flexible Work, Flexible Workers: The Restructuring of Clerical Work in a Large Telecommunications Company." *Studies in Political Economy* 60(Autumn): 59–84.

Fox, Elizabeth R, Gillian Pascall, and T. Warren 2009 "Work–Family Policies, Participation and Practices: Fathers and Childcare in Europe." *Community, Work and Family* 12(3): 313–26.

Frager, Ruth A. 1992 *Sweatshop Strife: Class, Ethnicity, and Gender in the Jewish Labour Movement of Toronto 1900–1939.* Toronto: University of Toronto Press.

Franke, Richard Herbert, and James D. Kaul 1978 "The Hawthorne Experiments: First Statistical Interpretation." *American Sociological Review* 43: 623–43.

Fraser, Nancy 1997 "After the Family Wage: A Post-Industrial Thought Experiment." In Nancy Fraser, *Justice Interruptus: Critical Reflections on the "Postsocialist" Condition.* New York: Routledge.

Freeman, Bill 1982 *1005: Political Life in a Union Local.* Toronto: James Lorimer.

Freeman, Richard B. 1995 "The Future for Unions in Decentralized Collective Bargaining Systems: U.S. and U.K. Unionism in an Era of Crisis." *British Journal of Industrial Relations* 33: 519–36.

Freeman, Richard B., and J. L. Medoff 1984 *What Do Unions Do?* New York: Basic Books.

Frege, Carola 2005 "The Discourse of Industrial Democracy: Germany and the U.S. Revisited." *Economic and Industrial Democracy* 26(1): 151–75.

Frenette, Marc 2001 "Overqualified? Recent Graduates, Employer Needs." *Perspectives on Labour and Income* 13(Spring): 45–53.

———— **2003** *Access to College and University: Does Distance Matter?* Analytical Studies Branch Research Paper no. 201. Ottawa: Statistics Canada.

———— **2007a** *Why Are Youth from Lower-Income Families Less Likely to Attend University?* Analytical Studies Branch Research Paper no. 295. Ottawa: Statistics Canada.

———— 2007b "Life after High Tech." *Perspectives on Labour and Income* 19(3): 21–29.

Frenkel, Stephen J., Marek Korczynski, Karen A. Shire, and May Tam 1999 *On the Front Line: Organization of Work in the Information Economy*. Ithaca, NY: ILR Press.

Friedman, Andrew L. 1977 *Industry and Labour: Class Struggle at Work and Monopoly Capitalism*. London: Macmillan.

Friedman, Thomas L. 2000 *The Lexus and the Olive Tree*. New York: Anchor Books.

———— 2005 *The World Is Flat: A Brief History of the 21st Century*. New York: Farrar, Strauss, Giroux.

Friendly, Martha, and Jane Beach 2005 *Early Childhood Education and Care in Canada 2004*. Toronto: Childcare Resource and Research Unit, University of Toronto.

Friendly, Martha, Shani Halfon, Jane Beach, and Barry Forer 2013 *Early Childhood Education and Care in Canada 2012*. Toronto: Childcare Research and Resource Unit.

Fudge, Judy, and Patricia McDermott, eds. 1991 *Just Wages: A Feminist Assessment of Pay Equity*. Toronto: University of Toronto Press.

Fudge, Judy, and Rosemary Owens, eds. 2006 *Precarious Work, Women and the New Economy: The Challenge to Legal Norms*. Oxford, England: Hart Publishing.

Fudge, Judy, and Leah F. Vosko 2001 "Gender, Segmentation and the Standard Employment Relationship in Canadian Labour Law, Legislation and Policy." *Economic and Industrial Democracy* 22(2): 271–310.

Fuller, Linda, and Vicki, Smith 1991 "Consumers' Reports: Management by Customers in a Changing Economy." *Work, Employment & Society* 5: 1–16.

Fuller, Sylvia 2008 "Job Mobility and Wage Trajectories for Men and Women in the United States." *American Sociological Review* 73: 158–83.

Fuller, Sylvia, and Todd F. Martin 2012 "Predicting Immigrant Employment Sequences in the First Years of Settlement." *International Migration Review* 46(1): 138–90.

Fuller, Sylvia, and Leah F. Vosko 2008 "Temporary Employment and Social Inequality in Canada: Exploring Intersections of Gender, Race and Immigration Status." *Social Indicators Research* 88: 31–50.

Gabriel, Yiannis, David E. Gray, and Harshita Goregaokar 2013 "Job Loss and Its Aftermath among Managers and Professionals: Wounded, Fragmented and Flexible." *Work, Employment & Society* 27(1): 56–72.

Galarneau, Diane 2005 "Earnings of Temporary versus Permanent Employees." *Perspectives on Labour and Income* 17(Spring): 40–53.

———— 2010 "Temporary Employment in the Downturn." *Perspectives on Labour and Income* (November): 5–17.

Galarneau, Diane, and René Morissette 2009 "Immigrants' Education and Required Job Skills." *Perspectives on Labour and Income* 21(1): 5–18.

Galarneau, Diane, and Marian Radulescu 2009. "Employment among the Disabled." *Perspectives on Labour and Income* 21(2): 31–41.

Galarneau, Diane, and Thao Sohn 2013 "Long Term Trends in Unionization." Statistics Canada, *Insights on Canadian Society*, Cat. No. 75-006-X.

Gallie, Duncan 1978 *In Search of the New Working Class: Automation and Social Integration within the Capitalist Enterprise*. Cambridge: Cambridge University Press.

———— 1983 *Social Inequality and Class Radicalism in France and Britain*. Cambridge: Cambridge University Press.

———— 2013 "Direct Participation and the Quality of Work." *Human Relations* 66(4): 453–73.

Gallie, Duncan, Alan Felstead, and Francis Green 2012 "Job Preferences and the Intrinsic Quality of Work: The Changing Attitudes of British Employees 1992–2006." *Work, Employment & Society* 26(5): 806–21.

Gandolfi, Franco 2009 "Executing Downsizing: The Experiences of Executioners." *Contemporary Management Research* 5(2): 185–200.

Gannagé, Charlene 1995 "Union Women in the Garment Industry Respond to New Managerial Strategies." *Canadian Journal of Sociology* 20(4): 469–95.

Ganster, Daniel C., Christa E. Kiersch, Rachel E. Marsh, and Angela Bowen 2011 "Performance-based Rewards and Work Stress." *Journal of Occupational Behavior and Management* 31: 221–35.

Gardell, B. 1977 "Autonomy and Participation at Work." *Human Relations* 30: 515–33.

Garver, Paul, Kirill Buketov, Hyewon Chong, and Beatriz Sosa Martinez 2007 "Global Labor Organizing in Theory and Practice." *Labor Studies Journal* 32(3): 237–56.

Garvin, David A. 2000 *Learning in Action: A Guide to Putting the Learning Organization to Work.* Boston: Harvard Business School Press.

Gaskell, Jane 1992 *Gender Matters from School to Work.* Milton Keynes, England: Open University Press.

Gazso, Amber 2007 "Balancing Expectations for Employability and Family Responsibilities While on Social Assistance: Low-Income Mothers' Experiences in Three Canadian Provinces." *Family Relations* 56(5): 454–66.

Gazso, Amber 2012 "Moral Codes of Mothering and the Introduction of Welfare-to-Work in Ontario." *Canadian Review of Sociology* 49(1): 26–49.

Gazso, Amber, and Harvey Krahn 2008 "Out of Step or Leading the Parade? Public Opinion about Income Support Policy in Alberta, 1995 and 2004." *Journal of Canadian Studies* 42(1): 154–78.

George, Jennifer M., and Gareth R. Jones 1997 "Experiencing Work Values, Attitudes, and Moods." *Human Relations* 50(4): 393–416.

Gephart, Martha A., Victoria J. Marsick, Mark E. Van Buren, and Michelle S. Spiro 1996 "Learning Organizations Come Alive." *Training & Development* (December): 35–45.

Gera, Surendra, ed. 1991 *Canadian Unemployment: Lessons from the 80s and Challenges for the 90s.* Ottawa: Economic Council of Canada.

Gerber, Theodore P., and Michael Hout 1998 "More Shock Than Therapy: Market Transition, Employment, and Income in Russia, 1991–1995." *American Journal of Sociology* 104(1): 1–50.

Gherardi, Silvia 1999 "Learning as Problem-Driven or Learning in the Face of Mystery?" *Organization Studies* 20(1): 101–23.

Giles, Anthony 1996 "Globalization and Industrial Relations." In Anthony Giles, Anthony E. Smith, and Gilles Trudeau, eds., *The Globalization of the Economy and the Worker.* Selected Papers from the 32nd Annual Canadian Industrial Relations Association Conference, Laval, QC.

Gillespie, Richard 1991 *Manufacturing Knowledge: A History of the Hawthorne Experiments.* New York: Cambridge University Press.

Gindin, Sam 1995 *The Canadian Auto Workers: The Birth and Transformation of a Union.* Toronto: James Lorimer.

Gingras, Yves, and Richard Roy 2000 "Is There a Skills Gap in Canada?" *Canadian Public Policy* (July Supplement): S159–74.

Gioia, Ted 2006 *Work Songs.* Durham and London: Duke University Press.

Gjerustad, Cay, and Tilmann von Soest 2012 "Socio-Economic Status and Mental Health—The Importance of Achieving Occupational Aspirations." *Journal of Youth Studies* 15: 890–908.

Glauber, Rebecca 2012 "Women's Work and Working Conditions: Are Mothers Compensated for Lost Wages?" *Work and Occupations* 39(2): 115–38.

Globe and Mail 2013a "Editorial: The Loss of Clarity on Poverty." September 13: A10.

——— **2013b** "How Much Canada's Top 100 CEOs Got Paid in 2012." May 27.

Godard, John 1994 *Industrial Relations: The Economy and Society.* Toronto: McGraw-Hill Ryerson.

——— **1997** "Managerial Strategies, Labour and Employment Relations and the State: The Canadian Case and Beyond." *British Journal of Industrial Relations* 35(3): 399–426.

——— **2001** "Beyond the High Performance Paradigm? An Analysis of Variation in Canadian Managerial Perceptions of Reform Programme Effectiveness." *British Journal of Industrial Relations* 39(1): 25–52.

——— **2004** "A Critical Assessment of the High-Performance Paradigm." *British Journal of Industrial Relations* 42(2): 349–78.

Goldfield, Michael, and Amy Bromsen 2013 "The Changing Landscape of U.S. Unions in Historical and Theoretical Perspective." *Annual Review of Political Science* 16: 231–57.

Goldin, Claudia 2014 "AEA President Address: A Grand Gender Convergence: Its Last Chapter." *American Economic Review* 104 (March): 1–30.

Goldin, Claudia, and Cecilia Rouse 2000 "Orchestrating Impartiality: The Impact of 'Blind' Auditions on Female Musicians." *American Economic Review* (September): 715–41.

Goldrick-Rab, Sara 2006 "Following Their Every Move: An Investigation of Social Class

Differences in College Pathways." *Sociology of Education* 79(1): 61–79.

Goldstein, Adam 2012 "Revenge of the Managers: Labor Cost-Cutting and the Paradoxical Resurgence of Managerialism in the Shareholder Value Era, 1984 to 2001." *American Sociological Review* 77(2): 268–94.

Goldthorpe, John H., D. Lockwood, F. Bechhofer, and J. Platt 1969 *The Affluent Worker in the Class Structure*. Cambridge: Cambridge University Press.

Gomez, Rafael, and David Foot 2013 "The Destiny of Demographic Change." *Policy Options* (April–May): 55–57.

Gordon, Brett R. 1994 "Employee Involvement in the Enforcement of the Occupational Safety and Health Laws of Canada and the United States." *Comparative Labor Law and Policy Journal* 15: 527–60.

Gordon, David M., R. Edwards, and M. Reich 1982 *Segmented Work, Divided Workers: The Historical Transformation of Labor in the United States*. New York: Cambridge University Press.

Gorham, Deborah 1994 " 'No Longer an Invisible Minority': Women Physicians and Medical Practice in Late Twentieth-Century North America." In Dianne Dodd and Deborah Gorham, eds., *Caring and Curing: Historical Perspectives on Women and Healing in Canada*. Ottawa: University of Ottawa Press.

Gorman, Elizabeth, and Julie A. Kmec 2009 "Hierarchical Rank and Women's Organizational Mobility: Glass Ceilings in Corporate Law Firms." *American Journal of Sociology* 114(5): 1428–74.

Gornick, Janet C., and Marcia K. Meyers 2009 *Gender Equality: Transforming Family Divisions of Labor*. Real Utopias Project Series. London: Verso Books.

Gorz, Andre 1982 *Farewell to the Working Class: An Essay on Post-industrial Socialism*. London, England: Pluto Press.

——— 1999 *Reclaiming Work: Beyond the Wage-Based Society*. Malden, MA: Polity Press.

Gougeon, Philippe 2009 "Shifting Pensions." *Perspectives on Labour and Income* (May): 16–23.

Gouldner, Alvin W. 1954 *Patterns of Industrial Bureaucracy*. New York: Free Press.

——— 1955 *Wildcat Strike*. New York: Free Press.

Goyder, John, and Kristyn Frank 2007 "A Scale of Occupational Prestige in Canada, Based on NOC Major Groups." *Canadian Journal of Sociology* 32(1): 63–83.

Grabb, Edward G. 2002 *Theories of Social Inequality*. 4th ed. Toronto: Harcourt Canada.

——— 2009 "Corporate Concentration, Foreign Ownership, and State Involvement in the Canadian Economy." In Edward Grabb and Neil Guppy, eds., *Social Inequality in Canada: Patterns, Problems, and Policies*. 5th ed. Toronto: Pearson/Prentice Hall.

Graham, Hilary 1991 "The Concept of Caring in Feminist Research: The Case of Domestic Service." *Sociology* 25(1): 25–61.

Graham, Laurie 1995 *On the Line at Subaru–Isuzu: The Japanese Model and the American Worker*. Ithaca, NY: ILR Press.

Grandey, Alicia, James Diefendorff, and Deborah Rupp 2013 *Emotional Labor in the 21st Century: Diverse Perspectives on the Psychology of Emotion Regulation at Work*. New York: Routledge.

Green, Archie ed. 1993 *Songs About Work: Essays in Occupational Culture for Richard A. Reuss*. Bloomington IN: Folklore Institute, Indiana University.

Green, David, Thomas Lemieux, Kevin Milligan, Craig Riddell, and Nicole Fortin 2011 "The Forces That Are Driving Income Inequality." *Vancouver Sun*, December 16: A15.

Green, Francis 2001 "It's Been a Hard Day's Night: The Concentration and Intensification of Work in Late Twentieth-Century Britain." *British Journal of Industrial Relations* 39(1): 53–80.

——— 2006 *Demanding Work: The Paradox of Job Quality in the Affluent Economy*. Princeton, NJ: Princeton University Press.

Green, Francis, and David Ashton 1992 "Skill Shortages and Skill Deficiency: A Critique." *Work, Employment & Society* 6: 287–301.

Green, Francis, and Yu Zhu 2010 "Overqualification, Job Dissatisfaction, and Increasing Dispersion in the Returns to Graduate Education." *Oxford Economic Papers* 62(4): 740–63.

Green, William C., and Ernest J. Yanarella, eds. 1996 *North American Auto Unions in Crisis: Lean Production as Contested Terrain*. Albany, NY: State University of New York Press.

Greenhaus, Jeffrey H., and Nicholas J. Beutell 1985 "Sources of Conflict between Work and Family Roles." *Academy of Management Review* 10(1): 76–88.

Greenhaus, Jeffrey H., and Gary Powell 2006 "When Work and Family Are Allies: A Theory of Work–Family Enrichment." *Academy of Management Review* 31:72–92.

Grenier, S., S. Jones, J. Strucker, T. S. Murray, G. Gervais, and S. Brink 2008 *Learning Literacy in Canada: Evidence from the International Survey of Reading Skills.* Ottawa: Statistics Canada. Cat. no. 89-552-MIE—No. 19.

Grint, Keith 1991 *The Sociology of Work: An Introduction.* Cambridge: Polity Press.

Grün, Carola, Wolfgang Hauser, and Thomas Rhein 2010 "Is Any Job Better Than No Job? Life Satisfaction and Re-employment." *Journal of Labor Research* 31:285–306.

Gunderson, Morley 1994 *Comparable Worth and Gender Discrimination: An International Perspective.* Geneva: International Labour Office.

———— **1998** "Harmonization of Labour Policies under Trade Liberalization." *Relations industrielles/Industrial Relations* 53(1): 24–52.

Gunderson, Morley, and Douglas Hyatt 2009 "Union Impact on Compensation, Productivity, and Management of the Organization." In Morley Gunderson and Daphne Taras, eds., *Canadian Labour and Employment Relations* Toronto: Pearson Addison Wesley.

Gunderson, Morley, Douglas Hyatt, and Allen Ponak 1995 "Strikes and Dispute Resolution." In Morley Gunderson and Allen Ponak, eds., *Union–Management Relations in Canada.* 3rd ed. Don Mills, ON: Addison-Wesley Publishers.

Gunderson, Morley, Jeffrey Sack, James McCartney, David Wakely, and Jonathan Eaton 1995 "Employee Buyouts in Canada." *British Journal of Industrial Relations* 33:417–42.

Gunderson, Morley, Andrew Sharpe, and Steven Wald 2000 "Youth Unemployment in Canada, 1976–1998." *Canadian Public Policy* (July Supplement): S85–100.

Gupta, Sanjiv 2006 "The Consequences of Maternal Employment during Men's Childhood for Their Adult Housework Performance." *Gender and Society* 20(1): 60–86.

Gustafsson, Bjorn, and Mats Johansson 1999 "In Search of Smoking Guns: What Makes Income Inequality Vary over Time in Different Countries?" *American Sociological Review* 64: 585–605.

Guthrie, Doug 2006 *China and Globalization: The Social, Economic, and Political Transformation of Chinese Society.* New York: Routledge.

Guzda, Henry P. 1993 "Workplace Partnerships in the United States and Europe." *Monthly Labor Review* (October): 67–72.

Hagan, John, and Fiona Kay 1995 *Gender in Practice: A Study of Lawyers' Lives.* New York: Oxford University Press.

Hakanen, Jari J., Wilmar B. Schaufeli, and Kirsi Ahola 2008 "The Job Demands-Resources Model: A Three-Year Cross-Lagged Study of Burnout, Depression, Commitment, and Work Engagement." *Work & Stress* 22(3): 224–41.

Hakim, Catherine 2002 "Lifestyle Preferences as Determinants of Women's Differentiated Labor Market Careers." *Work and Occupations* 29(4): 428–59.

———— **2006** "Women, Careers, and Work–Life Preferences." *British Journal of Guidance & Counselling* 34(3): 279–94.

Halpern, Norman 1984 "Sociotechnical Systems Design: The Shell Sarnia Experience." In J. B. Cunningham and T. H. White, eds., *Quality of Working Life: Contemporary Cases.* Ottawa: Labour Canada.

Halrynjo, Sigtona 2009 "Men's Work–Life Conflict, Career, Care and Self-Realization: Patterns of Privileges and Dilemmas." *Gender, Work & Organization* 16(1): 98–125.

Hamel, Gary 2007 *The Future of Management.* Boston: Harvard Business School Press.

Hammer, Michael, and James Champy 1993 *Reengineering the Corporation: A Manifesto for Business Revolution.* New York: HarperBusiness.

Hammer, Tove Helland, and Ariel Avgar 2005 "The Impact of Unions on Job Satisfaction, Organizational Commitment, and Turnover." *Journal of Labor Research* 26(2): 241–66.

Hamper, Ben 1986 *Rivethead: Tales from the Assembly Line.* New York: Warner Books.

Hampson, Ian 1999 "Lean Production and the Toyota Production System—or, the Case of the Forgotten Production Concepts." *Economic and Industrial Democracy* 20(3): 369–91.

Hancock, Philip 2009 "Introduction." In Philip Hancock and Melissa Tyler, *The Management of Everyday Life*. Basingstoke, England: Palgrave Macmillan.

Handel, Michael J. 2003 "Skills Mismatch in the Labor Market." *Annual Review of Sociology* 29: 135–65.

Hansen, Susan 2004 "From 'Common Observation' to Behavioural Risk Management: Workplace Surveillance and Employee Assistance 1914–2003." *International Sociology* 19(2): 151–71.

Harchaoui, Tarek M., F. Tarkani, C. Jackson, and P. Armstrong 2002 "Information Technology and Economic Growth in Canada and the U.S." *Monthly Labor Review* 125(10): 3–12.

Harley, Bill, Belinda C. Allen, and Leisa D. Sargent 2007 "High Performance Work Systems and Employee Experience of Work in the Service Sector: The Case of Aged Care." *British Journal of Industrial Relations* 45(3): 607–33.

Harrison, Bennett 1997 *Lean and Mean: Why Large Corporations Will Continue to Dominate the Global Economy*. New York: Guilford Press.

Harrison, Trevor 2005 *The Return of the Trojan Horse: Alberta and the New World (Dis) Order*. Montreal: Black Rose Books.

Hartmann, Heidi 1976 "Capitalism, Patriarchy, and Job Segregation by Sex." *Signs* 1: 137–69.

Hauser, Robert M., John Robert Warren, Min-Hsiung Huang, and Wendy C. Carter 2000 "Occupational Status, Education, and Social Mobility in the Meritocracy." In Kenneth Arrow, Samuel Bowles, and Steven Durlauf, eds., *Meritocracy and Economic Inequality*. Princeton, NJ: Princeton University Press.

Hausknecht, John P., Nathan J. Hiller, and Robert J. Vance 2008 "Work-Unit Absenteeism: Effects of Satisfaction, Commitment, Labor Market Conditions, and Time." *Academy of Management Journal* 51(6): 1223–45.

Hayden, Anders 1999 *Sharing the Work, Sparing the Planet: Work Time, Consumption, and Ecology*. Toronto: Between the Lines.

Hays, Sharon 1996 *The Cultural Contradictions of Motherhood*. New Haven, CT: Yale University Press.

Hearn, Jeff, Deborah L. Sheppard, Peta Tancred-Sheriff, and Gibson Burrell, eds. 1989 *The Sexuality of Organization*. London, England: Sage.

Hedgewisch, Arianne, and Janet C. Gornick 2011 "The Impact of Work–Family Policies on Women's Employment." *Community, Work and Family* 14(2): 119–38.

Heil, Gary, Warren Bennis, and Deborah C. Stephens 2000 *Douglas McGregor, Revisited: Managing the Human Side of the Enterprise*. New York: John Wiley & Sons.

Heinzl, John 1997 "Nike's Hockey Plans Put Bauer on Thin Ice." *Globe and Mail*, July 2, B2.

Heisig, Ulrich 2009 "The Deskilling and Upskilling Debate." In Rupert Maclean and David N. Wilson, eds., *International Handbook of Education for the Changing World of Work*. Dordrecht, Netherlands: Springer.

Heisz, Andrew 2005 "The Evolution of Job Stability in Canada: Trends and Comparisons with U.S. Results." *Canadian Journal of Economics* 38(1): 105–27.

Heisz, Andrew, and Sebastien LaRochelle-Côté 2007 "Work Hours Instability." *Perspectives on Labour and Income* 19: 18–21.

Held, Virginia 2006 *The Ethics of Care: Personal, Political, and Global*. Oxford and New York: Oxford University Press.

Helfen, Markus, and Michael Fichter 2013 "Building Transnational Union Networks across Global Production Networks: Conceptualizing a New Arena of Labour–Management Relations." *British Journal of Industrial Relations* 51(3): 553–76.

Hennebry, J. L., and J. McLaughlin 2012 " 'The Exception That Proves the Rule': Structural Vulnerability, Health Risks, and Consequences for Temporary Migrant Farm Workers in Canada." In Patti T. Lenard and Christine Straehle, eds., *Legislated Inequality: Temporary Labour Migration in Canada*. Montreal and Kingston: McGill-Queen's University Press.

Henson, Kevin D. 1996 *Just a Temp*. Philadelphia: Temple University Press.

Heron, Craig 1980 "The Crisis of the Craftsmen: Hamilton's Metal Workers in the Early Twentieth Century." *Labour/Le Travail* 6: 7–48.

——— **1989** *The Canadian Labour Movement: A Short History*. Toronto: James Lorimer.

Heron, Craig, and Bryan Palmer 1977 "Through the Prism of the Strike: Industrial Conflict in Southern Ontario, 1910–14." *Canadian Historical Review* 58:423–58.

Herzberg, Frederick 1966 Work and the Nature of Man. New York: World.

Hessing, Melody 1991 "Talking Shop(ping): Office Conversations and Women's Dual Labour." *Canadian Journal of Sociology* 16:23–50.

Higgins, Chris A., Linda E. Duxbury, and Sean T. Lyons 2010 "Coping with Overload and Stress: Men and Women in Dual-Earner Families." *Journal of Marriage and Family* 72:847–59.

Hilbrecht, Margo, Susan Shaw, Laura Johnson, and Jean Andrey 2013 "Remixing Work, Family and Leisure: Teleworkers' Experiences of Everyday Life." *New Technology, Work, and Employment* 28(2): 130–44.

Hill, Jeffrey E., Nicole Timmons Mead, Lukas Ray Dean, Dawn M. Hafen, Robyn Gadd, Alexis A. Palmer, and Maria S. Ferris 2006 "Researching the 60-Hour Dual-Earner Workweek: An Alternative to the 'Opt-Out Revolution.'" *American Behavioral Scientist* 49(9): 1184–1203.

Hill, Stephen 1981 *Competition and Control at Work*. London, England: Heinemann.

——— **1988** "Technology and Organizational Culture: The Human Imperative in Integrating New Technology into Organization Design." *Technology in Society* 10:233–53.

Hillman, Amy, Christine Shropshire, and Albert A. Cannella Jr. 2007 "Organizational Predictors of Women on Corporate Boards." *Academy of Management Journal* 50(4): 941–52.

Hilton, Rodney, ed. 1976 *The Transition from Feudalism to Capitalism*. London, England: New Left Books.

Hipple, Steven 2010 "Self-Employment in the United States." *Monthly Labor Review* (September): 17–32.

Hironimus-Wendt, Robert 2008 "The Human Costs of Worker Displacement." *Humanity and Society* 32(1): 71–93.

Hirschman, A. O. 1970 *Exit, Voice, and Loyalty*. Cambridge, MA: Harvard University Press.

Hirst, Paul, and Grahame Thompson 1995 "Globalization and the Future of the Nation State." *Economy and Society* 24:408–42.

Hjalmarsson, Marie 2009 "New Technology in Home Help Services—A Tool for Support or an Instrument of Subordination?" *Gender, Work & Organization* 16(3): 368–84.

Hochschild, Arlie 1983 *The Managed Heart: The Commercialization of Human Feeling*. Berkeley: The University of California Press.

——— **1989** *The Second Shift: Working Parents and the Revolution at Home*. New York: Viking Penguin.

——— **1997** *The Time Bind: When Work Becomes Home and Home Becomes Work*. New York: Henry Holt and Company.

——— **2009** "Through the Crack in the Time Bind: From Market Management to Family Management." In Philip Hancock and Melissa Tyler, eds., *The Management of Everyday Life*. Basingstoke, Hampshire: Palgrave Macmillan.

——— **2012** *The Outsourced Self: Intimate Life in Market Times*. New York: Metropolitan Books.

Hodson, Randy 1996 "Dignity in the Workplace under Participative Management: Alienation and Freedom Revisited." *American Sociological Review* 61:719–38.

——— **2001** *Dignity at Work*. Cambridge: Cambridge University Press.

——— **2004** "Work Life and Social Fulfillment: Does Social Affiliation at Work Reflect a Carrot or a Stick?" *Social Science Quarterly* 85(2): 221–39.

Hodson, Randy, and Robert L. Kaufman 1982 "Economic Dualism: A Critical Review." *American Sociological Review* 47:727–39.

Hollister, Matissa 2011 "Employment Stability in the U.S. Labor Market: Rhetoric versus Reality." *Annual Review of Sociology* 37:305–24.

Holzer, Boris 2000 "Miracles with a System: The Economic Rise of East Asia and the Role of Sociocultural Patterns." *International Sociology* 15(3): 455–78.

Holzer, Harry J. 1996 *What Employers Want: Job Prospects for Less-Educated Workers*. New York: Russell Sage Foundation.

Homans, George C. 1950 *The Human Group*. New York: Harcourt, Brace and World.

Hook, Jennifer 2006 "Care in Context: Men's Unpaid Work in 20 Countries, 1965–2003." *American Sociological Review* 71(4): 639–60.

Hoque, Kim, and Ian Kirkpatrick 2003
"Non-standard Employment in the
Management and Professional Workforce:
Training, Consultation and Gender
Implications." *Work, Employment & Society*
17(4): 667–89.
House, J. D. 1980 *The Last of the Free
Enterprisers: The Oilmen of Calgary.* Toronto:
Macmillan.
**HRSDC [Human Resources and Skills
Development Canada]** 2007 *Compassionate
Care Leave Provisions in Employment Standards
Legislation.* Ottawa: HRSDC. http://www
.hrsdc.gc.ca/eng/lp/spila/clli/ eslc/Compass
.pdf.
——— **2009** *Employment Equity Report 2008.*
Ottawa: HRSDC. Cat. no. HS21-1/2008.
——— **2012** *Indicators of Well-Being in Canada:
Financial Security—Low Income Incidence.*
Ottawa: HRSDC. http://www4
.hrsdc.gc.ca/.3ndic.1t.4r@-eng.jsp?iid=23#M_8.
——— **2013** *Aboriginal Labour Market Bulletin:
Spring 2013.* http://www.esdc.gc.ca/eng/jobs/
aboriginal/bulletins/spring2013.shtml.
Hsiung, Ping-Chun 1996 *Living Rooms as
Factories: Class, Gender, and the Satellite
Factory System in Taiwan.* Philadelphia:
Temple University Press.
**Huddart Kennedy, Emily, Harvey Krahn,
and Naomi Krogman 2013** "Downshifting:
An Exploration of Motivations, Quality
of Life, and Environmental Practices."
Sociological Forum 28(4): 764–83.
Hudson, Kenneth 2007 "The New Labor
Market Segmentation: Labor Market Dualism
in the New Economy." *Social Science Research*
36(1): 286–312.
**Hufbauer, Gary Clyde, and Jeffrey J. Schott
2005** *NAFTA Revisited: Achievements and
Challenges.* Washington, DC: Institute for
International Economics.
Hughes, Karen D. 1995 "Women in Non-
traditional Occupations." *Perspectives on
Labour and Income* (Autumn): 14–19.
——— **1996** "Transformed by Technology? The
Changing Nature of Women's 'Traditional' and
'Non-traditional' White-Collar Work." *Work,
Employment & Society* 10: 227–50.
——— **2000** *Women and Corporate
Directorships in Canada: Trends and Issues.*
Discussion Paper no. CPRN-01. Ottawa:
Canadian Policy Research Networks.

——— **2001** "Restructuring Work,
Restructuring Gender: The Movement of
Women into Non-traditional Occupations
in Canada." In Victor W. Marshall, Walter
R. Heinz, Helga Krüger, and Anil Verma,
eds., *Restructuring Work and the Life Course.*
Toronto: University of Toronto Press.
——— **2005** *Female Enterprise in the New
Economy.* Toronto: University of Toronto
Press.
——— **2010** "Canadian Women
Entrepreneurs." In Sandra Fielden and
Marilyn Davidson, eds., *International Research
Handbook on Successful Women Entrepreneurs.*
Cheltenham, England: Edward Elgar.
**Hughes, Karen D., and Graham S. Lowe
2000** "Surveying the 'Post-industrial'
Landscape: Information Technologies and
Labour Market Polarization in Canada."
Canadian Review of Sociology and Anthropology
37(1): 29–53.
**Hughes, Karen D., Graham S. Lowe, and
Grant Schellenberg 2003** *Men's and Women's
Quality of Work in the New Canadian
Economy.* Ottawa: Canadian Policy Research
Networks.
**Hughes, Karen D. and J. E. Jennings, eds.
2012** *Global Women's Entrepreneurship: Diverse
Settings, Questions, Approaches.* Cheltenham,
England: Edward Elgar.
Hughes, Karen D., and Vela Tadic 1998 "
'Something to Deal With': Customer Sexual
Harassment and Women's Retail Work in
Canada." *Gender, Work & Organization* 5(4):
207–19.
**Hulchanski, David, Robert Murdie, Alan
Walks and Larry Bourne (2013).** "Canada's
Voluntary Census is Worthless. Here's why",
Globe and mail, October 4.
**Human Resources Development Canada
2000a** *Statistical Analysis: Occupational Injuries
and Fatalities Canada.* Hull, QC: HRDC.
——— **2000b** *Occupational Injuries and Their
Cost in Canada 1993–1997.* Hull, QC:
HRDC.
**Human Resources Development Canada
and Statistics Canada 2002** *Results from the
Survey of Self-Employment in Canada.* Ottawa:
Applied Research Branch, Human Resources
Development Canada.
Humphrey, James H. 1998 *Job Stress.* Boston:
Allyn and Bacon.

Humphries, Jane 1977 "Class Struggle and the Persistence of the Working Class Family." *Cambridge Journal of Economics* 1: 241–58.

Hunter, Alfred A., and Michael C. Manley 1986 "On the Task Content of Work." *Canadian Review of Sociology and Anthropology* 23: 47–71.

Hurst, Matt 2008 "Work-Related Training." *Perspectives on Labour and Income* (Summer): 25–31.

Huxley, Christopher 1979 "The State, Collective Bargaining and the Shape of Strikes in Canada." *Canadian Journal of Sociology* 4: 223–39.

Hyman, Richard 1978 *Strikes*. 2nd ed. Glasgow: Fontana.

Iaffaldano, Michelle T., and Paul M. Muchinsky 1985 "Job Satisfaction and Job Performance: A Meta-analysis." *Psychological Bulletin* 97: 251–73.

Ibrahim, Mariam 2013 "Labour Bills Violate Rights, Union Charges." *Edmonton Journal*, November 29, A4.

Idle, Thomas R., and Arthur J. Cordell 1994 "Automating Work." *Society* 36(September–October): 65–71.

Ilies, Remus, Kelly Schwind Wilson, and David T. Wagner 2009 "The Spillover of Daily Job Satisfaction onto Employees' Family Lives: The Facilitating Role of Work–Family Integration." *Academy of Management Journal* 52(1): 87–102.

Ilg, Randy E. 1995 "The Changing Face of Farm Employment." *Monthly Labor Review* (April): 3–12.

Immen, Wallace 2013 "Students Seek More Fulfilling Jobs in Green Fields." *Globe and Mail*, April 22. http://www.theglobeandmail .com/report-on-business/careers/ students-seek-more-fulfilling-jobs-in-green-fields/ article11449129/.

Industry Canada 2009 *Key Small Business Statistics, January 2009*. Ottawa: Industry Canada. http://www.ic.gc.ca/eic/site/ sbrp-rppe.nsf/vwapj/KSBS-PSRPE_ Jan2009_ eng.pdf/$FILE/KSBS-PSRPE_ Jan2009_eng .pdf.

International Centre for Human Rights and Democratic Development 1997 *Commerce with Conscience? Human Rights and Corporate Codes of Conduct*. Montreal: ICHRDD.

International Labour Office (ILO) 1997 *World Employment Report 1997–98: Industrial Relations, Democracy and Stability*. Geneva: ILO.

——— **1999** *Decent Work*. Geneva: ILO.

Isaksen, Lise Widding, Sambasivan Uma Devi, and Arlie Hochschild 2008 "Global Care Crisis: A Problem of Capital, Care Chain, or Commons?" *American Behavioral Scientist* 52(3): 405–25.

Jackson, Andrew 2005 *Work and Labour in Canada: Critical Issues*. Toronto: Canadian Scholars' Press.

Jackson, Andrew, David Robinson, Bob Baldwin, and Cindy Wiggins 2000 *Falling Behind: The State of Working Canada, 2000*. Ottawa: Canadian Centre for Policy Alternatives.

Jacobs, Jerry, and Kathleen Gerson 2004 *The Time Divide: Work, Family and Gender Inequality*. Cambridge, MA: Harvard University Press.

Jacoby, Sanford M. 1985 *Employing Bureaucracy: Managers, Unions, and the Transformation of Work in American Industry, 1900–1945*. New York: Columbia University Press.

——— **1997** *Modern Manors: Welfare Capitalism since the New Deal*. Princeton, NJ: Princeton University Press.

——— **2005** *The Embedded Corporation: Corporate Governance and Employment Relations in Japan and the United States*. Princeton, NJ: Princeton University Press.

Jahoda, M. 1982 *Employment and Unemployment: A Social–Psychological Approach*. Cambridge: Cambridge University Press.

Jain, Hem C. 1990 "Worker Participation in Canada: Current Developments and Challenges." *Economic and Industrial Democracy* 11: 279–90.

Jamieson, Stuart Marshall 1971 *Times of Trouble: Labour Unrest and Industrial Conflict in Canada, 1900–66*. Ottawa: Queen's Printer.

Jarman, Jennifer, Robert M. Blackburn, and Girts Racko 2012 "The Dimensions of Occupational Gender Segregation in Industrial Countries." *Sociology* 46(6): 1003–19.

Jenness, Diamond 1977 *Indians of Canada*. 7th ed. Toronto: University of Toronto Press.

Jenson, Jane 1989 "The Talents of Women, the Skills of Men: Flexible Specialization and Women." In Stephen Wood, ed., *The*

Transformation of Work? Skill, Flexibility and the Labour Process. London: Unwin Hyman.

Jermier, John M. 1998 "Introduction: Critical Perspectives on Organizational Control." *Administrative Science Quarterly* 43(2): 235–56.

Jex, Steve 1998 *Stress and Job Performance: Theory, Research, and Implications for Managerial Practice.* Thousand Oaks, CA: Sage.

Jha, Prem Shankar 2002 *The Perilous Road to the Market: The Political Economy of Reform in Russia, India and China.* London: Pluto Press.

Jiang, Shanhe, Richard H. Hall, Karyn L. Loscocco, and John Allen 1995 "Job Satisfaction Theories and Job Satisfaction: A China and U.S. Comparison." *Research in the Sociology of Work* 5: 161–78.

Jin, Jane 2008 "Trends in Employment and Wages, 2002 to 2007." *Perspectives on Labour and Income* 20(Winter): 5–15.

Johnson, Chalmers 1982 *MITI and the Japanese Miracle: The Growth of Industrial Policy, 1925–1975.* Stanford: Stanford University Press.

Johnson, Holly 1994 "Work-Related Sexual Harassment." *Perspectives on Labour and Income* (Winter): 9–12.

Johnson, Jeffrey V. 1989 "Control, Collectivity and the Psychosocial Work Environment." In S. L. Sauter, J. J. Hurrell Jr., and C. L. Cooper, eds., *Job Control and Worker Health.* New York: Wiley.

Johnson, Monica K., and Jeylan T. Mortimer 2011 "Origins and Outcomes of Judgments about Work." *Social Forces* 89(4): 1239–60.

Johnson, Monica K., Rayna A. Sage, and Jeylan T. Mortimer 2012 "Work Values, Early Career Difficulties, and the U.S. Economic Recession." *Social Psychology Quarterly* 75: 242–67.

Johnston, David W., and Wang-Sheng Lee 2013 "Extra Status and Extra Stress: Are Promotions Good for Us?" *Industrial and Labor Relations Review* 66(1): 32–64.

Jones, Bryn 1996 "The Social Constitution of Labour Markets: Why Skills Cannot Be Commodities." In Rosemary Crompton, Duncan Gallie, and Kate Purcell, eds., *Changing Forms of Employment: Organisations, Skills, and Gender.* London and New York: Routledge.

Jones, Charles, Lorna Marsden, and Lorne Tepperman 1990 *Lives of Their Own: The Individualization of Women's Lives.* Don Mills, ON: Oxford University Press.

Jones, Melanie, and Victoria Wass 2013 "Understanding Changing Disability-Related Employment Gaps in Britain 1998–2011." *Work, Employment & Society* 27(6): 982–1003.

Jones, Oswald 2000 "Scientific Management, Culture and Control: A First-Hand Account of Taylorism in Practice." *Human Relations* 53(5): 631–53.

Jones, Stephen R. G. 1990 "Worker Interdependence and Output: The Hawthorne Studies Reevaluated." *American Sociological Review* 55: 176–90.

Jonsson, Berth 1980 "The Volvo Experiences of New Job Design and New Production Technology." *Working Life in Sweden* 18(September).

Judge, Timothy A., Joyce E. Bono, Carl J. Thoresen, and Gregory K. Patton 2001 "The Job Satisfaction–Job Performance Relationship: A Qualitative and Quantitative Review." *Psychological Bulletin* 127(3): 376–407.

Juillerat, Tina L. 2010 "Friends, Not Foes: Work Design and Formalization in the Modern Work Context." *Journal of Organizational Behavior* 31: 216–39.

Jütting, Johannes P., and Juan R. de Laiglesia, eds. 2009 *Is Informal Normal? Towards More and Better Jobs in Developing Countries.* Paris: OECD.

Kalleberg, Arne L. 1977 "Work Values and Job Rewards: A Theory of Job Satisfaction." *American Sociological Review* 42: 124–43.

——— **2001** "Organizing Flexibility: The Flexible Firm in a New Century." *British Journal of Industrial Relations* 39(4): 479–504.

——— **2008** "The Mismatched Worker: When People Don't Fit Their Jobs." *Academy of Management Perspectives* 22(1): 24–40.

——— **2009** "Precarious Work, Insecure Workers: Employment Relations in Transition." *American Sociological Review* 74(1): 1–22.

——— **2011** *Good Jobs, Bad Jobs: The Rise of Polarized and Precarious Employment Systems in the United States, 1970s to 2000s.* New York: Russell Sage Publications.

Kalleberg, Arne, and Karyn A. Loscocco 1983 "Aging, Values and Rewards: Explaining Age Differences in Job Satisfaction." *American Sociological Review* 48: 78–90.

Kalleberg, Arne L., Peter V. Marsden, Jeremy Reynolds, and David Knoke 2006

References

"Beyond Profit? Sectoral Differences in High-Performance Work Practices." *Work and Occupations* 33(3): 271–302.

Kalleberg, Arne, Barbara F. Reskin, and Ken Hudson 2000 "Bad Jobs in America: Standard and Nonstandard Employment Relations and Job Quality in the United States." *American Sociological Review* 65: 256–78.

Kalleberg, Arne L., and Mark E. Van Buren 1996 "Is Bigger Better? Explaining the Relationship between Organization Size and Job Rewards." *American Sociological Review* 61: 47–66.

Kamata, Satoshi 1983 *Japan in the Passing Lane: An Insider's Account of Life in a Japanese Factory.* New York: Pantheon.

Kan, Man Yee, Oriel Sullivan, and Jonathan Gershuny 2011 "Gender Convergence in Domestic Work: Discerning the Effects of Interactional and Institutional Barriers from Large-Scale Data." *Sociology* 45: 234–51.

Kanter, Rosabeth M. 1977 *Men and Women of the Corporation.* New York: Basic Books.

——— **1989** *When Giants Learn to Dance: Mastering the Challenges of Strategy, Management, and Careers in the 1990s.* New York: Simon & Schuster.

Kapstein, Ethan B. 1996 "Workers and the World Economy." *Foreign Affairs* 75: 16–37.

Karasek, Robert 1979 "Job Demands, Job Decision Latitude and Mental Health Implications for Job Redesign." *Administrative Science Quarterly* 24: 285–308.

Karasek, Robert, and Töres Theorell 1990 *Healthy Work: Stress, Productivity, and the Reconstruction of Working Life.* New York: Basic Books.

Kashefi, Max 2011 "High Performance Work Organizations and Job Rewards in Manufacturing and Service Economies." *International Sociology* 26(4): 547–70.

——— **2012** "Social Capital in High Performance Work Organizations." *International Review of Modern Sociology* 38(1): 65–91.

Kay, Fiona, and Elizabeth Gorman 2008 "Gender in the Legal Profession." *Annual Review of Law and Social Sciences* 4: 299–332.

Kay, Fiona M., and Elizabeth H. Gorman 2012 "Developmental Practices, Organizational Culture, and Minority Representation in Organizational Leadership: The Case of Partners in Large U.S. Law Firms." *The Annals of the American Academy of Political and Social Science* 639: 91–113.

Kay, Tamara 2011 *NAFTA and the Politics of Labor Transnationalism.* Cambridge, NY: Cambridge University Press.

Kazemipur, Abdolmohammad, and Shiva S. Halli 2001 "The Changing Colour of Poverty in Canada." *Canadian Review of Sociology and Anthropology* 38(2): 217–38.

Kealey, Gregory S. 1980 *Toronto Workers Respond to Industrial Capitalism, 1867–1892.* Toronto: University of Toronto Press.

——— **1981** "The Bonds of Unity: The Knights of Labour in Ontario, 1880–1900." *Histoire sociale/Social History* 14: 369–411.

——— **1986** "Work Control, the Labour Process, and Nineteenth-Century Canadian Printers." In Craig Heron and Robert Storey, eds., *On the Job: Confronting the Labour Process in Canada.* Montreal and Kingston: McGill–Queen's University Press.

——— **1995** *Workers and Canadian History.* Montreal and Kingston: McGill–Queen's University Press.

Keenoy, Tom 1985 *Invitation to Industrial Relations.* Oxford: Basil Blackwell.

Keister, Lisa A. 2007 "Upward Wealth Mobility: Exploring the Roman Catholic Advantage." *Social Forces* 85(3): 1195–1225.

Kelan, Elisabeth K. 2008 "Emotions in a Rational Profession: The Gendering of Skills in ICT Work." *Gender, Work & Organization* 15(1): 49–71.

Kelly, Erin L., Ellen Ernst Kossek, Leslie B. Hammer, Mary Durham, Jeremy Bray, Kelly Chermack, Lauren A. Murphy, and Dan Kaskubar 2008 "Getting There from Here: Research on the Effects of Work–Family Initiatives on Work–Family Conflict and Business Outcomes." *The Academy of Management Annals* 2(1): 305–49.

Kerr, Clark, J. T. Dunlop, F. H. Harbison, and C. A. Myers 1973 *Industrialization and Industrial Man.* London, England: Penguin.

Kerr, Clark, and Abraham Siegel 1954 "The Interindustry Propensity to Strike: An International Comparison." In Arthur Kornhauser, Robert Dubin, and Arthur M. Ross, eds., *Industrial Conflict.* New York: McGraw-Hill.

Kettler, David, James Struthers, and Christopher Huxley 1990 "Unionization and Labour Regimes in Canada and the United States." *Labour/Le Travail* 25: 161–87.

Kim, Young-Mi 2013 "Diverging Top and Converging Bottom: Labour Flexibilization and Changes in Career Mobility in the USA." *Work, Employment & Society* 27(5): 860–79.

Kimeldorf, Howard 2013 "Worker Replacement Costs and Unionization: Origins of the U.S. Labor Movement." *American Sociological Review* 78(6): 1033–62.

Kimmel, Jean, and Lisa M. Powell 1999 "Moonlighting Trends and Related Policy Issues in Canada and the United States." *Canadian Public Policy* 25(2): 207–31.

King, W. L. Mackenzie 1918 *Industry and Humanity: A Study in the Principles Underlying Industrial Reconstruction.* Toronto: Thomas Allen.

Kinnie, Nick, Sue Hutchinson, and John Purcell 2000 " 'Fun and Surveillance': The Paradox of High Commitment Management in Call Centres." *The International Journal of Human Resource Management* 11(5): 967–85.

Kinnunen, Ulla, Saija Mauno, and Marjo Siltaloppi 2010 "Job Insecurity, Recovery and Well-Being at Work: Recovery Experiences as Moderators." *Economic and Industrial Democracy* 31(2): 179–94.

Knight, Rolf 1978 *Indians at Work: An Informal History of Native Indian Labour in British Columbia 1858–1930.* Vancouver: New Star Books.

Knighton, Tamara, Filsan Hujaleh, Joe Iacampo, and Gugsa Werkneh 2009 *Lifelong Learning among Canadians Aged 18 to 64 Years Old: First Results from the 2008 Access and Support to Education and Training Survey (ASETS).* Ottawa: Statistics Canada. http:// www.statcan .gc.ca/pub/81-595-m/ 81-595-m2009079-eng.pdf.

Knights, David, Hugh Willmott, and David Collison, eds. 1985 *Job Redesign: Critical Perspectives on the Labour Process.* Aldershot, England: Gower.

Kochan, Thomas A. 1979 "How American Workers View Labor Unions." *Monthly Labor Review* 102(April): 23–31.

Kochan, Thomas, Russell Lansbury, and John Paul MacDuffle, eds. 1997 *After Lean Production: Evolving Practices in the World Auto Industry.* Ithaca, NY: ILR Press.

Kochan, Thomas A., and Paul Osterman 1994 *The Mutual Gains Enterprise: Forging*

a Winning Partnership among Labor, Management, and Government. Boston: Harvard Business School Press.

Kohn, Melvin L., and Carmi Schooler 1983 *Work and Personality: An Inquiry into the Impact of Social Stratification.* Norwood, NJ: Ablex.

Kompier, M., E. Degier, P. Smulders, and D. Draasisma 1994 "Regulations, Policies and Practices Concerning Work Stress in Five European Countries." *Work and Stress* 8: 296–318.

Kopinak, Kathryn 1996 *Desert Capitalism: Maquiladoras in North America's Western Industrial Corridor.* Tucson: University of Arizona Press.

Korabik, Karen, Donna S. Lero, and Denise L. Whitehead 2008 *Handbook of Work–Family Integration: Research, Theory and Best Practices.* London: Academic Press (Elsevier).

Korczynski, Marek 2013 "The Customer in the Sociology of Work: Different Ways of Going beyond the Management–Worker Dyad." *Work Employment & Society* [E-special issue]: 1–7.

Korczynski, Marek, Randy Hodson, and Paul Edwards, eds. 2006 *Social Theory at Work.* Oxford: Oxford University Press.

Korczynski, Marek, and Cameron Lynne Macdonald 2009 *Service Work: Critical Perspectives.* London: Routledge.

Korczynski, Marek, Michael Pickering, and Emma Robertson 2013 *Rhythms of Labour, Music at Work in Britain.* Cambridge: Cambridge University Press.

Koski, Pasi, and Anu Järvensivu 2010 "The Innovation Diffusion Paradox in the Light of 'Shop Floor Games' and Micro-Politics." *Economic and Industrial Democracy* 31(3): 345–63.

Kosny, Agnieszka, and Ellen MacEachan 2010 "Gendered, Invisible Work in Non-profit Social Service Organizations: Implications for Worker Health and Safety." *Gender, Work & Organization* 17(4): 359–80.

Kossek, Ellen E., and Cynthia Ozeki 1998 "Work–Family Conflict, Policies and the Job-Life Satisfaction Relationship: A Review and Directions for Organizational Behavior– Human Resources Research." *Journal of Applied Psychology* 83(2): 139–49.

Kotkin, Joel. 2013 "Marissa Mayer's Misstep and the Unstoppable Rise of Telecommuting." *Forbes*, March 26.

Krahn, Harvey 1992 *Quality of Work in the Service Sector.* General Social Survey Analysis Series 6. Ottawa: Statistics Canada. Cat. no. 11-612E—No. 6.

———— **1995** "Non-standard Work on the Rise." *Perspectives on Labour and Income* (Winter): 35–42.

———— **1997** "On the Permanence of Human Capital: Use It or Lose It." *Policy Options* 18(6): 17–21.

———— **2009** "Choose Your Parents Carefully: Social Class, Post-secondary Participation, and Occupational Outcomes." In Edward Grabb and Neil Guppy, eds., *Social Inequality in Canada: Patterns, Problems, and Policies.* 5th ed. Toronto: Pearson/Prentice Hall.

Krahn, Harvey, Tracey Derwing, Marlene Mulder, and Lori Wilkinson 2000 "Educated and Underemployed: Refugee Integration into the Canadian Labour Market." *Journal of International Migration and Integration* 1(Winter): 59–84.

Krahn, Harvey, and Nancy Galambos 2014 "Work Values and Beliefs of 'Generation X' and 'Generation Y.'" *Journal of Youth Studies* 17(1): 92–112.

Krahn, Harvey, and Trevor Harrison 1992 "Self-Referenced Relative Deprivation and Economic Beliefs: The Effects of the Recession in Alberta." *Canadian Review of Sociology and Anthropology* 29: 191–209.

Krahn, Harvey, Andrea Howard, and Nancy Galambos 2012 "Exploring or Floundering? The Meaning of Employment and Educational Fluctuations in Emerging Adulthood." *Youth & Society* (September 10). doi:10.1177/0044118X12459061.

Krahn, Harvey, and Julie Hudson 2006 *Pathways of Alberta Youth through the Post-secondary System into the Labour Market, 1996–2003.* Pathways to the Labour Market Series, Report No. 2. Ottawa: Canadian Policy Research Networks.

Krahn, Harvey, and Graham S. Lowe 1999 "Literacy in the Workplace." *Perspectives on Labour and Income* (Summer): 38–44.

Krahn, Harvey, Graham S. Lowe, and Wolfgang Lehmann 2002 "Acquisition of Employability Skills by High School Students." *Canadian Public Policy* 28(2): 259–80.

Krause-Jensen, Jacob 2010 "Values at Work: Ambivalent Situations and Human Resource Embarrassment." *Social Analysis* 54(3): 126–38.

Krinsky, John, and Ellen Reese 2006 "Forging and Sustaining Labor–Community Coalitions: The Workfare Justice Movement in Three Cities." *Sociological Forum* 21(4): 623–58.

Kristal, Tali 2013 "The Capitalist Machine: Computerization, Workers' Power, and the Decline in Labor's Share within U.S. Industries." *American Sociological Review* 78(3): 361–89.

Krogman, Naomi, and Tom Beckley 2002 "Corporate 'Bail-Outs' and Local 'Buyouts': Pathways to Community Forestry." *Society and Natural Resources* 15(2): 109–27.

Ku, Manwai D. 2011 "When Does Gender Matter? Gender Differences in Speciality Choice among Physicians." *Work and Occupations* 38(2): 221–62.

Kuhn, Thomas S. 1970 *The Structure of Scientific Revolutions.* 2nd ed. Chicago: University of Chicago Press.

Kumar, Krishnan 1995 *From Post-industrial to Post-modern Society: New Theories of the Contemporary World.* Oxford, England: Blackwell.

Kumar, Pradeep 1995 *Unions and Workplace Change in Canada.* Kingston, ON: IRC Press.

Kunda, Gideon, and Galit Ailon-Souday 2005 "Managers, Markets, and Ideologies: Design and Devotion Revisited." In Stephen Ackroyd, R. Batt, P. Thompson, and P. S. Tolbert, eds., *The Oxford Handbook of Work and Organization.* Oxford, England: Oxford University Press.

Kunze, Florian, Stephan A. Boehm, and Heike Bruch 2011 "Age Diversity, Age Discrimination Climate and Performance Consequences—A Cross Organizational Study." *Journal of Organizational Behavior* 32: 264–90.

Labour Canada 1986 *Women in the Labour Force, 1985 -86 Edition.* Ottawa: Labour Canada, Women's Bureau.

Labour Market Ministers 2000 *Profile of Canadian Youth in the Labour Market: Second Annual Report to the Forum of Labour Market Ministers.* Hull, QC: HRDC. Cat. no. RH61-1/2000E.

Lair, Craig, and George Ritzer 2009 "Metamanagement and the Outsourcing of Domestic Life." In Philip Hancock and Melissa Tyler, eds. *The Management of Everyday Life.* New York: Palgrave Macmillan.

Laliberte, Ron, and Vic Satzewich 1999 "Native Migrant Labour in the Southern Alberta Sugar-Beet Industry: Coercion and Paternalism in the Recruitment of Labour." *Canadian Review of Sociology and Anthropology* 36(1): 65–85.

Lam, Helen, and Yonatan Reshef 1999 "Are Quality Improvement and Downsizing Compatible? A Human Resources Perspective." *Relations industrielles/Industrial Relations* 54(4): 727–47.

Lamba, Navjot 2003 "The Employment Experiences of Canadian Refugees: Measuring the Impact of Human and Social Capital on Employment Outcomes." *Canadian Review of Sociology and Anthropology* 40(1): 45–64.

Land, Hillary 1980 "The Family Wage." *Feminist Review* 6: 55–77.

Landsbergis, Paul A., Janet Cahill, and Peter Schnall 1999 "The Impact of Lean Production and Related New Systems of Work Organization on Worker Health." *Journal of Occupational Health Psychology* 4(2): 108–30.

Langford, Tom 1996 "Effects of Strike Participation on the Political Consciousness of Canadian Postal Workers." *Relations industrielles/Industrial Relations* 51(3): 651–82.

Largacha-Martinez, Carlos 2011 "What Is Your Calling? SEMCO's Invitation to Participatory Management." In Ernst von Kimakowitz, Michael Pirson, Heiko Spitzeck, Claus Dierksmeier, and Wolfgang Amann, eds., *Humanistic Management in Practice* (pp. 215–30). New York: Palgrave Macmillan.

Laroche, Mireille, Marcel Merette, and G. C. Ruggeri 1999 "On the Concept and Dimensions of Human Capital in a Knowledge-Based Economy Context." *Canadian Public Policy* 25(1): 87–100.

LaRochelle-Côté, Sébastien 2013 *Employment Instability among Younger Workers*. Ottawa: Statistics Canada. Cat. No. 75-004-M—no. 002.

LaRochelle-Côté, S., and J. Gilmore 2009 "Canada's Employment Downturn." *Perspectives on Labour and Income* (December): 5–12.

LaRochelle-Côté, Sébastien, and Claude Dionne 2009 "International Differences in Low-Paid Work." *Perspectives on Labour and Income* 21(Autumn): 5–13.

Lash, Scott 1984 *The Militant Worker: Class and Radicalism in France and America*. London: Heinemann.

Lash, Scott, and John Urry 1987 *The End of Organized Capitalism*. Cambridge: Polity Press.

——— **2013** "Book Review Symposium: Response to Reviewers of *The End of Organized Capitalism*." *Work, Employment & Society* 27: 542–46.

Laslett, Barbara, and Johanna Brenner 1989 "Gender and Social Reproduction: Historical Perspectives." *Annual Review of Sociology* 15: 381–404.

Lautsch, Brenda A., and Maureen A. Scully 2007 "Restructuring Time: Implications of Work-Hours Reductions for the Working Class." *Human Relations* 60(5): 719–43.

Law Commission of Ontario 2012 *Vulnerable Workers and Precarious Work—Final Report*. Toronto: Law Commission of Ontario.

Lawler, Edward E., III, and Susan Albers Mohrman 2003 *Creating a Strategic Human Resources Organization: An Assessment of Trends and New Directions*. Stanford, CA: Stanford University Press.

Laxer, Gordon 1989 *Open for Business: The Roots of Foreign Ownership in Canada*. Don Mills, ON: Oxford University Press.

——— **1995** "Social Solidarity, Democracy and Global Capitalism." *Canadian Review of Sociology and Anthropology* 32: 287–313.

Leck, Joanne 2002 "Making Employment Equity Programs Work for Women." *Canadian Public Policy* 28: S85–S100.

Leckie, Norm, André Léonard, Julie Turcotte, and David Wallace 2001 *Employer and Employee Perspectives on Human Resource Practices*. The Evolving Workplace Series. Ottawa: Statistics Canada and Human Resources Development Canada. Cat. no. 71-584-MPE—No. 1.

Lee, Cheol Sung 2007 "Labor Unions and Good Governance: A Cross-National, Comparative Analysis." *American Sociological Review* 72(4): 585–609.

Lehmann, Wolfgang 2012 "Extra-Credential Experiences and Social Closure: Working-Class Students at University." *British Educational Research Journal* 38(2): 203–18.

Leicht, Kevin T., and Mary L. Fennell 2001 *Professional Work: A Sociological Approach*. Oxford, England: Blackwell.

Leidner, Robin 1993 *Fast Food, Fast Talk: Interactive Service Work and the Routinization of Everyday Life*. Berkeley, CA: University of California Press.

Lenski, Gerhard 1966 *Power and Privilege: A Theory of Social Stratification.* New York: McGraw-Hill.

Leonard, Andre 2013 *Employment Insurance: Ten Changes in 2012–13.* Background Paper. Ottawa: Library of Parliament. No. 2013-03-E.

Leontaridi, Marianthi 1998 "Segmented Labour Markets: Theory and Evidence." *Journal of Economic Surveys* 12(1): 103–9.

Lerner, Gerda 1986 *The Creation of Patriarchy.* New York: Oxford University Press.

Lévesque, Christian, and Gregor Murray 2010 "Trade Union Cross-Border Alliances within MNCs: Disentangling Union Dynamics at the Local, National and International Levels." *Industrial Relations Journal* 41(4): 312–32.

Levine, David I. 1995 *Reinventing the Workplace: How Business and Employees Can Both Win.* Washington, DC: Brookings Institution.

Levinson, Klas 2000 "Codetermination in Sweden: Myth and Reality." *Economic and Industrial Democracy* 21(4): 457–73.

Levitt, Howard 2014 "Why Internships Are Facing a Growing Backlash." *Financial Post,* March 11. http://business.financialpost.com/2014/03/11/why-unpaid-internships-are-facing-growing-backlash/.

Levitt, Kari Polanyi 2013 *From the Great Transformation to the Great Financialization: On Karl Polanyi and Other Essays.* Halifax: Fernwood Publishing.

Lewchuk, Wayne, A. Leslie Robb, and Vivienne Walters 1996 "The Effectiveness of Bill 70 and Joint Health and Safety Committees in Reducing Injuries in the Workplace: The Case of Ontario." *Canadian Public Policy* 22: 225–43.

Lewis, Jane 2009 *Work Family Balance, Gender and Policy.* Cheltenham, England: Edward Elgar.

Li, Peter S. 1982 "Chinese Immigrants on the Canadian Prairie, 1919–47." *Canadian Review of Sociology and Anthropology* 19: 527–40.

——— 2001 "The Market Worth of Immigrants' Educational Credentials." *Canadian Public Policy* 27(1): 23–38.

Liker, Jeffrey K. 2004 *The Toyota Way: 14 Management Principles from the World's Greatest Manufacturer.* New York: McGraw-Hill.

Lillie, Nathan 2005 "Union Networks and Global Unionism in Maritime Shipping."

Relations industrielles/Industrial Relations 60(1): 88–111.

Lin, Liang-Hung, Yu-Ling Ho, and Wei-Hsin Eugenia Lin 2013 "Confucian and Taoist Work Values: An Exploratory Study of the Chinese Transformational Leadership Behavior." *Journal of Business Ethics* 113: 91–103.

Lin, Nan 1999 "Social Networks and Status Attainment." *Annual Review of Sociology* 25: 467–87.

Lincoln, James R. 1990 "Japanese Organization and Organization Theory." *Research in Organizational Behavior* 12: 255–94.

Lincoln, James R., and Arne L. Kalleberg 1990 *Culture, Control, and Commitment: A Study of Work Organization and Work Attitudes in the United States and Japan.* Cambridge: Cambridge University Press.

Lincoln, James R., and Kerry McBride 1987 "Japanese Industrial Organization in Comparative Perspective." *Annual Review of Sociology* 13: 289–312.

Lindenfeld, Fran, and Pamela Wynn 1997 "Success and Failure of Worker Co-ops: The Role of Internal and External Environmental Factors." *Humanity and Society* 21(2): 148–61.

Lindsay, Sally 2007 "Gendering Work: The Masculinization of Nurse Anesthesia." *Canadian Journal of Sociology* 32(4): 429–48.

Linhart, Robert 1981 *The Assembly Line.* London, England: John Calder.

Lippmann, Stephen 2008 "Rethinking Risk in the New Economy: Age and Cohort Effects on Unemployment and Re-Employment." *Human Relations* 61(9): 1259–92.

Lipset, Seymour Martin 1990 *Continental Divide: The Values and Institutions of the United States and Canada.* New York: Routledge.

Lipset, Seymour M., and Noah M. Meltz 1997 "Canadian and American Attitudes toward Work and Institutions." *Perspectives on Work* 1(3): 14–19.

Lipshitz, Raanan 2000 "Chic, Mystique, and Misconception: Argyris and Schon and the Rhetoric of Organizational Learning." *Journal of Applied Behavioral Science* 36(4): 456–73.

Lipsig-Mummé, Carla 2009 "Trade Unions and Labour Relations Regimes: International Perspectives in a Globalizing World." In Morley Gunderson and Daphne Taras, eds.,

Canadian Labour and Employment Relations. Toronto: Pearson Addison Wesley.

Littler, Craig R., and Peter Innes 2003 "Downsizing and Deknowledging the Firm." *Work, Employment & Society* 17(1): 73–100.

Livingstone, David W. 1999 *The Education–Jobs Gap: Underemployment or Economic Democracy.* Toronto: Garamond Press.

———— 2005 *Basic Findings of the 2004 Canadian Learning and Work Survey.* http://lifelong.oise.utoronto.ca/papers/WALLBasicSummJune05.pdf.

————, ed. 2009 *Education & Jobs: Exploring the Gaps.* Toronto: University of Toronto Press.

Livingstone, David W., and David Guile 2012 *The Knowledge Economy and Lifelong Learning: A Critical Reader.* Rotterdam, The Netherlands: Sense Publishers.

Livingstone, David W., and Meg Luxton 1996 "Gender Consciousness at Work: Modification of the Male Breadwinner Norm." In David W. Livingstone and J. Marshall Mangan, eds., *Recast Dreams: Class and Gender Consciousness in Steeltown.* Toronto: Garamond Press.

Livingstone, David W., and Antonie Scholtz 2007 "Contradictions of Labour Processes and Workers' Use of Skills in Advanced Capitalist Economies." In Vivian Shalla and Wallace Clement, eds., *Work in Tumultuous Times: Critical Perspectives.* Montreal and Kingston: McGill–Queen's University Press.

Lizardo, Omar 2012 The Three Phases of Bourdieu's U.S. Reception: Comment on Lamont. *Sociological Forum* 27: 238–44.

Locke, Edwin A. 1982 "The Ideas of Frederick W. Taylor: An Evaluation." *The Academy of Management Review* 7(1): 14–24.

Lockwood, David 1966 "Sources of Variation in Working Class Images of Society." *Sociological Review* 14: 249–67.

Logue, John 1981 "Saab/Trollhattan: Reforming Work Life on the Shop Floor." *Working Life in Sweden* 23(June).

Logue, John, and Jacquelyn S. Yates 1999 "Worker Ownership American Style: Pluralism, Participation and Performance." *Economic and Industrial Democracy* 20(2): 225–52.

Long, Richard J. 1989 "Patterns of Workplace Innovation in Canada." *Relations industrielles/Industrial Relations* 44: 805–26.

———— 1995 "Employee Buyouts: The Canadian Experience." *Canadian Business Economics* (Summer): 28–41.

Looise, Jan Kees, and Michiel Drucker 2003 "Dutch Works Councils in Times of Transition: The Effects of Changes in Society, Organizations and Work on the Position of Works Councils." *Economic and Industrial Democracy* 24(3): 379–409.

Looker, E. Dianne, and Peter Dwyer 1998 "Education and Negotiated Reality: Complexities Facing Rural Youth in the 1990s." *Journal of Youth Studies* 1(1): 5–22.

Lopez, Steve 2006 "Emotional Labor and Organized Emotional Care: Conceptualizing Nursing Home Care Work." *Work and Occupations* 33(2): 133–60.

———— 2010 "Workers, Managers, and Customers: Triangles of Power in Work Communities." *Work and Occupations* 37(3): 251–71.

Lopez-Pacheco, Alexandra 2014 "A Little-Used Model." *Edmonton Journal,* January 2, B3.

Lorinc, John 2013 "State of the Unions." *The Walrus* (December): 24–31.

Lowe, Graham S. 1981 "Causes of Unionization in Canadian Banks." *Relations industrielles/Industrial Relations* 36: 865–92.

———— 1987 *Women in the Administrative Revolution: The Feminization of Clerical Work.* Toronto: University of Toronto Press.

———— 1998 "The Future of Work: Implications for Unions." *Relations industrielles/Industrial Relations* 53(2): 235–57.

———— 2000 *The Quality of Work: A People-Centred Agenda.* Don Mills, ON: Oxford University Press.

———— 2001 *Employer of Choice? Workplace Innovation in Government: A Synthesis Report.* Ottawa: Canadian Policy Research Networks.

———— 2007 *21st Century Job Quality: Achieving What Canadians Want.* Ottawa: Canadian Policy Research Networks. http://www.cprn.org.

Lowe, Graham S., and Harvey Krahn 1985 "Where Wives Work: The Relative Effects of Situational and Attitudinal Factors." *Canadian Journal of Sociology* 10: 1–22.

———— 1999 "Reconceptualizing Youth Unemployment." In Julian Barling and E. Kevin Kelloway, eds., *Young Workers: Varieties of Experience.* Washington, DC: American Psychological Association.

References

——— 2000 "Work Aspirations and Attitudes in an Era of Labour Market Restructuring: A Comparison of Two Canadian Youth Cohorts." _Work, Employment & Society_ 14(1): 1–22.

Lowe, Graham S., Harvey Krahn, and Jeff Bowlby 1997 _1996 Alberta High School Graduate Survey: Report of Research Findings._ Edmonton: Population Research Laboratory, University of Alberta.

Lowe, Graham S., and Herbert C. Northcott 1986 _Under Pressure: A Study of Job Stress._ Toronto: Garamond Press.

Lowe, Graham S., and Grant Schellenberg 2001 _What's a Good Job? The Importance of Employment Relationships._ CPRN Study W-05. Ottawa: Canadian Policy Research Networks.

Lowen, Aaron, and Paul Sicilian 2009 "Family-Friendly Fringe Benefits and the Gender Wage Gap." _Journal of Labor Research_ 30: 101–19.

Lucas, Rex A. 1971 _Minetown, Milltown, Railtown._ Toronto: University of Toronto Press.

Luce, Stephanie 2004 _Fighting for a Living Wage._ Ithaca, NY: Cornell University Press.

Luffman, Jacqueline 2003 "Taking Stock of Equity Compensation." _Perspectives on Labour and Income_ 15(Summer): 26–33.

Luffman, Jacqueline, and Deborah Sussman 2007 "The Aboriginal Labour Force in Western Canada." _Perspectives on Labour and Income_ 19(1): 30–44.

Lund, John, and Christopher Wright 2009 "Enabling 'Managed Activism': The Adoption of Call Centres in Australian, British and US Trade Unions." _New Technology, Work and Employment_ 24(1): 43–59.

Luong, May 2010 "The Financial Impact of Student Loans." _Perspectives on Labour and Income_ (January): 5–18.

Lupton, Ben 2006 "Explaining Men's Entry into Female-Concentrated Occupations: Issues of Masculinity and Social Class." _Gender, Work & Organization_ 13(2): 103–28.

Luxton, Meg, 1980 _More Than a Labour of Love._ Toronto: Women's Press.

Luxton, Meg, ed. 1997 _Feminism and Families._ Halifax: Fernwood Publishing.

Macarov, David 1982 _Worker Productivity: Myths and Reality._ Beverly Hills, CA: Sage.

Macey, William H., and Benjamin Schneider 2008 "The Meaning of Employee Engagement." _Industrial and Organizational Psychology_ 1(1): 3–30.

Macdonald, Keith M. 1995 _The Sociology of the Professions._ Thousand Oaks, CA: Sage.

Macdonald, Martha 1991 "Post-Fordism and the Flexibility Debate." _Studies in Political Economy_ 36: 177–201.

Mackenzie, Hugh 2012 _Canada's CEO Elite 100: The 0.01%._ Ottawa: Canadian Centre for Policy Alternatives.

MacLean, Brian K., and Lars Osberg, eds. 1996 _The Unemployment Crisis: All for Nought?_ Montreal and Kingston: McGill–Queen's University Press.

Macleod, Gus 1997 _From Mondragon to America: Experiments in Community Economic Development._ Sydney, NS: University College of Cape Breton Press.

MacPhail, Fiona, and Paul Bowles 2009 "Corporate Social Responsibility as Support for Employee Volunteers: Impacts, Gender Puzzles and Policy Implications in Canada." _Journal of Business Ethics_ 84(3): 405–16.

Mahon, Rianne 1984 _The Politics of Industrial Restructuring: Canadian Textiles._ Toronto: University of Toronto Press.

——— 1987 "From Fordism To? New Technology, Labour Markets and Unions." _Economic and Industrial Democracy_ 8: 5–60.

Mahon, Rianne, with Sonya Michel 2002 _Child Care Policy at the Crossroads: Gender and Welfare State Restructuring._ London, England: Routledge.

Mainiero, Lisa, and Kevin Jones 2013 "Sexual Harassment versus Workplace Romance: Social Media Spillover and Textual Harassment in the Workplace." _Academy of Management Perspectives_ 27(3): 187–203.

Mandel, Hadas 2013 "Up the Down Staircase: Women's Upward Mobility and the Wage Penalty for Occupational Feminization, 1970–2007." _Social Forces_ 91(4): 1183–1207.

Mann, Michael 1970 "The Social Cohesion of Liberal Democracy." _American Sociological Review_ 35: 423–39.

Mann, Sandi, and Lynn Holdsworth 2003 "The Psychological Impact of Teleworking: Stress, Emotions and Health." _New Technology, Work and Employment_ 18(3): 196–211.

Manser, Marilyn E., and Garnett Picot 1999 "Self-Employment in Canada and the United States." *Perspectives on Labour and Income* (Autumn): 37–44.

Marchak, M. Patricia 1981 *Ideological Perspectives on Canada*. 2nd ed. Toronto: McGraw-Hill Ryerson.

Marin, Alexandra 2012 "Don't Mention It: Why People Don't Share Job Information, When They Do, and Why It Matters." *Social Networks* 34: 181–92.

Marquardt, Richard 1998 *Enter at Your Own Risk: Canadian Youth and the Labour Market*. Toronto: Between the Lines.

Marshall, Katherine 1989 "Women in the Professional Occupations: Progress in the 1980s." *Canadian Social Trends* (Spring): 13–16.

—— 1993 "Dual Earners: Who's Responsible for Housework?" *Canadian Social Trends* (Winter): 11–14.

—— 1996 "A Job to Die For." *Perspectives on Labour and Income* (Summer): 26–31.

—— 1997 "Job Sharing." *Perspectives on Labour and Income* (Summer): 6–10.

—— 2000 "Incomes of Young Retired Women: The Past 30 Years." *Perspectives on Labour and Income* 12(Winter): 9–17.

—— 2001 "Working with Computers." *Perspectives on Labour and Income* 13(Summer): 9–15.

—— 2003 "Benefits of the Job." *Perspectives on Labour and Income* 15(Summer): 7–14.

—— 2006 "Converging Gender Roles." *Perspectives on Labour and Income* (July): 5–17.

—— 2009 "The Family Work Week." *Perspectives on Labour and Income* (April): 5–13.

—— 2011 "Generational Change in Paid and Unpaid Work." *Canadian Social Trends* (Summer): 13. Statistics Canada Cat. no. 11-008-X. http://www.statcan.gc.ca/pub/11-008-x/2011002/article/11520-eng.htm.

Marshall, Victor W., and Margaret M. Mueller 2002 *Rethinking Social Policy for an Aging Society: Insights from the Life Course Perspective*. Ottawa: Canadian Policy Research Networks. http://www.cprn.org.

Martin, D'Arcy 1995 *Thinking Union: Activism and Education in Canada's Labour Movement*. Toronto: Between the Lines Press.

Martin, Gary 2000 "Employment and Unemployment in Mexico in the 1990s." *Monthly Labor Review* (November): 3–18.

Martin, Jack K., and Paul M. Roman 1996 "Job Satisfaction, Job Reward Characteristics, and Employees' Problem Drinking Behaviors." *Work and Occupations* 23: 4–25.

Martin, Jack K., and Constance L. Shehan 1989 "Education and Job Satisfaction: The Influences of Gender, Wage-Earning Status, and Job Values." *Work and Occupations* 16: 184–99.

Martin, Joanne 2002 *Organizational Culture: Mapping the Terrain*. Thousand Oaks, CA: Sage Publications.

Maslach, Christina, and Michael P. Leiter 1997 *The Truth about Burnout: How Organizations Cause Personal Stress and What to Do about It*. San Francisco: Jossey-Bass.

Massoni, Kelly 2004 "Modeling Work: Occupational Messages in *Seventeen* Magazine." *Gender and Society* 18(1): 47–65.

Matthews, Roy A. 1985 *Structural Change and Industrial Policy: The Redeployment of Canadian Manufacturing, 1960–80*. Ottawa: Supply and Services Canada.

Maximova, Katerina, and Harvey Krahn 2005 "Does Race Matter? Earnings of Visible Minority Graduates from Alberta Universities." *Canadian Journal of Higher Education* 35(1): 85–110.

Mayer-Ahuja, Nicole, and Harald Wolf 2007 "Beyond the Hype: Working in the German Internet Industry." *Critical Sociology* 33(1–2): 73–99.

Maynard, Douglas C., Todd Allen Joseph, and Amanda M. Maynard 2006 "Underemployment, Job Attitudes, and Turnover Intentions." *Journal of Organizational Behaviour* 27: 509–36.

Mayo, Elton 1945 *The Social Problems of an Industrial Civilization*. Cambridge, MA: Harvard University Press.

McBride, Anne 2011 "Lifting the Barriers? Workplace Education and Training, Women and Job Progression." *Gender, Work & Organizations* 18(5): 528–47.

McCabe, Darren 1999 "Total Quality Management: Anti-union Trojan Horse or Management Albatross?" *Work, Employment & Society* 13(4): 665–91.

McCormack, A. Ross 1978 *Reformers, Rebels and Revolutionaries: The Western Canadian Radical Movement, 1899–1919*. Toronto: University of Toronto Press.

McCormick, Chris, ed. 1998 *The Westray Chronicles: A Case Study of an Occupational Disaster.* Halifax: Fernwood Publishing.

Mcdonald, Judith A., and Robert J. Thornton 1998 "Private-Sector Experience with Pay Equity in Ontario." *Canadian Public Policy* 24(2): 185–208.

McDowell, Linda 2009 *Working Bodies: Interactive Service Employment and Workplace Identities.* Chichester, England: Wiley Blackwell.

McFarland, Janet 2007 "'Big Leavers' Lever Bigger Pay Packages." *Globe and Mail,* June 4, B5.

McFarlane, Seth, Roderic Beaujot, and Tony Haddad 2000 "Time Constraints and Relative Resources as Determinants of the Sexual Division of Domestic Work." *Canadian Journal of Sociology* 25(1): 61–82.

McGregor, Douglas 1960 *The Human Side of Enterprise.* New York: McGraw-Hill.

McGuigan, Jim 2009 *Cool Capitalism.* London, England: Pluto Press.

McIlwee, Judith S., and J. Gregg Robinson 1992 *Women in Engineering: Gender, Power, and Workplace Culture.* Albany, NY: State University of New York Press.

McKay, Shona 1996 "You're (Still) Hired." *Report on Business* magazine, December, 54–60.

McKenna, Barrie 2013 "Canada Post Gears Up for Pension Fight." *Globe and Mail,* December 17, B1.

McLuhan, Marshall 1964 *Understanding Media: The Extensions of Man.* New York: McGraw-Hill.

McMahon, Martha 2005 *Engendering Motherhood: Identity and Self-Transformation in Women's Lives.* New York: Guilford Press.

McMullin, Julie 2010 *Understanding Social Inequality: Intersections of Class, Age, Gender, Ethnicity, and Race in Canada.* 2nd ed. Don Mills, ON: Oxford University Press.

McRae, Susan 2003 "Constraints and Choices in Mothers' Employment Careers: A Consideration of Hakim's Preference Theory." *British Journal of Sociology* 54(3): 317–38.

Meissner, Martin 1971 "The Long Arm of the Job: A Study of Work and Leisure." *Industrial Relations* 10: 239–60.

Meissner, Martin, E. W. Humphreys, S. M. Meis, and W. J. Scheu 1975 "No Exit for Wives: Sexual Division of Labour and the Cumulation of Household Demands." *Canadian Review of Sociology and Anthropology* 12: 424–39.

Mendelsohn, Matthew 2012 "Changes to EI Leave the Job Unfinished." *Globe and Mail,* June 4.

Mendenhall, Ruby, Ariel Kalil, Laurel J. Spindel, and Cassandra M. D. Hart 2008 "Job Loss at Mid-Life: Managers and Executives Face the 'New Risk Economy'" *Social Forces* 87(1): 185–209.

Menzies, Heather 1996 *Whose Brave New World? The Information Highway and the New Economy.* Toronto: Between the Lines.

Merton, Robert K. 1952 "Bureaucratic Structure and Personality." In Robert K. Merton, A. P. Gray, B. Hockey, and H. C. Selvin, eds., *Reader in Bureaucracy.* New York: Free Press.

Meyer, Stephen 1981 *The Five Dollar Day: Labor Management and Social Control in the Ford Motor Company, 1908–1921.* Albany, NY: State University of New York Press.

Michels, Robert 1959 *Political Parties: A Sociological Study of the Oligarchical Tendencies of Modern Democracy.* New York: Dover Publications. (Orig. pub. 1915.)

Micklethwait, John, and Adrian Wooldridge 1996 *The Witch Doctors: Making Sense of the Management Gurus.* New York: Times Books.

Middleton, Chris 1988 "The Familiar Fate of the *Famulae*: Gender Divisions in the History of Wage Labour." In R. E. Pahl, ed., *On Work: Historical, Comparative and Theoretical Approaches.* Oxford, England: Basil Blackwell.

Milan, Anne, Leslie-Anne Keown, and Covadonga Robies Urquijo 2011 "Families, Living Arrangements, and Unpaid Work." In *Women in Canada: A Gender-Based Statistical Report.* Ottawa: Statistics Canada. Catalogue no. 89-503-X.

Milan, Anne, and Kelly Tran 2004 "Blacks in Canada: A Long History." *Canadian Social Trends* (Spring): 2–7.

Milanovic, Branko 2011 *The Haves and the Have-Nots: A Brief and Idiosyncratic History of Global Inequality.* New York: Basic Books.

Milkman, Ruth 1991 *Japan's California Factories: Labor Relations and Economic Globalization.* Los Angeles: Institute of Industrial Relations, University of California at Los Angeles.

——— 1997 *Farewell to the Factory: Auto Workers in the Late Twentieth Century.* Berkeley: University of California Press.

Miller, Danny, and Jon Hartwick 2002 "Spotting Management Fads." *Harvard Business Review*, October, 26–27.

Miller, Gloria 2004 "Frontier Masculinity in the Oil Industry: The Experience of Women Engineers." *Gender, Work & Organization* 11(1): 47–73.

Miller, Karen A., Melvin L. Kohn, and Carmi Schooler 1985 "Educational Self-Determination and the Cognitive Functioning of Students." *Social Forces* 63(4): 923–44.

Mills, C. Wright 1948 *The New Men of Power.* New York: Harcourt-Brace.

——— **1956** *White Collar: The American Middle Classes.* New York: Oxford University Press.

Mills, Melinda 2004 "Demand for Flexibility or Generation of Insecurity: The Individualization of Risk, Irregular Work Shifts and Canadian Youth." *Journal of Youth Studies* 7(2): 115–39.

Milner, Henry 1989 *Sweden: Social Democracy in Practice.* Oxford: Oxford University Press.

Mintzberg, Henry 1989 *Mintzberg on Management: Inside Our Strange World of Organizations.* New York: Free Press.

Mirchandani, Kiran 1999 "Legitimizing Work: Telework and the Gendered Reification of the Work–Nonwork Dichotomy." *Canadian Review of Sociology and Anthropology* 36(1): 87–107.

Mirchandani, Kiran 2012 *Phone Clones: Authenticity Work in the Transnational Service Economy.* Ithica and London: Cornell University Press.

Mishel, Lawrence, and Jared Bernstein 2003 "Wage Inequality and the New Economy in the US: Does IT-Led Growth Generate Wage Inequality?" *Canadian Public Policy* 29(S1): S203–S221.

Mishra, Aneil K., and Gretchen M. Spreitzer 1998 "Explaining How Survivors Respond to Downsizing: The Roles of Trust, Empowerment, Justice, and Work Redesign." *Academy of Management Review* 23(3): 567–88.

Mitchell, Alanna 1997 "The Poor Fare Worst in Schools." *Globe and Mail*, April 18, A1.

Moen, P., E. Kelly, and K. Chermack 2008 "Learning from a Natural Experiment: Studying a Corporate Work-Time Policy Initiative." In A. C. Crouter and A. Booth, eds.,

Work-Life Policies That Make a Real Difference for Individuals, Families, and Organizations. Washington, DC: Urban Institute Press.

Moen, Phyllis, Jack Lam, Samantha Ammons, and Erin Kelly 2013 "Time Worked by Overworked Professionals: Strategies in Response to the Stress of Higher Status." *Work and Occupations* 40(2): 79–114.

Mohamed, Norshidah, Nor Shahriza Abdul Karim, and Ramiah Hussein 2010 "Linking Islamic Work Ethic to Computer Use Ethics, Job Satisfaction and Organisational Commitment in Malaysia." *Journal of Business Systems, Governance and Ethics* 5(1): 13–22.

Mohr, Robert D., and Cindy Zoghi 2008 "High-Involvement Work Design and Job Satisfaction." *Industrial and Labor Relations Review* 61(3): 275–96.

Morgan, Gareth 1997 *Images of Organization.* Thousand Oaks, CA: Sage Publications.

Morissette, René 1997 "Declining Earnings of Young Men." *Canadian Social Trends* (Autumn): 8–12.

Morissette, René, and Yuri Ostrovky 2007 *Income Instability of Lone Parents, Singles and Two-Parent Families in Canada, 1984 to 2004.* Analytical Studies Branch Research Paper No. 297. Ottawa: Statistics Canada. Cat. no. 11F0019MIE—No. 297.

Morissette, René, Grant Schellenberg, and Anick Johnson 2005 "Diverging Trends in Unionization." *Perspectives on Labour and Income* 16(April): 5–12.

Morissette, René, Grant Schellenberg, and Cynthia Silver 2004 "Retaining Older Workers." *Perspectives on Labour and Income* 16(Winter): 33–38.

Morissette, René, and Rizwan Sultan 2013 "Twenty Years in the Careers of Immigrant and Native-Born Workers." *Economic Insights,* Issue 32 (November): 1–4. Statistics Canada Cat. no. 11-626-X.

Morissette, René, and Xuelin Zhang 2005 "Escaping Low Earnings." *Perspectives on Labour and Income* 17(Summer): 37–44.

——— **2007** "Revisiting Wealth Inequality." *Perspectives on Labour and Income* 19(1): 6–17.

Morita, Masaya 2001 "Have the Seeds of Japanese Teamworking Taken Root Abroad?" *New Technology, Work and Employment* 16(3): 178–90.

Morton, Desmond 2007 *Working People: An Illustrated History of the Canadian Labour*

Movement. 5th ed. Montreal and Kingston: McGill-Queen's University Press.

Moss-Racusin, Corinne A., John F. Dovidio, Victoria L. Brescoll, Mark J. Graham, and Jo Handelsman 2012 "Science Faculty's Subtle Gender Biases Favor Male Students." *Proceedings of the National Academy of Sciences* 109(41): 16474–79.

Mueller, Frank, Raffaella Valsecchi, Chris Smith, Jonathan Gabe, and Mary Ann Elston 2008 " 'We Are Nurses, We Are Supposed to Care for People': Professional Values among Nurses in NHS Direct Call Centres." *New Technology, Work and Employment* 23(1–2): 2–16.

Mueller, Steffen 2012 "Works Councils and Establishment Productivity." *Industrial and Labor Relations Review* 65(4): 880–98.

Muhlhausen, David B. 2005 "Do Job Programs Work? A Review Article." *Journal of Labor Research* 26(2): 299–322.

Murphy, Brian, Paul Roberts, and Michael Wolfson 2007 "High-Income Canadians." *Perspectives on Labour and Income* 19(4): 7–19.

Murphy, Brian, Xuelin Zhang, and Claude Dionne 2012 *Low Income in Canada: A Multi-line and Multi-index Perspective.* Ottawa: Statistics Canada Cat. no. 75F0002M—No. 001.

Mustard, Cam, John N. Lavis, and Aleck Ostry 2005 "Work and Health: New Evidence and Enhanced Understandings." In Jody Heymann, C. Hertzman, M. Barer, and R. Evans, eds., *Creating Healthier Societies: From Analysis to Action.* Oxford: Oxford University Press.

Muszynski, Alicja 1996 *Cheap Wage Labour: Race and Gender in the Fisheries of British Columbia.* Montreal and Kingston: McGill–Queen's University Press.

Myles, John 1988 "The Expanding Middle: Some Canadian Evidence on the Deskilling Debate." *Canadian Review of Sociology and Anthropology* 25: 335–64.

——— **2000** "Incomes of Seniors." *Perspectives on Labour and Income* 12(Winter): 23–32.

Myles, John, and Jill Quadagno, eds. 2005 *States, Labour Markets and the Future of Old Age Policy.* Philadelphia: Temple University Press.

Mythen, Gabe 2005 "Employment, Individualization and Insecurity: Rethinking the Risk Society Perspective." *The Sociological Review* 53(1): 129–49.

Neale, Deborah 1992 "Will Bob Rae Deliver on His Promise?" *Policy Options* (January–February): 25–28.

Neckerman, Kathryn M., and Florencia Torche 2007 "Inequality: Causes and Consequences." *Annual Review of Sociology* 33: 335–57.

Nelson, Daniel 1980 *Frederick W. Taylor and the Rise of Scientific Management.* Madison, WI: University of Wisconsin Press.

Nelson, Fiona 1996 *Lesbian Motherhood: An Exploration of Canadian Lesbian Families.* Toronto: University of Toronto Press.

Nelson, Joel I. 1995 *Post-industrial Capitalism: Exploring Economic Inequality in America.* Thousand Oaks, CA: Sage.

Niezen, Ronald 1993 "Power and Dignity: The Social Consequences of HydroElectric Development for the James Bay Cree." *Canadian Review of Sociology and Anthropology* 30: 510–29.

Nilsson, Tommy 1996 "Lean Production and White Collar Work: The Case of Sweden." *Economic and Industrial Democracy* 17: 447–72.

Nishman, Robert F. 1995 *Worker Ownership and the Restructuring of Algoma Steel in the 1990s.* Kingston, ON: IRC Press.

Noack, Andrea M., and Leah F. Vosko 2011 *Precarious Jobs in Ontario: Mapping Dimensions of Labour Market Insecurity by Workers' Social Location and Context* [Commissioned Research Report]. Toronto: Law Commission of Ontario. http://www.lco-cdo.org/en/vulnerable-workers-call-for-papers-noack-vosko.

Noble, David 1995 *Progress without People: New Technology, Unemployment, and the Message of Resistance.* Toronto: Between the Lines.

Noël, Alain, and Keith Gardner 1990 "The Gainers Strike: Capitalist Offensive, Militancy, and the Politics of Industrial Relations in Canada." *Studies in Political Economy* 31: 31–72.

Nolan, Peter, and P. K. Edwards 1984 "Homogenise, Divide and Rule: An Essay on Segmented Work, Divided Workers." *Cambridge Journal of Economics* 8(2): 197–215.

Noonan, Mary C. and Jennifer L. Glass 2012 "The Hard Truth about Telecommuting." *Monthly Labor Review* (June): 38–45.

Northcott, Herbert C., and Graham S. Lowe 1987 "Job and Gender Influences in the

Subjective Experience of Work." *Canadian Review of Sociology and Anthropology* 24: 117–31.

Nussbaum, Karen, and Virginia duRivage 1986 "Computer Monitoring: Mismanagement by Remote Control." *Business and Society Review* 56(Winter): 16–20.

Oakes, Leslie S., Barbara Townley, and David J. Cooper 1998 "Business Planning as Pedagogy: Language and Control in a Changing Institutional Field." *Administrative Science Quarterly* 43: 257–92.

OECD [Organisation for Economic Co-operation and Development] 2004 *OECD Employment Outlook 2004.* Paris: OECD. IXBN 92-64-01045-9.

——— **2010** *OECD Harmonised Unemployment Rates.* News Release. February 8. http://www.oecd.org/dataoecd/17/54/44563975.pdf.

——— **2011** *Divided We Stand: Why Inequality Keeps Rising.* Paris: OECD http://www.oecd.org/document/51/0,3746,en_2649_33933_49147827_1_1_1_1,00.html.

——— **2012** *OECD Factbook 2011–12.* Paris: OECD.

OECD and Statistics Canada 2011 *Literacy for Life: Further Results from the Adult Literacy and Life Skills Survey Second International ALL Report.* Ottawa: Statistics Canada. Cat. no. 89-604-XWE-2011001.

O'Faircheallaigh, Ciaran, and Tony Corbett 2005 "Indigenous Participation in Environmental Management of Mining Projects: The Role of Negotiated Agreements." *Environmental Politics* 14(5): 629–47.

Oldham, Greg R., and J. Richard Hackman 2010 "Not What It Was and Not What It Will Be: The Future of Job Redesign Research." *Journal of Organizational Behavior* 31: 463–79.

Ollivier, Michèle 2000 " 'Too Much Money off Other People's Backs': Status in Late Modern Societies." *Canadian Journal of Sociology* 25(4): 441–70.

Olsen, Gregg 1999 "Half Empty or Half Full? The Swedish Welfare State in Transition." *Canadian Review of Sociology and Anthropology* 36(2): 241–67.

——— **2008** "Labour Market Policy in the United States, Canada and Sweden:

Addressing the Issue of Convergence." *Social Policy & Administration* 42(4): 323–41.

Olson, Mancur 1965 *The Logic of Collective Action.* Cambridge, MA: Harvard University Press.

O'Neill, Jeff 1991 "Changing Occupational Structure." *Canadian Social Trends* (Winter): 8–12.

Ontario 2014 *Report and Final Recommendations of the Ontario Minimum Wage Advisory Panel.* Toronto: Ontario Ministry of Labour.

Orme, W. A., Jr. 1996 *Understanding NAFTA: Mexico, Free Trade, and the New North America.* Austin: University of Texas Press.

Orr, Julian E. 1996 *Talking about Machines: An Ethnography of a Modern Job.* Ithaca, NY: ILR Press.

Osberg, Lars 2008 *A Quarter Century of Economic Inequality in Canada: 1981–2006.* Toronto: Canadian Centre for Policy Alternatives.

Osberg, Lars, Fred Wein, and Jan Grude 1995 *Vanishing Jobs: Canada's Changing Workplace.* Toronto: Lorimer.

Ospina, Sonia 1996 *Illusions of Opportunity: Employee Expectations and Workplace Inequality.* Ithaca and London: Cornell University Press.

Osterman, Paul 2000 "Work Reorganization in an Era of Restructuring: Trends in Diffusion and Effects on Employee Welfare." *Industrial and Labor Relations Review* 53(2): 179–96.

——— **2010** "Job Design in the Context of the Job Market." *Journal of Organizational Behavior* 31: 401–11.

Osterman, Paul, and M. Diane Burton 2005 "Ports and Ladders: The Nature and Relevance of Internal Labor Markets in a Changing World." In Stephen Ackroyd, R. Batt, P. Thompson, and P. S. Tolbert, eds., *The Oxford Handbook of Work and Organization.* Oxford: Oxford University Press.

Osterman, Paul, and Beth Shulman 2011 *Good Jobs America: Making Work Better for Everyone.* New York: Russell Sage Foundation.

Ostroff, Frank 1999 *The Horizontal Organization: What the Organization of the Future Actually Looks Like and How It Delivers Value to Customers.* New York: Oxford University Press.

Ostry, Sylvia 1968 *The Female Worker in Canada*. Ottawa: Queen's Printer.

O'Toole, James, ed. 1977 *Work, Learning and the American Future*. San Francisco: Jossey-Bass.

Otto, Kathleen, Anja Hoffmann-Biencourt, and Gisela Mohr 2010 "Is There a Buffering Effect of Flexibility for Job Attitudes and Work-Related Strain under Conditions of High Job Insecurity and Regional Unemployment Rate?" *Economic and Industrial Democracy* 32(4): 609–30.

Ouchi, William 1981 *Theory Z: How American Business Can Meet the Japanese Challenge*. Reading, MA: Addison-Wesley.

Owram, Doug 1996 *Born at the Right Time: A History of the Baby Boom Generation*. Toronto: University of Toronto Press.

Page, Marianne E. 2004 "New Evidence on the Intergenerational Correlation in Welfare Participation." In Miles Corak, ed., *Generational Income Mobility in North America and Europe*. Cambridge: Cambridge University Press.

Palameta, Boris 2004 "Low Income among Immigrants and Visible Minorities." *Perspectives on Labour and Income* 16(Summer): 32–37.

Palmer, Bryan 1975 "Class, Conception and Conflict: The Thrust for Efficiency, Managerial Views of Labor and the Working Class Rebellion, 1902–22." *Radical Review of Political Economics* 7: 31–49.

——— 1979 *A Culture in Conflict: Skilled Workers and Industrial Capitalism in Hamilton, Ontario, 1860–1914*. Montreal and Kingston: McGill–Queen's University Press.

——— 1986 *The Character of Class Struggle: Essays in Canadian Working Class History, 1850–1985*. Toronto: McClelland & Stewart.

——— 1992 *Working Class Experience: Rethinking the History of Canadian Labour, 1800–1991*. 2nd ed. Toronto: McClelland & Stewart.

Palmer, Craig, and Peter Sinclair 1997 *When the Fish Are Gone: Ecological Disaster and Fishers in Northwestern Newfoundland*. Halifax: Fernwood Publishing.

Panitch, Leo, and Donald Swartz 1993 *The Assault on Trade Union Freedoms: From Wage Controls to Social Contract*. Toronto: Garamond.

Paris, Hélène 1989 *The Corporate Response to Workers with Family Responsibilities*. Report 43-89. Ottawa: Conference Board of Canada.

Park, Jungwee 2012 "Job-Related Training of Older Workers." *Perspectives on Labour and Income* (Summer): 27–36.

Parker, Jane, and Janice Foley 2010 "Progress on Women's Equality with U.K. and Canadian Trade Unions: Do Women's Structures Make a Difference?" *Relations Industrielles/Industrial Relations* 65(2): 281–303.

Parr, Joy 1990 *The Gender of Breadwinners: Women, Men and Change in Two Industrial Towns 1880–1950*. Toronto: University of Toronto Press.

Parreñas, Rhacel Salazar 2001 *Servants of Globalization: Women, Migration and Domestic Work*. Stanford, CA: Stanford University Press.

Parthasarathy, Balaji 2004 "India's Silicon Valley or Silicon Valley's India? Socially Embedding the Computer Software Industry in Bangalore." *International Journal of Urban and Regional Research* 28(3): 664–85.

Patterson, E. Palmer, II 1972 *The Canadian Indian: A History since 1500*. Don Mills, ON: Collier-Macmillan.

Payne, Jonathan 2009 "Emotional Labour and Skill: A Reappraisal." *Gender, Work & Organization* 16(3): 348–67.

Pendleton, Andrew, and Andrew Robinson 2010 "Employee Stock Ownership, Involvement, and Productivity: an Interaction-Based Approach." *Industrial and Labor Relations Review* 64(1): 3–29.

Pentland, H. Claire 1979 "The Canadian Industrial Relations System: Some Formative Factors." *Labour/Le Travail* 4: 9–23.

——— 1981 *Labour and Capital in Canada, 1650–1860*. Toronto: James Lorimer.

Perales, Francisco 2013 "Occupational Sex-Segregation, Specialized Human Capital and Wages: Evidence from Britain." *Work Employment & Society* 27(4): 600–620.

Perlow, Leslie 2012 *Sleeping with Your Smartphone: How to Break the 24/7 Habit and Change the Way You Work*. Boston: Harvard Business School Publishing.

Perusse, Dominique 2008 *Aboriginal People Living Off-Reserve and the Labour Market:*

Estimates from the Labour Force Survey. Ottawa: Statistics Canada (Labour Division). Cat. no. 71-588-X.

Peters, Thomas J., and Robert H. Waterman Jr. 1982 *In Search of Excellence.* New York: Warner.

Peters, Tom 1987 *Thriving on Chaos: Handbook for a Management Revolution.* New York: Alfred A. Knopf.

Petersen, Trond, Ishak Saporta, and Marc-David L. Seidel 2000 "Offering a Job: Meritocracy and Social Networks." *American Journal of Sociology* 106:763–816.

Pfeffer, Jeffrey 1994 *Competitive Advantage through People: Unleashing the Power of the Workforce.* Boston: Harvard University Press.

Pfeffer, Jeffrey, and Robert I. Sutton 2000 *The Knowing–Doing Gap: How Smart Companies Turn Knowledge into Action.* Boston: Harvard Business School Press.

Phelan, Jo 1994 "The Paradox of the Contented Female Worker: An Assessment of Alternative Explanations." *Social Psychology Quarterly* 57:95–107.

Picot, Garnett 1987 "The Changing Industrial Mix of Employment, 1951–1985." *Canadian Social Trends* (Spring): 8–11.

——— **1998** "What Is Happening to Earnings Inequality and Youth Wages in the 1990s?" *Canadian Economic Observer* (September): 3.1–3.18.

——— **2008** *Immigrant Economic and Social Outcomes in Canada: Research and Data Development at Statistics Canada.* Ottawa: Statistics Canada. Cat. no. 11F0019M—No. 319.

Picot, Garnett, and Andrew Heisz 2000 "The Performance of the 1990s Canadian Labour Market." *Canadian Public Policy* 26(Supplement): 7–25.

Pierce, Jennifer 1995 *Gender Trials: Emotional Lives in Contemporary Law Firms.* Berkeley and Los Angeles: University of California Press.

Pierson, Ruth Roach 1986 *They're Still Women After All: The Second World War and Canadian Womanhood.* Toronto: McClelland and Stewart.

Piketty, Thomas 2014 *Capital in the Twenty-first Century.* Boston: Harvard University Press.

Piore, Michael J., and Charles F. Sabel 1984 *The Second Industrial Divide: Possibilities for Prosperity.* New York: Basic Books.

Pirson, Michael A., and Paul R. Lawrence 2010 "Humanism in Business—Towards a Paradigm Shift?" *Journal of Business Ethics* 93(4): 553–65.

Piva, Michael J. 1979 *The Condition of the Working Class in Toronto, 1900–1921.* Ottawa: University of Ottawa Press.

Pocock, Barbara 2003 *Work–Life Collision.* Sydney, Australia: The Federation Press.

Podolny, Joel M., and Karen L. Page 1998 "Network Forms of Organization." *Annual Review of Sociology* 24:57–64.

Polanyi, Karl 1957 *The Great Transformation.* Boston: Beacon Press.

Pollert, Anna 1988 "The Flexible Firm: Fixation or Fact?" *Work, Employment & Society* 2:281–316.

Ponak, Allen, and Daphne Taras 1995 *Right-to-Work.* Submission to Alberta Economic Development Authority Joint Review Committee.

Popper, Micha, and Raanan Lipshitz 2000 "Organizational Learning: Mechanisms, Culture, and Feasibility." *Management Learning* 31(2): 181–96.

Portes, Alejandro 2005 "The Informal Economy and Its Paradoxes." In Neil Smelser and Richard Swedberg, eds., *The Handbook of Economic Sociology.* 2nd ed. Princeton, N.J.: Princeton University Press.

Poutsma, Erik, John Hendrickx, and Fred Huijgen 2003 "Employee Participation in Europe: In Search of the Participative Workplace." *Economic and Industrial Democracy* 24(1): 45–76.

Powell, Gary N., and Laura Graves 2011 *Women and Men in Management.* 4th ed. Thousand Oaks, CA: Sage.

Powell, Jason L., and Cook, Ian G. 2009 "Global Ageing in Comparative Perspective: A Critical Discussion." *International Journal of Sociology and Social Policy* 29(7–8): 388–400.

Pratt, Courtney 2007 "'New Big Thing' Could Put Brakes on CEO Pay." *Globe and Mail,* June 11, B2.

Presser, Harriet 2003. *Working in the 24/7 Economy: Challenges for American Families.* New York: Russell Sage Foundation.

Price, Christine A. 2000 "Women and Retirement: Relinquishing Professional Identity." *Journal of Aging Studies* 14(1): 81–101.

Prince, Michael J. 2004 "Canadian Disability Policy: Still a Hit-and-Miss Affair." *Canadian Journal of Sociology* 29(1): 59–82.

Pringle, Rosemary 1989 "Bureaucracy, Rationality and Sexuality: The Case of Secretaries." In Jeff Hearn, Deborah L. Sheppard, Peta Tancred-Sheriff, and Gibson Burrell, eds., *The Sexuality of Organization.* London: Sage.

Pruijt, Hans 2003 "Teams between Neo-Taylorism and Anti-Taylorism." *Economic and Industrial Democracy* 24(1): 77–101.

Pugh, D. S., D. J. Hickson, and C. R. Hinings 1985 *Writers on Organizations.* Beverly Hills, CA: Sage.

Pupo, Norene 1997 "Always Working, Never Done: The Expansion of the Double Day." In Ann Duffy, Daniel Glenday, and Norene Pupo, eds., *Good Jobs, Bad Jobs, No Jobs: The Transformation of Work in the 21st Century.* Toronto: Harcourt-Brace Canada.

Pupo, Norene J., and Andrea Noack 2010 "Dialling for Service: Transforming the Public-Sector Workplace in Canada." In Norene J. Pupo and Mark P. Thomas, eds., *Interrogating the New Economy: Restructuring Work in the 21st Century.* Toronto: University of Toronto Press.

Pupo, Norene J., and Mark P. Thomas, eds., 2010 *Interrogating the New Economy: Restruturing Work in the 21st Century.* Toronto: University of Toronto Press.

Pyle, Kenneth 1996 *The Making of Modern Japan.* 2nd ed. Lexington: D.C. Heath and Company.

Radl, Jonas 2012 "Too Old to Work, or Too Young to Retire? The Pervasiveness of Age Norms in Western Europe." *Work, Employment & Society* 26(5): 775–71.

Randle, Keith 1996 "The White-Coated Worker: Professional Autonomy in a Period of Change." *Work, Employment & Society* 10: 737–53.

Rankin, Tom 1990 *New Forms of Work Organization: The Challenge for North American Unions.* Toronto: University of Toronto Press.

Ranson, Gillian 1998 "Education, Work and Family Decision-Making: Finding the 'Right Time' to Have a Baby." *Canadian Review of Sociology and Anthropology* 35(4): 517–33.

Ranson, Gillian 2010 *Against the Grain: Couples, Gender, and the Reframing of Parenting.* Toronto: University of Toronto Press.

Rashid, Abdul 1994 "High Income Families." *Perspectives on Labour and Income* (Winter): 46–57.

Ray, Carol Axtell 1986 "Corporate Culture: The Last Frontier of Control?" *Journal of Management Studies* 23: 287–97.

Rayman, Paula M. 2001 *Beyond the Bottom Line: The Search for Dignity at Work.* New York: Palgrave.

Reich, Robert B. 1991 *The Work of Nations: Preparing Ourselves for 21st-Century Capitalism.* New York: Alfred A. Knopf.

——— **2000** *The Future of Success.* New York: Alfred A. Knopf.

Reid, Frank 1982 "Wage-and-Price Controls in Canada." In John Anderson and Morley Gunderson, eds., *Union–Management Relations in Canada.* Don Mills, ON: Addison-Wesley.

Reimer, Neil 1979 "Oil, Chemical and Atomic Workers International Union and the Quality of Working Life: A Union Perspective." *Quality of Working Life: The Canadian Scene* (Winter): 5–7.

Reiter, Ester 1991 *Making Fast Food: From the Frying Pan into the Fryer.* Montreal and Kingston: McGill–Queen's University Press.

Reitz, Jeffrey G. 2007a "Immigrant Employment Success in Canada, Part I: Individual and Contextual Causes." *Journal of International Migration and Integration* 8: 11–36.

Reitz, Jeffrey G. 2007b "Immigrant Employment Success in Canada, Part II: Understanding the Decline." *Journal of International Migration and Integration* 8: 37–62.

Reitz, Jeffrey G., and Anil Verma 2004 "Immigration, Race, and Labor: Unionization and Wages in the Canadian Labor Market." *Industrial Relations* 43(4): 835–54.

Reshef, Yonatan, and Sandra Rastin 2003 *Unions in the Time of Revolution: Government Restructuring in Alberta and Ontario.* Toronto: University of Toronto Press.

Reskin, Barbara 1998 *The Realities of Affirmative Action in Employment.* Washington, DC: American Sociological Association.

Reskin, Barbara F., and Debra B. McBrier 2000 "Why Not Ascription? Organizations' Employment of Male and Female Managers." *American Sociological Review* 65: 210–33.

Reskin, Barbara, and Irene Padavic 2002 *Men and Women at Work.* 2nd ed. Thousand Oaks, CA: Pine Forge Press.

Reynolds, John R., and Chardie L. Baird. 2010 "Is There a Downside to Shooting for the Stars? Unrealized Educational Expectations and Symptoms of Depression." *American Sociological Review* 75: 151–72.

Richards, James 2008 " 'Because I Need Somewhere to Vent': The Expression of Conflict through Work Blogs." *New Technology, Work and Employment* 23(1–2): 95–110.

Richardson, Charley 1996 "Computers Don't Kill Jobs, People Do: Technology and Power in the Workplace." *Annals of the American Academy of Political and Social Science* (March): 167–79.

Riddell, W. Craig 1985 "Work and Pay: The Canadian Labour Market: An Overview." In W. Craig Riddell, ed., *Work and Pay: The Canadian Labour Market.* Toronto: University of Toronto Press.

Riddell, W. Craig, and Andrew Sharpe 1998 "The Canada–U.S. Unemployment Rate Gap: An Introduction and Overview." *Canadian Public Policy* (February Supplement): S1–S37.

Riddell, W. Craig, and France St-Hilaire, eds. 2000 *Adapting Public Policy to a Labour Market in Transition.* Montreal: Institute for Research on Public Policy.

Ridgeway, Cecilia 2011 *Framed by Gender: How Gender Inequality Persists in the Modern World.* Oxford and New York: Oxford University Press.

Rifkin, Jeremy 1995 *The End of Work: The Decline of the Global Labor Force and the Dawn of the Post-market Era.* New York: Putnam.

Rinehart, James 1978 "Contradictions of Work-Related Attitudes and Behaviour: An Interpretation." *Canadian Review of Sociology and Anthropology* 15: 1–15.

———— 1984 "Appropriating Workers' Knowledge: Quality Control Circles at a General Motors Plant." *Studies in Political Economy* 14: 75–97.

———— 2006 *The Tyranny of Work: Alienation and the Labour Process.* 5th ed. Toronto: Thomson Nelson.

Rinehart, James, Christopher Huxley, and David Robertson 1997 *Just Another Car Factory: Lean Production and Its Discontents.* Ithaca, NY: ILR Press.

Rivera, Lauren A. 2012 "Hiring as Cultural Matching: The Case of Elite Professional Firms." *American Sociological Review* 77(6): 999–1022.

Roberts, Alasdair 2012 "Why the Occupy Movement Failed." *Public Administration Review* 72(5): 754–62.

Roberts, Karen, Doug Hyatt, and Peter Dorman 1996 "The Effect of Free Trade on Contingent Work in Michigan." In Karen Roberts and Mark I. Wilson, eds., *Policy Choices: Free Trade among NAFTA Nations.* East Lansing, MI: Michigan State University Press.

Roberts, Wayne 1990 *Cracking the Canadian Formula: The Making of the Energy and Chemical Workers Union.* Toronto: Between the Lines.

Robertson, David, James Rinehart, Christopher Huxley, and the CAW Research Group on CAMI 1992 "Team Concept and Kaizen: Japanese Production Management in a Unionized Canadian Auto Plant." *Studies in Political Economy* 39 (Autumn): 77–107.

Robertson, David, and Jeff Wareham 1987 *Technological Change in the Auto Industry.* Willowdale, ON: Canadian Auto Workers (CAW).

Rodrik, Dani 2007 *One Economics, Many Recipes.* Princeton and Oxford: Princeton University Press.

Roethlisberger, F. J., and W. J. Dickson 1939 *Management and the Worker.* Cambridge, MA: Harvard University Press.

Rollings-Magnusson, Sandra 2000 "Canada's Most Wanted: Pioneer Women on the Western Prairies." *Canadian Review of Sociology and Anthropology* 37(2): 223–38.

Rollings-Magnusson, Sandra, Harvey Krahn, and Graham S. Lowe 1999 *Does a Decade Make a Difference? Education and Work among 1985 and 1996 University Graduates.* Edmonton: Population Research Laboratory, University of Alberta.

Rónas-Tas, Ákos 1994 "The First Shall Be Last? Entrepreneurship and Communist Cadres in the Transition from Socialism." *American Journal of Sociology* 100: 40–69.

Roscigno, Vincent J., Sherry Mong, Reginald Byron, and Griff Tester 2007 "Age Discrimination, Social Closure and Employment." *Social Forces* 86(1): 313–34.

Rose, Joseph 2001 "From Softball to Hardball: The Transition in Labour–Management Relations in the Ontario Public Service." In Gene Swimmer, ed., *Public-Sector*

Labour Relations in an Era of Restraint and Restructuring. Toronto: Oxford University Press.

Rose, Joseph B., and Gary N. Chaison 2001 "Unionism in Canada and the United States in the 21st Century: The Prospects for Revival." *Relations industrielles/Industrial Relations* 56(1): 34–62.

Rosenthal, Patrice, Stephen Hill, and Riccardo Peccei 1997 "Checking Out Service: Evaluating Excellence, HRM and TQM in Retailing." *Work, Employment & Society* 11(3): 481–503.

Ross, Peter, Greg J. Bamber, and Gillian Whitehouse 1998 "Employment, Economics and Industrial Relations: Comparative Statistics." In Greg J. Bamber and Russell D. Lansbury, eds., *International and Comparative Employment Relations*. 3rd ed. Thousand Oaks, CA: Sage Publications.

Ross-Smith, Anne and Kate Huppatz 2010 "Management, Women, and Gender Capital." *Gender, Work & Organization* 17(5): 547–66.

Rothstein, Jeffrey 2005 "Selective Participation: Controlling Workers' Input at General Motors." *Research in the Sociology of Work* 16: 151–75.

Rowe, Reba, and William E. Snizek 1995 "Gender Differences in Work Values: Perpetuating the Myth." *Work and Occupations* 22: 215–29.

Roy, Donald 1952 "Quota Restriction and Goldbricking in a Machine Shop." *American Journal of Sociology* 57: 427–42.

——— **1959–60** " 'Bananatime': Job Satisfaction and Informal Interaction." *Human Organization* 18: 158–68.

Roychowdhury, Supriya 2003 "Public Sector Restructuring and Democracy: The State, Labour and Trade Unions in India." *The Journal of Development Studies* 39(3): 29–50.

Rubery, Jill 1996 "The Labour Market Outlook and the Outlook for Labour Market Analysis." In Rosemary Crompton, Duncan Gallie, and Kate Purcell, eds., *Changing Forms of Employment: Organisations, Skills and Gender*. London and New York: Routledge.

Rubery, Jill, and Colette Fagan 1995 "Gender Segregation in Societal Context." *Work, Employment & Society* 9: 213–40.

Rubery, Jill, and Damian Grimshaw 2001 "ICTs and Employment: The Problem of Job Quality." *International Labour Review* 140(2): 165–92.

Ruddick, Sara 1995 *Maternal Thinking: Towards a Politics of Peace*. Boston: Beacon Press.

Russell, Bob 1990 *Back to Work? Labour, State, and Industrial Relations in Canada*. Scarborough, ON: Nelson.

——— **1997** "Rival Paradigms at Work: Work Reorganization and Labour Force Impacts in a Staple Industry." *Canadian Review of Sociology and Anthropology* 34: 25–52.

——— **1999** *More with Less: Work Reorganization in the Canadian Mining Industry*. Toronto: University of Toronto Press.

Ryerson, Stanley B. 1968 *Unequal Union: Confederation and the Roots of Conflict in the Canadas, 1815–1873*. Toronto: Progress Books.

Sallaz, Jeffrey J. 2004 "Manufacturing Concessions: Attritionary Outsourcing at GM's Lordstown, USA Assembly Plant." *Work, Employment & Society* 18(4): 687–708.

Sanchez, Laura, and Elizabeth Thomson 1997 "Becoming Mothers and Fathers: Parenthood, Gender and the Division of Labor." *Gender and Society* 11(6): 747–72.

Sandberg, Ake 1994 " 'Volvoism' at the End of the Road?" *Studies in Political Economy* 45: 170–82.

Sangster, Joan 1978 "The 1907 Bell Telephone Strike: Organizing Women Workers." *Labour/Le Travail* 3: 109–30.

——— **1995** "Doing Two Jobs: The Wage-Earning Mother, 1945–70." In Joy Parr, ed., *A Diversity of Women: Ontario, 1945–1980*. Toronto: University of Toronto Press.

——— **2010** *Transforming Labour: Women and Work in Postwar Canada*. Toronto: University of Toronto Press.

Sargent, Timothy C. 2000 "Structural Unemployment and Technological Change in Canada, 1990–1999." *Canadian Public Policy* 26(S1): 109–23.

Sass, Robert 1986 "Workplace Health and Safety: Report from Canada." *International Journal of Health Services* 16: 565–82.

——— **1995** "A Conversation about the Work Environment." *International Journal of Health Services* 25: 117–28.

Sassen, Saskia 2002 "Global Cities and Survival Circuits." In Barbara Ehrenreich and Arlie Russell Hochschild, eds., *Global Woman: Nannies, Maids, and Sex Workers in the New Economy*. New York: Metropolitan Books.

Satzewich, Vic, ed. **1998** *Racism and Social Inequality in Canada: Concepts, Controversies and Strategies of Resistance.* Toronto: Thompson Educational Publishing.

Saul, John R. **1995** *The Unconscious Civilization.* Toronto: Anansi.

Sauvé, Roger **2006** *The Current State of Canadian Family Finances: 2005 Report.* Ottawa: Vanier Institute of the Family.

Schalk, René, and Adriënne van Rijckevorsel **2007** "Factors Influencing Absenteeism and Intention to Leave in a Call Centre." *New Technology, Work and Employment* 22(3): 260–74.

Schecter, Stephen, and Bernard Paquet **1999** "Contested Approaches in the Study of Poverty: The Canadian Case and the Argument for Inclusion." *Current Sociology* 47(3): 43–64.

Schein, Edgar H. **2004** *Organizational Culture and Leadership.* 3rd ed. San Francisco: Jossey-Bass.

Schellenberg, Grant, and Hélène Maheux **2007** "Immigrants' Perspectives on Their First Four Years in Canada: Highlights from Three Waves of the Longitudinal Survey of Immigrants to Canada." *Canadian Social Trends* (Special Edition): 2–17.

Schellenberg, Grant, and Yuri Ostrovsky **2008** "The Retirement Plans and Expectations of Older Workers." *Canadian Social Trends* (Winter): 11–34.

Schellenberg, Grant, and Cynthia Silver **2004** "You Can't Always Get What You Want: Retirement Preferences and Experiences." *Canadian Social Trends* (Winter): 2–7.

Schissel, Bernard, and Terry Wotherspoon **2003** *The Legacy of School for Aboriginal People: Education, Oppression, and Emancipation.* Don Mills, ON: Oxford University Press.

Schooler, Carmi **1984** "Psychological Effects of Complex Environments during the Life Span: A Review and Theory." *Intelligence* 8: 259–81.

——— **1996** "Cultural and Social-Structural Explanations of Cross-National Psychological Differences." *Annual Review of Sociology* 22: 323–49.

Schor, Juliet **1991** *The Overworked American: The Unexpected Decline of Leisure.* New York: Basic Books.

——— **1998** *The Overspent American.* New York: Basic Books.

Schott, Jeffrey, and Gary Hufbauer **2007** "NAFTA Revisited." *Policy Options* (October): 83–88.

Schouteten, Roel, and Jos Benders **2004** "Lean Production Assessed by Karasek's Job Demand–Job Control Model." *Economic and Industrial Democracy* 25(3): 347–73.

Schuetze, Hans **2012** "Large Archipelago, Small Bridges, and Infrequent Ferries: Lifelong Learning and Canadian Higher Education." In Maria Slowey and Hans Schuetze, eds., *Global Perspectives on Higher Education and Lifelong Learners* (pp. 135–56). New York: Routledge.

Sciadas, George **2002** *The Digital Divide in Canada.* Ottawa: Statistics Canada. Cat. no. 56F0009XIE.

Scott, Robert E., Carlos Salas, and Bruce Campbell **2006** *Revisiting NAFTA: Still Not Working for North America's Workers.* Economic Policy Institute Briefing Paper no. 173. http://epi.3cdn.net/6def605657a958c3da_85m6ibu0h.pdf.

Seeman, Melvin **1967** "On the Personal Consequences of Alienation in Work." *American Sociological Review* 32: 273–85.

——— **1975** "Alienation Studies." *Annual Review of Sociology* 1: 91–125.

Segal, David **2012** "Apple's Retail Army, Long on Loyalty but Short on Pay." *New York Times,* June 23.

Selmi, Michael, and Sonia Weil **2013** "Can All Women Be Pharmacists? A Critique of Hanna Rosin's The End of Men." *Boston University Law Review* 93(3): 851–70.

Senge, Peter M. **1990** *The Fifth Discipline: The Art and Practice of the Learning Organization.* New York: Doubleday.

Sennett, Richard **1998** *The Corrosion of Character: The Personal Consequences of Work in the New Capitalism.* New York: W.W. Norton.

Sennett, Richard, and Jonathan Cobb **1972** *The Hidden Injuries of Class.* New York: Knopf.

Sev'er, Aysan **1999** "Sexual Harassment." Special Issue. *Canadian Review of Sociology and Anthropology* 36(4).

Sewell, Graham **1998** "The Discipline of Teams: The Control of Team-Based Industrial Work through Electronic and Peer Surveillance." *Administrative Science Quarterly* 43: 397–428.

Sewell, Graham, and Barry Wilkinson **1992** "Someone to Watch Over Me: Surveillance,

Discipline and Just-in-Time Labour Process." *Sociology* 26(2): 271–89.

Shaker, Erica, and David Macdonald (with Nigel Wodrich) 2013 *Degrees of Uncertainty: Navigating the Changing Terrain of University Finance.* Ottawa: Canadian Centre for Policy Alternatives.

Shalla, Vivian 2002 "Jettisoned by Design? The Truncated Employment Relationship of Customer Sales and Service Agents under Airline Restructuring." *Canadian Journal of Sociology* 27(1): 1–32.

——— 2004 "Time Warped: The Flexibilization and Maximization of Flight Attendant Working Time." *The Canadian Review of Sociology and Anthropology* 41(3): 345–68.

——— 2007a "Theoretical Reflections on Work: A Quarter-Century of Critical Thinking." In Vivian Shalla and Wallace Clement, eds., *Work in Tumultuous Times: Critical Perspectives.* Montreal and Kingston: McGill–Queen's University Press.

——— 2007b "Shifting Temporalities: Economic Restructuring and the Politics of Working Time." In Vivian Shalla and Wallace Clement, eds., *Work in Tumultuous Times: Critical Perspectives.* Montreal and Kingston: McGill–Queen's University Press.

Shalla, Vivian, and Wallace Clement, eds. 2007 *Work in Tumultuous Times: Critical Perspectives.* Montreal and Kingston: McGill–Queen's University Press.

Shanahan, Michael J. 2000 "Pathways to Adulthood in Changing Societies: Variability and Mechanisms in Life Course Perspective." *Annual Review of Sociology* 26: 667–92.

Sharman, Shalendra D. 2009 *China and India in the Age of Globalization.* Cambridge: Cambridge University Press.

Sharp, Isadore 2009 *Four Seasons: The Story of a Business Philosophy.* Toronto: Viking Canada.

Sharpe, Andrew, and Jill Hardt 2006 *Five Deaths a Day: Workplace Fatalities 1993–2005.* Ottawa: Centre for the Study of Living Standards.

Sheikh, Munir 2013 "Good Government and Statistics Canada: The Need for True Independence." *Academic Matters: The Journal of Higher Education* (May).

Sherman, Barrie, and Phil Judkins 1995 *Licensed to Work.* London, England: Cassel.

Shewell, Hugh 2004 *"Enough to Keep Them Alive": Indian Welfare in Canada, 1873–1965.* Toronto: University of Toronto Press.

Shieh, G. S. 1992 *"Boss" Island: The Subcontracting Network and Micro-entrepreneurship in Taiwan's Development.* New York: Peter Lang.

Shields, Margot 2000 "Long Working Hours and Health." *Perspectives on Labour and Income* 12(Spring): 49–56.

Shildrick, Tracy, Robert MacDonald, Colin Webster, and Kayleigh Garthwaite 2013 *Poverty and Insecurity: Life in Low-Pay, No-Pay Britain.* Cambridge: Polity Press.

Shorter, Edward, and Charles Tilly 1974 *Strikes in France, 1830–1968.* Cambridge, MA: Cambridge University Press.

Sidani, Yusuf and Dima Jamali 2010 "The Egyptian Worker: Work Beliefs and Attitudes." *Journal of Business Ethics* 92: 433–50.

Sidani, Yusuf, and Jon Thornberry 2009 "The Currrent Arab Work Ethic: Antecedents, Implications, and Potential Remedies." *Journal of Business Ethics* 91: 35–49.

Siltanen, Janet 1994 *Locating Gender: Occupational Segregation, Wages and Domestic Responsibilities.* London, England: UCL Press.

Siltanen, Janet, Alette Willis and Willow Scobie 2009 "Flows, Eddies, Swamps and Whirlpools: Inequality and the Experience of Work Change." *Canadian Journal of Sociology* 34(4): 1003–32.

Singh, Parbudyal, and Natasha Loncar 2010 "Pay Satisfaction, Job Satisfaction, and Turnover Intent." *Relations Industrielles/Industrial Relations* 65(3): 470–90.

Sinha, M. 2013 *Portrait of Caregivers, 2012.* Ottawa: Minister of Industry.

Skof, Karl 2010 "Trends in the Trades: Registered Apprenticeship Total Registrations, Completions and Certification, 1991 to 2007." *Education Matters: Insights on Education, Learning and Training in Canada* 6(6). Statistics Canada Cat. no. 81-004-X.

Skrypnek, Berna J., and Janet E. Fast 1996 "Work and Family Policy in Canada." *Journal of Family Issues* 17: 793–812.

Slowey, Maria, and Hans Schuetze 2012, eds. *Global Perspectives on Higher Education and Lifelong Learners.* New York: Routledge.

Smith, Adam 1976 *The Wealth of Nations.* Chicago: University of Chicago Press. (Orig. pub. 1776.)

Smith, Michael R. 1978 "The Effects of Strikes on Workers: A Critical Analysis." *Canadian Journal of Sociology* 3: 457–72.

———— 1999 "The Production of Flexible Attitudes in the Canadian Pulp and Paper Industry." *Relations industrielles/Industrial Relations* 54(3): 581–608.

———— 2001 "Technological Change, the Demand for Skills, and the Adequacy of Their Supply." *Canadian Public Policy* 27(1): 1–22.

Smith, Vicki 1994 "Braverman's Legacy: The Labour Process Tradition at 20." *Work and Occupations* 21: 403–21.

———— 1997 "New Forms of Work Organization." *Annual Review of Sociology* 23: 315–39.

———— 2006 " 'It's the End of Work as We Know It … But Maybe Not.' " *Work and Occupations* 33(3): 303–6.

Smith, Vicki, and Esther Neuwirth 2008 *The Good Temp*. Ithaca, NY: ILR Press.

Smucker, Joseph 1980 *Industrialization in Canada*. Scarborough, ON: Prentice-Hall.

Smucker, Joseph, Axel van den Berg, Michael R. Smith, and Anthony C. Masi 1998 "Labour Deployment in Plants in Canada and Sweden: A Three-Industry Comparison." *Relations industrielles/Industrial Relations* 53(3): 430–56.

Sonnenfeld, Jeffrey A. 1985 "Shedding Light on the Hawthorne Studies." *Journal of Occupational Behaviour* 6: 111–30.

Sosteric, Mike 1996 "Subjectivity and the Labour Process: A Case Study in the Restaurant Industry." *Work, Employment & Society* 10: 297–318.

Spalding, Derek 2010 "The New Face of Business." *Nanaimo Daily News*, January 29, A1.

Spencer, Dale, and Niki Carlan 2008 "The Complexities of the Automotive Industry: Positive and Negative Feedbacks in Production Systems." *Canadian Journal of Sociology* 33(2): 265–90.

Spenner, Kenneth I. 1983 "Deciphering Prometheus: Temporal Change in the Skill Level of Work." *American Sociological Review* 48: 824–37.

Spilerman, Seymour 2000 "Wealth and Stratification Processes." *Annual Review of Sociology* 26: 497–524.

Spitzer, Denise, Anne Neufeld, Margaret Harrison, Karen D. Hughes, and Miriam

Stewart 2003 "My Wings Have Been Cut, Where Can I Fly? Gender, Migration and Caregiving—Chinese and South Asian Canadian Perspectives." *Gender and Society* 17(2): 267–86.

Staber, Udo 1993 "Worker Cooperatives and the Business Cycle: Are Cooperatives the Answer to Unemployment?" *The American Journal of Economics and Sociology* 52: 129–43.

Stabler, Jack C., and Eric C. Howe 1990 "Native Participation in Northern Development: The Impending Crisis in the NWT." *Canadian Public Policy* 16: 262–83.

Stanford, Jim 2005 "Revisiting the 'Flexibility Hypothesis.'" *Canadian Public Policy* 31(1): 109–16.

Stansfeld, Stephen, and Bridget Candy 2006 "Psychosocial Work Environment and Mental Health—A Meta-analytic Review." *Scandinavian Journal of Work Environment & Health* 32(6): 443–62.

Stasiulis, Daiva, and Abigail B. Bakan 2003 *Negotiating Citizenship: Migrant Women in Canada and the Global System*. New York: Palgrave MacMillan.

Statistics Canada 1995 "Moving with the Times: Introducing Change to the LFS." *The Labour Force* (December): C2–C19.

———— 2000 *Women in Canada 2000: A Gender-Based Statistical Report*. Ottawa: Statistics Canada. Cat. no. 89-503-XPE.

———— 2002 Childcare Service Industry, *The Daily*, April 2–3, 2002.

———— 2003 *Canada's Ethnocultural Portrait: The Changing Mosaic*. 2001 Census Analysis Series. http://www .statcan.gc.ca.

———— 2004a "Childcare Arrangements." *Perspectives on Labour and Income* 16(Summer): 54–58.

———— 2004b "The Near-Retirement Rate." *Perspectives on Labour and Income* 16(Spring): 68–72.

———— 2005 *Women in Canada: A Gender-Based Statistical Report*. Ottawa: Statistics Canada. Cat. no. 89-503-XIE. http:// www. statcan.gc.ca/bsolc/olc-cel/olc-cel?catno=89-503-x&lang=eng.

———— 2006 *Income and Earnings, 2006 Census*. Ottawa: Statistics Canada. Cat. no. 97-563-XWE2006062. http://www.statcan .gc.ca/bsolc/olc-cel/olc-cel?catno=97-563-X2006062&lang=eng.

———— **2007a** *The Canadian Labour Market at a Glance.* Ottawa: Statistics Canada. Cat. no. 71-222-X.

———— **2007b** *Participation and Activity Limitation Survey 2006: Analytical Report.* Ottawa: Statistics Canada. Cat. no. 89-628-XIE—No. 002. http://www .statcan.gc.ca/ pub/89-628-x/89-628-x2007002-eng.pdf.

———— **2008a** *Labour Force Historical Review 2008.* Ottawa: Statistics Canada. Cat. no. 71F0004XCB.

———— **2008b** *Canada's Changing Labour Force, 2006 Census.* Ottawa: Statistics Canada. Cat. no. 97-559-X. http://www12.statcan .gc.ca/english/census06/analysis/labour/ pdf/97-559-XIE2006001.pdf.

———— **2008c** *Canada's Ethnocultural Mosaic, 2006 Census.* Ottawa: Statistics Canada. Cat. no. 97-562-X. http:// www12.statcan. ca/census-recensement/ 2006/as-sa/97-562/ pdf/97-562-XIE2006001.pdf.

———— **2008d** *Education, 2006 Census.* Ottawa: Statistics Canada. Cat. no. 97-560-XIE.

———— **2008e** *The Aboriginal Labour Force Analysis Series.* Cat. no. 71-588-XWE.

———— **2008f** *Workplace and Employee Survey Compendium 2005.* Cat. no. 71-585-X.

———— **2008g** *2006 Census: Aboriginal Peoples in Canada in 2006: Inuit, Métis, and First Nations, 2006 Census: Findings.* Ottawa: Statistics Canada. Cat. no. 97-558-XIE2006001. http://www12.statcan.ca/ census-recensement/2006/ as-sa/ 97-558/index-eng.cfm?CFID=3488 61&CFTOKEN=58769179.

———— **2008h** Chapter 19, "Information and Communications Technology." *Canada Year Book 2008.* Ottawa: Statistics Canada. Cat. no. 11-402-XWE.

———— **2008i** "Unionization." *Perspectives on Labour and Income* (Autumn): 70–79.

———— **2009a** *The Canadian Labour Market at a Glance 2007.* Ottawa: Statistics Canada. Cat. no. 71-222-X. http://www .statcan.gc.ca/ pub/71-222-x/71-222-x2008001-eng.pdf.

———— **2009b** *Lifelong Learning among Canadians Aged 18 to 64 Years: First Results from the 2008 Access and Support to Education and Training Survey.* Ottawa: Statistics Canada. Cat. no. 81-595-M2009079.

———— **2010** *Projections of the Diversity of the Canadian Population 2006 to 2031.* Ottawa:

Statistics Canada. Cat. no. 91-551-X. http:// www.statcan.gc.ca/ pub/91-551-x/ 91-551-x2010001-eng. pdf.

———— **2011** *Guide to the Labour Force Survey.* Ottawa: Statistics Canada. Cat. no. 71-543-G.

———— **2012** *National Occupational Classification 2011.* Ottawa: Statistics Canada. Cat. no. 12-583-X.

———— **2013a** *Guide to the Labour Force Survey.* Ottawa: Statistics Canada. Cat. no. 71-543-G. http://www.statcan.gc.ca/pub/ 71-543-g/71-543-g2013001-eng.pdf.

———— **2013b** *Portrait of Canada's Labour Force.* Ottawa: Statistics Canada. Cat. no. 99-012-X2011002. http://www12.statcan .gc.ca/nhs-enm/2011/as-sa/99-012-x/ 99-012-x2011002-eng.pdf.

———— **2013c** *Immigration and Ethnocultural Diversity in Canada.* Ottawa: Statistics Canada. Cat. no. 99-010-X2011001. http:// www12.statcan.gc.ca/nhs-enm/2011/as-sa/ 99-010-x/99-010-x2011001-eng.pdf.

———— **2013d** *Aboriginal Peoples in Canada: First Nations People, Métis and Inuit.* Ottawa: Statistics Canada. Cat. no. 99-011-X2011001. http://www12.statcan.gc.ca/ nhs-enm/2011/as-sa/99-011-x/ 99-011-x2011001-eng.pdf.

———— **2013e** The Educational Attainment of Aboriginal Peoples in Canada: National Household Survey (NHS). Ottawa: Statistics Canada. Cat. no. 99-012-X2011003. http://www12.statcan.gc.ca/ nhs-enm/2011/as-sa/99-012-x/99-012-x2011003_3-eng.pdf.

———— **2013f** *Low Income Lines 2011–12.* Ottawa: Statistics Canada. Cat. no. 75F0002M—No. 002.

———— **2013g** *Commuting to Work: National Household Survey (NHS) 2011 Brief.* Ottawa: Statistics Canada. Cat. no. 99-012-X2011003.

———— **2013h** 2011 National Household Survey. Data Tables: Occupation. Cat. no. 99-102-X2011033. https://www12.statcan .gc.ca/nhs-enm/2011/dp-pd/dt-td/Index-eng .cfm.

———— **2013i** 2011 National Household Survey. Data Tables: Employment Income Statistics in 2010 by National Occupational Classification. Catalogue no. 99-014-X2011042. https://www12.statcan.gc.ca/ nhs-enm/2011/dp-pd/dt-td/Index-eng.cfm.

Steinberg, Ronnie J. 1990 "Social Construction of Skill: Gender, Power, and Comparable Worth." *Work and Occupations* 17: 449–82.

Stern, Robert N. 1976 "Intermetropolitan Pattern of Strike Frequency." *Industrial and Labor Relations Review* 29: 218–35.

Stewart, A., and R. M. Blackburn 1975 "The Stability of Structured Inequality." *Sociological Review* 23: 481–508.

Stiglitz, Joseph 2006 *Making Globalization Work*. New York: W.W. Norton and Company.

Stiglitz, Joseph 2012 *The Price of Inequality: How Today's Divided Society Endangers Our Future*. New York: W.W. Norton.

Stinson, Jane 2010 "Labour Casualization in the Public Sector" In Norene J. Pupo and Mark P. Thomas, eds., *Interrogating the New Economy: Restructuring Work in the 21st Century*. Toronto: University of Toronto Press.

Stinson, John F., Jr. 1997 "New Data on Multiple Jobholding Available from the CPS." *Monthly Labor Review* (March): 3–8.

Stone, Leroy O., ed. 2008 *New Frontiers of Research on Retirement*. Ottawa: Statistics Canada. Cat. no. 75-511-XWE.

Stone, Pamela 2007 *Opting Out? Why Women Really Quit Careers and Head Home*. Berkeley, CA: University of California Press.

Stonebridge, C. 2013 *Future Care for Canadians—Why It Matters*. Ottawa: Conference Board of Canada.

Storey, Robert 1983 "Unionization versus Corporate Welfare: The Dofasco Way." *Labour/Le Travail* 12: 7–42.

Storey, Robert 2009a "From Invisibility to Equality? Women Workers and the Gendering of Workers' Compensation in Ontario, 1900–2005." *Labour/Le Travail* 64: 75–106.

Storey, Robert 2009b " 'They Have All Been Faithful Workers': Injured Workers, Truth, and Workers' Compensation in Ontario, 1970–2008." *Journal of Canadian Studies* 43(1): 154–85.

Storey, Robert, and Wayne Lewchuk 2000 "From Dust to DUST to Dust: Asbestos and the Struggle for Worker Health and Safety at Bendix Automotive." *Labour/Le Travail* 45(Spring): 103–40.

Strong-Boag, Veronica 1988 *The New Day Recalled: Lives of Girls and Women in English Canada, 1919–1939*. Markham, ON: Penguin Books.

Strong-Boag, Veronica, and A. Fellman, eds. 1997 *Rethinking Canada: The Promise of Women's History*. 3rd ed. Don Mills, ON: Oxford University Press.

Stubblefield, Al 2005 *The Baptist Health Care Journey to Excellence: Creating a Culture That WOWs!* Hoboken, NJ: John Wiley & Sons.

Sugiman, Pamela 1992 " 'That Wall's Comin' Down': Gendered Strategies of Worker Resistance in the UAW Canadian Region (1963–1970)." *Canadian Journal of Sociology* 17: 24–27.

Sullivan, Maureen 1996 "Rozzie and Harriet? Gender and Family Patterns of Lesbian Coparents." *Gender and Society* 10(6): 747–67.

Sullivan, Terrance, ed. 2000 *Injury and the New World of Work*. Vancouver and Toronto: UBC Press.

Sunter, Deborah 2001 "Demography and the Labour Market." *Perspectives on Labour and Income* 13(Spring): 28–39.

Sunter, Deborah, and Geoff Bowlby 1998 "Labour Force Participation in the 1990s." *Perspectives on Labour and Income* (Autumn): 15–21.

Super, Donald E., and Branimir Šverko, eds. 1995 *Life Roles, Values, and Careers: International Findings of the Work Importance Study*. San Francisco: Jossey-Bass.

Suplee, Curt 1997 "Robot Revolution." *National Geographic*, July, 76–93.

Sussman, Deborah 1998 "Moonlighting: A Growing Way of Life." *Perspectives on Labour and Income* (Summer): 24–31.

——— 2000 "Unemployment Kaleidoscope." *Perspectives on Labour and Income* 12(Autumn): 9–15.

Swanson, Jean 2001 *Poor-Bashing: The Politics of Exclusion*. Toronto: Between the Lines.

Swift, Jamie 1995 *Wheel of Fortune: Work and Life in the Age of Falling Expectations*. Toronto: Between the Lines.

Synder, Karrie Ann, and Adam Isaiah Green 2008 "Revisiting the Glass Escalator: The Case of Gender Segregation in a Female Dominated Occupation." *Social Problems* 55(2): 271–99.

Szelényi, Iván, and Eric Kostello 1996 "The Market Transition Debate: Toward a Synthesis?" *American Journal of Sociology* 10: 1082–96.

Tal, Benjamin 2012 "The Haves and Have Nots of the Canadian Labour Market." *CIBC In Focus*, December 3.

Tanner, Julian 1984 "Skill Levels of Manual Workers and Beliefs about Work, Management, and Industry: A Comparison of Craft and Non-craft Workers in Edmonton." *Canadian Journal of Sociology* 9:303–18.

Tanner, Julian, and Rhonda Cockerill 1986 "In Search of Working-Class Ideology: A Test of Two Perspectives." *Sociological Quarterly* 27:389–402.

Tanner, Julian, Rhonda Cockerill, Jan Barnsley, and A. P. Williams 1999 "Flight Paths and Revolving Doors: A Case Study of Gender Desegregation in Pharmacy." *Work, Employment & Society* 13(2): 275–93.

Tanner, Julian, Harvey Krahn, and Timothy F. Hartnagel 1995 *Fractured Transitions from School to Work: Revisiting the Dropout Problem*. Don Mills, ON: Oxford University Press.

Tapscott, Don 1996 *The Digital Economy: Promise and Peril in the Age of Networked Intelligence*. San Francisco: McGraw-Hill.

Taras, Daphne G. 2002 "Alternative Forms of Employee Representation and Labour Policy." *Canadian Public Policy* 28(1): 105–16.

Taras, Daphne G., Allen Ponak, and Morley Gunderson 2005 "Introduction to Canadian Industrial Relations." In Morley Gunderson, Allen Ponak, and Daphne G. Taras, eds., *Union–Management Relations in Canada*, 5th ed. Toronto: Pearson Addison Wesley.

Taylor, Alison 2001 *The Politics of Educational Reform in Alberta*. Toronto: University of Toronto Press.

Taylor, Alison, Jason Foster, and Carolina Cambre 2012 "Training 'Expendable' Workers: Temporary Foreign Workers in Nursing." *Globalization, Societies and Education* 10(1): 95–117.

Taylor, Alison, and Harvey Krahn 2013 "Living Through our Children: Exploring the Education and Career 'Choices' of Racialized Immigrant Youth in Canada." *Journal of Youth Studies* 16(8): 1000–1021.

Taylor, Frederick Winslow 1911 *The Principles of Scientific Management*. New York: Norton.

Taylor, Philip, and Peter Bain 2001 "Trade Unions, Workers' Rights and the Frontier of Control in UK Call Centres." *Economic and Industrial Democracy* 22(1): 39–66.

———— **2003** "'Subterranean Worksick Blues': Humour as Subversion in Two Call Centres." *Organization Studies* 24(9): 1487–1509.

Teasdale, Nina 2013 "Fragmented Sisters: The Implications of Flexible Employment Policies for Professional Women's Workplace Relationships." *Gender, Work & Organization* 20(4): 397–412.

Teeple, Gary 1972 "Land, Labour and Capital in Pre-Confederation Canada." In Gary Teeple, ed., *Capitalism and the National Question in Canada*. Toronto: University of Toronto Press.

Tehrani, Noreen 2004 "Bullying: A Source of Chronic Traumatic Stress?" *British Journal of Guidance & Counselling* 32(3): 357–66.

Terkel, Studs 1971 *Working*. New York: Pantheon.

Therrien, Pierre, and André Léonard 2003 *Empowering Employees: A Route to Innovation*. The Evolving Workplace Series. Ottawa: Statistics Canada and Human Resources Development Canada. Cat. no. 71-584-MEI—No. 8.

Thomas, Derrick 2009 "The Impact of Working in a Non-official Language on the Occupations and Earnings of Immigrants in Canada." *Canadian Social Trends* (Summer): 12–20.

Thomas, Derrick 2010 "Foreign Nationals Working Temporarily in Canada." *Canadian Social Trends* (June).

Thomas, Mark 2010 "Labour Migration and Temporary Work: Canada's Foreign-Worker Programs in the 'New Economy.'" In Norene J. Pupo and Mark P. Thomas, eds., *Interrogating the New Economy: Restructuring Work in the 21st Century*. Toronto: University of Toronto Press.

Thomason, Terry, and Silvana Pozzebon 2002 "Determinants of Firm Workplace Health and Safety and Claims Management Practices." *Industrial and Labor Relations Review* 55(2): 286–307.

Tilly, Charles 1979 *From Mobilization to Revolution*. Reading, MA: Addison-Wesley.

Timpson, Annis May 2001 *Driven Apart: Women's Employment Equality and Child Care in Canadian Public Policy*. Vancouver and Toronto: University of British Columbia Press.

Titus, Marvin A. 2006 "Understanding College Degree Completion of Students with Low Socioeconomic Status: The Influence of the Institutional Financial Context." *Research in Higher Education* 47(4): 371–98.

Todeschini, Maya Morioka 2011 "'Webs of Engagement': Managerial Responsibility in a Japanese Company." *Journal of Business Ethics* 101: 45–59.

Toffler, Alvin 1980 *The Third Wave*. New York: Bantam.

Tomlinson, Michael 2007 "Graduate Employability and Student Attitudes and Orientations to the Labour Market." *Journal of Education and Work* 20(4): 285–304.

Torres, Sara, Denise L. Spitzer, Karen D. Hughes, Jacqueline Oxman-Martinez, and Jill Hanley 2012 "From Temporary Worker to Resident: The Live-in Caregiver Program (LCP) and Its Impact through an Intersectional Lens." In Patti Lenard and Christine Straehle, eds., *Temporary Foreign Work in Canada*. Montreal and Kingson: McGill–Queen's University Press.

Towers, I., L. E. Duxbury, C. Higgins, and J. Thomas 2006 "Time Thieves and Space Invaders: Technology, Work and Organization." *Journal of Organizational Change Management* 19(5): 593–618.

Townley, Barbara 1993 "Foucault, Power/Knowledge and Its Relevance for Human Resource Management." *Academy of Management Review* 18(3): 518–45.

——— **1994** *Reframing Human Resource Management: Power, Ethics and the Subject at Work*. London, England: Sage Publications.

Tran, Kelly 2004 "Visible Minorities in the Labour Force: 20 Years of Change." *Canadian Social Trends* (Summer): 7–11.

Treathaway, Natasha 2000 *Domestic Work: Poems*. Minneapolis, MN: Graywolf Publishing.

Trist, E. L., and K. W. Bamforth 1951 "Some Social and Psychological Consequences of the Longwall Method of Coal-Getting." *Human Relations* 4: 3–38.

Tronto, Joan 1993 *Moral Boundaries: A Political Argument for an Ethic of Care*. New York and London: Routledge.

Tucker, Eric 1992 "Worker Participation in Health and Safety Regulation: Lessons from Sweden." *Studies in Political Economy* 37: 95–127.

——— **2003** "Diverging Trends in Worker Health and Safety Protection and Participation in Canada, 1985–2000." *Relations industrielles/Industrial Relations* 58(3): 395–424.

Tufts, Steven, and John Holmes 2010 "Student Workers and the 'New Economy' of Mid-Sized Cities: The Cases of Peterborough and Kingston, Ontario." In Norene J. Pupo and Mark P. Thomas, eds., *Interrogating the New Economy: Restructuring Work in the 21st Century*. Toronto: University of Toronto Press.

Turcotte, Martin 2010 "Working at Home: An Update." *Canadian Social Trends* (December): 3–11.

——— **2011a** "Intergenerational Education Mobility: University Completion in Relation to Parents' Education Level." *Canadian Social Trends* (Winter): 38–44.

——— **2011b** "Women and Education." In *Women in Canada: A Gender-Based Statistical Report*. Ottawa: Statistics Canada. Catalogue no. 89-503-X.

——— **2013** *Family Caregiving: What Are the Consequences?* Ottawa: Minister of Industry.

Underhill, Cathy 2006 "Training through the Ages." *Perspectives on Labour and Income* 18(4): 26–36.

United Nations Economic Commission for Europe 2010 *Measuring Quality Employment: Country Pilot Reports*. Geneva: United Nations. http://www.unece.org/fileadmin/DAM/publications/oes/STATS_Measuring QualityEmployment.E.pdf.

Uppal, Sharanjit 2011 "Unionization 2011." *Perspectives on Labour and Income* (Winter): 3–12.

Urry, John 2007 *Mobilities*. Cambridge, England: Polity Press.

Usalcas, Jeannine 2008 "Hours Polarization Revisited." *Perspectives on Labour and Income* (March): 5–15.

Usalcas, Jeannine 2011 *Aboriginal People and the Labour Market: Estimates from the Labour Force Survey 2008-10*. Ottawa: Statistics Canada. Catalogue No. 71-588-X, no. 3.

U.S. Bureau of Labor Statistics 2012 *Charting International Labor Comparisons*.

U.S. Bureau of Labor Statistics 2013 *International Comparisons of Annual Labor Force Statistics, 1970–2012*. Full Series by Indicator and Underlying Levels. http://www.bls.gov/fls/#laborforce.

Uttal, Lynet 2009 "(Re)Visioning Family Ties to Communities and Contexts." In Sally A. Lloyd, April L. Few, and Katherine R. Allen, eds., *Handbook of Feminist Family Studies*. Thousand Oaks, CA: Sage Publications.

Vahtera, Jussi, Mika Kivimäki, Jaana Pentti, Anne Linna, Marianna Virtanen, Pekka Virtanen, and Jane E. Ferrie 2004 "Organisational Downsizing, Sickness Absence, and Mortality: 10-Town Prospective Cohort Study." *British Medical Journal* 328(7439): 555. http://www.bmj.com.

Vaisey, Stephen 2006 "Education and Its Discontents: Overqualification in America, 1972–2002." *Social Forces* 85(2): 835–64.

Vallas, Steven Peter 2003 "Why Teamwork Fails: Obstacles to Workplace Change in Four Manufacturing Plants." *American Sociological Review* 68: 223–50.

van den Berg, Annette, Yolanda Grift, and Arjen van Witteloostuijn 2011 "Works Councils and Organizational Performance: The Role of Top Managers' and Works Councils' Attitudes in Bad vis-à-vis Good Times." *Journal of Labor Research* 32: 136–56.

van den Berg, Axel, and Joseph Smucker, eds. 1997 *The Sociology of Labour Markets: Efficiency, Equity, Security.* Scarborough, ON: Prentice-Hall.

Van Houten, Donald R. 1990 "The Political Economy and Technical Control of Work Humanization in Sweden during the 1970s and 1980s." *Work and Occupations* 14: 483–513.

Van Kirk, Sylvia 1980 *Many Tender Ties: Women in Fur-Trade Society, 1670–1870.* Winnipeg: Watson and Dwyer.

Varghese, Jeji, Naomi T. Krogman, Thomas M. Beckley, and Solange Nadeau 2006 "Critical Analysis of the Relationship between Local Ownership and Community Resiliency." *Rural Sociology* 71(3): 505–27.

Vaughan, Diane 1999 "The Dark Side of Organizations: Mistake, Misconduct, and Disaster." *Annual Review of Sociology* 25: 271–305.

Veltmeyer, Henry 1983 "The Development of Capitalism and the Capitalist World System." In J. Paul Grayson, ed., *Introduction to Sociology: An Alternative Approach.* Toronto: Gage.

Vézina, Mireille, and Susan Crompton 2012 "Volunteering in Canada." *Canadian Social Trends* 93: 37–55.

Vidal, Matt 2007 "Lean Production, Worker Empowerment, and Job Satisfaction: A Qualitative Analysis and Critique." *Critical Sociology* 33: 247–278.

Viswesvaran, Chockalingam, Juan I. Sanchez, and Jeffrey Fisher 1999 "The Role of Social Support in the Process of Work Stress: A Meta-analysis." *Journal of Vocational Behavior* 54(2): 314–34.

Vogel, David 2005 *The Market for Virtue: The Potential and Limits of Corporate Social Responsibility.* New York: The Brookings Institute.

Vosko, Leah F. 1998 "Regulating Precariousness? The Temporary Employment Relationship under the NAFTA and the EC Treaty." *Relations industrielles/Industrial Relations* 53(1): 123–53.

——— 2000 *Temporary Work: The Gendered Rise of a Precarious Employment Relationship.* Toronto: University of Toronto Press.

——— 2002 "The Pasts (and Futures) of Feminist Political Economy in Canada: Reviving the Debate." *Studies in Political Economy* 68: 55–83.

——— 2010 *Managing the Margins: Gender, Citizenship, and the International Regulation of Precarious Employment.* Oxford, England: Oxford University Press.

———, ed. 2005 *Precarious Employment: Understanding Labour Market Insecurity in Canada.* Montreal and Kingston: McGill–Queen's University Press.

Vosko, Leah, Nancy Zukewich, and Cynthia Cranford 2003 "Precarious Jobs: Towards a New Typology." *Perspectives on Labour and Income* 15(Winter): 39–49.

Voss, Kim 1994 *The Making of American Exceptionalism: The Knights of Labor and Class Formation in the Nineteenth Century.* Ithaca, NY: Cornell University Press.

Voss, Kim, and Rachel Sherman 2000 "Breaking the Iron Law of Oligarchy: Union Revitalization in the American Labor Movement." *American Journal of Sociology* 106(2): 303–49.

Vrankulj, Sam 2012 *Finding Their Way: Second Round Report on the CAW Worker Adjustment Tracking Project.* http://www.caw.ca/assets/images/phase-Two-Tracking-study.pdf.

Walby, Sylvia 1990 *Theorizing Patriarchy.* Oxford, England: Basil Blackwell.

Waldie, Paul 2005 "How Health Costs Hurt the Big Three." *Globe and Mail,* March 22, B1.

Walker, C. R., and R. H. Guest 1952 *Man on the Assembly Line.* Cambridge, MA: Harvard University Press.

Wallace, Jean, and Fiona Kay 2012 "Tokenism, Organizational Segregation, and

Coworker Relations in Law Firms." *Social Problems* 59(3): 389–410.

Walmsley, Ann 1992 "Trading Places." *Report on Business Magazine*, March 17–27.

Walsworth, Scott, and Richard J. Long 2012 "Is the Union Employment Suppression Effect Diminishing? Further Evidence from Canada." *Relations Industrielles/Industrial Relations* 67(4): 654–80.

Walters, David 2006 "One Step Forward, Two Steps Back: Worker Representation and Health and Safety in the United Kingdom." *International Journal of Health Services* 36(1): 87–111.

Wannell, Ted 2007 "Public Pensions and Work." *Perspectives on Labour and Income* 8(8): 12–19.

Wanner, Richard A. 1999 "Expansion and Ascription: Trends in Educational Opportunity in Canada, 1920–1994." *Canadian Review of Sociology and Anthropology* 36(3): 409–42.

——— 2009 "Social Mobility in Canada: Concepts, Patterns, and Trends." In Edward Grabb and Neil Guppy, eds., *Social Inequality in Canada: Patterns, Problems, and Policies*. 5th ed. Toronto: Pearson/Prentice Hall.

Warhurst, Chris, Françoise Carré, Patricia Findlay, and Chris Tilly, eds. 2012 *Are Bad Jobs Inevitable? Trends, Determinants and Responses to Job Quality in the Twenty-First Century*. Basingstoke, England: Palgrave Macmillan.

Warren, Tracey 2011 "Researching the Gender Division of Unpaid Domestic Work: Practices, Relationships, Negotiation, and Meaning." *The Sociological Review* 59(1): 129–48.

Washington Post 2010 "Obama's Ambitious Export Plan May Rekindle Free-Trade Battle." March 12.

Watkins, Mel 1991 "A Staples Theory of Economic Growth." In Gordon Laxer, ed., *Perspectives on Canadian Economic Development*. Toronto: Oxford University Press.

Weaver, Robert D., Nazim Habibov, and Lida Fan 2010 "Devolution and the Poverty Reduction Effectiveness of Canada's Provincial Social Welfare Programs: Results from a Time-Series Investigation of a Canadian National Survey." *Journal of Policy Practice* 9(2): 80–95.

Weber, Max 1946 "Bureaucracy." In H. H. Gerth and C. Wright Mills, eds., *From Max Weber*. New York: Oxford University Press.

——— 1958 *The Protestant Ethic and the Spirit of Capitalism*. New York: Scribner.

Weiss, David 2003 *In Search of the Eighteenth Camel: Discovering a Mutual Gains Oasis for Unions and Management*. Kingston, ON: Industrial Relations Centre, Queen's University.

Weiss, Donald D. 1976 "Marx versus Smith on the Division of Labour." *Monthly Review* 28: 104–18.

Weller, Sally A. 2012 "Financial Stress and the Long-Term Outcomes of Job Loss." *Work, Employment & Society* 26(1): 10–25.

Wellesley Institute 2013 *Shadow Economies: Economic Survival Strategies of Toronto Immigrant Communities*. Toronto: Wellesley Institute.

Wells, Donald M. 1997 "When Push Comes to Shove: Competitiveness, Job Security and Labour–Management Cooperation in Canada." *Economic and Industrial Democracy* 18(2):

Weyzig, Francis 2009 "Political and Economic Arguments for Corporate Social Responsibility: Analysis and a Proposition Regarding the CSR Agenda." *Journal of Business Ethics* 86(4): 417–28.

Wharton, Amy 1993 "The Affective Consequences of Service Work: Managing Emotions on the Job." *Work and Occupations* 20(2): 205–32.

——— 2009 "The Sociology of Emotional Labor." *Annual Review of Sociology* 35: 147–65.

Wheeler, Hoyt N. 2008 "A New Frontier for Labor: Collective Action by Worker Owners." *Labor Studies Journal* 33(2): 163–78.

White, Jerry P. 1990 *Hospital Strike: Women, Unions, and Public Sector Conflict*. Toronto: Thompson Educational Publishing.

White, Julie 1990 *Mail and Female: Women and the Canadian Union of Postal Workers*. Toronto: Thompson Educational Publishing.

White, Lynn, Jr. 1962 *Medieval Technology and Social Change*. Oxford, England: Oxford University Press.

White, Michael, Stephen Hill, Patrick McGovern, Colin Mills, and Deborah Smeaton 2003 "'High-Performance' Management Practices, Working Hours and Work–Life Balance." *British Journal of Industrial Relations* 41(2): 175–95.

Whitehead, T. N. 1936 *Leadership in a Free Society*. Cambridge, MA: Harvard University Press.

Whittaker, D. H. 1990 "The End of Japanese-Style Employment?" *Work, Employment & Society* 4:21–47.

Whittal, Michael, Herman Knudson, and Herman Huijgen, eds. 2007 *Towards a European Labour Identity: The Case of the European Work Council.* New York: Routledge.

Whyman, Philip 2004 "An Analysis of Wage-Earner Funds in Sweden: Distinguishing Myth from Reality." *Economic and Industrial Democracy* 25(3): 411–45.

Whyte, Martin King 2009 "Paradoxes of China's Economic Boom." *Annual Review of Sociology* 35:371–92.

Whyte, William Foote, and Kathleen King Whyte 1988 *Making Mondragon: The Growth and Dynamics of the Worker Cooperative Complex.* Ithaca, NY: ILR Press.

Wiatrowski, William 2012 "The Last Private Industry Pension Plans: A Visual Essay." *Monthly Labor Review* (December): 3–18.

Wilensky, Jeanne L., and Harold L. Wilensky 1951 "Personnel Counseling: The Hawthorne Case." *American Journal of Sociology* 57: 265–80.

Wilkinson, Richard, and Kate Pickett 2009 *The Spirit Level: Why Greater Equality Makes Societies Stronger.* London: Penguin Books.

Williams, Alison, Valorie A. Crooks, Melissa Giesbrecht, Sarah Dykeman 2010 *Evaluating Canada's Compassionate Care Benefit from the Perspective of Family Caregivers.* Hamilton, ON: McMaster University.

Williams, Cara 2003 "Sources of Workplace Stress." *Perspectives on Labour and Income* 15(Autumn): 23–30.

——— 2008 "Work–Life Balance of Shift Workers." *Perspectives on Labour and Income* 9(August): 5–16.

——— 2010 "Economic Well-Being." In *Women in Canada: A Gender-Based Statistical Report.* Ottawa: Statistics Canada. Cat. no. 89-503-X.

Williams, Christine L. 1989 *Gender Differences at Work: Women and Men in Nontraditional Occupations.* Berkeley, CA: University of California Press.

——— 1992 "The Glass Escalator: Hidden Advantages for Men in the 'Female Professions.'" *Social Problems* 39(3): 253–67.

——— 1995 *Still a Man's World: Men Who Do "Women's Work."* Berkeley, CA: University of California Press.

——— 2011 "The Glass Escalator Revisited: Gender Inequality in Neoliberal Times." *Gender and Society* 27(5): 609–29.

Williams, Christine, Chandra Muller, and Kristine Kilanski 2012 "Gendered Organizations in the New Economy." *Gender and Society* 26: 549–71.

Williams, Joan C. 2010 *Reshaping the Work–Family Debate.* Cambridge, MA: Harvard University Press.

Williams, Joan C., Mary Blair-Loy, and Jennifer L. Berdahl 2013 "Cultural Schemas, Social Class, and the Flexibility Stigma." *Journal of Social Issues* 69(2): 209–34.

Williams, Joan C., and Amy Cuddy 2012 "Will Working Mothers Take Your Company to Court?" *Harvard Business Review* 90(9): 94–100.

Williams, Joan C., and Rachel Dempsey 2014 *What Works for Women at Work.* New York and London: New York University Press.

Williams, Joan C., Jessica Manvell, and Stephanie Bornstein 2007 *"Opt Out" or Pushed Out? How the Press Covers Work/Family Conflict.* San Francisco: University of California, Hastings College of the Law, The Center for WorkLife Law. http://www.uchastings.edu/site_files/ WLL/ OptOutPushedOut.pdf.

Wilson, Daniel, and David Macdonald 2010 *The Income Gap between Aboriginal Peoples and the Rest of Canada.* Ottawa: Canadian Centre for Policy Alternatives.

Wilson, John 2000 "Volunteering." *Annual Review of Sociology* 26(1): 215–40.

Wingrove, Josh, and Dawn Walton 2013 "Alberta Jail Guard Wildcat Strike Leaves Main Courthouses in Gridlock." *Globe and Mail* [online], April 29.

Winson, Anthony, and Belinda Leach 2002 *Contingent Work, Disrupted Lives: Labour and Community in the New Rural Economy.* Toronto: University of Toronto Press.

Winters, L. Alan, and Shahid Yusuf, eds. 2007 *Dancing with Giants: China, India and the Global Economy.* Washington, DC: World Bank.

Wirth, Linda 2004 *Breaking Through the Glass Ceiling: Women in Management: Update.* Geneva: International Labour Office.

Witz, Ann 1992 *Professions and Patriarchy.* London, England: Routledge.

Womack, James P., Daniel T. Jones, and Daniel Roos 1990 *The Machine That Changed the World.* New York: Harper Perennial.

Wood, Linda Solomon 2013 "Hard Work, High Pay in the Tar Sands 'Hell.'" *Vancouver Observer*, July 9.

Wood, Stephen 1989a "The Japanese Management Model." *Work and Occupations* 16: 446–60.

———, ed. 1989b *The Transformation of Work? Skill, Flexibility and the Labour Process.* London: Unwin Hyman.

Wood, Stephen, David Holman, and Christopher Stride 2006 "Human Resource Management and Performance in U.K. Call Centres." *British Journal of Industrial Relations* 44(1): 99–124.

Woodward, Joan 1980 *Industrial Organization: Theory and Practice.* 2nd ed. Oxford, England: Oxford University Press.

Workers Uniting 2010 http://www.worker-suniting.org.

World Bank 1991 *World Development Report 1991: The Challenge of Development.* Oxford: World Bank and Oxford University Press. http://wdronline.worldbank.org/worldbank/a/c.html/world_development_report_1991/chapter_1_world_economy_transition

World Bank 1993 *The East Asian Miracle: Economic Growth and Public Policy.* New York: Oxford University Press.

——— 2001 *Rethinking the East Asian Miracle.* New York: Oxford University Press and the World Bank.

——— 2005a *World Development Indicators 2005.* http://www.worldbank.org/data/wdi2005/wditext/Cover.htm.

——— 2005b *East Asia Update, April 2005.* http://siteresources.worldbank.org/INTEAPHALFYEARLYUPDATE/Resources/eapupdate.pdf.

World Commission on Environment and Development 1987 *Our Common Future.* Oxford, England: Oxford University Press.

World Trade Organization (WTO) 2013 *International Trade Statistics, 2012.* http://www.wto.org/english/res_e/statis_e/its2012_e/its2012_e.pdf.

Worth, Sean 2005 "Beating the 'Churning' Trap in the Youth Labour Market." *Work, Employment & Society* 19(2): 403–14.

Wray-Lake, Laura, A. K. Syverson, L. Briddell, D. W. Osgoode, and C. A. Flanagan 2011 "Exploring the Changing Meaning of Work for American High School Seniors from 1976 to 2005." *Youth & Society* 43: 1110–35.

Wrege, Charles D., and Richard M. Hodgetts 2000 "Frederick W. Taylor's 1899 Pig Iron Observations: Examining Fact, Fiction, and Lessons for the New Millennium." *Academy of Management Journal* 43(6): 1283–91.

Wright, Erik Olin 1997 *Class Counts: Comparative Studies in Class Analysis.* Cambridge: Cambridge University Press.

——— 2009 "Understanding Class: Toward an Integrated Analytic Approach." *New Left Review* 60: 101–16.

Wright, Erik Olin, C. Costello, D. Hachen, and J. Sprague 1982 "The American Class Structure." *American Sociological Review* 47: 709–26.

Wu, Xiaogang, and Yu Xie 2002 "Does the Market Pay Off? Earnings Returns to Education in Urban China." *American Sociological Review* 68: 425–42.

Wylie, William N. T. 1983 "Poverty, Distress, and Disease: Labour and the Construction of the Rideau Canal, 1826–1832." *Labour/Le Travail* 11: 7–30.

Yalnizyan, Armine 2010 *The Rise of Canada's Richest 1%.* Ottawa: Canadian Centre for Policy Alternatives (CCPA).

Yates, Charlotte 1990 "The Internal Dynamics of Union Power: Explaining Canadian Autoworkers' Militancy in the 1980s." *Studies in Political Economy* 31: 73–105.

——— 1998 "Unity and Diversity: Challenges to an Expanding Canadian Autoworkers' Union." *Canadian Review of Sociology and Anthropology* 35(1): 93–118.

——— 2000 "Staying the Decline in Union Membership: Union Organizing in Ontario, 1985–1999." *Relations industrielles/Industrial Relations* 55(4): 640–71.

——— 2006 "Challenging Misconceptions about Organizing Women into Unions." *Gender, Work & Organization* 13(6): 565–84.

Yates, Charlotte, Wayne Lewchuk, and Paul Stewart 2001 "Empowerment as a Trojan Horse: New Systems of Work Organization in the North American Automobile Industry." *Economic and Industrial Democracy* 22(4): 517–41.

Yeates, Nicola 2009 *Globalizing Care Economies and Migrant Workers: Explorations in Global Care Chains.* Basingstoke, England: Palgrave Macmillan.

Yoder, Janice D. 1991 "Rethinking Tokenism: Looking beyond Numbers." *Gender and Society* 5(2): 178–92.

Young, Marisa C. 2010 "Gender Differences in Precarious Work Settings." *Relations industrielles/Industrial Relations* 65(1): 74–97.

Youngdahl, Jay 2008 "Mapping the Future: Cross-Border Unionizing Strategies." *New Labor Forum* 17(2): 71–81.

Yuen, Jennifer 2010 "Job-Education Match and Mismatch: Wage Differentials." *Perspectives on Labour and Income* 11(4): 16–26.

Zbaracki, Mark J. 1998 "The Rhetoric and Reality of Total Quality Management." *Administrative Science Quarterly* 43(3): 602–36.

Zeitlin, Irving M. 1968 *Ideology and the Development of Sociological Theory.* Englewood Cliffs, NJ: Prentice-Hall.

Zeitlin, M. 1974 "Corporate Ownership and Control." *American Journal of Sociology* 79: 1073–1119.

Zetka, James R., Jr. 1992 "Work Organization and Wildcat Strikes in the U.S. Automobile Industry, 1946–1963." *American Sociological Review* 57: 214–26.

Zeytinoglu, Isik U., and Gordon B. Cooke 2005 "Non-standard Work and Benefits: Has Anything Changed since the Wallace Report?" *Relations industrielles/Industrial Relations* 60(1): 29–63.

Zeytinoglu, Isik U., Gordon B. Cooke, Karlene Harry, and James Chowhan 2008 "Low-Paid Workers and On-the-Job Training in Canada." *Relations industrielles/Industrial Relations* 63(1): 5–29.

Zeytinoglu, Isik U., Margaret Denton, Sharon Davies, Andrea Baumann, Jennifer Blythe, and Linda Boos 2007 "Associations between Work Intensification, Stress and Job Satisfaction: The Case of Nurses in Ontario." *Relations industrielles/Industrial Relations* 62(2): 201–25.

Zeytinoglu, Isik U., and Jacinta K. Muteshi 2000 "Gender, Race and Class Dimensions of Nonstandard Work." *Relations industrielles/Industrial Relations* 55(1): 133–65.

Zimmerman, Mary K., Jacquelyn S. Litt, and Christine E. Bose 2006 *Global Dimensions of Gender and Carework.* Stanford, CA: Stanford University Press.

Zuberi, Dan 2013 *Cleaning Up: How Hospital Outsourcing Is Hurting Workers and Endangering Patients.* Ithaca, NY: Cornell University Press.

Zuberi, Daniyal 2011 "Contracting Out Hospital Support Jobs: The Effects of Poverty Wages, Excessive Workload, and Job Insecurity on Work and Family Life." *American Behavioral Scientist* 55(7): 920–40.

Zuboff, Shoshana 1988 *In the Age of the Smart Machine: The Future of Work and Power.* New York: Basic Books.

INDEX